**‘… TO SEE TAKES TIME,
LIKE TO HAVE A FRIEND TAKES TIME.’**

GEORGIA O’KEEFFE

**‘THERE IS NO SUBJECT–OBJECT
RELATION BETWEEN HUMANS AND ART.
THE ART IS A PART OF YOU, AND YOU ARE
A PART OF THE ART.’**

REVEREND TAKAFUMI ZENRYU KAWAKAMI

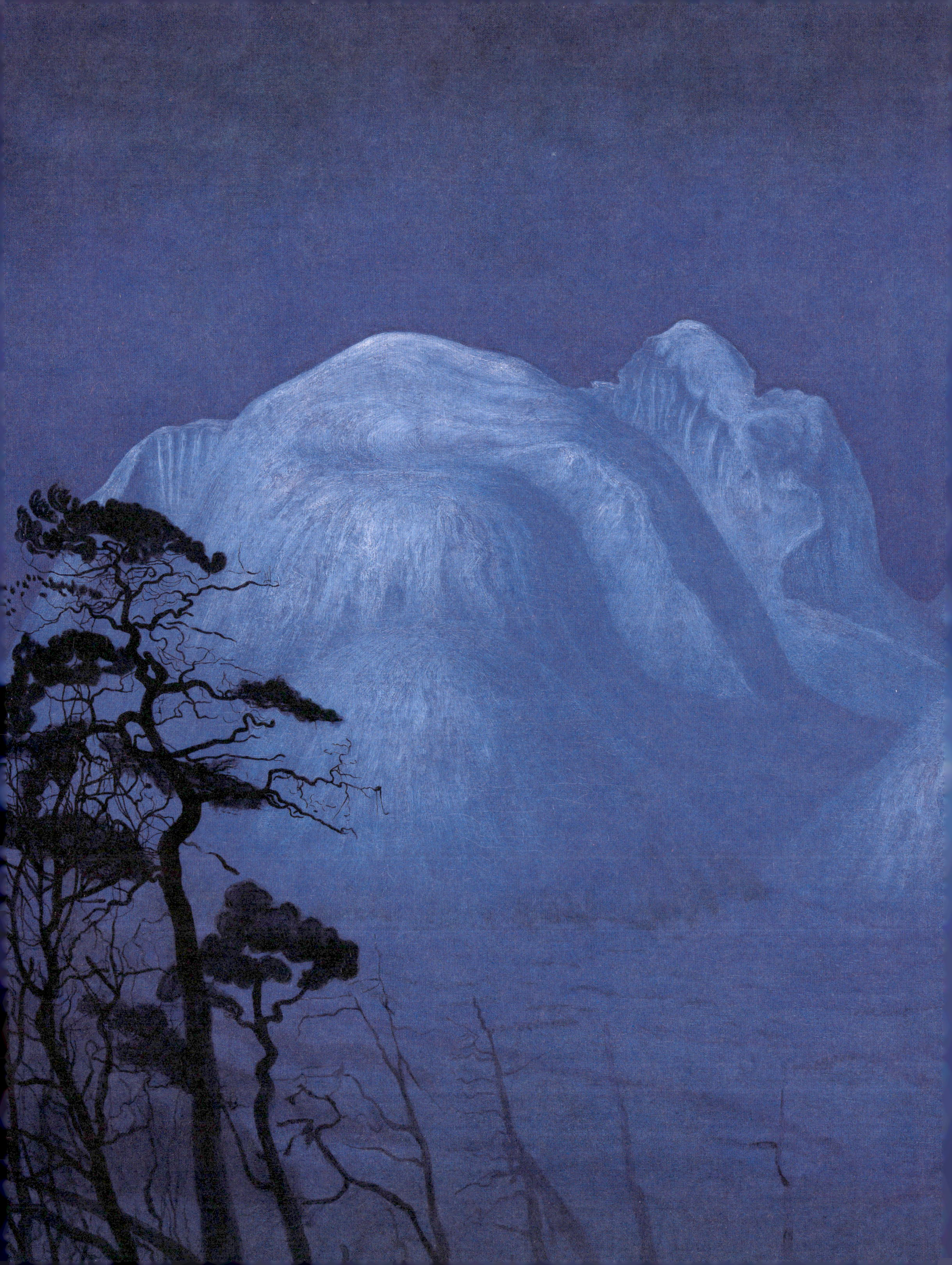

OLIVIA MEEHAN

SLOW LOOKING
THE ART OF NATURE

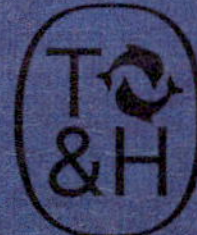

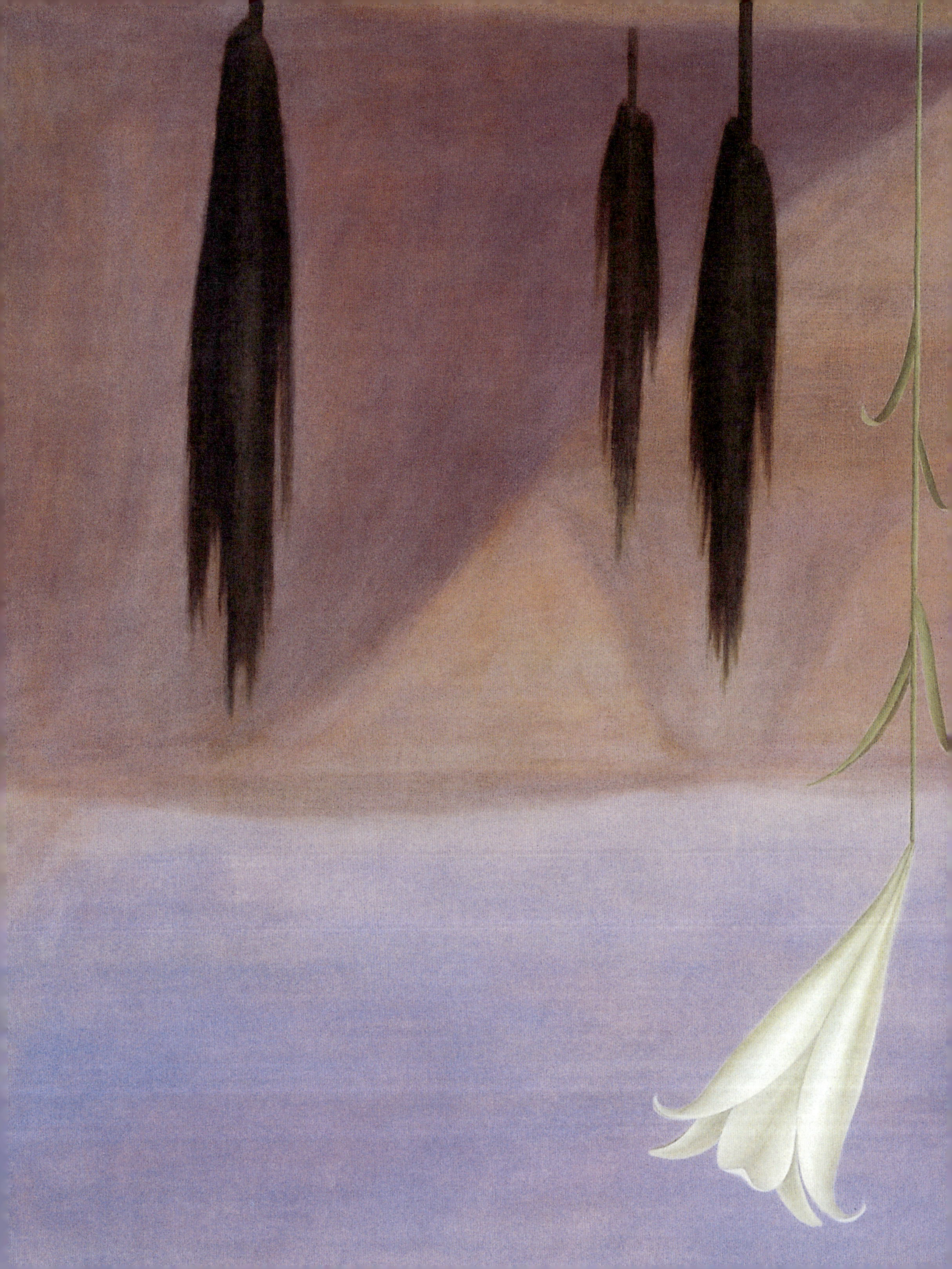

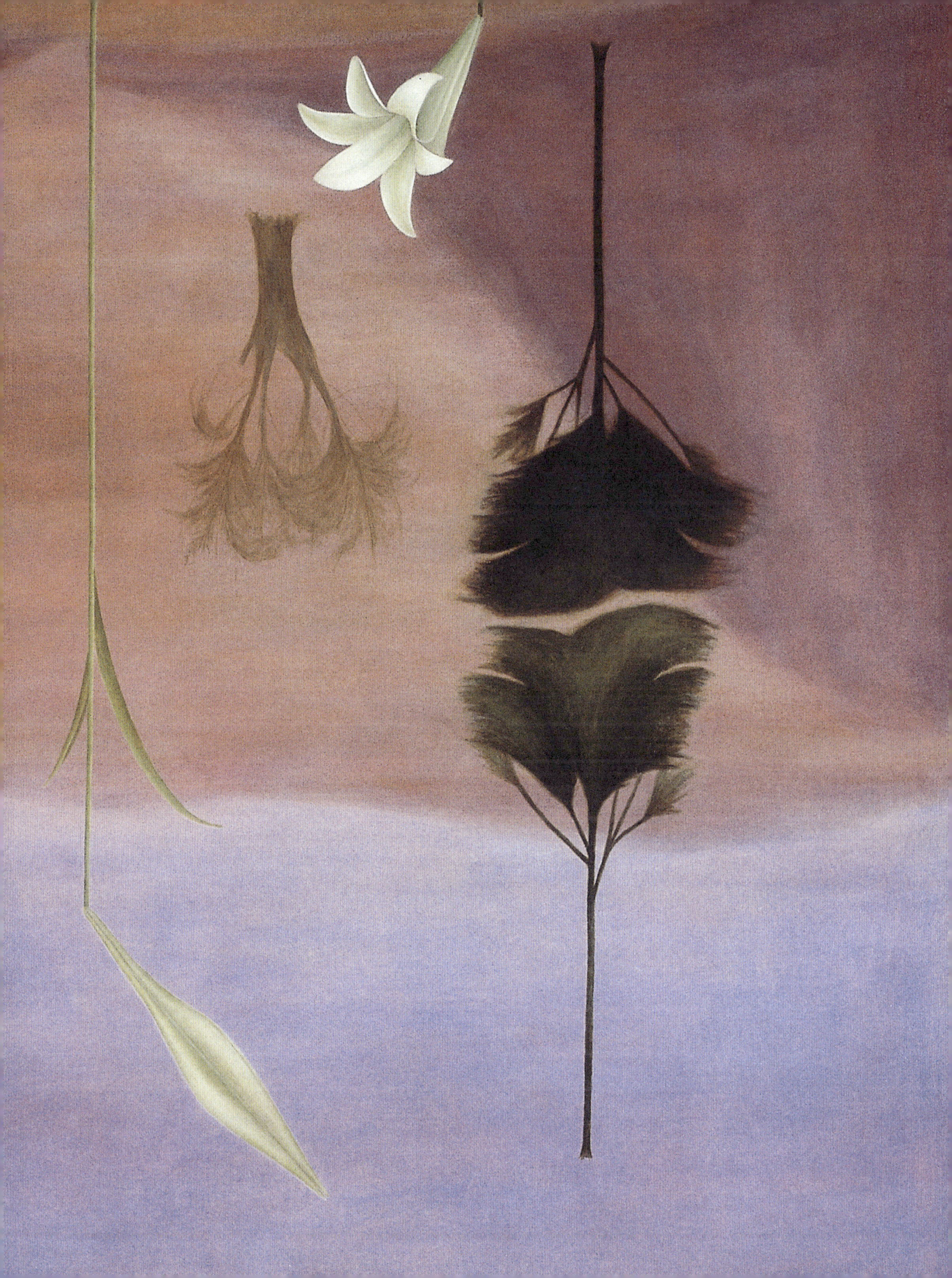

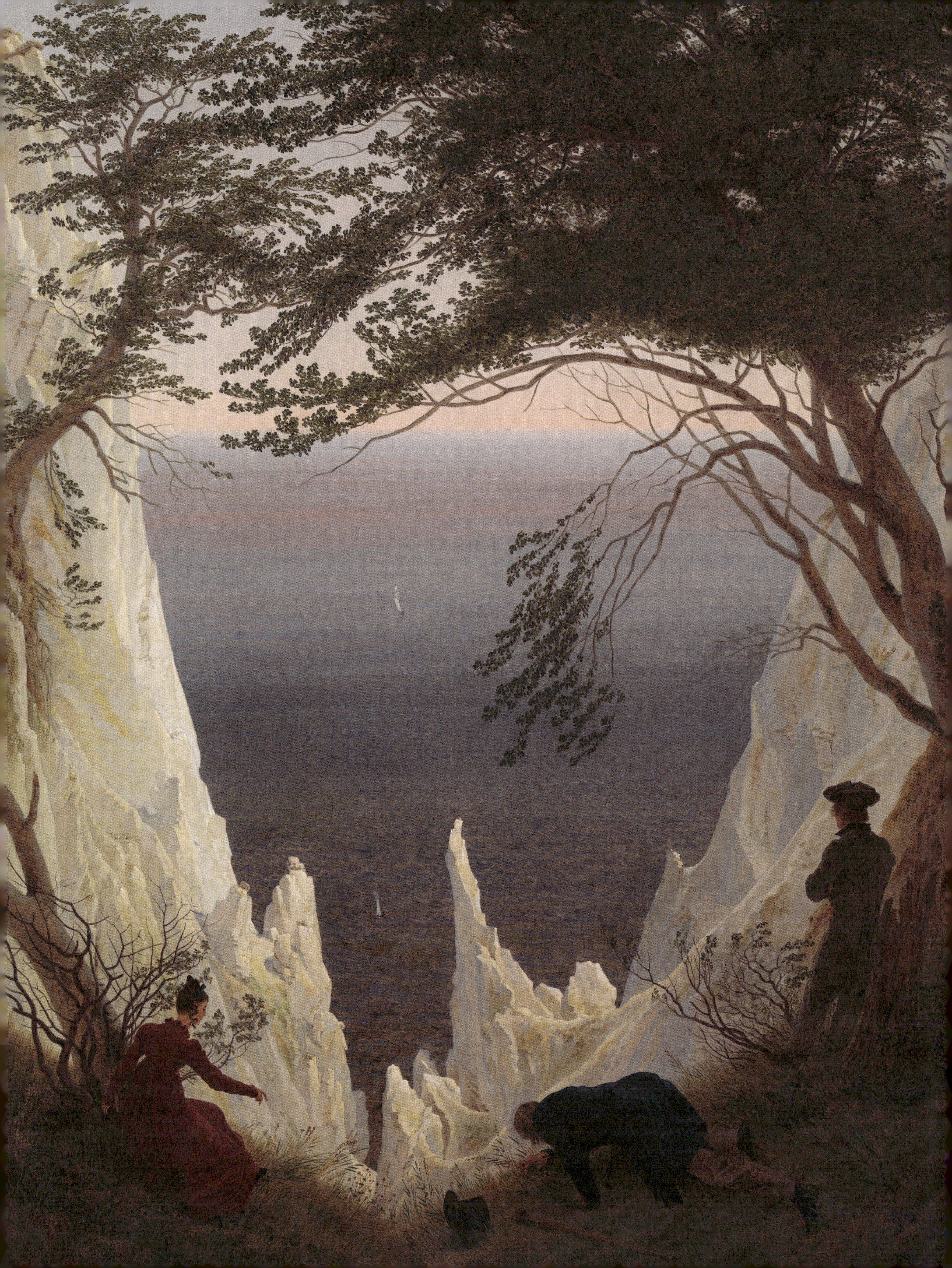

INTRODUCTION

–

THE PRACTICE OF SLOW LOOKING

Olivia Meehan

THE ART OF NATURE INVITES US TO IMAGINE THE NATURAL WORLD OVER CENTURIES AND ACROSS CULTURES, THROUGH THE EYES AND SENSES OF HUNDREDS OF ARTISTS, REVEALING NEW AND IMAGINATIVE WAYS OF SEEING THE NATURAL WORLD. THESE IMAGININGS ARE THE GREAT GIFT ARTISTS CONTINUE TO SHARE WITH US AS WE BEHOLD THE BEAUTY OF ART AND NATURE, ACROSS LAND, SEA AND SKY.

THE CASE FOR BEAUTY

Have you considered your looking practice? What do you notice about your immediate environment? Our surroundings are in a constant state of change. Many of these variations are perceived through our senses; we might observe changing light, sound, temperature or smell. But as we increasingly attempt to control our environment to live in an 'on-demand' world, natural changes such as the gradual and subtle turn to autumn have become imperceivable and perhaps inconsequential to many. This outlook has an impact not only on our attitude towards the environment, but on our senses, which are in danger of being dulled by the din of 21st-century life.

There are many obvious advantages to the technological progress we are making and the role it plays in our daily lives, but at what cost to being human? Sharp observational skills can help us discern risk and notice ambiguities; they also help us see beauty. To look upwards and outwards carries the potential for real transformation. It also inspires enquiry, curiosity and empathy – things that live beyond the strictures of algorithms and pre-emptive text.

The practice of slow looking has emerged as an antidote to our fast-paced times and has found a special place within museums and galleries.

EMOTIONS AND ART

To observe beauty in art requires a willingness to be moved emotionally. French author Stendhal (Marie-Henri Beyle) (1783–1842) wrote about his experience of being struck by an overwhelming sensation when he travelled to Florence and saw works of infinite beauty. He described the feeling as a sort of ecstasy that manifested itself physically by way of faintness and heart palpitations. In his book *Rome, Naples, and Florence* (1817) he wrote of the feeling: 'Absorbed in the contemplation of sublime beauty, I could perceive its very essence close at hand; I could, as it were, feel the stuff of it beneath my fingertips. I had attained to that supreme degree of sensibility where the divine intimations of art merge with the impassioned sensuality of emotion.' This reaction to objects and works of art in Florence is now referred to as 'Stendhal syndrome' or 'Florence syndrome', and it is said that many people have noted similar experiences in the city. Of course it is impossible to predict the emotional response to close encounters with beauty. Direct experience must count for something though, especially in an age of digital dependency, and slow looking offers a practice for deep engagement. Beauty can be perceived and expressed in different ways – it can be a private or shared experience.

The art historian James Elkins explored the way paintings move us, sometimes to tears, in his brilliant book *Pictures and Tears: A History of People Who Have Cried in Front of Paintings* (2001). Elkins outlines the causes of changes to the way we react to works of art, in particular painting, and explains how those reactions have evolved over time, leading us finally to a place where very few people are moved to cry, when encountering paintings. He is critical of the traditionally 'cool' training of art historians, which might foster a passion for art and an intellectual connection with it, but also demands a sort of 'professional detachment'.

Previous – *Chalk Cliffs on Rügen*, 1818, oil on canvas, Caspar David Friedrich (German)

The Japanese art historian and critic Sōetsu Yanagi (1889–1961) explained that he was preoccupied with the ability to see beauty in things. He defined seeing as 'something directly connected to the object', whereas knowing belongs to the context surrounding it, something that can be taught or learned. In explaining that 'knowing is not accompanied by seeing', he is specifically talking about imparting knowledge without reference to the skill and instinct required for seeing.

The key to seeing beauty is to be in immediate contact with the painting or object. What does the object tell you? The beauty will not automatically reveal itself. Beauty, as Yanagi suggests, is invisible, something embedded deep within a thing and requires an 'intuitive insight' to recognise it. The pursuit of the slow looking practice is to activate the potential for discovering the invisible component of the work of art. For example, in Monet's *Water Lilies* (see page 200), at first glance it looks as though he has used only shades of pink, green and brown. But go up close and you can see various shades of yellow, orange, purple and more in the foliage and water. The natural world in these paintings is a living, breathing entity. It's almost as though you can feel and hear the heartbeat of those paintings in those softly lit rooms in which they are housed.

This method has inevitably entered the world of museums and galleries, and shaped a certain type of linear looking and thinking about the art. As Elkins suggests, we have become comfortable in the structure and feel safe in the distance placed between us, the objects, and those who care for them and tell their histories.

Contemplation and deep reflection also invite daydreaming and imaginative thinking. Engaging in such meditative exercise with a work of art can always be enhanced with expertise or knowledge, but also offers a chance to hone our instinct for connection. How are we to build rapport with a work of art, to discover its invisible beauty, its essence, if we do not spend time with it, looking at it closely?

A SACRED OUTLOOK ON NATURE

There are myriad mythologies that elaborate on our connection to nature. Religion and philosophy have also played a role in the development of iconography featuring nature, sometimes coded and sometimes made explicit. Zen priest, thinker and head monk of Shunkoin Temple Kyoto, Reverend Takafumi Zenryu Kawakami, offers a superb insight into the concept of nature from a Buddhist perspective and the changing nature of Japanese landscape painting. In so doing he articulates another way of conceiving of nature and how it is reflected in art.

Highlighting the point of difference between Judeo-Christian thought and the Buddhist perception of nature and humankind, Kawakami says, 'In Buddhism, the self is understood as an ever-changing and interdependent collection of conditions, with no permanent or separate essence (no-self). In Taoism everything is one, but humankind likes to names things, to categorise them for convenience. Originally it had no name and was not separated. There is no human–nature dichotomy.' He notes that prior to Western influence in the 19th century, the human trace in Japanese landscape painting can be found in the presence of a small boat on the river, or a tiny shack on the side of the mountain. Kawakami astutely observes how the untouched and wild landscapes in Western paintings of the late 17th and early 18th century

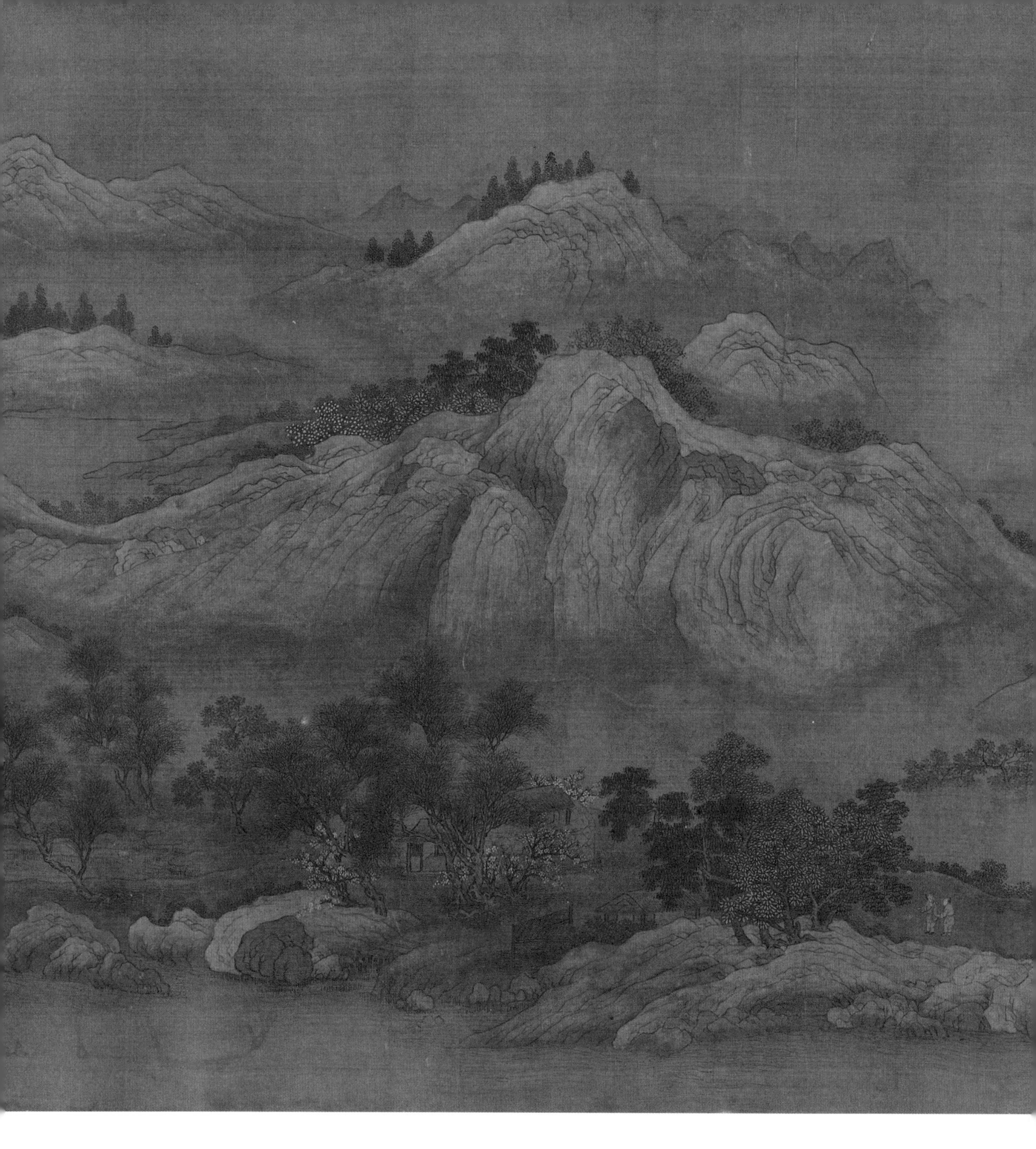

12 *Springtime Mountains*, c. 1644–1911, ink and colour on silk, formerly attributed to Zhao Bosu (Chinese)

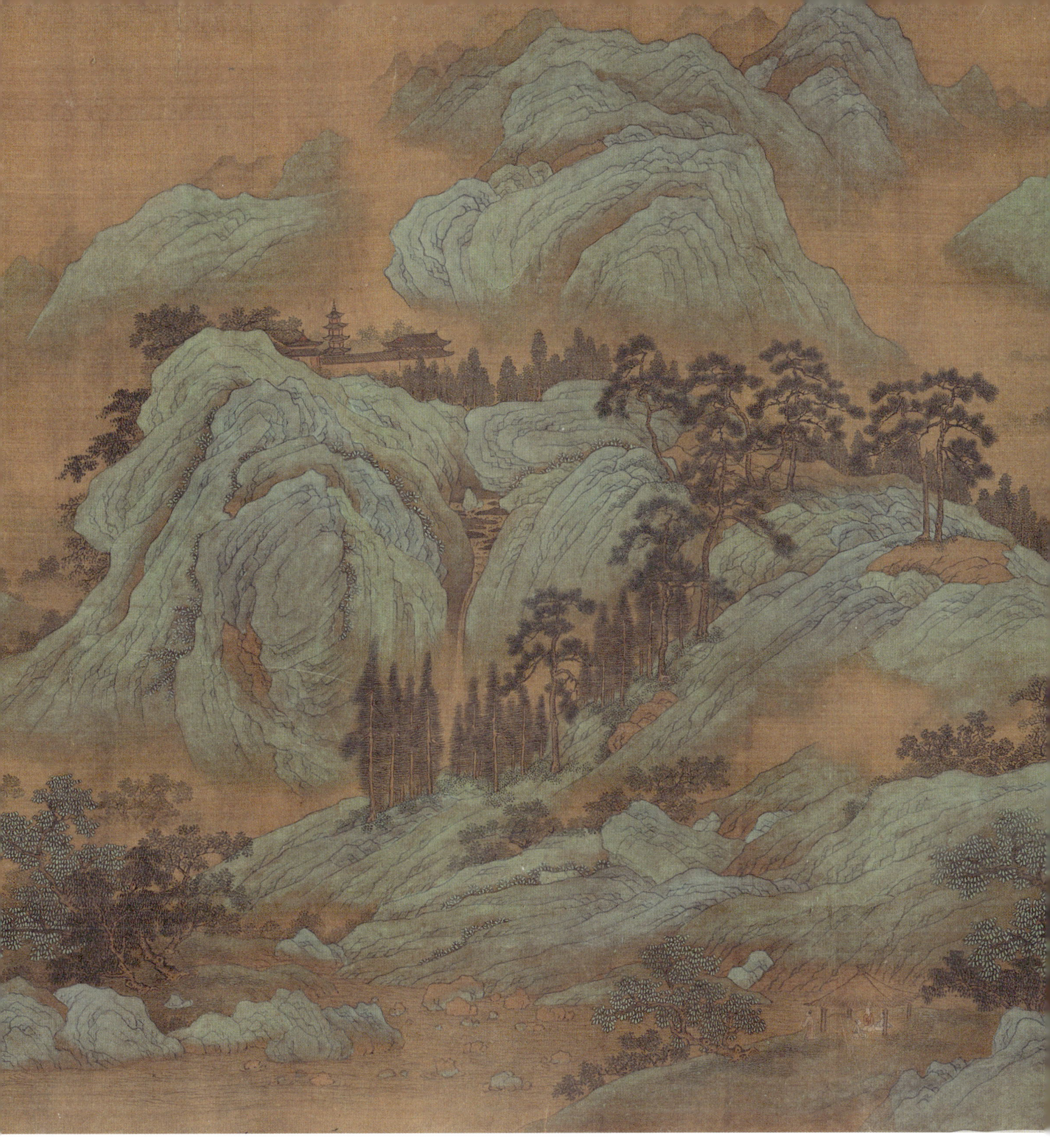

reflect the Enlightenment view of 'nature as a distinct, often majestic entity separate from human activity'. When considering traditional Japanese art and design created around the same time, he observes that it avoids a central focal point; this avoidance allows a more authentic sense of balance in painting, garden design and other forms of art. Ultimately, Kawakami's view arises from within the Buddhist context: 'There is no subject–object relation between humans and art. The art is a part of you, and you are a part of the art.'

Human presence is often found in the art of nature because people are nature. Humans are not separate from or simply surrounded by nature. Art is an expression of our existence. And not only that – but our existence is discoverable through the intangible aspects of art, the essence of what lies within and beyond a piece of art. It rests with us to find ways to discover this life force, and deep contemplation is one way to challenge ourselves to look inside the artwork, beyond its material form and surface.

Shifting our gaze from the West, the mythical legend of the Tang dynasty, painter Wu Daozi (also known as Wu Tao-Tzu) (c.680–740 CE), unfolds for us a powerful sense of transcendence and the mystical bond between artist and nature. Wu Daozi painted a stunning mural for Emperor Xuanzong, filled with scenes from nature – flowers, mountains and valleys. The artist revealed that within the mountain cave resided a spirit. As he clapped his hands, Daozi entered the painting and disappeared into the cave, taking the entire artwork with him. This evocative myth, which blends imagination and reality, inspired Sven Lindqvist's meditative book *The Myth of Wu Tao-Tzu* (1967), exploring themes of self-discovery and artistic immersion.

Ideally, the experience of this book will engender a practice that can be adapted to daily life. A walk in nature may now be enhanced by new and imaginative ways of seeing, but even daily walks in the urban environment can provide surprise encounters with the natural world. This is the great gift artists continue to give us: we need only look up, and look closely.

CHALLENGING THE MAINSTREAM NARRATIVE

Rather than focusing solely on lesser-known voices, or those omitted from art history, this collection is a feast of both familiar artworks and little-known works from across the world. The selection invites new readings and fosters unique intersections within the world of art.

Women and non-Western artists, historically marginalised and excluded in the canon of art history, are now finding their place in the contemporary analyses of fine art. Long forgotten, these artists are resurfacing, to reshape our understanding of art and the natural world, challenging the well-worn perspectives surrounding (largely male) artists' representation of nature.

Contemporary writers and poets have been invited here to respond to these varied paintings, prints, drawings and objects. Through their individual voices, fresh ideas about landscapes, locality and environment emerge. These perspectives encourage a broader understanding of art, as we experience familiar works anew and take the opportunity to explore diverse cultural and philosophical contexts.

Relooking at the art of land, sea and sky challenges the mainstream narrative, mostly dominated by male voices and overwhelmingly from a Western perspective. This re-examination invites deeper engagement with how artists from different cultures and eras have interpreted the natural world. Through this lens, nature's spiritual and symbolic roles are emphasised, allowing viewers to appreciate the profound connection between nature and the human consciousness.

A LINEAR PERSPECTIVE

To chart the representation of nature in art is a complex and near-impossible task. Through the history of art, we can identify key movements and narratives in which nature plays a central role. Both in subject matter and in the material aspects of artmaking, the presence of the natural world can be found in the earliest creations, when humankind sought to communicate their relationship with animals, the land, and constellations through rock art, painting and carvings. There are numerous early examples of the representation of connections to nature, and through history, one finds examples not only in works of art, but in architectural ornament and everyday design.

The idea of 'paradise', both earthly and heavenly, has preoccupied artistic imagination for centuries, from the grandest of scales to the tiniest miniatures. Frescoed murals of landscapes and gardens decorated the walls of villas in Ancient Roman times. Roses ramble and birds perch in the margins of illuminated manuscripts. Woven from silk and wool, European tapestries of the Middle Ages were decorated in a *millefleurs*, a pattern of many small flowers and plants. Herbals, or botanical illustrated books, were used in medieval and Renaissance times as guides for identifying, plants and flowers. Early Netherlandish painters of the 16th century, such as the unknown artist of *Shepherd and Shepherdess Making Music* (c. 1500–30), depicted some of the most intricately painted landscapes in religious painting.

In Western art historical terms, the hierarchy of genres in painting emerged around the 16th century, coinciding with the formal establishment of academies dedicated to training in the fine arts. Landscape painting ranked around third on the list, behind history painting and portraiture, with still-life painting relegated towards the bottom. Yet the rendering of landscape often represented more than just a physical impression.

HUMAN PRESENCE IN NATURE

As Reverend Takafumi Zenryu Kawakami has explained, Chinese literati painting invariably placed a tiny human presence within towering landscapes, to indicate humanity as nature. And the trees, hills and streams, birds and animals, depicted in Japanese screen painting reveal the role that nature played in that traditional practice. The 'schools' within which such artists worked dictated strict rules regarding both style and content.

In the 18th century, German Romanticism conveyed an inextricable connection to nature and the divine. Caspar David Friedrich (1774–1840) communicated the divine through creative expression, notably his compositions that depict man gazing into the landscape (see pages 8 & 280). Such paintings demonstrate the meditative practice required for a meaningful affinity with the divine. A group of American landscape painters of the mid 19th century, known as the Hudson River School, were greatly influenced by the Romantic movement in Europe. Members of the school, such as Frederic Edwin Church (see page 303) and Martin Johnson Heade (see page 239), used their canvases to depict the Adirondack and Catskill mountain ranges and the Hudson River Valley outside of New York.

John Constable (1776–1837) (see pages 151 & 258) belonged to the English Romantic movement. He was most famous for his depictions of rural and pastoral landscapes. In 1803 he attended a lecture entitled 'Essay on the Modification of Clouds' presented by the young meteorologist Luke Howard. Constable was fascinated by Howard's proposition that clouds could be named and classified by type and formation. The cloudscapes present in Constable's canvases were based on his artistic training in the academy (see page 225). It is thought that the lecture inspired Constable to create oil sketches of various atmospheric conditions, and these 'cloud studies' became a significant turning point in his practice.

The later works of Joseph Mallord William Turner's (1775–1851) (see pages 173 & 215) characterise a significant shift in the vision of nature in painting. In these works there is a notable atmosphere that sets them apart from other paintings of the time. Through a clever use of colour and broad brushstroke he captured the play of light on his subject matter, creating a unique atmospheric effect. Turner is a good example of an artist who worked within, or was aware of, the wider movement of art in his time, yet went beyond it: such exceptions would come to include Vincent van Gogh (1853–90) (see pages 77, 231 & 295), Georgia O'Keeffe (1887–1986) (see pages 20–1, 33, 157, 169 & 177), Barbara Hepworth (1903–75) (see pages 127 & 129), and David Hockney (b.1937) (see pages 92–3 & 128), all of whom took inspiration from the natural world.

Working in the mid 19th century, the Barbizon School, a group of French painters including Théodore Rousseau (1812–67) (see page 86) and Charles-François Daubigny (1817–78) (see page 28–9), also broke from the strictures of academic painting when they set up camp in the hamlets surrounding the forest of Fontainebleau, Paris. Painting outdoors in a loose and naturalist manner, they documented the subtle ecosystems of the forest over many years and their contribution is considered the forerunner to the Impressionist movement. The painters were active in setting up the Friends of Fontainebleau (Les Amis de la Forêt de Fontainebleau) and in 1852 Rousseau petitioned Emperor Napoleon III to protect the forest from deforestation and further damage in the wake of rapid industrialisation and unfettered tourism. The artists and environmental activists were successful in their campaign and as a result the first nature reserve of its kind was founded. They are considered to be the first of the modern environmental activists.

Founded in France in the late 19th century, the Impressionist movement exemplified the practice of painting outdoors, *en plein air*, to create works with a new outlook, use of colour and visible broad brushstrokes. Working around the same time as their European counterparts, a group of Australian painters began working outdoors. They aimed to capture the dazzling atmosphere and light of the Australian bush and coastline with a distinct colour palette that included soft ochre yellow, eucalypt green, and brilliant topaz blue. And in the 20th century, The Group of Seven was formed by Canadian landscape painters who endeavoured to convey the essence and uniqueness of the Canadian land.

While artmaking itself has long been free of conventional codes, it is widely argued that the thinking around, and reading of, landscapes would now benefit from a more nuanced approach, one that reckons with both long-held colonial points of view and the critical impact of climate change. There is important work being done in the space of environmental humanities and ecocriticism, to underscore the current and future threats facing the natural world. Site-specific environmental art with sculptural or performative elements, such as Judy Chicago's renowned atmosphere works staged in Californian landscape in the 1960s and 70s, inspire new ways of seeing the land (see page 222).

Tracing some of the key art movements in the canon of Western art history with a focus on nature is an interesting exercise but it only emphasises the cultures and stories not mentioned. There are multiple influences between cultures, and many are accounted for in this publication, as are the many influential and important female artists working on and in nature. Discovering more stories and insights into the works of art presented in this book will hopefully inspire further reading and exploration.

A GUIDE TO SLOW LOOKING

Works of art provide an excellent platform for practicing slow looking techniques and the development of visual intelligence.

Research in art galleries and museums has shown that most people will spend around 8–15 seconds looking at a work of art. Most people will spend 15 seconds reading (or gazing at) the extended wall text, then glance at the work of art for around 3 seconds. In some instances they will move on without looking at the work itself. Given the rise of engagement with social media platforms it makes sense that attention spans are being further reduced, equating to the average swipe-away mark of 2–3 seconds. If this is the case, the formation of our skills in visual literacy, which are not just confined to 'reading' an image but also how one 'sees' an image, are becoming increasingly limited.

To slow down our looking takes training. It is not easy, but it can be rewarding. When we first approach a work of art, it is customary to look at the label or caption: we feel compelled to know the title, who painted it and when it was painted. All this information is interesting, often important, and can provide context for the circumstances and the history surrounding the work, but how does it guide our looking?

Slow looking necessitates a return to looking at what is before us: the object or work of art itself.

In the spirit of engaging in slow looking practice, try not to take your phone out. This will help focus your attention on the work of art and its placement in relation to surrounding objects, and other things that may be taking place in the gallery: everything is vying for your attention. Acknowledging your surroundings will support your looking and possibly even enhance it. In some galleries, along with works of art and objects on display, there is the exhibition design to consider and often a curated soundtrack, together offering an immersive experience.

When first approaching a work of art, resist reading the caption. What do you see? Take note of what first draws your eye. Examine the entire canvas, page, or object, the total surface of the thing. We can never fully exhaust the work with our eyes and our first look will reveal only part of what it has to offer. In the first instance, remove all pressure of learning something or acquiring knowledge and simply return to the work of art. Find descriptive ways to name the colour as you perceive it. Does it remind you of something? The same could be applied to describing the subject matter or place represented. In the process of slow looking there is always room for new discoveries and wonder, even if the work is familiar to you. There is no immediate need to share your reaction or response with others. Allow it to settle.

CASE STUDY: SLOW LOOKING AT GEORGIA O'KEEFFE'S *UNTITLED (RED AND YELLOW CLIFFS)*

Looking at the artwork on pages 20–1, what is the first thing you notice? It might be colour. If you begin by looking at the lower register in the foreground of the canvas, you will notice a tapered strip painted in a minty green colour, representing what looks like small trees or shrubbery, together with a mix of colours including pistachio green and patches of pale yellow extending to the edges of the image. This section of the picture, although narrow, contains depth and texture. Casting our eye upwards to the blush of the pinkish hills, a spectacular cascading green effect spills from the furrowed terrain of the hillside. Capped by cliffs painted in bands of yellow and chalky white, the range extends upwards, beyond the picture plane. In the upper lefthand corner a small block of turquoise signifies a vast horizon. O'Keeffe achieves a sense of scale and magnificence by pushing the subject matter up close to the viewer; it occupies almost every inch of the canvas. This visual effect has us looking upwards, in awe of the radiance and majesty of the natural formation before us. Stepping back from the image, the rolling surface of the hills could easily be mistaken for the soft crimpled skin of a creature, with its hefty, undulating form leaning over a pool of water. What do you see in this work? Does it remind you of a place you have visited or seen before? How would you describe the weather conditions? How would you describe the colour of the sky compared with the colours of the cliff? A slow looking practice begins with observation, leading to the kind of visual analysis that can prompt further questions and enquiry.

SEE WHAT YOU CAN SEE

This book will guide you through millennia, to known and unknown places, presenting accomplished artists who evoke the power of the natural world. it invites us to explore art from every continent through more than 300 works and gives us the opportunity to extend our gaze beyond a mere glimpse. These pieces are inspired by nature, highlighting its diversity of expression, connection to philosophical thought and its reflection of the human spirit.

Slow Looking: The Art of Nature is an invitation to clap your hands and disappear into the essence of land, sea and sky. In the abstract forms of a Qing Dynasty Scholar's rock (see page 112), discover the symbolism of Daoist ideas of humans' relationship to nature; on a Stringybark canvas (see page 293), behold a universe of stars mapped onto a river. Intersections are everywhere, a testament to the way nature contests the limitations of classification and type.

In land, sea and sky, art and nature intersect across time and cultures. The pages that follow delicately but deliberately extend an invitation for close looking and observation of the natural world as depicted by artists, but also for looking again at the world around us. Careful and unhurried observation may yield new and exciting connections. Modern and abstract works of art may challenge your perception of how nature is represented: try slow looking, see what you can find. Some works will delight you, many will move you, all have the potential to inspire you. In art there is a place to contemplate, to be still and to rest for a while, perhaps to rediscover beauty or become acquainted with it for the first time, to see what you can see.

The works of art selected here can be found in public collections around the world. Seeing them face to face would be a treasured experience, but in the absence of that particular pleasure, we all live within landscapes, seascapes and skies. Even cityscapes have trees, weeds, birds and flowers. Studies in neuroscience and visual perception have demonstrated that being in nature, especially around the colour green, is beneficial to our health and wellbeing. In an uncertain age, when conflict and division can take a toll on the human spirit, taking time may feel like a luxury but it also affords kindness. Time offers a chance to breathe, to reconnect, to see things afresh, sometimes even more critically than before.

Following – *Untitled (Red and Yellow Cliffs)*, 1940, oil on canvas, Georgia O'Keeffe (American)

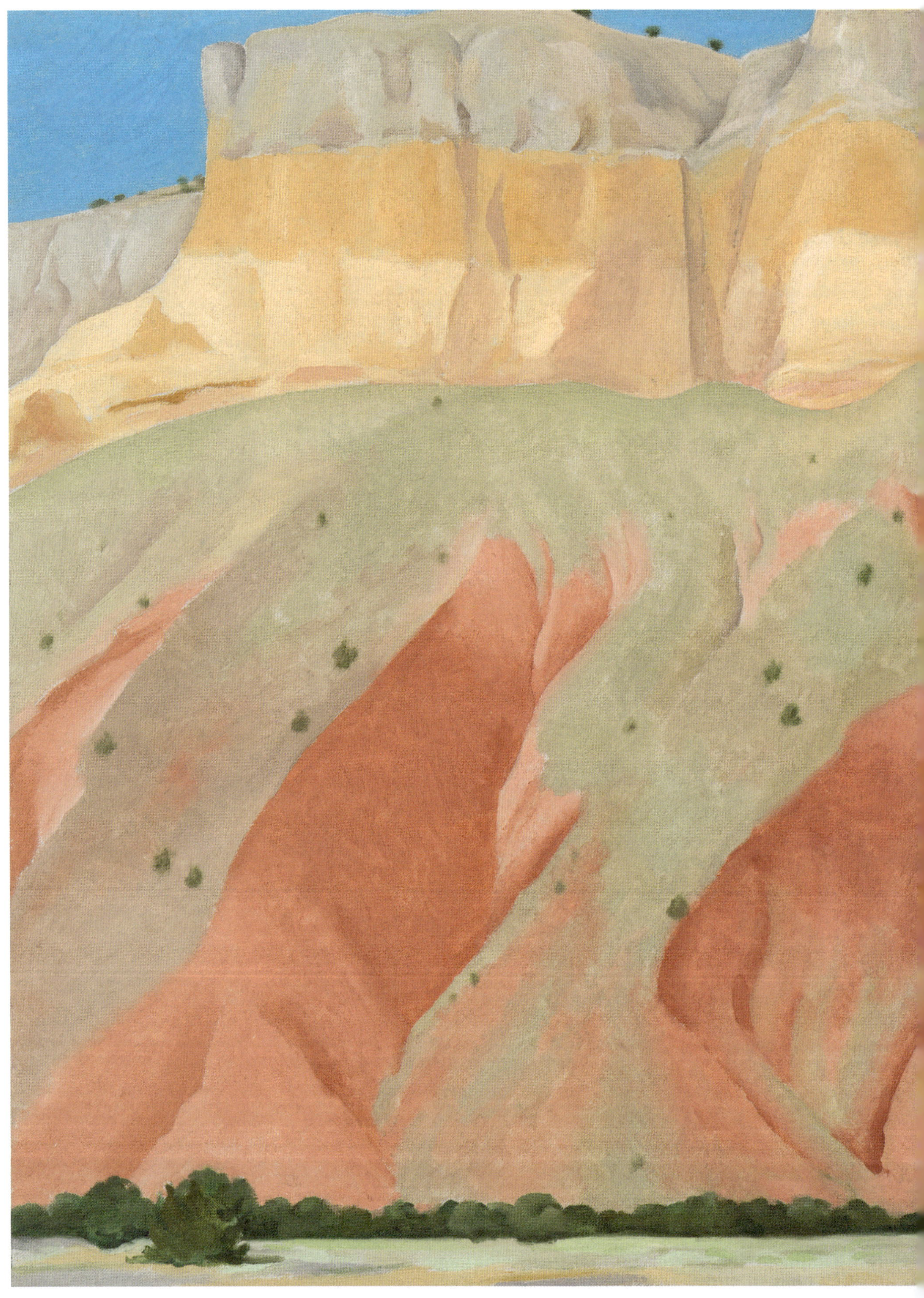

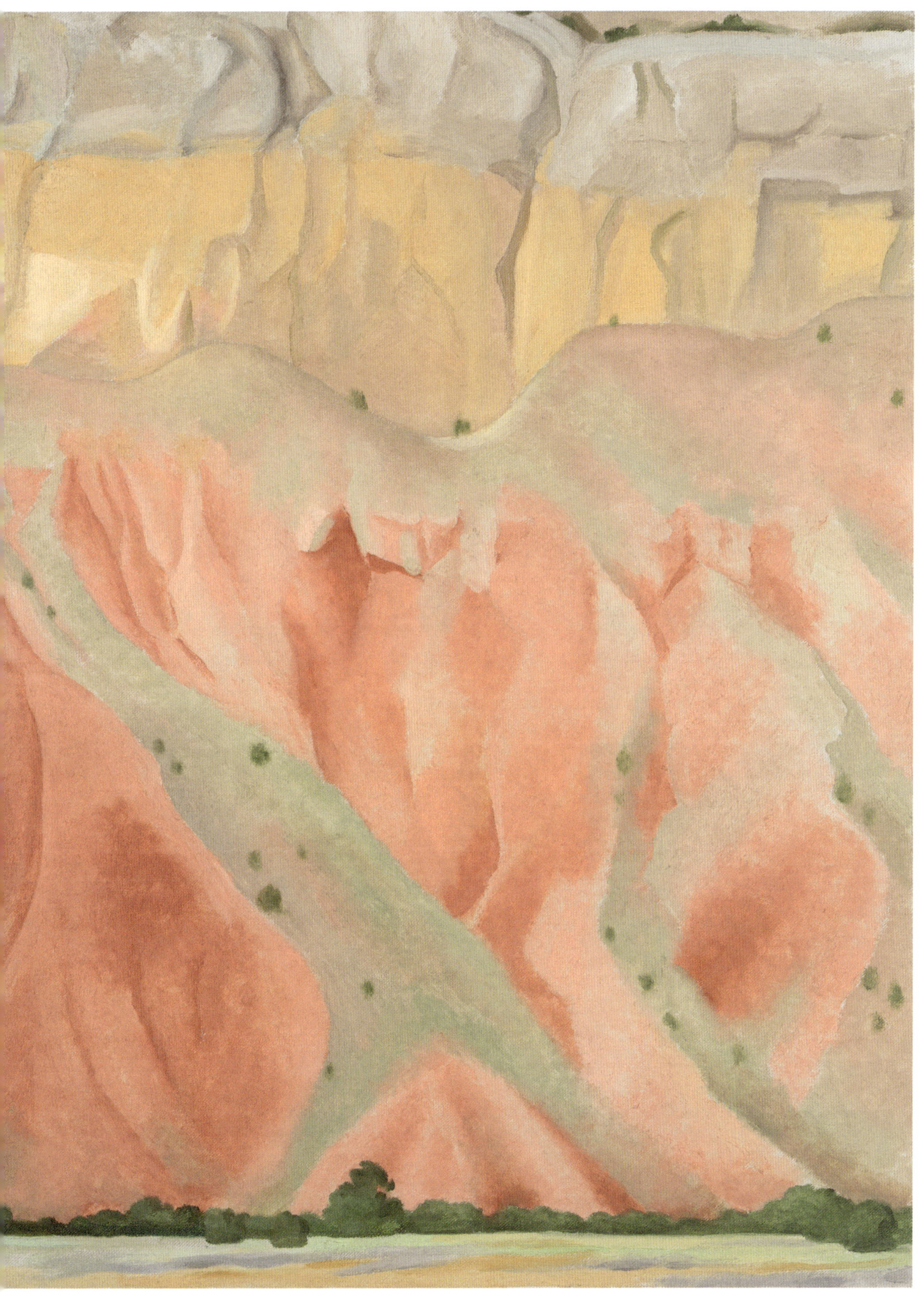

LAND

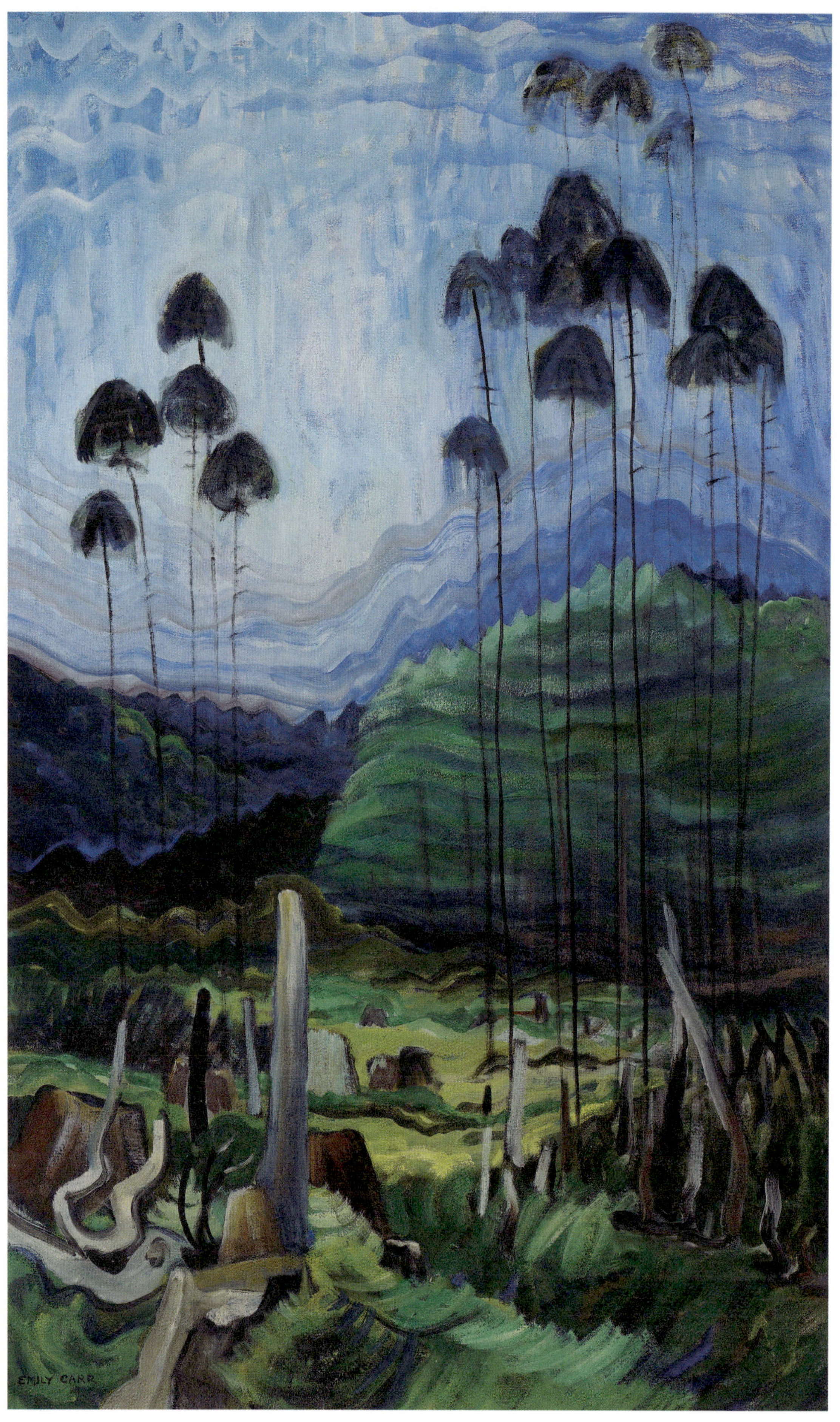
EMILY CARR

LAND

THE CONCEPT OF LAND IN ART IS ALMOST LITERALLY SYNONYMOUS WITH LANDSCAPE. HERE YOU WILL FIND MOUNTAINS, INFINITE WILDFLOWER MEADOWS, DENSE FORESTS AND VAST DESERTS. BUT THERE IS SO MUCH MORE TO DISCOVER. LANDSCAPE PAINTING IS NOT MERELY ABOUT CAPTURING A VIEW. IT IS OFTEN AN EXPRESSION OF EMOTION AND FEELING, AND ALONG WITH THE CONVENTIONAL CHARACTERISTICS OF THE GENRE, THERE WILL INVARIABLY BE SOME ELEMENT OF HUMAN EFFORT AND SPIRIT TO BE FOUND ON THE PAGE.

Listening to the land demands careful attention. Many of the artistic endeavours gathered here on the broad theme of land express a connection, or disconnection, to land. They may convey tradition passed down through generations, they may utter the consequences of war and conflict, or they may be a gesture of love contained in the smallest keepsake.

Scottish modernist and writer Nan (Anna) Shepherd (1893–1981) devoted herself to finding what she called 'essential nature' in the wilds of the Cairngorms, a mountain range in the eastern highlands of Scotland. During the Second World War she scribed her now well-known meditation, *The Living Mountain*. Unlike many of her male counterparts, her quest in walking this terrain was never to reach the summit of a mountain, instead she was looking for the 'essence' within and around the mountain. Nan Shepherd's practice of tracing all aspects of a landscape with an observant eye can easily be applied to looking at art:

> ***The air is part of the mountain, which does not come to an end with its rock and its soil. It has its own air: and it is to the quality of its air that is due the endless diversity of its colourings. Brown for the most part in themselves, as soon as we see them clothed in air the hills become blue. Every shade of blue, from opalescent milky-white to indigo, is there. They are the most opulently blue when rain is in the air. Then the gullies are violet. Gentian and delphinium hues, with fire in them, lurk in the folds. These sultry blues have more emotional effect than a dry air can produce ... the violet range of colours can trouble the mind like music ... Rain in the air has also the odd power of letting one see things in the round, as though stereoscopically.***

The artistic endeavour needed to embed the stories and lives connected to place is no ordinary feat. The blue-green colour found in Chinese paintings of mountains is thought to denote cosmic realms occupied by immortals. The incandescent mineral pigment in these paintings is suggestive of some sort of supernatural property contained within the landscape, and the painting itself. *Travelers on the Road to Shu*, a painting formerly attributed to the great master Qiu Ying (c. 1494–1552), is radiant with blue-green mountains (see page 105). The sharp and towering peaks are embraced by coiling clouds which help to soften their rocky outer appearance. The scene represents the journey to Shu, an excursion which saw travellers cross dangerous ravines and steep mountain ranges. The Tang poet Li Bai (701–762 CE) wrote 'Oh, whew, my! How steep it is and high! Hard is the road to Shu, harder than ascending the clear blue sky!'

During the First World War, artists in Britain were demonised, and at times detained, following the revelation that some had been making topographical drawings featuring landmarks to pass on to the enemy state. Sketching outdoors, especially along the coastline, was effectively prohibited. At the same time the British government initiated a scheme to appoint official war artists to record events in conflict, a scheme that continues in some countries, Australia for example, to this day. Appointed an official war artist in 1940, Evelyn Dunbar (1906–60) was commissioned to chronicle

Previous – *Trees in the Sky*, 1939, oil on canvas, Emily Carr (Canadian)

the women's effort on the home front, specifically the Women's Land Army and the Women's Voluntary Service. Dunbar's painting *A Land Girl and the Bail Bull* (1945) is set on the Hampshire Downs and shows an imagined scene of the land girls working at an outdoor dairy (see page 72–3). With the epic and patterned sky and undulating fields, the painting conveys an awe for nature while also giving prominence to the land girl who dominates the foreground of the picture.

The rabbiters (1947) by Russell Drysdale (1912–81) documents the drought-stricken landscape west of New South Wales (see page 97). When he arrived in Australia from England in the early 1920s, Drysdale abandoned the stylistic conventions of his art school training in Paris to make way for a more appropriate colour palette and expression of form. In *The rabbiters* the heat haze located in the centre of the painting settles like a halo around the colossal, uprooted tree that is cradled by the rocks and boulders framing the picture. Two small figures forage in the foreground of the picture. Their shadows have been cast on the surface of the smooth pale stones, giving the illusion of more people in the space. The landscape is described from a low vantage point, which emphasises the oppressive heat of a ruinous long drought.

While landscapes are often considered to be portraits of nature devoid of human beings, the above-mentioned examples highlight the ways in which the human form is integral to the story of the land. What is observed on the surface of things is only one aspect to land, for there is life beneath, seismic activity and low frequency vibrations that we only notice when they threaten to break through.

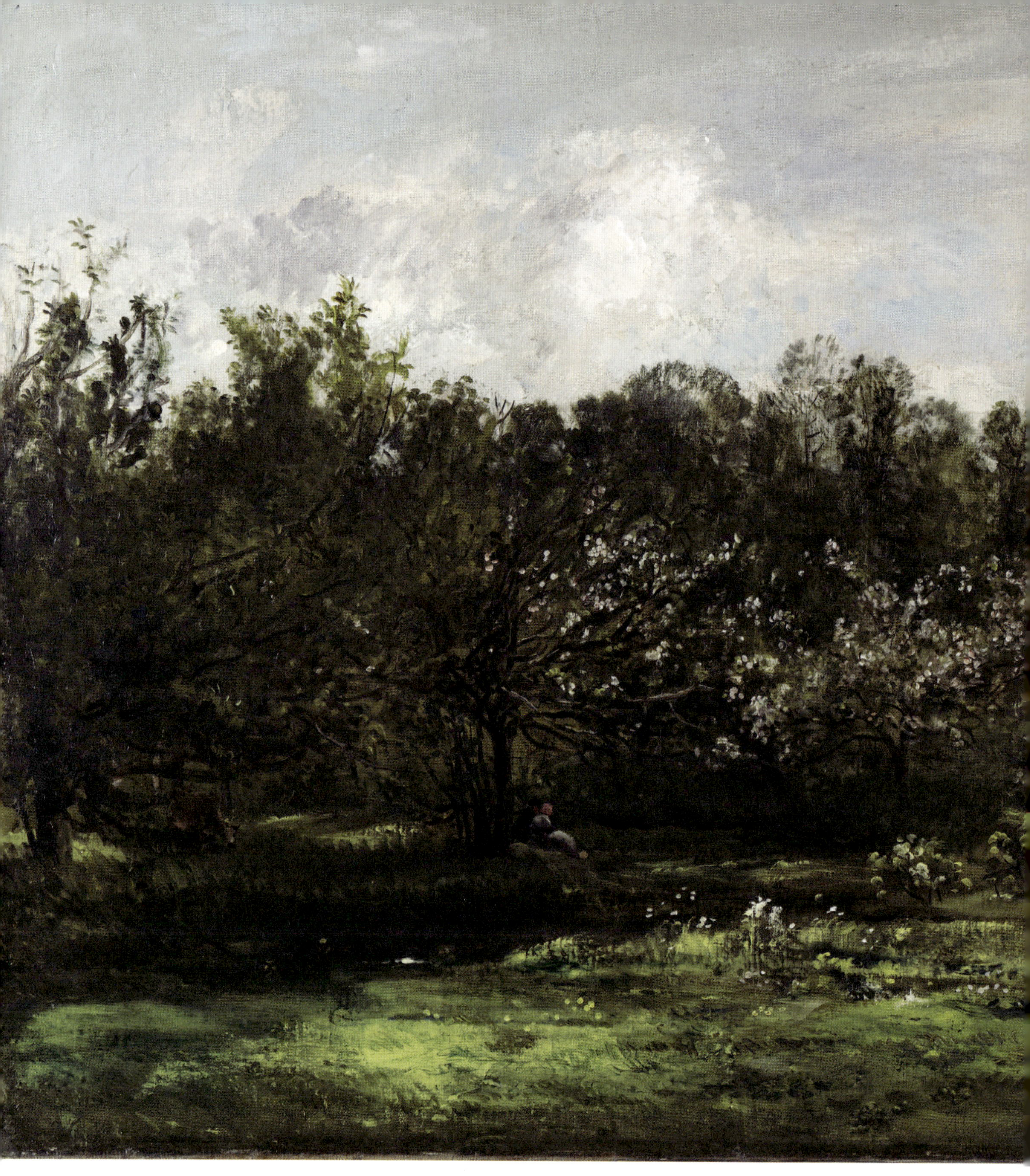

 Apple Trees in Blossom, 1874, oil on canvas, Charles-François Daubigny (French)

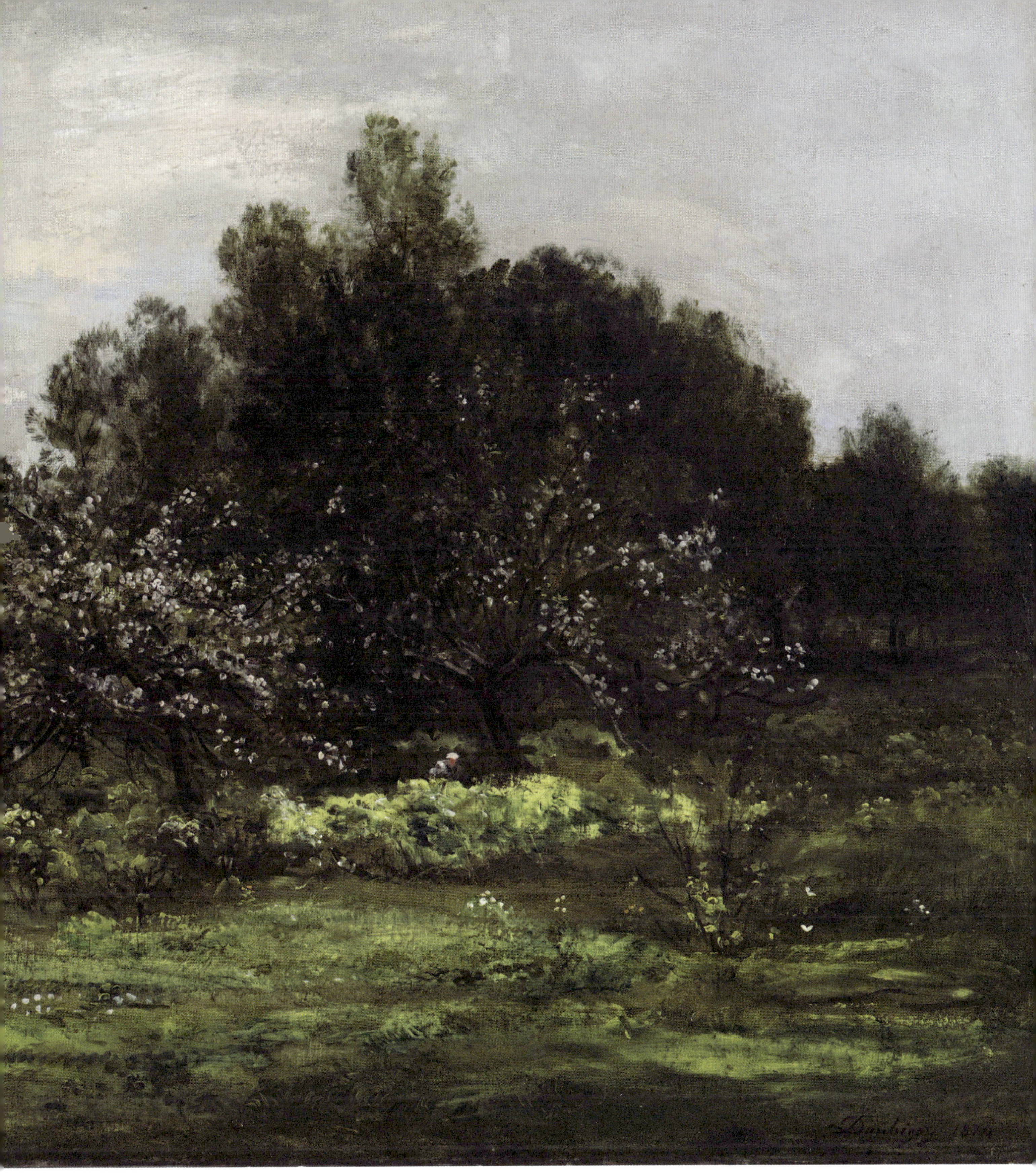

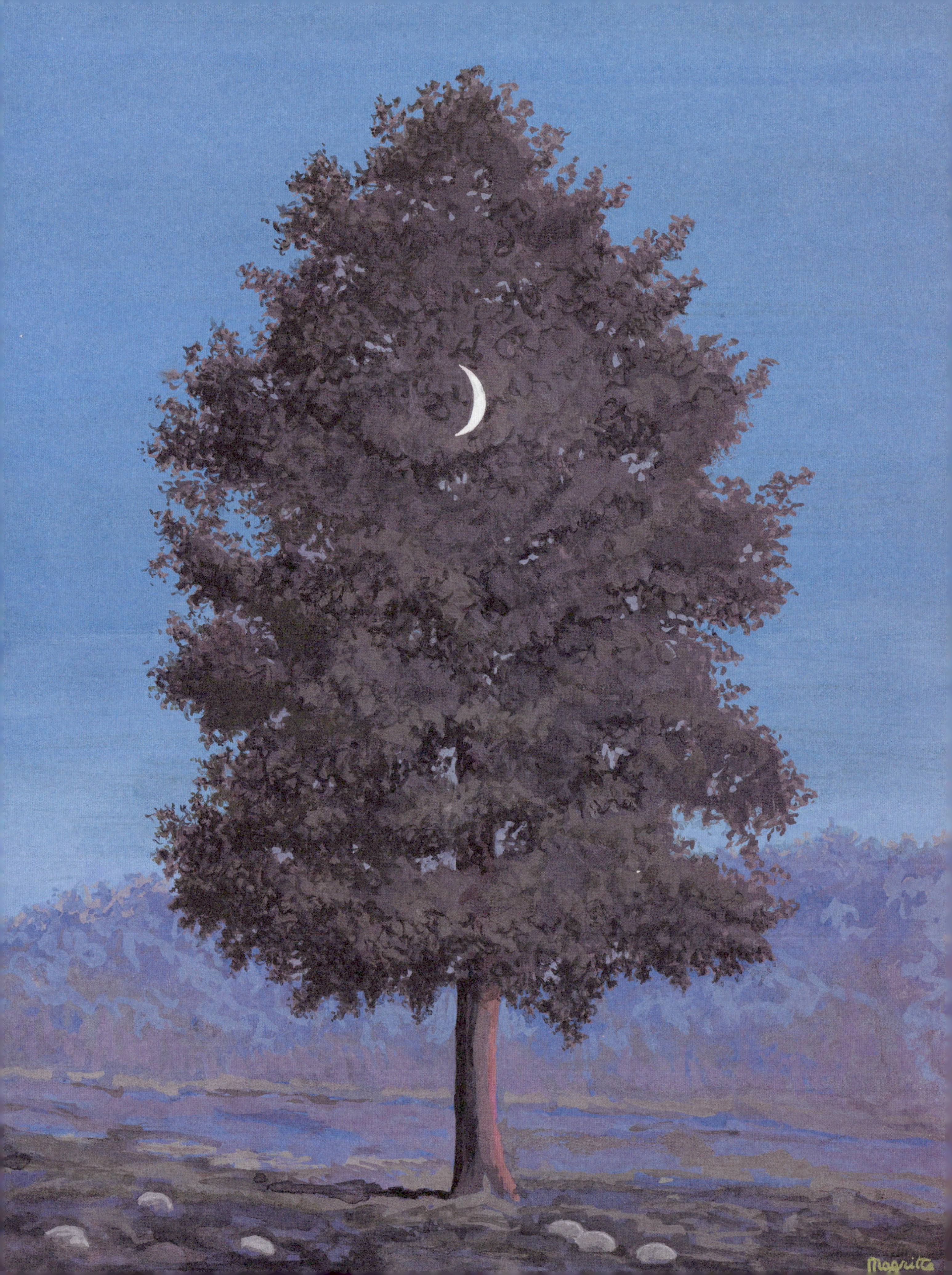
Magritte

TREES

TREE PORTRAITS CAN OFTEN BE READ AS EXPRESSIONS OF AFFECTION TOWARDS A PARTICULAR TREE OR SPECIES. SOME REPRESENTATIONS PLACE PROMINENCE ON SCALE, OR THE UNIQUE FORM OF BRANCHES, WHILE OTHERS MAY FOCUS ON THE ANCIENT AND MYTHOLOGICAL CHARACTERISTICS OF A TREE.

Opposite – *The Sixteenth of September*, c. 1956–58, gouache over graphite on paper, René Magritte (Belgian)

Top – *Moon Pine, Ueno*, 1857, woodblock print; ink and colour on paper, Utagawa Hiroshige (Japanese)

Bottom – *Laurel tree*, c. 1930, oil on board, Cedric Savage (New Zealander)

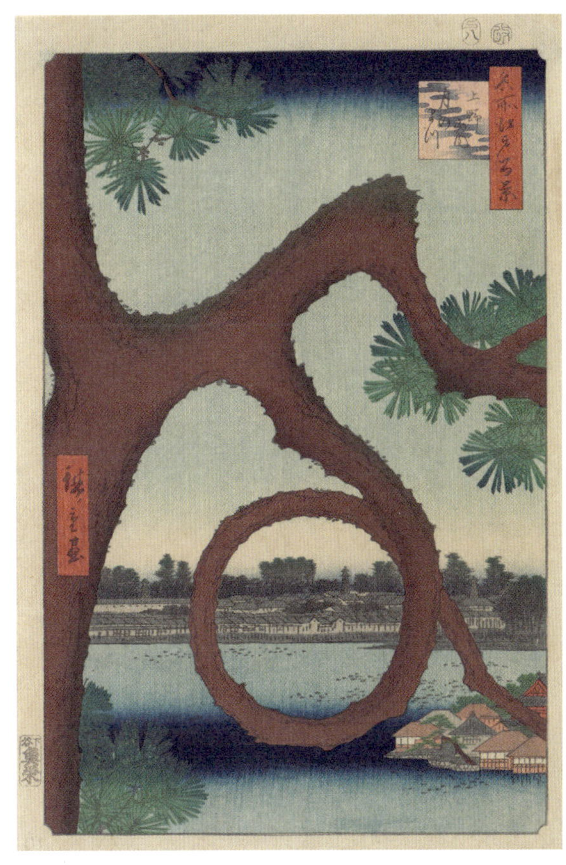

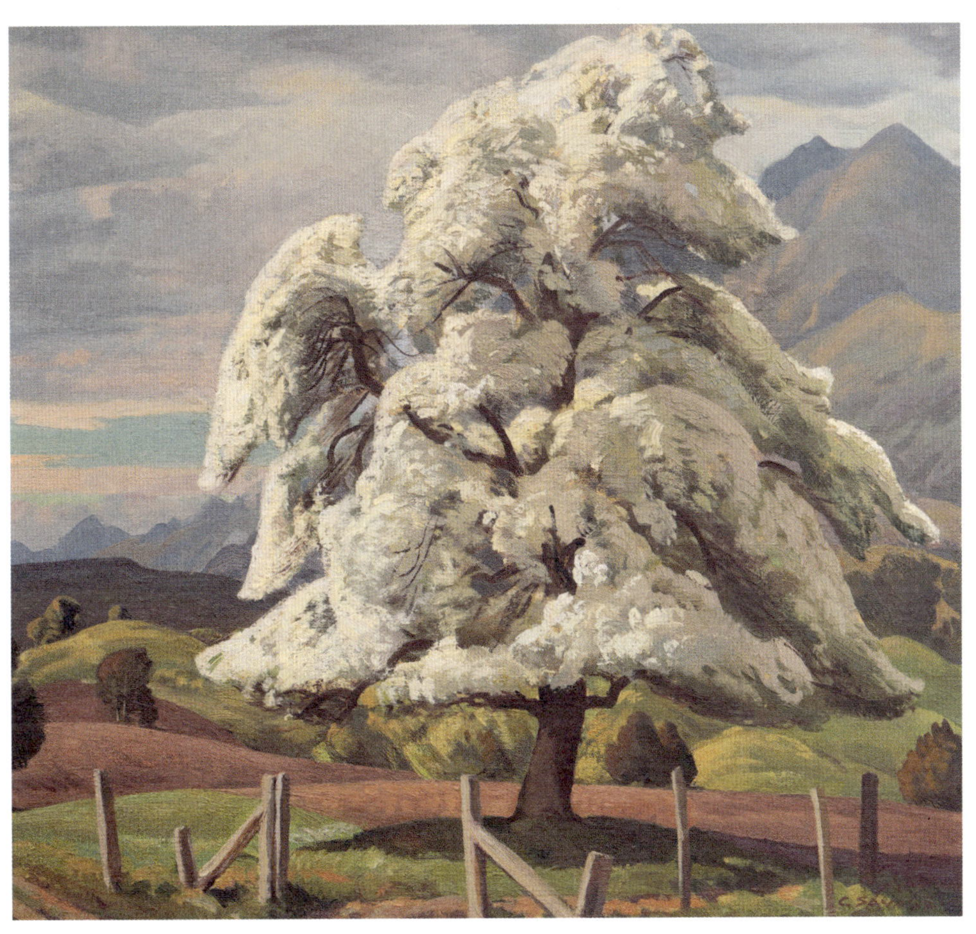

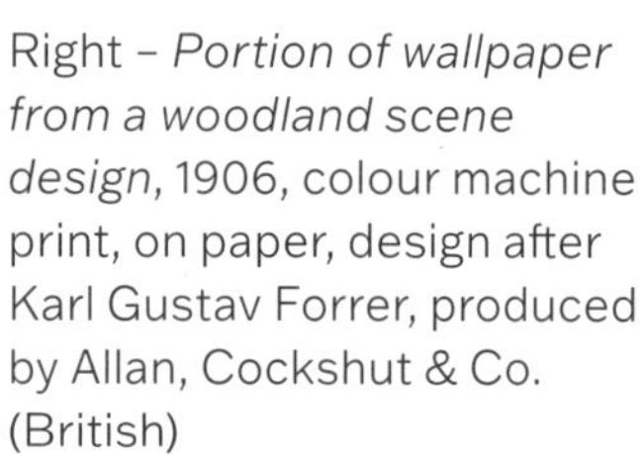

Right – *Portion of wallpaper from a woodland scene design*, 1906, colour machine print, on paper, design after Karl Gustav Forrer, produced by Allan, Cockshut & Co. (British)

Opposite top left – *Jar with pine tree*, c. 1900, stoneware, overglaze, Unknown artist (Japanese)

Opposite top right – *Forest scene with oak trees*, early 19th century, oil on canvas, John Crome (British)

Opposite bottom – *The Lawrence Tree*, 1929, oil on canvas, Georgia O'Keeffe (American)

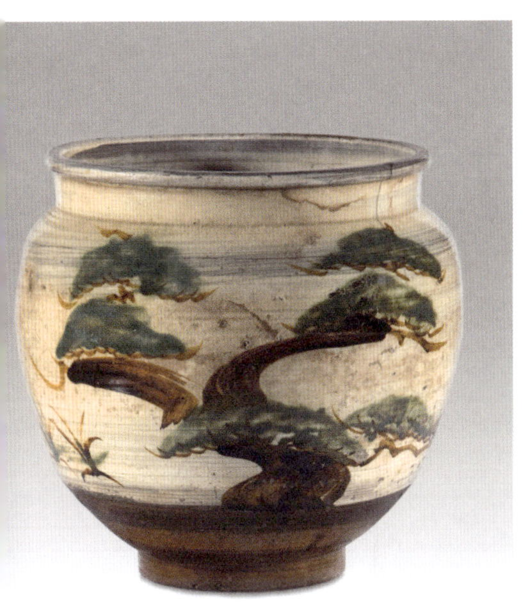

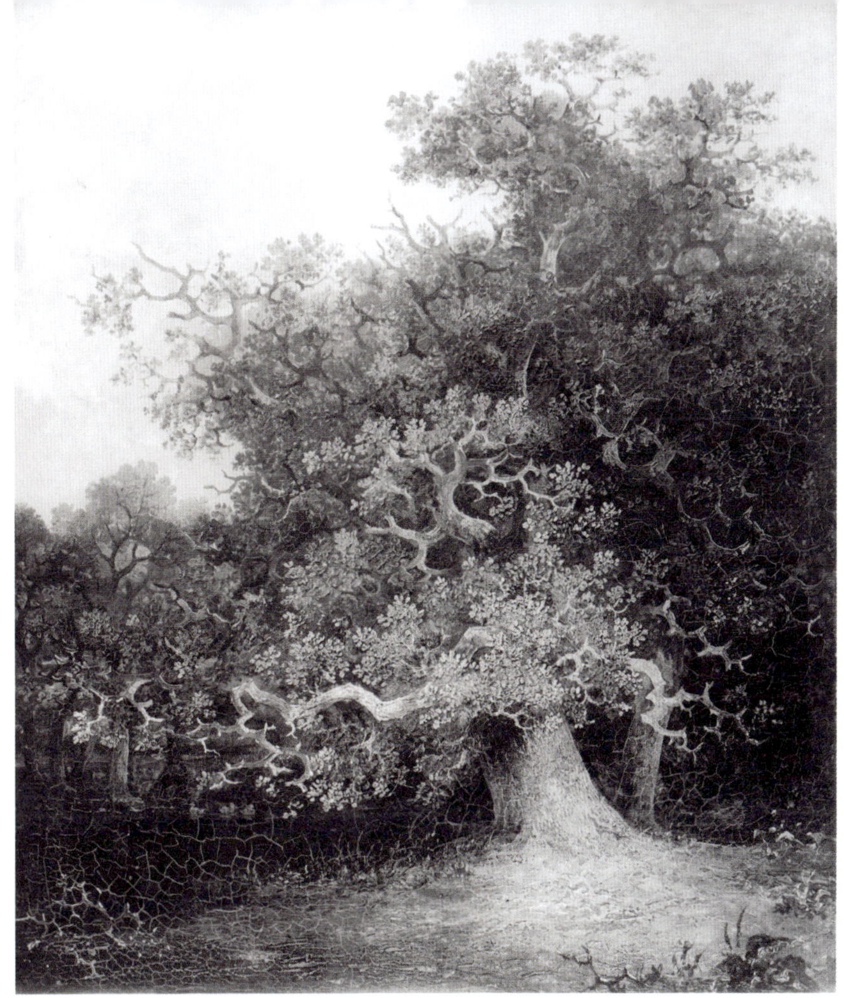

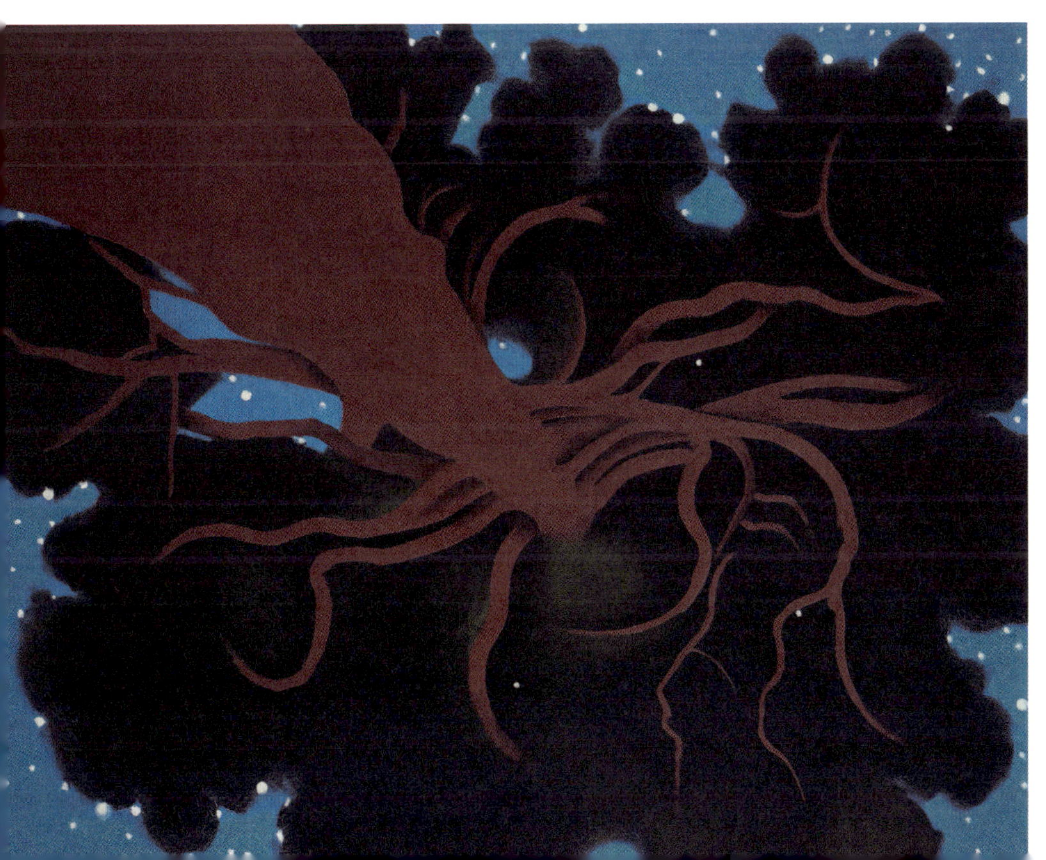

GEORGIA O'KEEFFE CREATED A PORTRAIT OF THE PONDEROSA PINE TREE LOCATED ON THE NEW MEXICO PROPERTY OF NOVELIST D H LAWRENCE AND HIS WIFE FRIEDA. SHE LAY BENEATH THE TREE JUST AS LAWRENCE DID, TO CAPTURE THIS TRULY MAGICAL PERSPECTIVE OF LOOKING UP AT THE STARRY SKY THROUGH ITS BOUGHS.

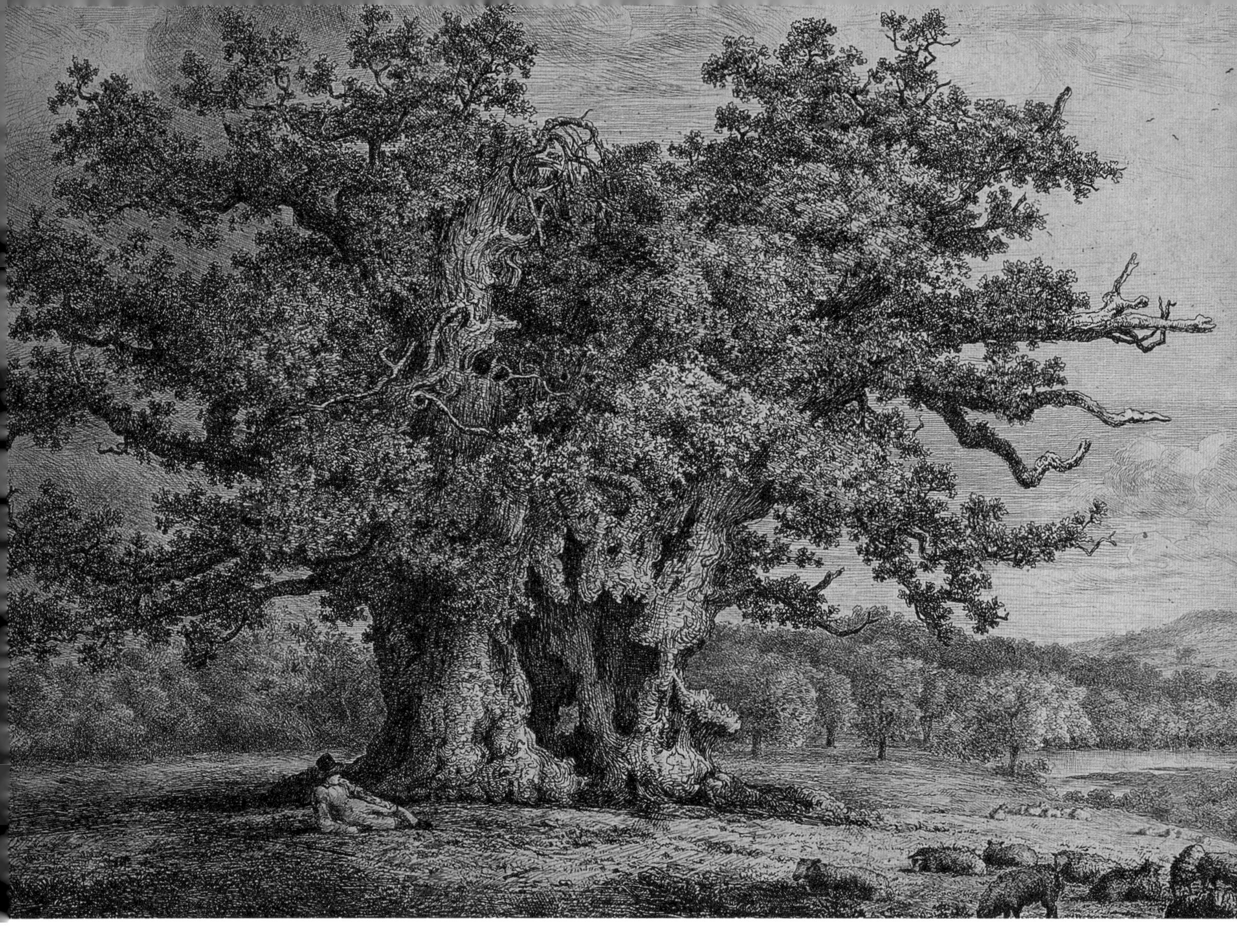

A gnarled and hollow old oak tree (Quercus robur L.) sheltering a shepherd and his sheep (detail), 1823, etching, Jacob George Strutt (British)

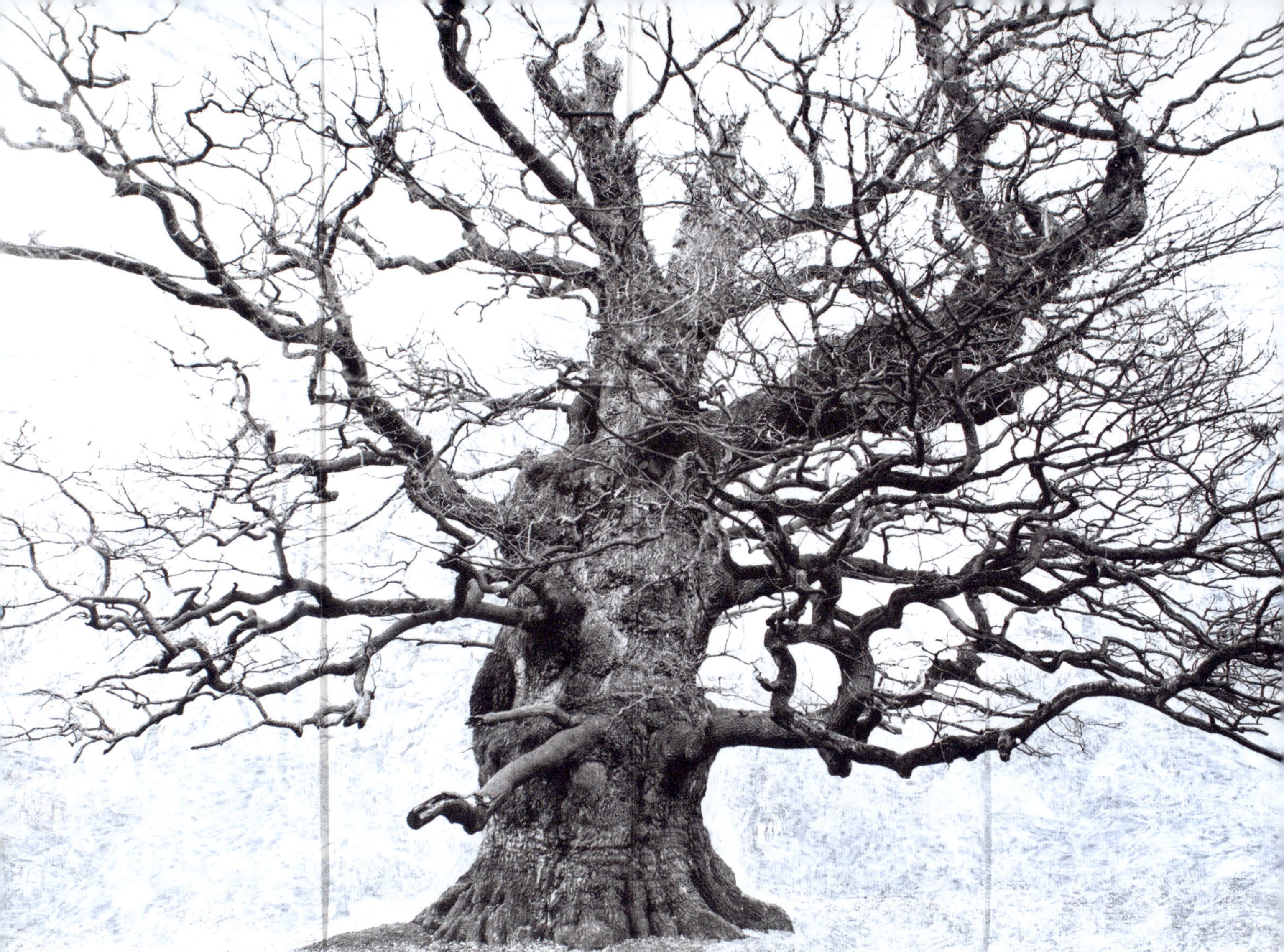

NOTICE THE REMARKABLE SILHOUETTE OF THE BOUGHS ON THE LEAFLESS OAK TREE COMPARED WITH THE APPEARANCE OF THE ONE ADORNED WITH LEAVES. IN BOTH IMAGES THE MAGNIFICENCE OF SCALE IS CONVEYED BY THE IMPRESSIVE CROWN THAT EXTENDS TO THE OUTER EDGES OF THE FRAMES.

IN CONTRAST, THE SMALL-SCALE TREES ON THE FOLLOWING PAGE, MADE OF JADE AND OTHER PRECIOUS MATERIALS, ARE REMINISCENT OF THE AESTHETIC IN TANG DYNASTY CHINA. THESE OBJECTS WERE USED AS TOOLS FOR CONTEMPLATION, AND AS A REMINDER OF THE INSEPARABLE CONNECTION BETWEEN HUMANKIND AND NATURE.

Majesty, 2006, gouache on photograph mounted on paper, Tacita Dean (British)

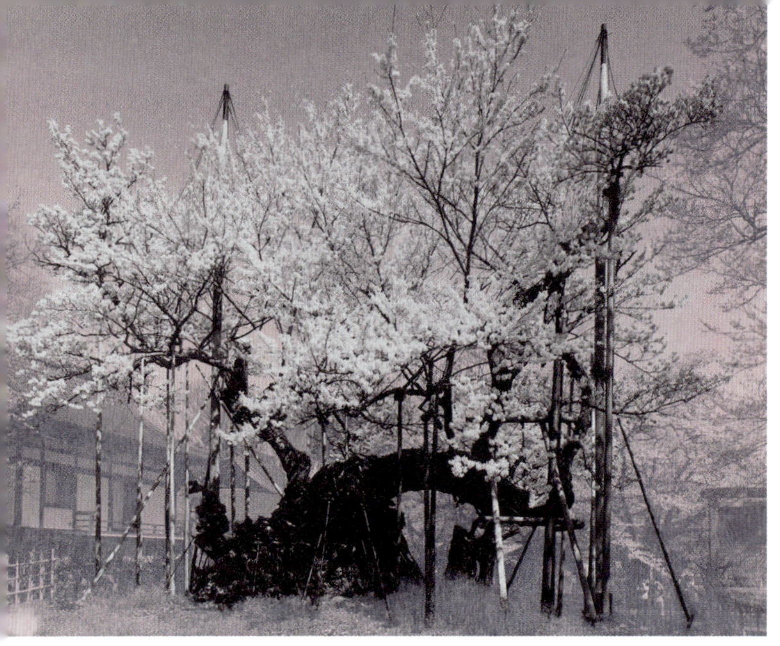

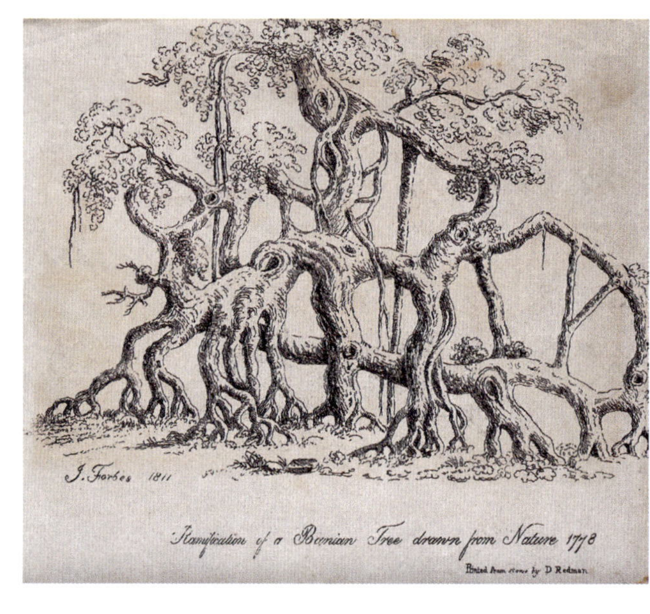

J. Forbes 1811
Ramification of a Banian Tree drawn from Nature 1778
Printed from stone by D Redman

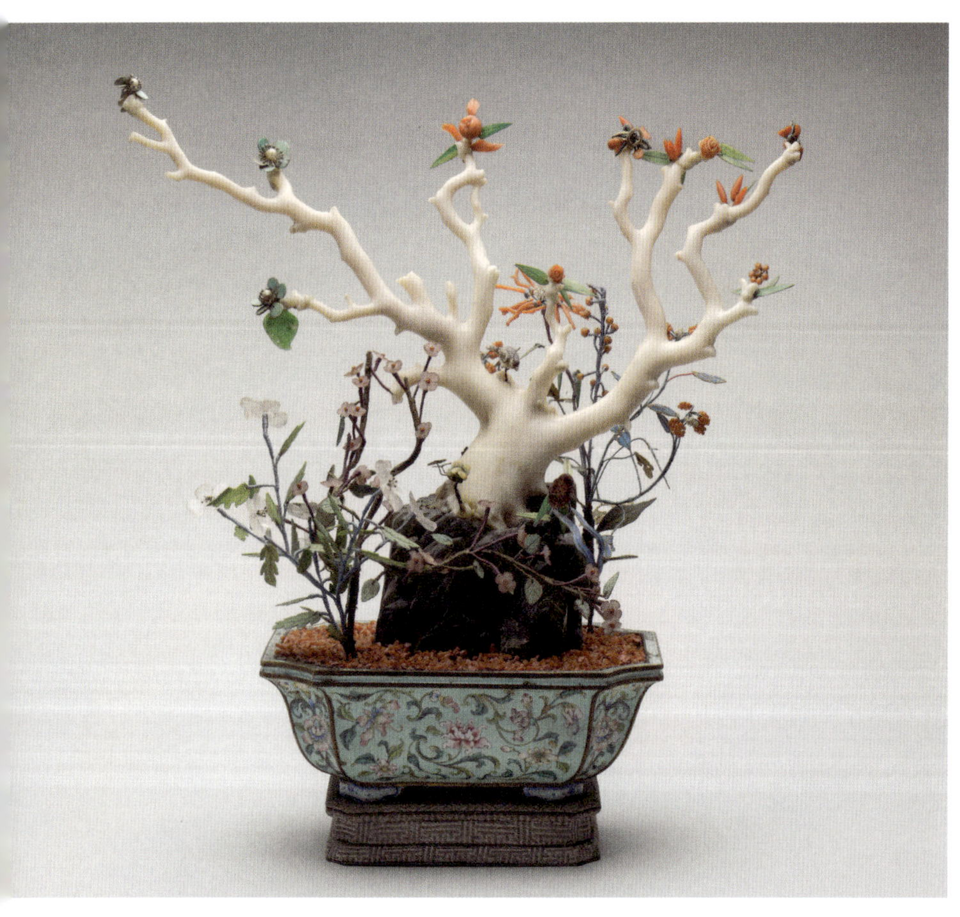

Opposite top – *Small Sakura Study (Jindai II)*, 2023, coloured pencil on handprinted Foma matte silver gelatin photograph mounted on paper, Tacita Dean (British)

Opposite middle – *Banyan tree (Ficus benghalensis L.) with many trunks*, 1811, lithograph, W Stoker (1811) after James Forbes (1778) (British)

Opposite bottom – *Pair of miniature trees in enamelled basins* (one of a pair), second half of 18th century, painted enamles on copper, coral, ivory and various stones, Unknown artist (Chinese)

Top – *Pine tree in bowl*, c. 1896–1908, painted matt gilt, wire and diamonds, Henrik Immanuel Wigström (Finnish)

Bottom – *Three Friends of Winter* (right of a pair), first half of 19th century, ink with flecks of gold pigment on paper, Yamamoto Baiitsu (Japanese)

Following – *The Forest Stream* (detail), c. 1660, oil on canvas, Jacob van Ruisdael (Dutch)

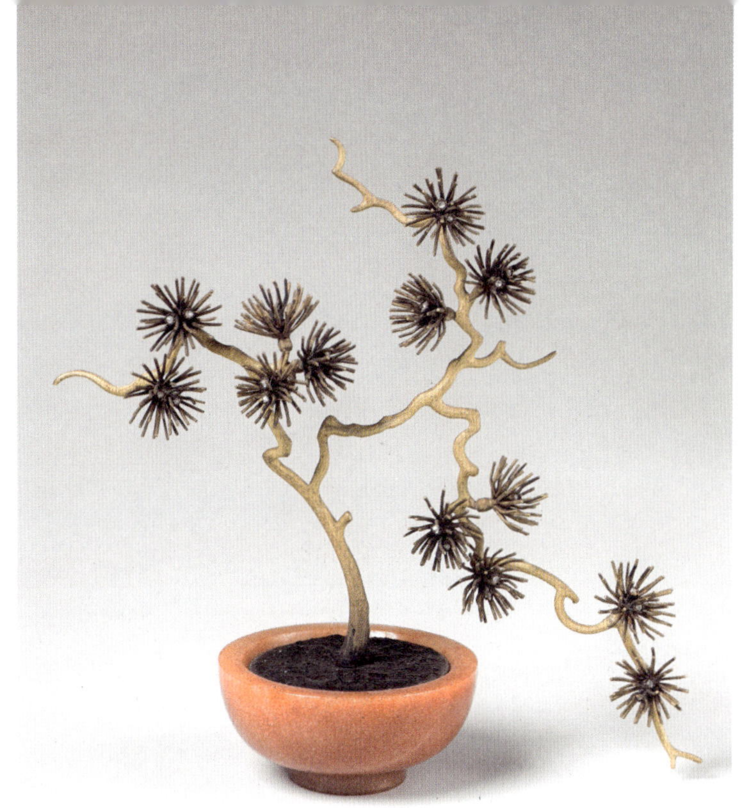

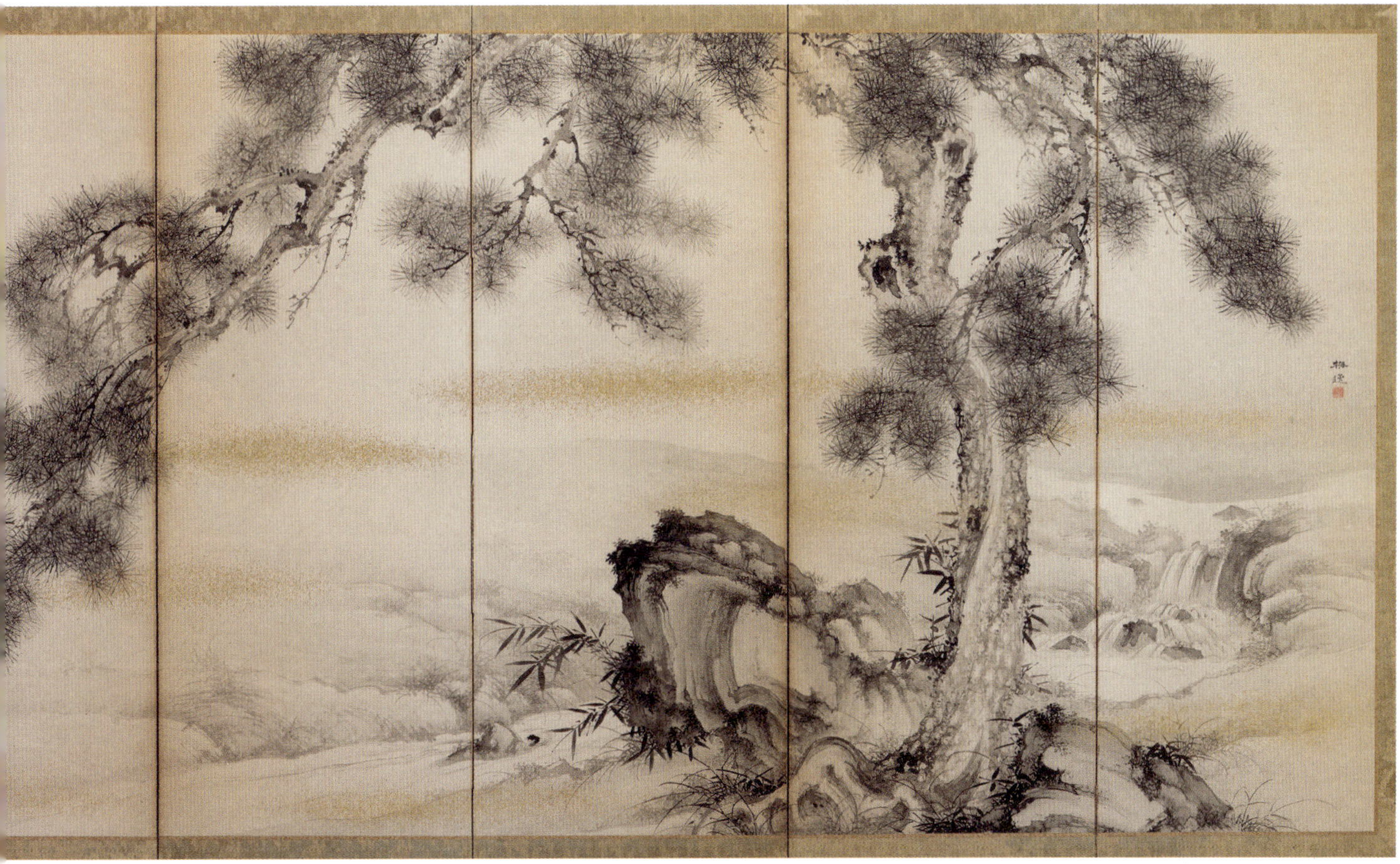

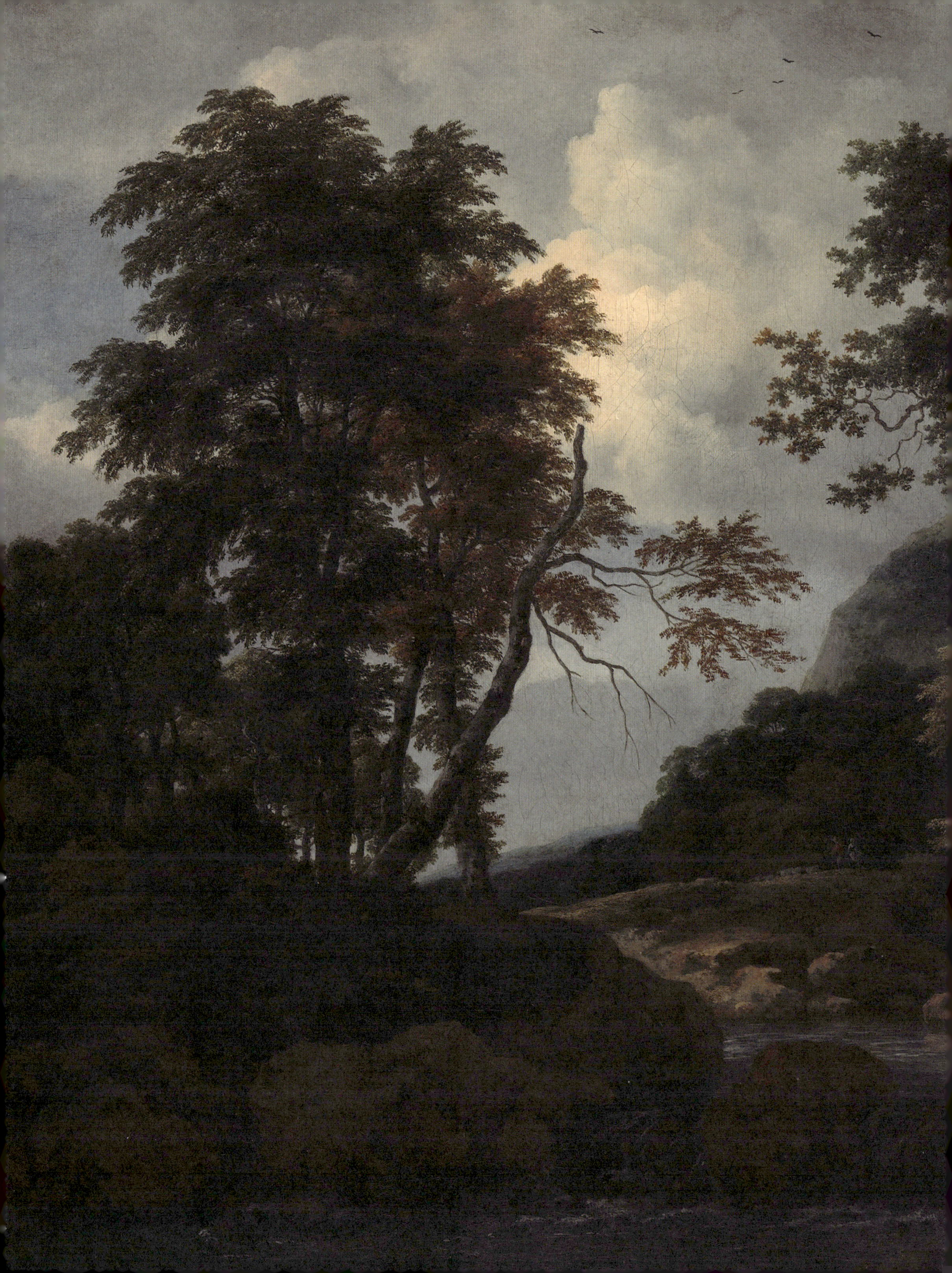

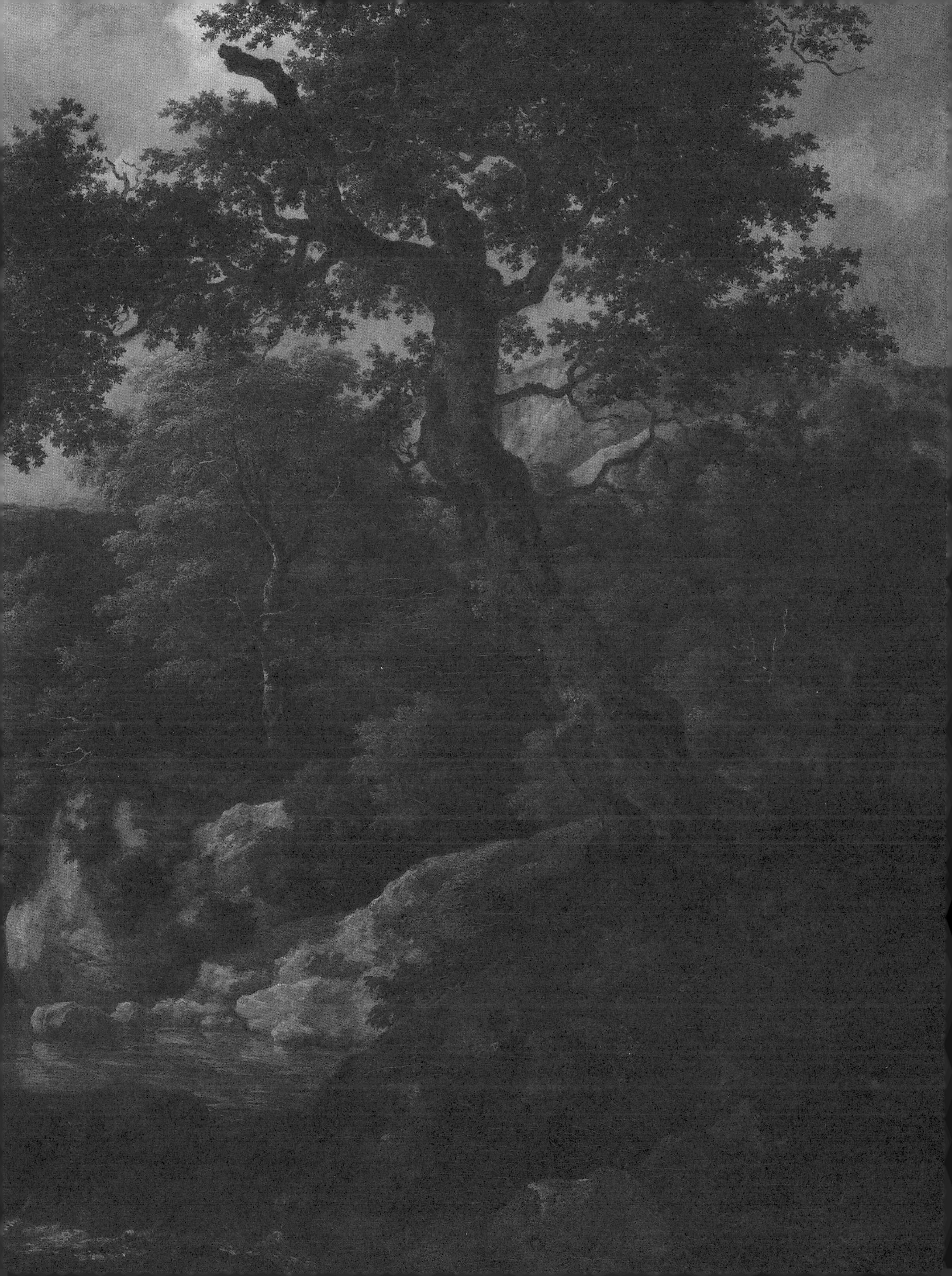

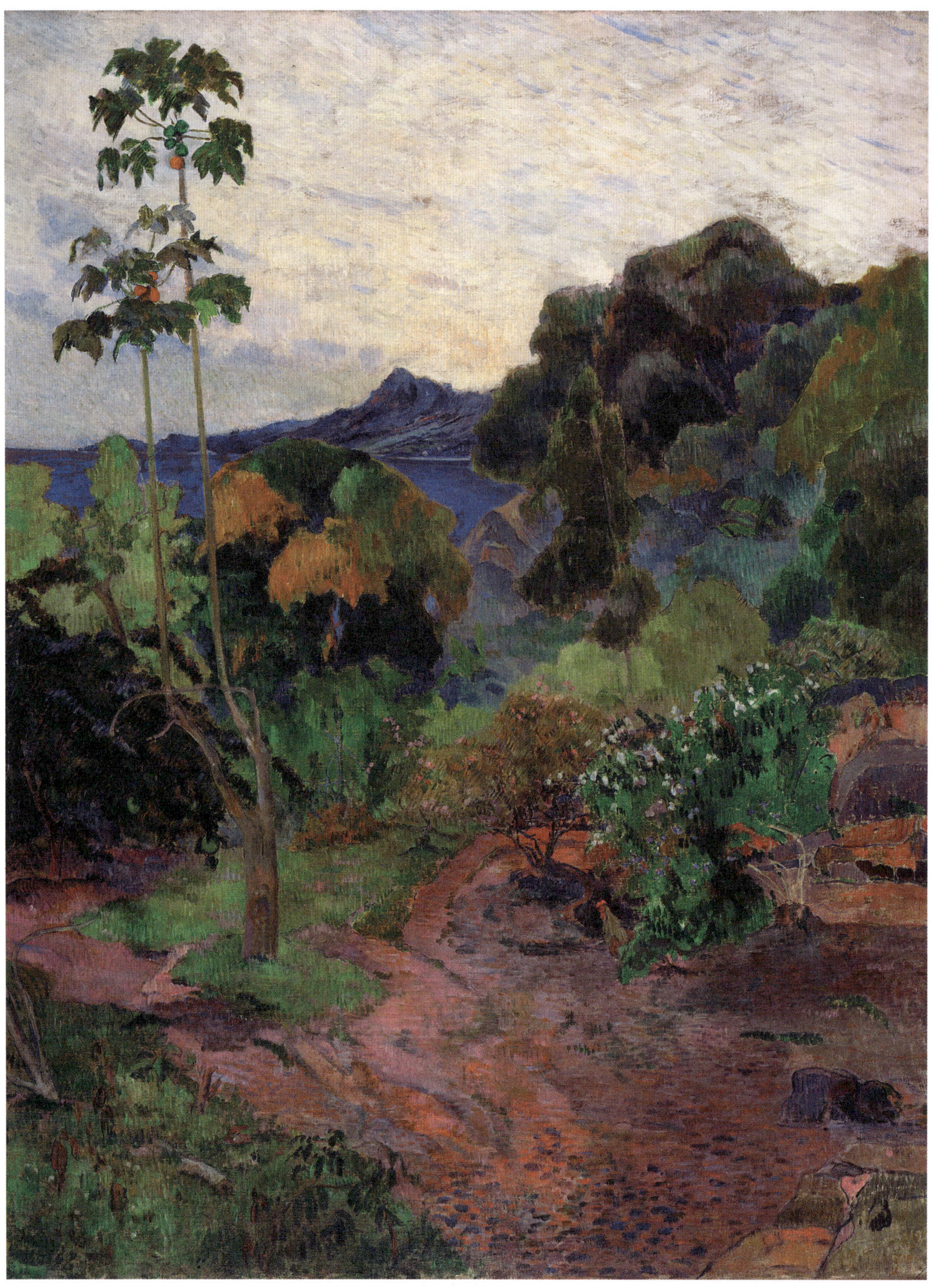

 Martinique Landscape, 1887, oil on canvas, Paul Gauguin (French)

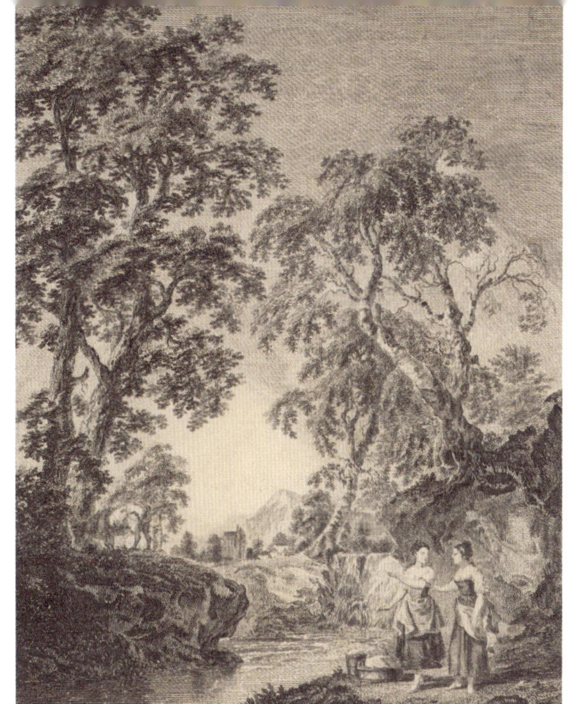

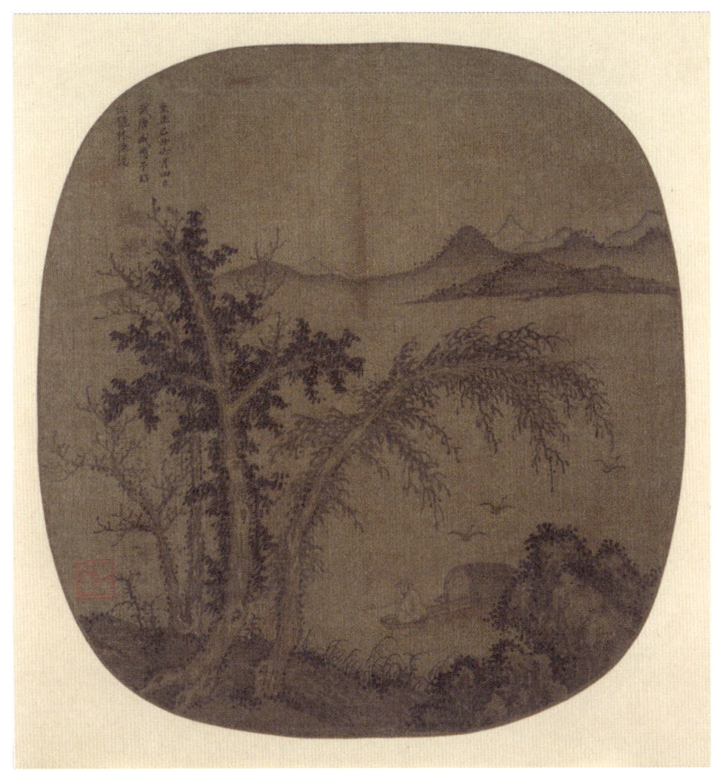

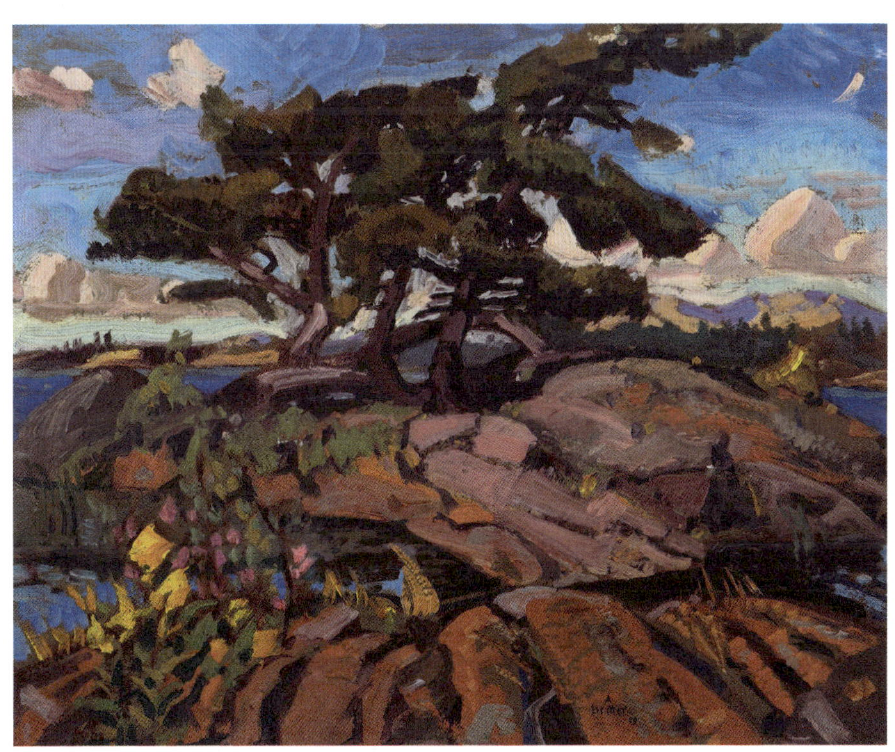

Top – *Peggy and Jenny,* 1758, illustration for *The Gentle Shepherd* by Allan Ramsay, Paul Sandby (etcher) & David Allan (draughtsman) (British)

Middle – *Recluse Fisherman, Autumn Trees*, c. 1349, fan mounted as an album leaf; ink and colour on silk, Sheng Mao (Chinese)

Bottom – *Little Island, MacGregor Bay*, 1929, oil on wood-pulp board, Arthur Lismer (Canadian)

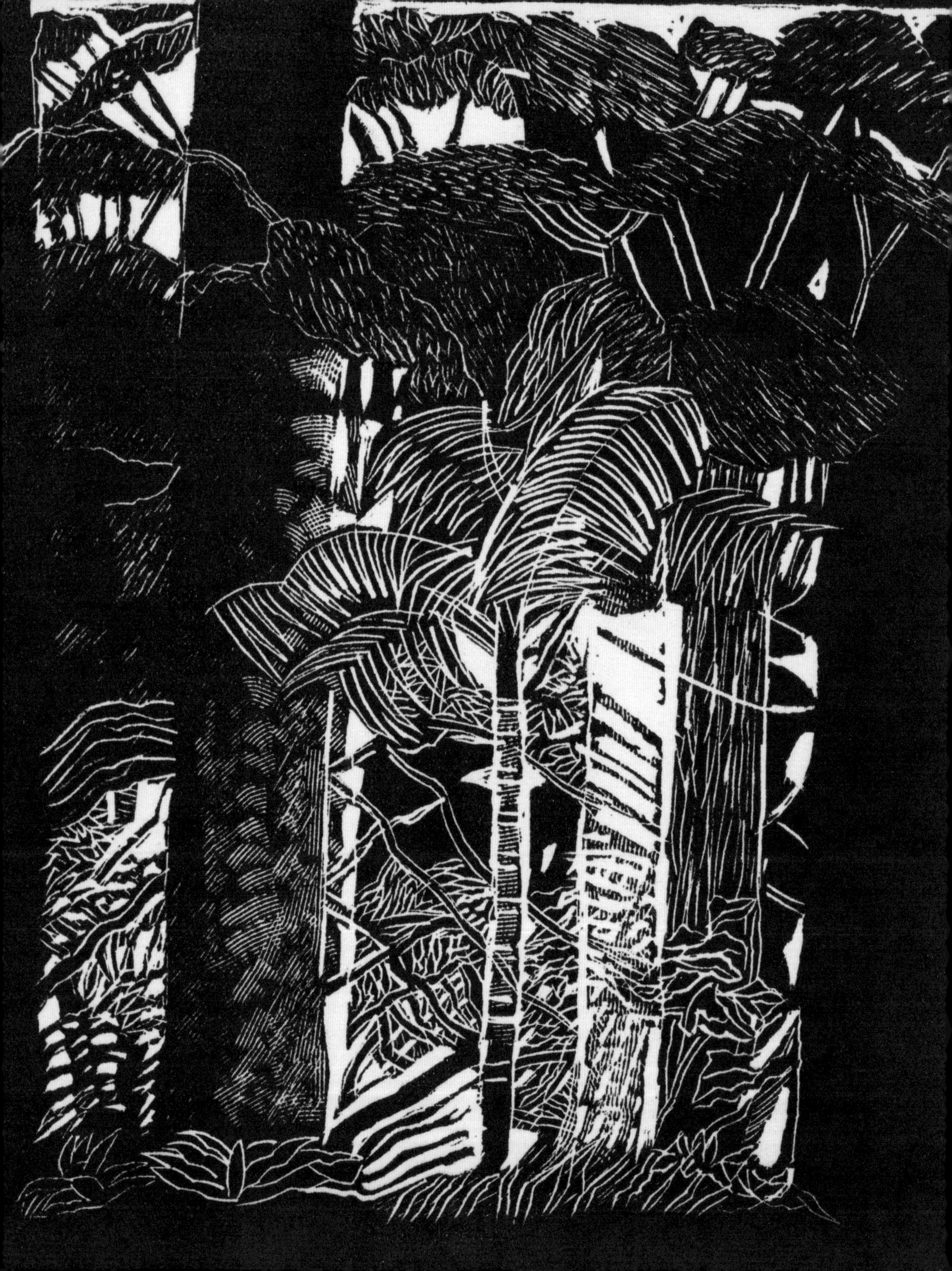

OBSERVE THE DISTINCT LINE WORK USED TO RENDER THE SHAPE OF THE TREE FERNS, PALMS AND SUGAR CANE BLOOM. USING DIFFERENT TECHNIQUES EACH ARTIST CONVEYS THE RECOGNISABLE AND UNIQUE FORM OF THESE TROPICAL SPECIES.

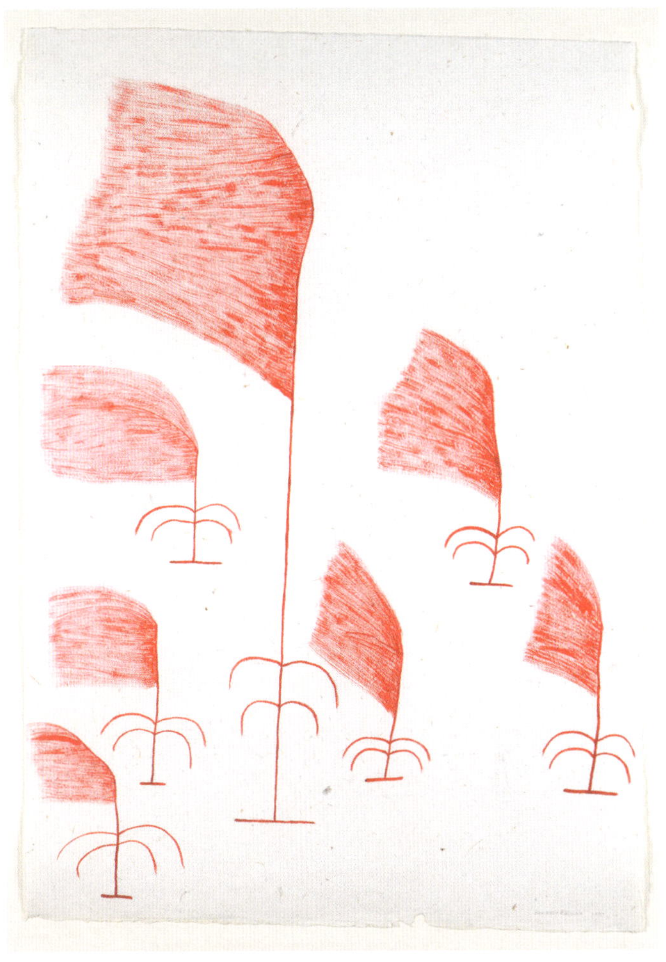

Opposite – *Winter Forest*, 2006, wood engraving printed in black ink on white wove paper, Ruth Burgess (Australian)

Top – *Shereka hemoshi*, 2020, acrylic on handmade cotton paper, Sheroanawe Hakihiiwe (Venezuelan)

Bottom – *Ferntree Gully, Dandenong Ranges, Victoria*, 1867, colour lithograph, Eugene von Guérard (Austrian)

Following – *Light over former times*, 1933, watercolour, Paul Klee (Swiss)

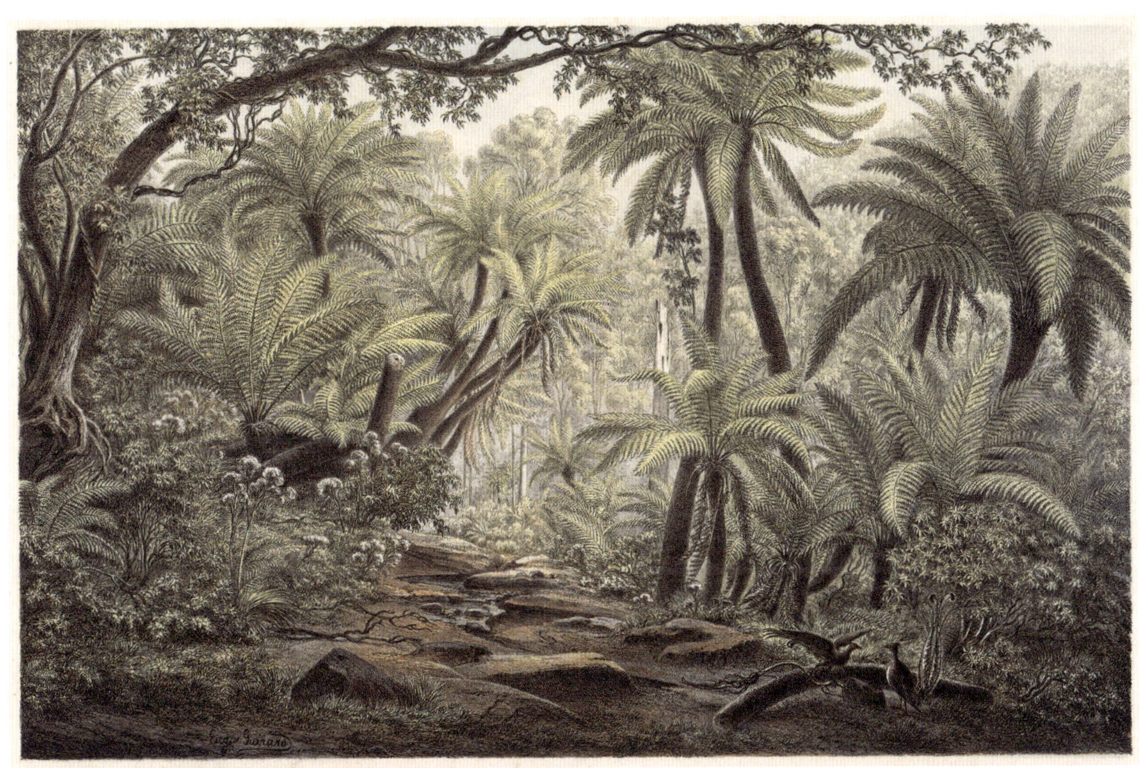

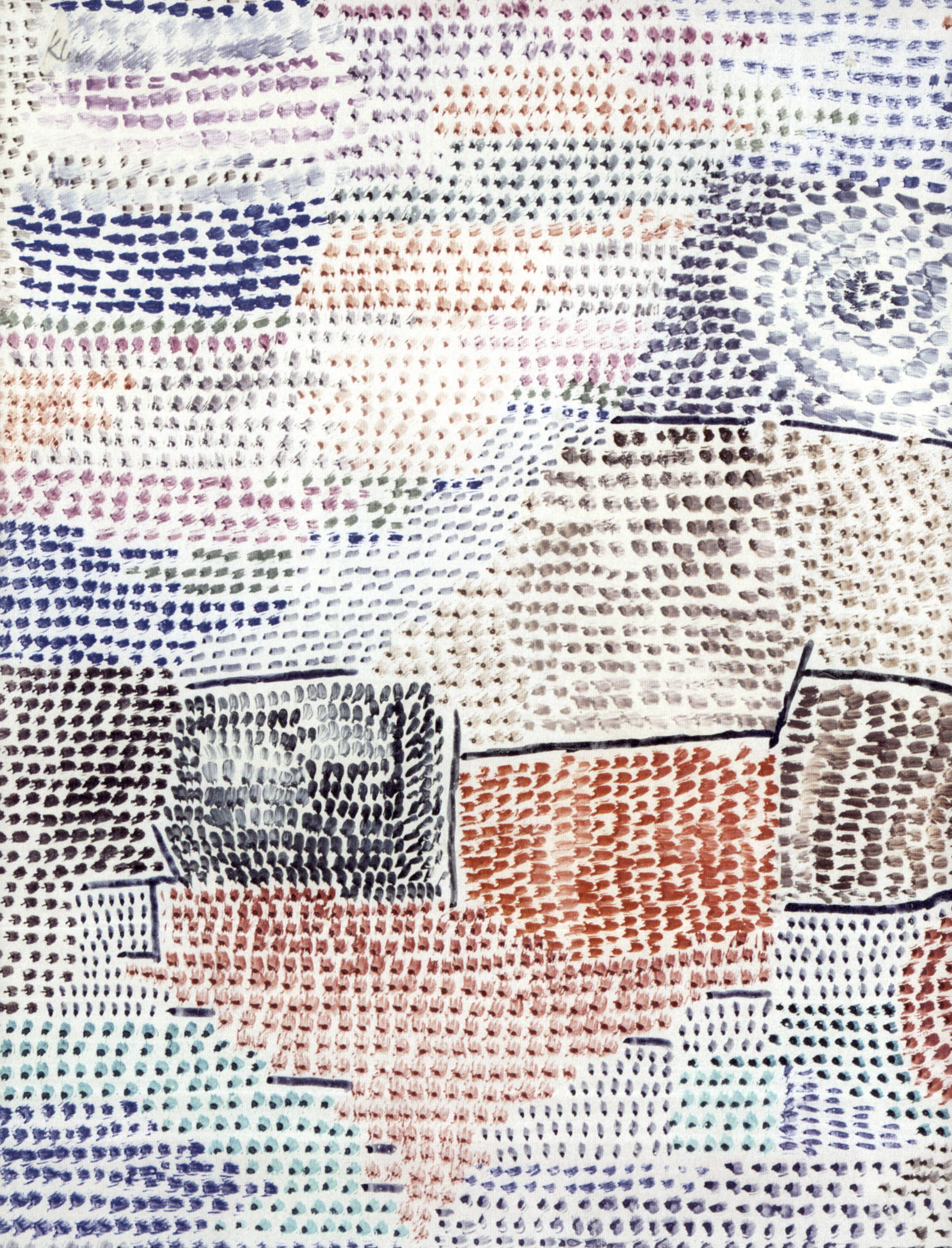
Klee

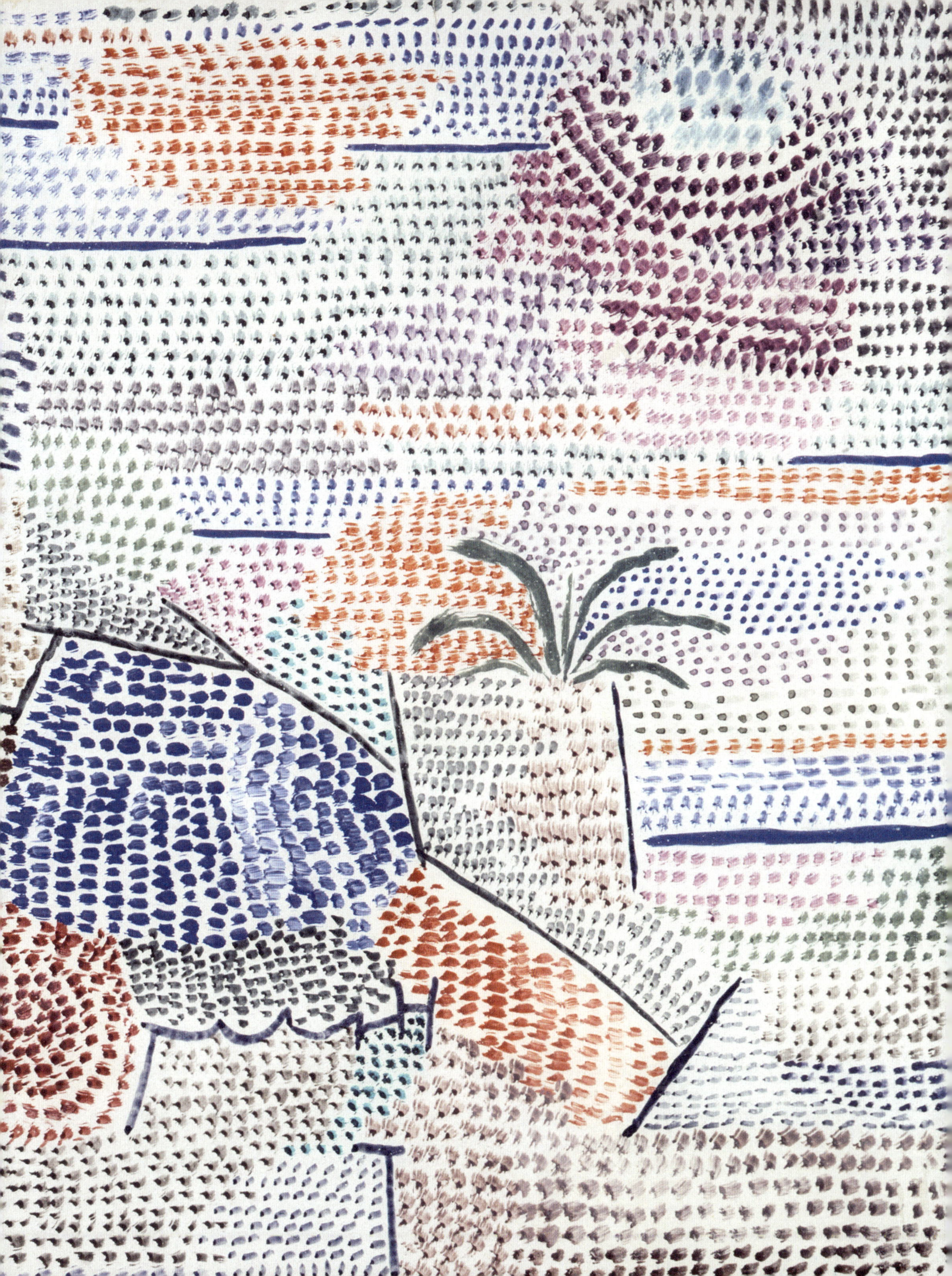

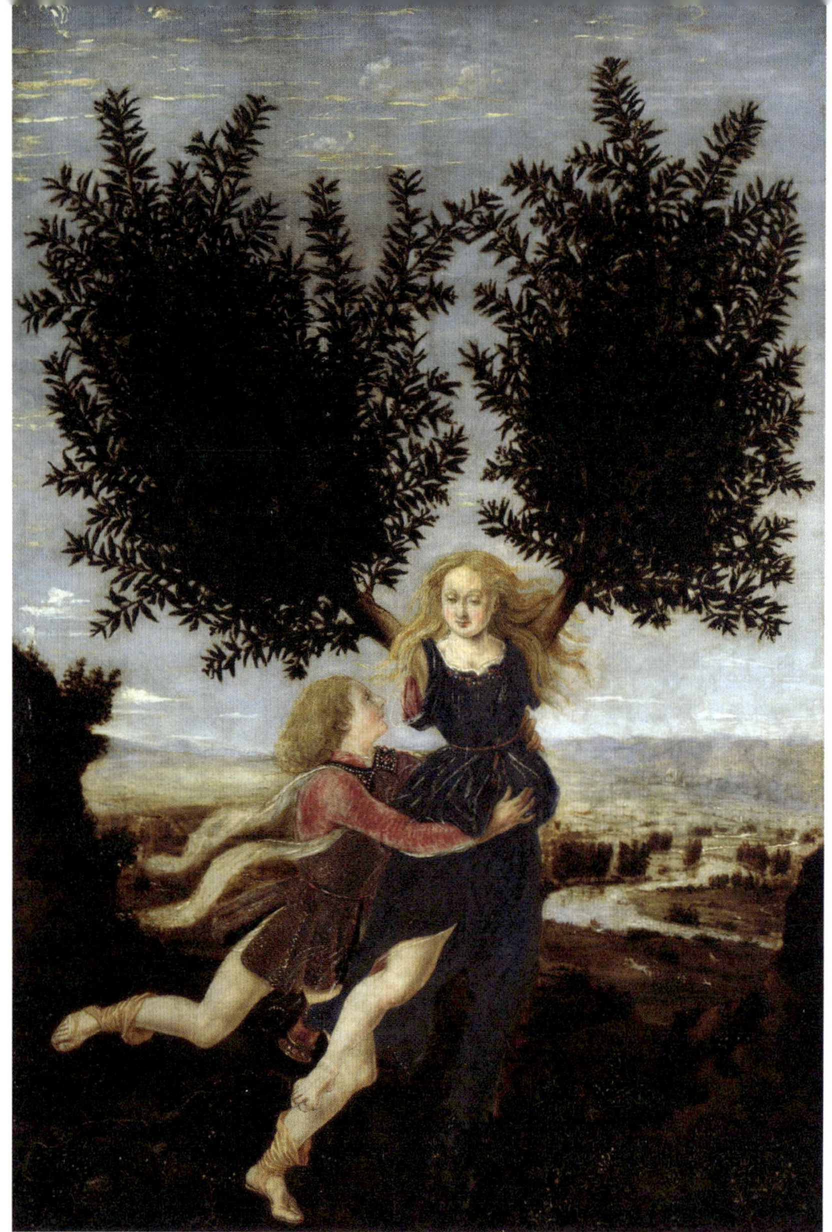

TREES PLAY AN ALLEGORICAL ROLE IN ART, OFTEN SYMBOLISING A MAGICAL TRANSFORMATION OR CHANGE.

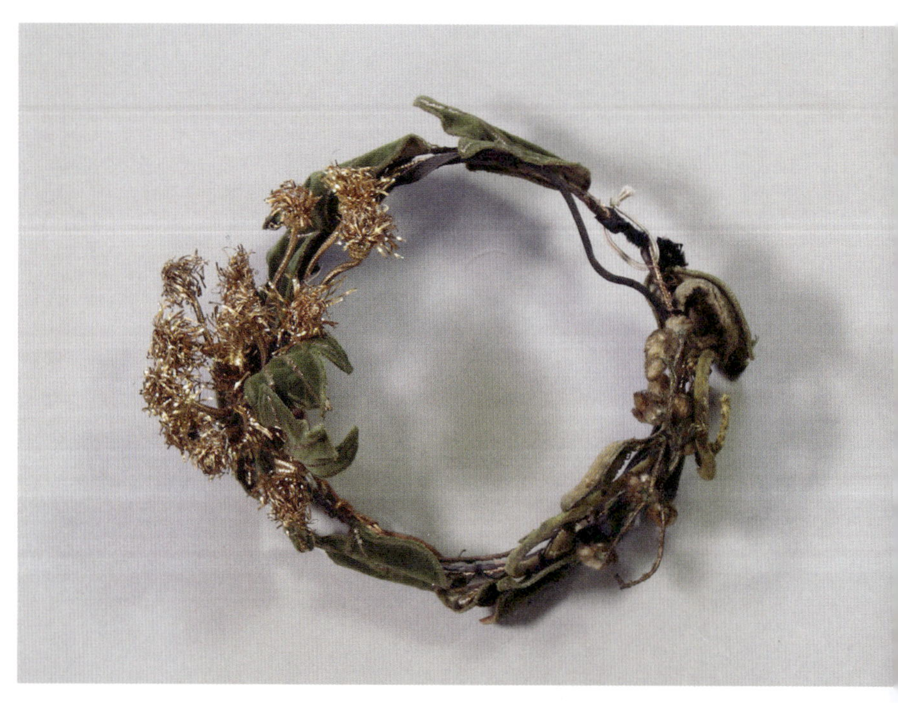

Top – *Apollo and Daphne*, c. 1470–80, oil on wood, Piero del Pollaiuolo (Italian)

Bottom – *Theatre costume (headdress for the Cavalier of the Fairy of the Woodland Glades in The Sleeping Beauty, Sadler's Wells Ballet, Convent Garden)*, 1960, millinery, Oliver Messel (designer) (British)

Opposite – *Vase*, c. 1820–25, hard-paste porcelain, Royal Porcelain Manufactory, Berlin (German)

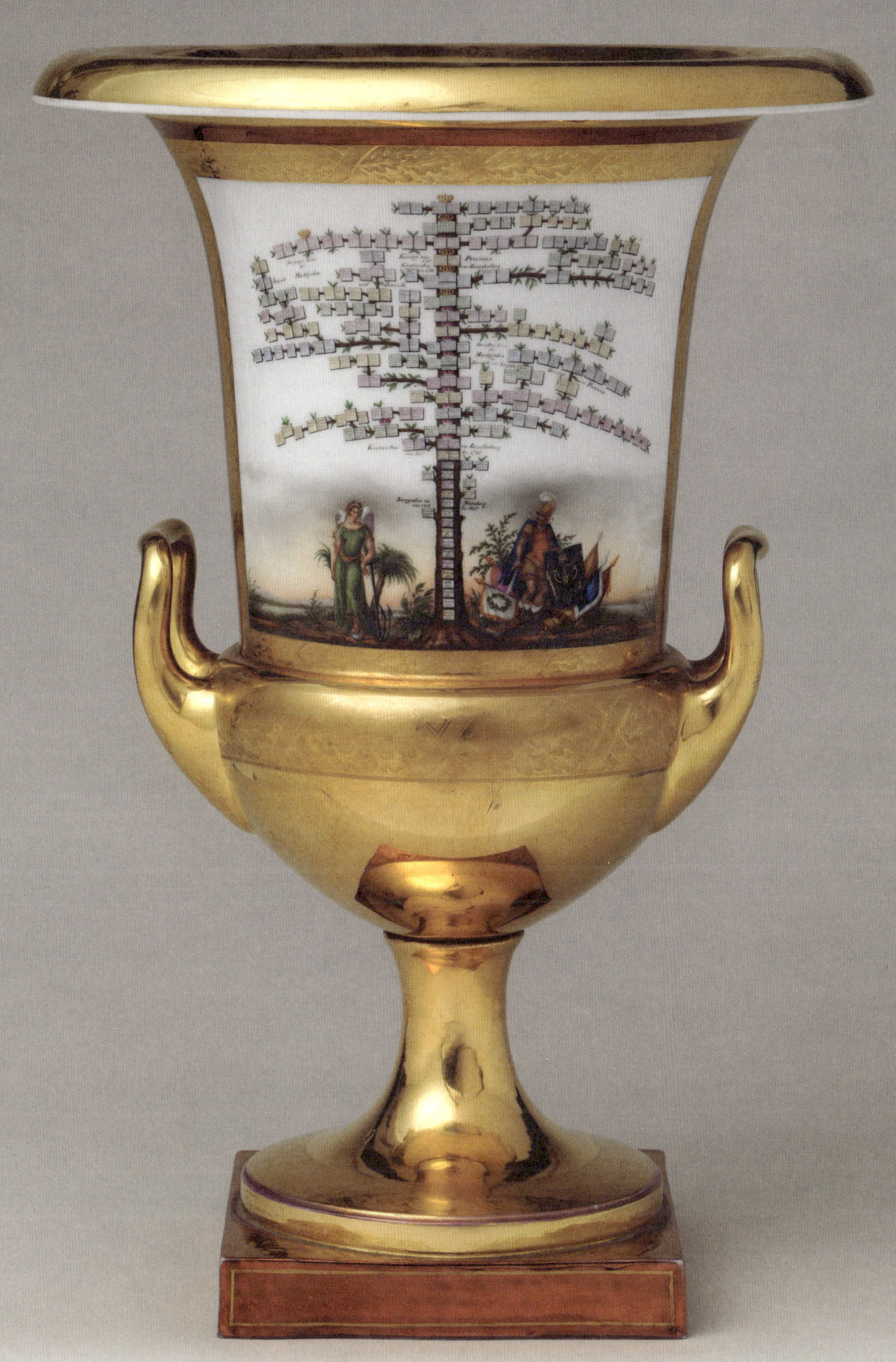

GUSTAV KLIMT HAD A FOND LOVE OF NATURE. IN *THE PARK* HE PRUDENTLY RENDERS DENSE FOLIAGE IN LUSH GREENS, VIOLET AND LAVENDER, WHICH CREATES A MESMERIC EFFECT. THE TREES SEEM COMPRESSED INTO THE SQUARE CANVAS, A FORMAT THAT EMERGED FROM HIS REGULAR USE OF A CARDBOARD VIEWFINDER WHEN LOOKING AT LANDSCAPES. THE SPECKLED OBJECTS IN THE FOREGROUND ARE DECEPTIVE. AT FIRST GLANCE THEY APPEAR TO BE FIGURES BENEATH THE LEAFY CROWN. UPON CLOSER INSPECTION THEY ARE TREE TRUNKS DECORATED IN KLIMT'S CHARACTERISTIC MOSAIC STYLE.

The Park, c. 1910, oil on canvas, Gustav Klimt (Austrian)

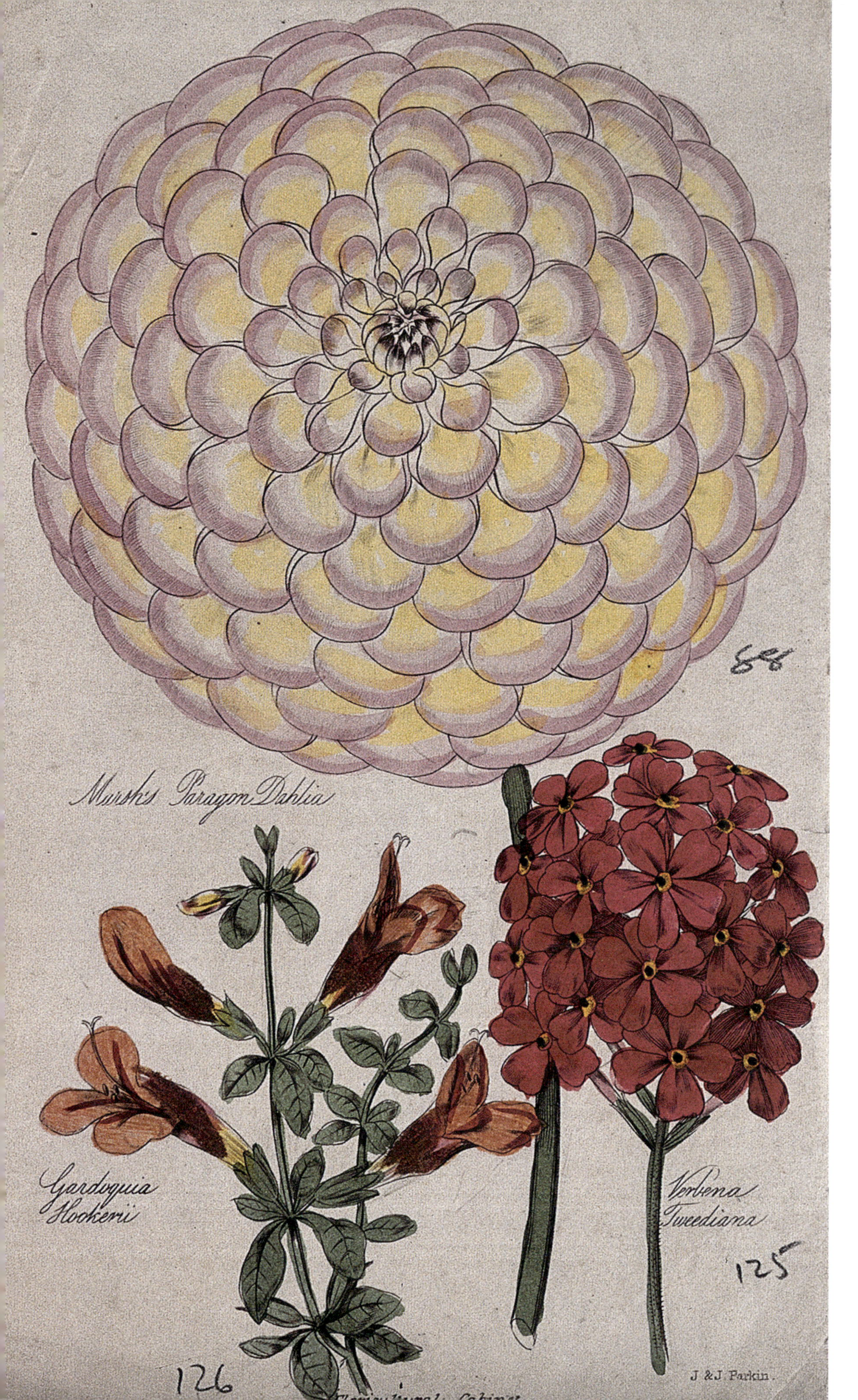
88
Marsh's Paragon Dahlia
Gardoquia
Hookerii
Verbena
Tweediana
125
126
J &J. Parkin.

PLANTS & FLOWERS

THE PORTRAYAL OF FLOWERS IN ART DEMANDS THE USE OF COLOUR. OBSERVE THE RANGE OF HUES AND TINTS APPLIED IN THE WORKS THAT FOLLOW AND INDULGE IN THE IMPACT THEY CAN HAVE ON MOOD AND FEELING.

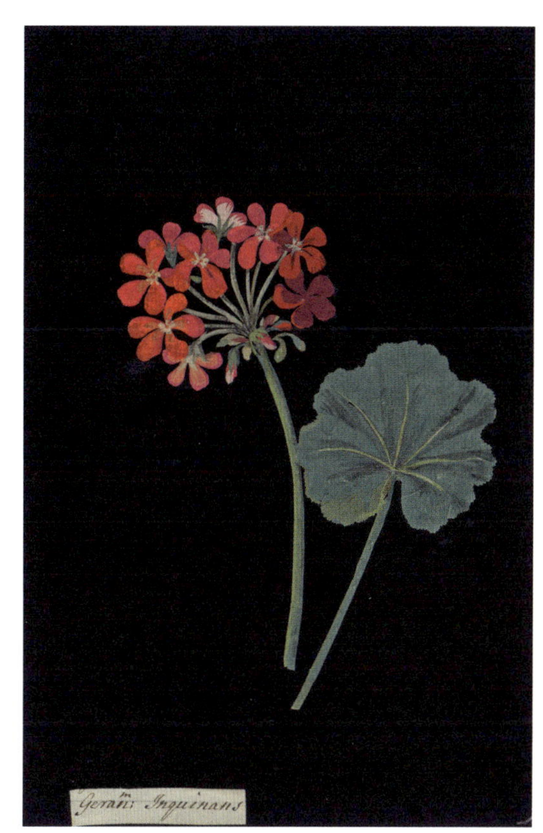

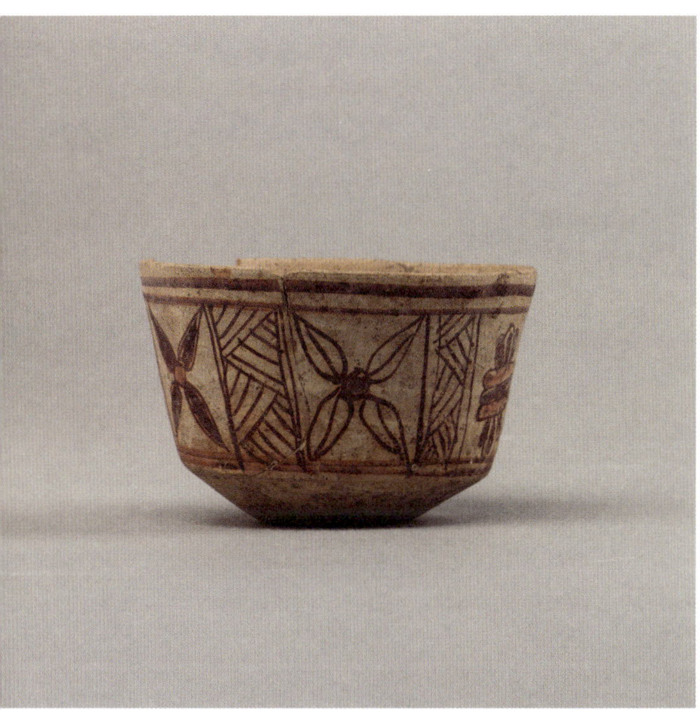

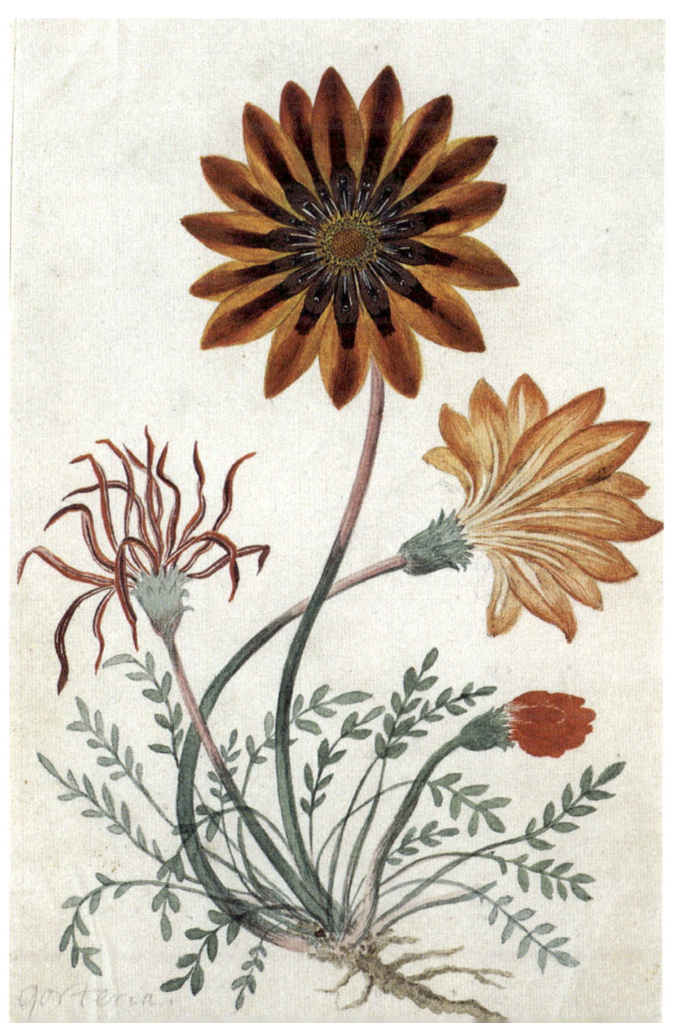

Opposite – *Three flowering plants: a garden dahlia (Dahlia cultivar), a calamint (Calamintha coccinea) and a verbena (Verbena tweediana)*, c. 1833–59, coloured engraving, J & J Parkin (British)

Top – *Geranium Inquinans, from an album (Vol.IV, 72)*, 1778, collage of coloured papers with bodycolour and watercolour on black ink background, Mary Delany (British)

Middle – *Bowl with floral and geometric designs*, c. 1st–3rd century, pottery and paint, Unknown artist (Sudanese)

Bottom – *Gorteria diffusa*, c. 1777–86, drawing, Robert Jacob Gordon (Dutch)

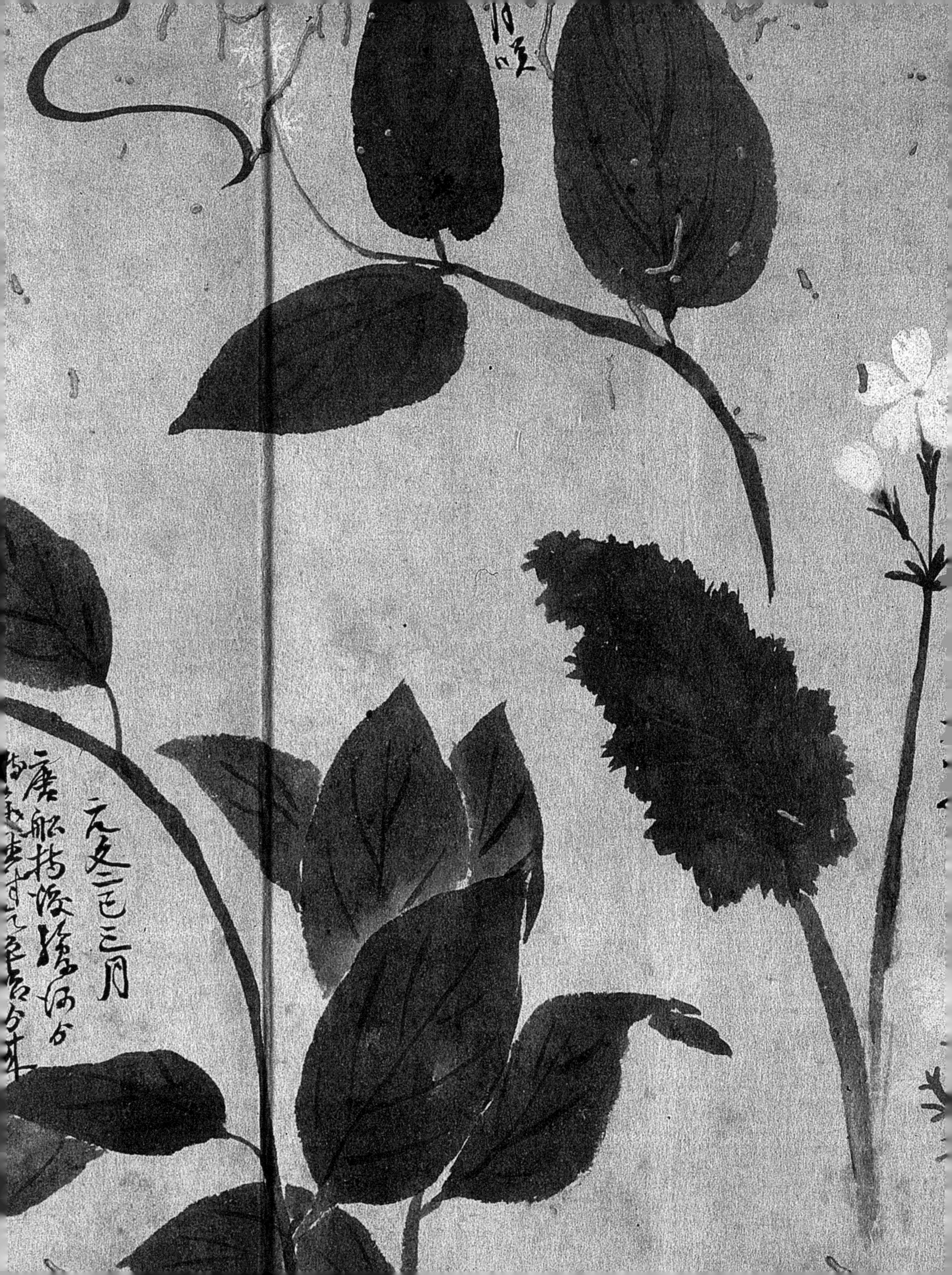
元文二巳三月

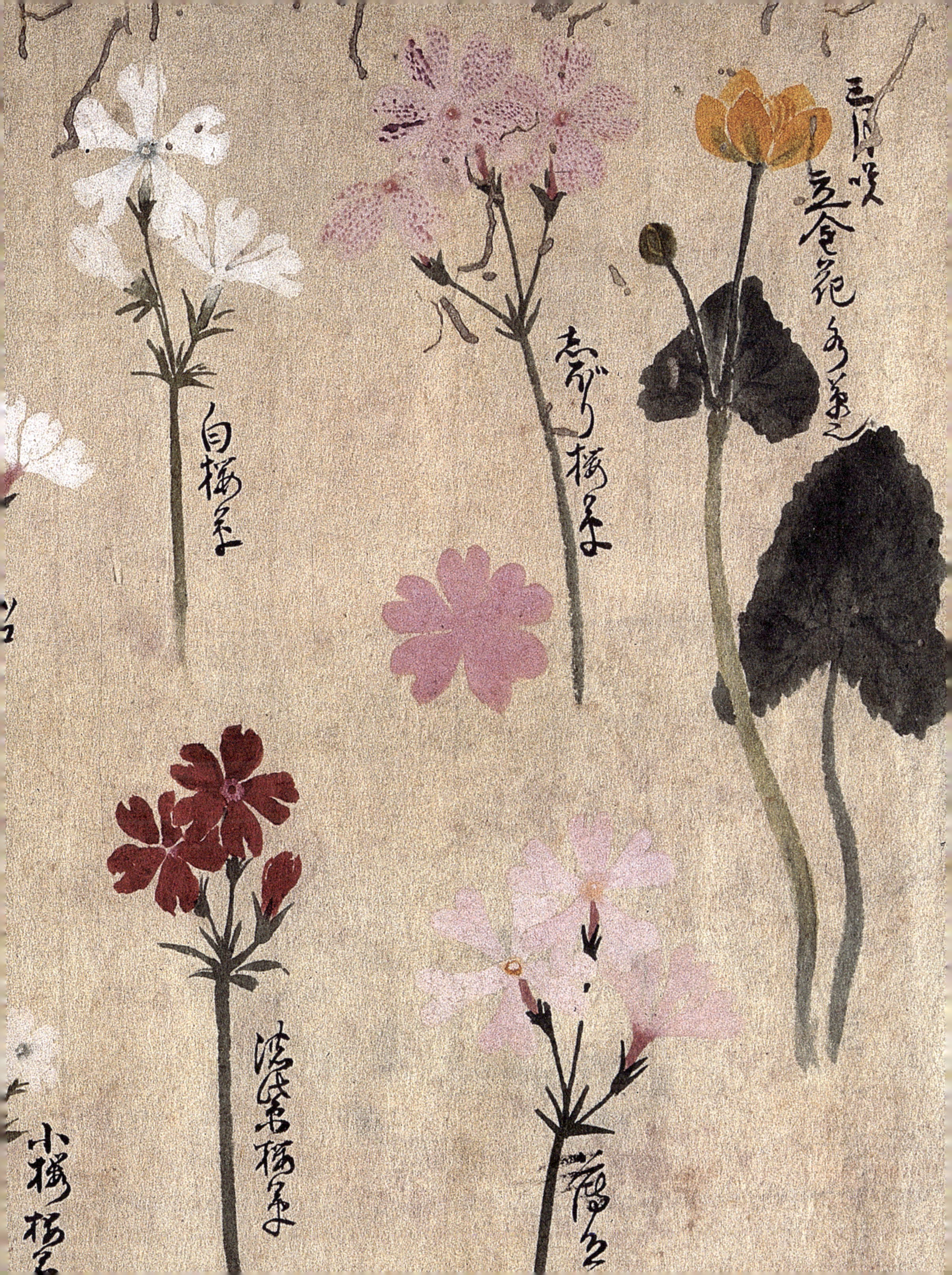
白桜草

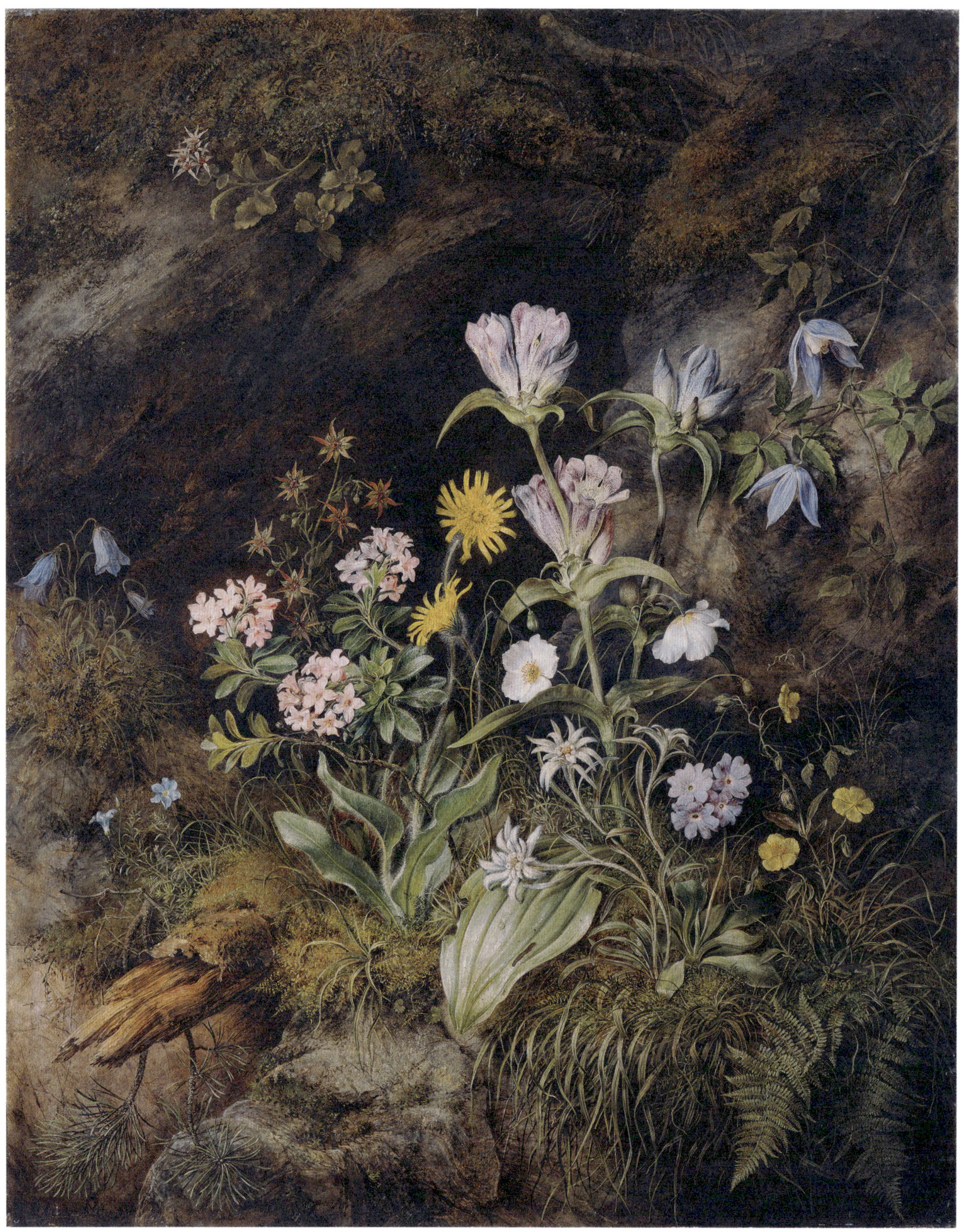

 Alpine Flora, 1853, oil on canvas, Theodor Josef Petter (Austrian)

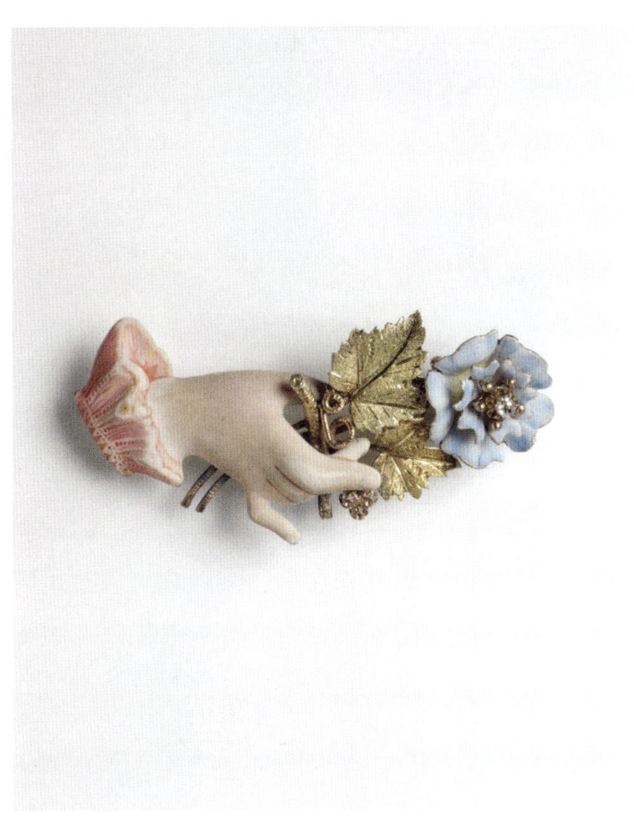

ALPINE FLOWERS CONVENE IN TUNDRA, OFTEN GATHERING IN A JEWEL-LIKE FORMATION OR CONSTELLATION. NOTICE HOW THE WARM UNDERTONES AND THE PALE BLUES CORRESPOND BETWEEN WORKS, PRODUCING A SENSE OF DELICACY AND CHARM.

Previous – *Seven flowering plants, one possibly a kingcup and six pinks (Dianthus species)* (detail), c. 1870, watercolour, Unknown artist (Japanese)

Top – *Brooch*, c. 1880–1900, gold, silver, diamond and enamel brooch, (likely American or British)

Bottom – *Untitled [flower in forest]*, 1968, gelatin silver print, Josef Sudek (Czech)

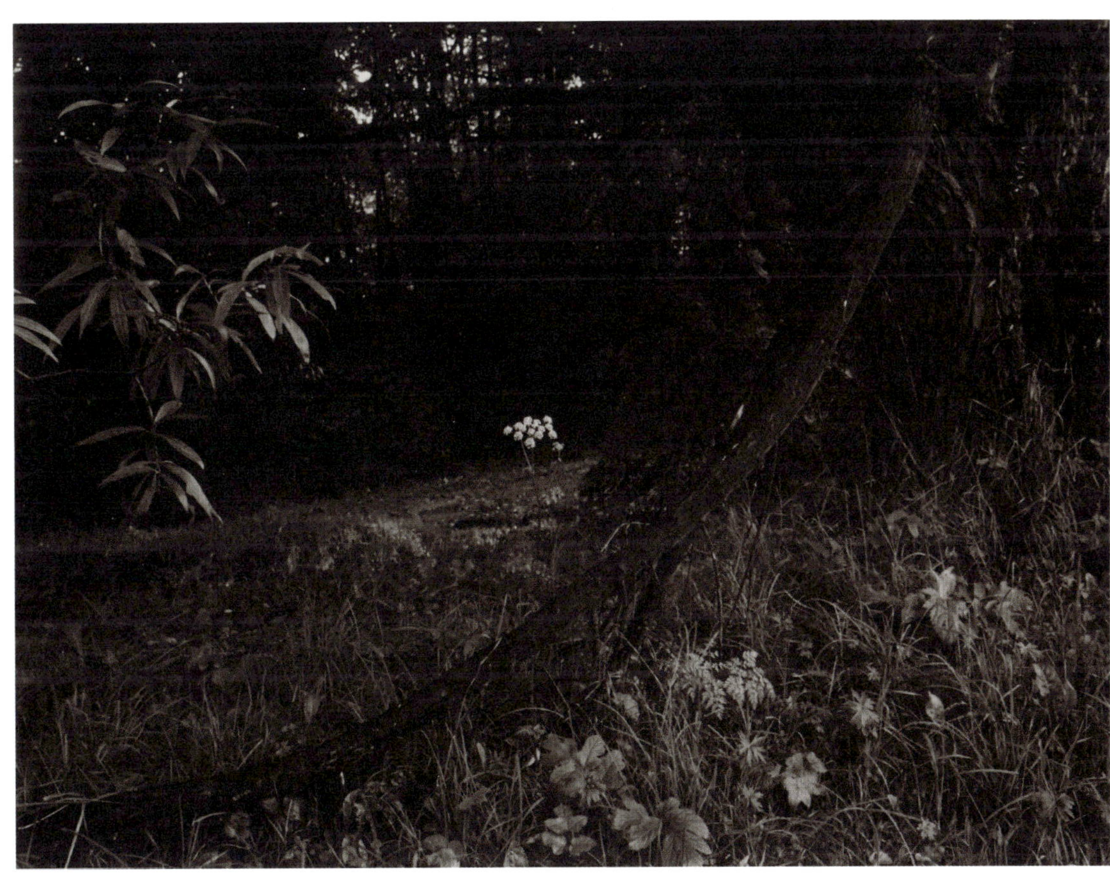

LILAC, ROSE AND TINY BRIGHT YELLOW FLORA CASCADE LIKE AN ANCIENT GLACIER DOWN A VERDANT HILLSIDE TO ARRIVE AT THE FEET OF THE VIEWER. THE VISUAL EFFECT OF THE FLOWERS SPILLING DOWN AND OFF THE PAGE GIVES THE IMPRESSION OF BEING ENVELOPED IN AN EXPANSIVE AND SOFT LANDSCAPE.

Beach Flowers (detail), 1990, reduction woodcut, Gordon Mortensen (American)

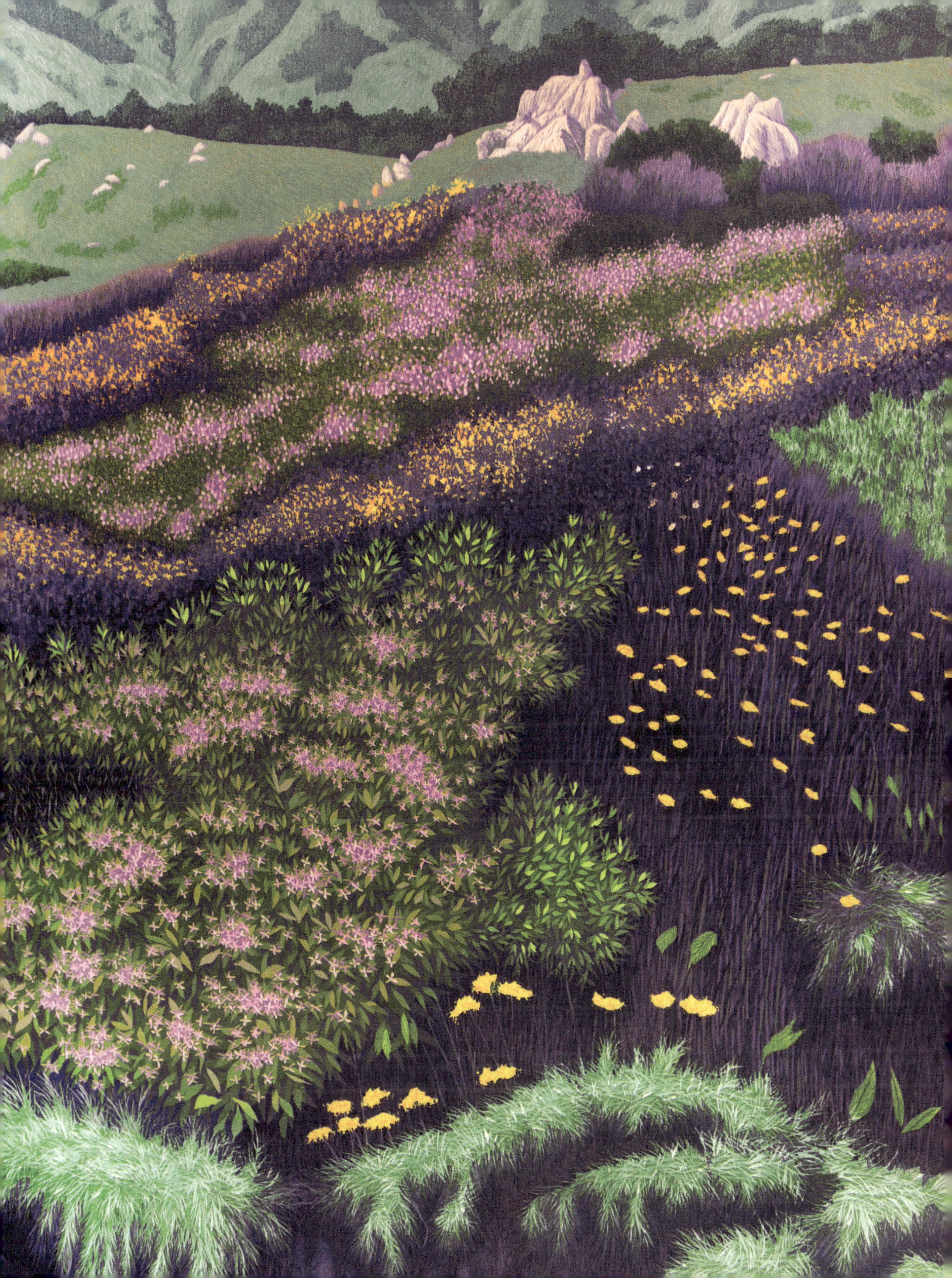

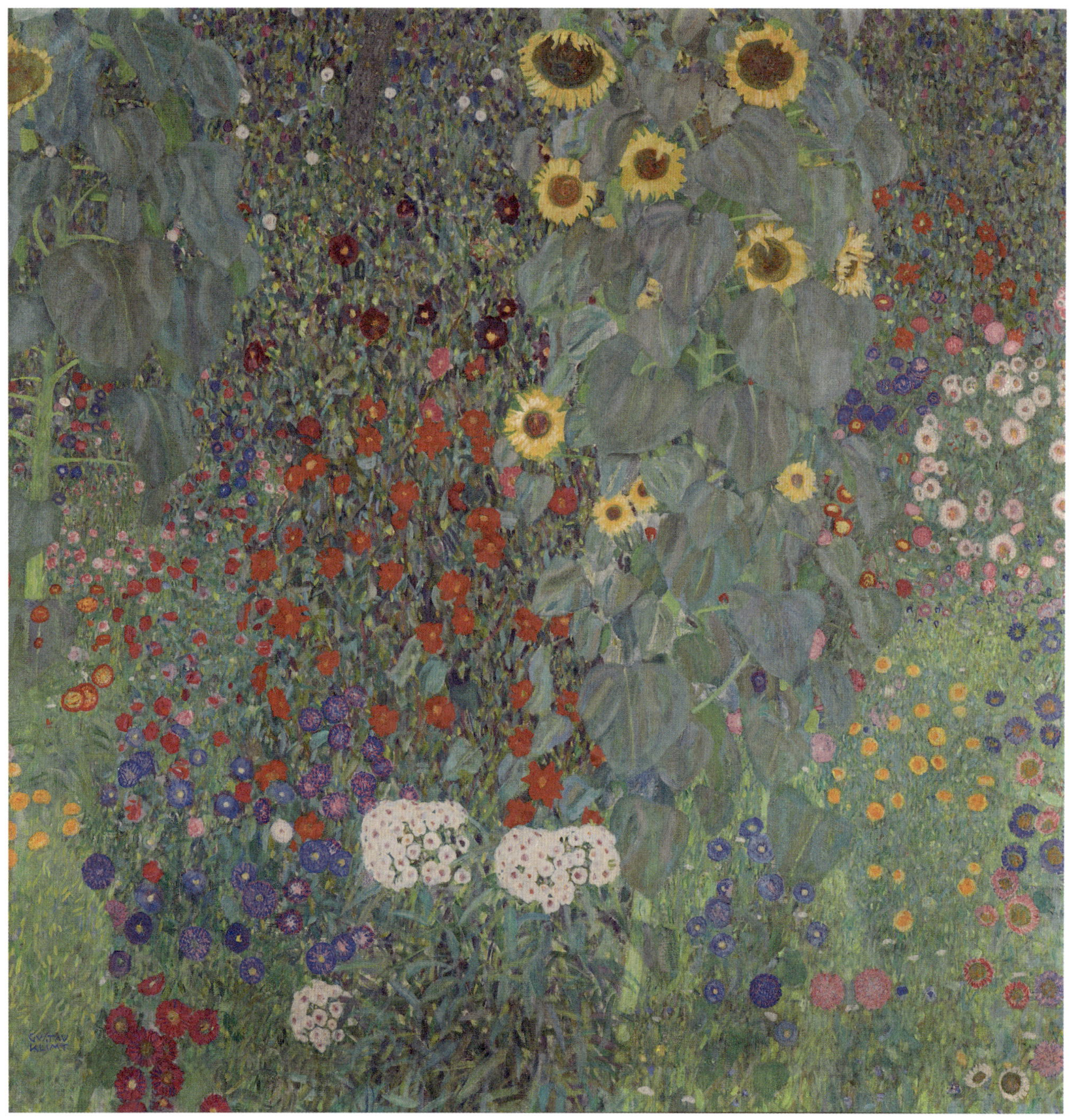

CONSIDER THE CORRESPONDING FORM BETWEEN THE IMAGES: THE FINE ARC OF THE AUTUMN GRASSES WITH THE MEANDERING TENDRILS OF PASSIONFLOWERS, OR THE HEART-SHAPED OUTLINE OF THE SUNFLOWER LEAF ALONGSIDE THE EARLY MODERN STUDY OF EGYPTIAN PLANTS.

 Farm Garden with Sunflowers, 1906, oil on canvas, Gustav Klimt (Austrian)

Top – *Plate with autumn grasses*, c. 17th–19th century, nabeshima ware, Unknown artist (Japanese)

Middle – *Four Egyptian plants in a landscape, including purging cassia, French jujube or Chinese date, and a taro species*, c. 1676, line engraving, Unknown artist (Dutch)

Bottom – *Restricted Storage Area*, 2019, pigment ink-jet print, Daniel Shipp (Australian)

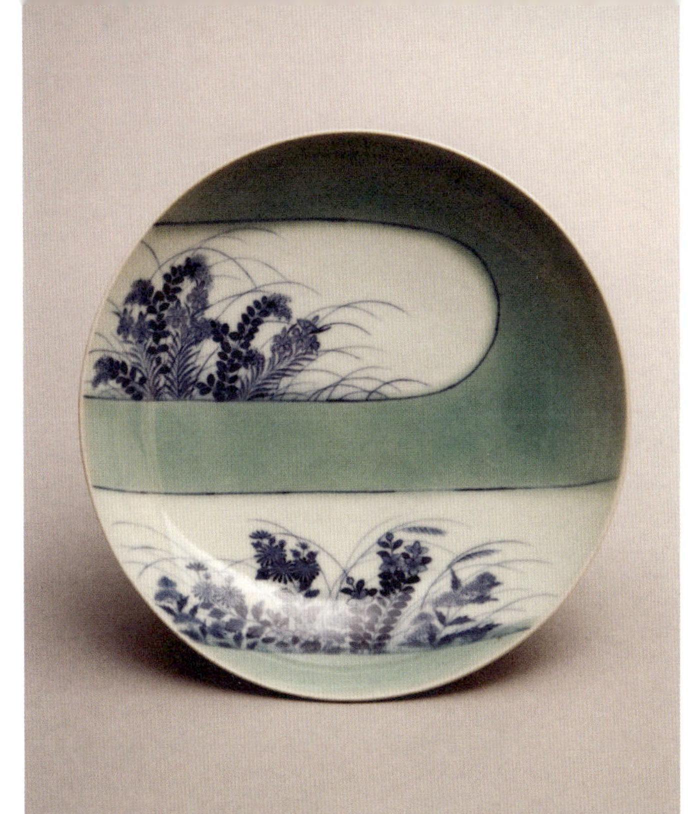

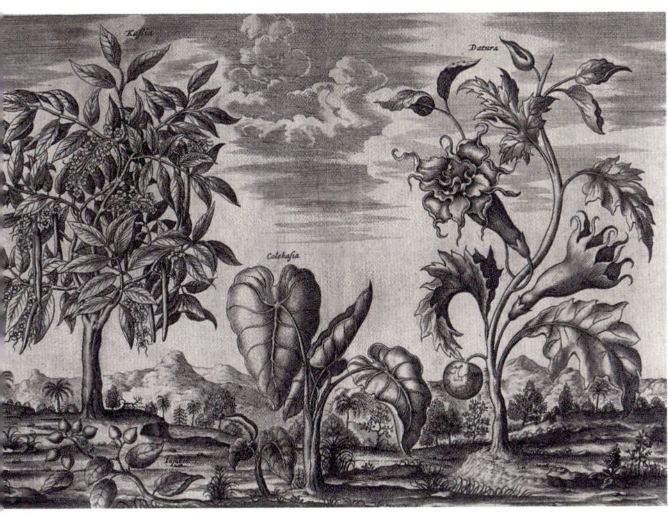

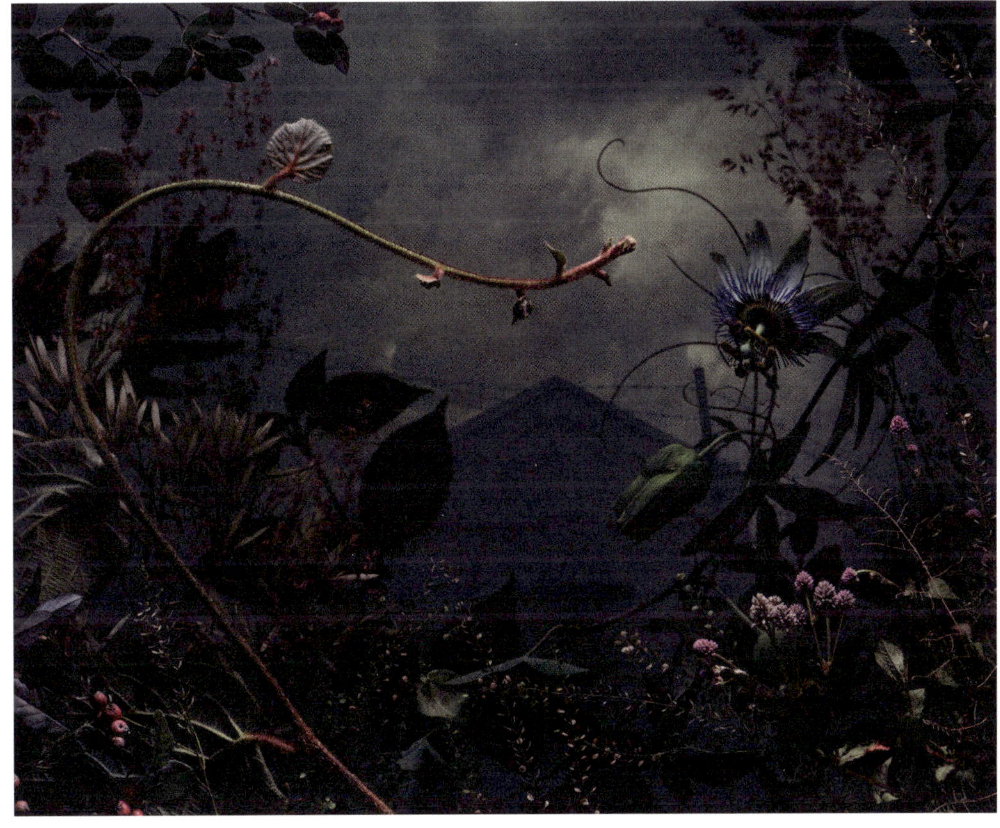

REGARDING FLOWERBEDS

HARRIET BAKER

The city in summer always puts me in mind of Virginia Woolf. Perhaps it is because there is a melancholiness to a season so briefly and sharply lived, and which invites a different kind of looking – late walks and open windows, glimpses into other people's lives.

When I lived in London, there was a patch I knew well by walking. In the afternoons, I would set out in search of green, navigating by flowerbeds as if hopping between islands in a tarmacked sea. From my flat, I visited the roses in Leathermarket Gardens, laid out in their municipal colours between gravel paths studded with wrought-iron benches in bottle green. On to Tabard Gardens, where hollyhocks pushed their way through cracks in the pavement by the Eastwell flats. At Trinity Church Square, and another garden behind railings, tangled and in a permanent state of elegant decay. There, children played outside their houses, drawing in coloured chalks on the pavement and abandoning their bicycles askew. Roses, again, outside the Imperial War Museum, planted in a circle around the guns. I visited once at midsummer, beneath a full moon. The roses glowed, their heads bobbing; moths filled the air. Home, by the river, or – if I was weary – the churchyard of St John's Waterloo.

Flowerbeds became my errand, the means by which I found my way. Walking and looking, I resembled a version of Woolf's street haunter (though, in that sketch of city life, the hour is dusk and the season winter), or one of her city women – Clarissa Dalloway, perhaps, walking through Westminster and noticing incidental things, from girls walking woolly dogs to ducks. I was recording the human life, too: the mothers with their prams, talking into their phones; the elderly women with their little dogs; a volunteer gardener pausing from her weeding to sip coffee from a chipped mug.

Cities fall easily to romance. I saw, too, the man running from the supermarket clutching nappies and washing detergent; avoided a trail of wet dog shit that went around the block. I was heart sick, I suppose, and a long way from home. In those moments, it was comforting to pass by the flowerbeds, and think of Clarissa visiting Miss Pym's shop, or Eleanor, standing up from the dining table in the final passages of *The Years*. As the guests leave, dusting crumbs from their evening clothes and grabbing bunches of flowers to take home, Eleanor watches from the window as, across the square, a young couple gets out of a taxi. A night has passed in the city. What of those stories, those unrecorded lives?

* * *

A story, and a painting. Virginia Woolf's short story 'Kew Gardens' begins with a flowerbed, oval-shaped, into which the light falls, daubing a pebble, a leaf, a snail's shell with bright spots of colour. Above, the flower stalks are stirred by the breeze and men and women walk in pairs through the gardens. Their movements, describes Woolf, are like those of the butterflies, irregular, aimless, zig-zagging from bed to bed. And their talk – reminiscent of the past, or shell-shocked, and so a little mad, or chiding and domestic – contributes to the wavering tissue of sound. First published in 1919, the story was the first in a series of 'short things' she was beginning to write, an attempt at

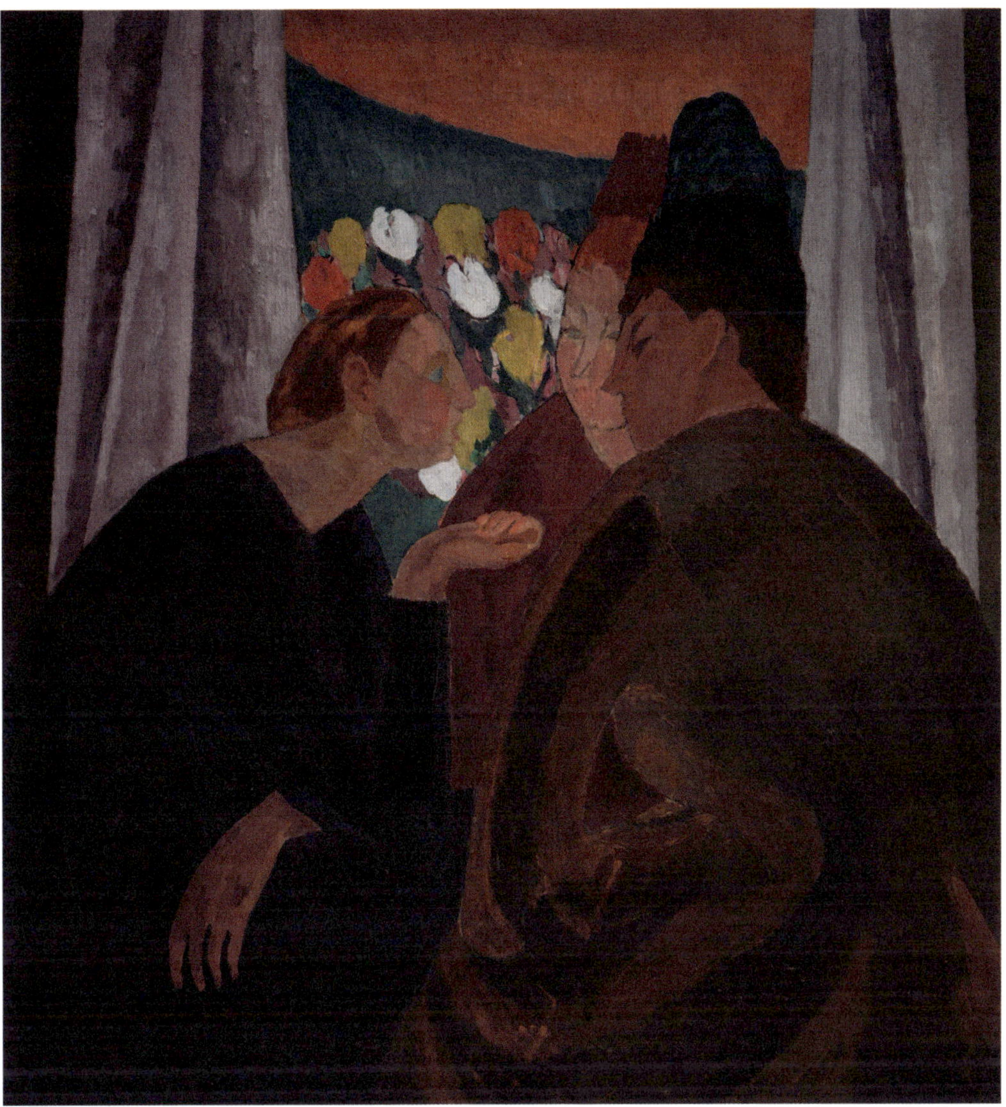

capturing the weave of human and animal life, of giving a sense impression of a garden in a city on a hot July day.

Her sister, the painter Vanessa Bell, worked on the woodcuts, producing a sketch for a frontispiece depicting two hatted women against a leafy background with flowers, and a tailpiece of a butterfly and a caterpillar. Virginia found the sketch of the women to be 'just in the mood I wanted'. In their letters, the women discussed how the woodcut put them in mind of an earlier work of Vanessa's, *A Conversation*, completed in 1916 (see above). It is my favourite of her paintings. I like the intimate, conspiratorial secrecy of the women's talk, just out of earshot; the hand proffered in emphasis, the speaker's face met by two intently listening faces, two narrowing pairs of eyes. Most of all, I like how these women's forms (forms, not figures, for Bell was approaching a radical new direction in her style) make me think of large insects – beetles, perhaps – so rounded are they, and painted in shining, earthy tones. Beyond these huddled forms, we can see the flowerbed, its oval shape, its blooms depicted in bright lozenges of colour.

A flowerbed, a short story, a woodcut: all are methods of constraint. The sisters staked out their boundaries, established the forms in which they could expand, experiment, create. One put sensations and feelings before words, the other made stories out of paint. Both come to mind when I look at flowerbeds, at the soil and heavy stems, while voices and city sounds murmur overhead. Dark recesses between stalks, yet teeming with life.

A Conversation, c. 1913–16, oil on canvas, Vanessa Bell (British)

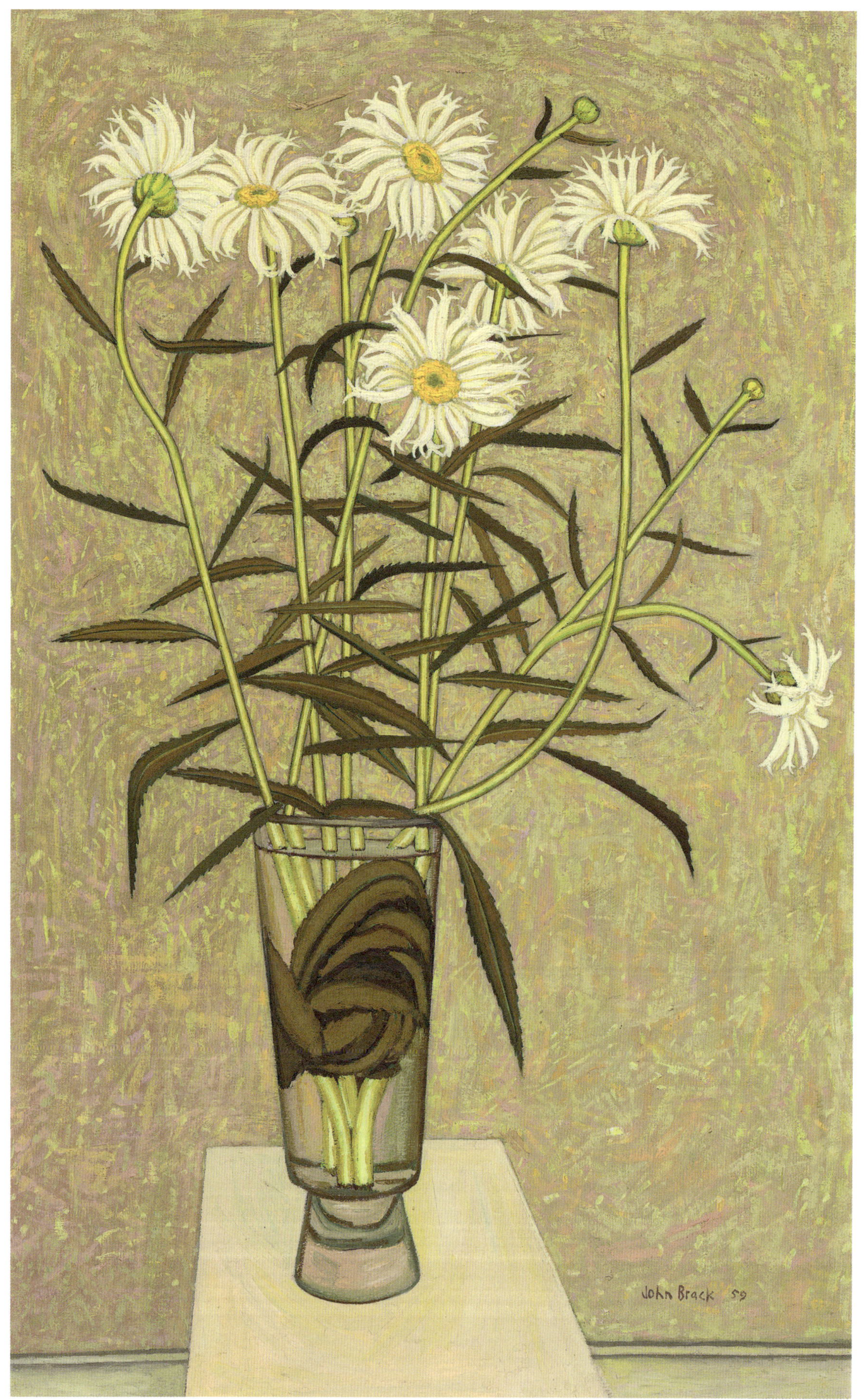
John Brack 59

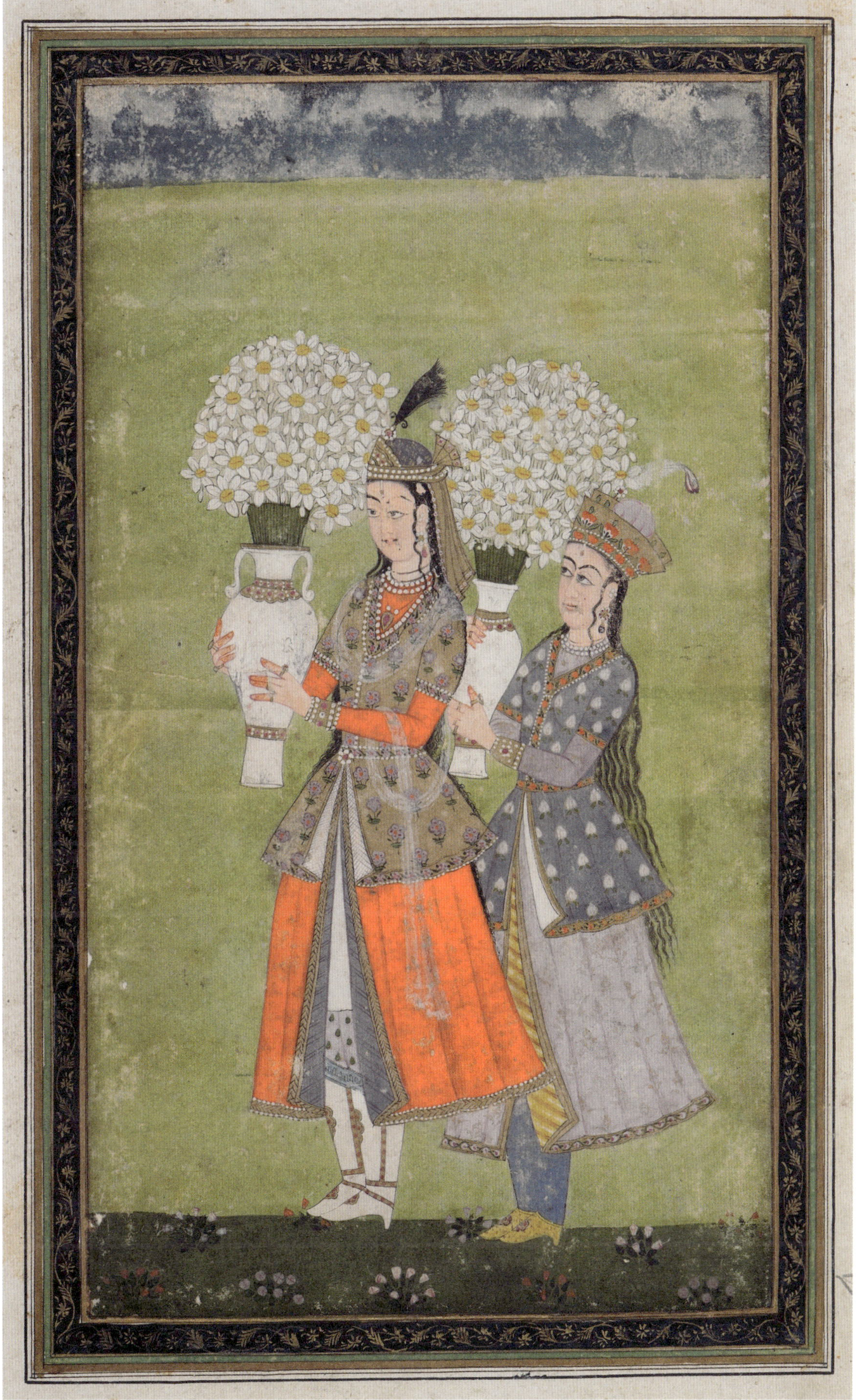

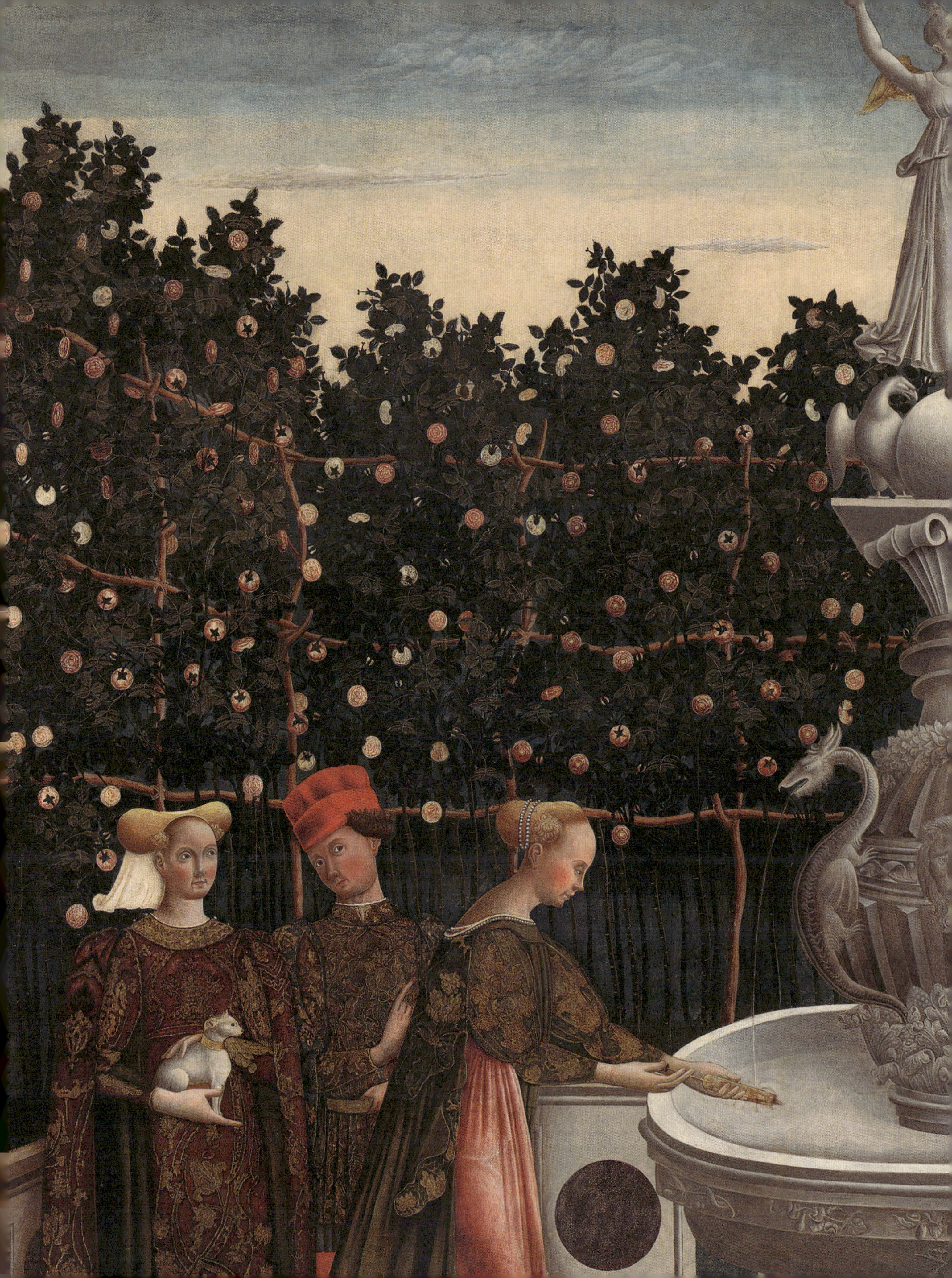

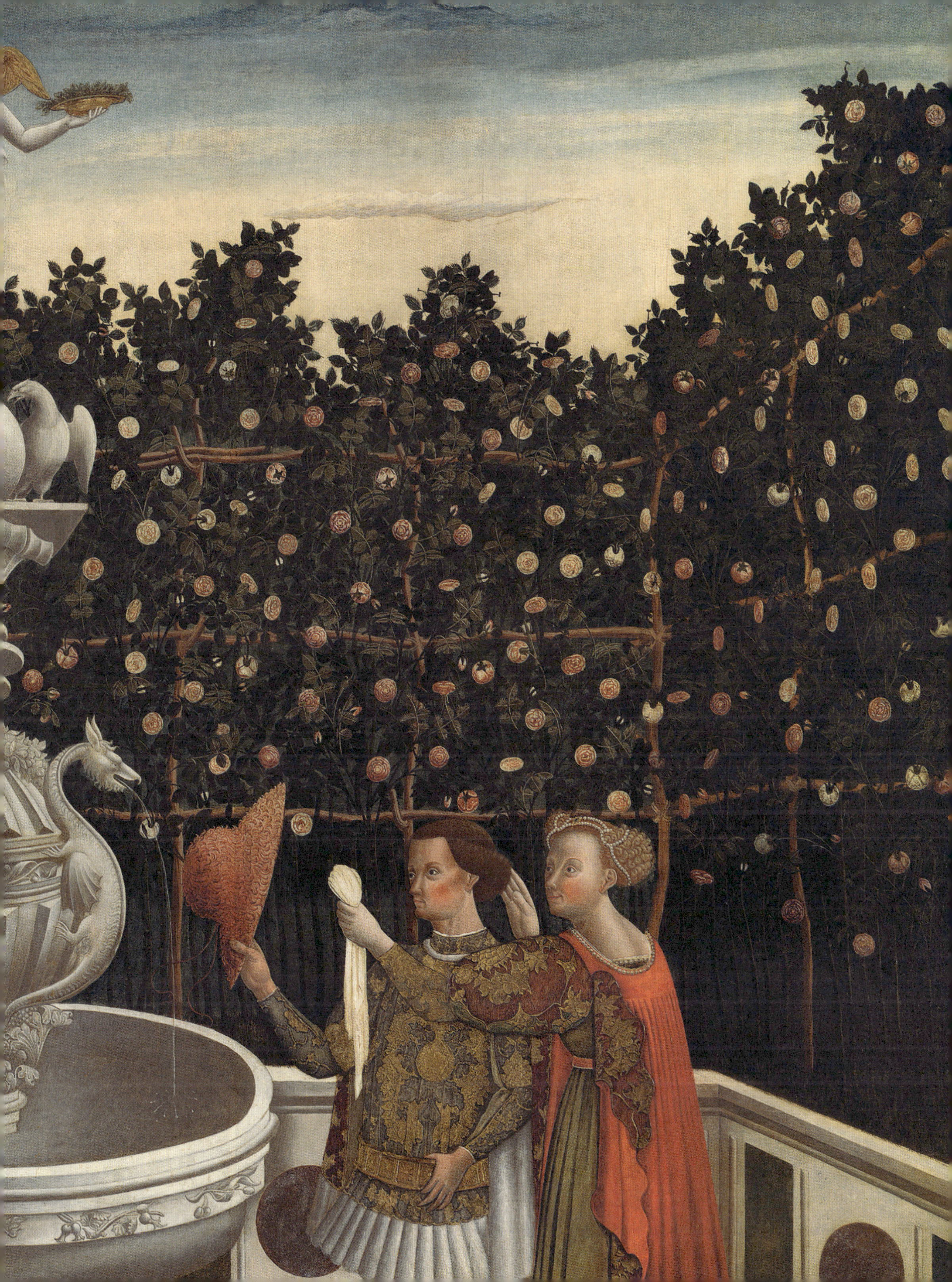

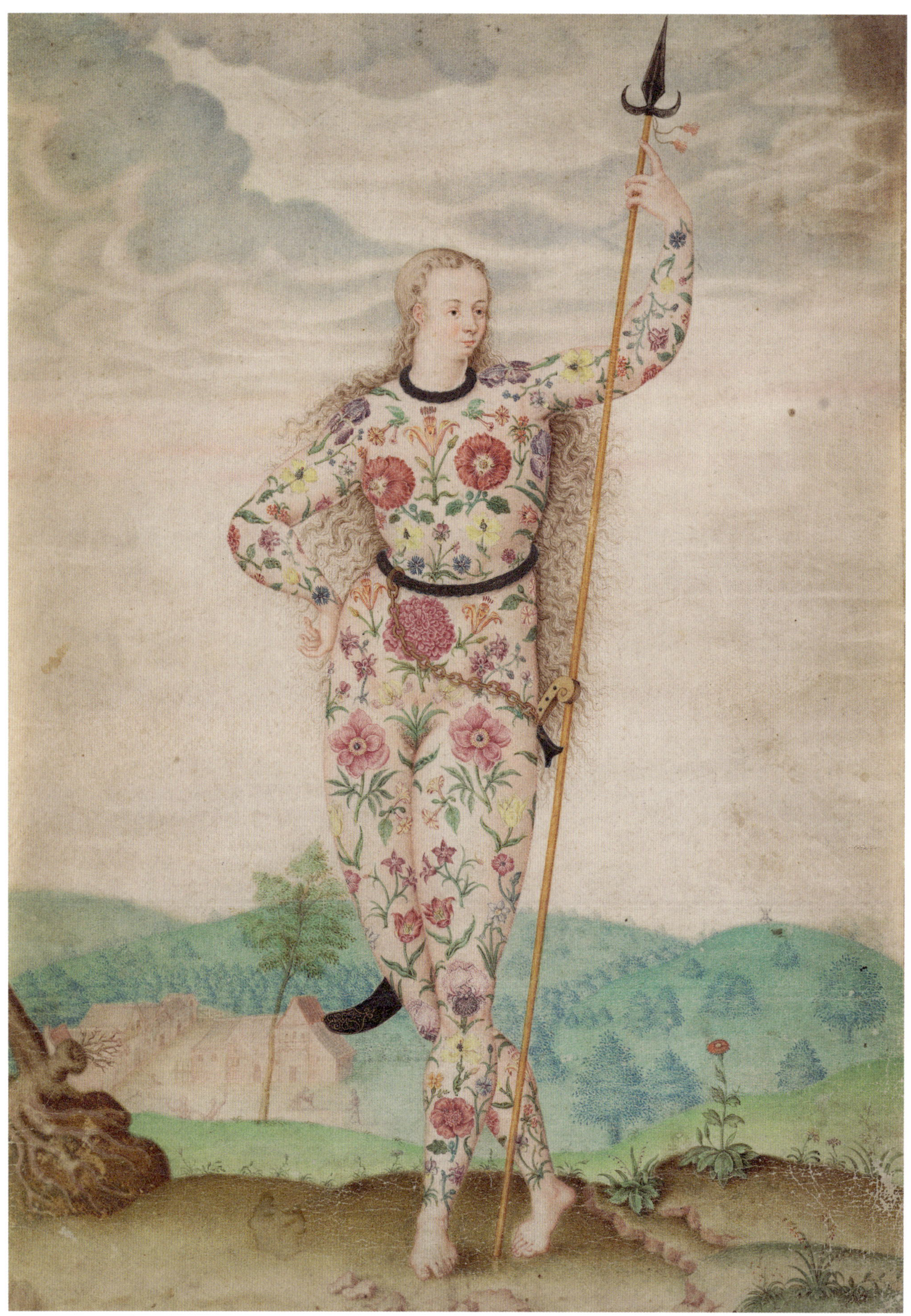

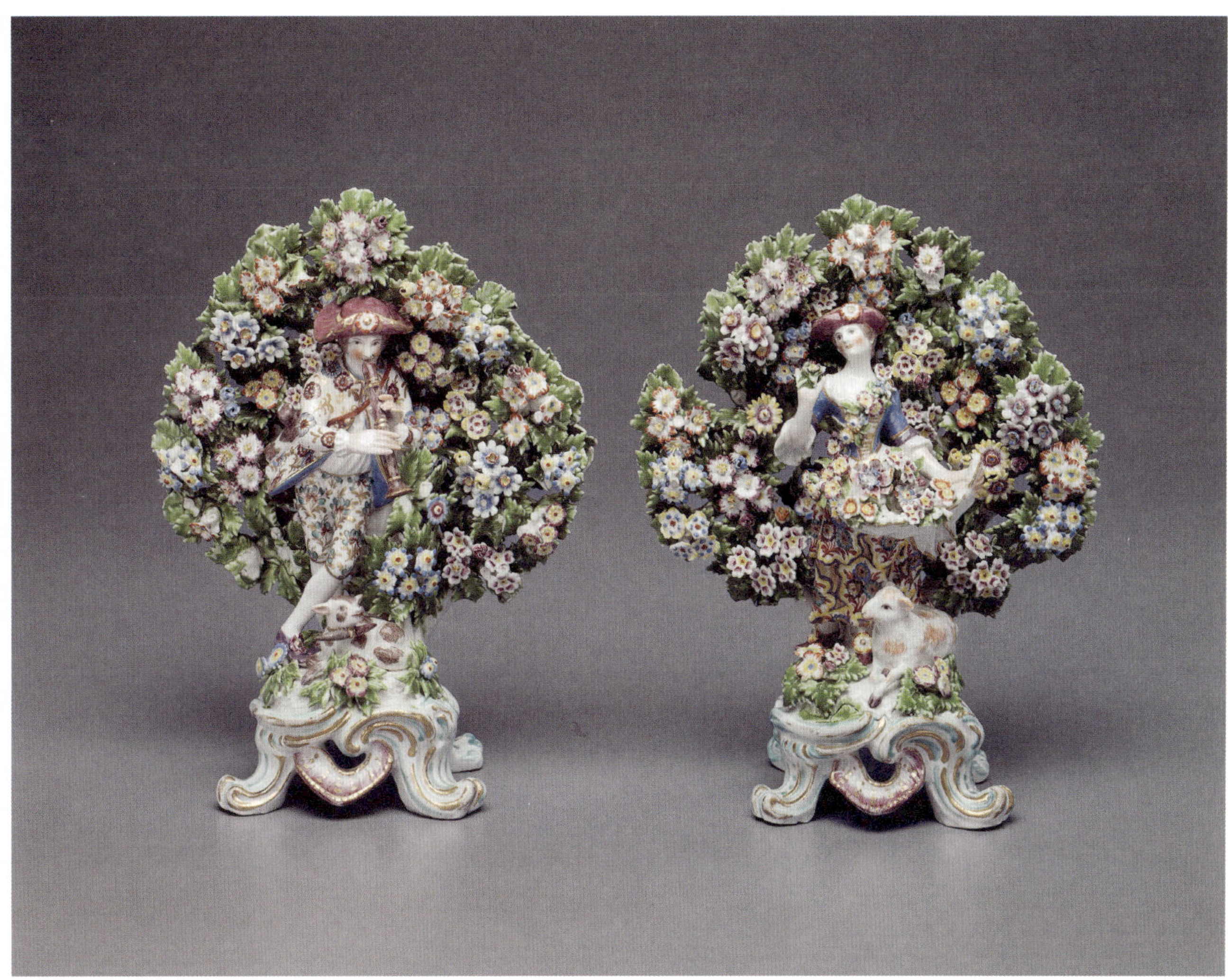

THE SHEPHERD AND SHEPHERDESS FIGURINES DEPICTED HERE ARE ADORNED WITH HALO-LIKE FLORAL ARRANGEMENTS AMPLIFYING THE PASTORAL IDEAL UPHELD IN THE 18TH CENTURY ROCOCO PERIOD. NOTICE A SIMILAR RADIANT EFFECT EMANATING FROM FLORAL DESIGNS TATTOOED ON THE WOMAN'S BODY IN THE MINIATURE PAINTING. BOTH WORKS CONVEY A LUMINOUS FORCE.

Page 62 – *Flowers* (*Shasta daisies*), 1959, oil on composition board, John Brack (Australian)

Page 63 – *Two ladies carry flowers*, 19th century, opaque watercolour and gold on paper, Unknown artist (Indian)

Previous – *The Garden of Love*, c. 1465–70, oil, tempera and gold on spruce panel, Antonio Vivarini (studio of) (Italian)

Opposite – *A Young Daughter of the Picts*, c. 1585, watercolour and gouache touched with gold on parchment, Jacques Le Moyne de Morgues, formerly attributed to John White (French)

Above – *Figures*, c. 1760, porcelain, Bow Porcelain Works, London (manufacturer) (British)

THE FRAGRANCED DUTCH FLOWER PAINTING

LIZZIE MARX

A good Dutch flower still life is deceivingly realistic. A botanist can identify with ease every flower that the artist recorded in oil paint. And yet they might also note the artist's cunning in the composition. Prior to advances in modern horticulture and floristry, living flowers could never be seen together in this way, at the same time, and in the same region. In Abraham Mignon's (1640–79) (Fig. 1) painted bouquet, a narcissus, heralder of spring, is united with the later bloomers of irises, morning glories, and white hydrangeas. Flower paintings were a sub-genre of the broader classification of still life, which could also depict ripe fruits, dead game, luxury objects, or indeed an entire banquet. The colours and the sensory experiences they offer make them beguiling works, even many centuries later.

Perhaps one of the most important flowers in the story of Dutch still-life painting is the tulip. In the early modern period, tulips were prized for their colours. Among the most important exemplars was the striped tulip, which carried a virus that caused them to produce an elegant pattern of striped petals. So coveted was the flower that it is credited as the cause of the first recorded economic bubble. Countless flower still lifes from the 17th century include tulips, immortalising the ephemeral flowers so that they could be enjoyed for longer than their fleeting lifespan. Though beautiful in appearance, a tulip is almost scentless.

By the middling decades of the 18th century, however, it was the double hyacinth that became one of the most desired flowers of its time. The overlaying of petals made it particularly rare, and what it lacked in the beautiful flares of the tulip was made up for in the evocative scent of the flower. In a canvas by the renowned Dutch still-life painter Rachel Ruysch (1664–1750), the striped tulip is juxtaposed with its 18th-century counterpart (Fig. 2). Perhaps this was to imply that the double hyacinth may risk reaching the same dangerous economic frenzy as the tulip.

It was at the same time in the early modern period that artists were immortalising the appearance of flowers, that the perfume industry was endeavouring to preserve a bloom's fragrance. The climate in the South of France became a favourable place to cultivate fragrant flowers including irises, orange blossoms, jasmine, and, later in the 17th century, tuberose. A newly developed technique could preserve their scent through '*enfleurage*', wherein fresh flowers were laid into purified lard or olive oil that was spread across glazed wooden frames.

Fig. 1 (following left) – *Still Life with Flowers and a Watch*, c. 1660–79, oil on canvas, Abraham Mignon (German)

The sight was not dissimilar to a framed still-life painting, though made of real flowers. After the fat fully absorbed the scent, it was heated and strained, resulting in a potent essence. Long after the flowers had faded, their souls lingered through this olfactory preservation. As artists were producing flower still lifes that defied reality, so too were perfumers developing fragrances whose compositions challenged the course of nature.

The artists of the Low Countries imbued flower still lifes and their corresponding scents with meaning. The renowned Dutch moralist Jacob Cats (1577–1660) expounded on flowers in his book of emblems, *Mirror of the Old and New Times*, first published in 1632. In one such example, an elderly woman recounts an Italian proverb to her young and fashionable companion: '*Ogni fiore al fin perde l'odore*' (Every flower loses its scent in the end). The youthful looks of the woman will, like the flower, wither in time. Artists alluded to this idea in their painted still lifes. Balthasar van der Ast (1593–1657) added a fly (among other critters) to his composition, which he goads the viewer to swat from the scene (Fig. 3). The insect's attraction suggests that the fragrance of the flower is on the cusp of transitioning from floral to indole (the faecal scent of flower rot), since flies were drawn to decay. The connection between the bouquet's imminent decline and the mortality of humans would not have been lost on the 17th-century audience. The flowers in these paintings were immortalised at the peak of their fragrance, but it was well understood that a scent would sour as the bouquet would eventually decompose. So too would every viewer meet the same fate.

The poets and great writers of the Dutch Republic praised still-life paintings that could stimulate sensory experiences beyond the visual. The artist-biographer Arnold Houbraken (1660–1719) equated the success of a flower painting with its ability to elicit fragrance. For instance, the Antwerp still lifes of Jan van Kessel (1626–79) could 'refresh the spirits by their pleasant and sweet smell, and caress the eyes pleasingly with charming beauty'. The poet Constantijn Huygens (1596–1687), who was, incidentally, an amateur perfumer, was similarly enchanted by the olfactory abilities of still-life artists. In a poem dedicated to the Antwerp artist Daniël Seghers (1590–1661), he wrote 'with oil Father Seegers creates, in his painting, the fragrance of roses'. The early modern viewing experience of flower still lifes was multi-sensory, and through seeing these ornate bouquets, the imagination was sparked to smell them too.

Our sensibilities have changed since the early modern period, and were we to dwell on mortality in the manner of our 17th-century counterparts, other imagery may come to mind before a painted vase overflowing with flowers. Nevertheless, our sense of imagination has remained, and these evocative artworks continue to conjure fragrances that linger centuries after the depicted blooms have wilted.

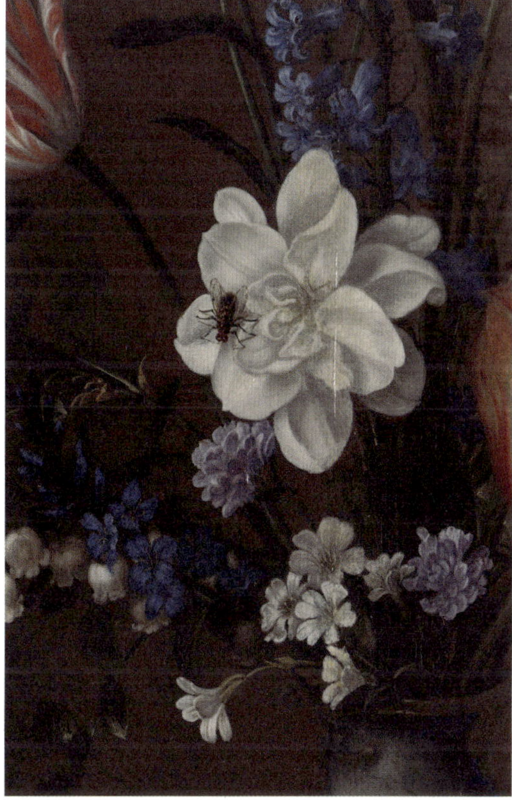

Fig. 3 – *Flowers in a Wan-Li Vase, with Shells* (detail), c. 1640–50, oil on canvas, Balthasar van der Ast (Dutch)

Fig. 2 (following right) – *Vase of Flowers with an Ear of Corn*, 1742, oil on canvas, Rachel Ruysch (Dutch)

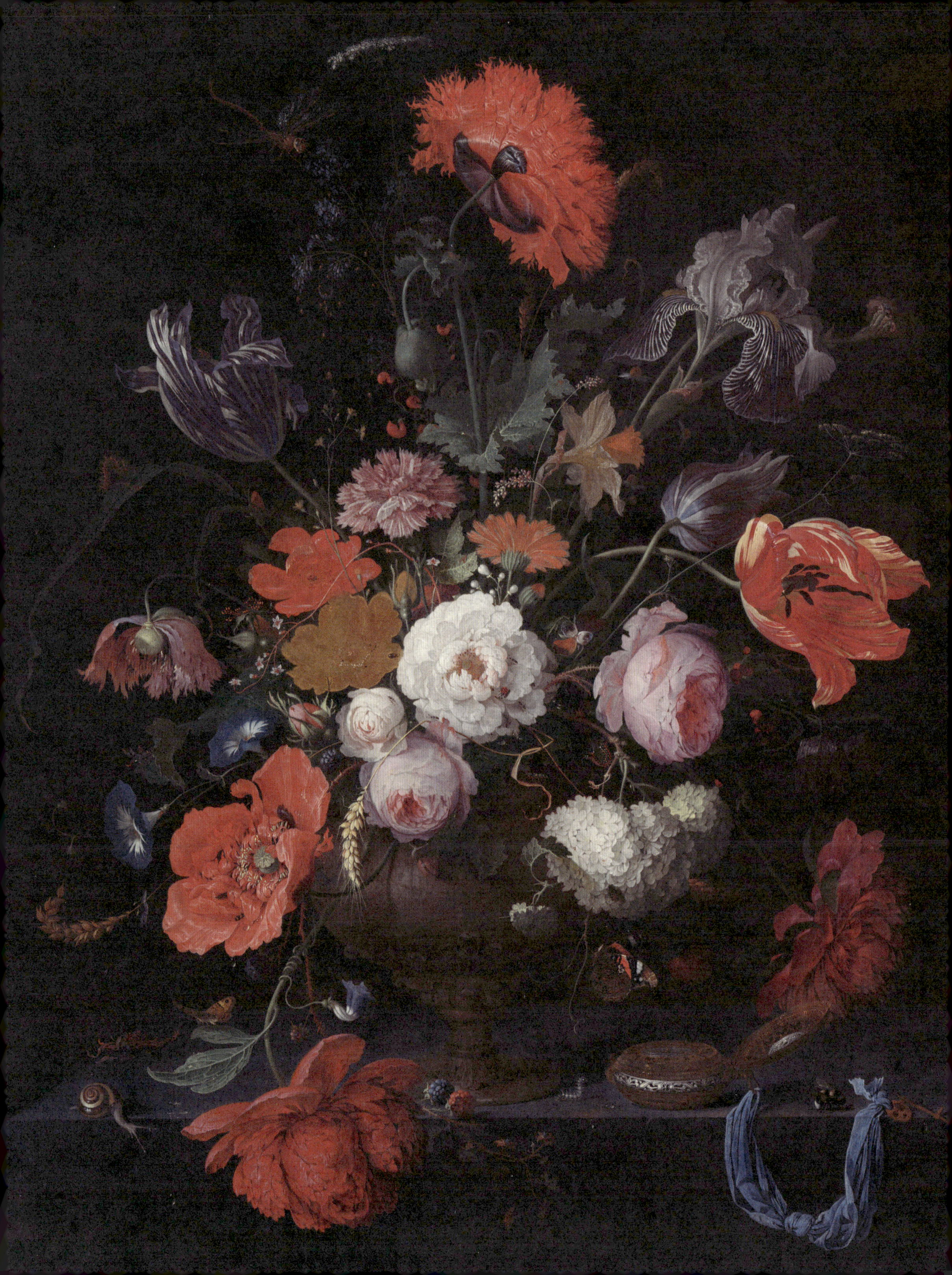

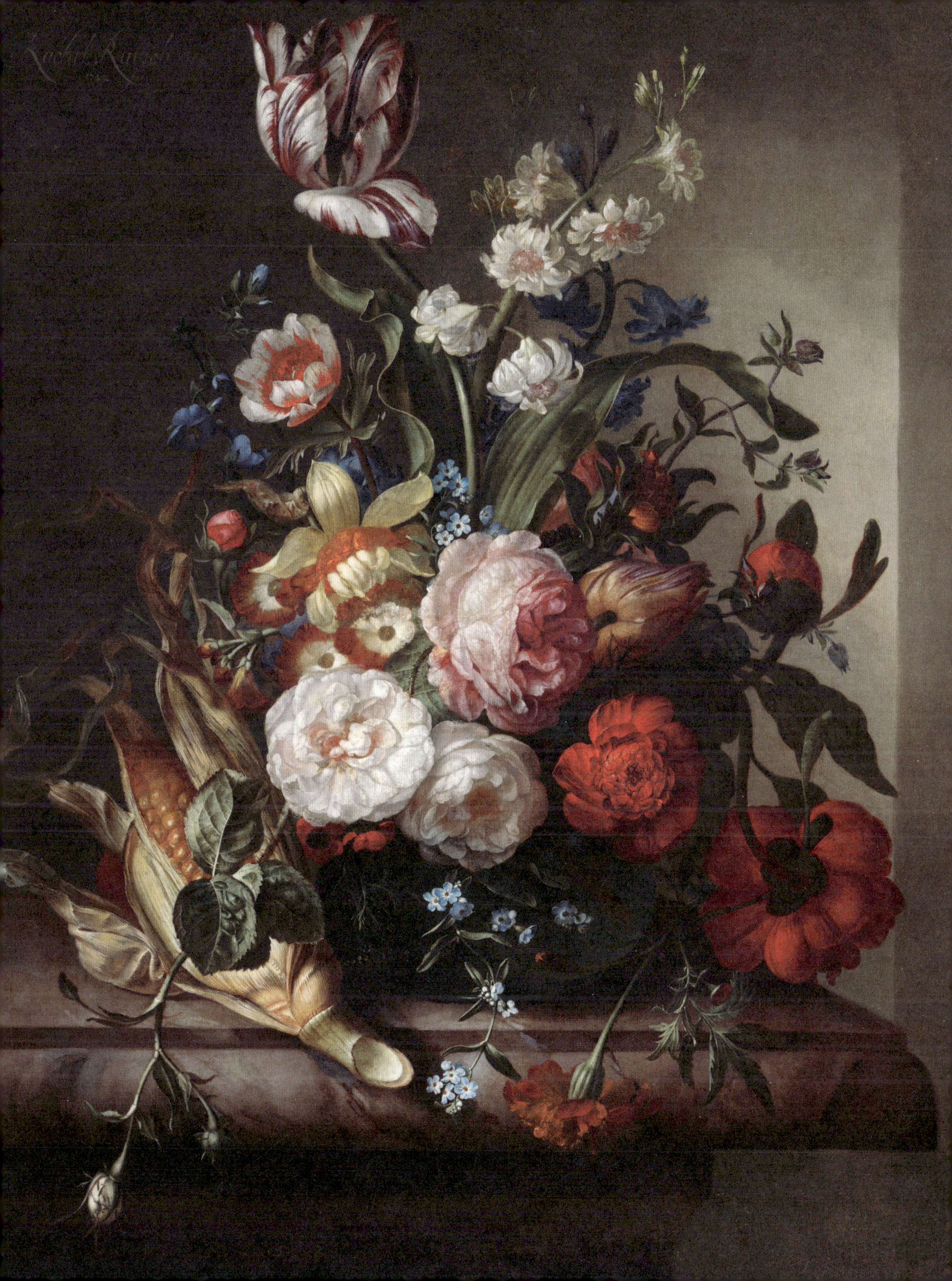

A Land Girl and the Bail Bull, 1945, oil paint on canvas, Evelyn Dunbar (British)

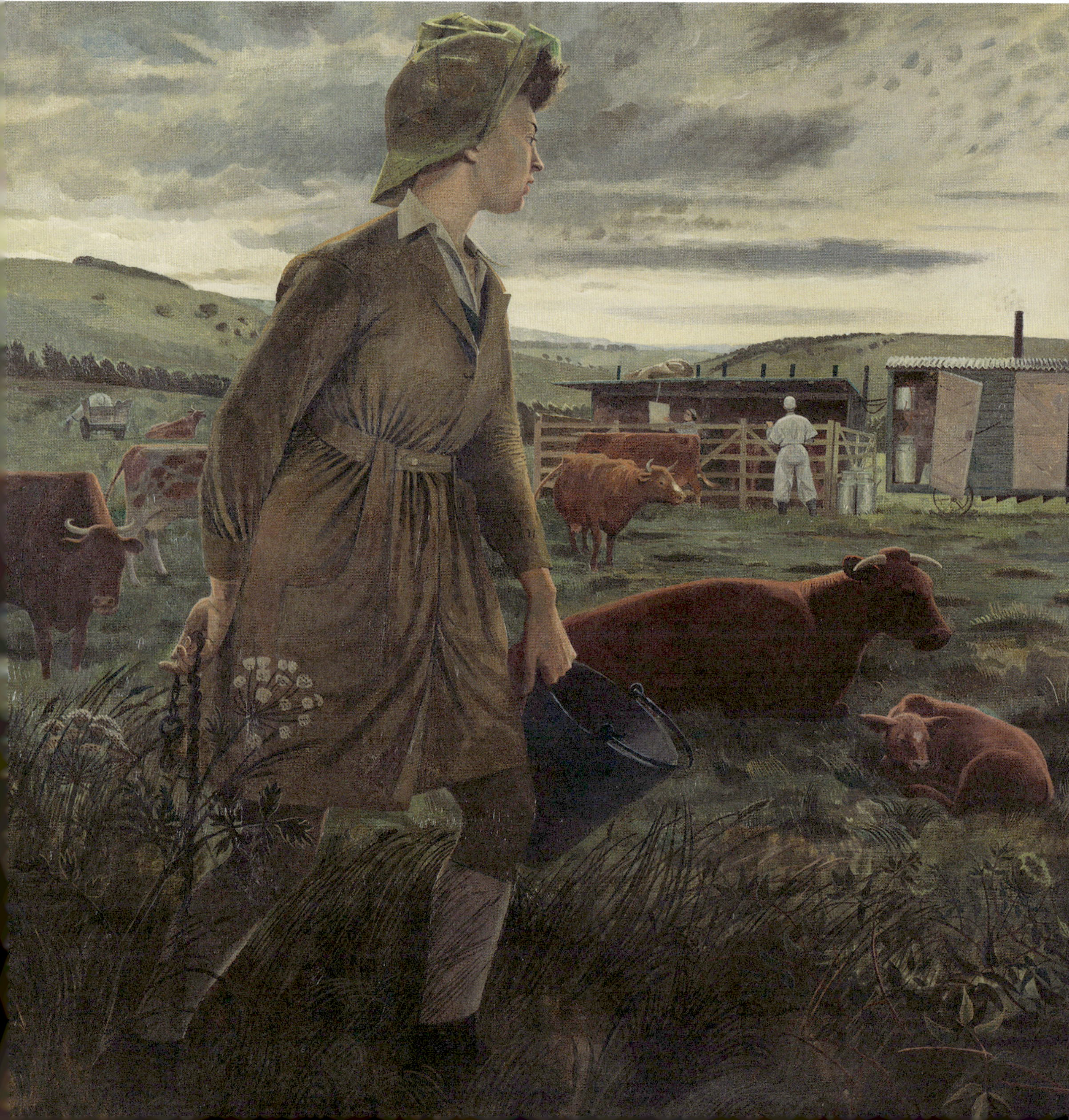

FARMING

LABOUR AND FARMING IS A WIDESPREAD THEME IN LANDSCAPE IMAGERY. THE PORTRAYAL OF LIFE ON THE LAND AND AGRICULTURAL SCENES ALSO DETAIL THE CONSIDERABLE CHANGE TO NATURAL HABITATS. THE STRUGGLE OF WORKING ON THE LAND IS OFTEN EXPRESSED THROUGH WEATHER CONDITIONS AND PHYSICAL CHALLENGES EXPERIENCED BY LABOURERS AND FARMERS. THREATENING SKIES AND GUSTY WINDS DOMINATE SCENES ON THE LAND.

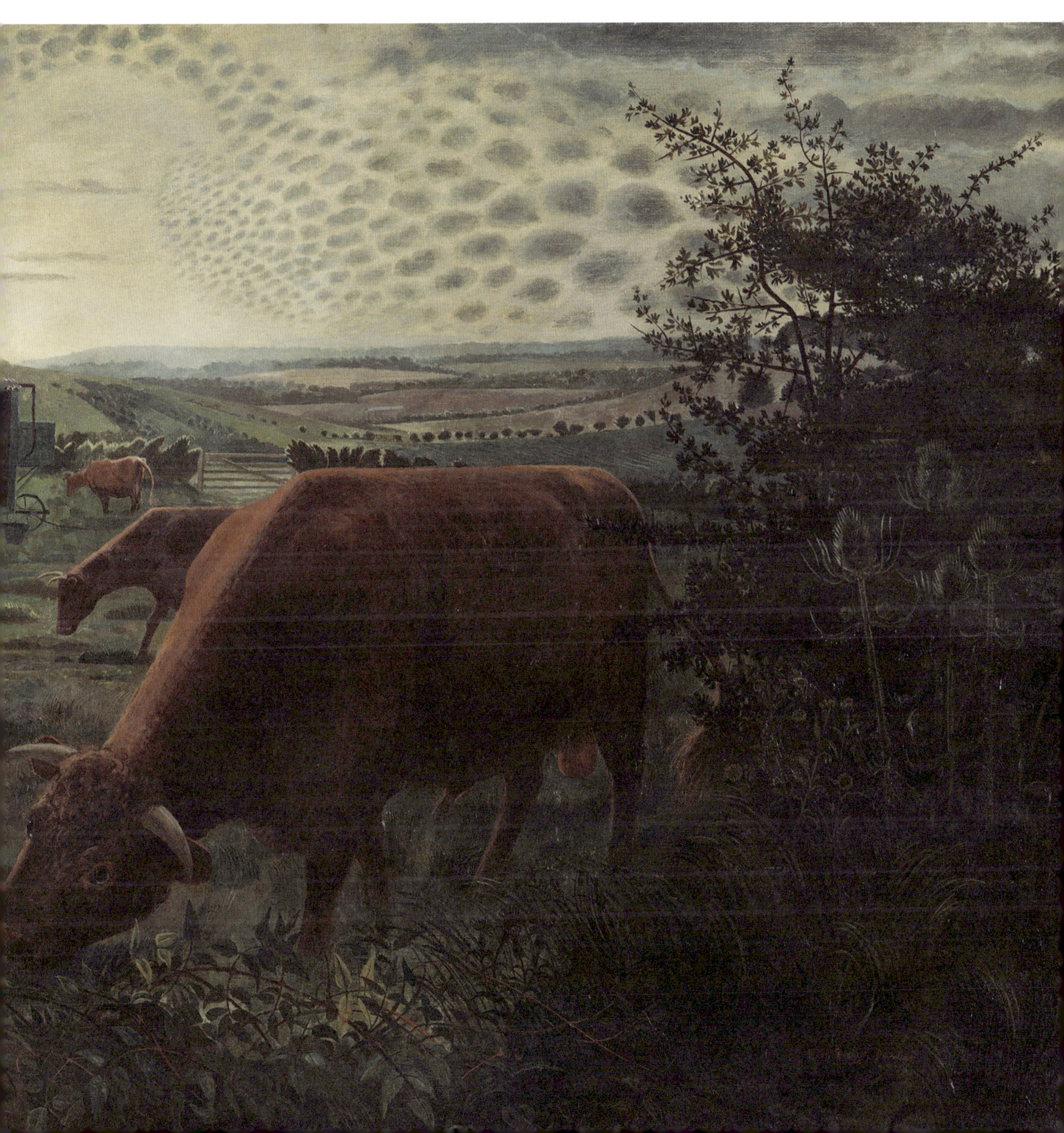

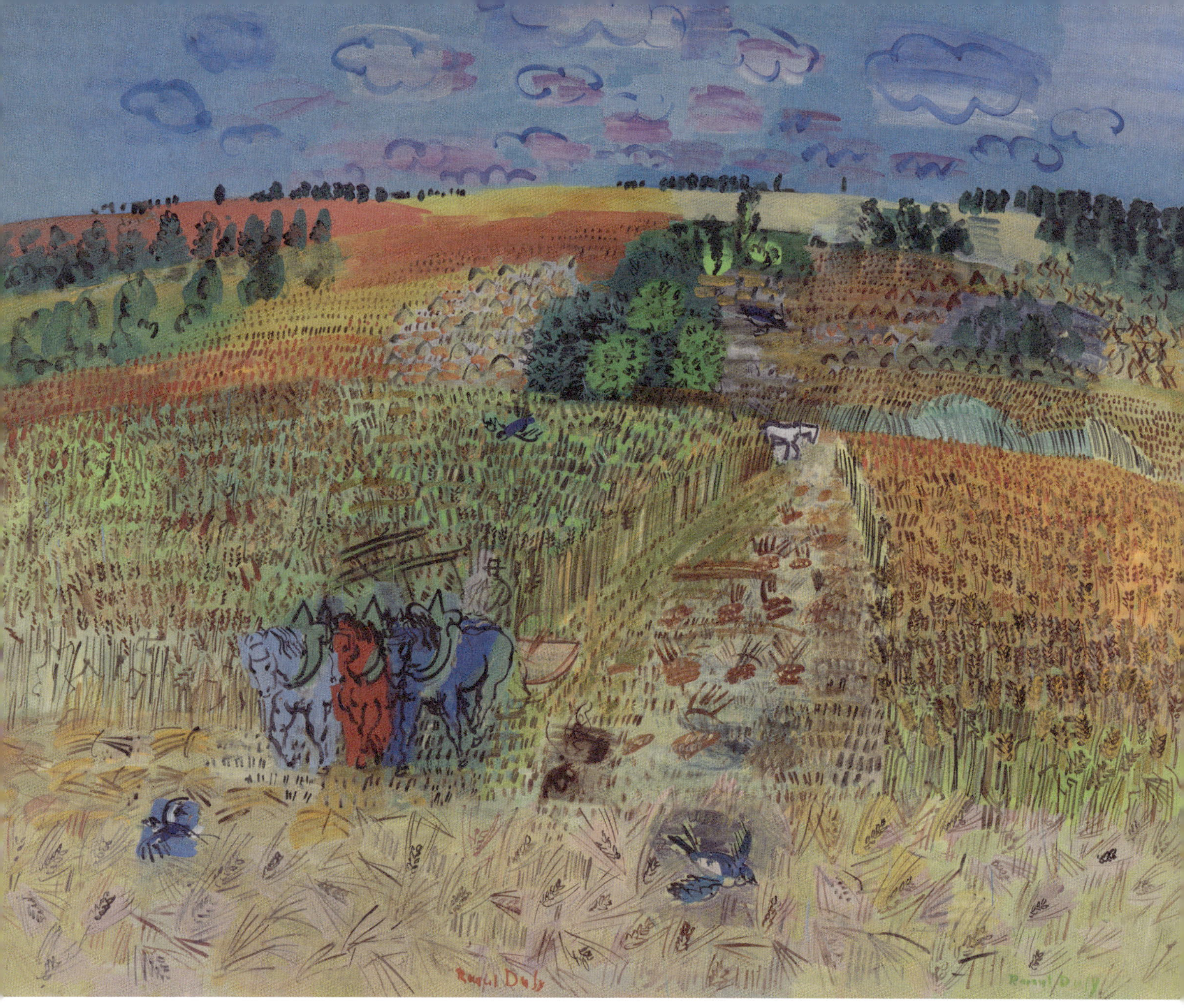

Above – *The Wheatfield*, 1929, oil paint on canvas, Raoul Dufy (French)

Opposite top – *Harvest time in autumn*, c. 1826–35, colour woodblock, Utagawa Toyokuni II (Japanese)

Opposite bottom – *Harvest-Time*, 1775, engraving, Francis Vivares (French), Peter Paul Rubens (after) (Dutch)

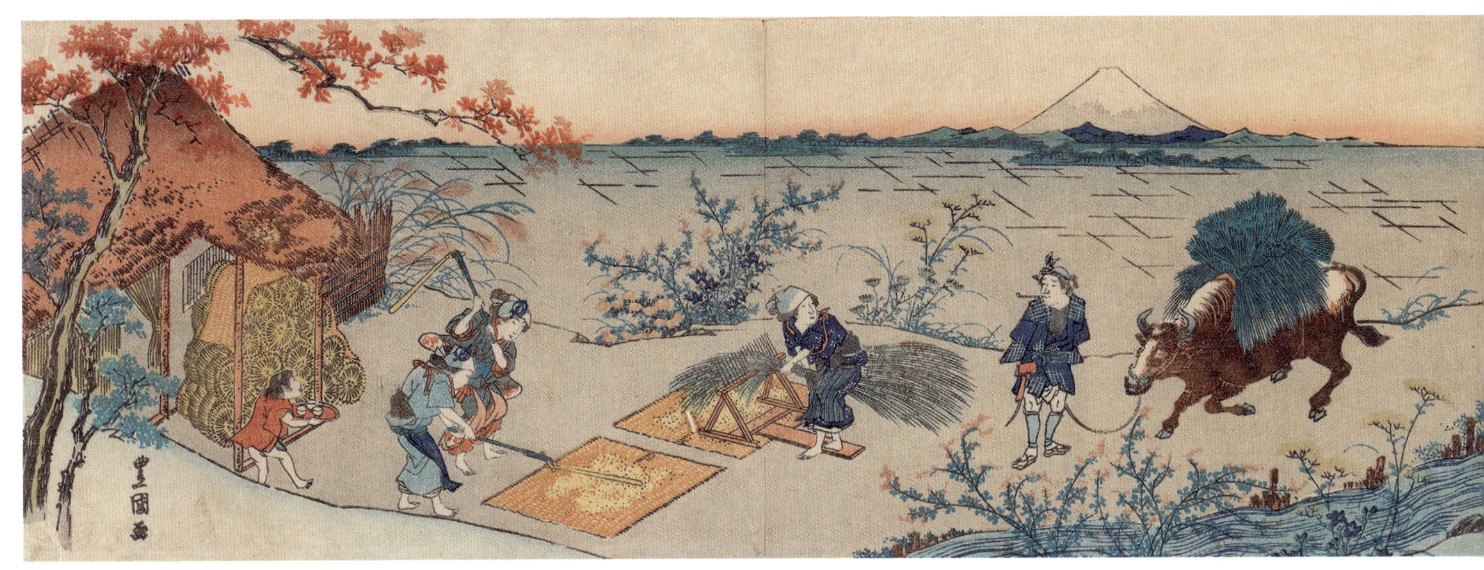

THE HARVEST REPRESENTS A TIME OF INDUSTRIOUS ACTIVITY. ANIMALS AND PEOPLE ARE WORKING HARD IN THE WARMTH OF THE AUTUMN SUN. OBSERVE THE SMALL DETAILS IN EACH PICTURE; NOTICE HOW THE LABOURERS HASTEN TO COMPLETE THEIR HARVEST BEFORE THE ONSET OF COLDER WINTER MONTHS AHEAD.

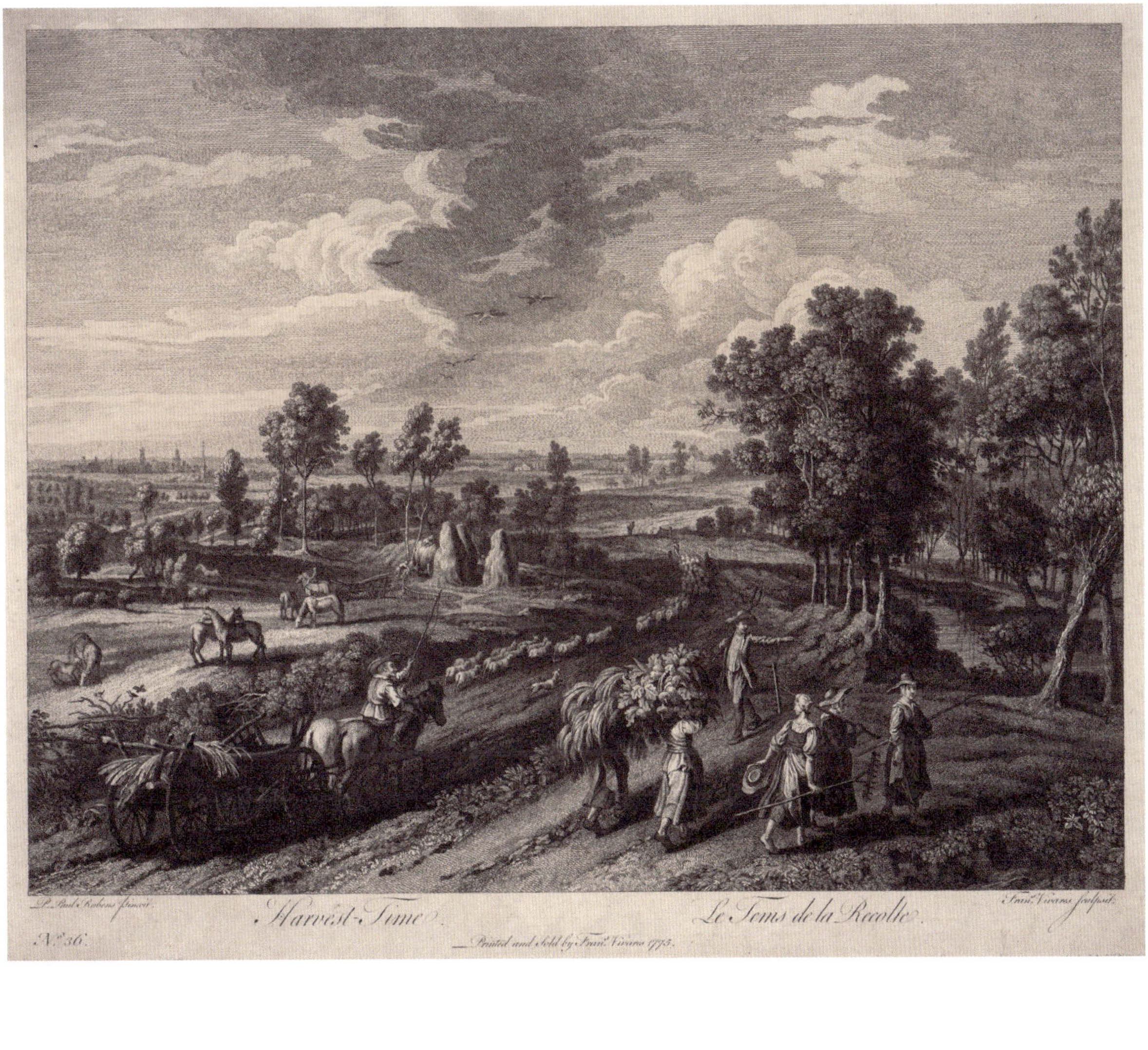

P. Paul Rubens pinxit. Harvest-Time. Le Tems de la Recolte. Fran. Vivares sculpsit.

No. 36. Printed and Sold by Fran. Vivares 1775.

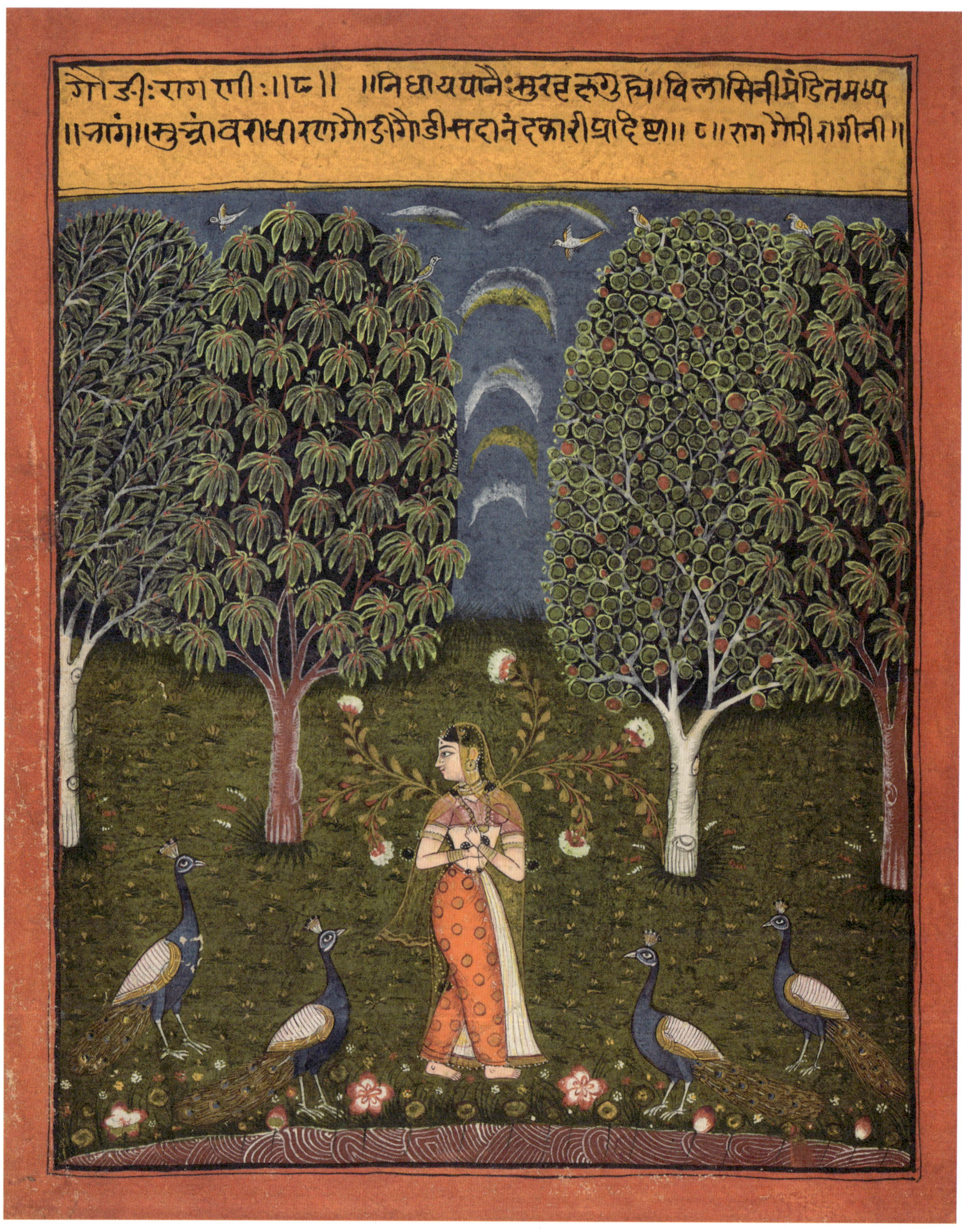

Gauri Ragini, Folio from a Ragamala, c. 1650, opaque watercolour and gold on paper, Unknown artist (Indian)

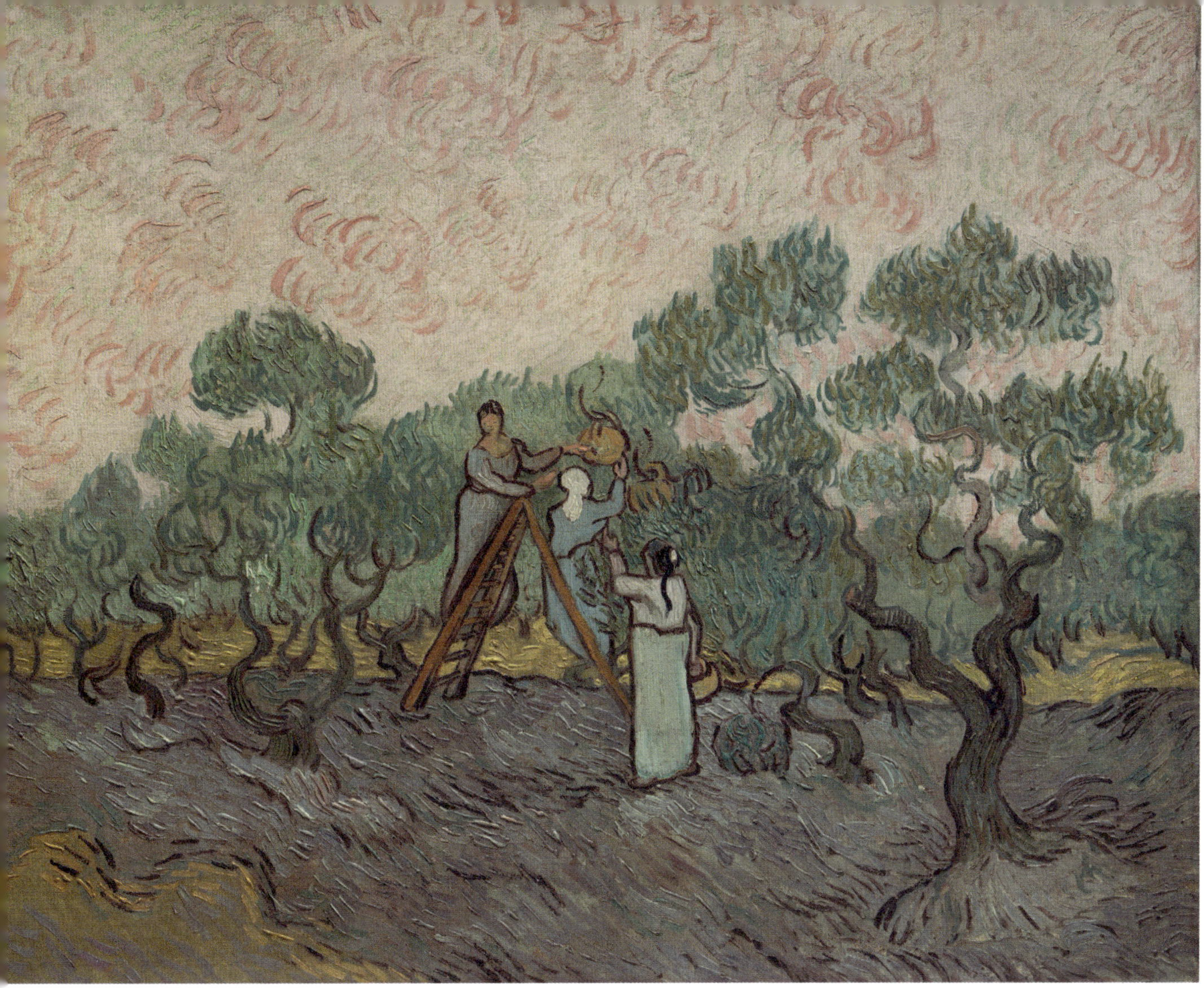

IN A LETTER TO HIS BROTHER THEO IN SEPTEMBER 1889, VINCENT VAN GOGH WROTE ' ... YOU KNOW THAT I CAME TO THE SOUTH AND THREW MYSELF INTO WORK FOR A THOUSAND REASONS. TO WANT TO SEE ANOTHER LIGHT, TO BELIEVE THAT LOOKING AT NATURE UNDER A BRIGHTER SKY CAN GIVE US A MORE ACCURATE IDEA OF THE JAPANESE WAY OF FEELING AND DRAWING.'

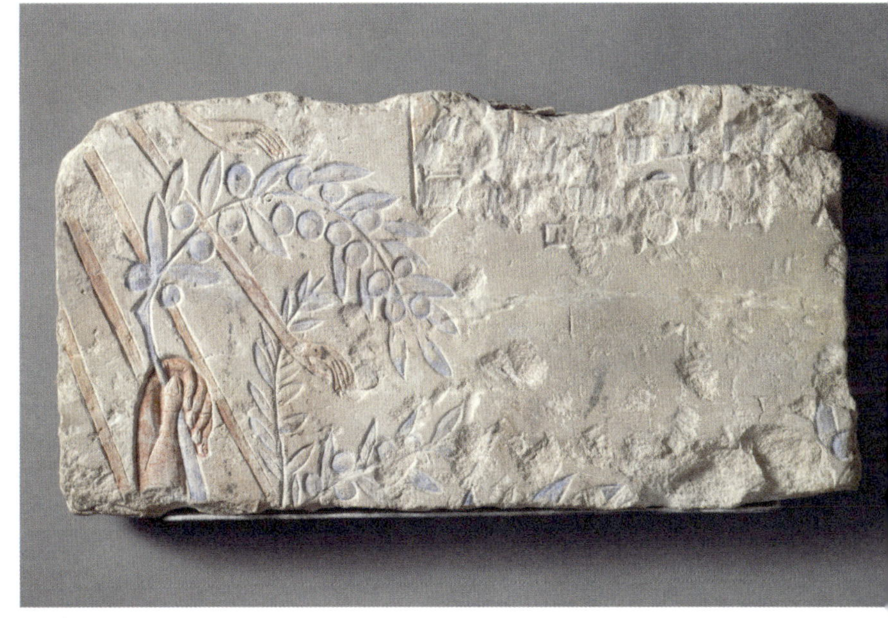

Top – *Women Picking Olives*, 1889, oil on canvas, Vincent van Gogh (Dutch)

Bottom – *Hand Clutching an Olive Branch*, limestone, c. 1353–1323 BC, limestone, Unknown artist (Ancient Egypt)

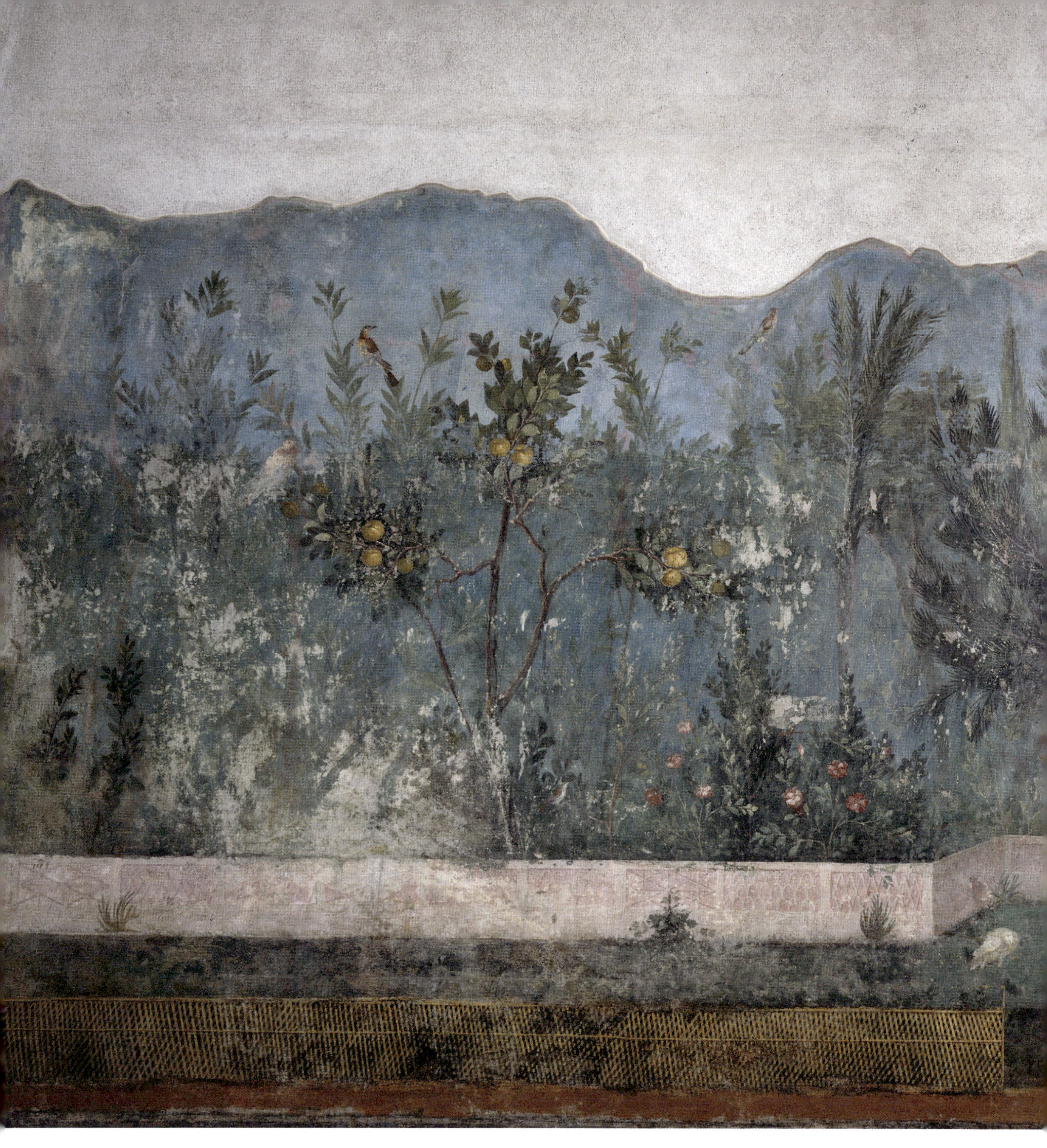

 The painted garden from the Villa of Livia, c. 40–20 BC, painted wall, Unknown artist (Roman)

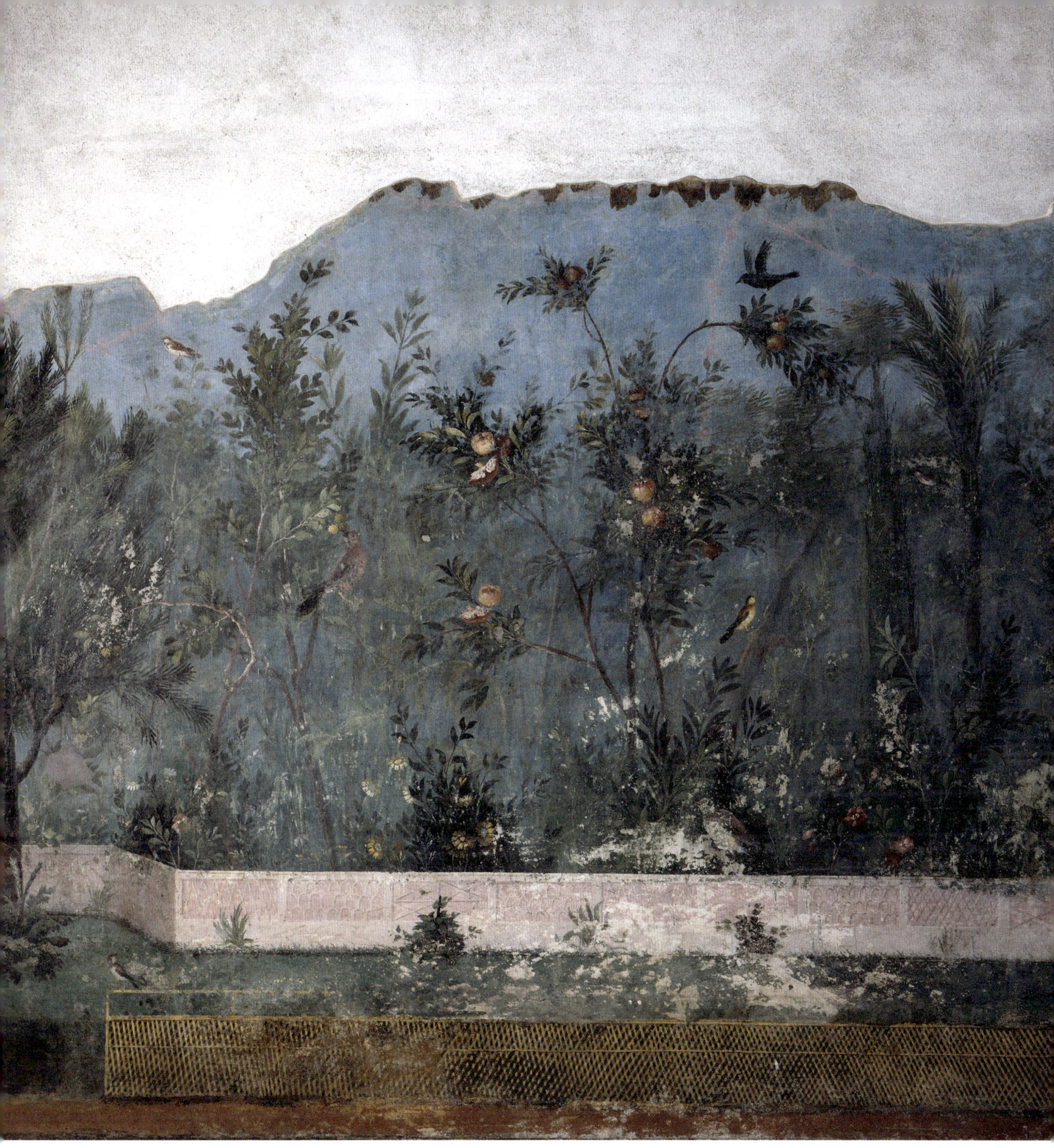

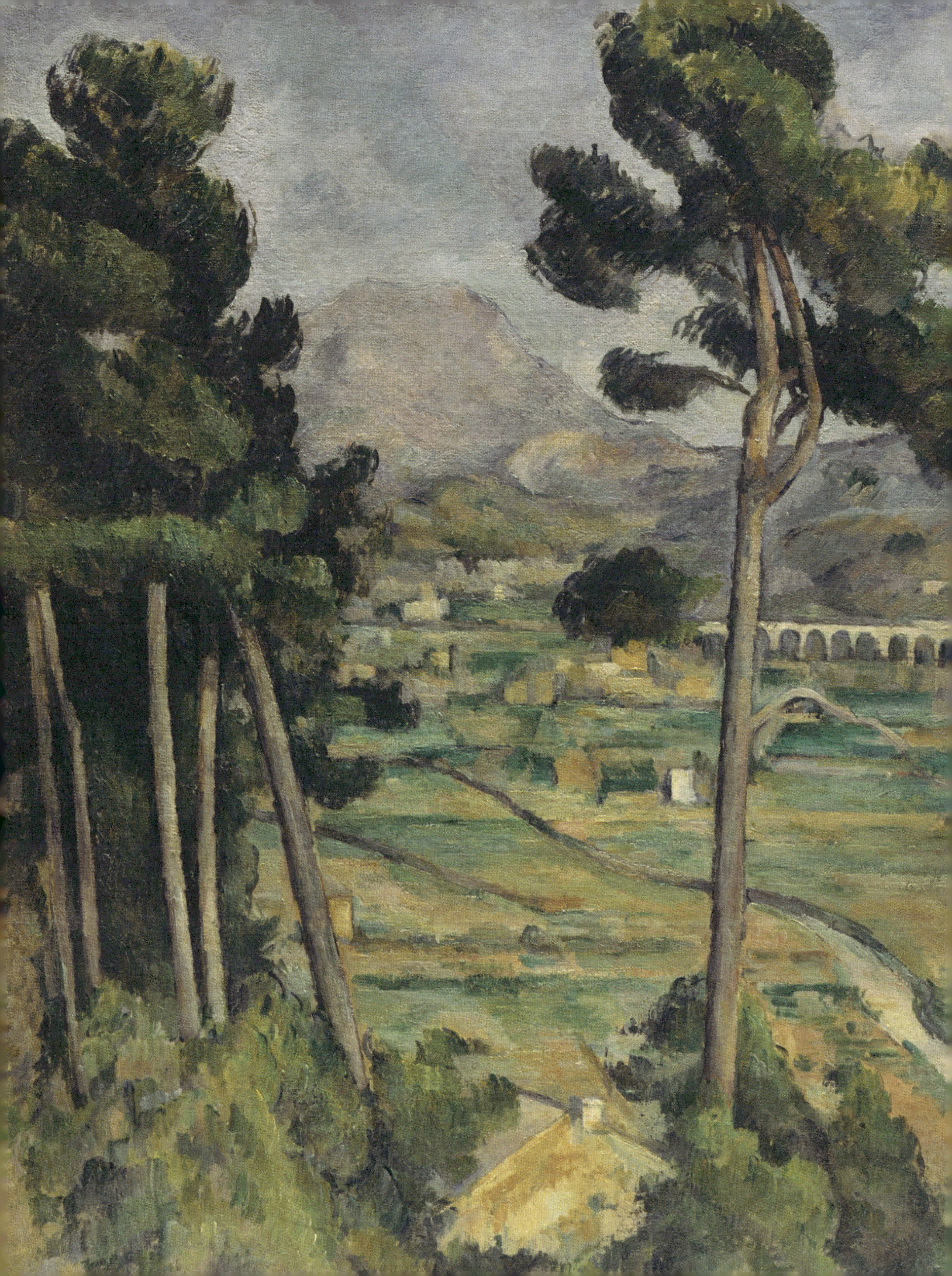

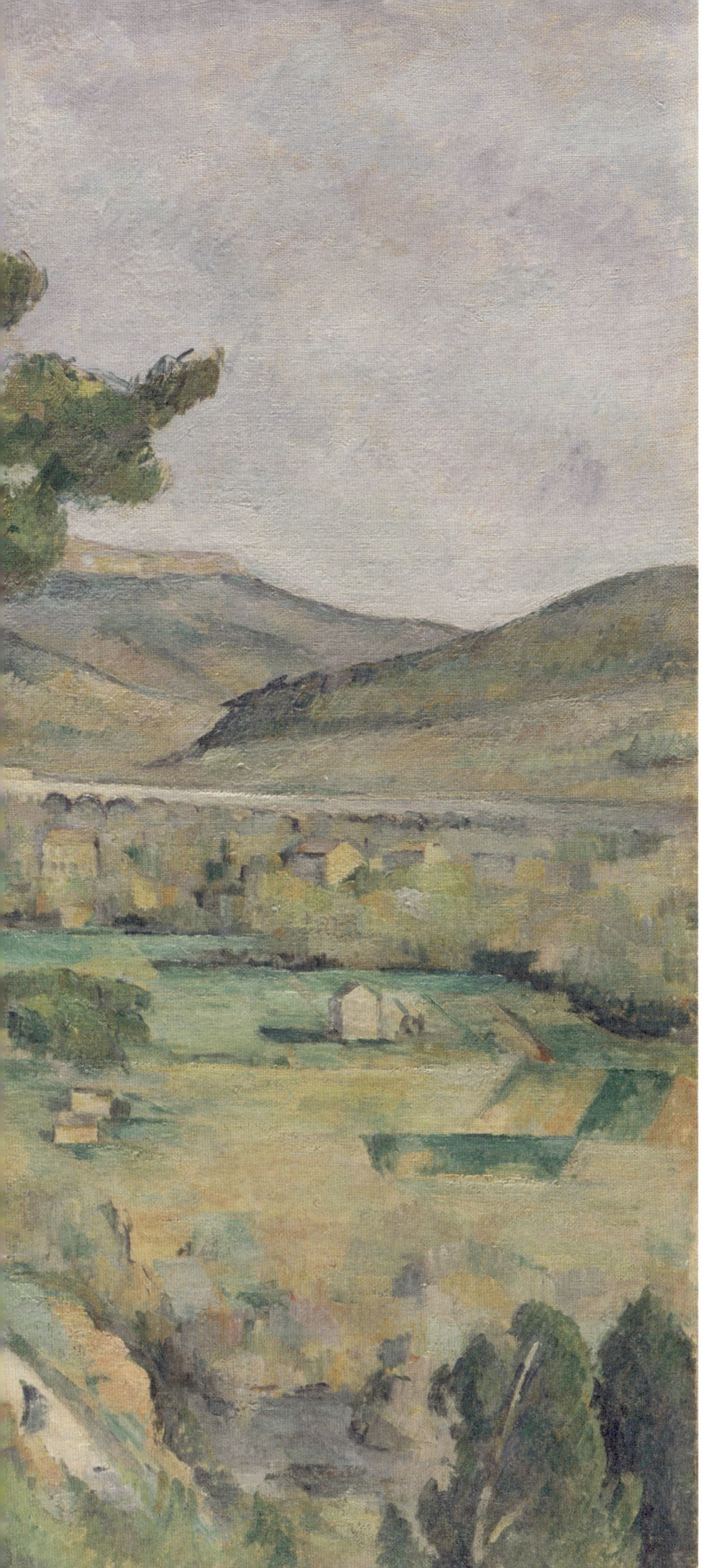

FIELDS

FIELDS PRESENT THE ARTIST WITH AN OPPORTUNITY TO ILLUSTRATE DISTINCTLY GEOMETRIC FORM AND PATTERN. LOOK FOR HORIZONTAL LINES THAT INTERSECT WITH THE IMPOSING VERTICAL LINES PROFILED AGAINST THE BLUE SKIES. OR AERIAL VIEWS OF PRAIRIES SEPARATED BY CORRIDORS AND FENCES.

Mont Sainte-Victoire and the Viaduct of the Arc River Valley, c. 1882–85, oil on canvas, Paul Cézanne (French)

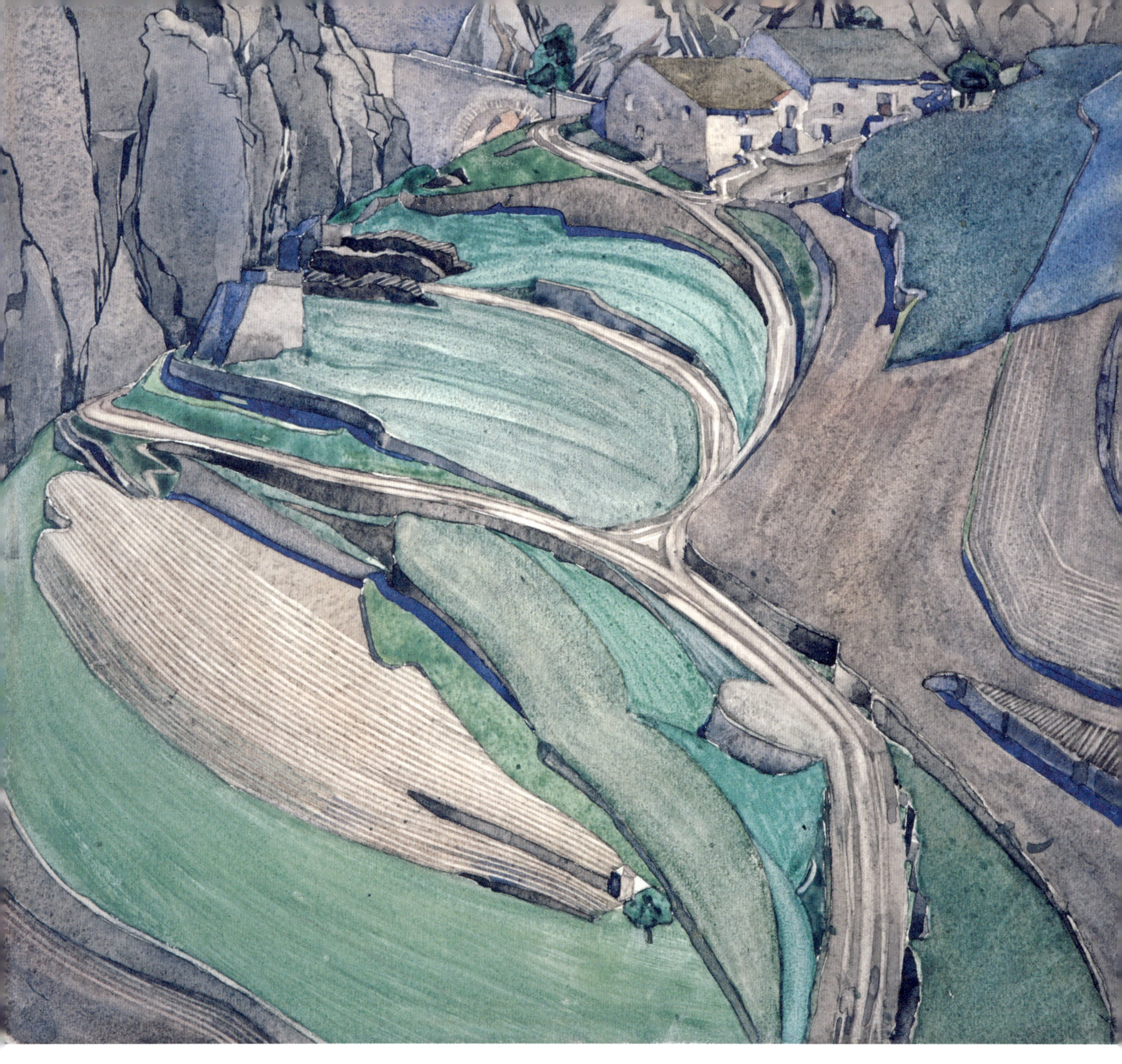

Above – *Mont Alba*, c. 1924–27, watercolour on paper, Charles Rennie Mackintosh (Scottish)

Opposite top – *An Idyllic Landscape: the sun shining on a meadow with a river and hills in the distance*, 1809, black chalk, pen and brown ink, brown and grey wash and watercolour, Johann Wilhelm Tischbein (German)

Opposite bottom – *Algarve*, 1971, coloured lithograph, Joan Williams (British)

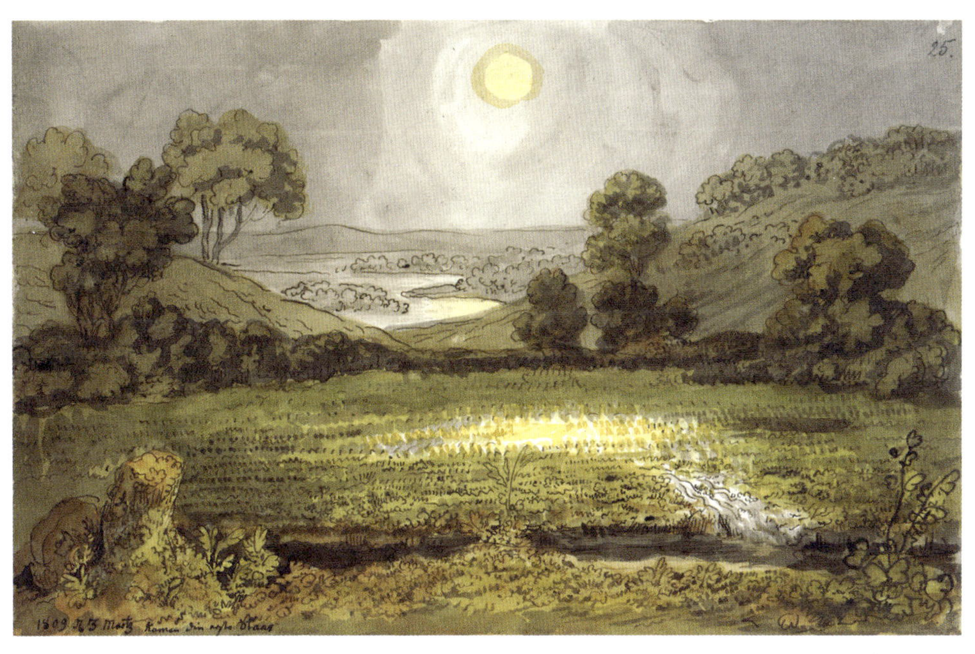
25.

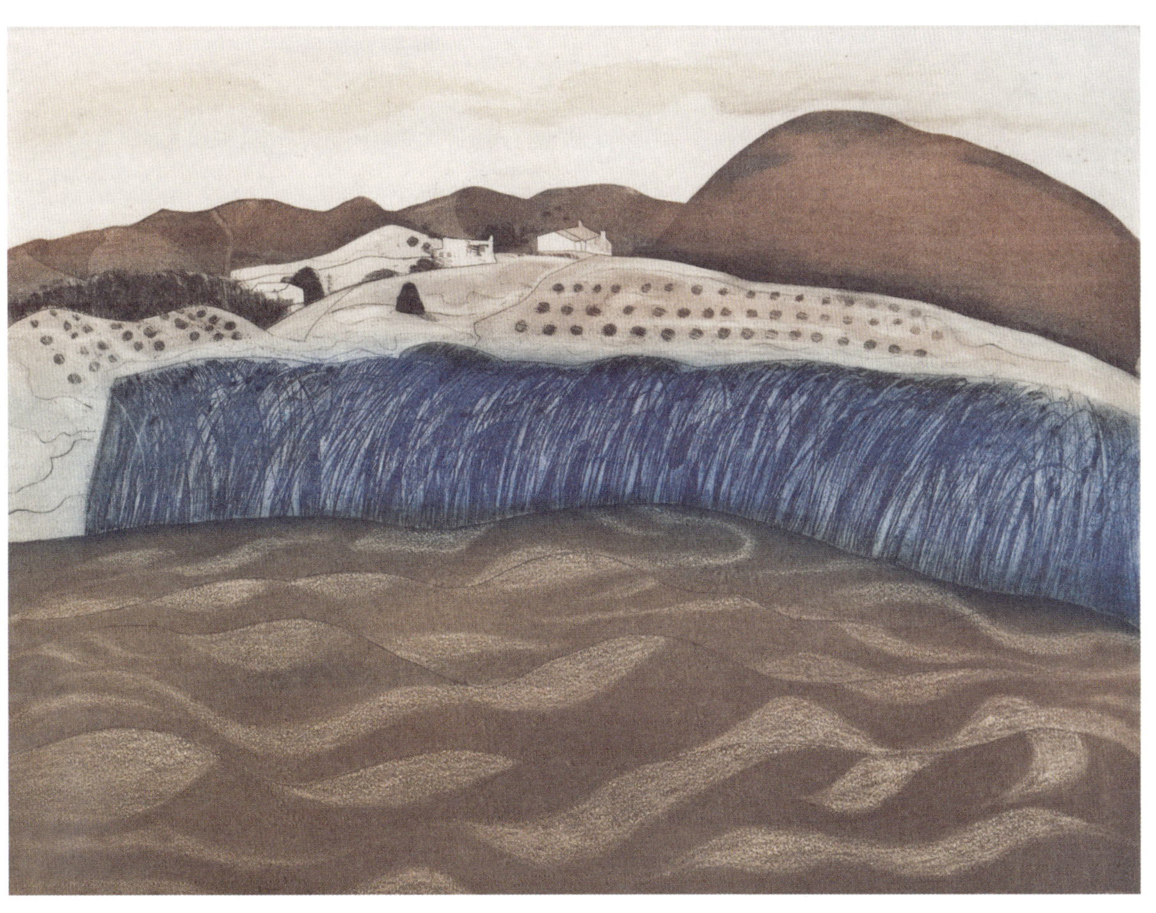

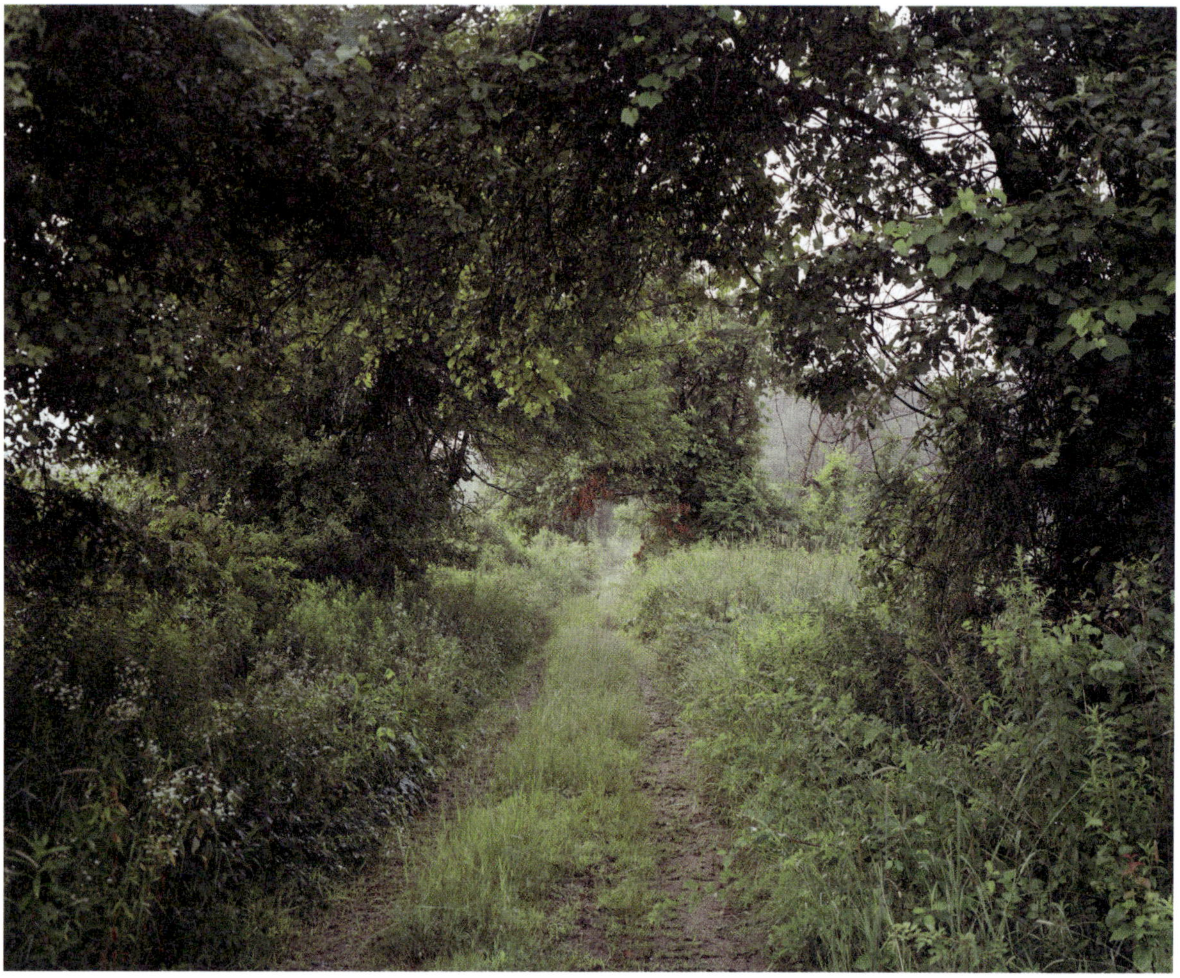

NOTICE THE OCCURRENCE OF PATHWAYS DEEPLY IMPRESSED ONTO MEADOWS OFTEN LEADING TO WOODED AREAS. IMAGINE WHAT LIES BEYOND THE TRAIL.

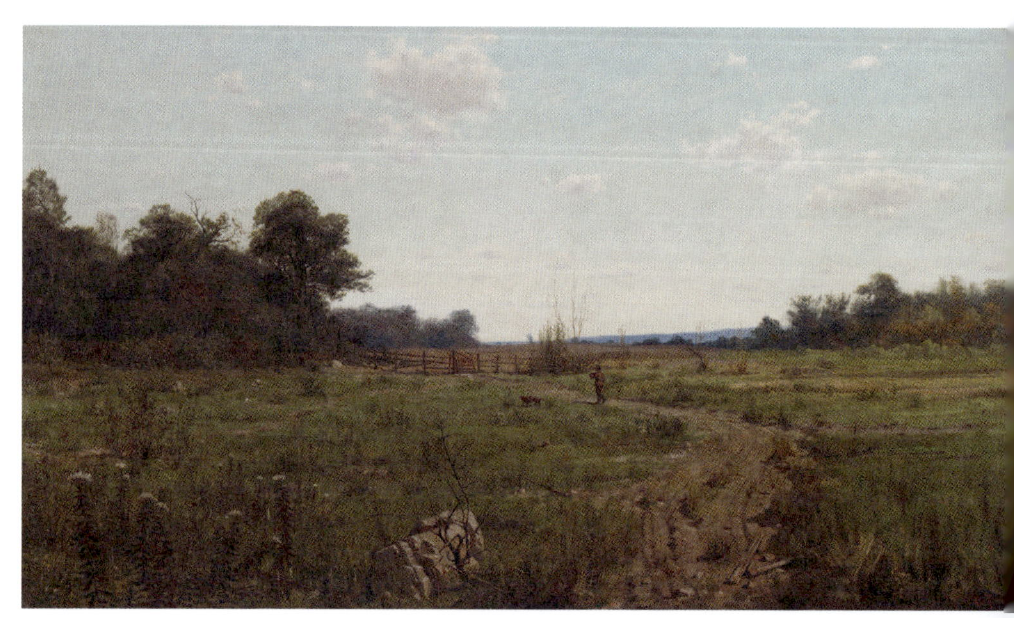

Top – *Untitled*, from the series *Meadow, Carlisle, Massachusetts*, 2004, chromogenic print, sheet and image, Barbara Bosworth (American)

Bottom – *September*, 1889, oil on canvas, Alexis Jean Fournier (American)

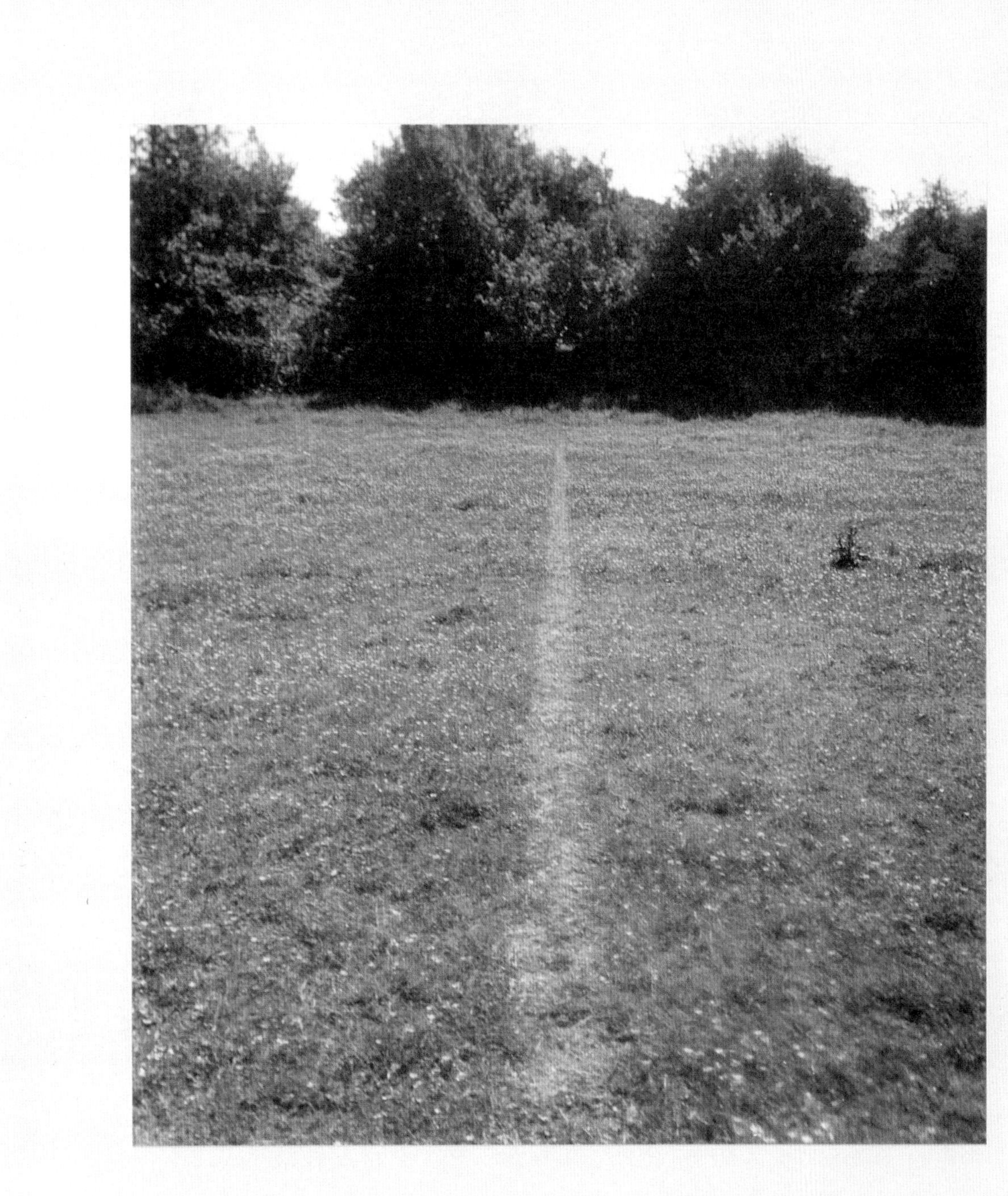

A Line Made by Walking, 1967, photograph, gelatin silver print on paper and graphite on board, Richard Long (British)

A FIGURE RESTS IN DAPPLED SUNLIGHT THAT GLIMMERS THROUGH THE CANOPY ABOVE. JEAN-BAPTISTE CAMILLE COROT CAPTURES A POETIC FEEL THROUGH HIS MASTERFUL USE OF CONTRAST AND THE DELICATE MIX OF COLOURS.

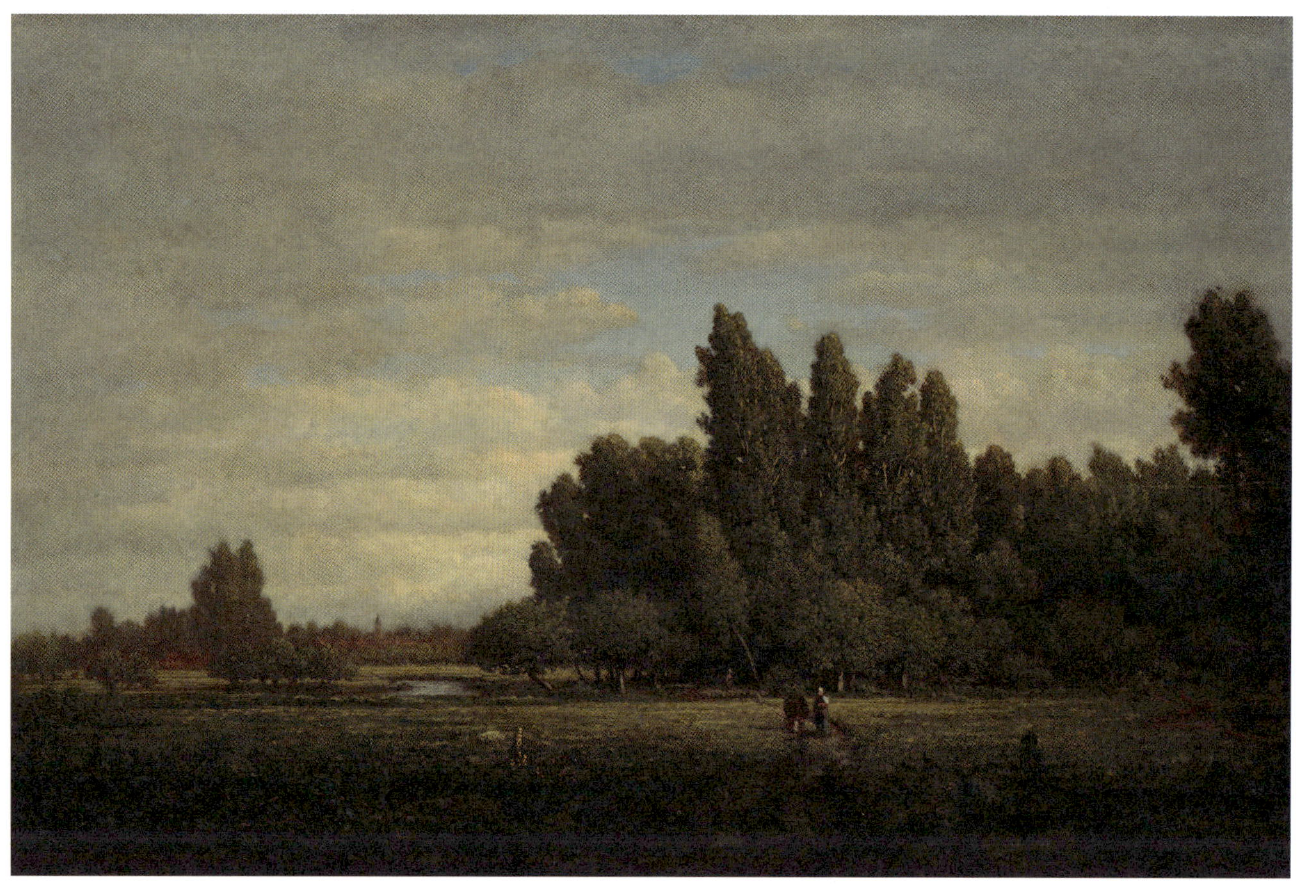

Above – *A Meadow Bordered by Trees,* c. 1845–60, oil on wood, Théodore Rousseau (French)

Opposite – *Ville-d'Avray: Entrance to the Wood,* c. 1823–25, oil on canvas, Jean-Baptiste Camille Corot (French)

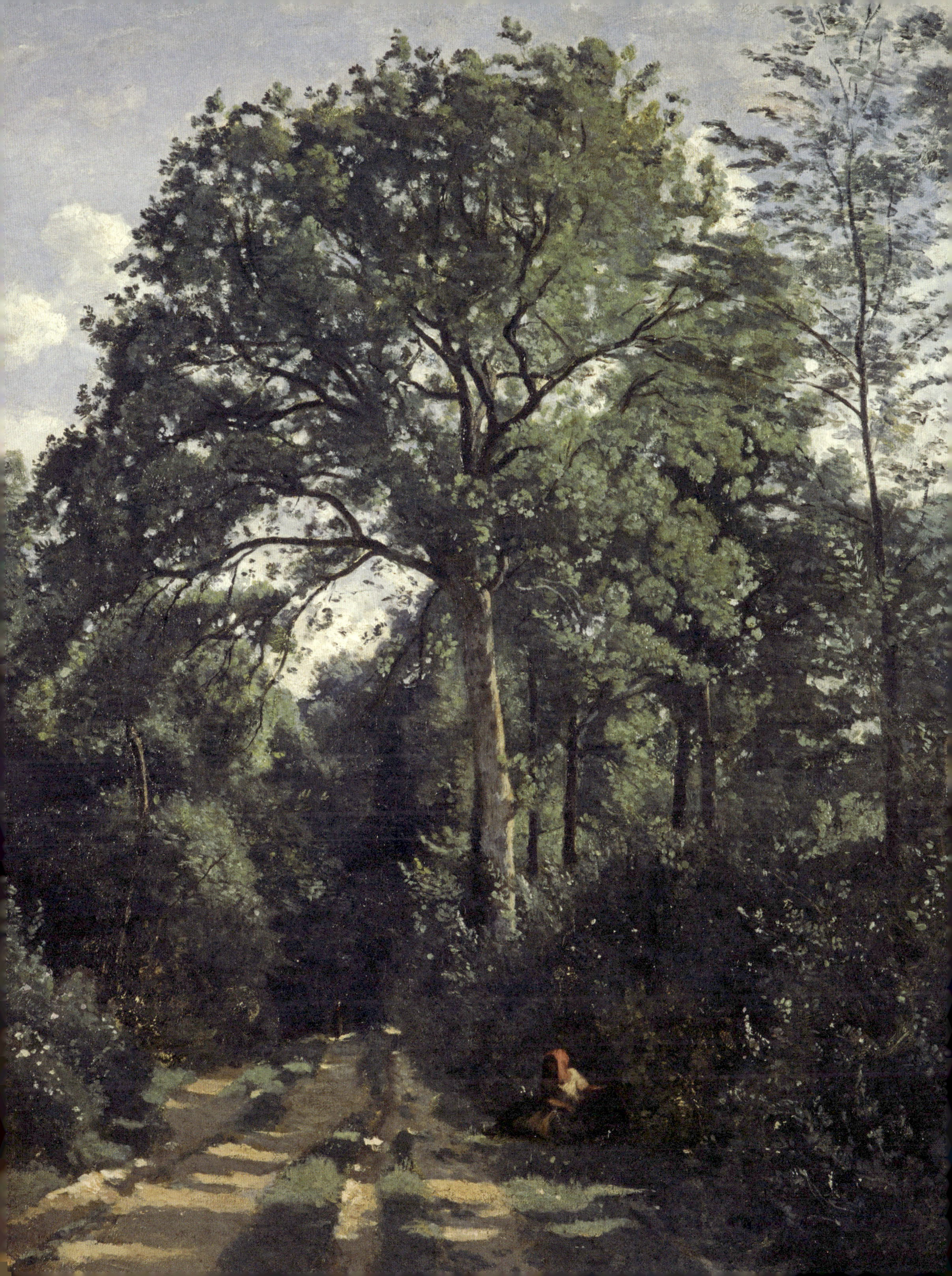

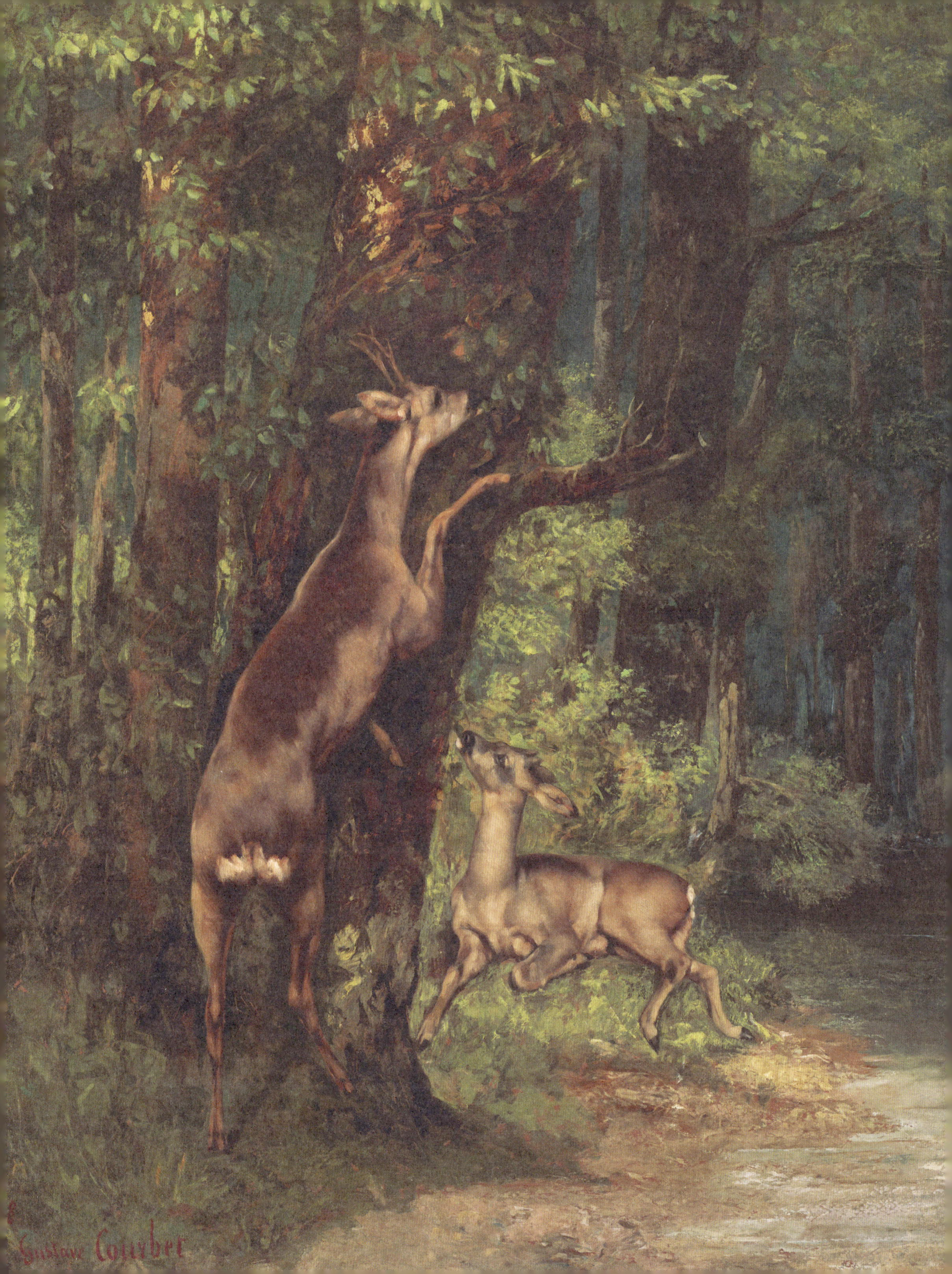
Gustave Courbet

FORESTS & WOODLANDS

THE FOREST IS ANIMATED WITH WOODLAND CREATURES AND INSECTS. ARTISTS HAVE FOUND CAPTIVATING AND WHIMSICAL WAYS OF INCLUDING THEM IN THEIR WORKS. GUSTAVE COURBET'S REALIST STYLE OF PAINTING IS EPITOMISED IN HIS LANDSCAPE WORKS, ESPECIALLY THOSE SET IN THE FOREST. THE DEER IN HIS PAINTING APPEAR TO MERGE WITH THE TREES, SLIDING IN AND OUT OF VIEW THE CLOSER YOU LOOK. A SOFT GOLDEN LIGHT TOUCHES THEIR FUR AND SOME OF THE LEAVES ON THE TREE CANOPY, INDICATING THE SCENE MIGHT TAKE PLACE AT DUSK.

THE FOREST BED IN KATAYAMA BOKUYŌ'S PAINTING IS COVERED IN FLOWERING FRESH MINT AND WILD STRAWBERRIES. A SLENDER WEASEL HUNTING UNDER THE GREENERY LOOKS UP AND OUTWARD, FOR A MOMENT HOLDING DIRECT GAZE WITH THE VIEWER.

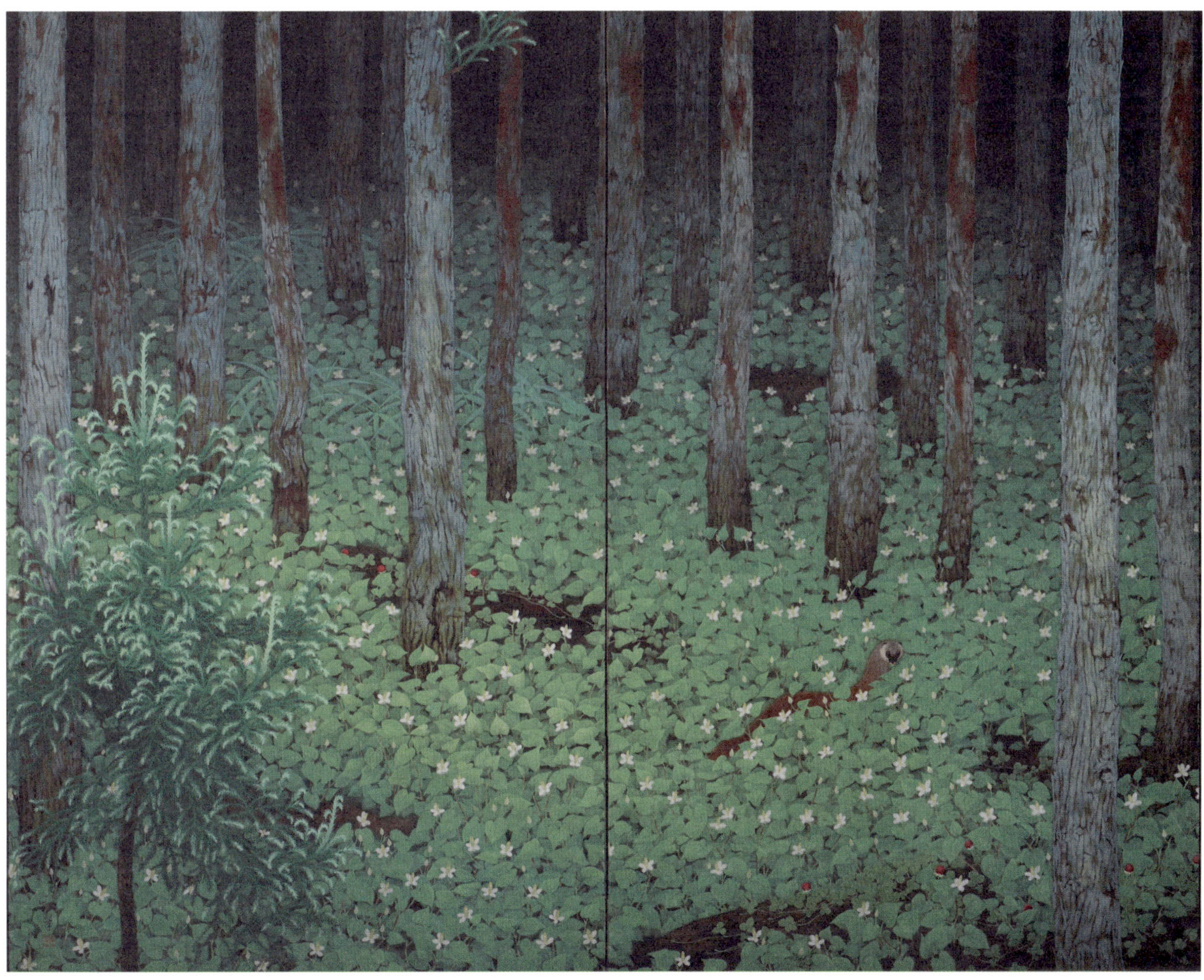

Opposite – *Deer in the Forest*, 1868, oil on canvas, Gustave Courbet (French)

Above – *Forest*, 1928, ink and mineral pigments on silk, Katayama Bokuyō (Japanese)

Following – *Shepherd and Shepherdess Making Music* (detail), c. 1500–30, wool warp, wool and silk wefts, Unknown artist (South Netherlandish)

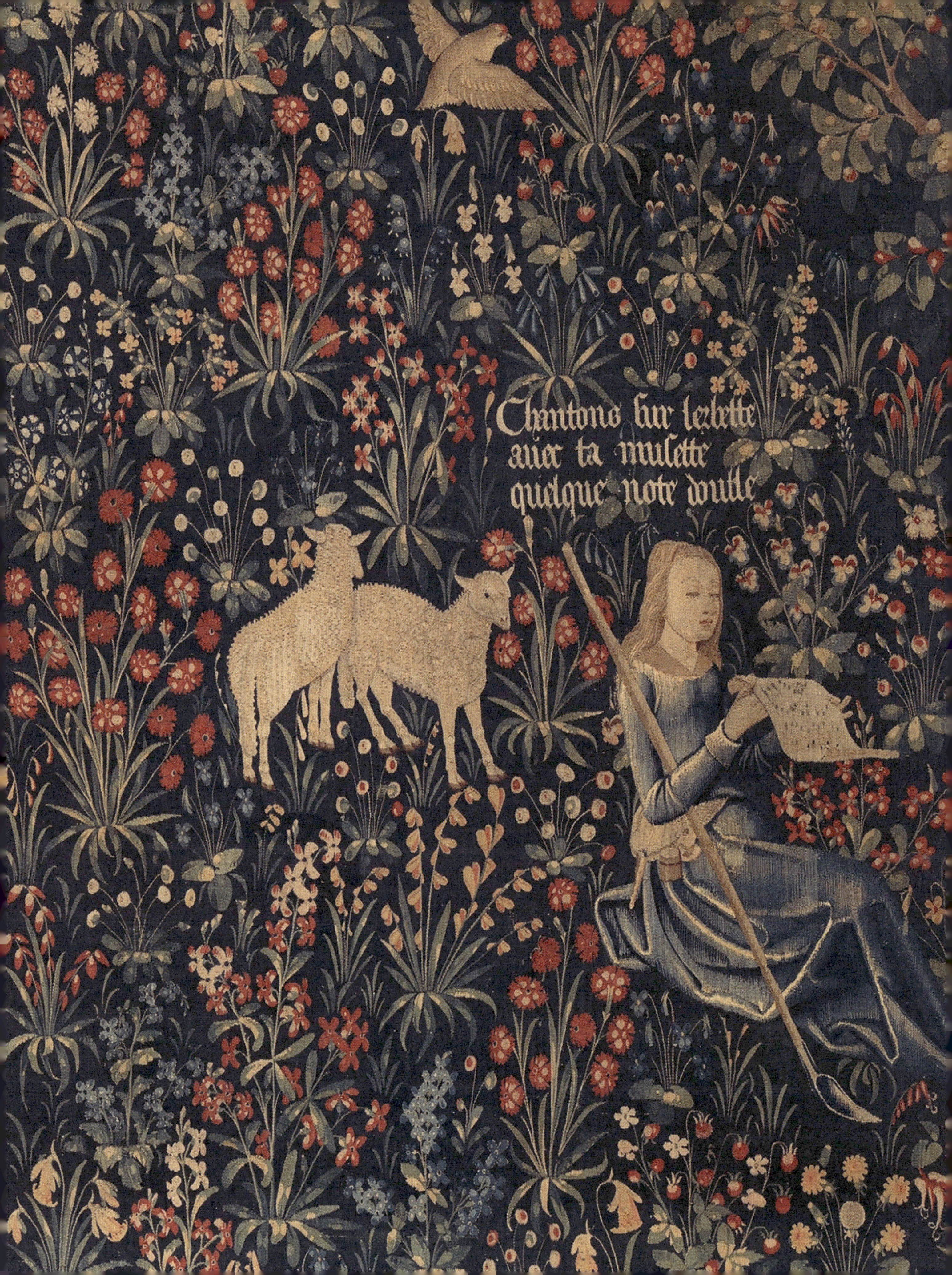
Chantons sur lerbette
auec ta musette
quelque note doulce

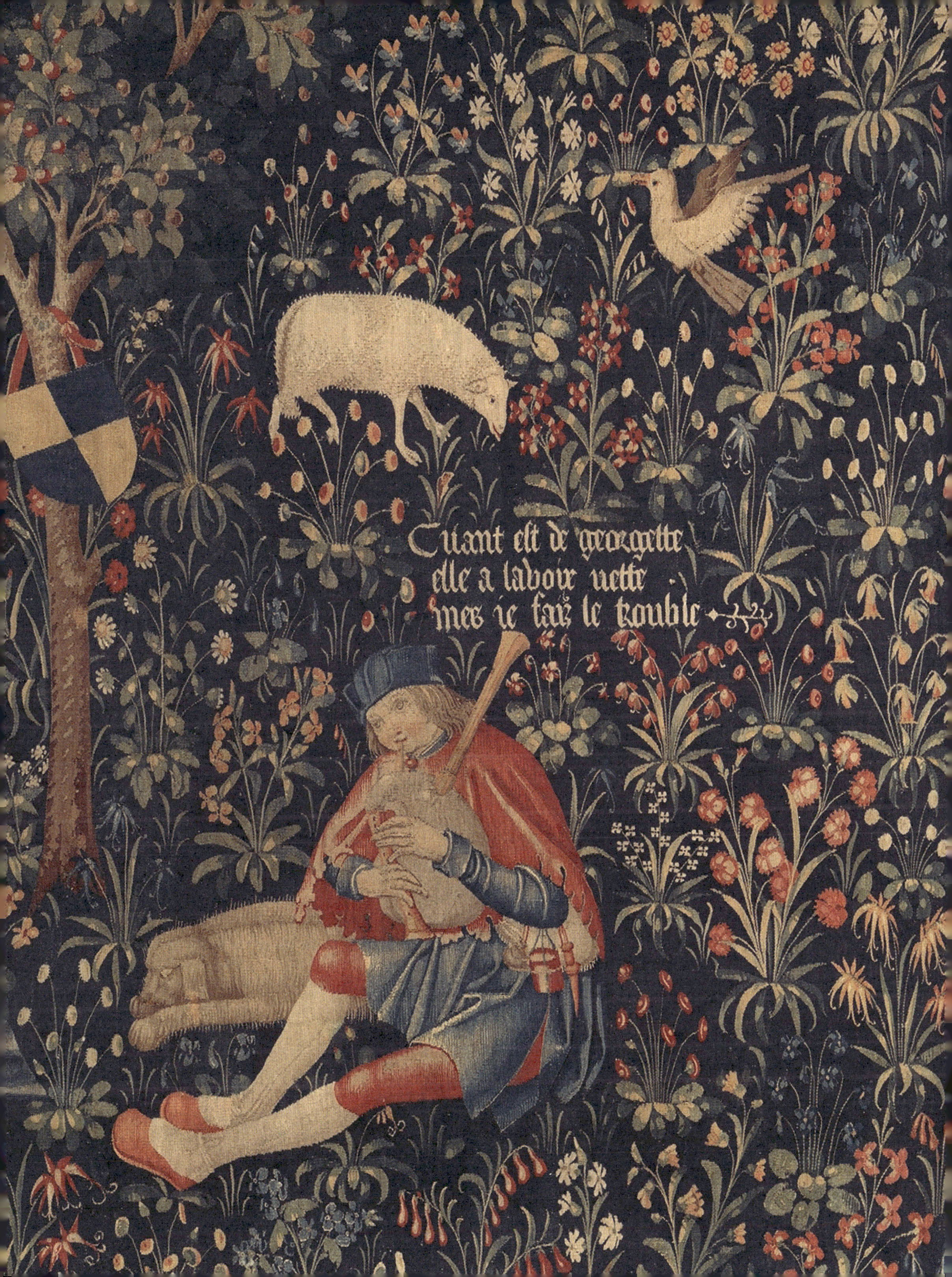
Cuant est de georgette
elle a labour nette
mes ie faiz le trouble

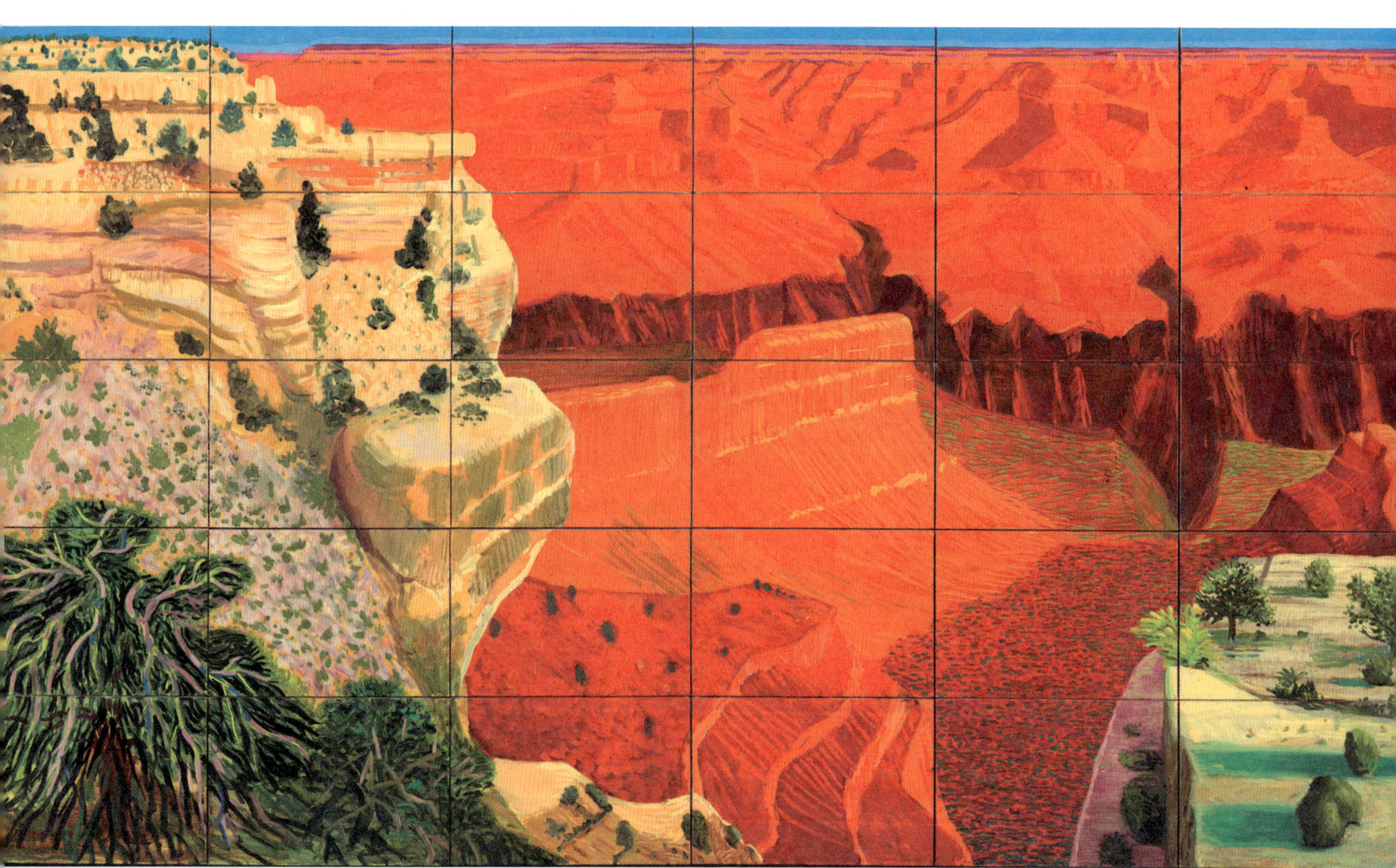

HOCKNEY'S LARGESCALE WORK *A BIGGER GRAND CANYON* COMPRISES SIXTY CANVASES. THIS COLOURFUL AND DETAILED PAINTING TAKES THE VIEWER TO THE SOUTH EDGE OF THIS IMMENSE CRATER. WHILE EMPHASISING VARIOUS CHARACTERISTICS OF THE DESERT LANDSCAPE, HOCKNEY HAS MANAGED TO CONVEY MULTIPLE VIEWPOINTS IN ONE WORK.

 A Bigger Grand Canyon, 1998, oil on sixty canvas, David Hockney (British)

ROCKS, MOUNTAINS & GORGES

GIVEN THE MANY AND VARIED VANTAGE POINTS FROM WHICH THEY MAY BE VIEWED, MOUNTAINS OFFER A SPECIAL SET OF CHALLENGES FOR AN ARTIST. WHEN CREATING A PORTRAIT OF A MOUNTAIN, IS IT POSSIBLE TO DETECT THE CHARACTER BY ITS SURFACE ALONE? ARTISTS ACROSS CULTURES AND TECHNIQUES HAVE ATTEMPTED TO CAPTURE THE ESSENCE OF MOUNTAINS FROM A CLOSE VANTAGE POINT, FROM A GREAT DISTANCE, OR THROUGH IMAGINATIVE PRACTICES AND STORIES. TO DESCRIBE THE SPIRIT OF THE MOUNTAIN, AND ITS SENSE OF TRUE LIVELINESS, AN ARTIST MAY RENDER VAPOURS, CREVASSES OR TROUGHS TO CREATE A SENSE OF DEPTH AND GREAT HEIGHT.

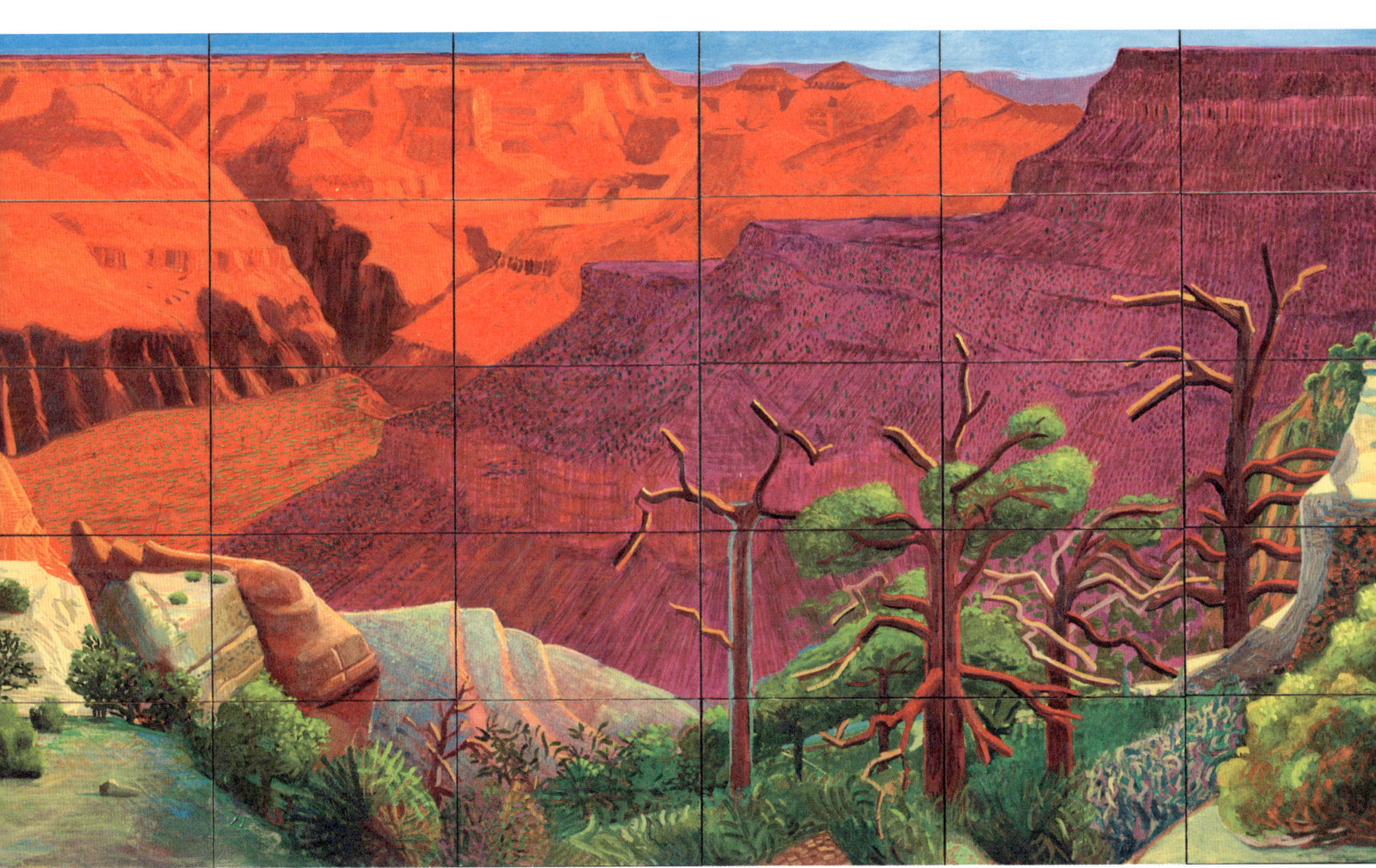

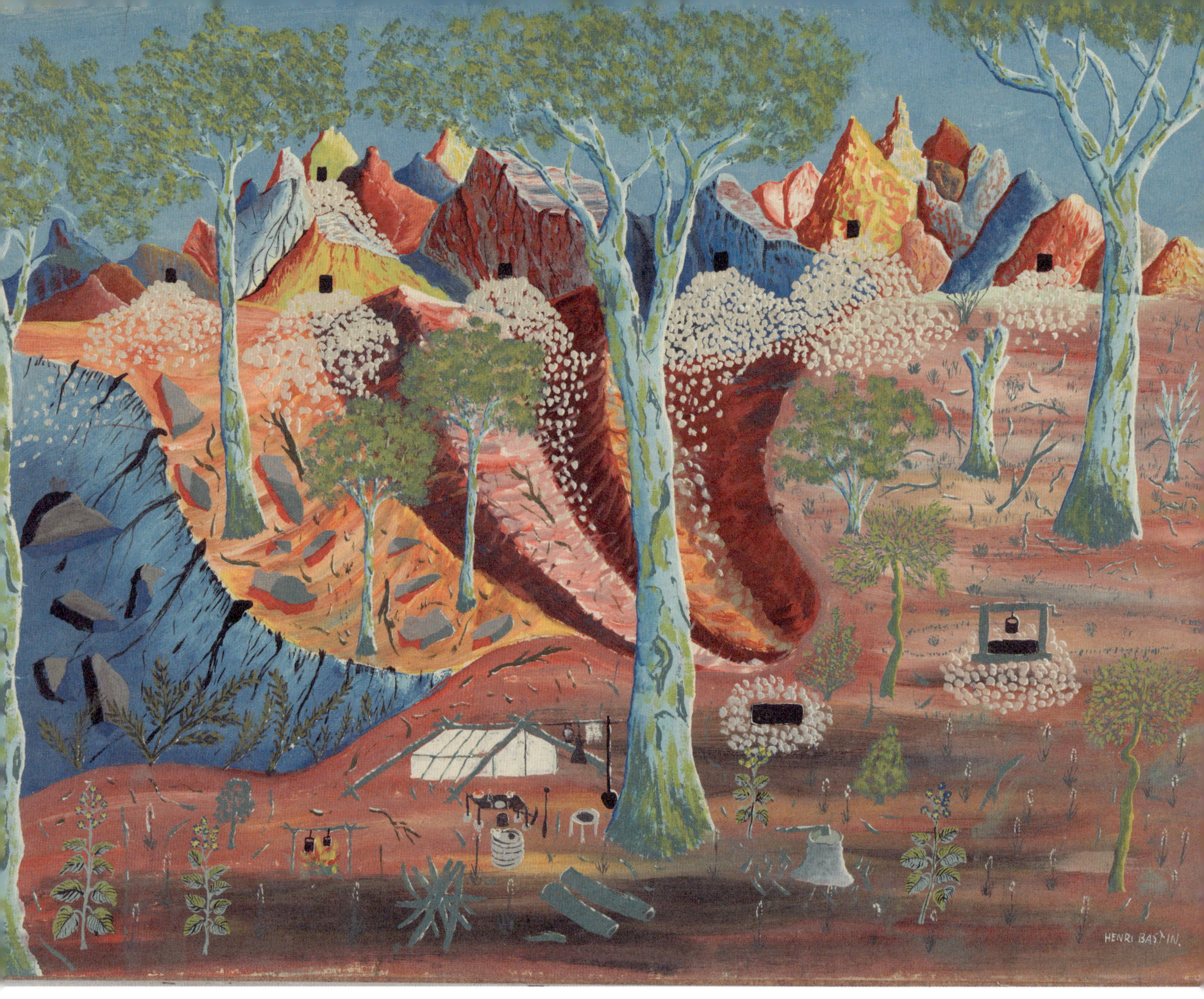

Above – *Opal miner's camp*, 1958, synthetic polymer paint on composition board, Henri Bastin (Belgian)

Opposite top – *Spanish Landscape with Mountains*, c. 1924, oil paint on canvas, Dora Carrington (British)

Opposite bottom – *Desert*, 1950, oil and enamel on composition board, Sidney Nolan (Australian)

Following – *The rabbiters*, 1947, oil on canvas, Russell Drysdale (Australian)

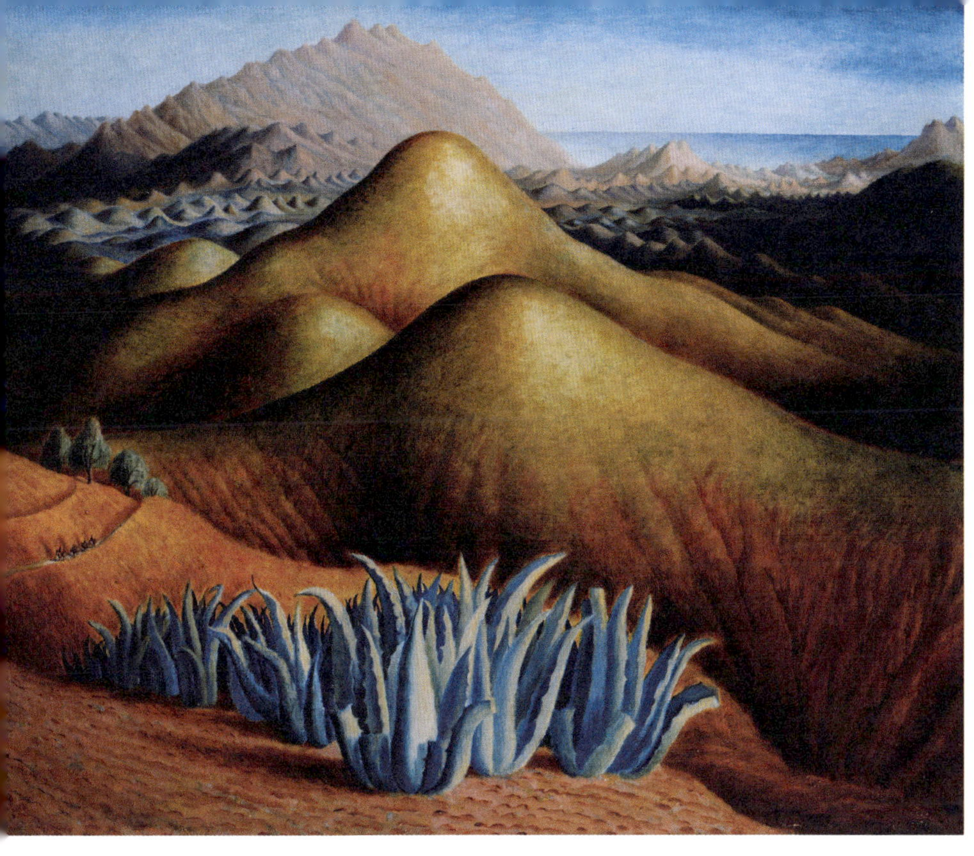

THE MONUMENTAL SCALE OF THE GOLDEN ROUNDED MOUNTAINTOPS OF THE ANDALUSIAN LANDSCAPE IS BRILLIANTLY HIGHLIGHTED BY THE TRAIL OF TINY TRAVELLERS HIKING ALONG THE SIDE OF A HILL. THE SPIKY BLUE GREEN AGAVE GATHERED IN THE FOREGROUND OF THE COMPOSITION ACTS LIKE A REFRESHING POOL IN AN OTHERWISE VAST AND DESERT-LIKE LANDSCAPE. IMAGINE THE HEAT OF THE DAY AND LONGING FOR A COOL REFRESHMENT AT THE END OF A LONG WALK.

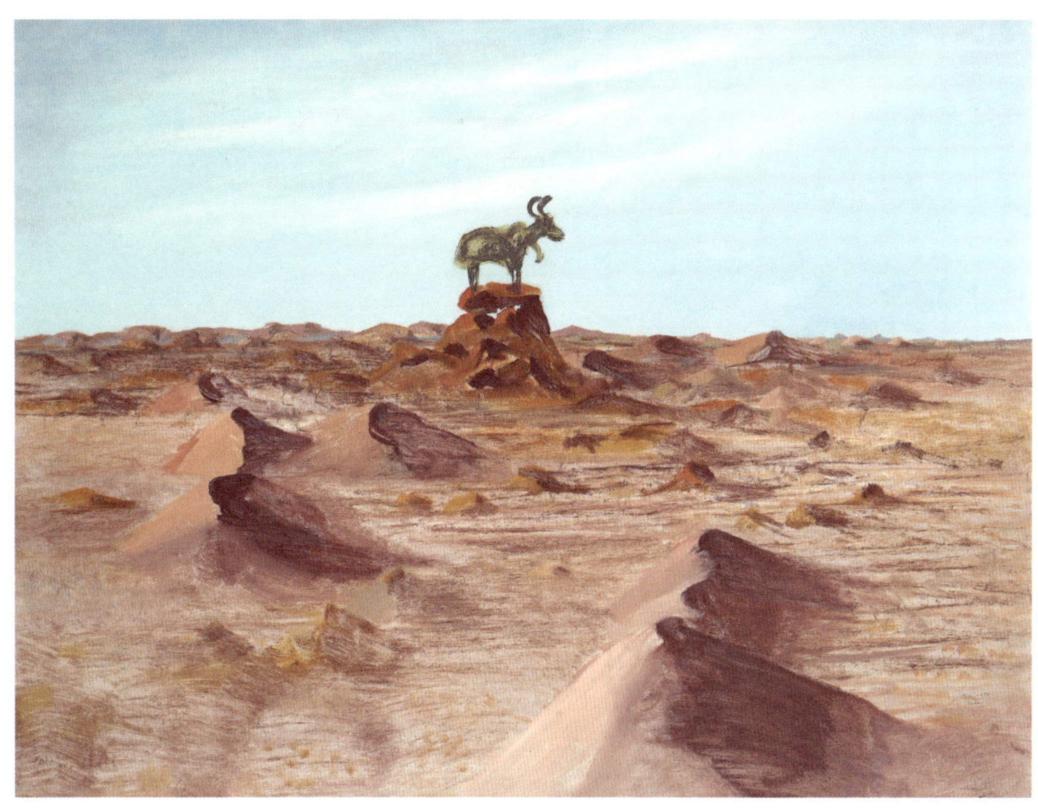

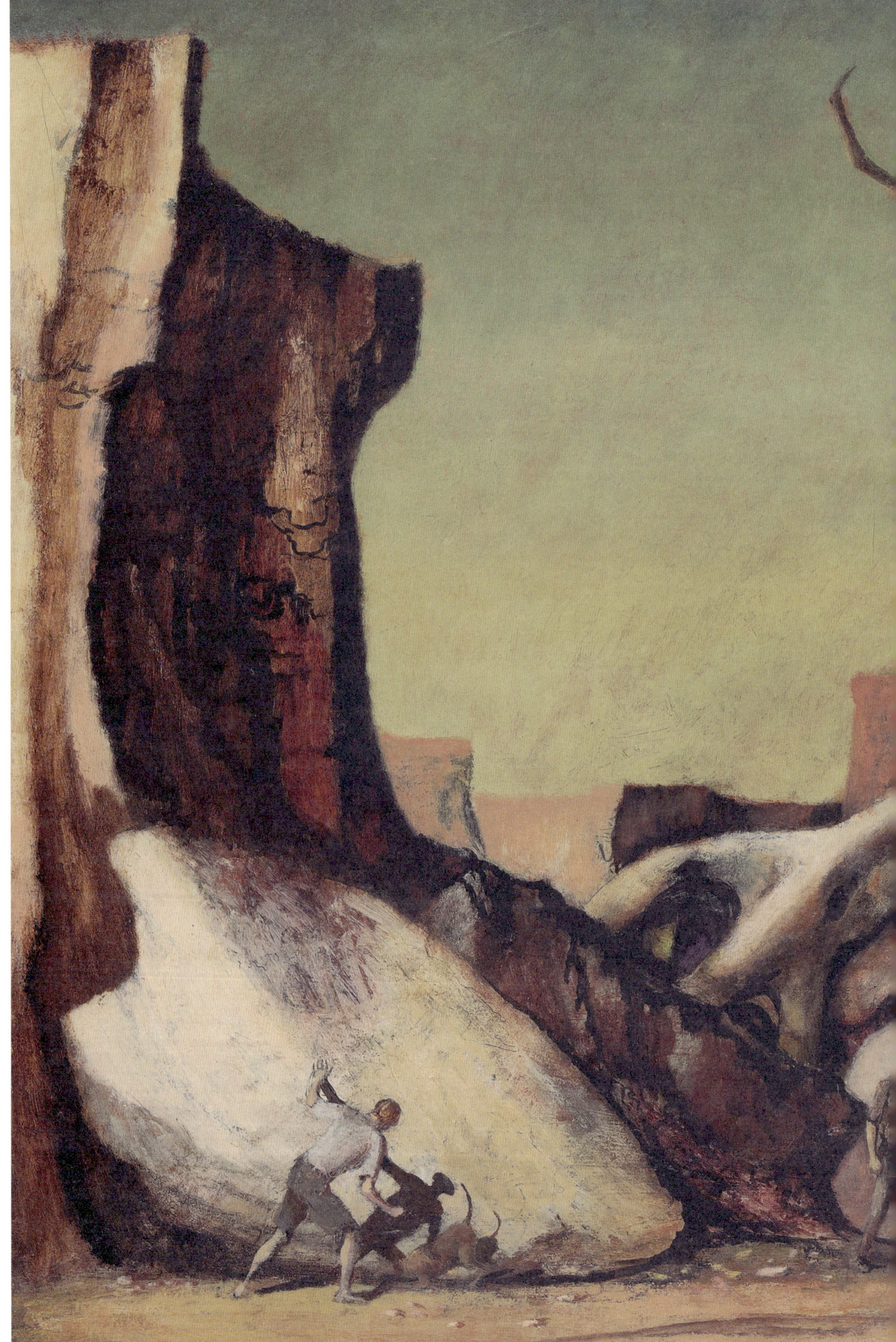

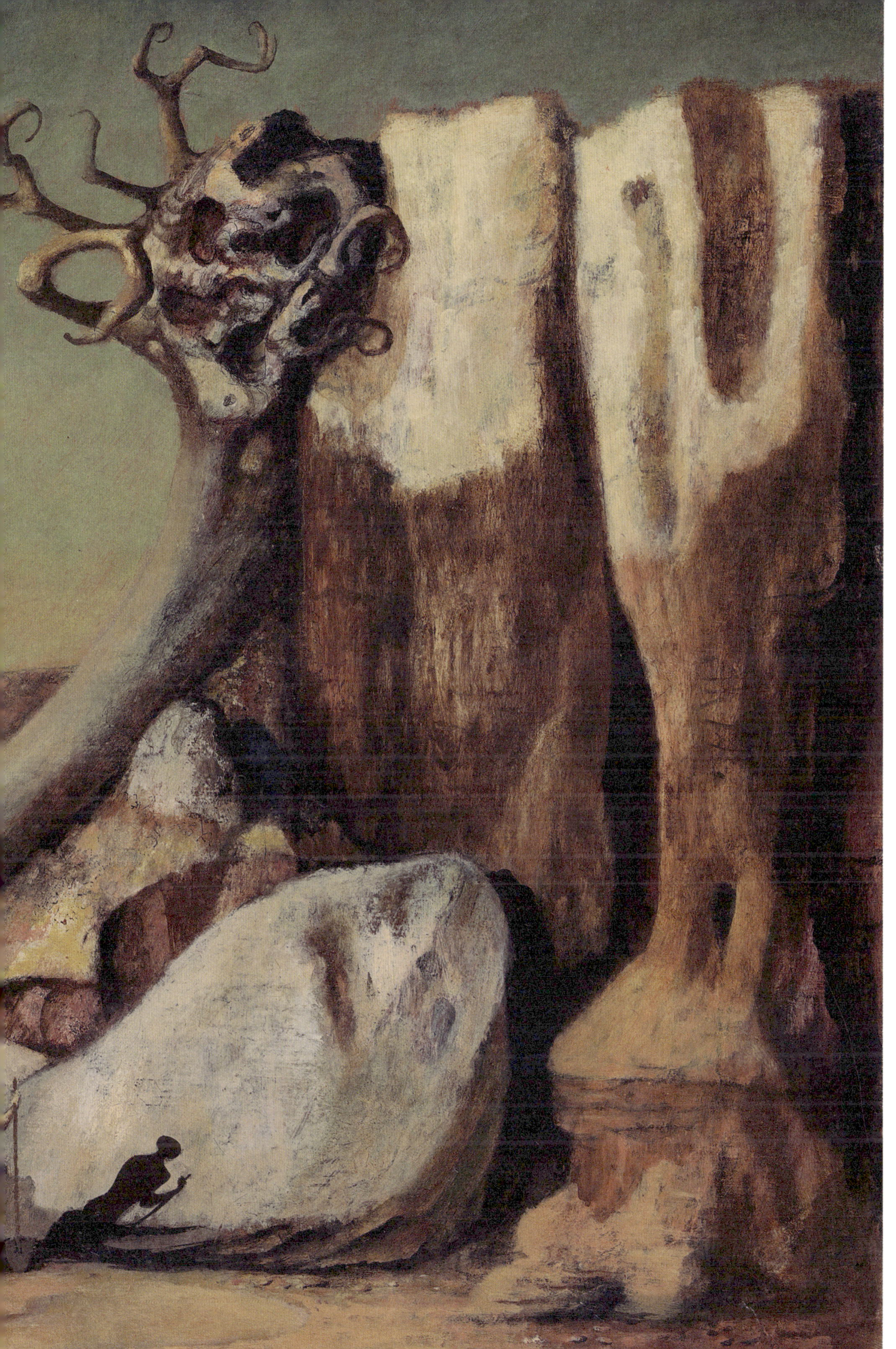

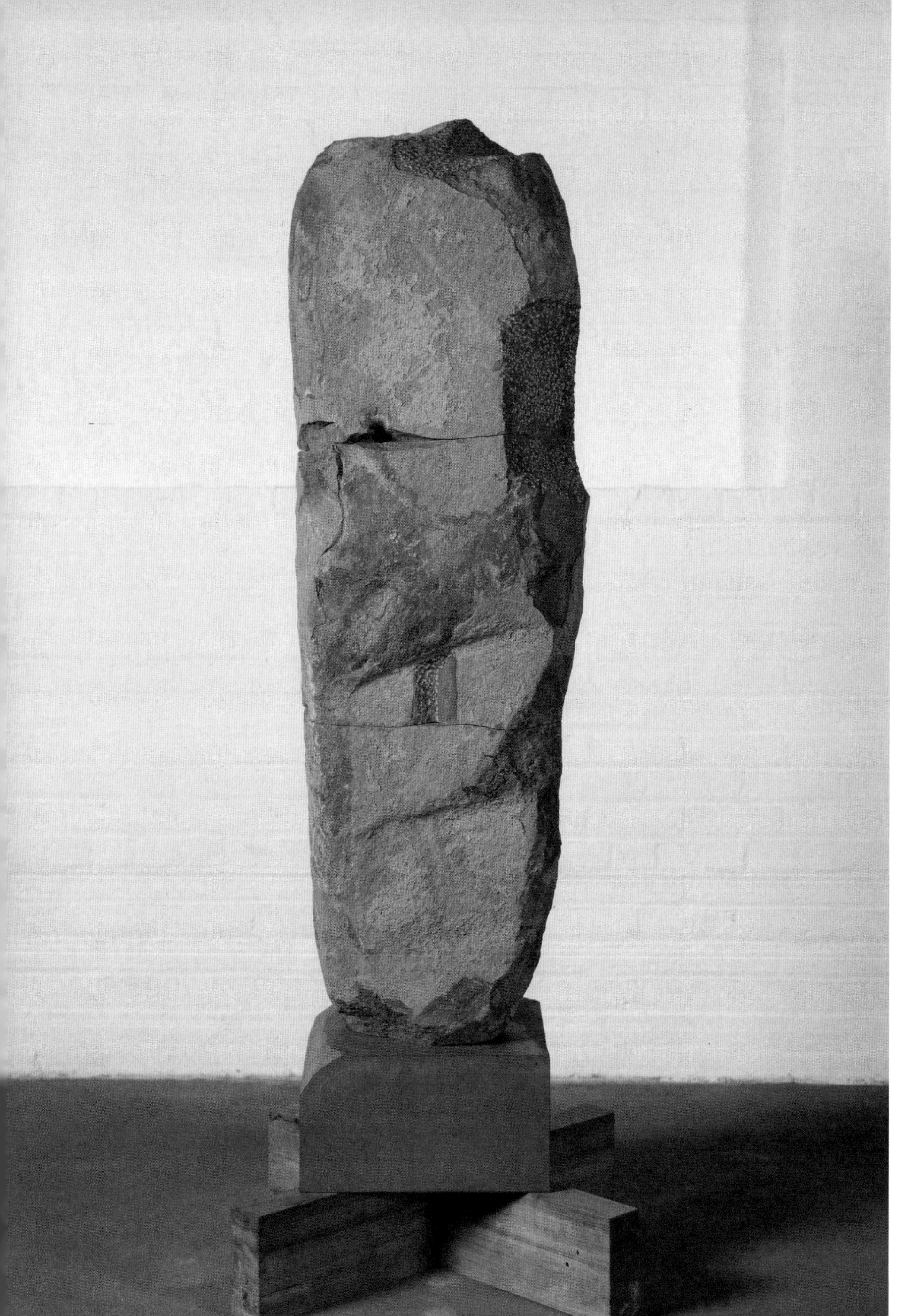

PERPENDICULAR FORM LEADS THE EYE SKYWARD; IT CAN ALSO ACT AS A CONDUIT BETWEEN THINGS. CONSIDER THE ARRANGEMENT OF FORM AND HOW IT IS USED TO DIRECT THE GAZE, AND TO SHAPE INTERPRETATION.

Opposite – *To Intrude on Nature's Way*, 1971, basalt with Japanese pine base, Isamu Noguchi (Japanese/American)

Below – *Vanquished*, 1930, oil on canvas, Emily Carr (Canadian)

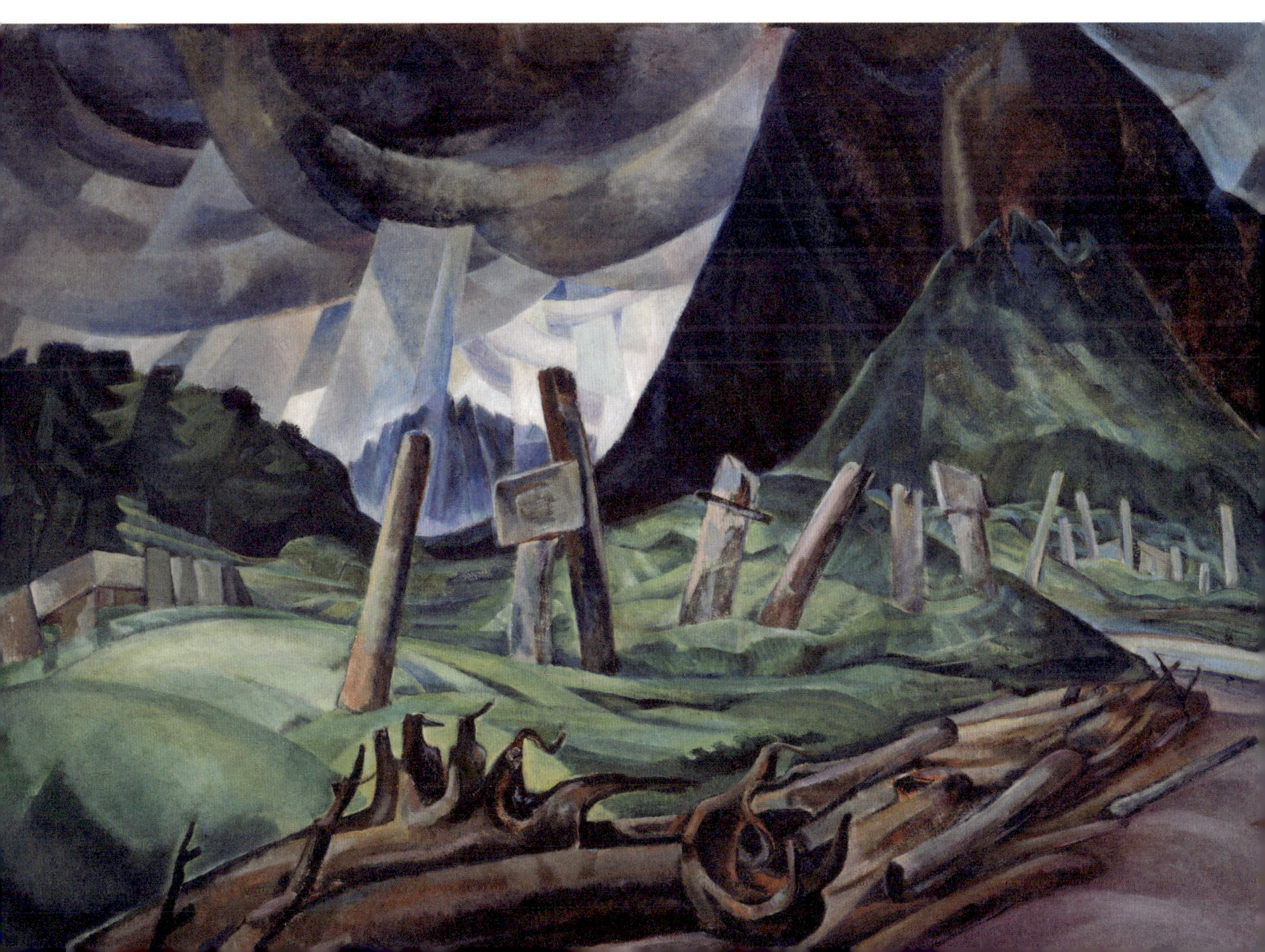

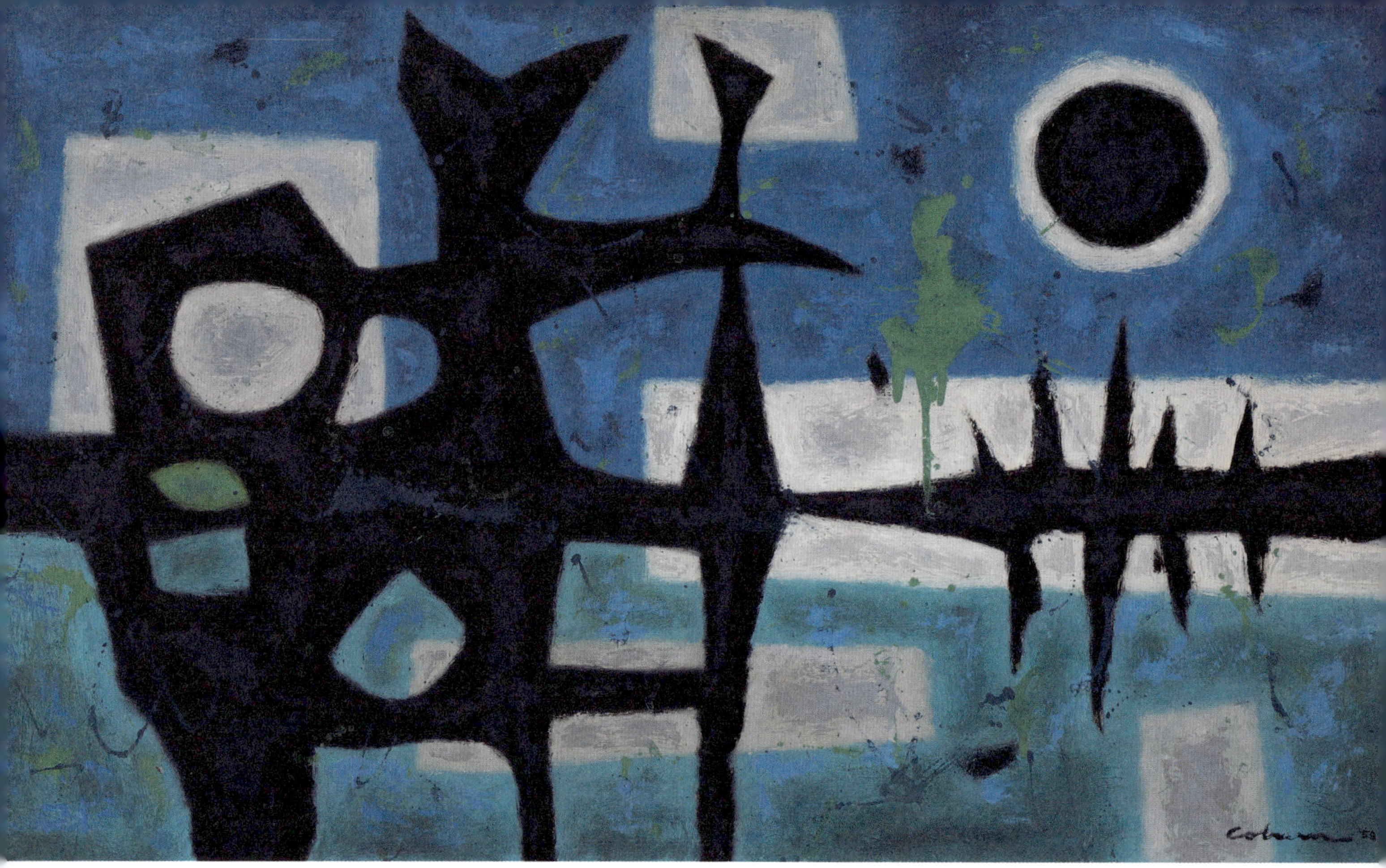

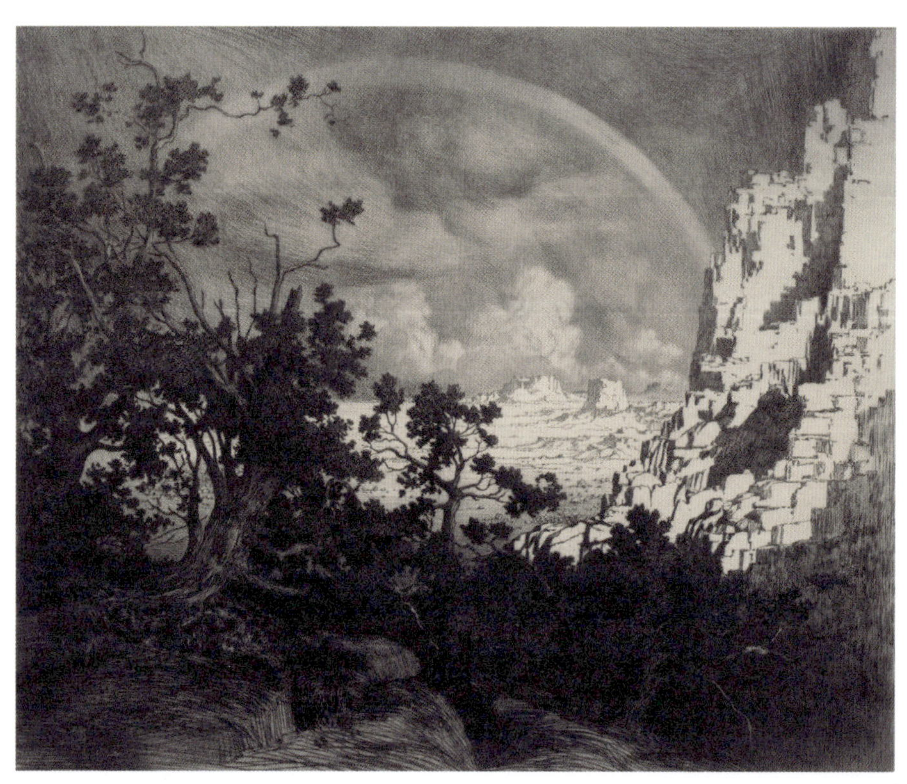

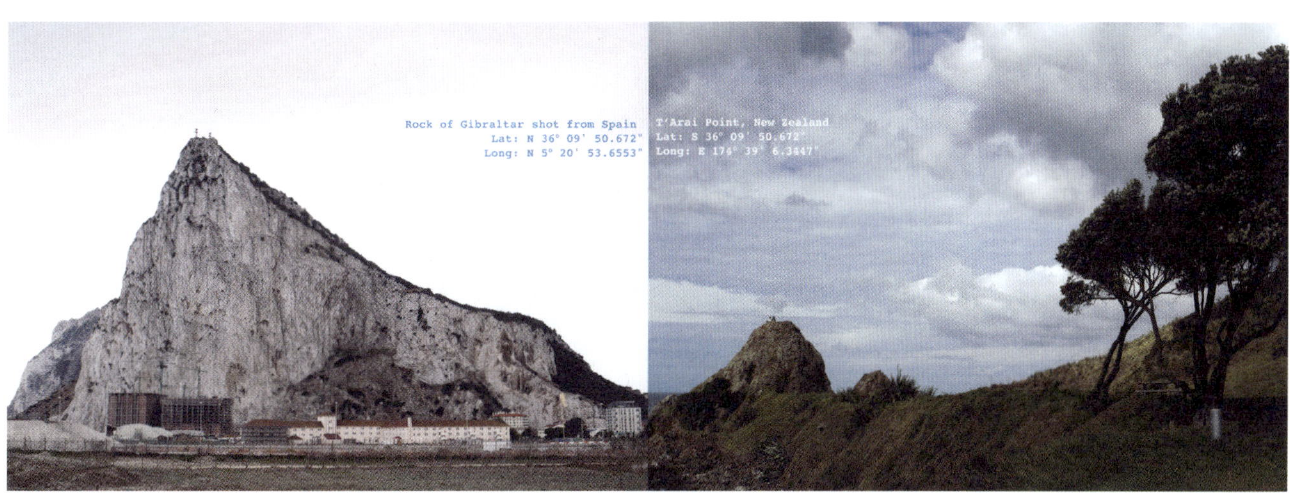

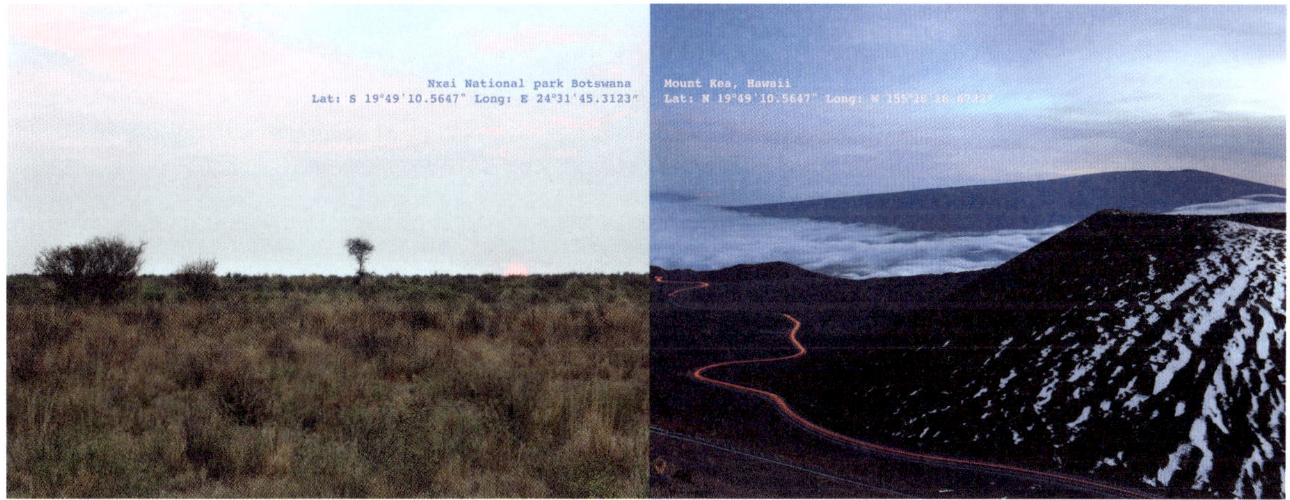

Opposite top – *Landscape*, 1958, oil on composition board, John Coburn (Australian)

Opposite bottom – *The Edge of the Desert, Arizona*, after 1924, etching and drypoint on paper, George Elbert Burr (American)

Above – From the *Antipodes* series, 2014, stills from film, Uta Kögelsberger (British)

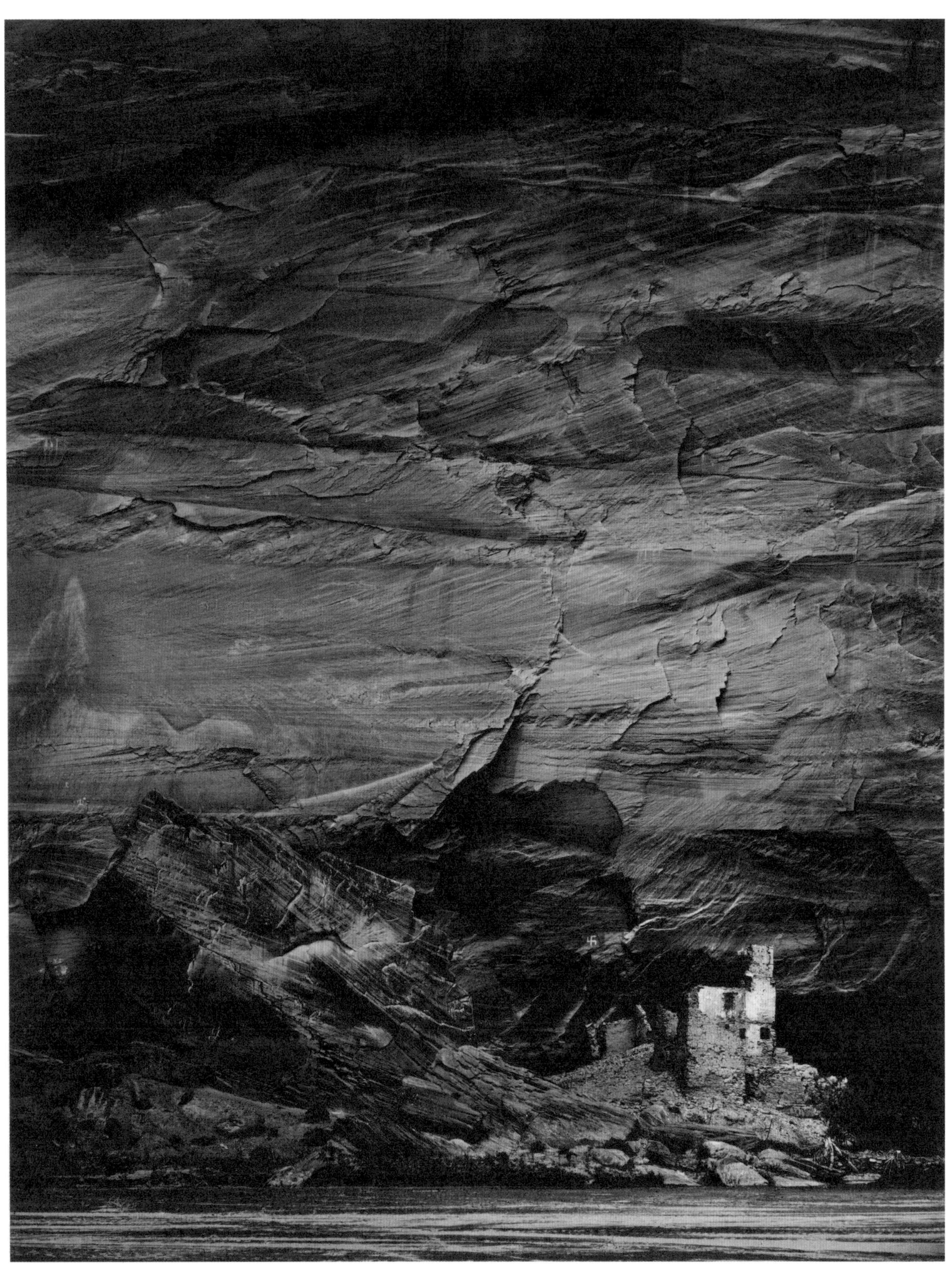

Antelope House ruin, Canyon de Chelly National Monument, Arizona, 1942, gelatin silver photograph, Ansel Adams (American)

NESTLED WITHIN A VAST MOUNTAINSCAPE, THE HUMAN PRESENCE MAY APPEAR DIMINUTIVE. A REMARKABLE CONTRAST IN SCALE AMPLIFIES THE SHEER MAGNITUDE OF THE NATURAL FORM.

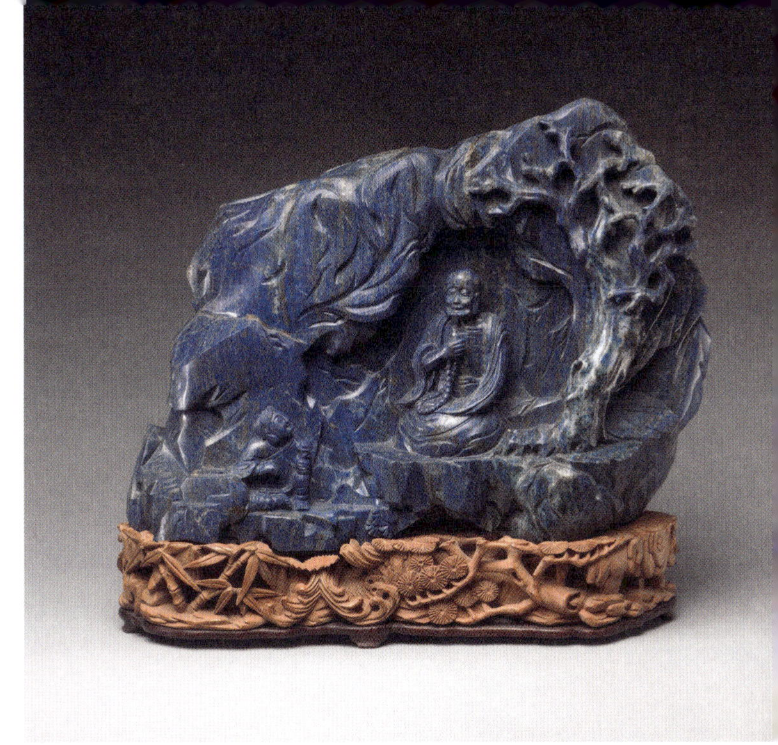

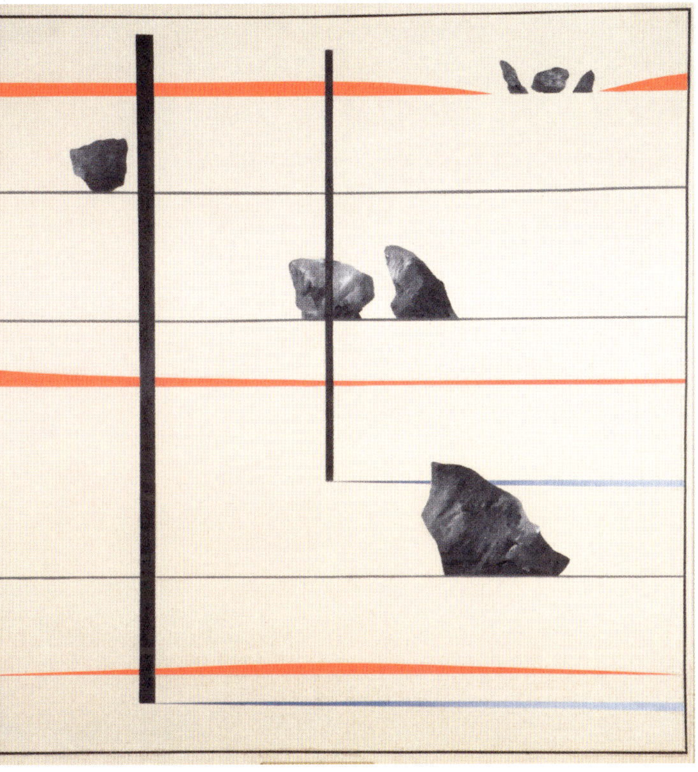

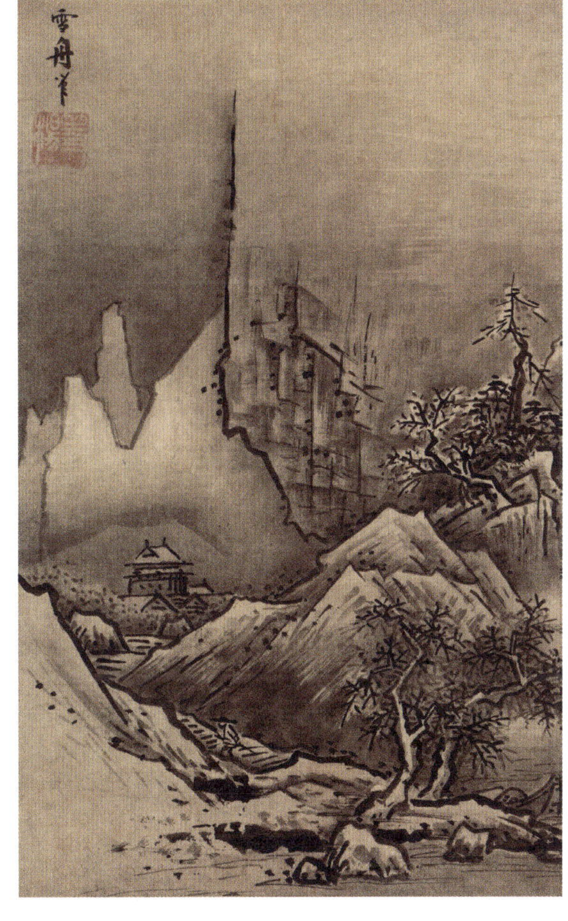

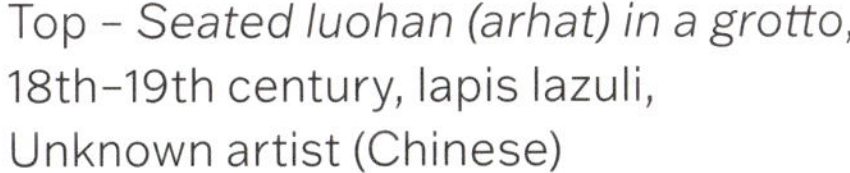

Top – *Seated luohan (arhat) in a grotto*, 18th–19th century, lapis lazuli, Unknown artist (Chinese)

Middle – *Avebury Series No. 4*, 1973, acrylic on canvas, Derek Jarman (British)

Bottom – *Autumn and Winter Landscapes* (one panel), c. late 15th–early 16th century, ink on washi paper, Sesshū Tōyō (Japanese)

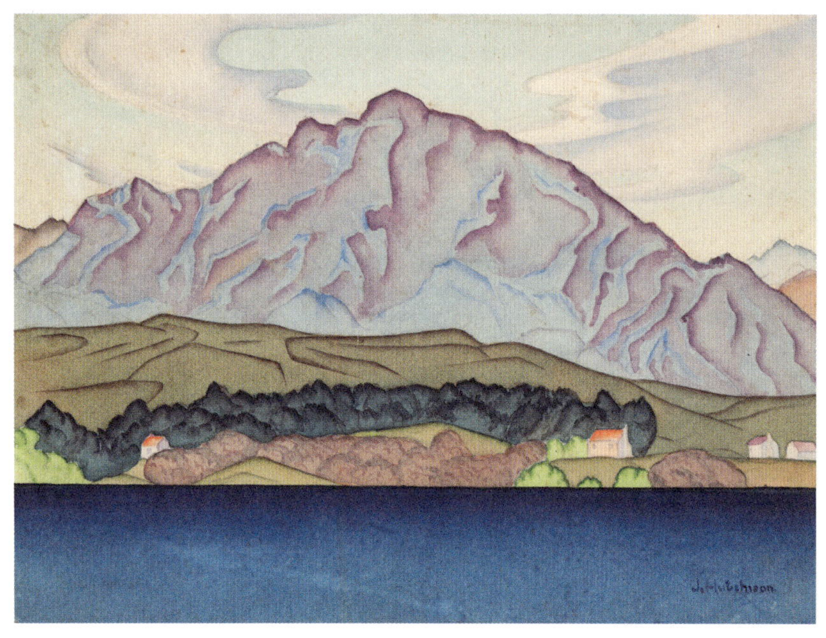

Top – *South Island lake and mountain*, c. 1910–87, watercolour, Jack Hutchison (New Zealander)

Bottom – *Lake O'Hara*, 1930, oil on canvas, J E H MacDonald (Canadian)

Opposite top – *Travelers on the Road to Shu* (detail), c. 16th–17th century, ink and colour on silk, formerly attributed to Qiu Ying (Chinese)

Opposite bottom – *Kerry Landscape*, 1949, oil on board, Ithell Colquhoun (British)

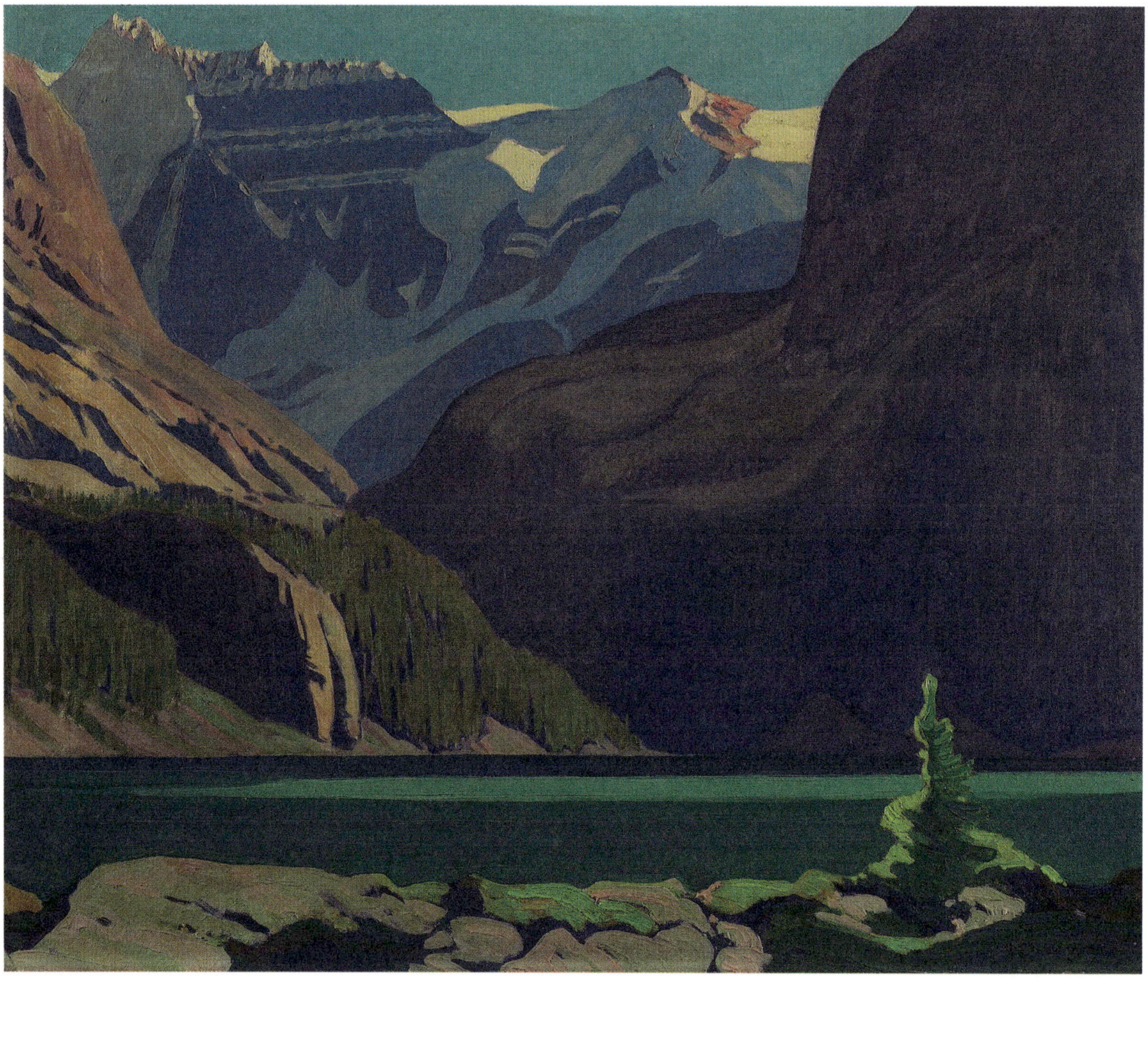

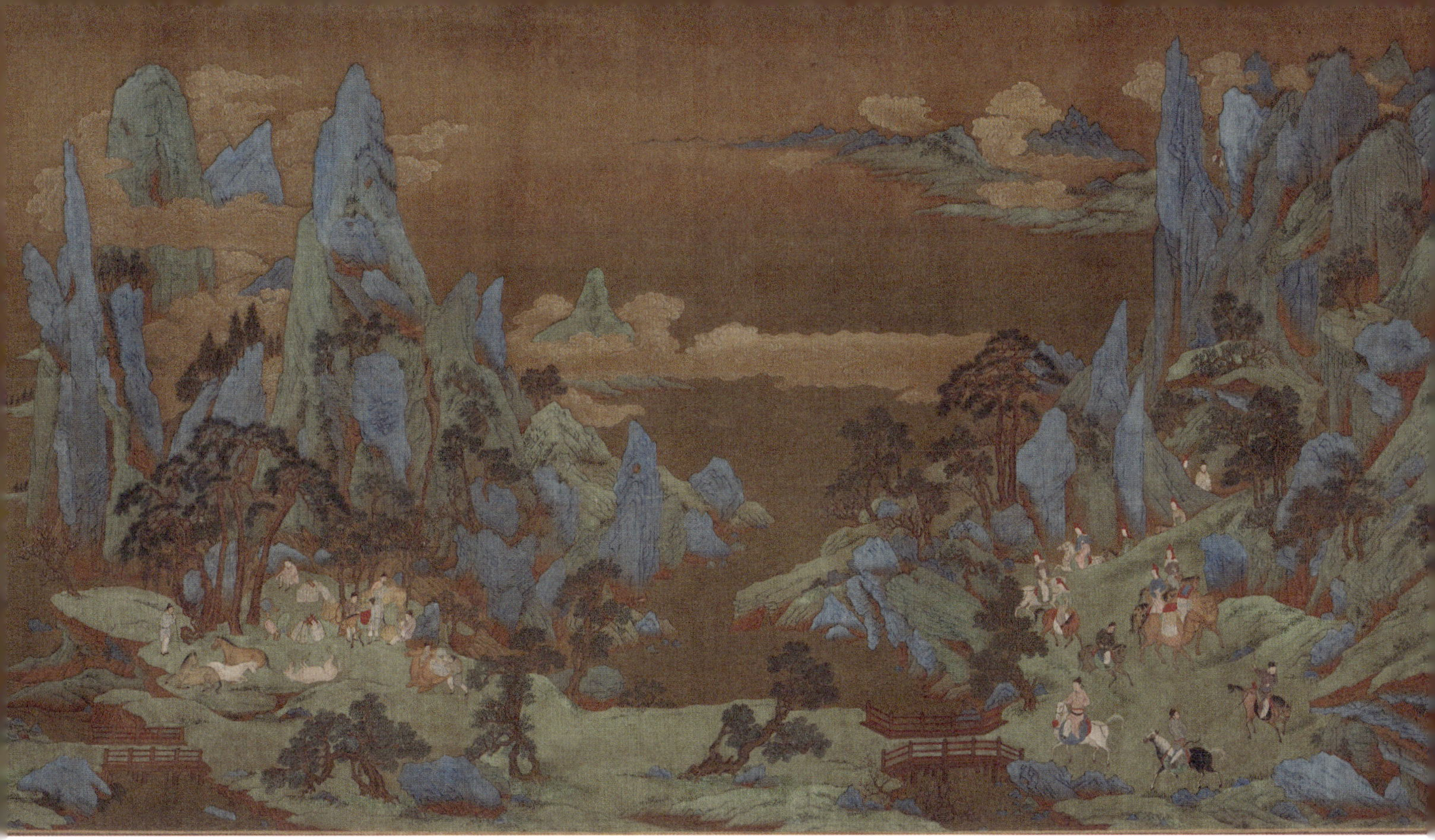

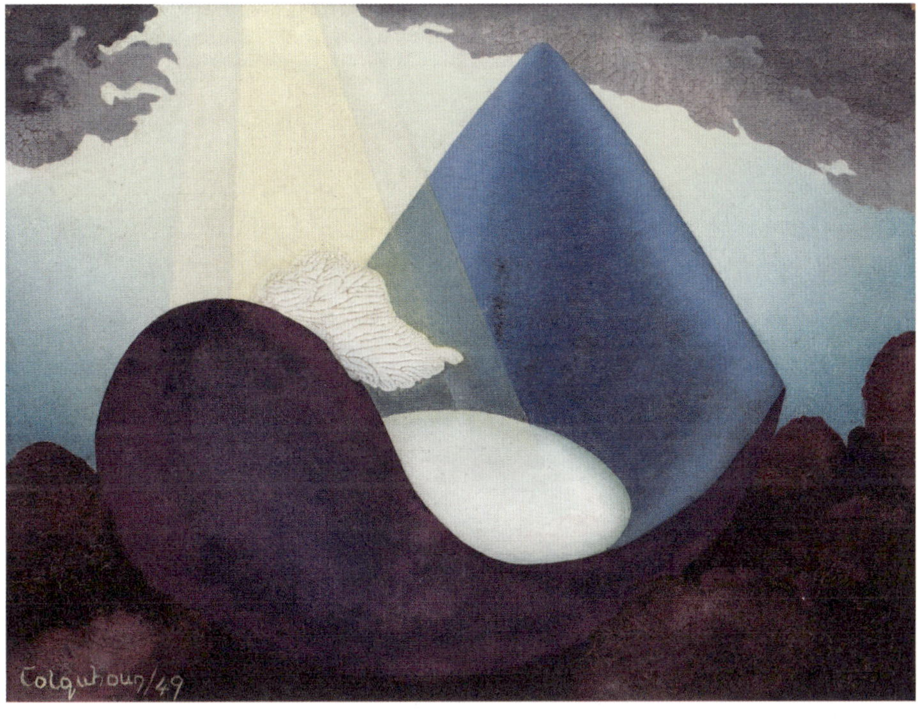
Colquhoun/49

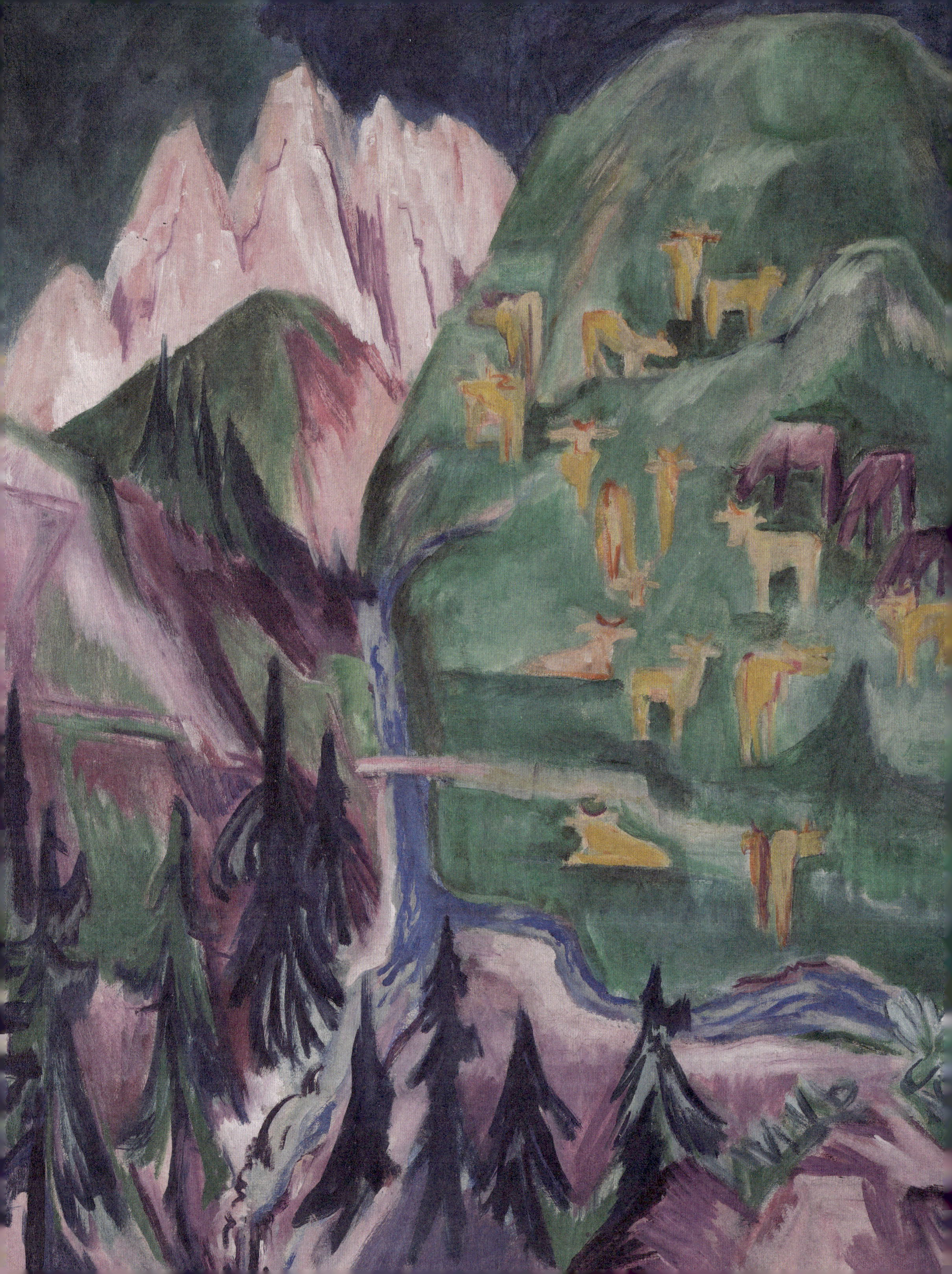

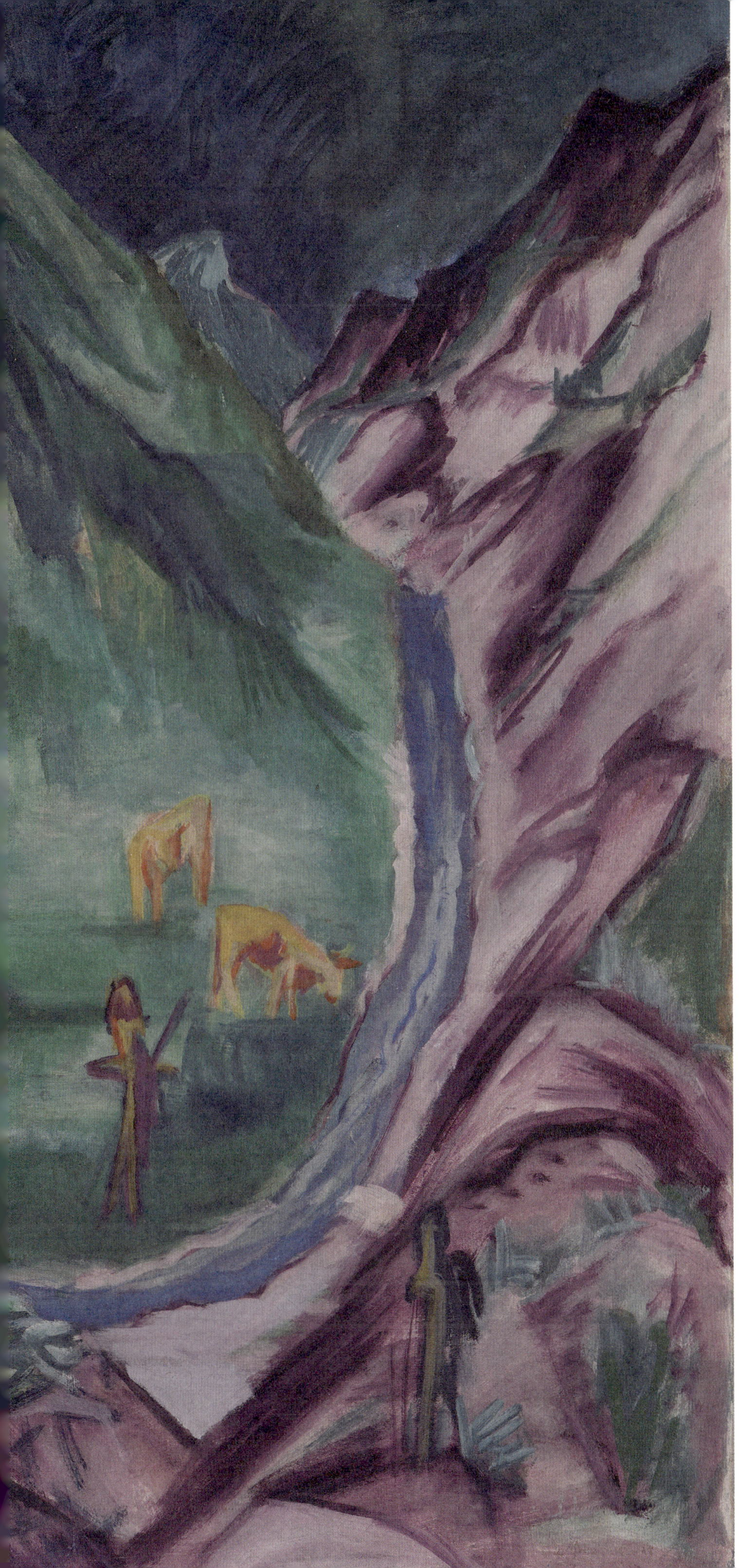

'IT SEEMS AS THOUGH THE GOAL OF MY WORK HAS ALWAYS BEEN TO DISSOLVE MYSELF COMPLETELY INTO THE SENSATIONS OF THE SURROUNDINGS IN ORDER TO THEN INTEGRATE THIS INTO A COHERENT PAINTERLY FORM.'

— ERNST LUDWIG KIRCHNER, C. 1913

Mountain with Cattle, 1918, oil on canvas, Ernst Ludwig Kirchner (German)

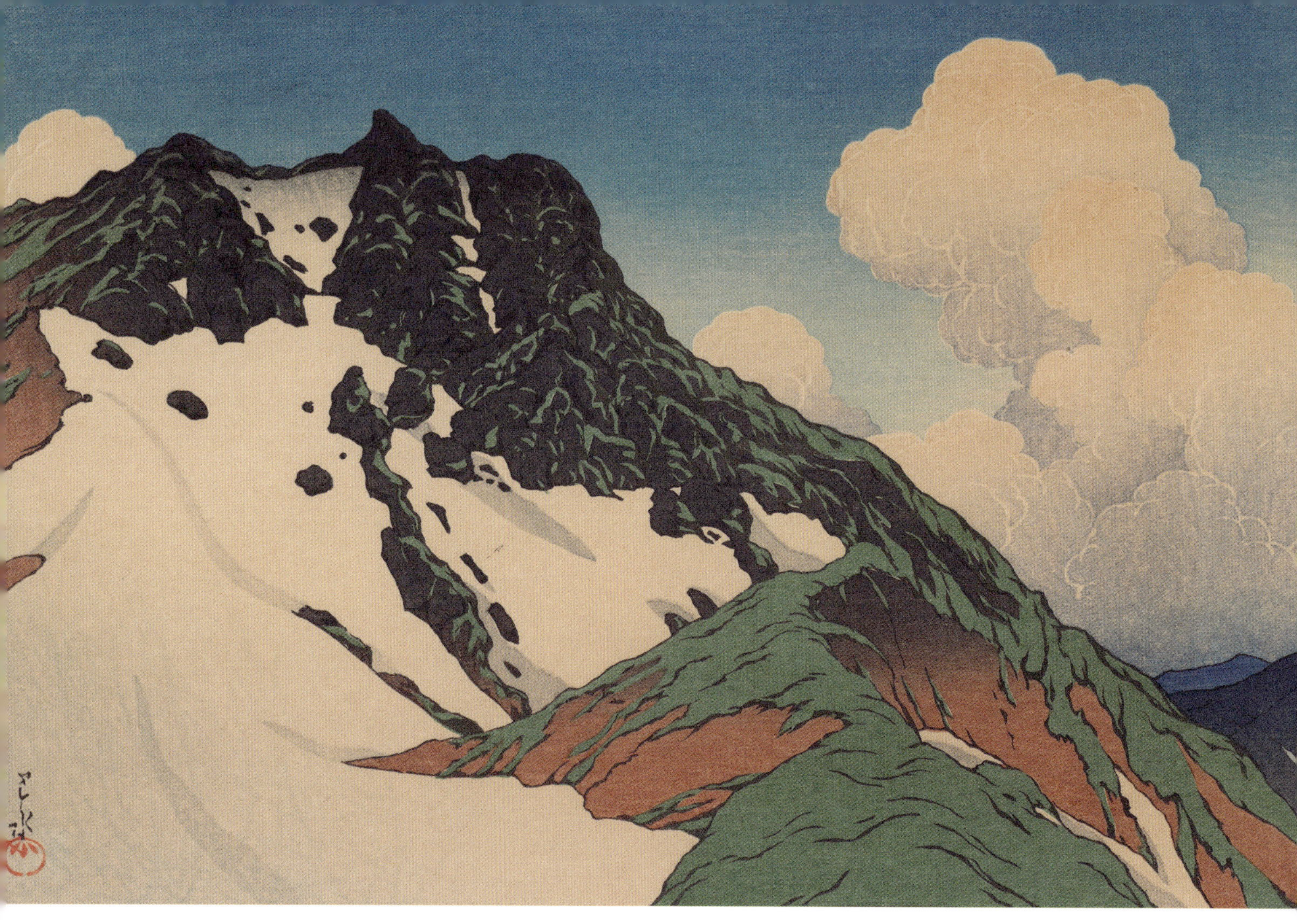

Above – *Asahi Peak Seen from Mt. Hakuba*, 1924, woodblock print, ink and colour on paper, Kawase Hasui (Japanese)

Opposite top – *Mt Sefton from near the Hermitage*, c. 1856–1945, watercolour, Charles Howorth (New Zealander)

Opposite bottom – *Glaciers, Rolleston Mountains*, c. 1886–1962, oil on canvas, Grace Butler (New Zealander)

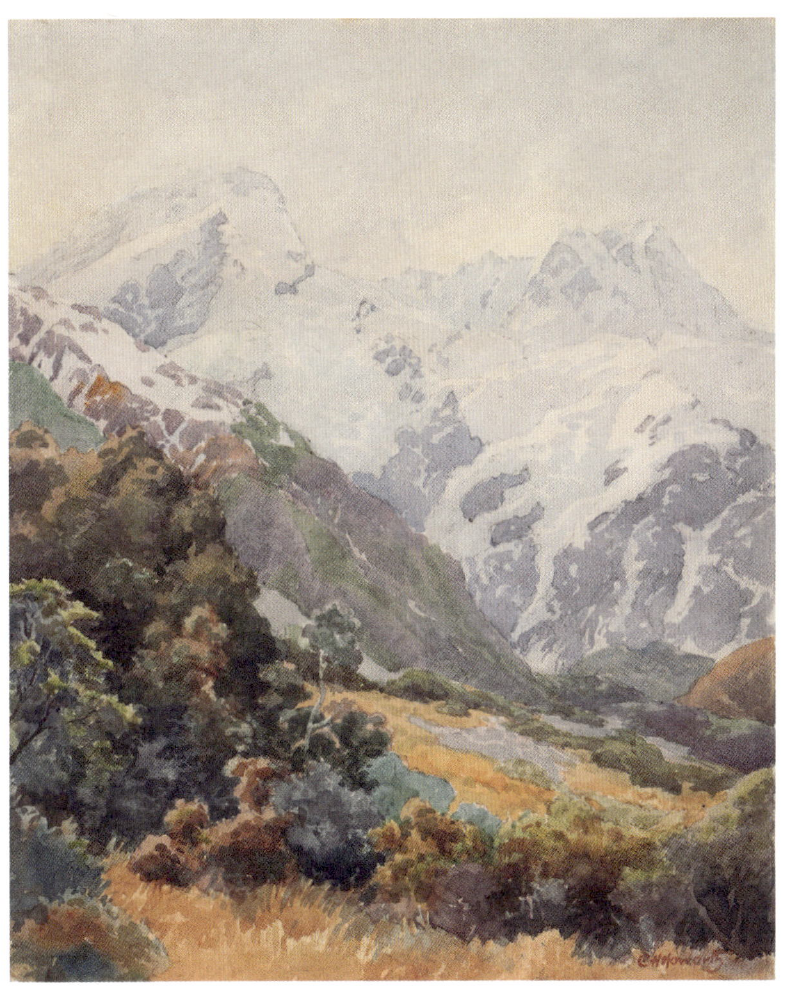

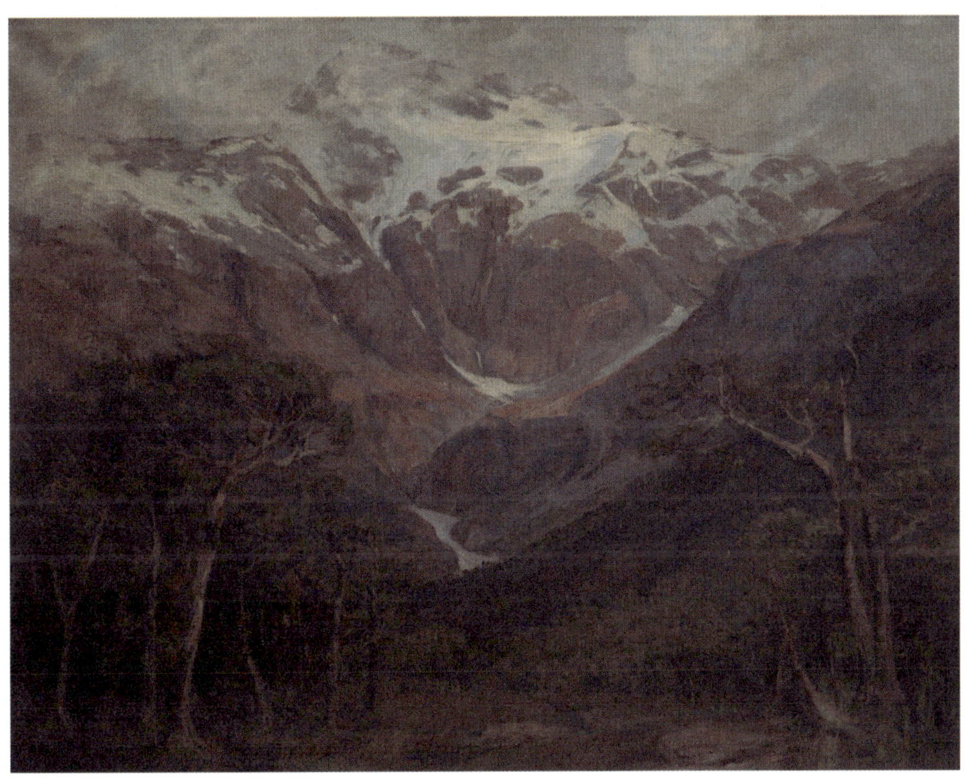

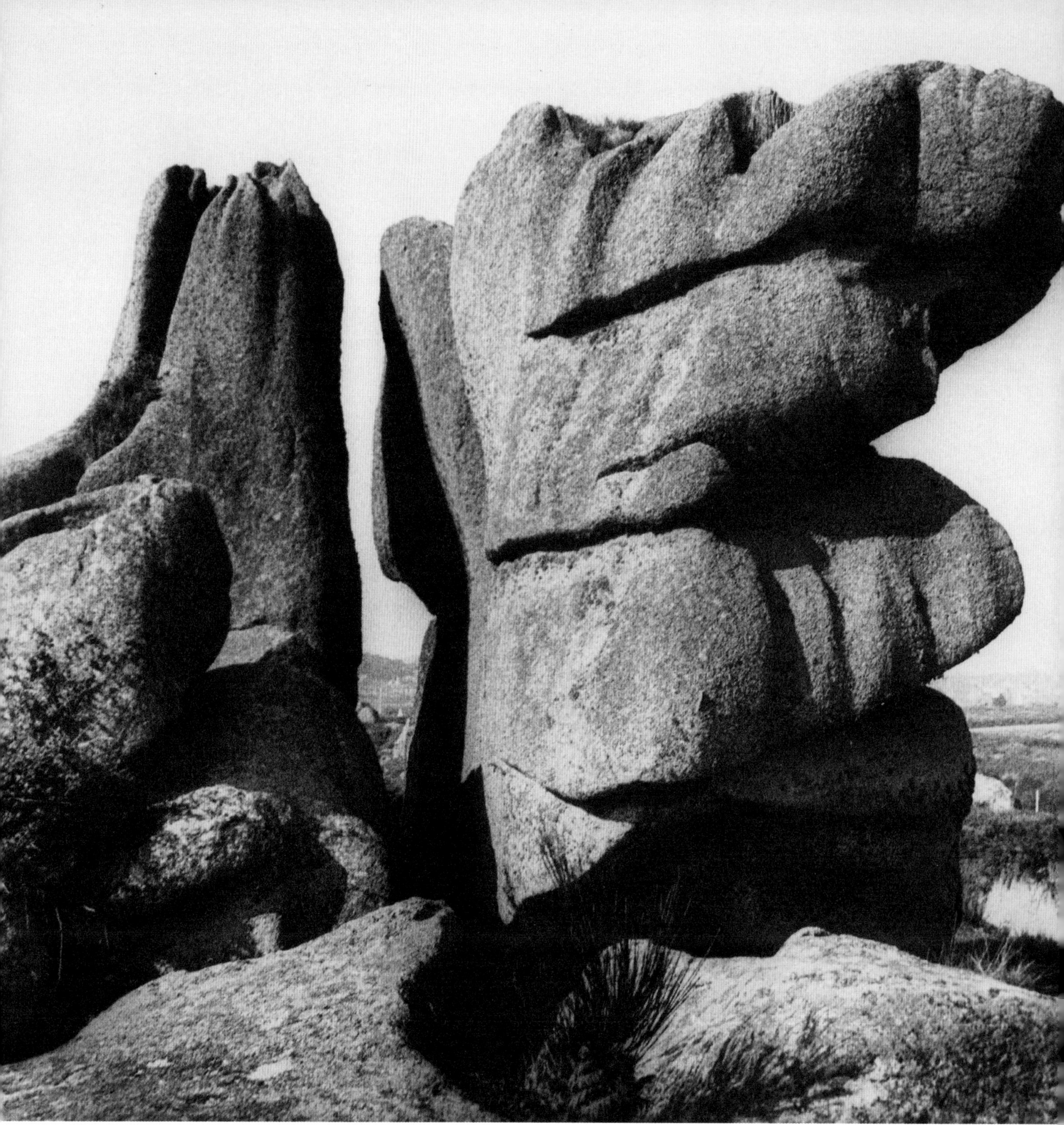

EILEEN AGAR TOOK AROUND SEVENTY PHOTOGRAPHS OF VARIOUS ROCKS IN ENGLAND AND FRANCE. HER ROCK PORTRAITS UNCOVER A SUPERB, AND AT TIMES QUIRKY, VIEW OF NATURAL FORMATIONS, COMPARED WITH VISUAL LANGUAGE USED BY CÉZANNE, WHICH EXERCISES A SOFTNESS AND WARM CONTRAST AT THE EDGES, BLURRING ANY HARSH LINES.

 Rocks at Ploumanach, Brittany, 1936, photograph, gelatin silver print, Eileen Agar (Argentine/British)

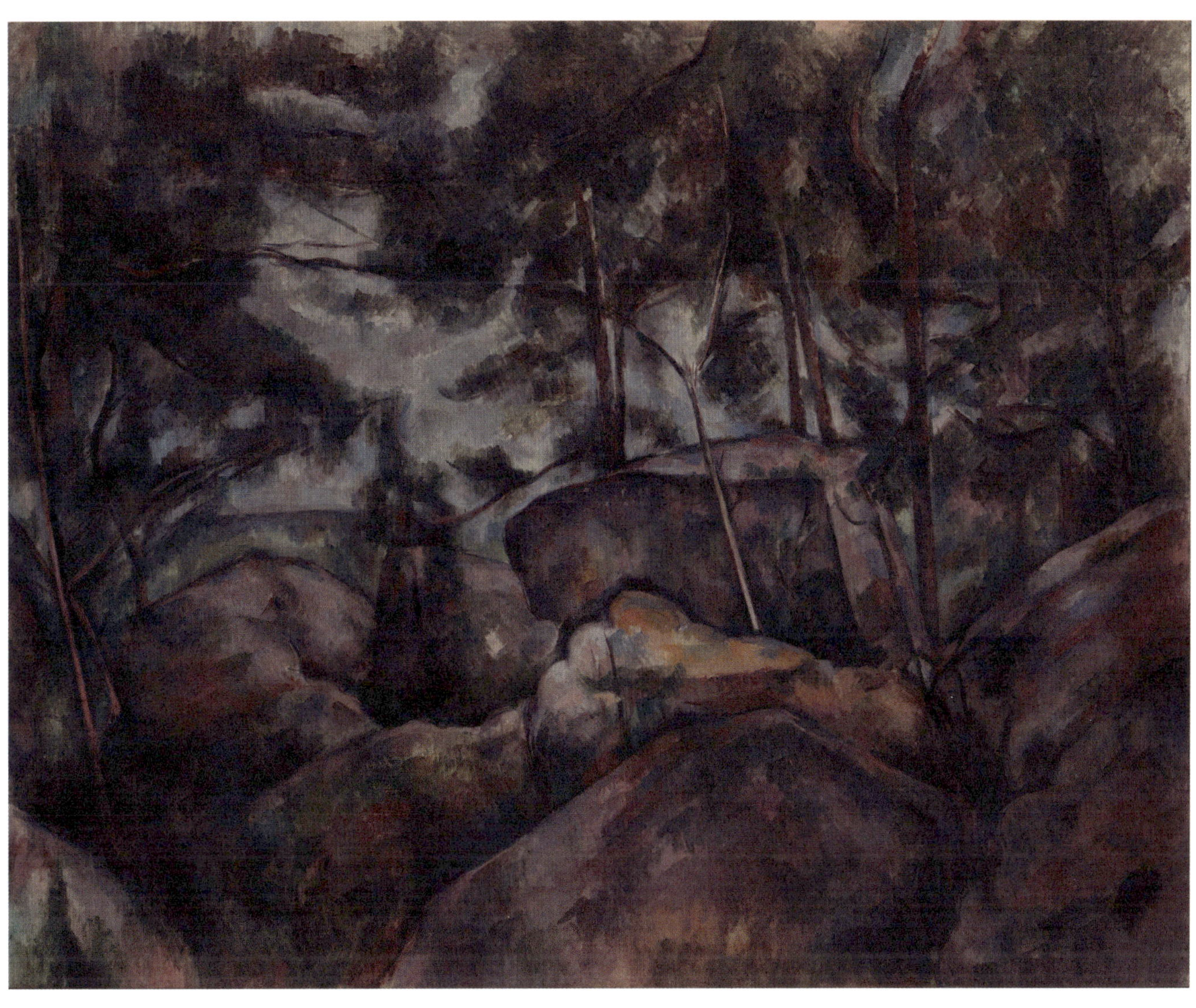

Rocks at Fontainebleau, c. 1890s, oil on canvas, Paul Cézanne (French)

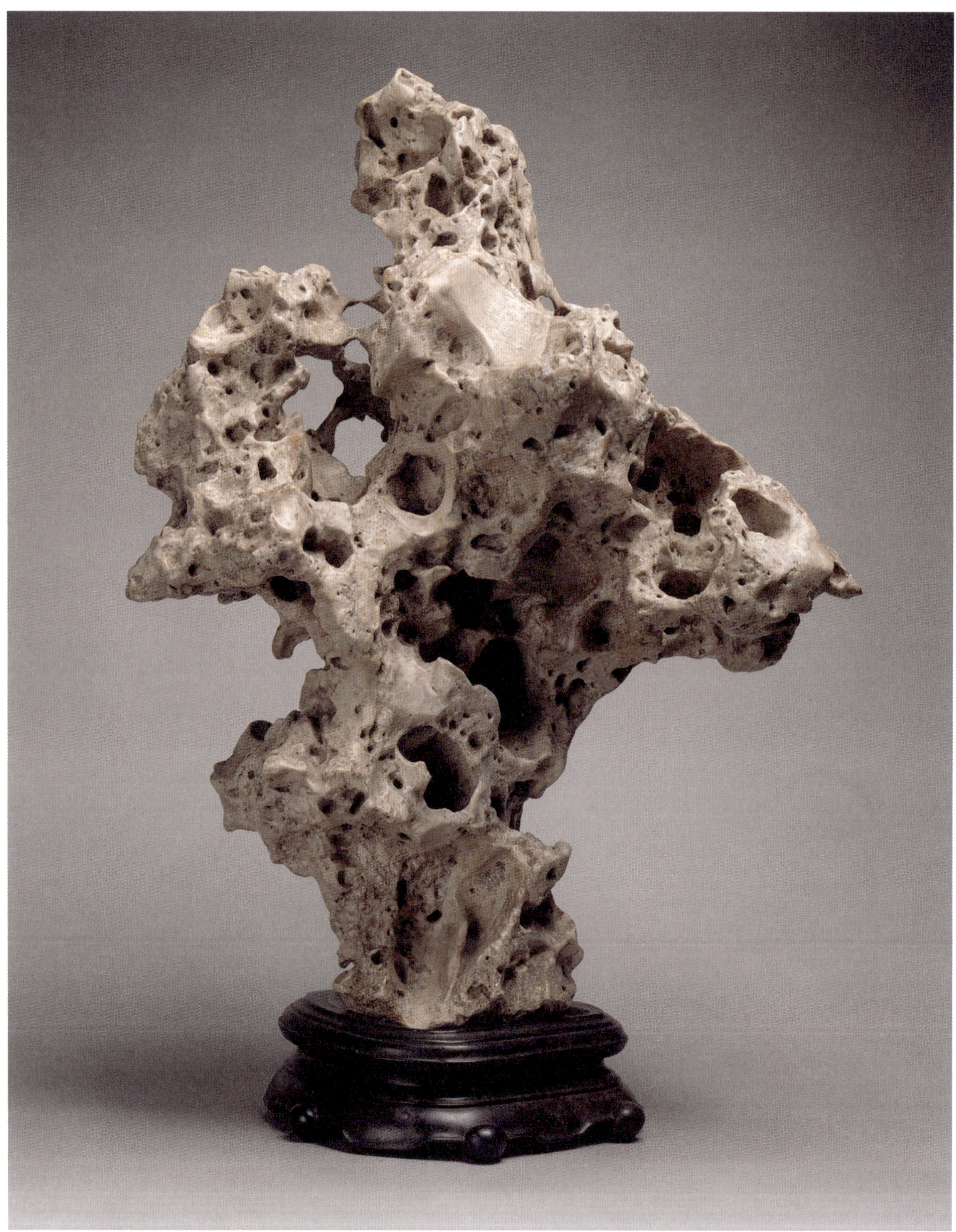

 Scholar's rock, c. 19th century, limestone, wood stand, Unknown artist (Chinese)

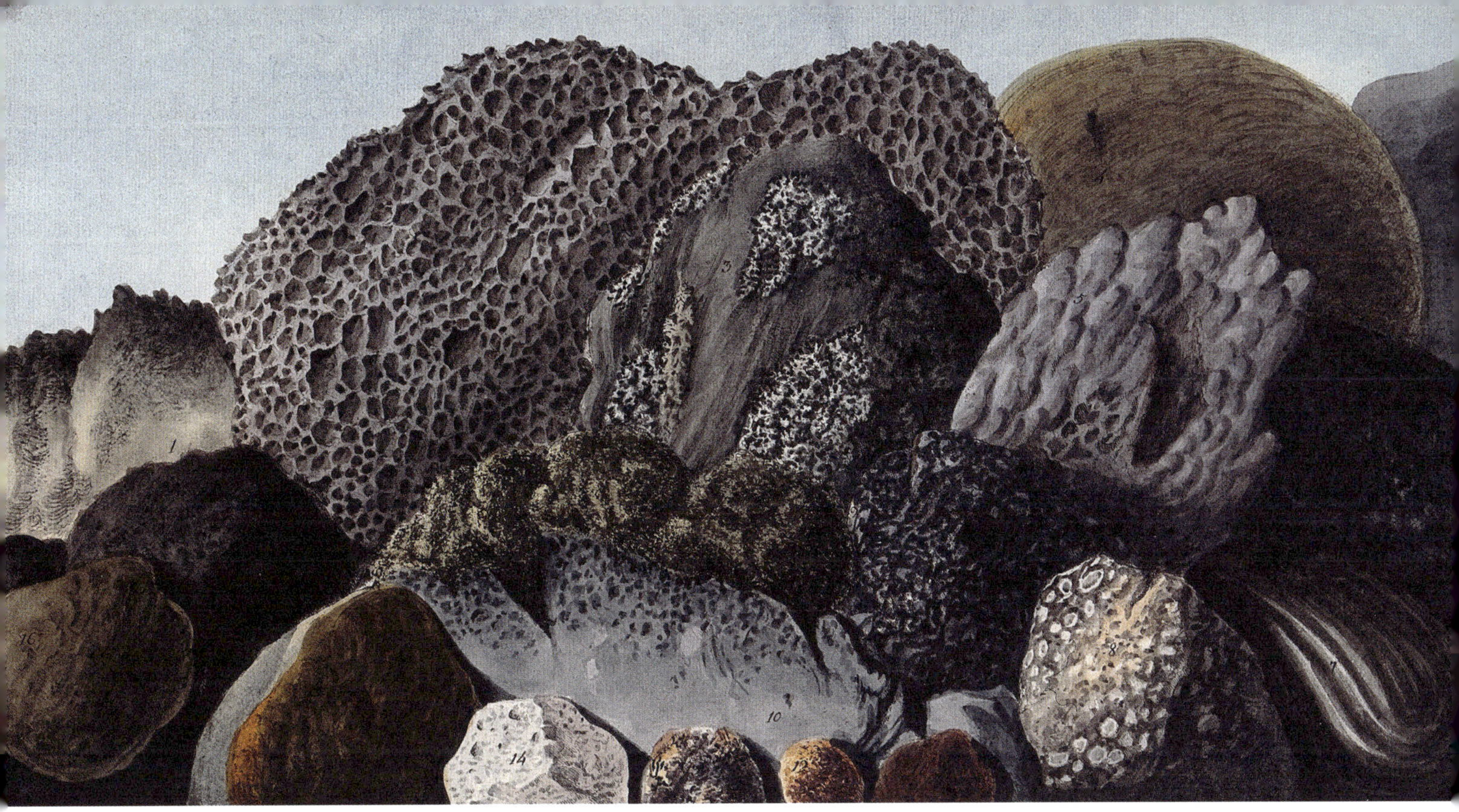

SCHOLAR'S ROCKS INSPIRE QUIET CONTEMPLATION OF SCALE AND BEAUTY FOUND IN NATURE. STUDY THE EXQUISITE CONTRAST OF LIGHT AND SHADE ON THE DIMPLED SURFACE OF THE VOLCANIC ROCK WITH THE DEEP-SET CRATER FORMATIONS ON THE LIMESTONE.

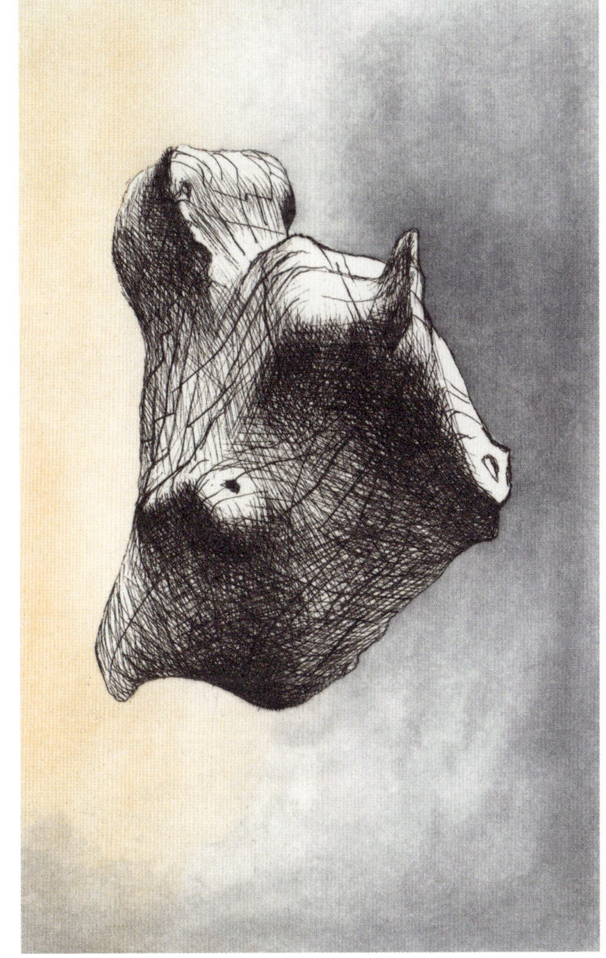

Top – *Lava, scoriae and pumice from Mount Vesuvius*, 1776, coloured etching with gouache, Pietro Fabris (Italian)

Bottom – *Dante Stones, Stone II*, 1977, etching on paper, Henry Moore OM, CH (British)

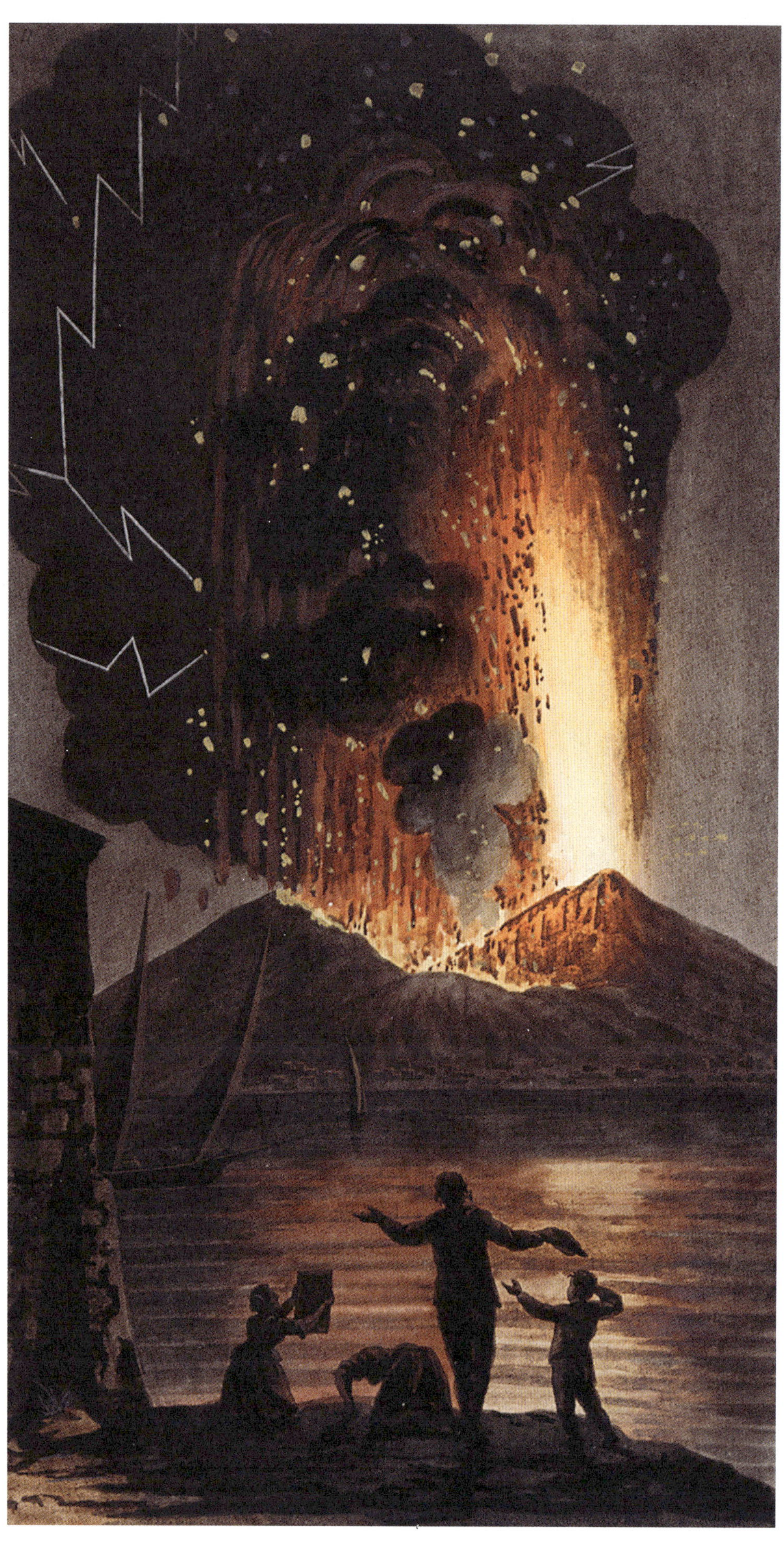

The Eruption of Mount Vesuvius in the Night of 8 August 1779, 1779, coloured etching on gouache, Pietro Fabris (Italian)

VOLCANOES

THE DRAMA OF AN ACTIVE VOLCANO BECAME A POPULAR PART OF VISUAL ICONOGRAPHY IN THE MID 1800S, BRINGING TOGETHER NOTIONS OF THE SUBLIME AND ROMANTIC. BY PLACING THE VIEWER AT THE EDGE OF THE CRATER OR SMOULDERING LAVA POOL, THESE WORKS CHARACTERISE A FASCINATION WITH THE POWER AND THREAT OF THE NATURAL WORLD. THERE IS ALSO REVERENCE FOUND IN THE REPRESENTATION OF DORMANT VOLCANOES, LIKE THE ICONIC MOUNT FUJI.

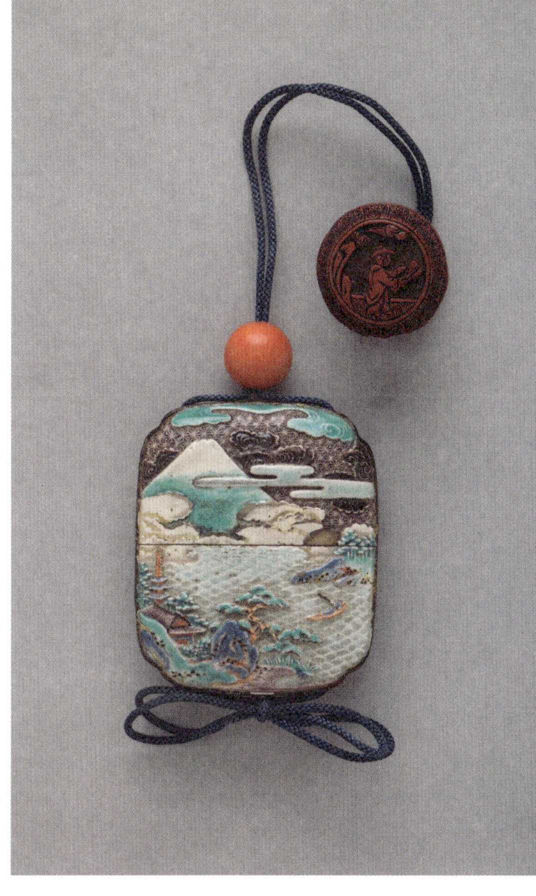

Top – *Case (Inrō) with Design of Deer and Maple Trees (obverse); Mount Fuji (reverse)*, c. 1820, lacquer with pottery plaques, Unknown artist (Japanese)

Bottom – *A volcanic eruption in Herculaneum, showing the advance of lava flow over walls, with Vesuvius visible in the background*, 1861, gouache painting, Unknown artist (Italian)

Following – *Volcano*, 1955, acquarell pencil on card, Erica McGilchrist (Australian)

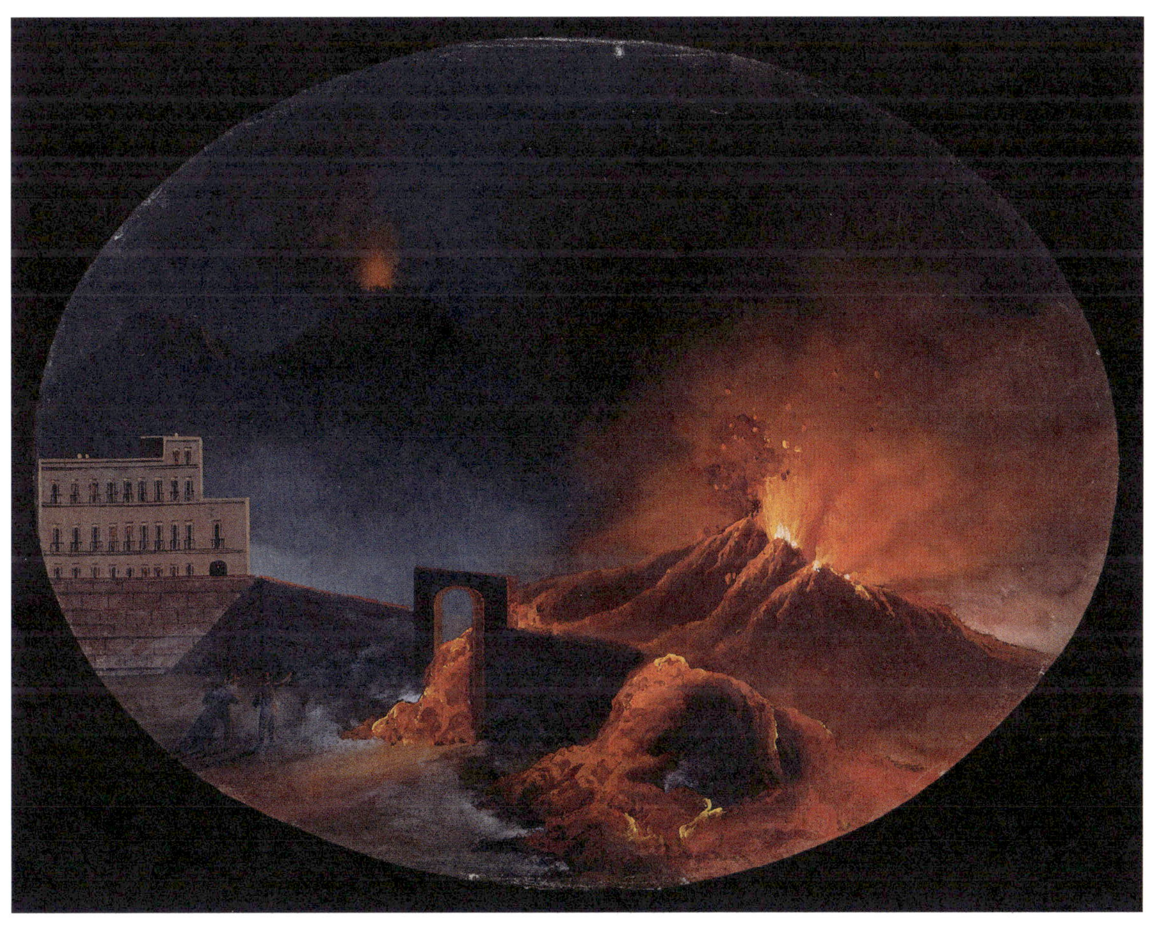

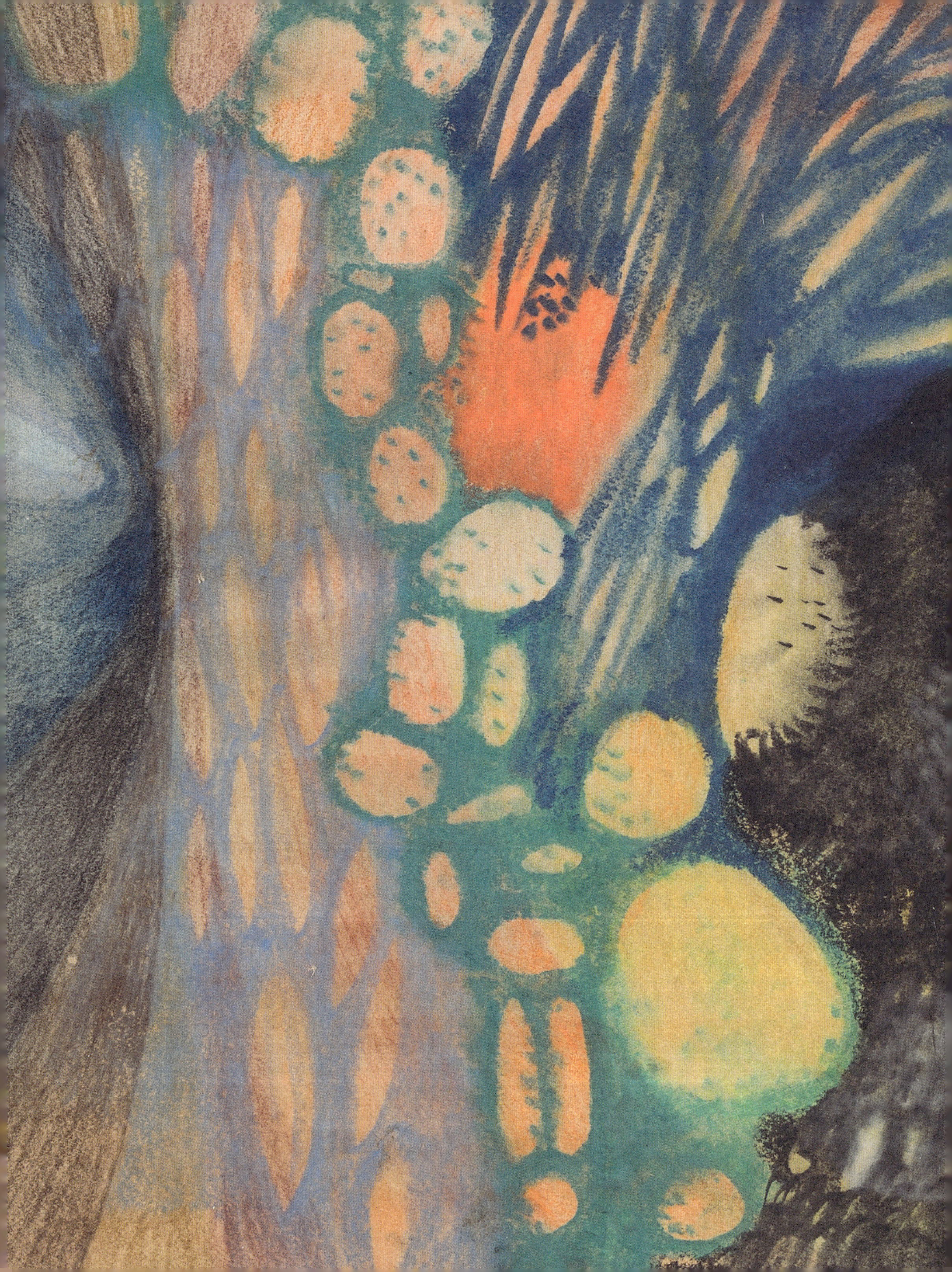

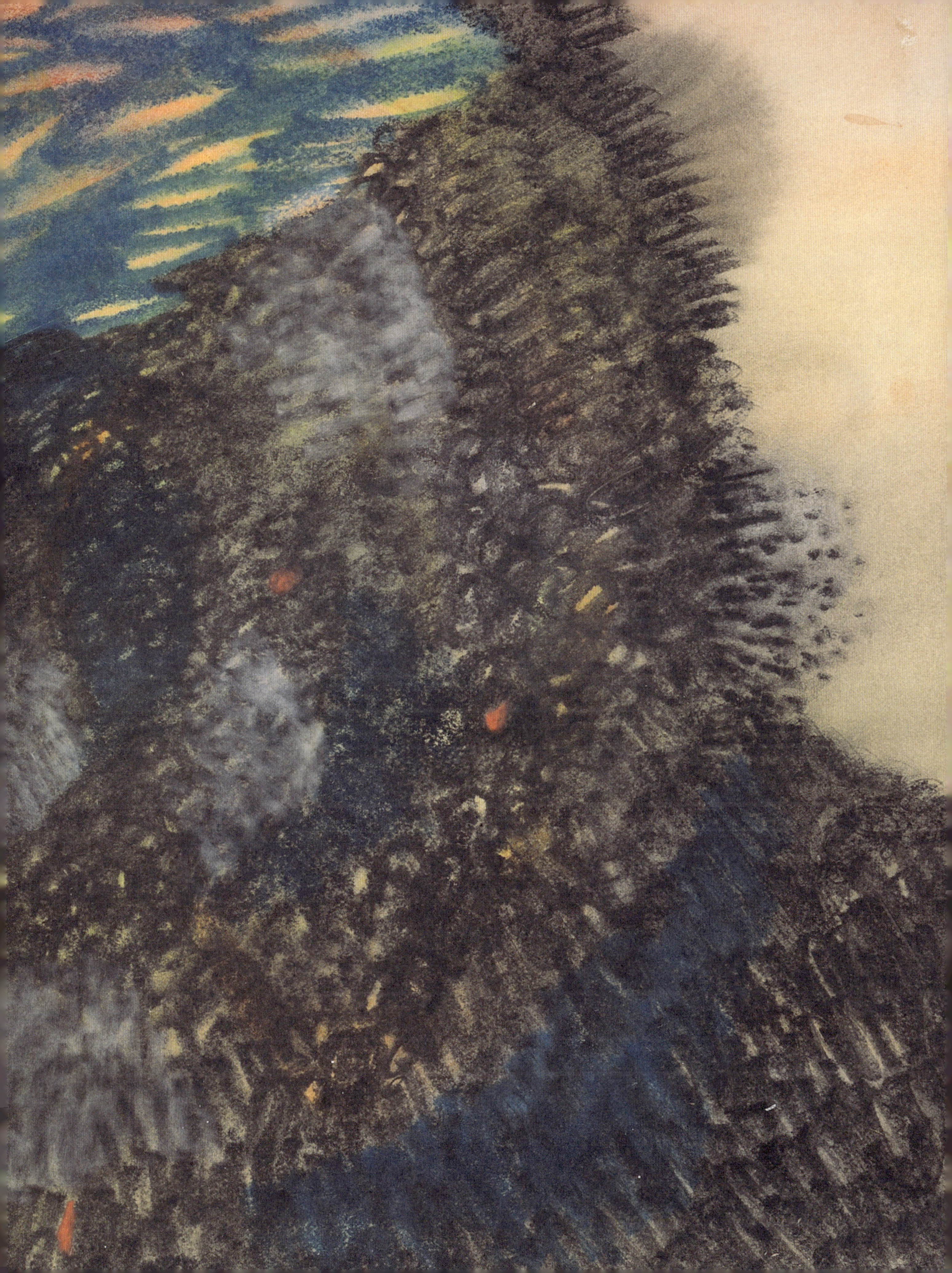

WATER

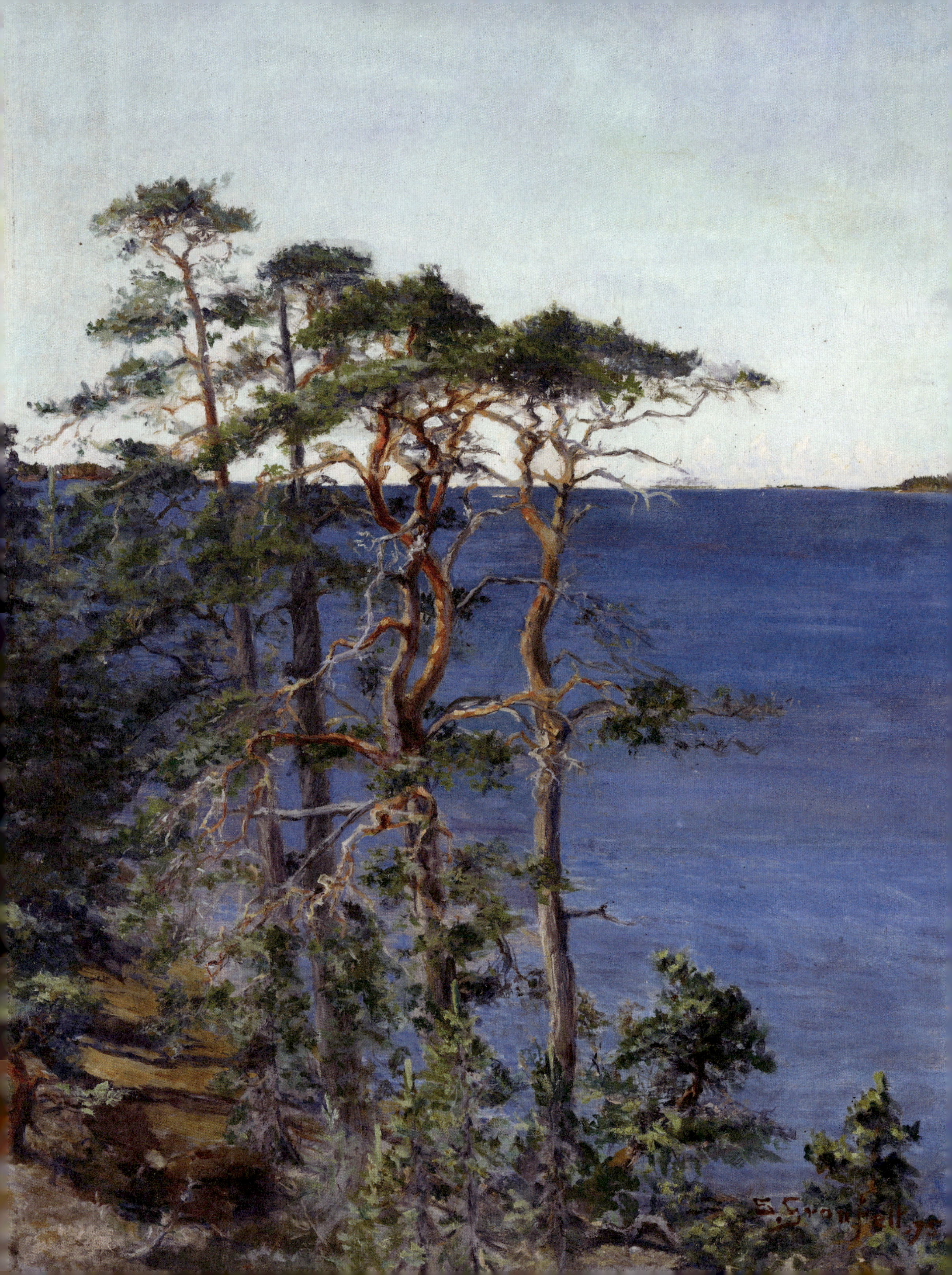

WATER

RIVERS, OCEANS, LAKES, WATERING HOLES, GLACIERS, WATERFALLS AND MORE HAVE BEEN DESCRIBED BY ARTISTS IN SO MANY WAYS. THE SURFACE OF WATER HOLDS AN ESPECIALLY ATTRACTIVE PROPOSITION FOR THE ARTIST: IT MAY BE THAT THE REFLECTIVE QUALITY OF A LAKE OR POND AFFORDS A SECOND SKY, OR THE STEADY FLOW OF A RIVER PROVIDES THE SENSE OF MOVEMENT TO A COMPOSITION.

Bodies of water indicate a life force necessary for all beings. In art they are depicted in a myriad of ways and from various vantage points: perched on a rugged coastline, located from inside a tumultuous sea, or from observing on high a glistening stream snake through a landscape. There is also life below the surface of water; seaweeds, corals and shells washed ashore or harvested, have become symbolic elements in art.

The sea separates and joins us, and is itself connected to other energies such as tidal forces governed by the Sun and the Moon. For over forty years now contemporary Japanese artist Hiroshi Sugimoto (b.1948) has photographed seascapes and vast horizons from around the world, and the effect of a prolonged exposure time is ethereal. He says, 'Mystery of mysteries, water and air are right there before us in the sea. Every time I view the sea, I feel a calming sense of security, as if visiting my ancestral home; I embark on a voyage of seeing.' In his small sculptural work *Five Elements: Sea of Japan, Hokkaido, 1986* (2011) made of optical-quality glass, he has created a five-tier stupa that represents the elements of the cosmos: earth, water, fire and air. Inside the sphere signifying water, he has placed a small photograph of the ocean (see page 124). Reflecting on medieval Buddhist tradition and the power yielded by aesthetic artefacts of faith, he identifies a diminished reverence for deity and Buddha in contemporary life. 'Perhaps the only object of devotion I have left is the origin of my consciousness, the sea. And so, in each of the Five-ring Pagoda made of optical glass, I enshrine a seascape within the water sphere.'

Australian artist Judy Watson (b.1959) was living in France when the subject for her work *two halves with bailer shell* (2002) appeared to her in a dream (see page 154). The shells are delicately sketched on an ultramarine and Prussian-blue canvas. She describes the significance of the bailer shell and water, and the connection to her people, the Waanyi people of north-west Queensland, known as running water people: 'There is a split of the female form, referring to my maternal side, which is Aboriginal. It refers to my grandmother and ancestors and to the culture that is embodied within ... the blue is memory, dreams, water being a carrier ... for culture.'

Sea Form (Porthmeor) (1958) created by Barbara Hepworth (1903–75) (see page 127) is cast in bronze with a textured organic appearance that reveals patination on the inner curves, while the outer edges of the sculpture are smooth and rounded. In this work Hepworth seizes the changing natural form of the sea as she observed it in St Ives, Cornwall. In a letter to the art historian Herbert Read she explained the 'extraordinary feeling being poised above the changing calligraphy of tide & water movement'. Hepworth's *Sea Form (Porthmeor)* is more than a study of the sea – it appears to be of the sea, from the sea.

Piero della Francesca's *Madonna and Child with Saints* (1472–74) (see page 152) has often been considered as a scene of deep contemplation. The enthroned Virgin's eyes are downcast, her hands clasped in a gesture of prayer as the Christ child sleeps on her lap in an arrangement suggestive of the lamentation or death of Christ. They are surrounded by saints, archangels and kneeling donor Federico da Montefeltro, who all assume a posture of reverie. While the connection to water is not immediate to the view, a slow looking approach rewards the curious. The infant is decorated with a pink-orange beaded necklace and coral pendant, while the architectural attributes of

 Previous – *Pines by the Sea* (detail), 1895, oil on canvas, Sigrid Granfelt (Finnish)

the apse include a large clam shell with an ostrich egg suspended by a golden chain. The egg alludes to the fruitfulness of the Virgin, and is also a feature of the Montefeltro heraldry. The Ancient Greeks and Romans commonly used coral for teething children and also as a talisman to protect the wearer from evil, a tradition upheld well into medieval and early modern times.

All of these works are elegies and tributes to water, in all its forms, to be recited, closely observed, and rediscovered here. The pattern and texture of water is conveyed according to style, tradition and the personal expression of an artist. Like land, water can most obviously be read with reverence and awe, but also careful and patient examination, in a politicised and polarising manner.

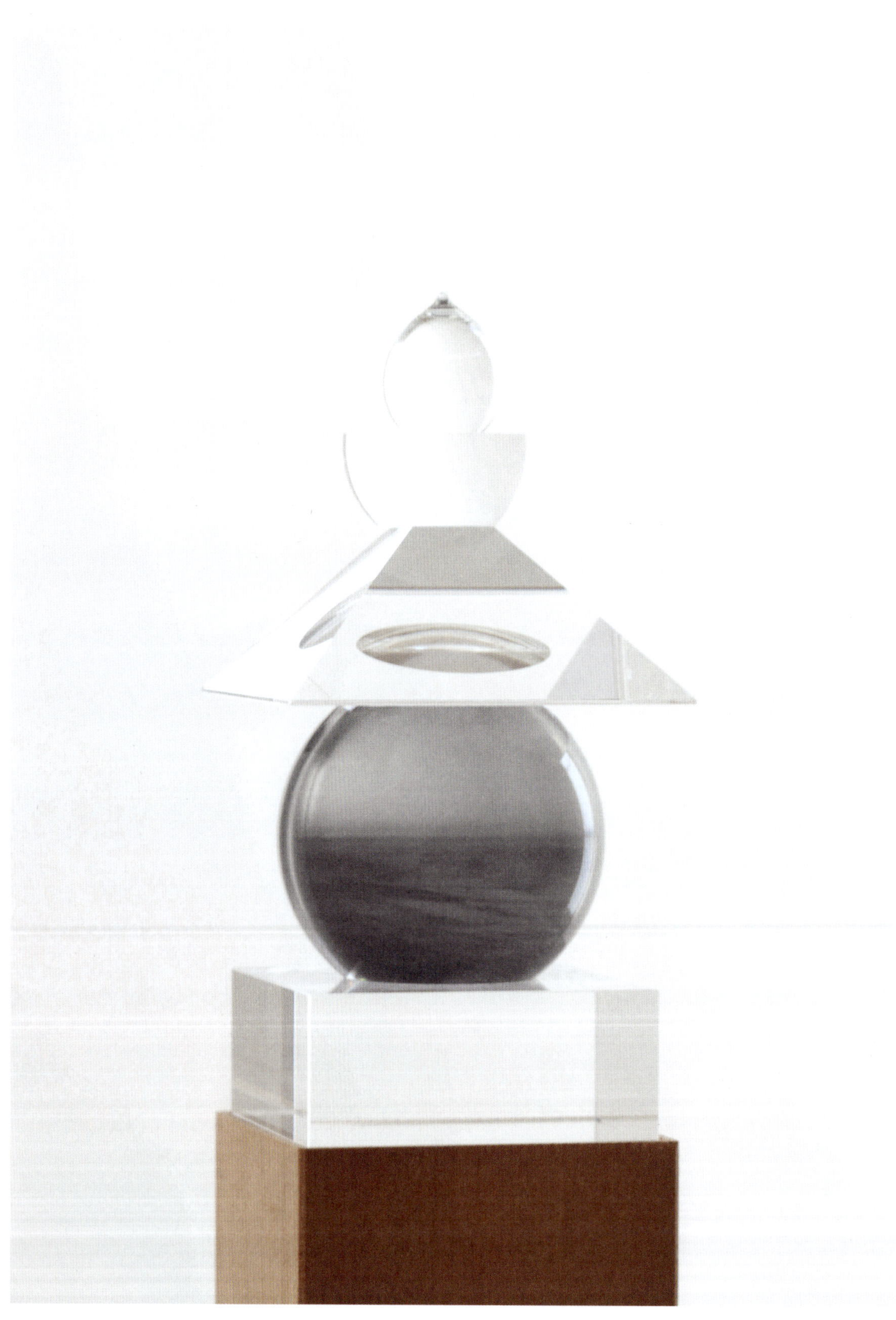

SEAS

IT IS ONLY EVER POSSIBLE TO REPRESENT A FRACTION OF THE SEA IN A PICTURE OR OBJECT. THE SURFACE OF THE SEA IS JUST ONE COMPONENT OF ITS FORM. CONSIDER WHAT IS UNSEEN, WHAT LIES BENEATH.

Opposite – *Five Elements: Sea of Japan, Hokkaido, 1986*, 2011, optical-quality glass with black-and-white film, Hiroshi Sugimoto (Japanese)

Bottom – *Winter Sea*, c. 1925–37, oil on canvas, Paul Nash (British)

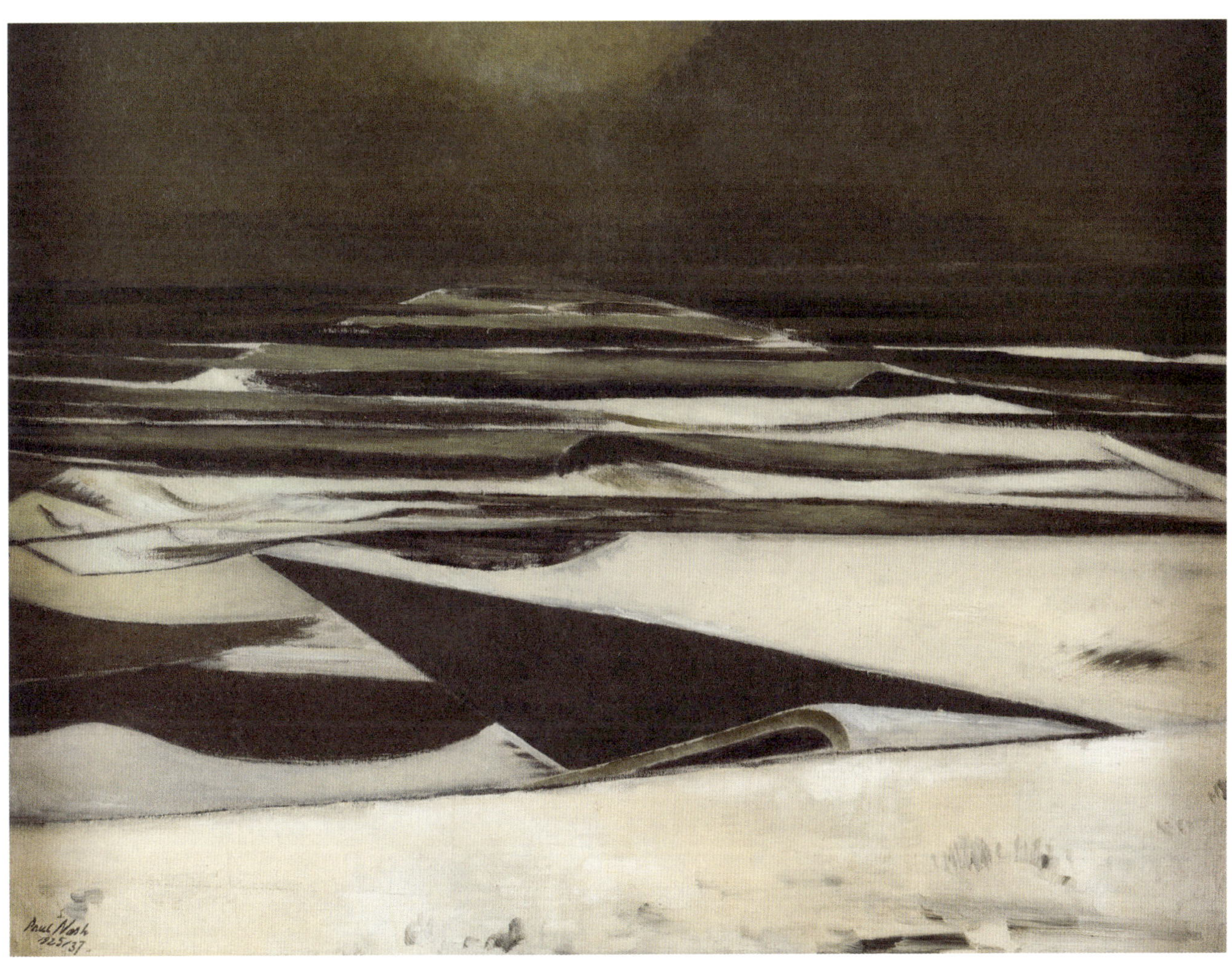

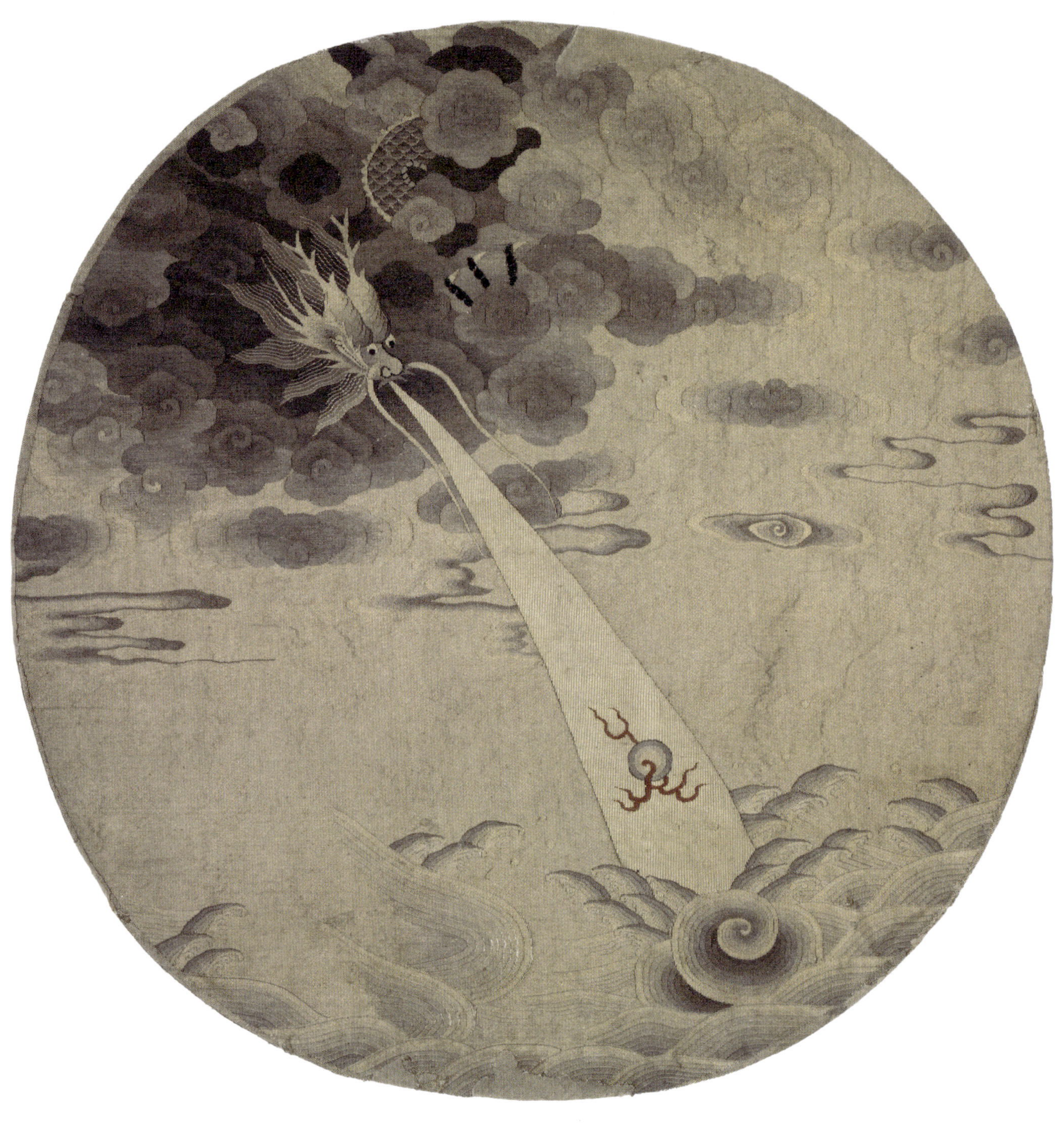

Above – *Fan with Dragon*, c. 17th century, silk tapestry, Unknown artist (Chinese)

Opposite top – *Sea Form (Porthmeor)*, 1958, bronze on wooden base, Dame Barbara Hepworth (British)

Opposite bottom – *Waves and Breakers in the Bay of Naples*, 1821, oil on cardboard, Johan Christian Dahl (Norwegian)

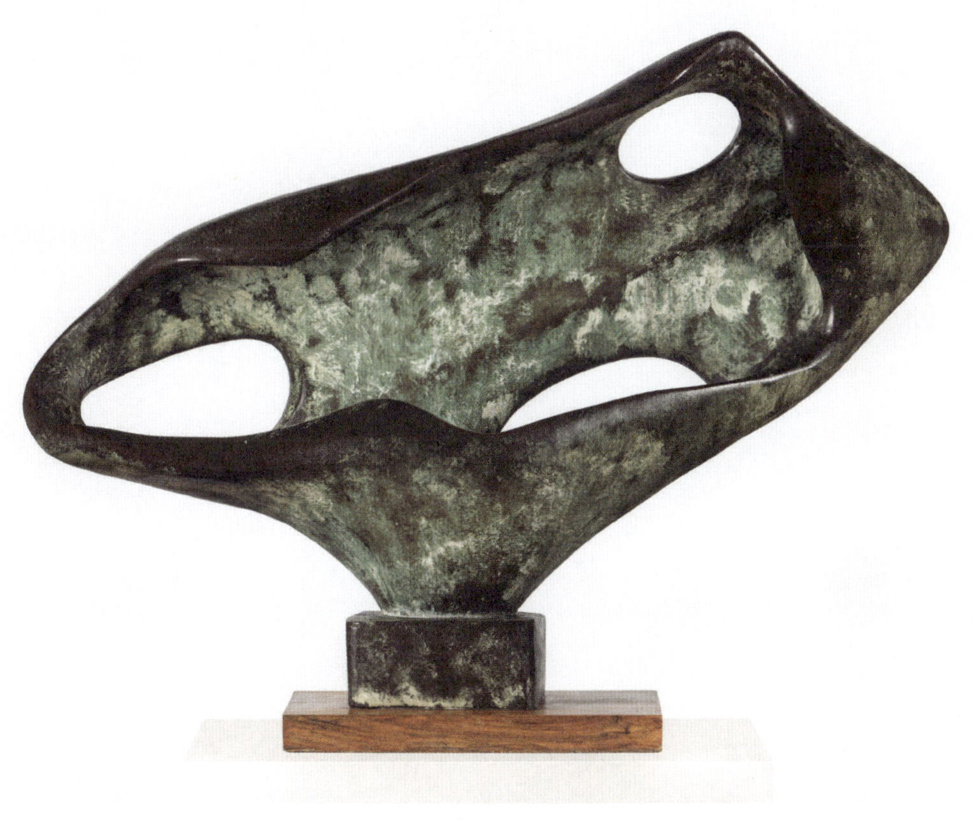

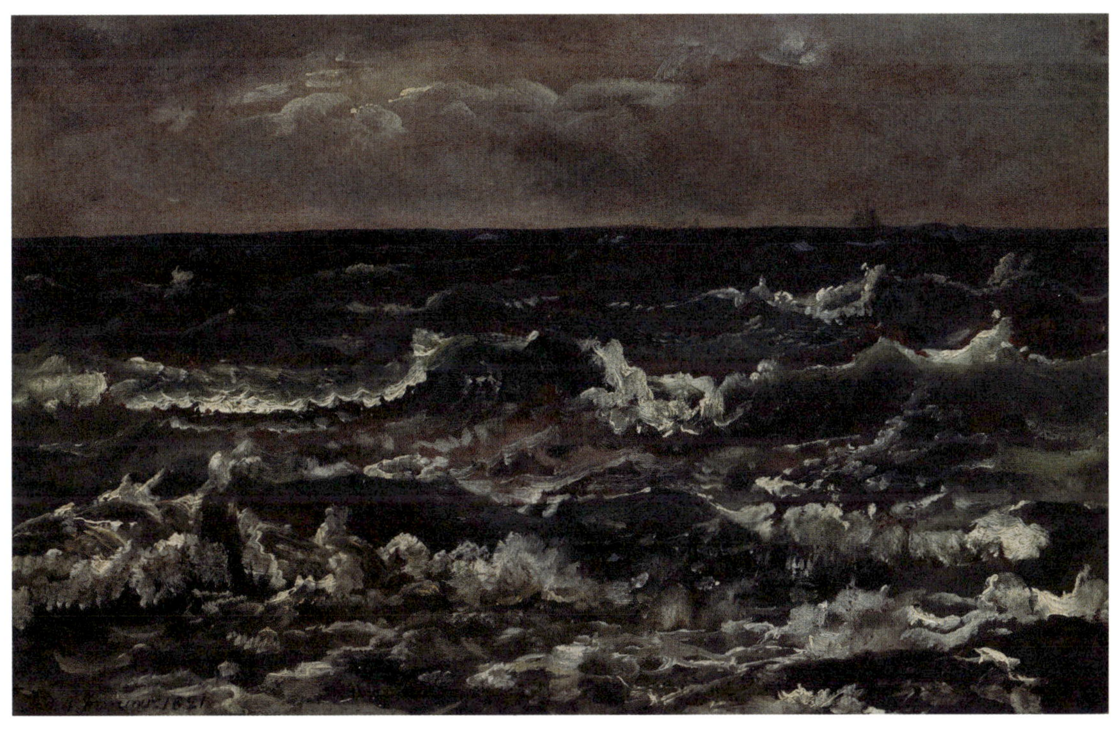

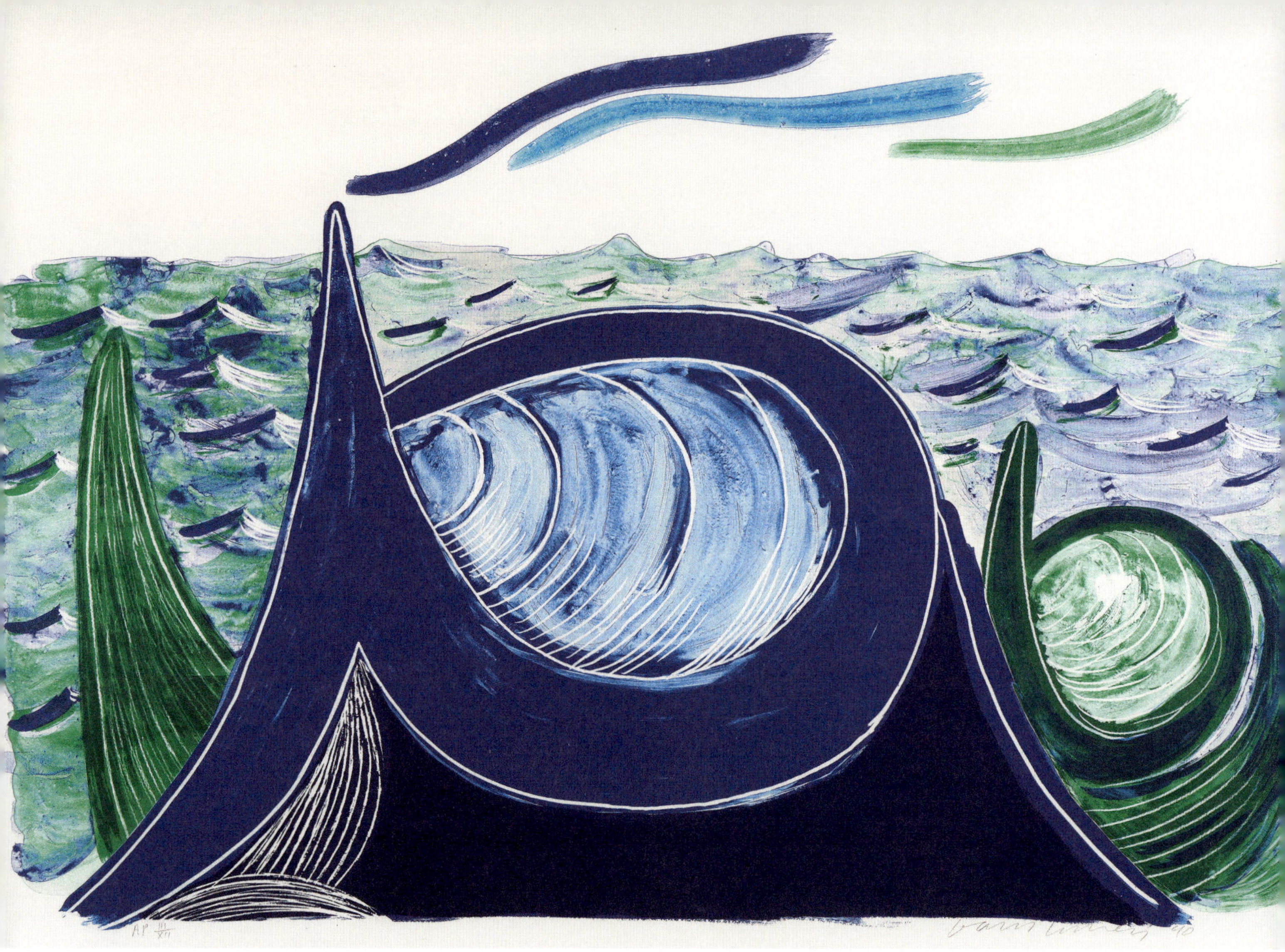

THE GEOMETRY OF AN OCEAN WAVE HAS BEEN EXPRESSED IN IMAGINATIVE WAYS BY ARTISTS. NOTICE HERE THE RECURRENT CIRCULAR FORMATION CREATED WHEN A WAVE TUCKS UNDER ITSELF – A FLEETING MOMENT THAT CONJURES A SENSE OF EXHILARATION BEFORE IT BREAKS AND CRASHES.

Above – *The Wave, A Lithograph*, 1990, lithograph on paper, David Hockney (British)

Opposite top – *Pelagos*, 1946, elm and strings on oak base, Dame Barbara Hepworth (British)

Opposite bottom – *The Wave*, 1917, oil on canvas, C R W Nevinson (British)

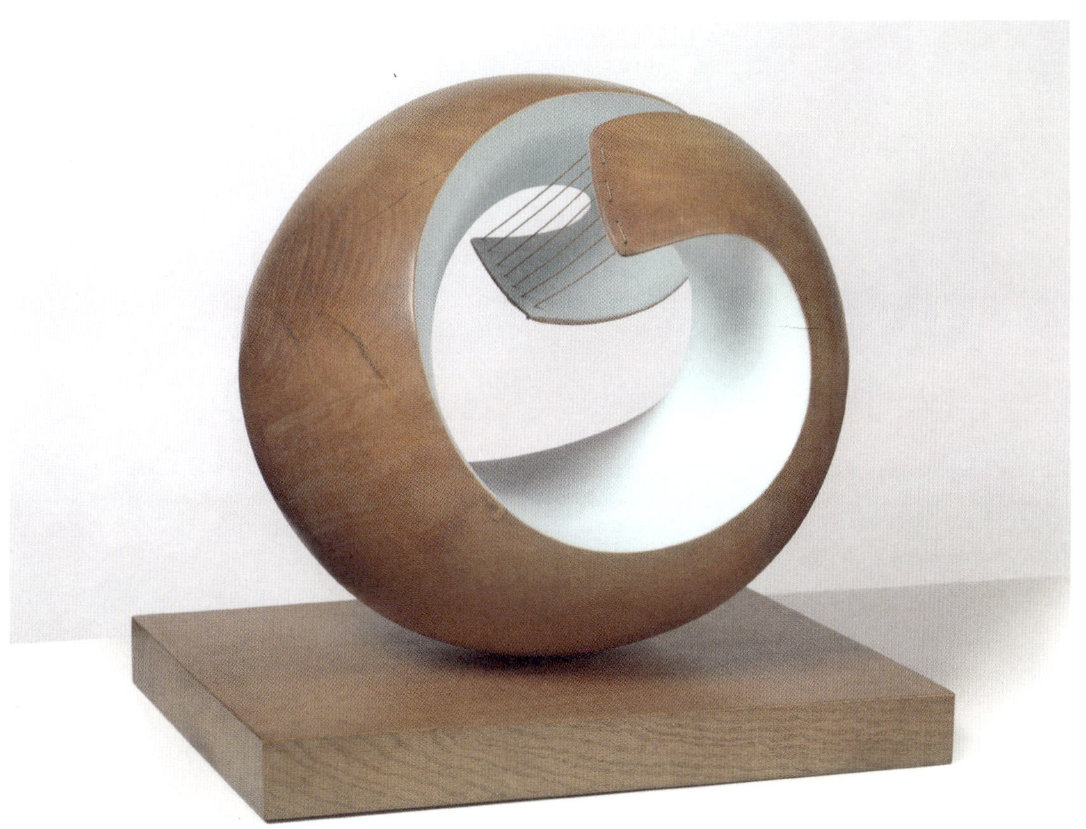

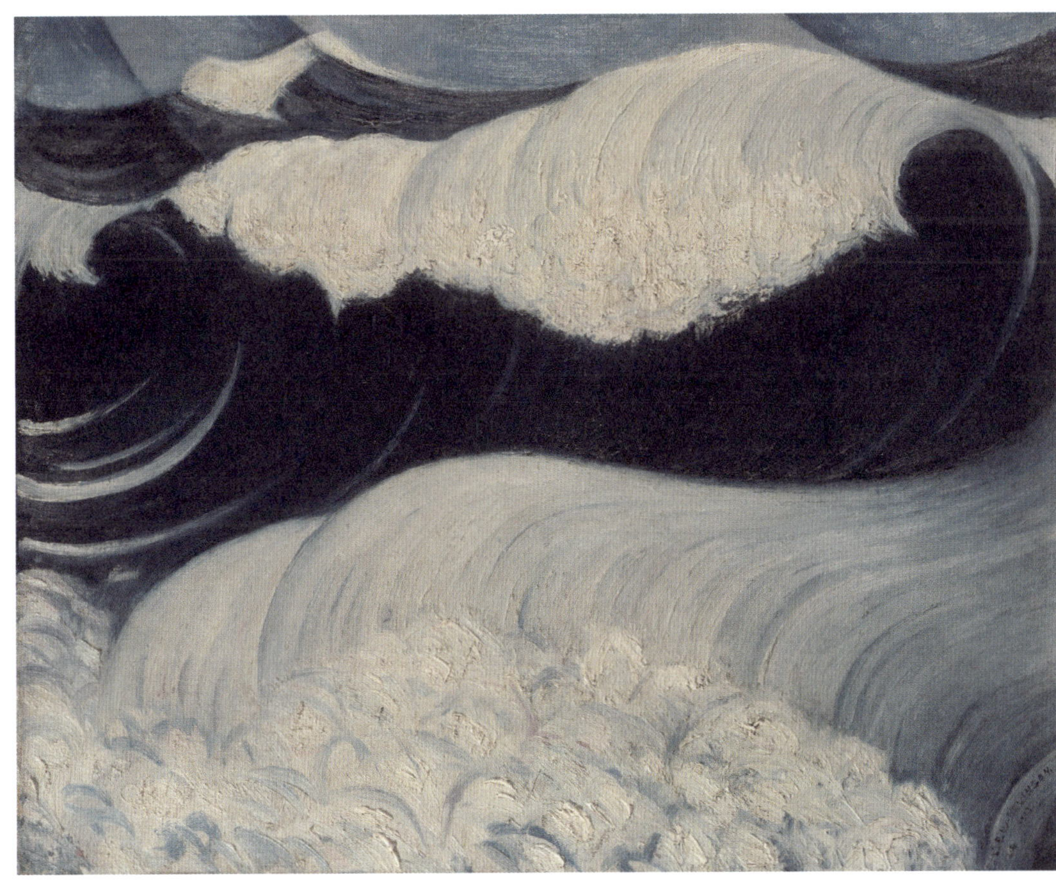

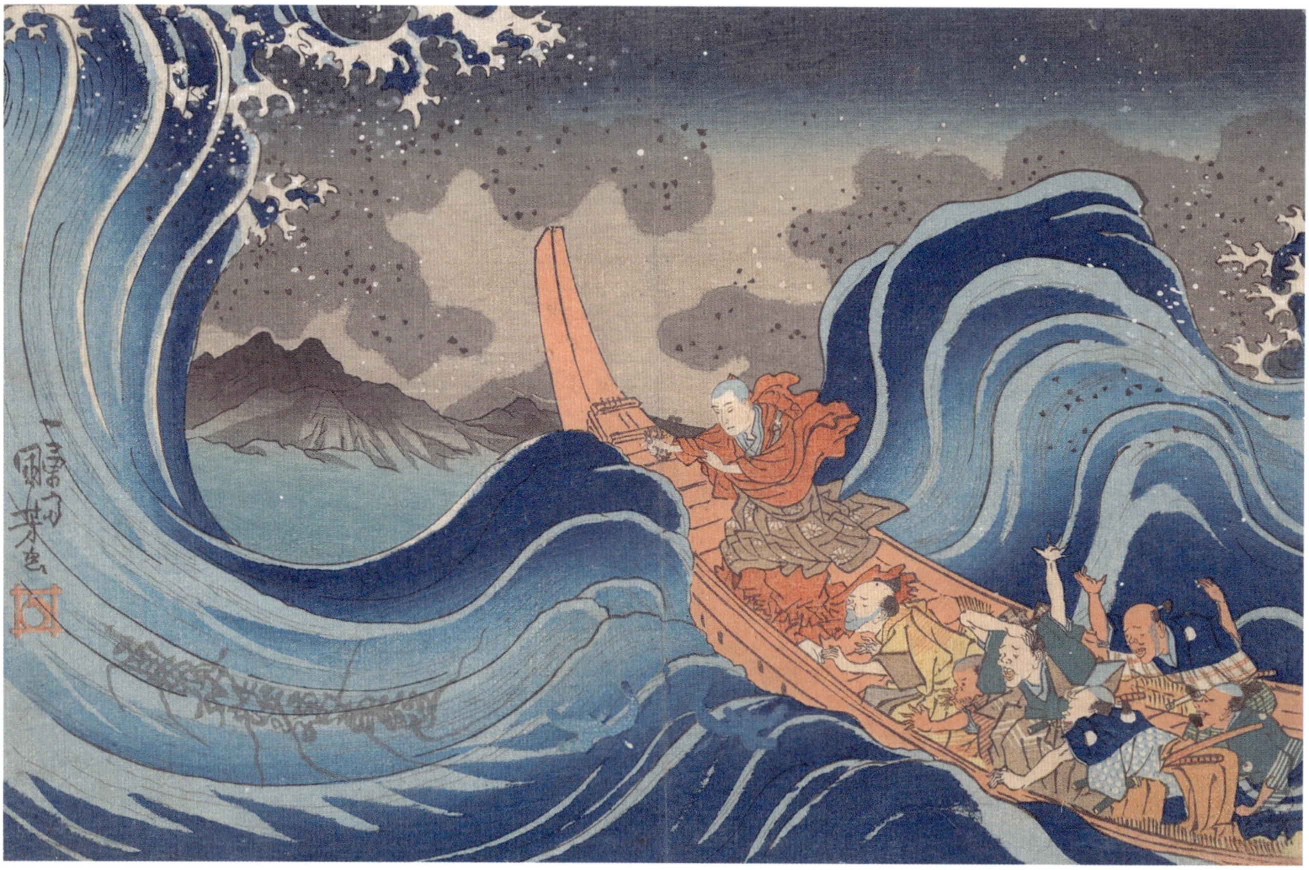

WILD SEAS! TAKE A SLOW LOOK AT THIS COLLECTION OF IMAGES SHOWING TREACHEROUS SEASCAPES. DOES THE PRESENCE OF HUMAN ACTIVITY AT SEA HELP EXALT THE POWER OF NATURE? OBSERVE HOW THE SKY AND THE SEA CONVERGE TO ENGULF THE BOATS.

Top – *Concise Illustrated Biography of Monk Nichiren: Calming the Stormy Sea at Tsunoda in Exile to Sado Island*, c. 1835–36, woodblock print; ink and colour on paper, Utagawa Kuniyoshi (Japanese)

Bottom – *Sailboat on a Raging Sea*, c. 1818–19, brush and brown wash, watercolour over black chalk, on brown laid paper, Théodore Géricault (French)

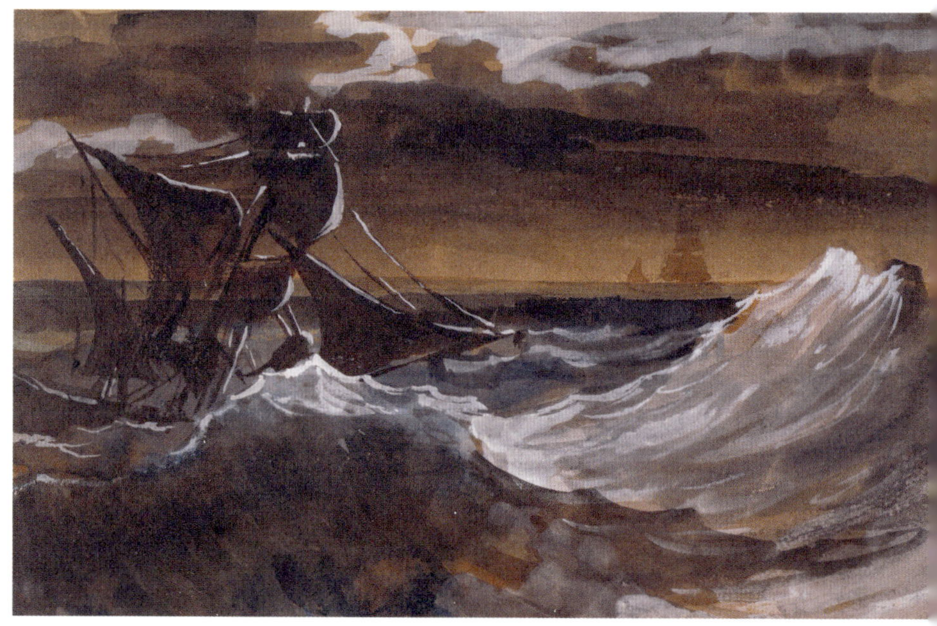

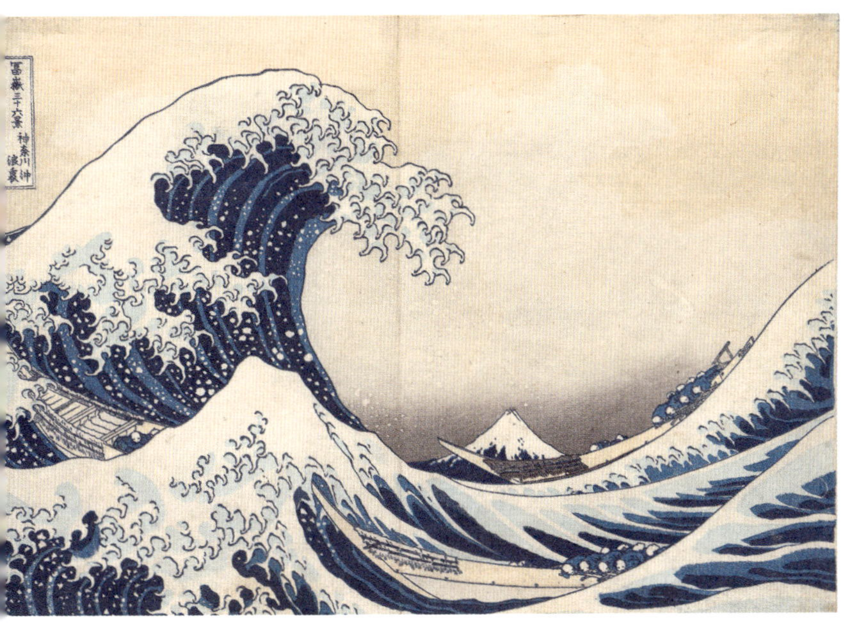

Top – *The Great Wave off Kanagawa*, c. 1830, colour woodblock, Katsushika Hokusai (Japanese)

Bottom – *Sailing ships in a storm*, c. 1609–70, oil on wood, Pieter Jansz van der Croos (Dutch)

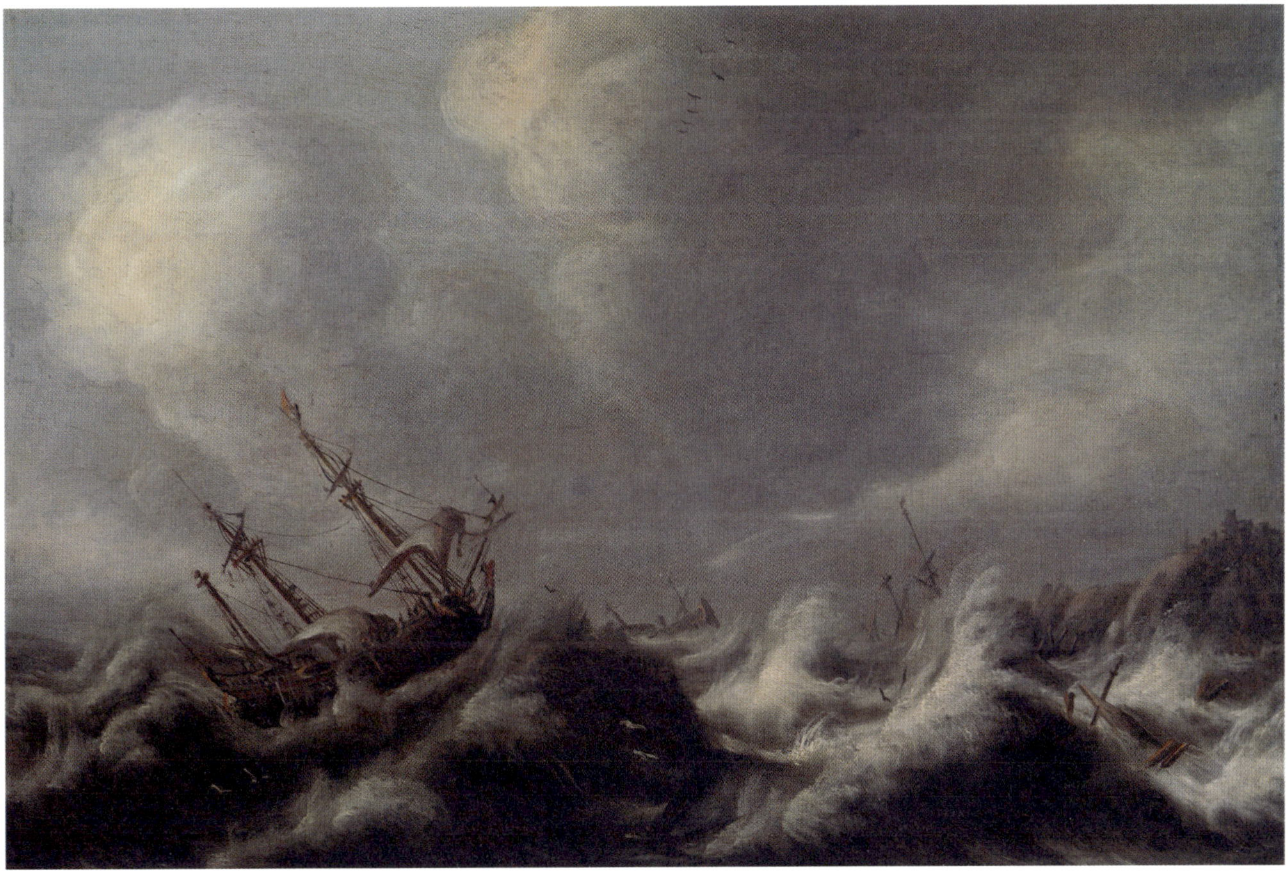

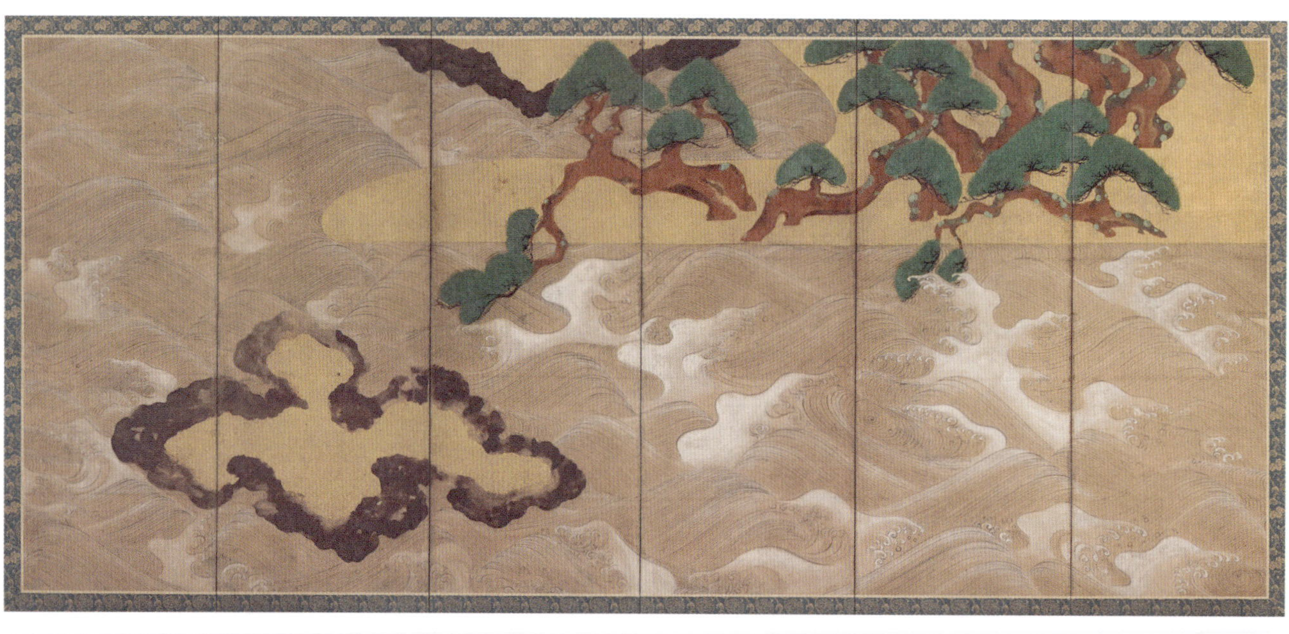

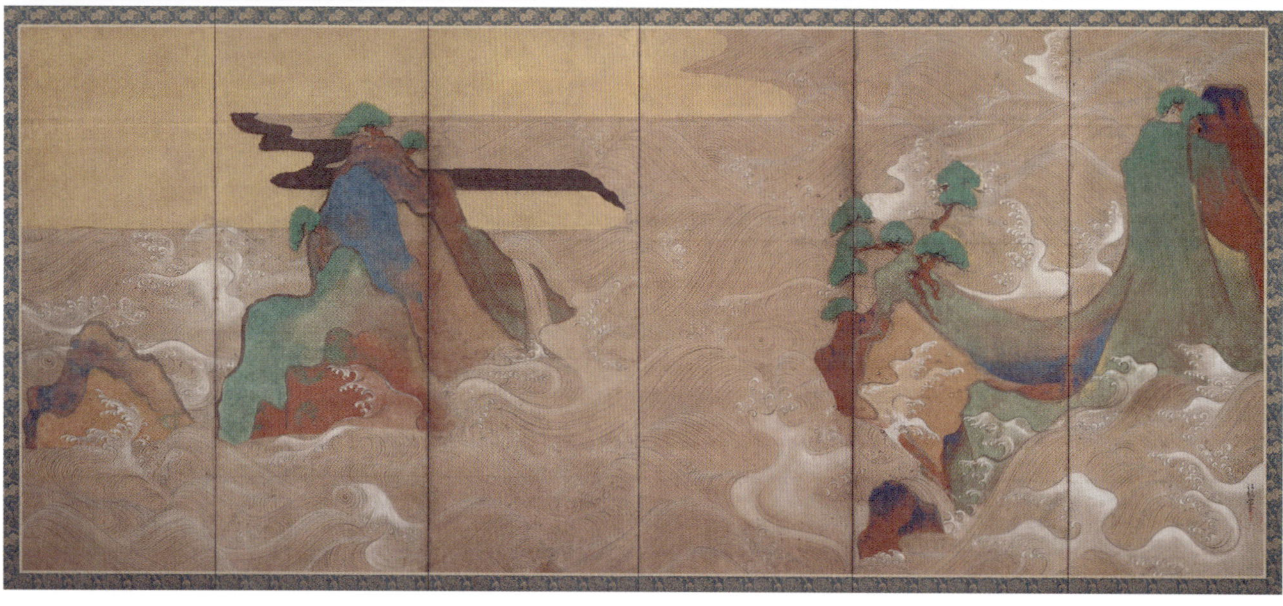

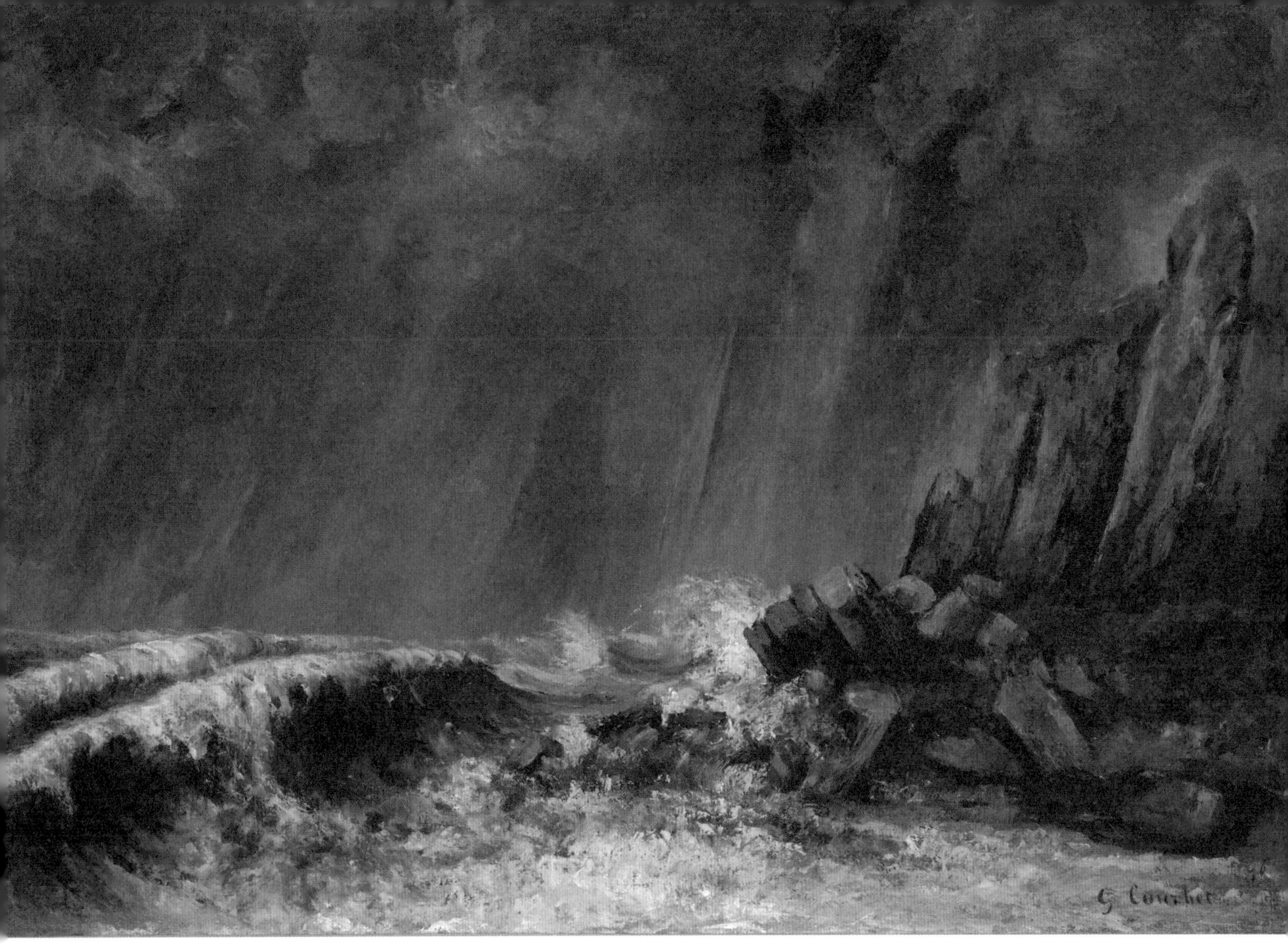

Opposite – *Waves at Matsushima*, c. 17th century, pair of folding screen paintings; ink, colour, gold, and silver on paper, Tawaraya Sotatsu (Japanese)

Above – *Marine: The Waterspout*, 1870, oil on canvas, Gustave Courbet (French)

Following – *Ligurian Sea, Riomagio*, 1993, gelatin-silver print,Hiroshi Sugimoto (Japanese)

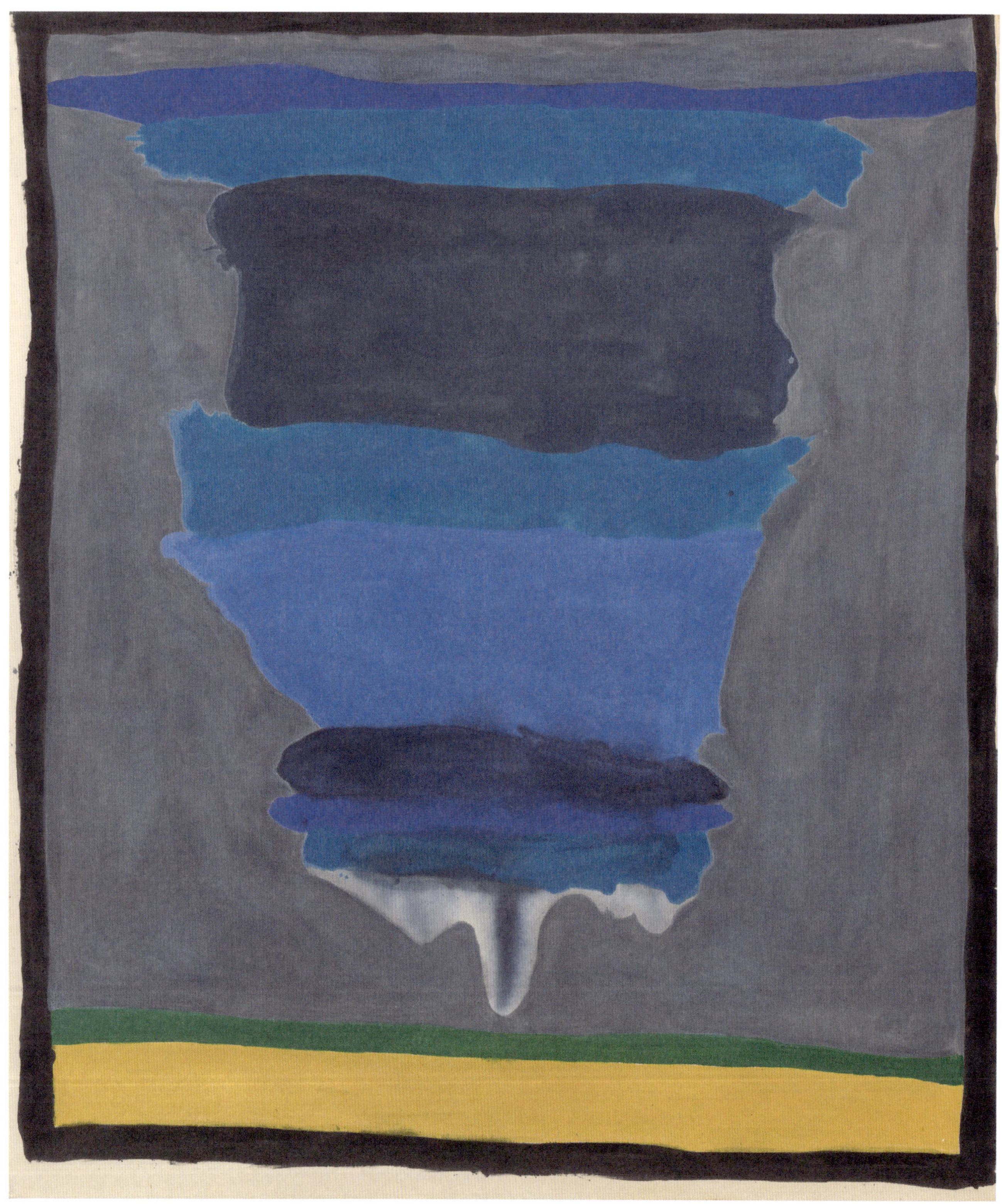

 Cape, (Provincetown), 1964, synthetic polymer paint and resin on canvas, Helen Frankenthaler (American)

COASTLINES

PERCHING THE VIEWER HIGH ON A BLUFF FACING OUT TO AN INFINITE OCEAN AND SKY INSPIRES A SOARING SENSATION. IMAGES THAT TAKE US TO THE EDGE OF ONE SPACE AND TO FACE ANOTHER CAN HAVE A POWERFUL EFFECT ON OUR IMAGINATION AND FEELING. FROM THIS VIEWPOINT, OUR PERSPECTIVE CAN EMBRACE ELEMENTS NOT FELT ON LOWER PLAINS. REFLECT ON HOW ARTISTS ELEVATE THE VIEWER TO GREAT HEIGHTS, WHILE AT THE SAME TIME CONVEYING A SENSE OF PLUNGING DEPTH.

Below – *(Rocks and Sea)*, c. 1916–19, oil on wood, Edward Hopper (American)

Following – *Coast scene*, c. late 1920s–early 1930s, watercolour over pencil, laid down, Edward Bawden (British)

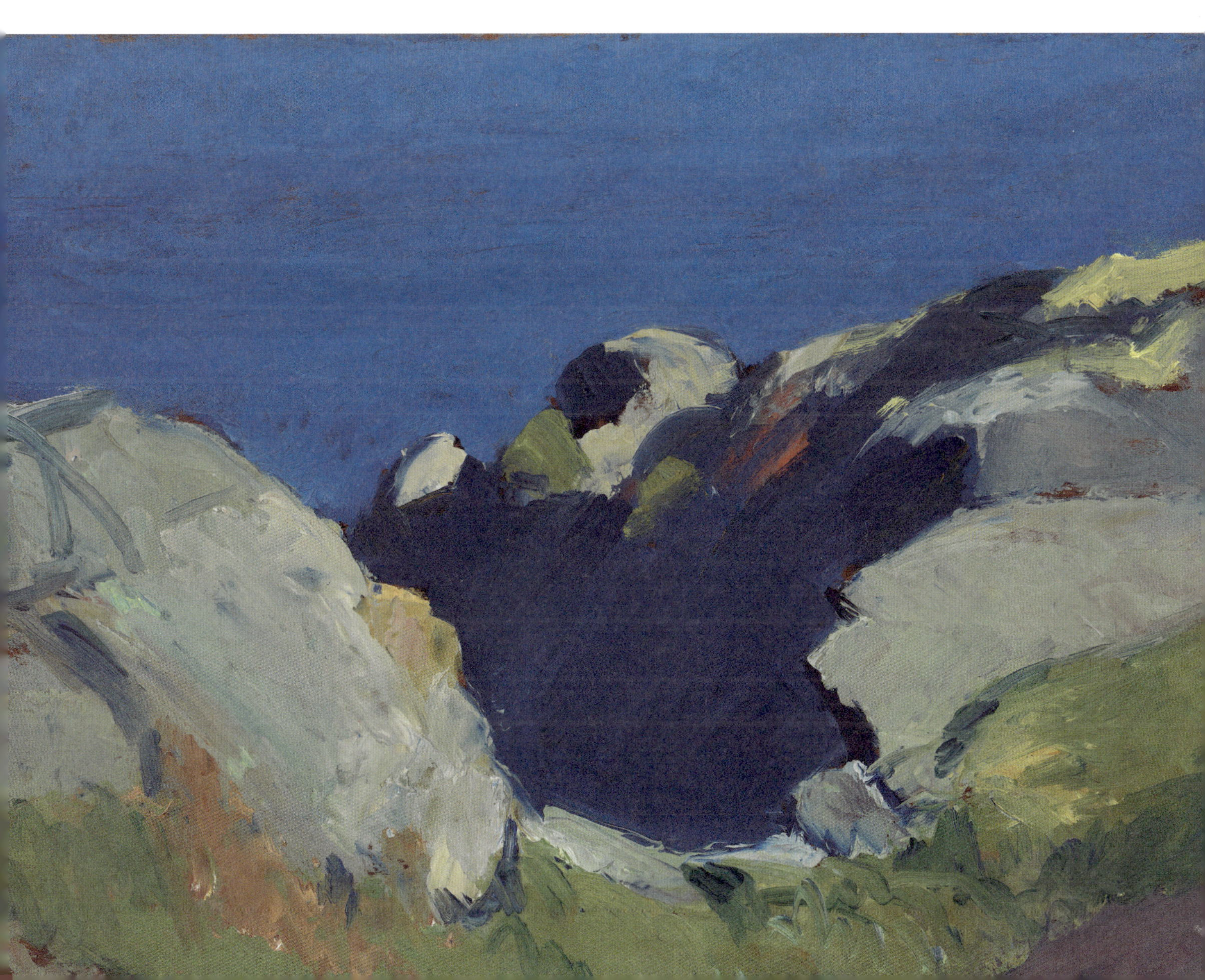

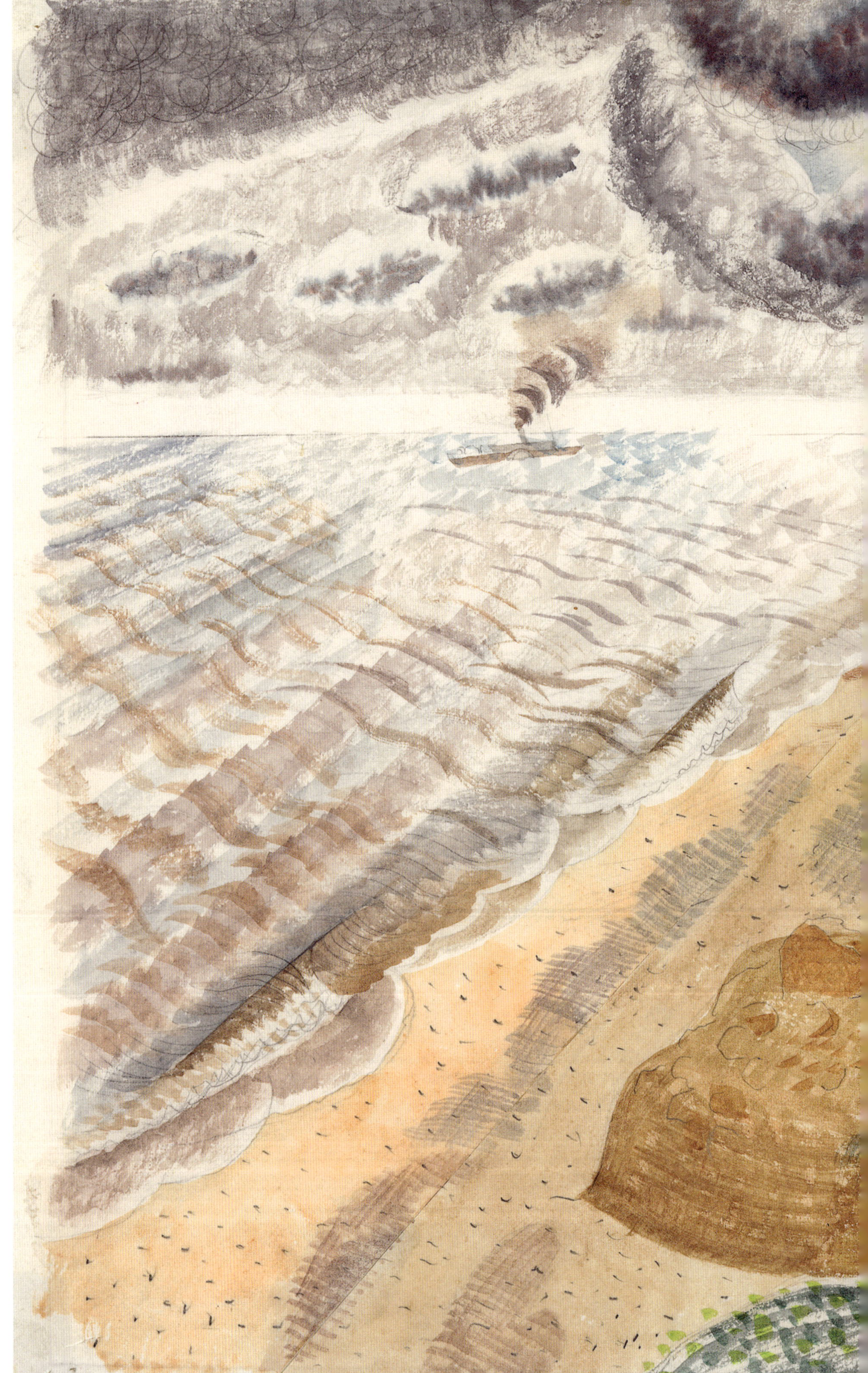

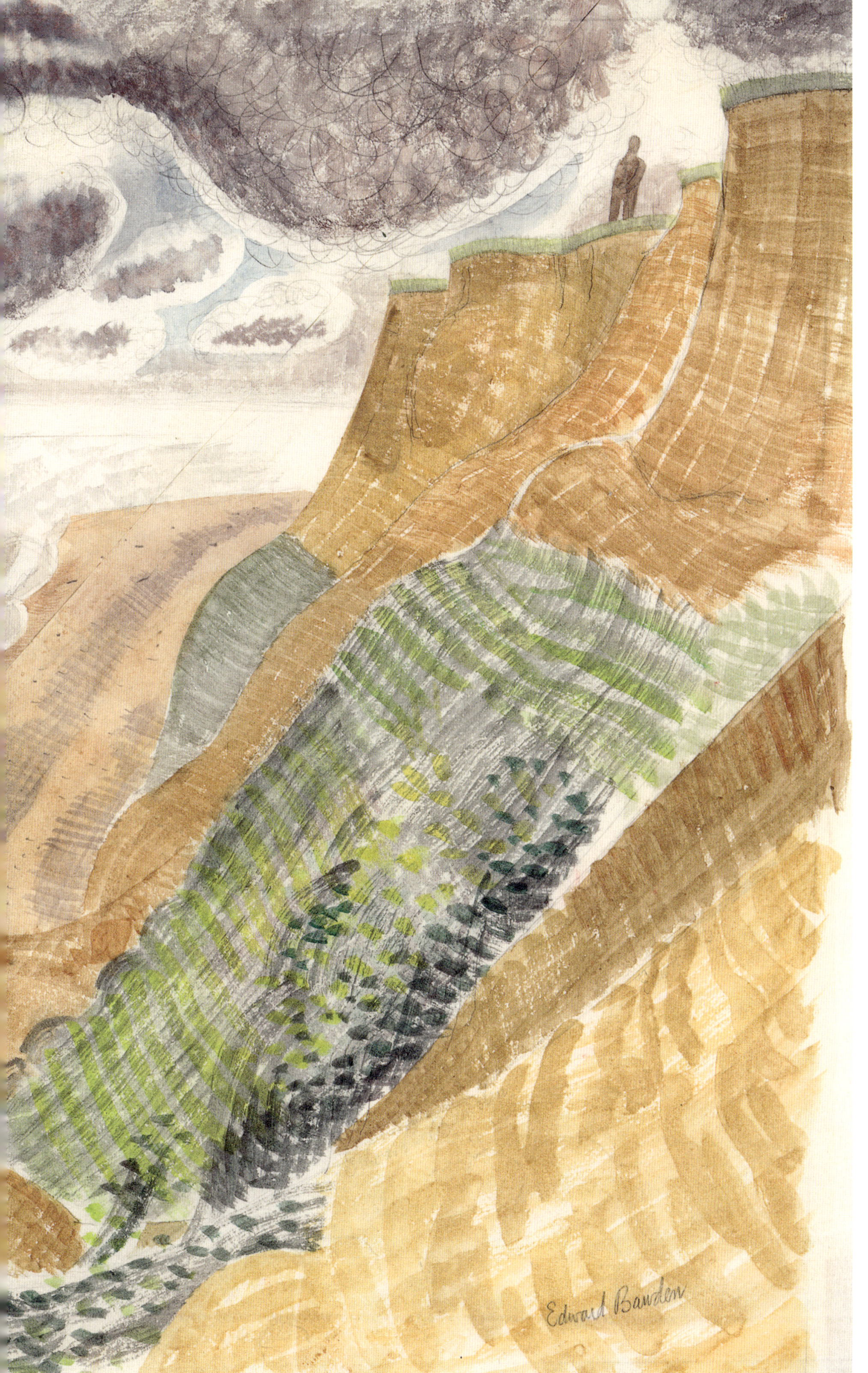
Edward Bawden

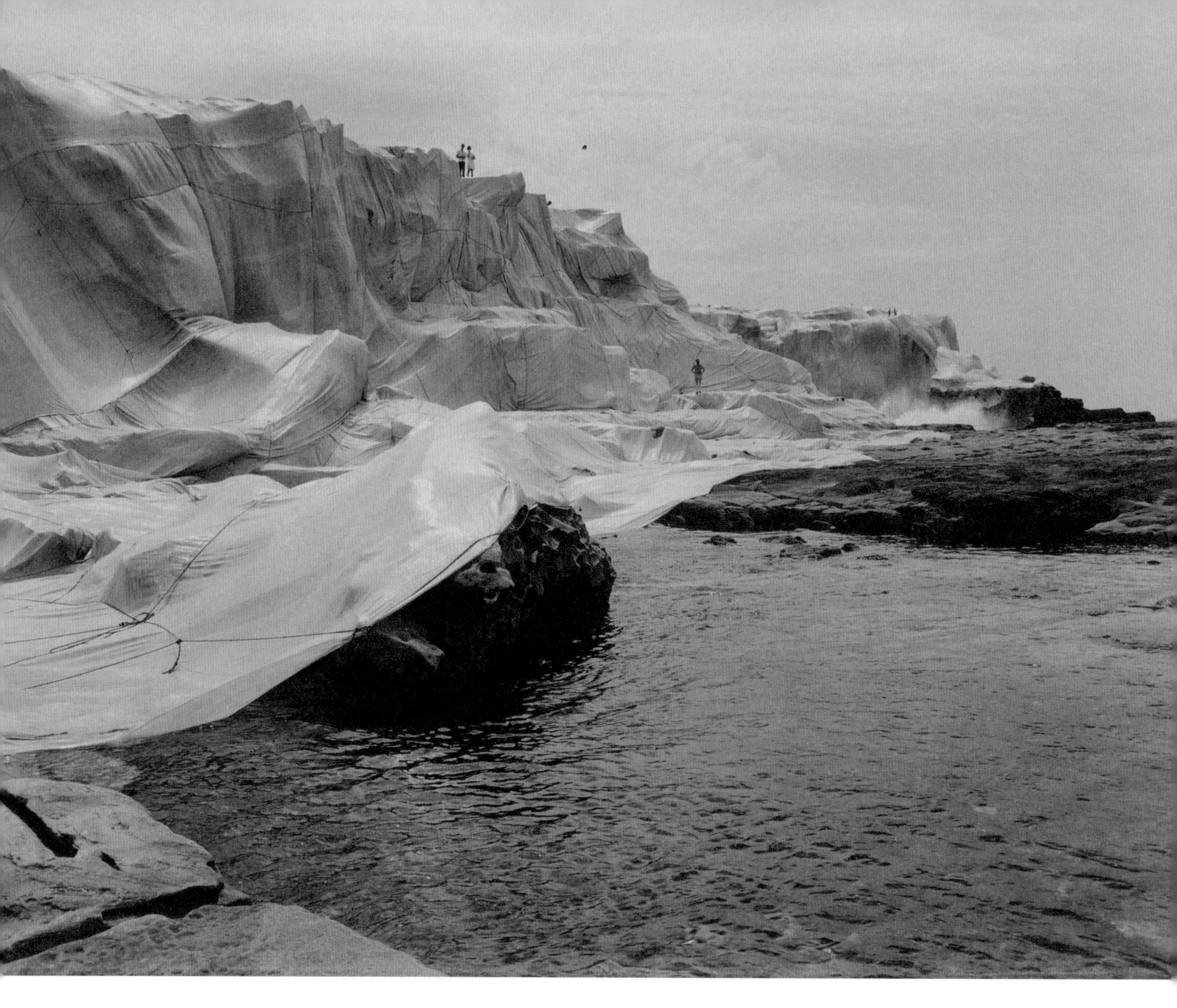

Wrapped Coast, Little Bay, Sydney, Australia, 1968–1969, 1969, colour photograph by Harry Shunk mounted on aluminium panel, Christo and Jeanne-Claude (American)

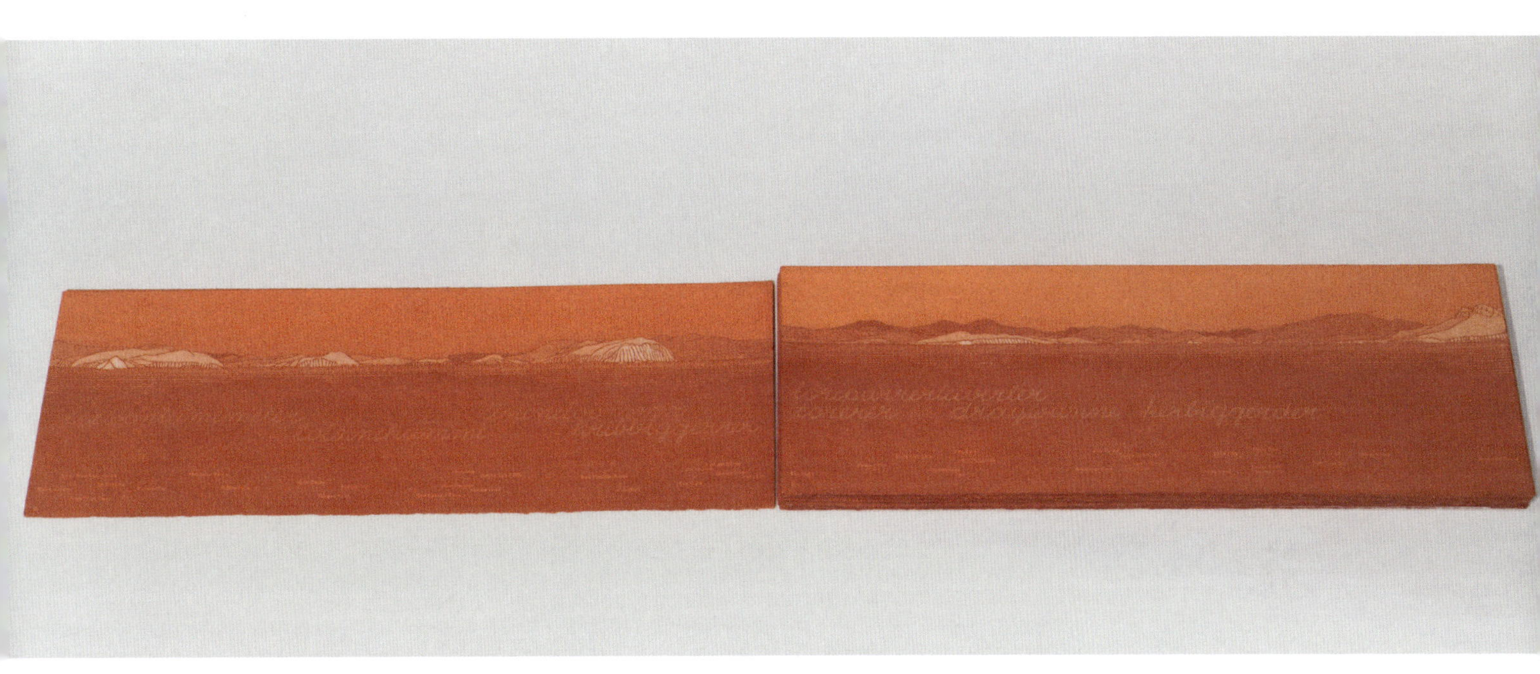

THE MAGNITUDE OF NATURE IN ART IS OFTEN CHARACTERISED BY THE PRESENCE OF HUMAN FIGURES WHO APPEAR MINUSCULE IN THEIR SETTING. NOTICE HOW MANY IMAGES INCLUDE PEOPLE AND HOW THEY WORK AS A PICTORIAL DEVICE TO INDICATE GREAT SCALE.

Terra Spiritus ... with a darker shade of pale, c. 1993–98, stencil, printed in hand-ground Launceston ochre, from multiple hand-cut mylar stencils; letterpress text blind printed; hand-written script, Bea Maddock (Australian)

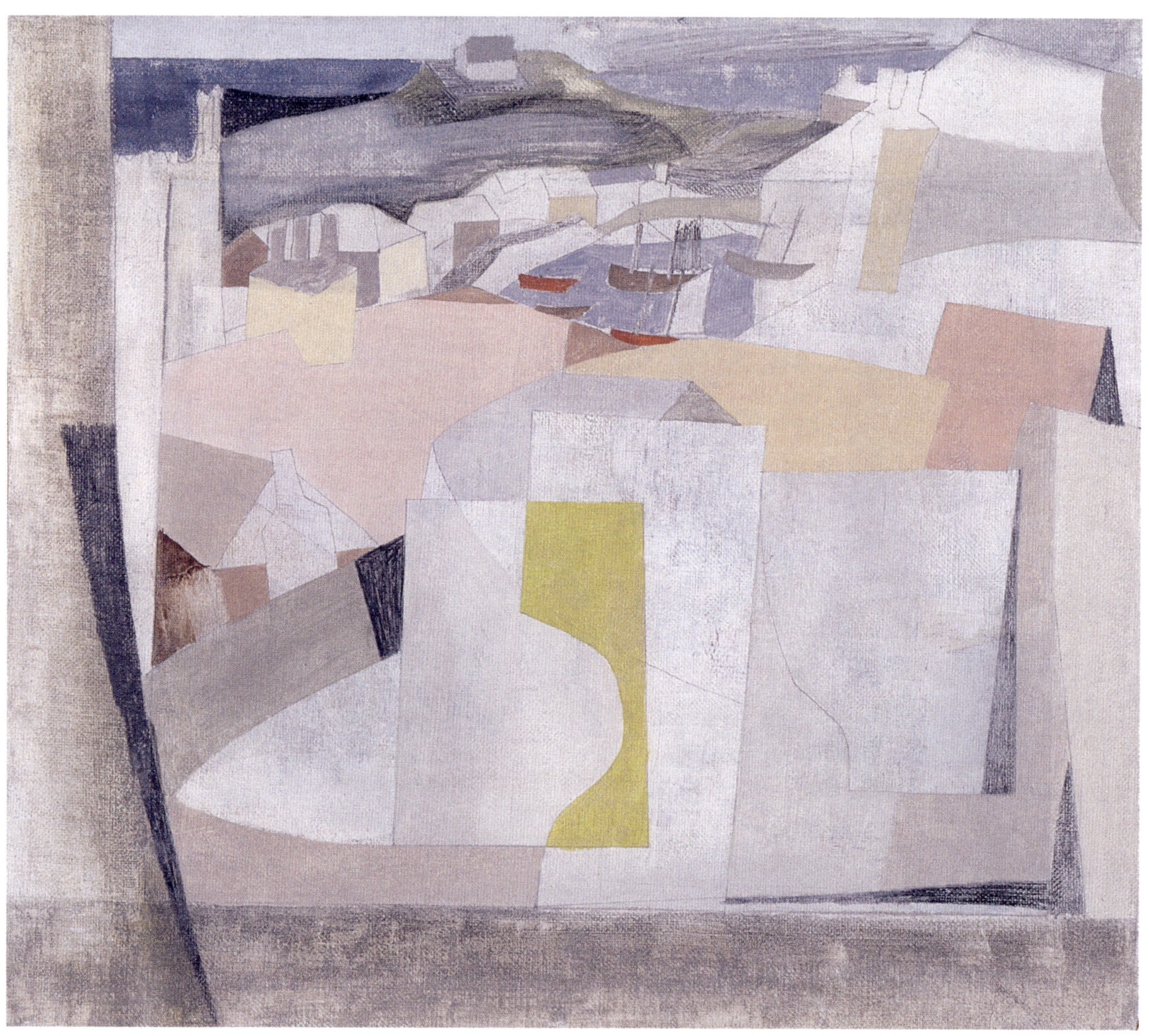

142 *July 15 1949 (St Ives harbour)*, 1949, oil and pencil on canvas, Ben Nicholson (British)

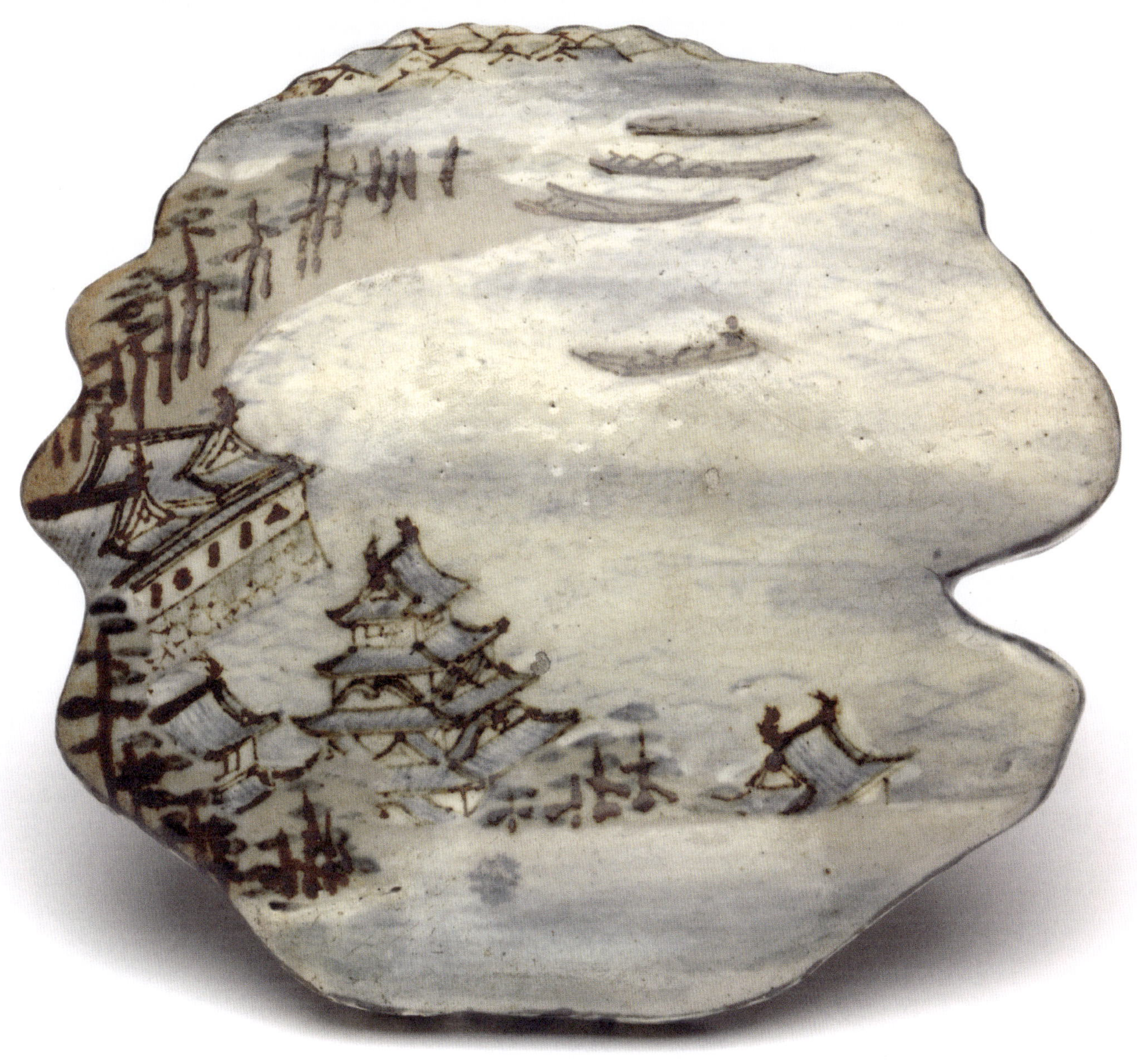

THIS INCENSE CONTAINER SHOWS WATER LAPPING AT THE HARBOUR SCENE WITH FISHING BOATS, BUILDINGS AND TREES LINING THE SHORE. THE TRANSLUCENT WHITE GLAZE TINTED WITH BLUE AND GOLD APPLIED TO THE SURFACE OF THE CONTAINER, ALONG WITH ITS SHELL-LIKE SHAPE, GIVE IT THE APPEARANCE OF A TREASURE THAT MIGHT WASH UP ON THE BEACH.

Japanese incense container, c. 1799, stoneware with glaze, Ogata Kenzan (Japanese)

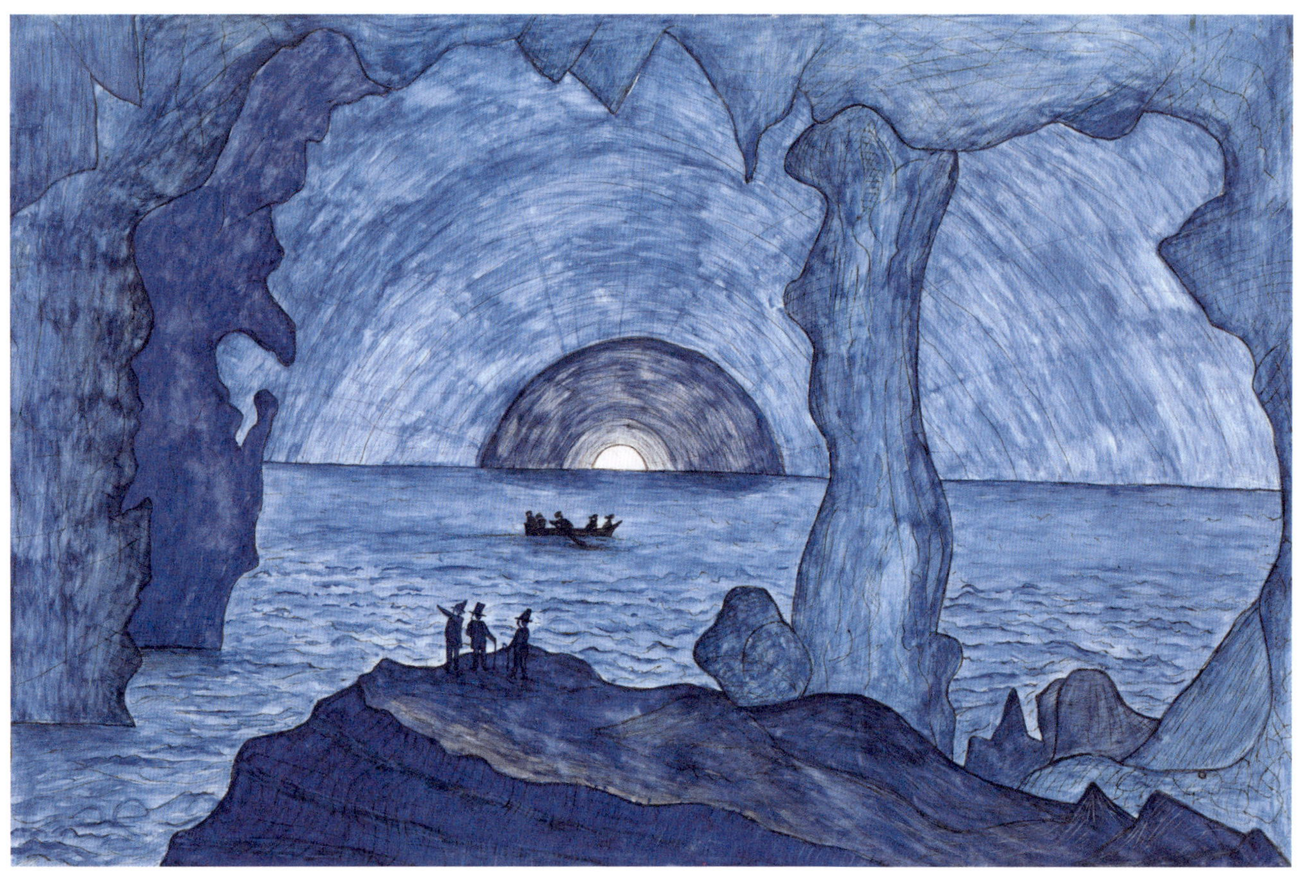

ULTRAMARINE, COBALT, NAVY, CERULEAN BLUE, INTERNATIONAL KLEIN BLUE. SUBMERGING INTO THE BLUES ON THE PAGE, TAKE A MOMENT TO REFLECT ON THE TONES OF BLUE AND HOW THEY CREATE A SENSE OF DEPTH, OR LIGHTNESS, ALONGSIDE CONTRASTING COLOURS AND INFLECTIONS OF WHITE.

Above – *The Blue Grotto*, c. 1880, watercolour on paper, Lawrence W Ladd (American)

Opposite – *Evening coming in on Sydney Harbour* (detail), 1975, oil on cotton on canvas, Brett Whiteley (Australian)

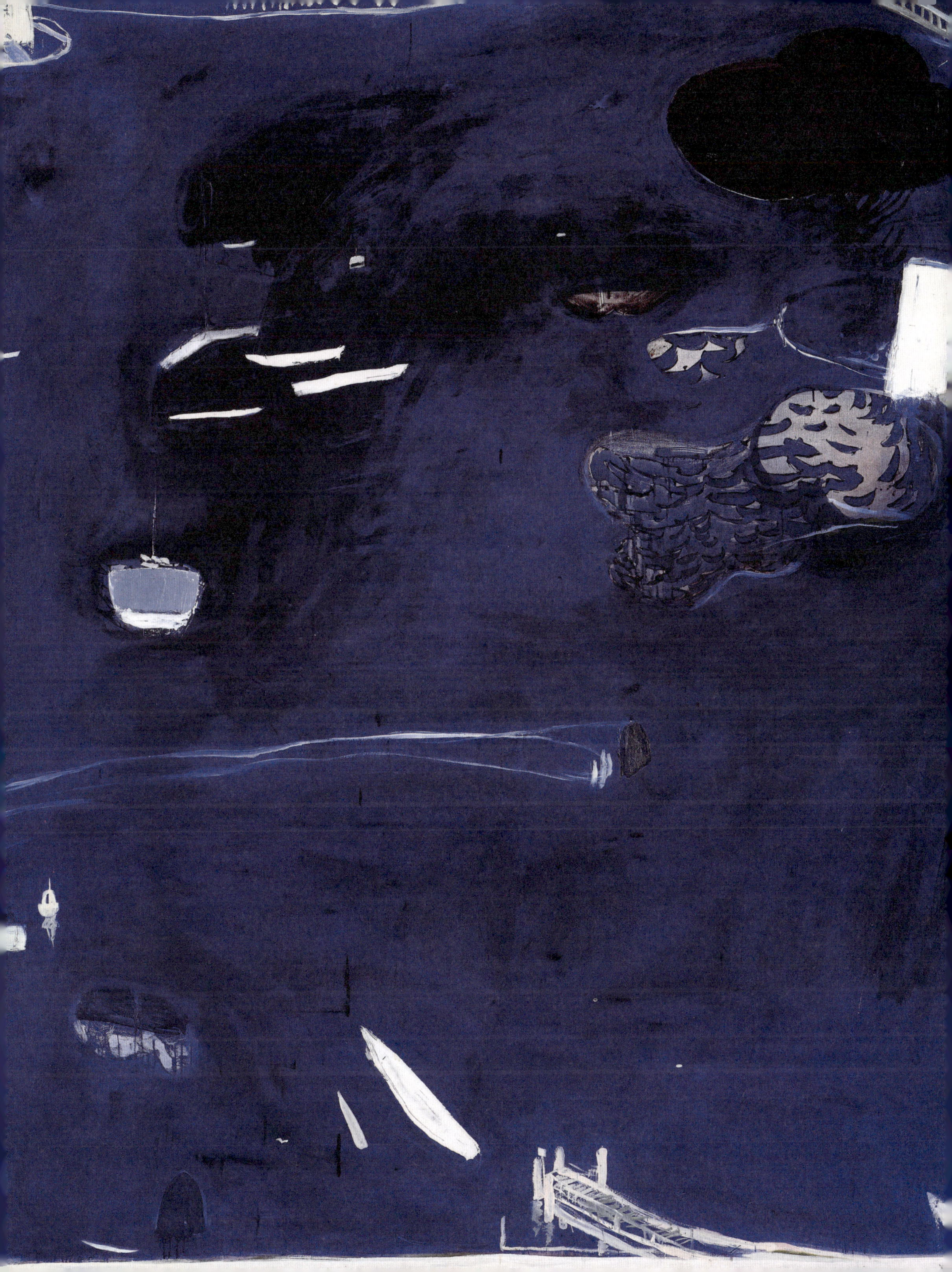

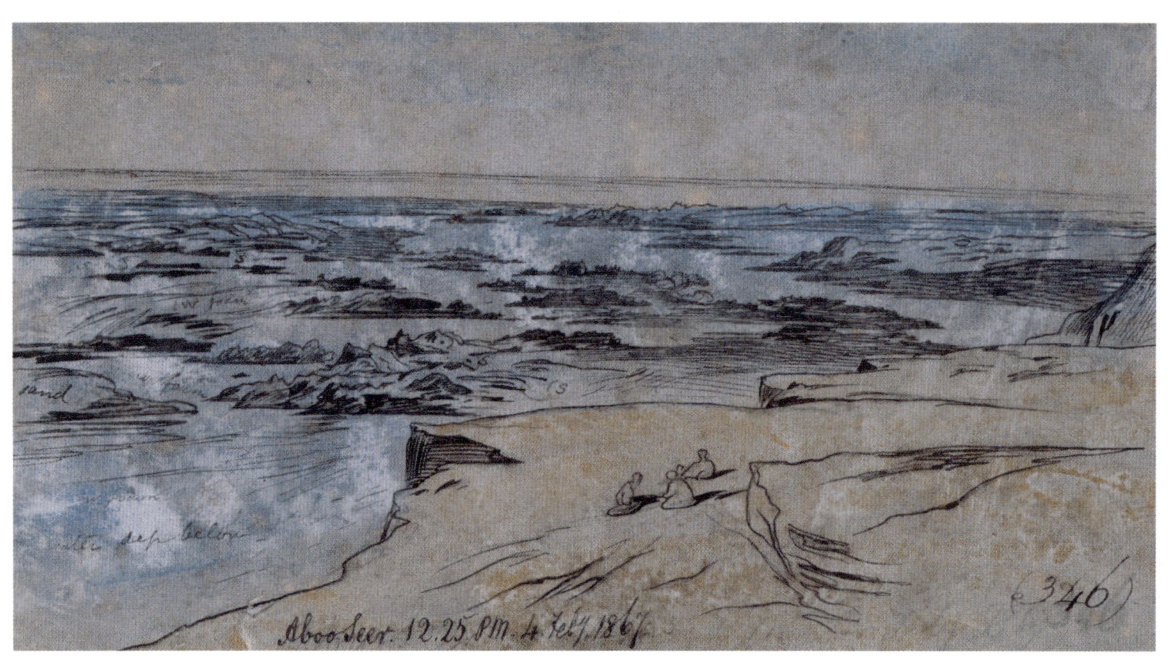
Aboo Seer. 12.25 PM. 4 Feby. 1867
(346)

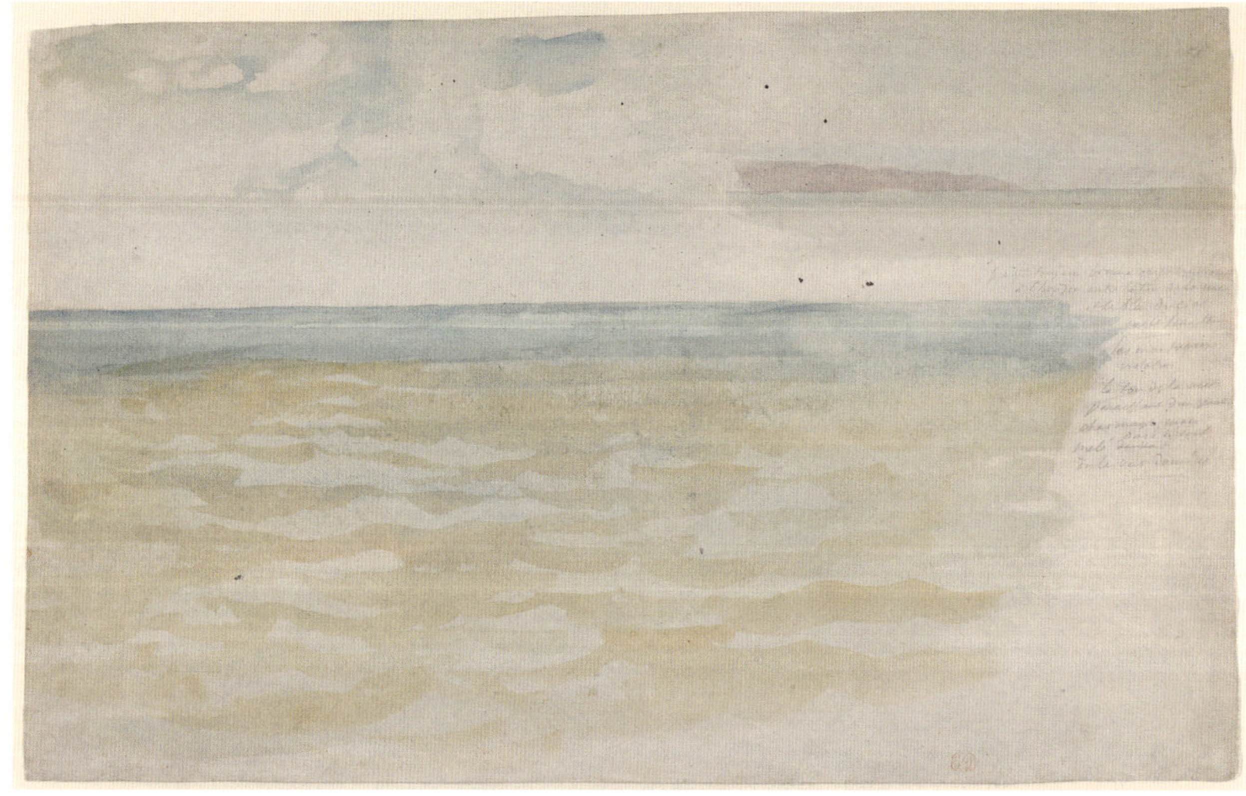

BEACHES

IMAGES OF SANDY SHORES AND BEACHES OFFER ANOTHER ANGLE THROUGH WHICH WE CONNECT WITH THE OCEAN. OBSERVE HOW PICTORIAL DEPTH IS ACHIEVED IN THE CALLIGRAPHIC INK WORK OF ABSTRACT EXPRESSIONIST PAINTER WILLEM DE KOONING COMPARED WITH THE SPIRITED BRUSH WORK OF ENGLISH ROMANTIC PAINTER JOHN CONSTABLE (SEE PAGES 148 & 152).

Opposite top – *Abu Seer*, 1867, watercolour, graphite, pen and black ink on medium, slightly textured, blue laid paper, Edward Lear (British)

Opposite bottom – *The Sea at Dieppe*, c. 1852–54, watercolour on laid paper, Eugène Delacroix (French)

Below – *Blue Coast 20*, 2006, acrylic on board, Vanessa Gardiner (British)

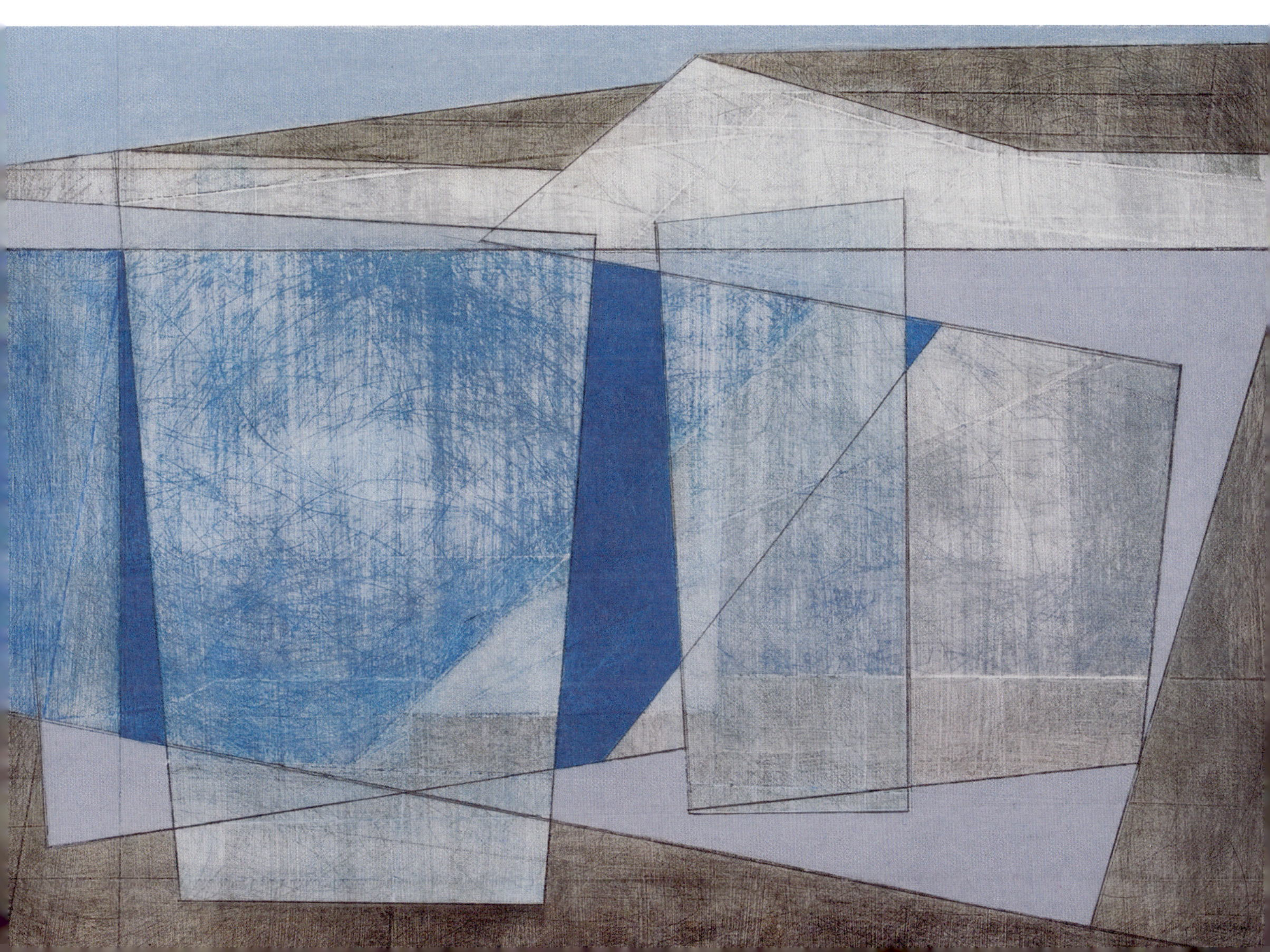

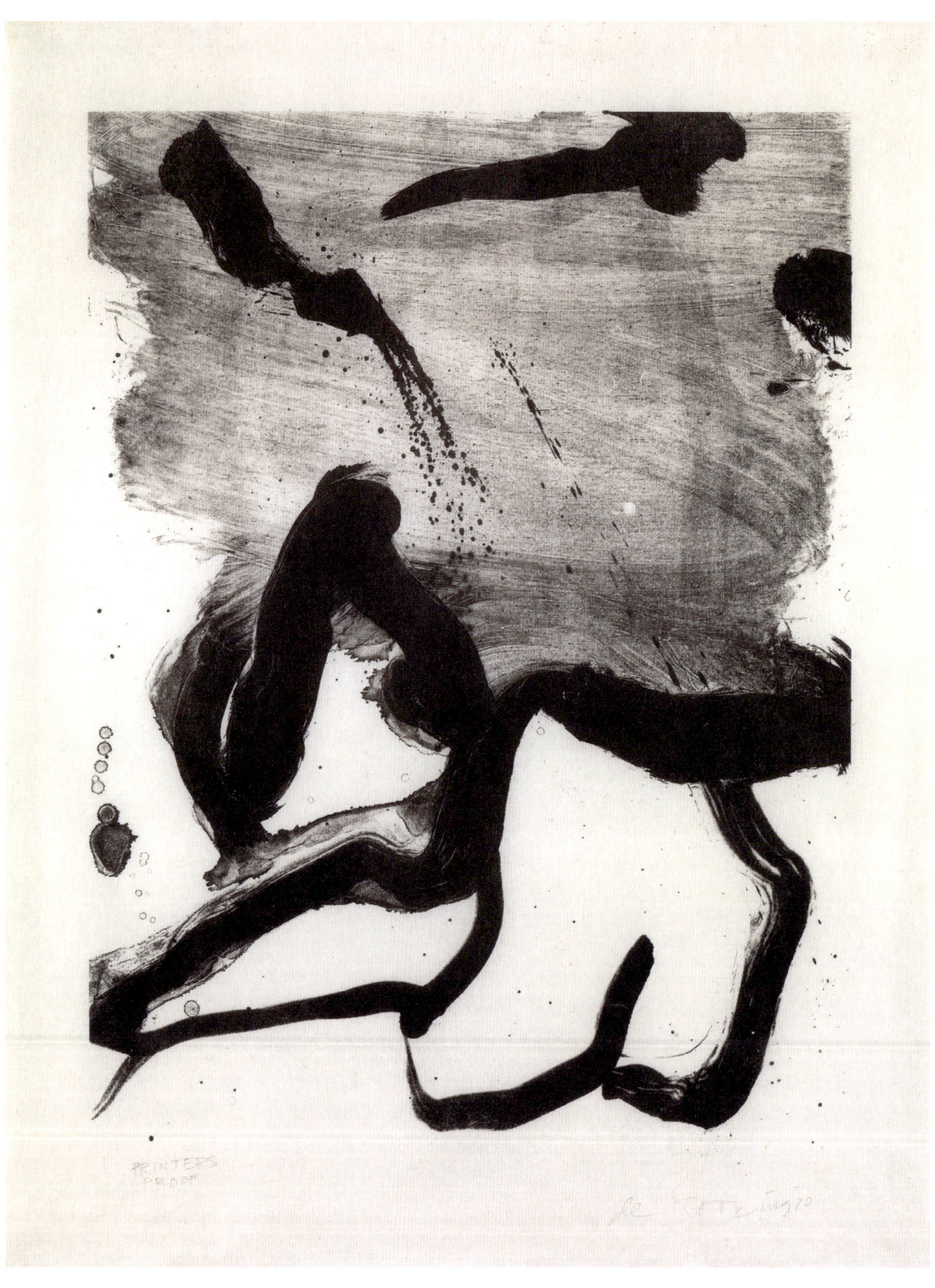

Above – *Beach scene*, 1970, lithograph, Willem de Kooning (American/Dutch)

Opposite – *Old horizon*, 1928, oil on canvas, Yves Tanguy (French)

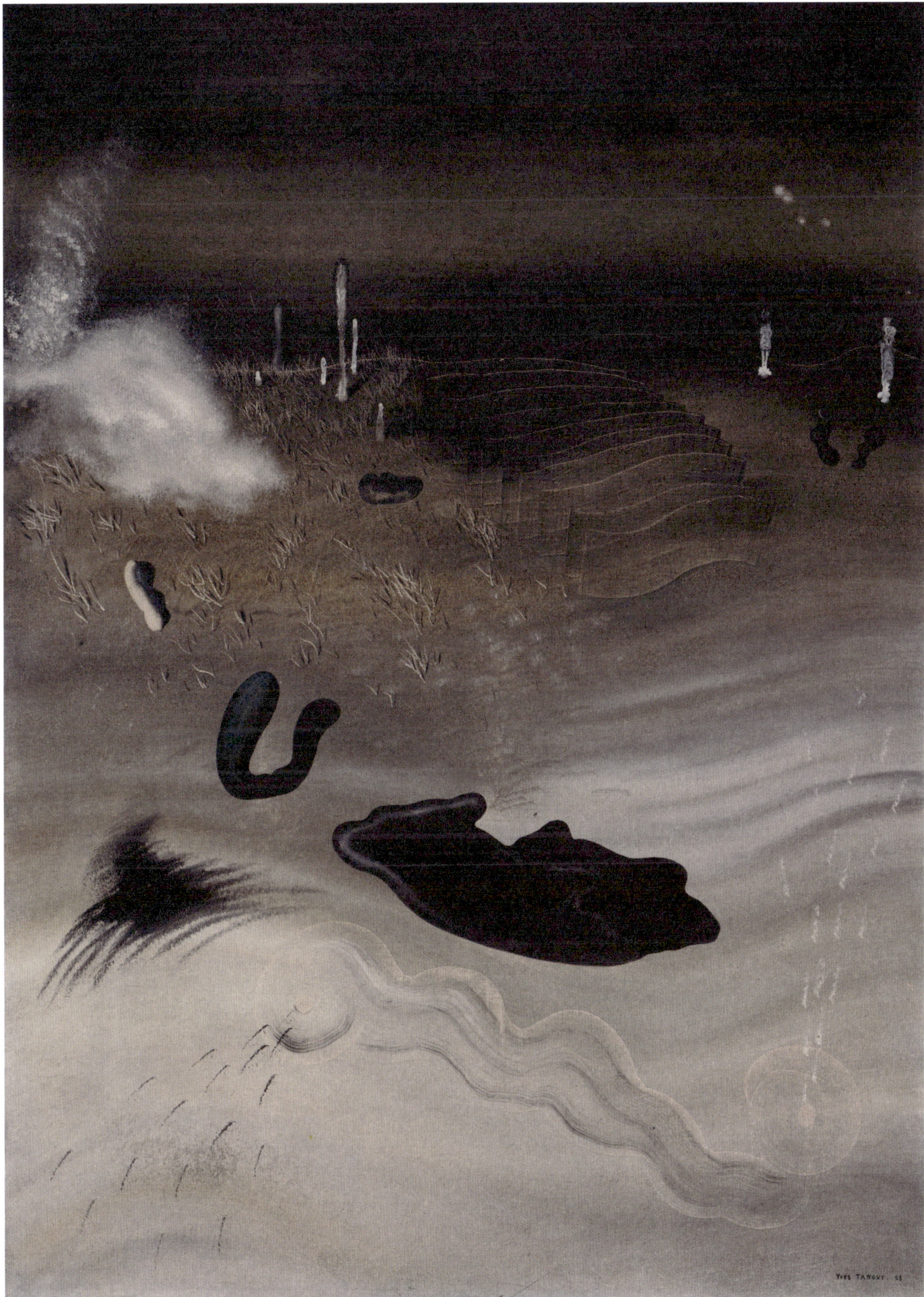
YVES TANGUY

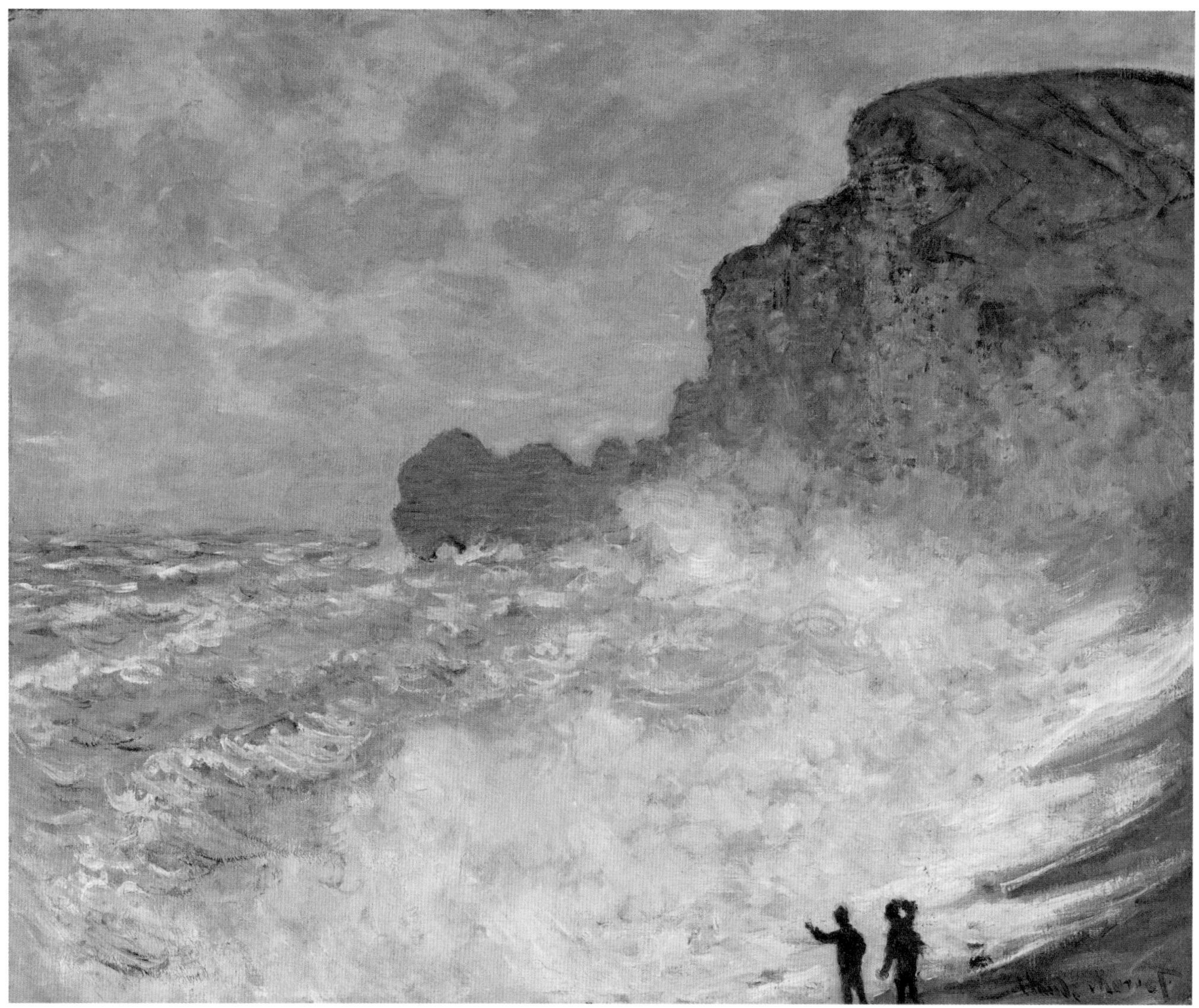

SEA SPRAY FROM SWEEPING WAVES FILL THE PICTORIAL SPACE IN THIS DRAMATIC SMALL PAINTING BY MONET OF THE BEACH AT ÉTRETAT ON THE NORTH COAST OF FRANCE. THE SMALL FIGURES WAVING IN THE FOREGROUND MAGNIFY THE POWERFUL FORCE OF THE SURF. WALKING TRACKS, OR DESIRE LINES, CAN BE SEEN ON THE PLATEAU OF CRAGGY MASS; THEY INDICATE THE PATHWAYS CREATED BY VISITORS SEEKING A SPECTACULAR COASTAL VIEW.

Above – *Rough weather at Étretat*, 1883, oil on canvas, Claude Monet (French)

Opposite top – *Weymouth Bay*, 1816, oil on canvas, John Constable (British)

Opposite bottom – *Weymouth Bay, Dorsetshire*, 1830, mezzotint and drypoint on chine collé, David Lucas (engraver) and John Constable (British)

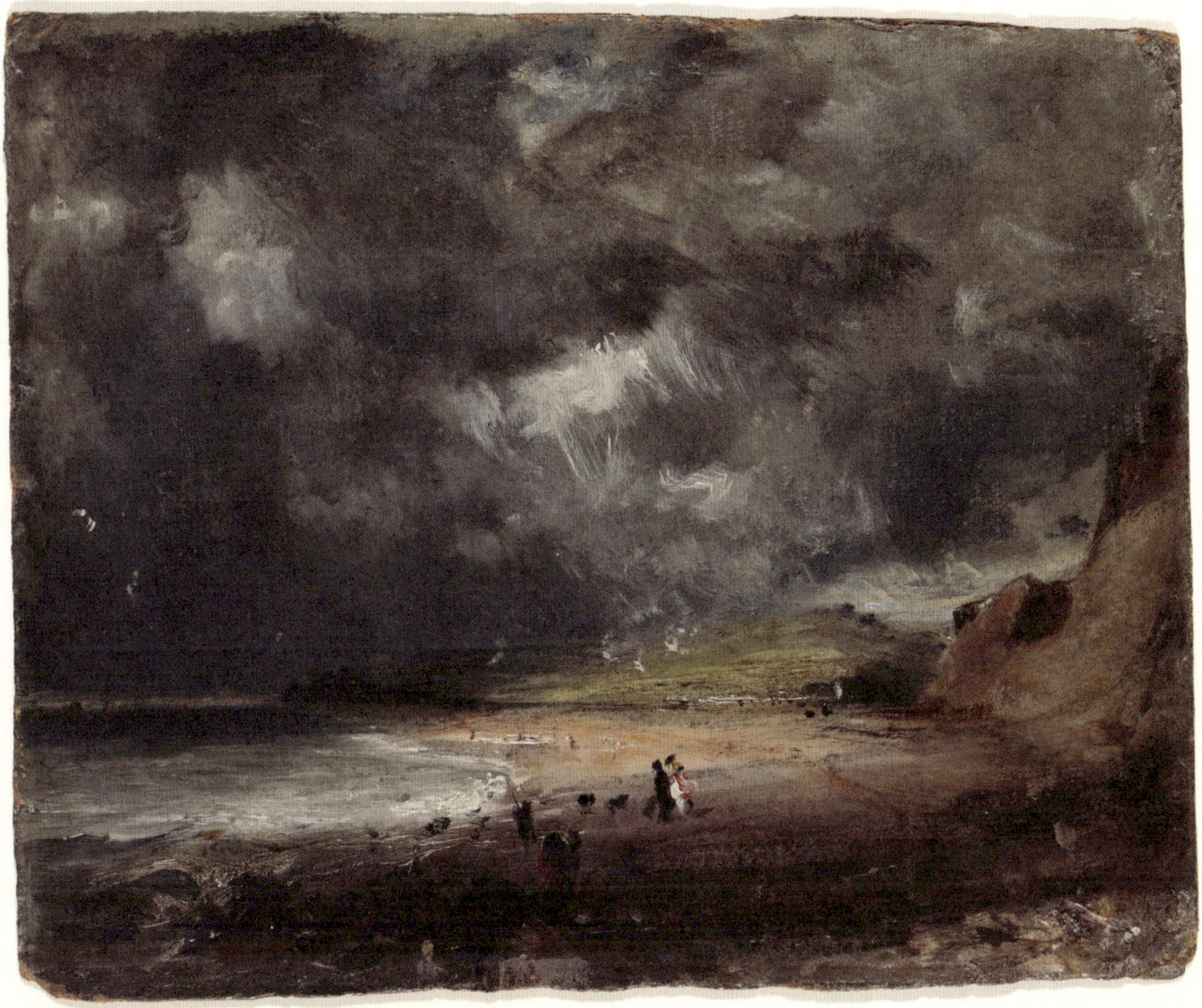

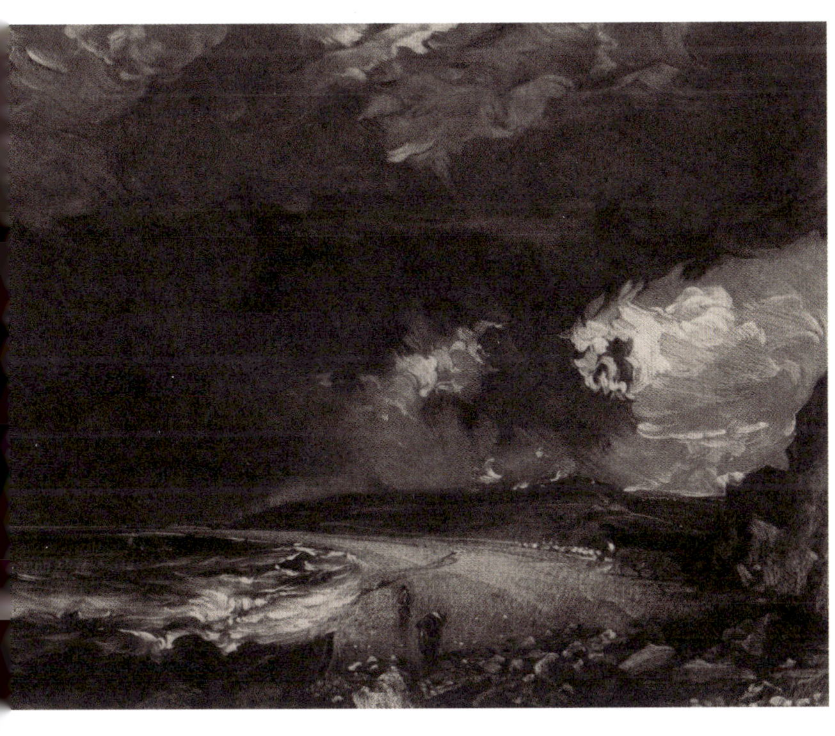

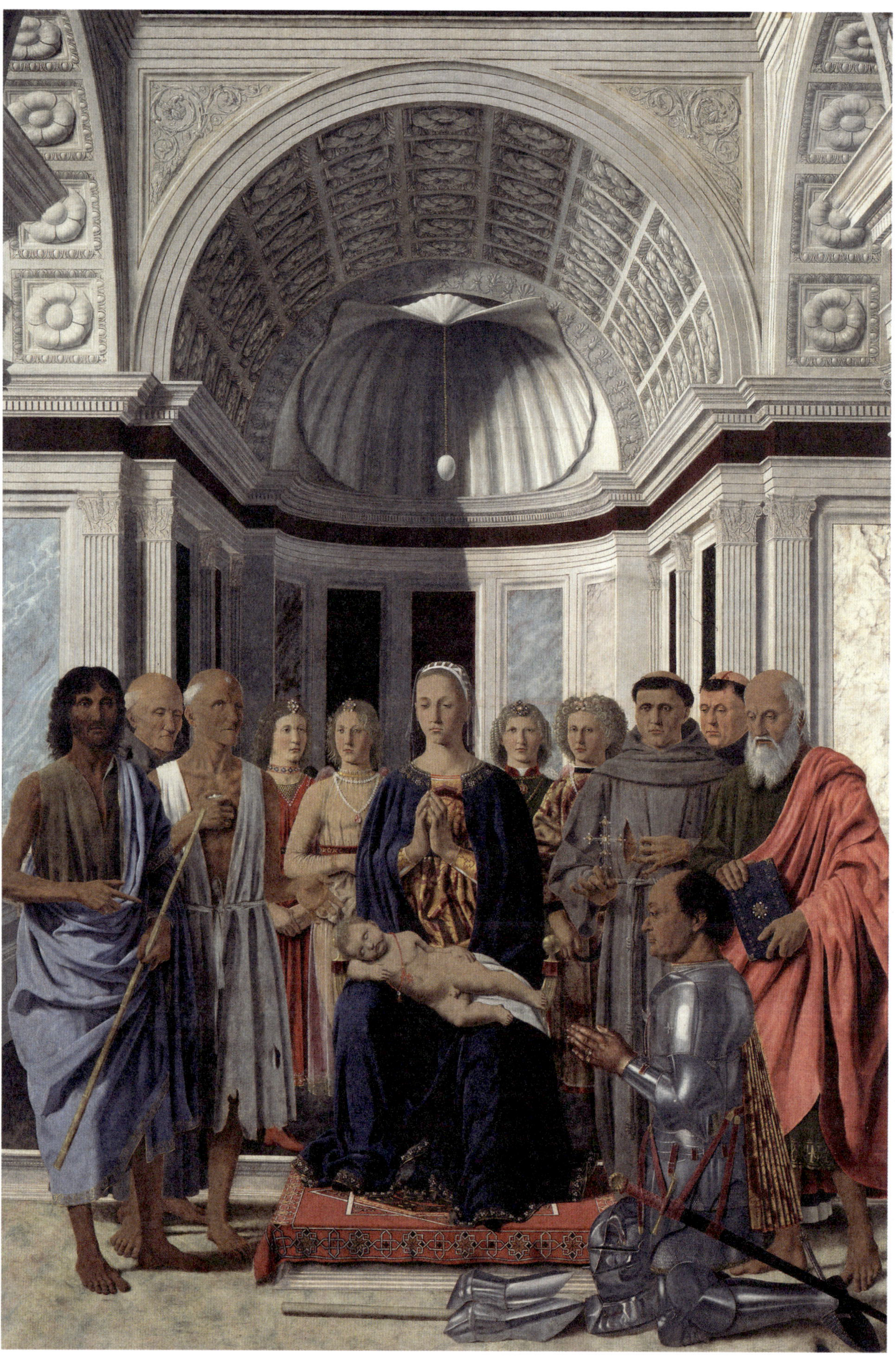

CORAL & SHELLS

ACROSS THE FOLLOWING PAGES, NOTE THE ACCENT OF COLOUR, FROM THE PINK-ORANGE CORALS IN PIERO DELLA FRANCESCA'S PAINTING TO THE BROWN MADDER AND BURNT SIENNA PIGMENTS USED BY GEORGIA O'KEEFFE IN HER WORK OF A CLAMSHELL AND SEAWEED. NOW OBSERVE THE GREYSCALE USED IN PICTURES OF THE CONCH SHELL, WHICH HIGHLIGHT THE LOGARITHMIC SPIRALS AND ARCHITECTURAL CHARACTERISTIC IN ITS FORM.

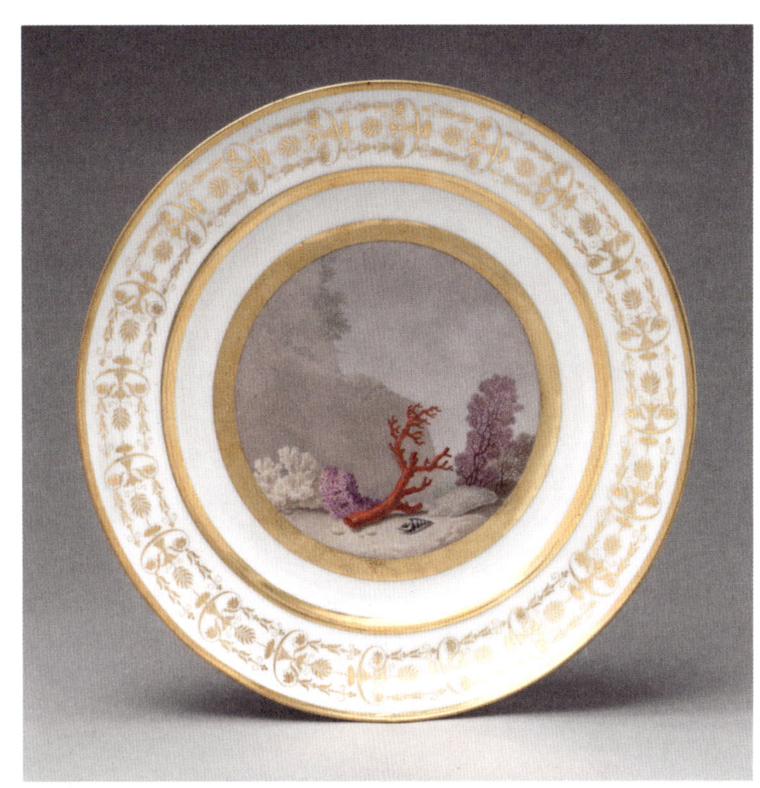

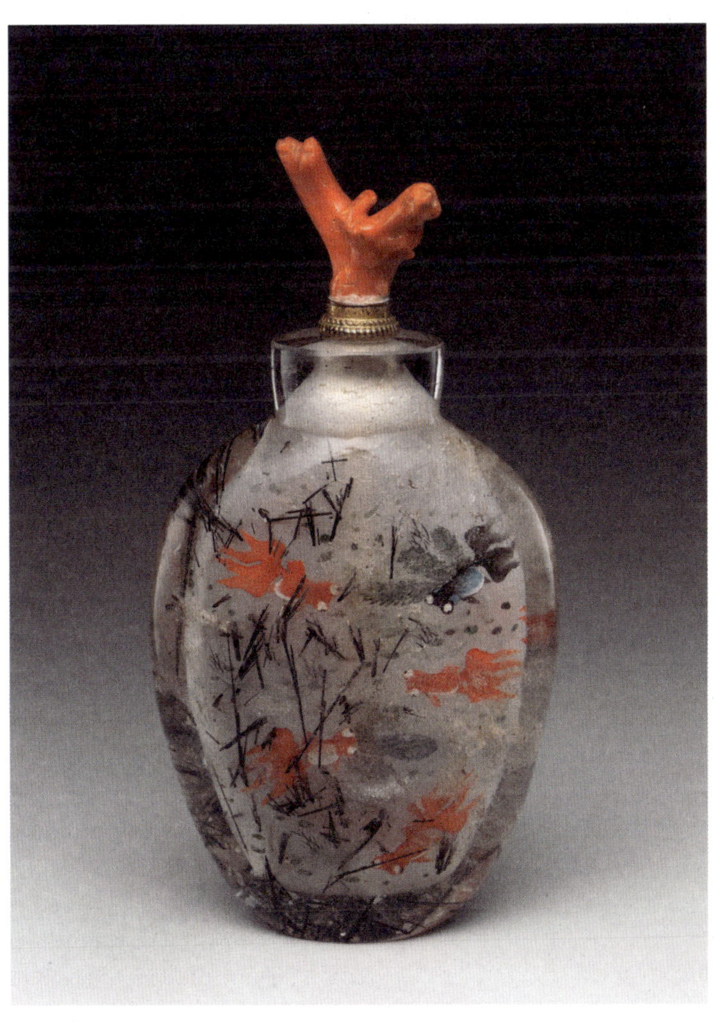

Opposite – *Madonna and Child with Saints (Montefeltro Altarpeice)*, c. 1472–74, tempera on panel, Piero della Francesca (Italian)

Top – *Plate with marine subject*, c. 1789–97, porcelain, Dihl et Guérhard (French)

Bottom – *Snuff Bottle*, c. 19th century, hair crystal, coral stopper, Unknown artist (Chinese)

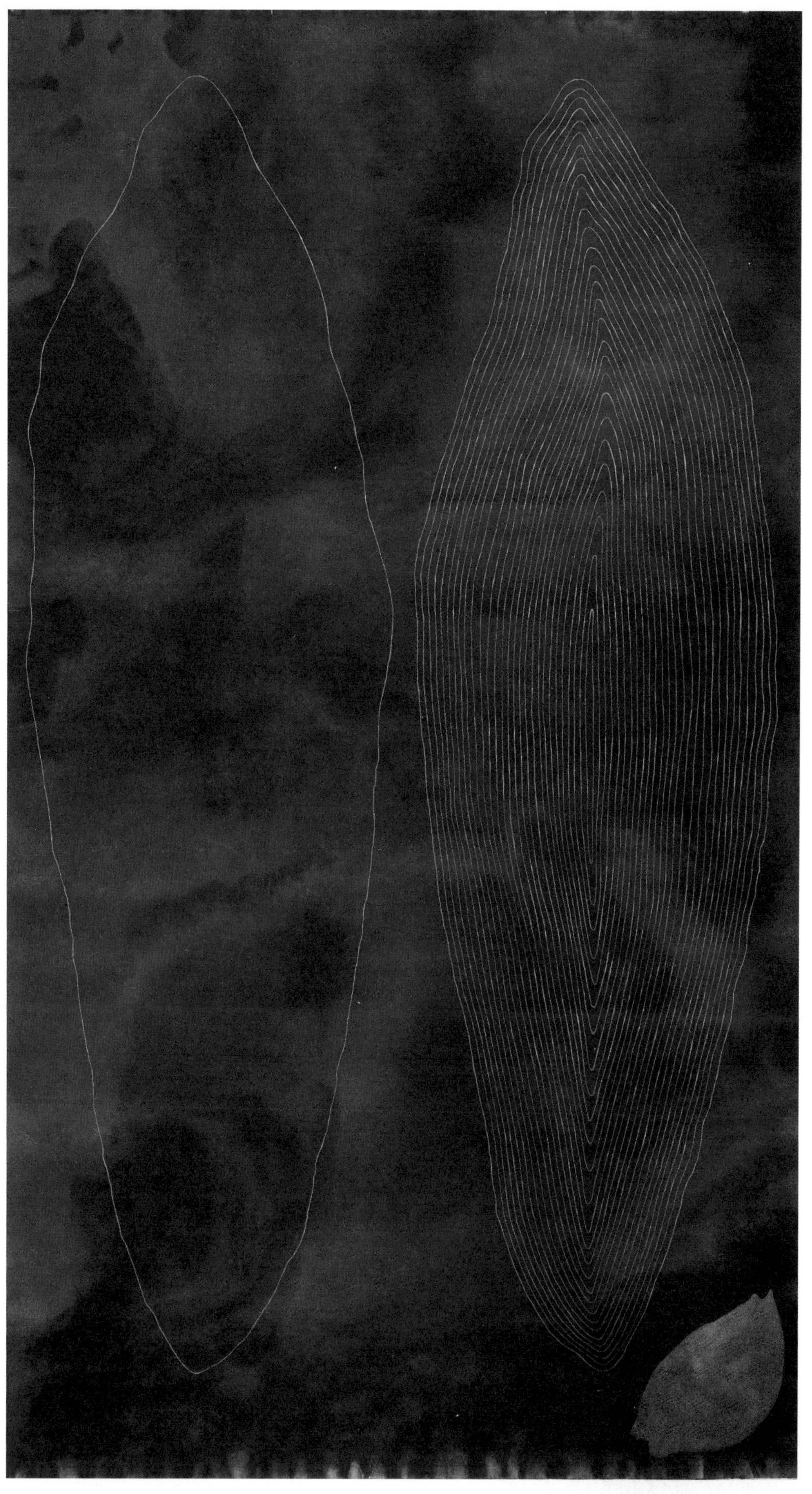

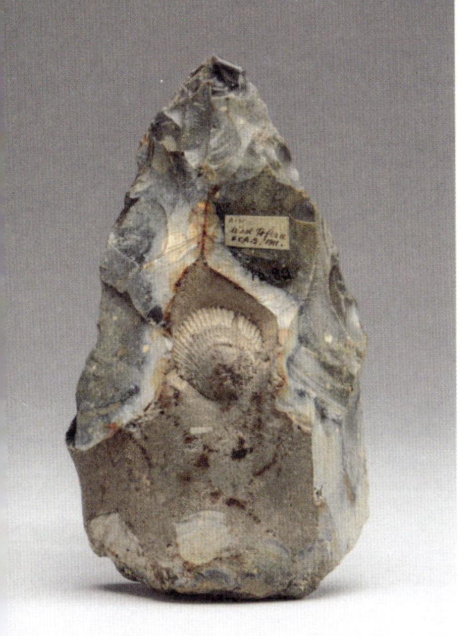

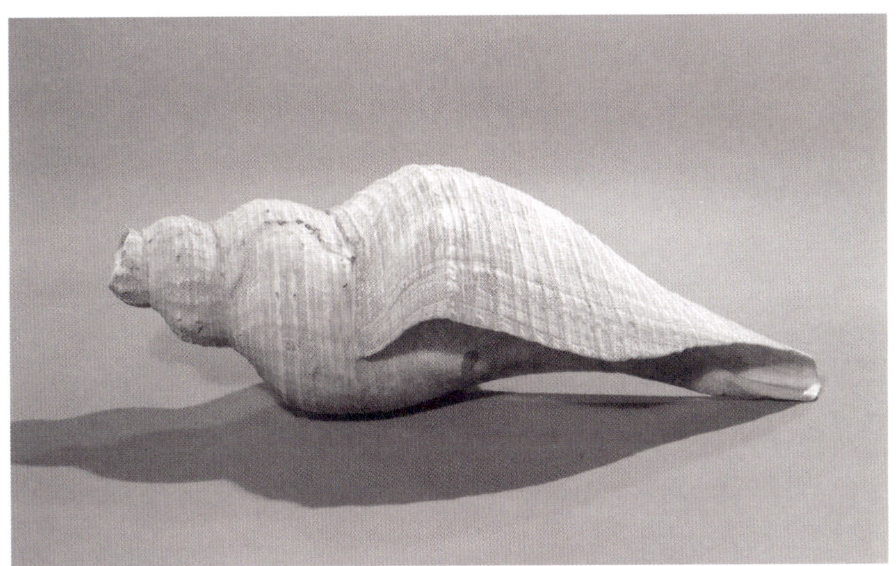

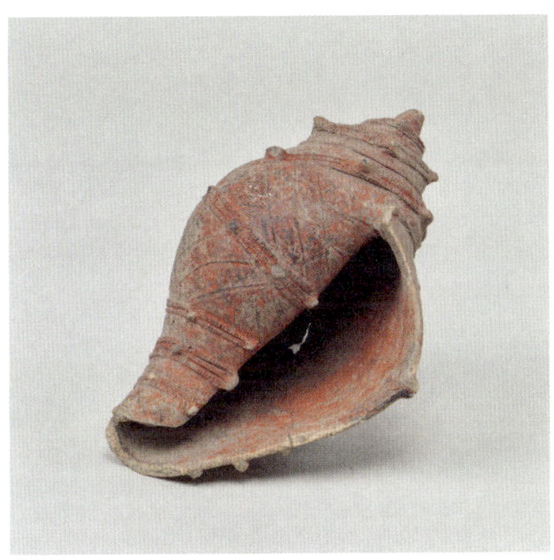

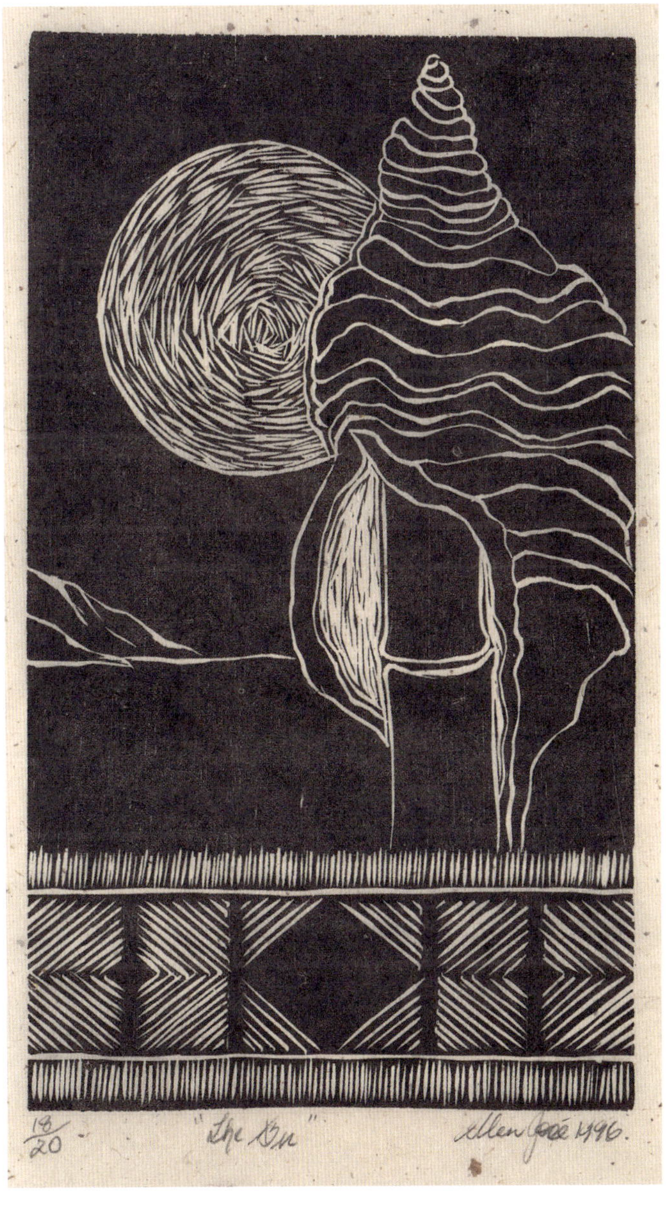

Opposite – *two halves with bailer shell*, 2002, pigment, synthetic polymer paint on canvas, Judy Watson (Waanyi people, Australian)

Top left – *Hand axe knapped around a fossil shell, located centrally on one face, identified as the Cretaceous bivalve mollusc Spondylus spinosus*, c. 500,000–300,000 BCE, stone, flint, shell, Unknown artist/maker

Top right – *Hai-Lo*, c. 19th century, sea shell, found object (Chinese)

Middle – *Conch-Shaped Clay Object*, Jōmon period, 2000–1000 BC, clay, Unknown artist (Japanese)

Bottom – *The bu (Trumpet shell)*, 1996, woodblock print on unryushi paper, Ellen José (Meriam Mir people, Australian)

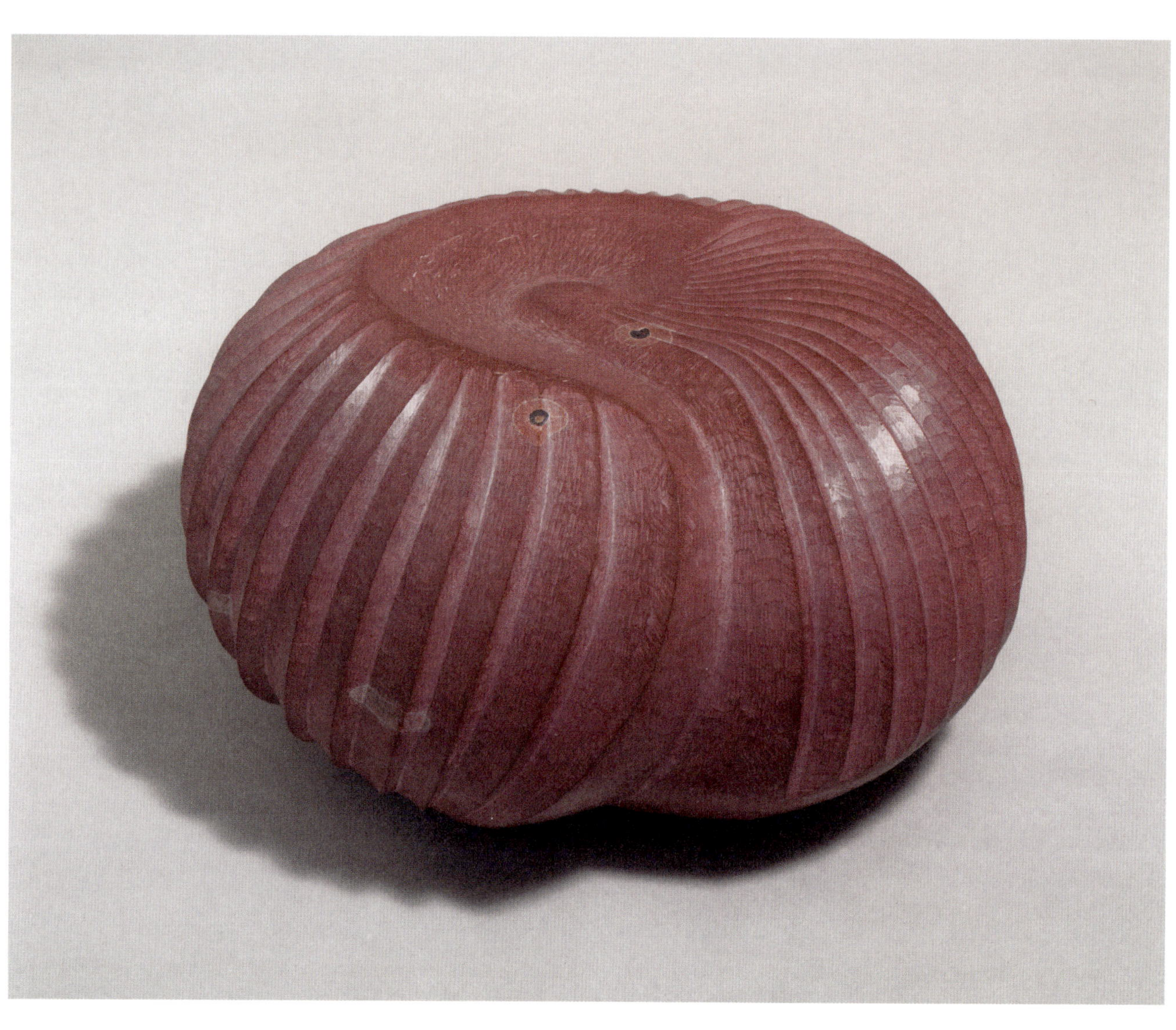

Above – *Red Stone*, c. 1964–65, stone, Naum Gabo (Russian)

Opposite – *Shell No. 2*, 1928, oil on board, Georgia O'Keeffe (American)

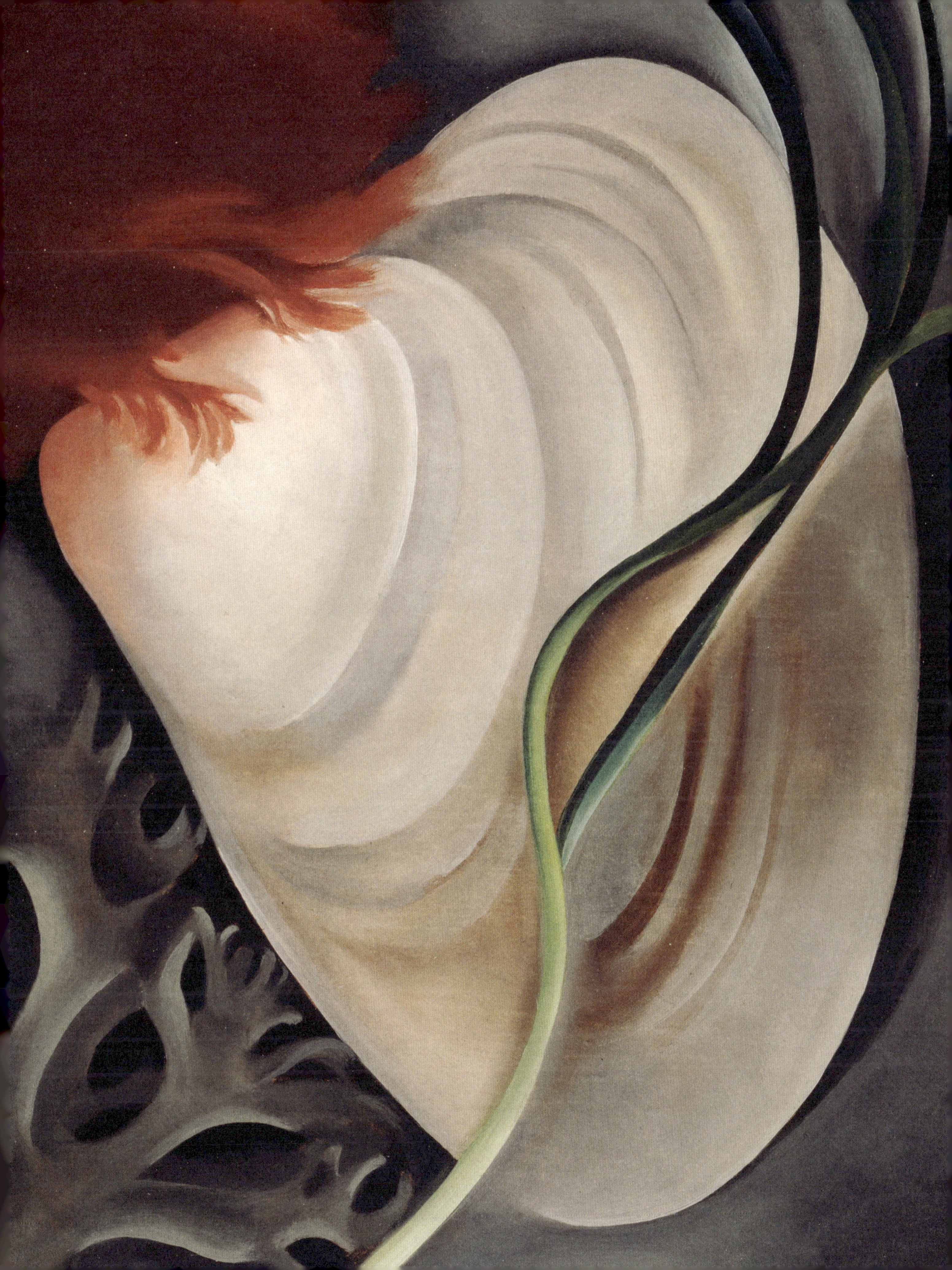

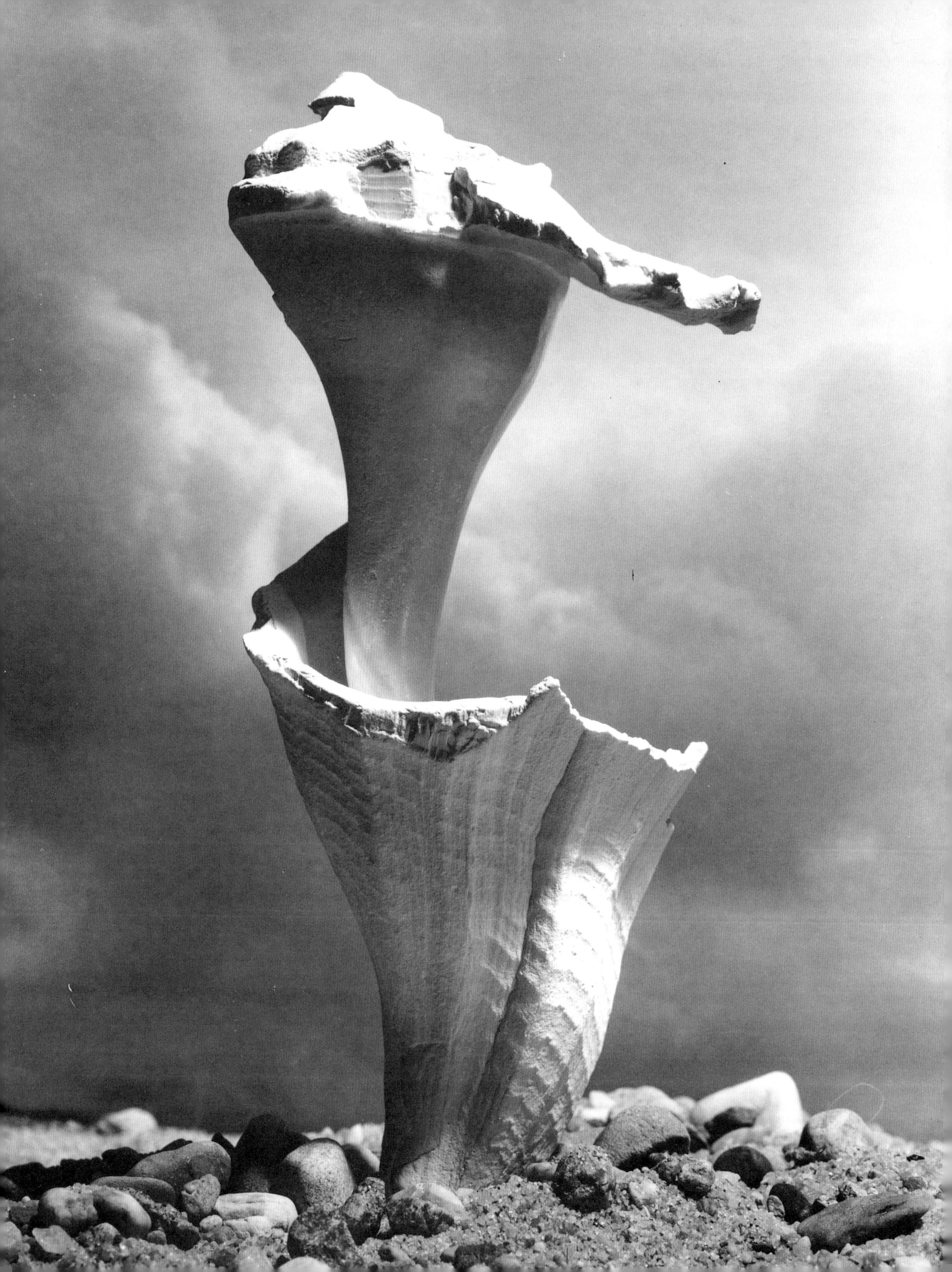

Opposite – *Broken Conch Shell*, c. 1977, gelatin silver print, Andreas Feininger (American)

Top – *City shell*, 1938; printed 1972, gelatin silver photograph, Barbara Morgan (American)

Bottom – *The shell*, c. 1935, gelatin silver photograph, Olive Cotton (Australian)

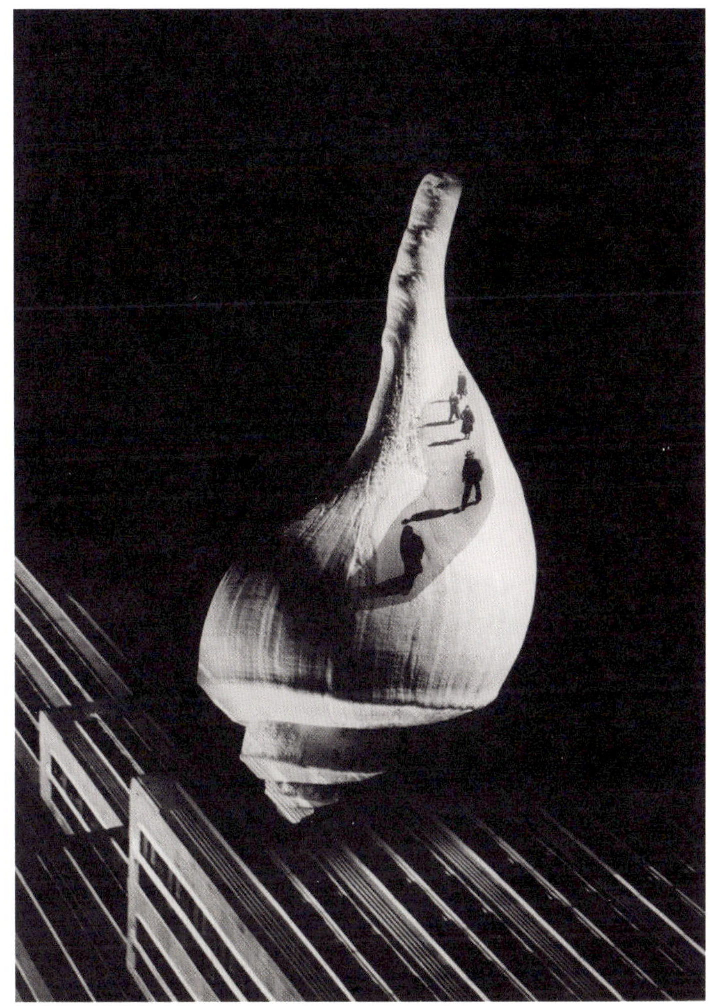

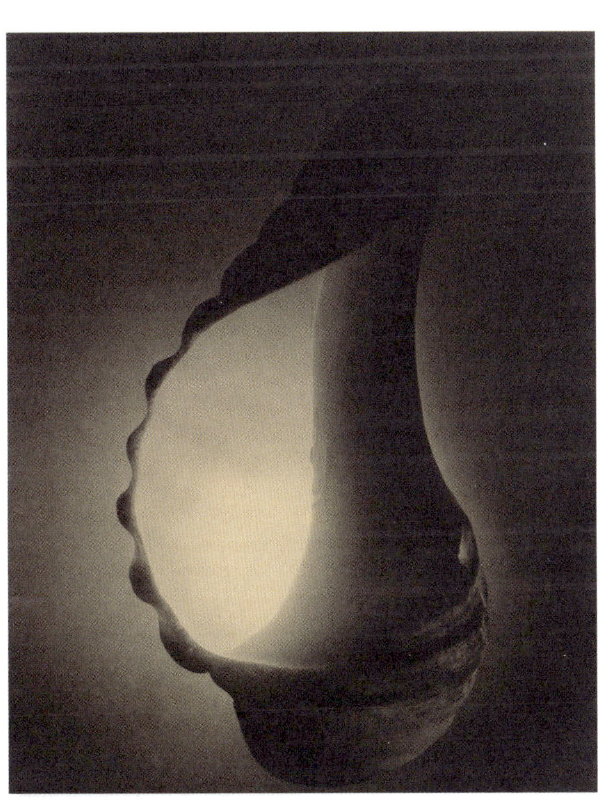

SEA CREATURES

THE REPRESENTATION OF MERMAIDS, SELKIES AND OTHER CREATURES OF THE SEA, LOCHS AND RIVERS, ABOUND IN ARTS AND CRAFTS. BELONGING TO CELTIC AND NORSE MYTHOLOGIES, SELKIES SHAPESHIFT BETWEEN HUMAN AND SEAL FORM. REFLECT ON THE VISUAL LANGUAGE OF PICTURES THAT REPRESENT LIFE UNDER OCEANS AND RIVERS, NOTICE THE SERPENTINE FORM AND BILLOWING SHAPE REPEATED ACROSS THE WORKS.

 Figure of mermaid with seal, c. 1947, modelled earthenware, Marguerite Mahood (Australian)

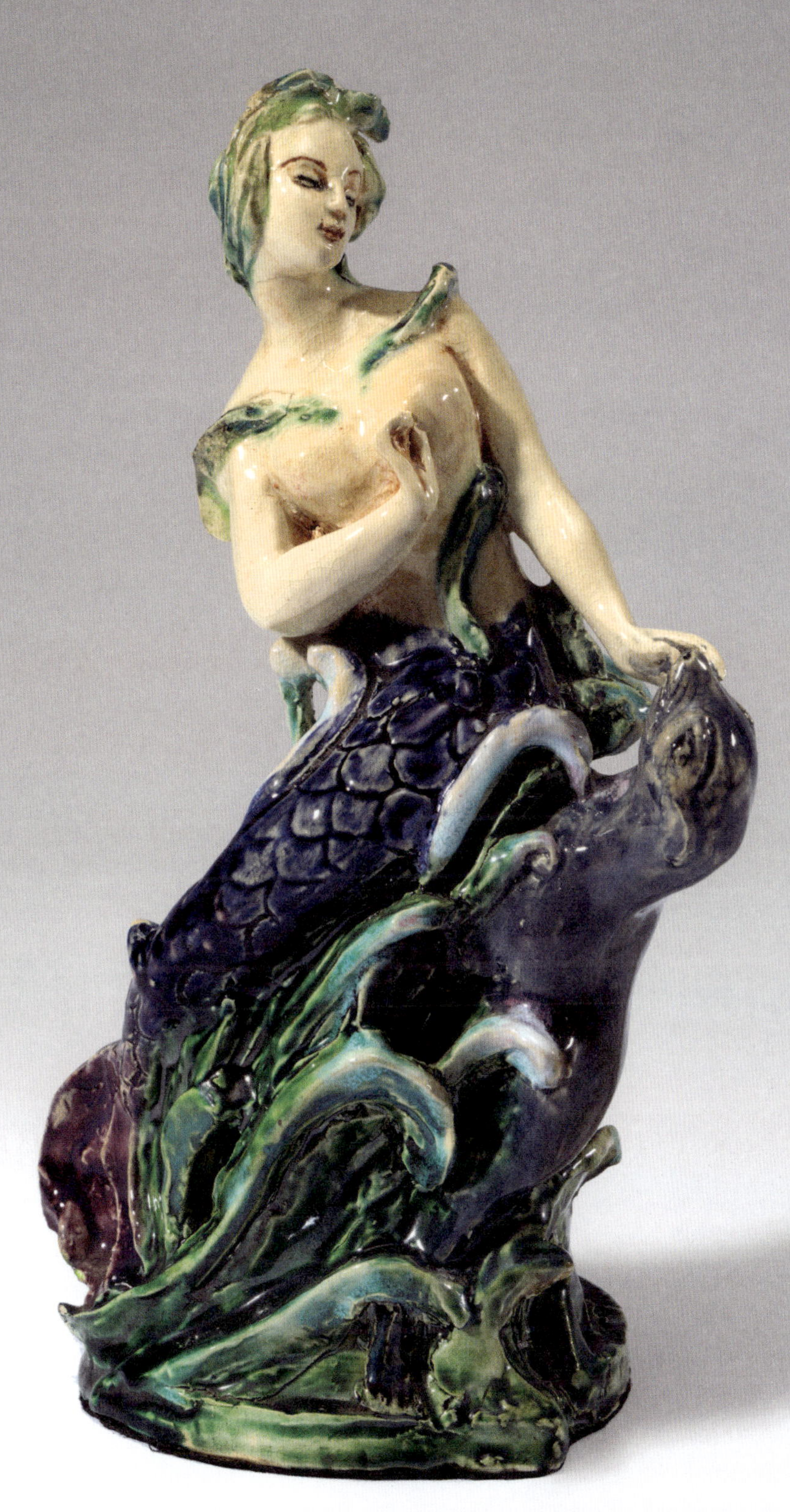

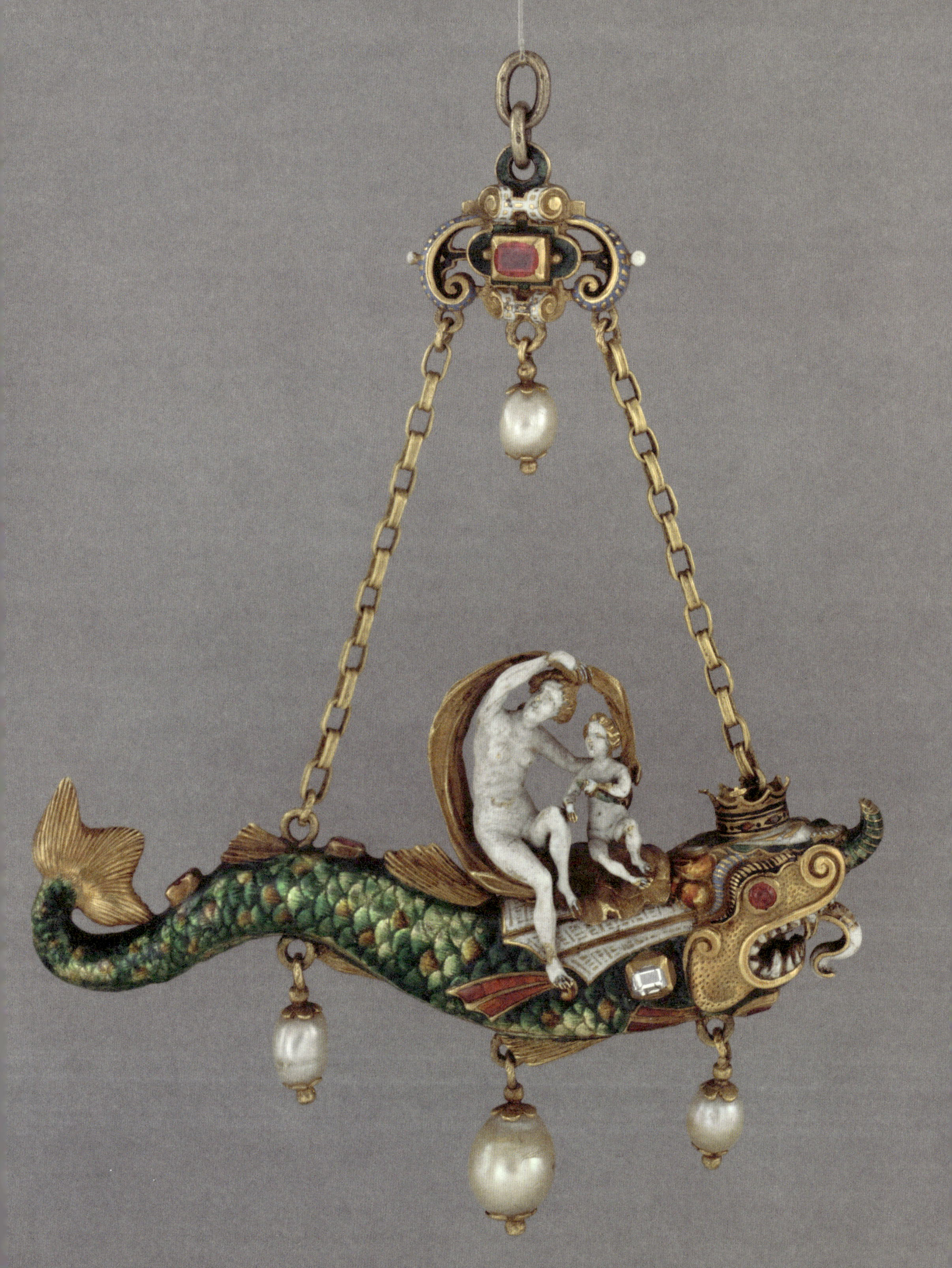

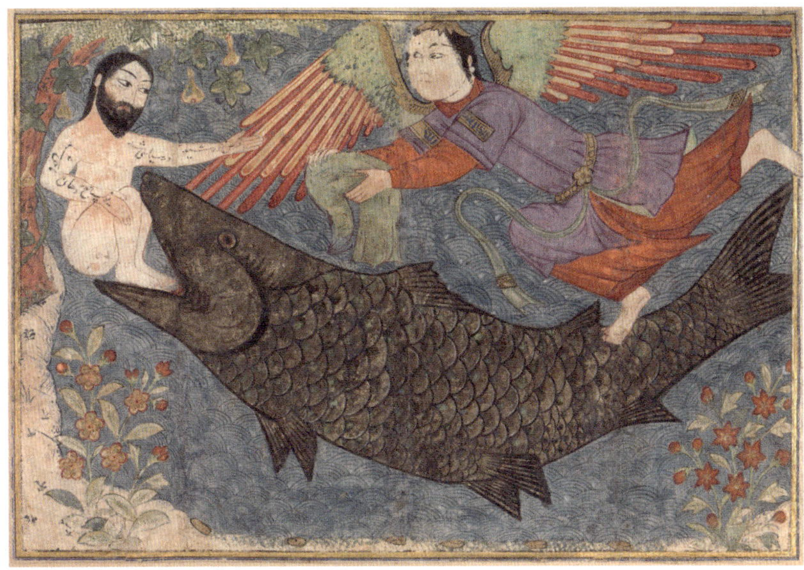

Opposite – *Pendant with Venus and Cupid on a Dolphin*, c. 1865–90, enamelled gold, rubies and pearls, perhaps made by Reinhold Vasters (German) or Alfred André (French)

Top – *'Jonah and the Whale'*, c. 1400, ink, opaque watercolour, gold, and silver on paper, Unknown artist (Iranian)

Middle – *Female Nude with Two Seahorses*, c. 1599–1622, engraving, engraved by Anonymous, after Battista Franco (Italian)

Bottom – *Parabaik. Burmese court manuscript* (detail), c. 1857–85, paint on paper, Unknown artist (Burmese)

Following – *Birth of Venus*, c. 1485, tempera on canvas, Sandro Botticelli (Italian)

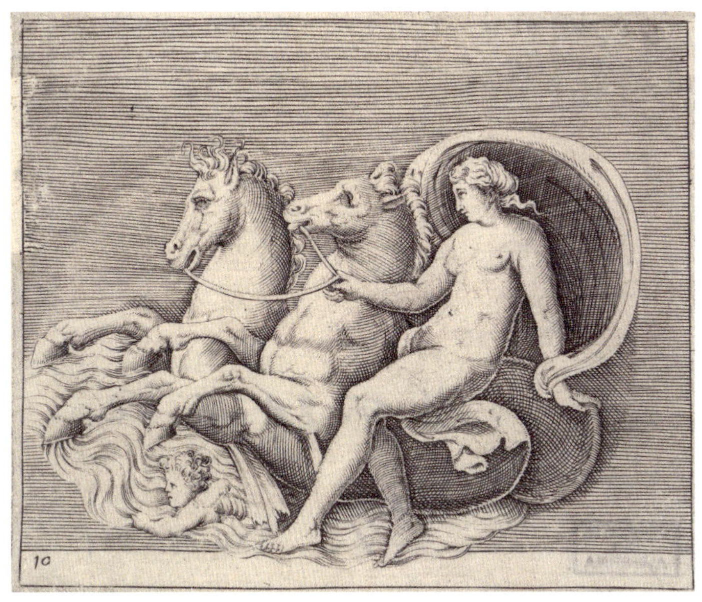

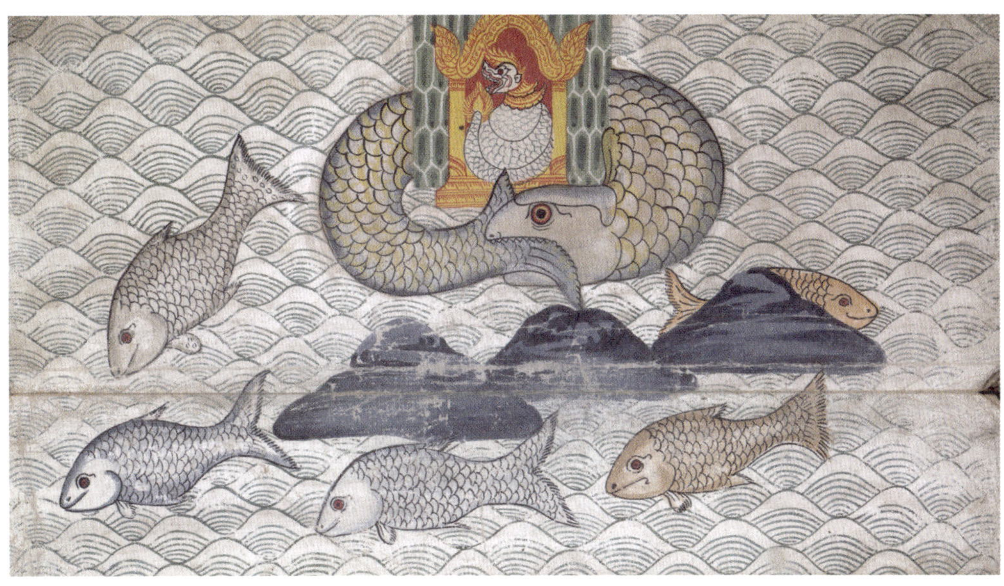

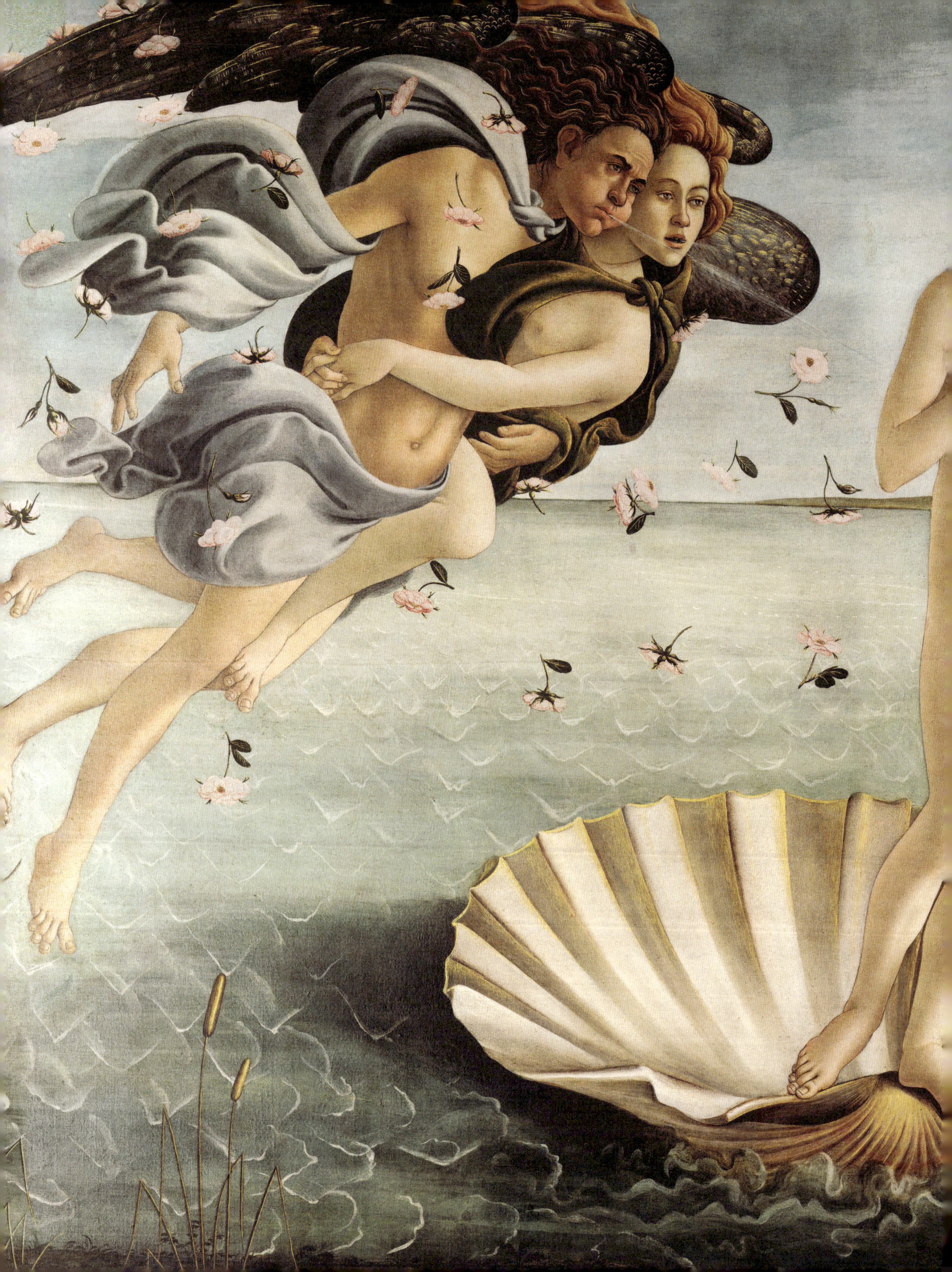

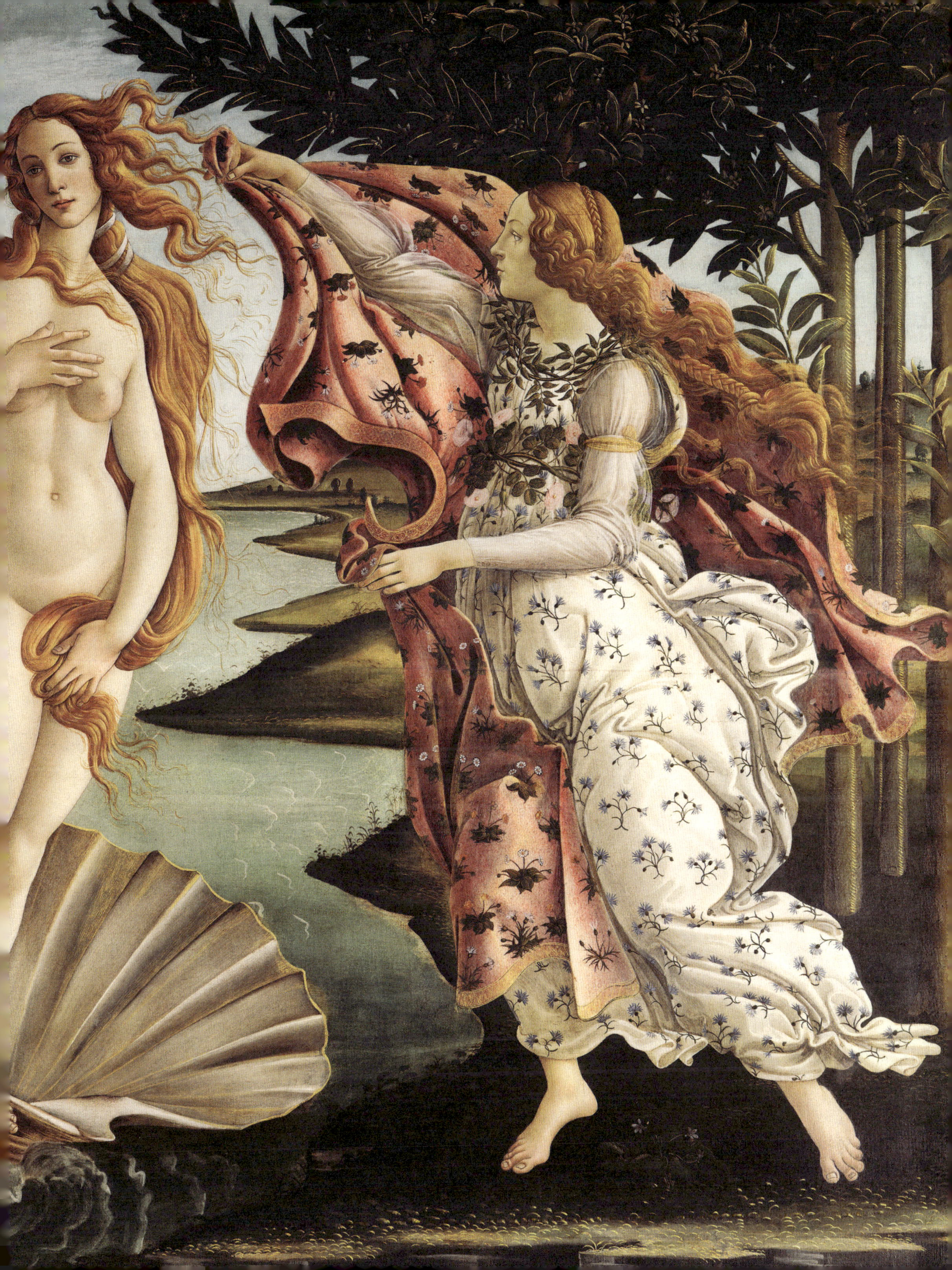

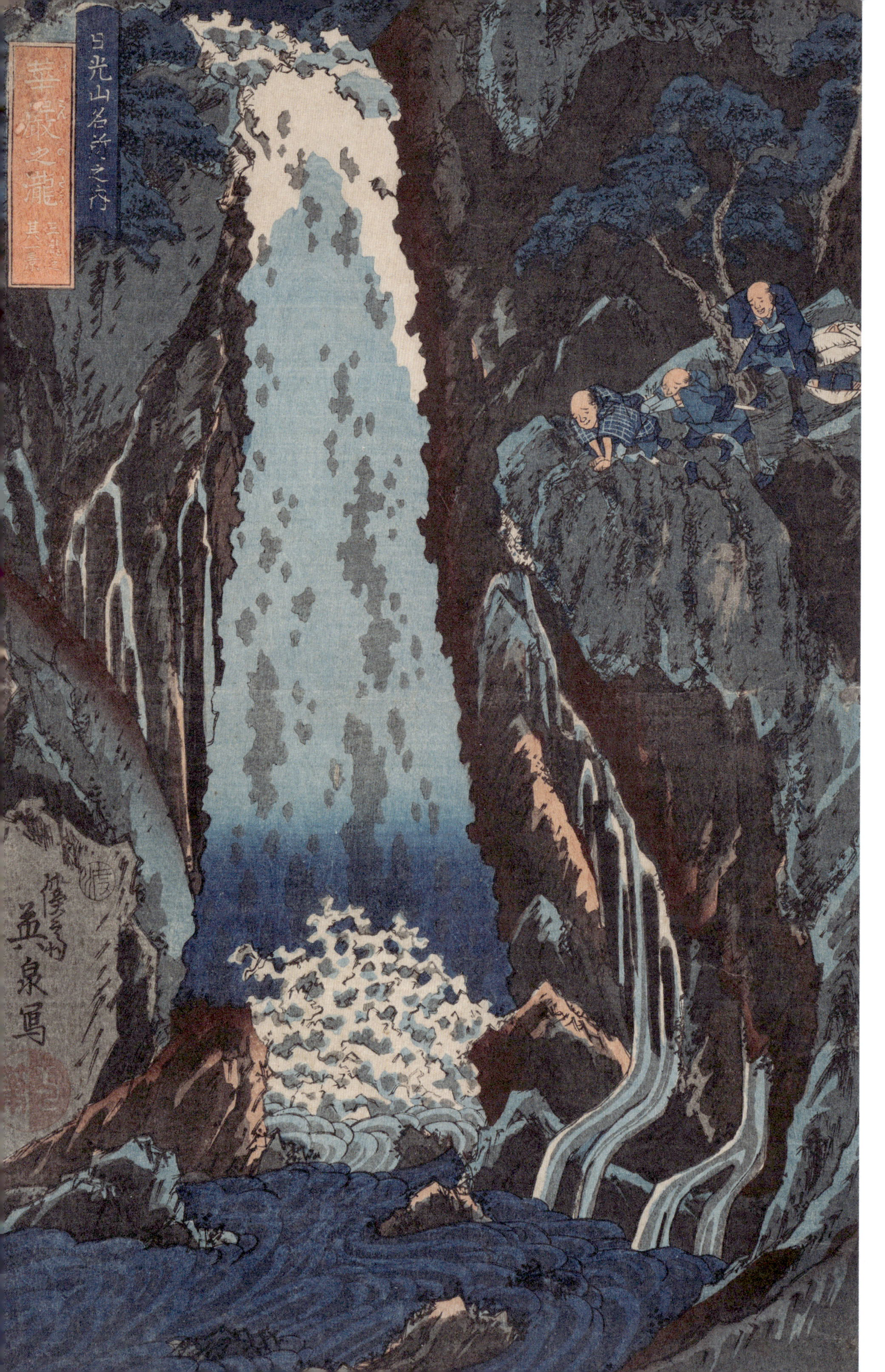
日光山名所之内
華厳之瀧
其一景
英泉冩

WATERFALLS

TAKE A SLOW LOOK AT THE ECHOES OF SHAPE AND COLOUR USED TO CREATE THE ILLUSION OF CASCADING WATER. FROM A WATERFALL DESIGN MADE OF DIAMONDS AND GOLD SO SMALL IT COULD FIT INSIDE YOUR HAND TO THE ABSTRACT WATERFALL DEPICTED IN EDDIE CLEMENS'S LINE WORK, IT IS POSSIBLE TO IMAGINE THE ROARING SOUND OF WATER AS IT RUSHES TOWARDS THE PLUNGE POOL BELOW.

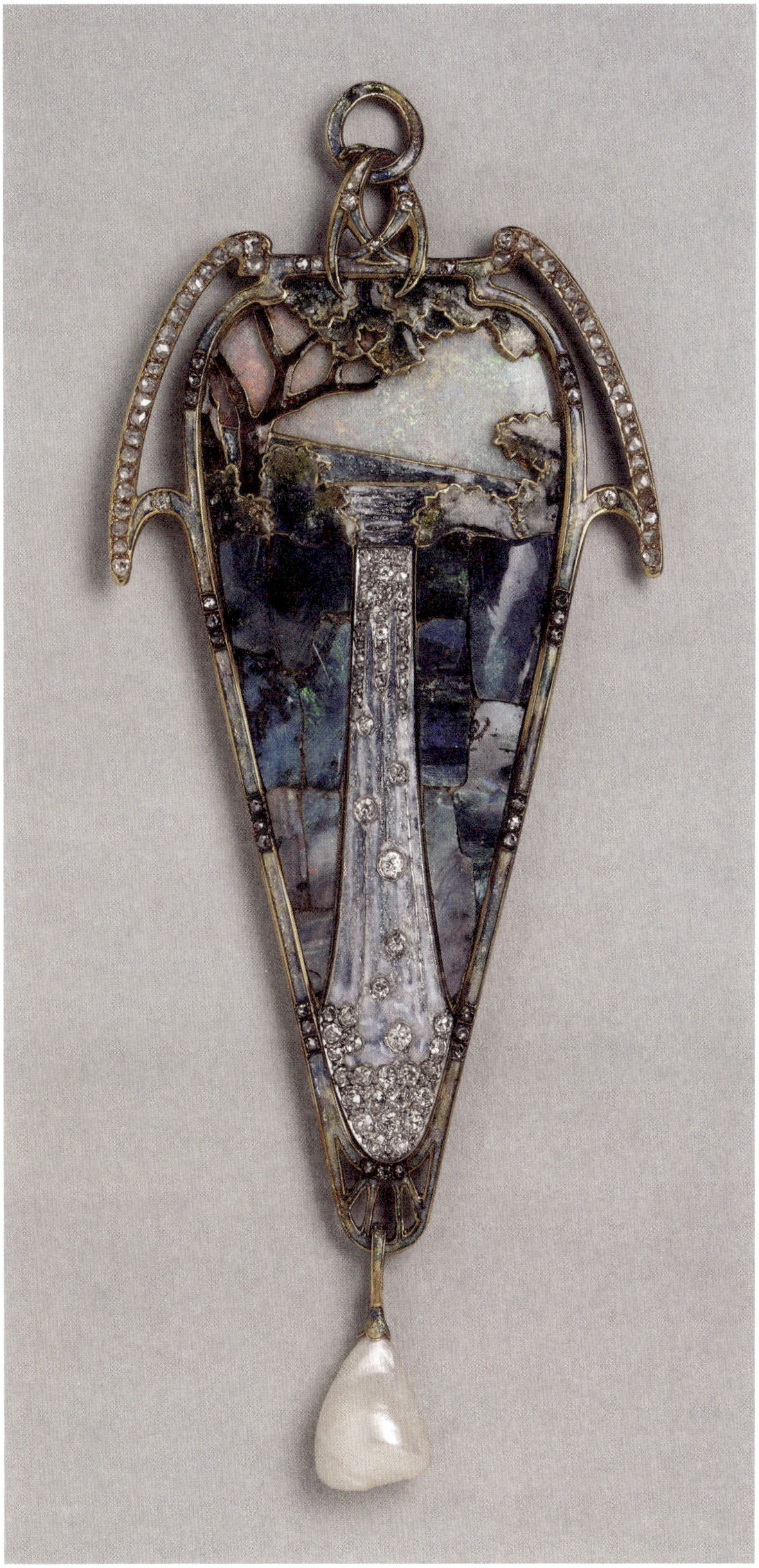

Opposite – *The Kegon Falls, One of the Three Waterfalls*, c. 1845, woodcut, nishiki-e (full colour) technique, Keisai Eisen (Japanese)

This page – *'Cascade' Pendant*, c. 1900, gold, open enamel on spangles, opals, diamonds and baroque pearl, Georges Fouquet (French)

Following left – *The End of the Waterfall (No. 2)* (detail), 2007, ink on paper (found receipt role ends), Eddie Clemens (New Zealander)

Following right – *Waterfall—End of Road—'Iao Valley* (detail), 1939, oil on canvas, Georgia O'Keeffe (American)

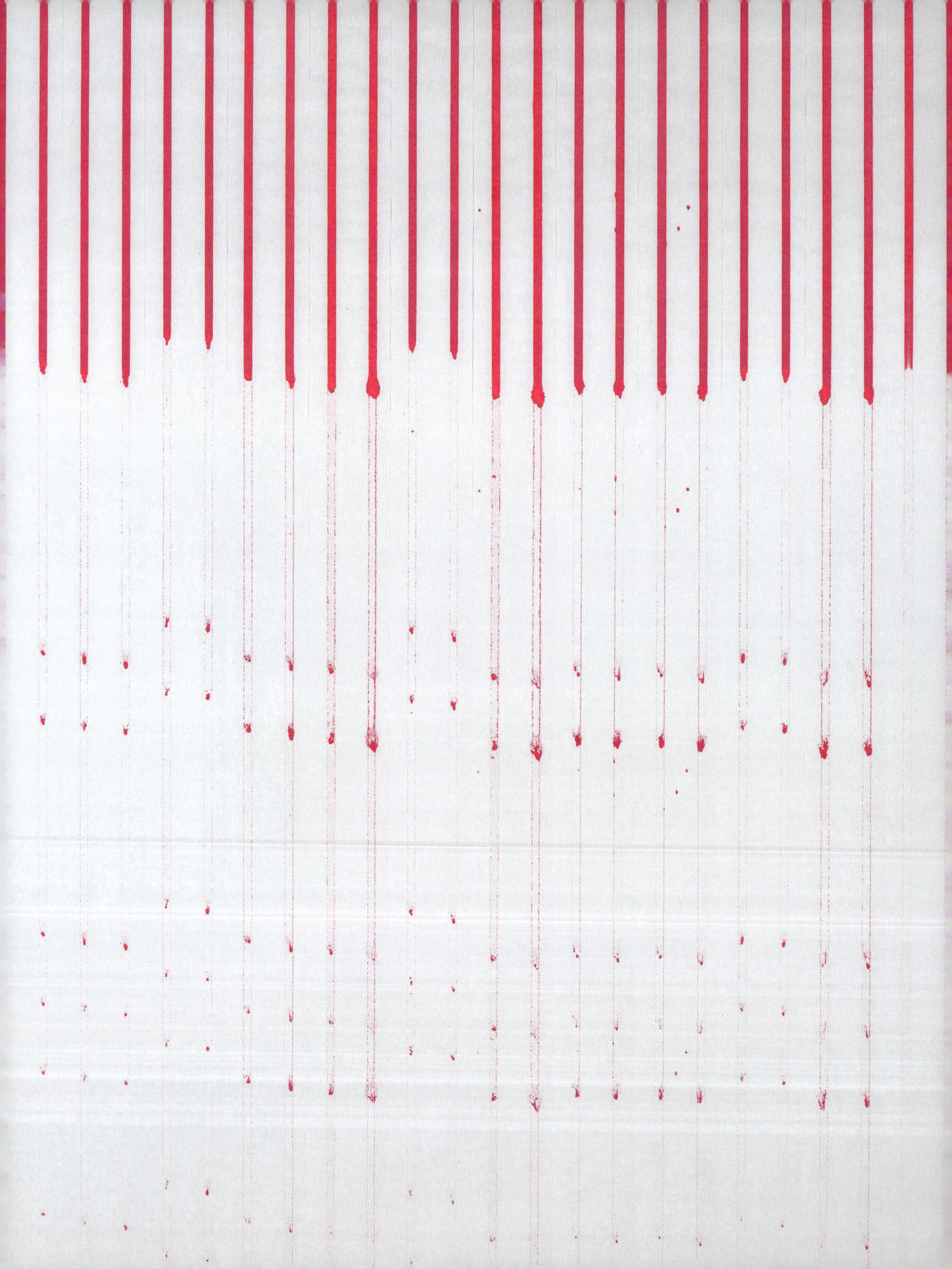

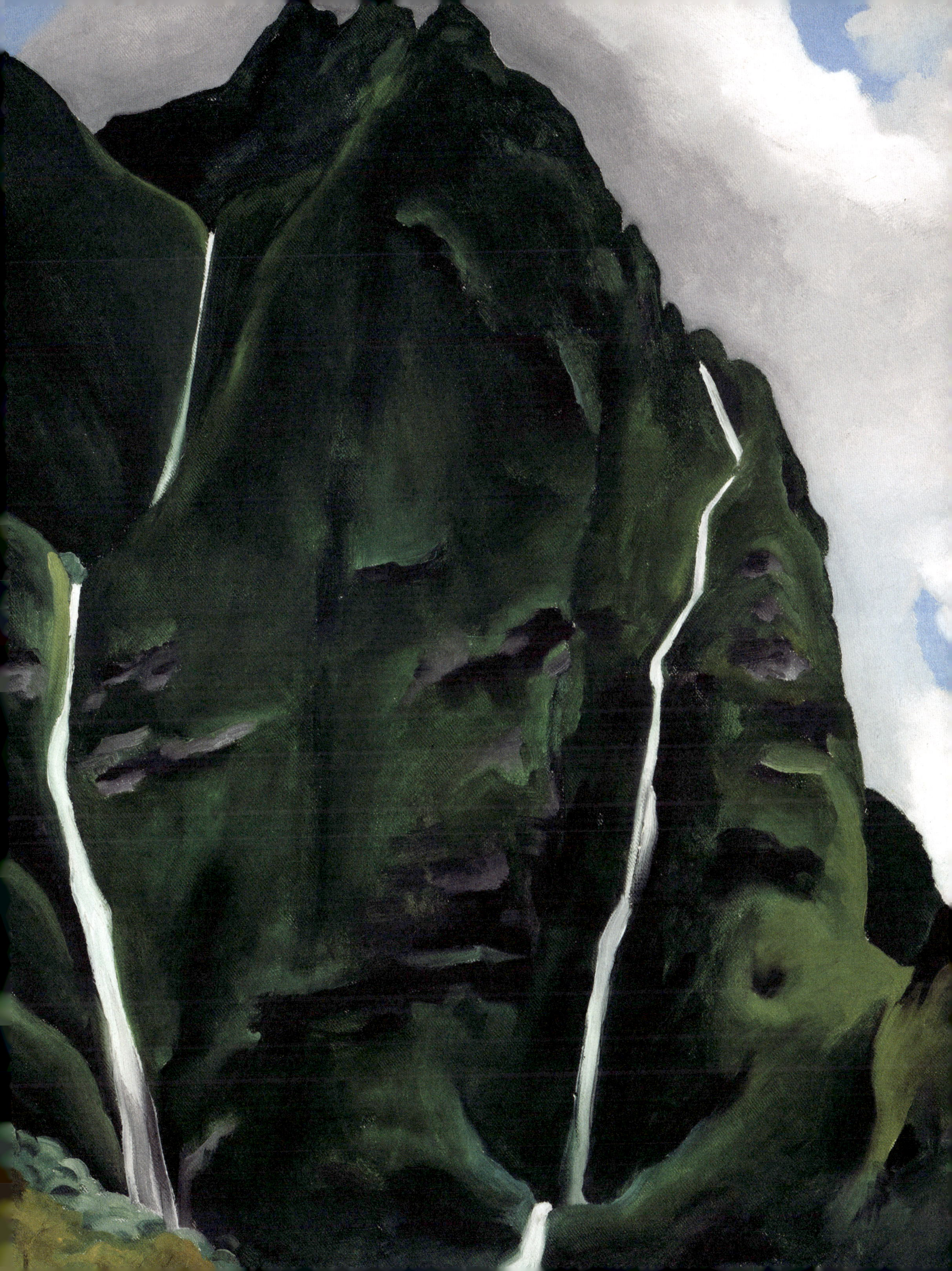

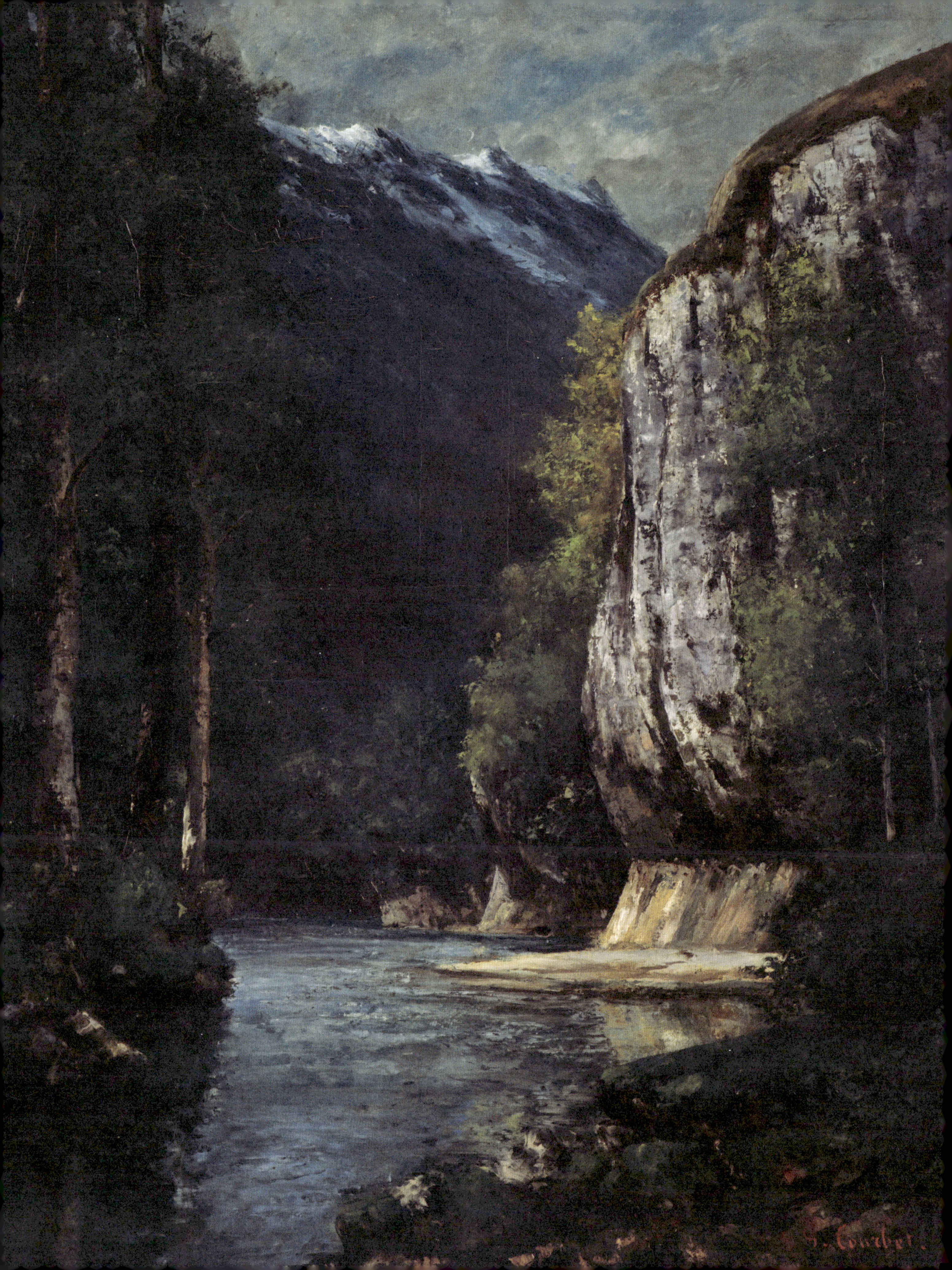
G. Courbet.

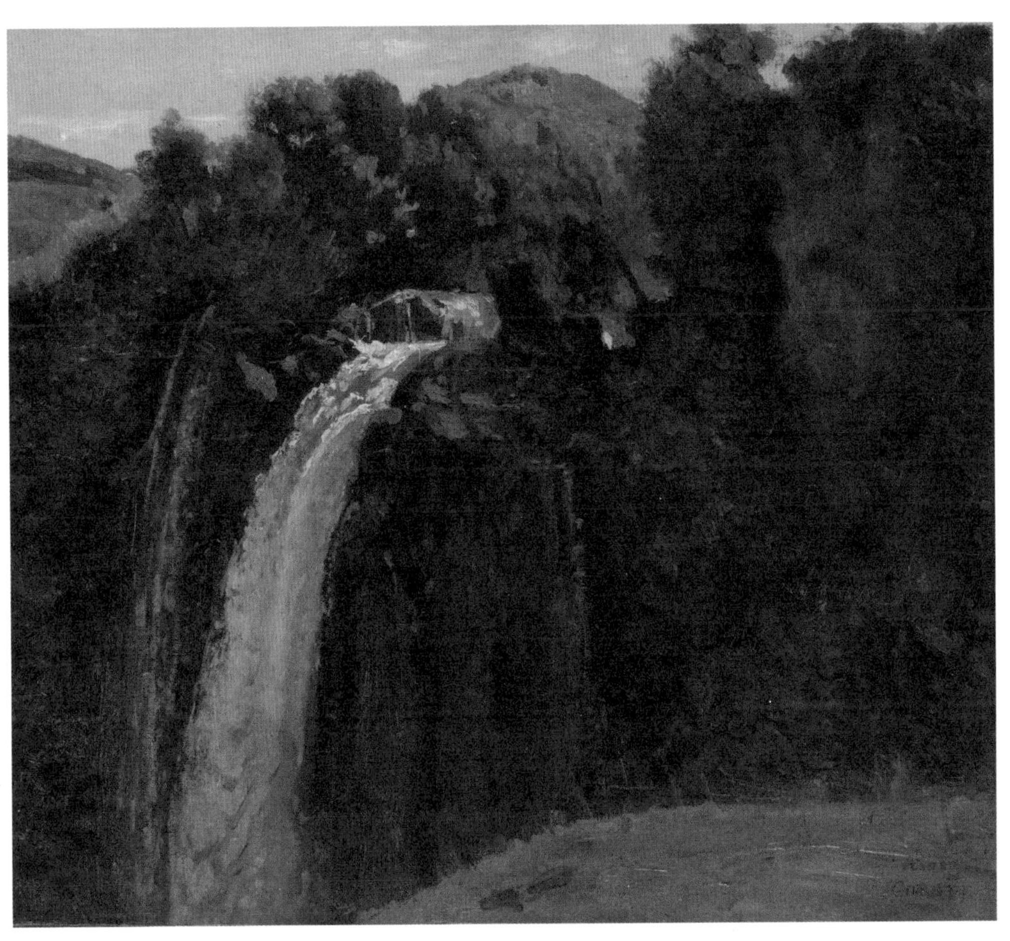

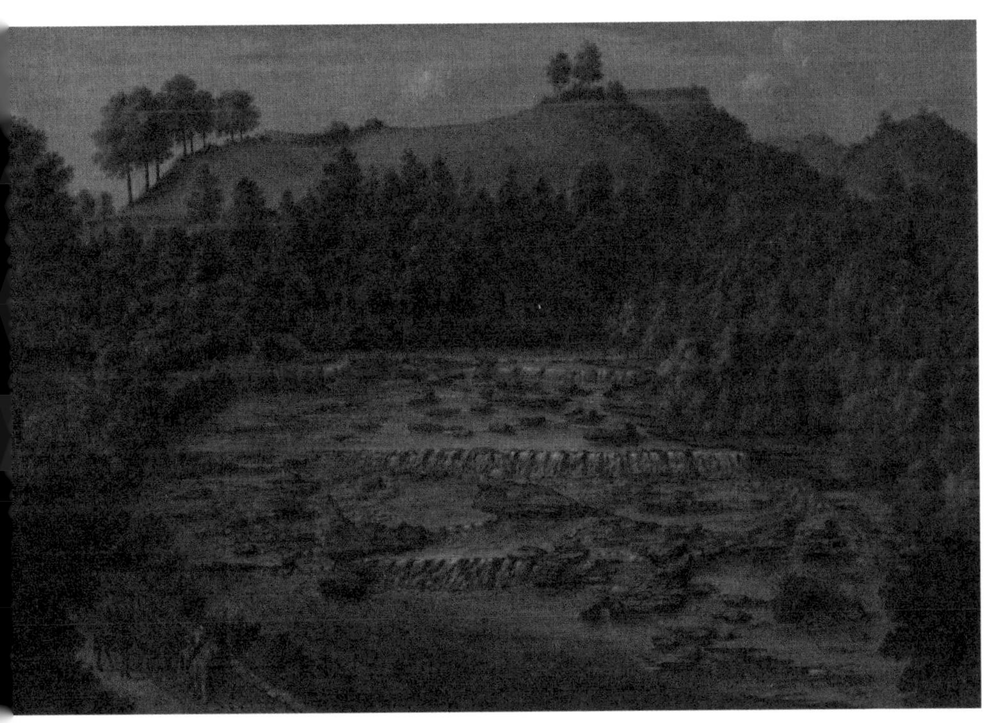

Opposite – *A River in a Mountain Gorge*, c. 1864–65, oil on canvas, Gustave Courbet (French)

Top – *Waterfall at Terni*, 1826, oil on paper, Camille Corot (French)

Bottom – *Aysgarth Falls, Yorkshire*, c. 1750–1762, oil on canvas, Balthazar Nebot (British)

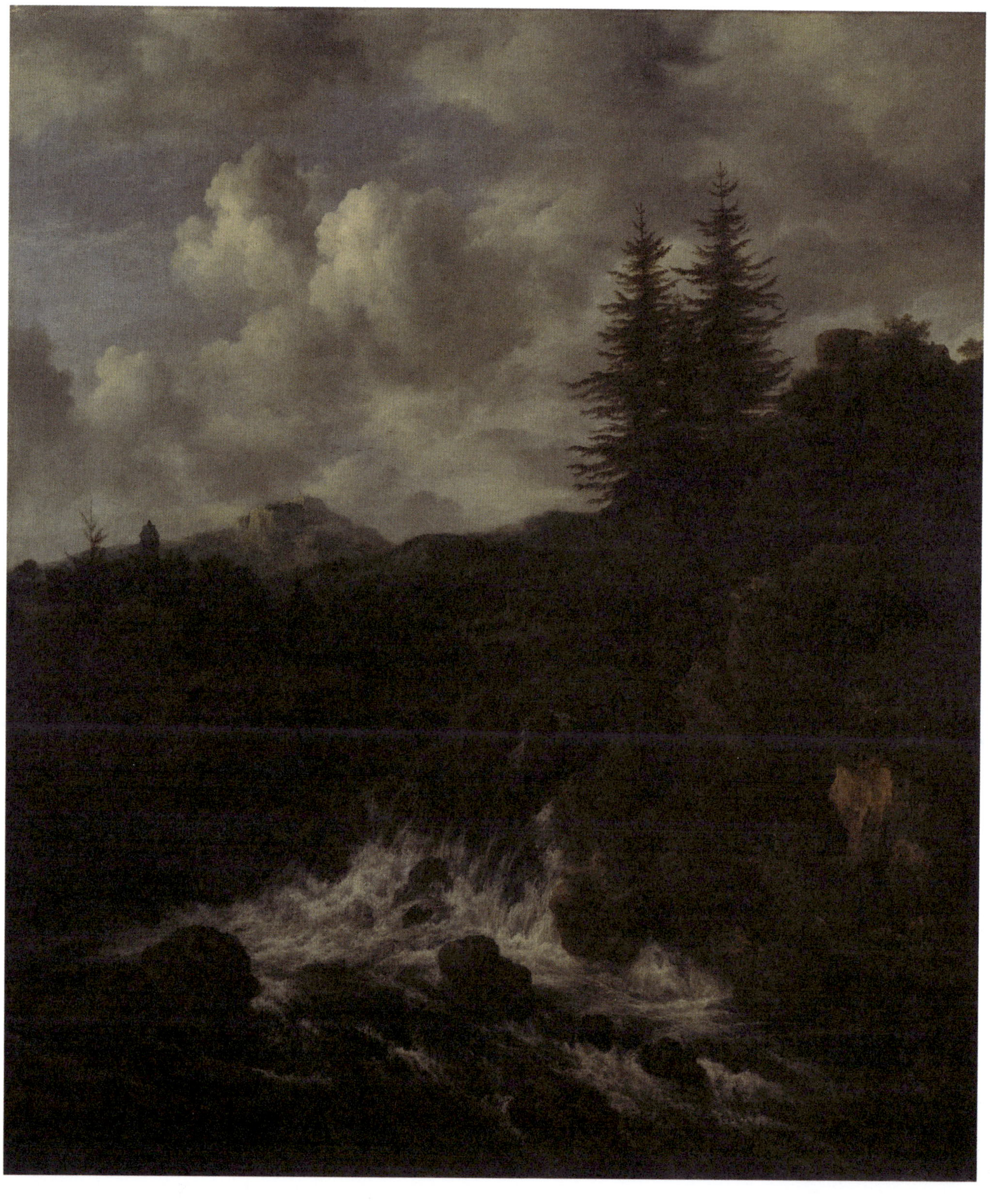

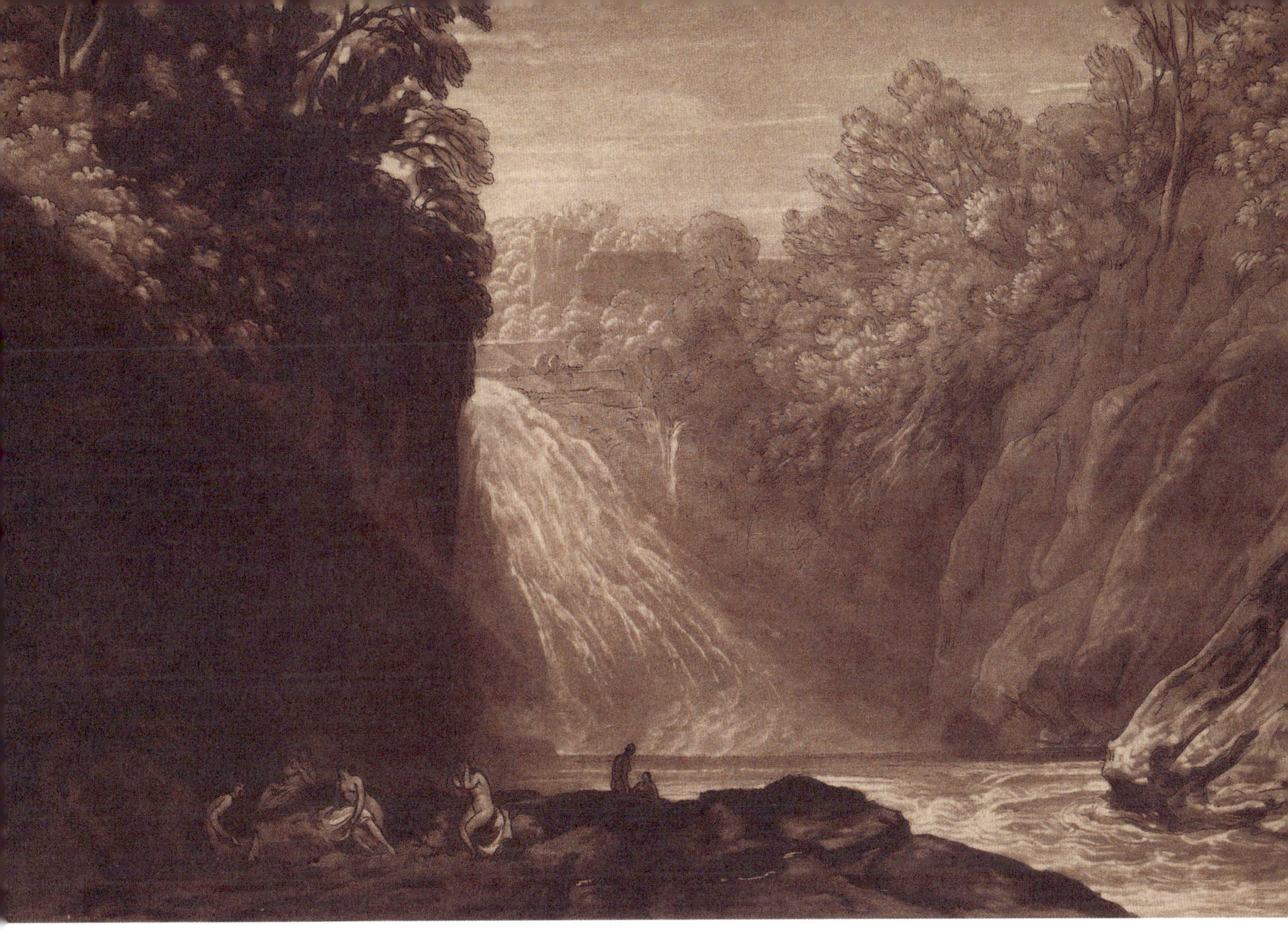

Opposite – *A Landscape with a Waterfall and a Castle on a Hill*, c. 1660–70, oil on canvas, Jacob van Ruisdael (Dutch)

Above – *Drawing of the Clyde (Liber Studiorum, part IV, plate 18)*, 1809, etching and mezzotint, Joseph Mallord William Turner (British)

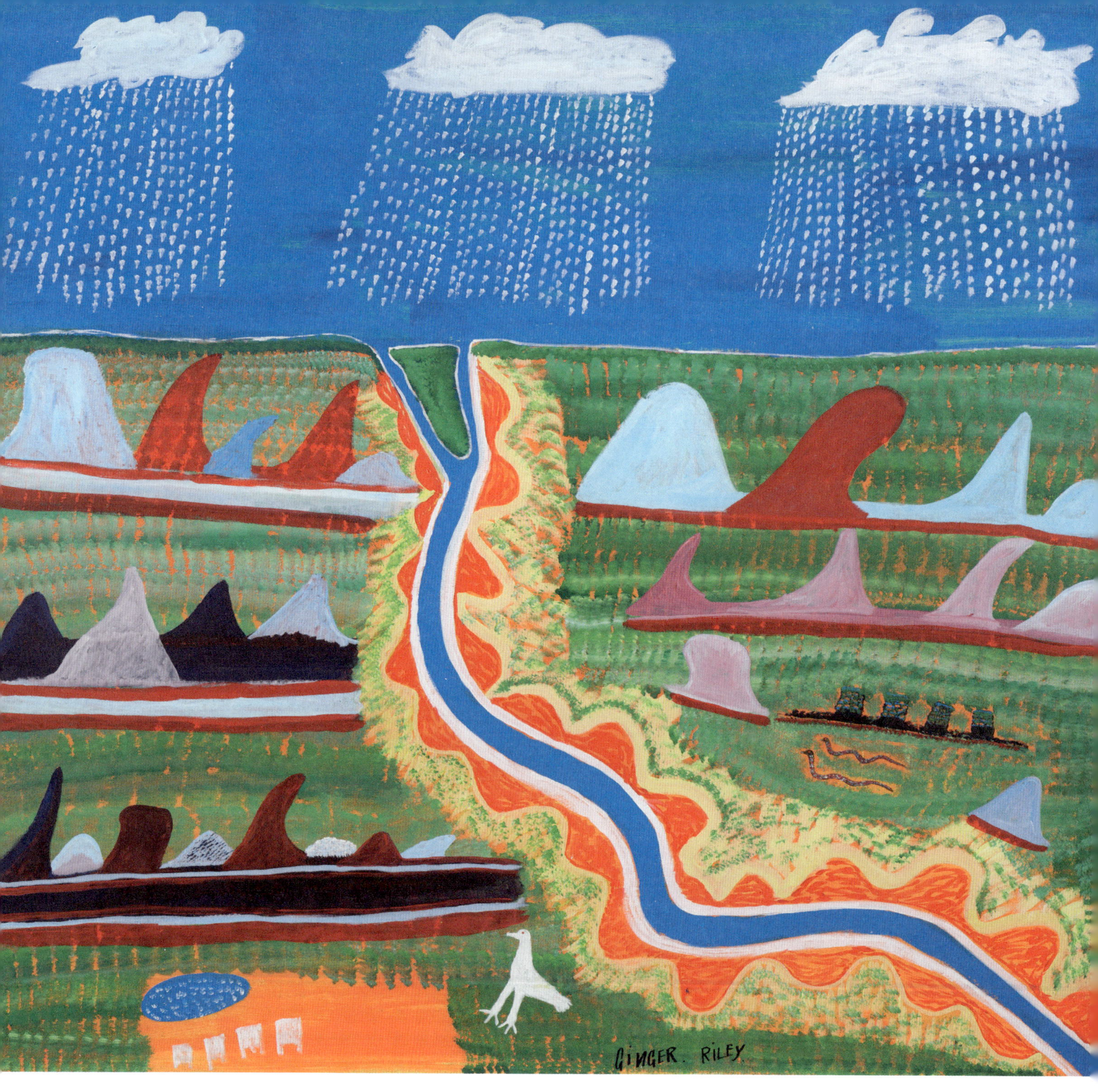

Nyamiyukanji, the river country, 1997, synthetic polymer paint on canvas, Ginger Riley Munduwalawala (Marra people, Australian)

RIVERS & WATERHOLES

A RIVER OR FJORD IS IN A CONSTANT STATE OF FLOW; ITS STEADY AND SOMETIMES FAST CURRENT SYMBOLISES CHANGE AND RENEWAL. A RIVER MEANDERS THROUGH LANDSCAPES, IT SPARKLES WHEN TOUCHED BY THE SUN AND SHIMMERS UNDER MOONLIGHT. THE POWERFUL FORCE OF THE RIVER IS STRENGTHENED BY THE LEGENDS OF GODS AND MONSTERS WHO INHABIT THEM. NOTICE THE DIFFERENT VIEWPOINTS TAKEN BY ARTISTS WHEN DEPICTING A RIVER IN ART.

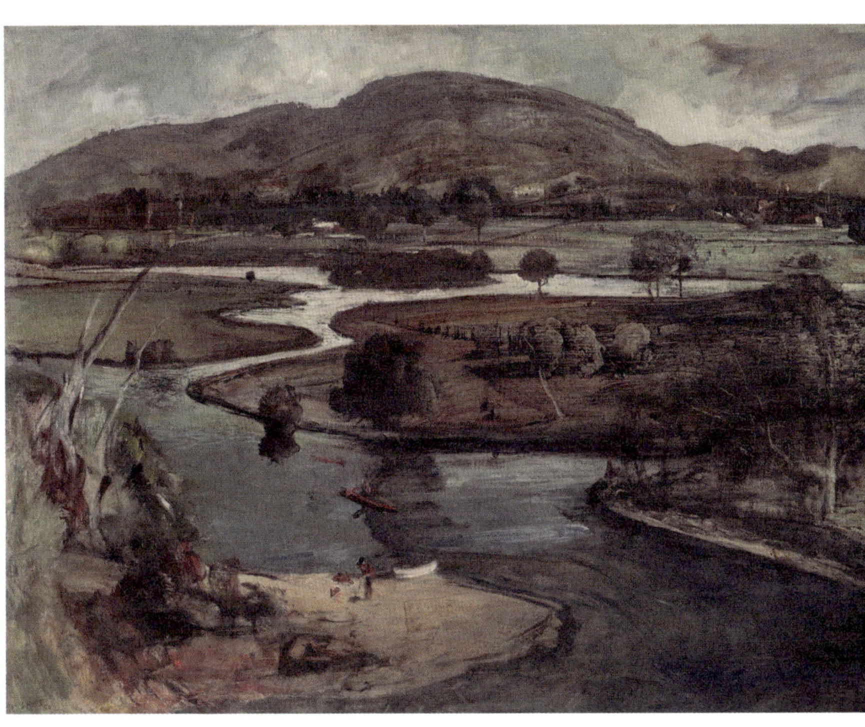

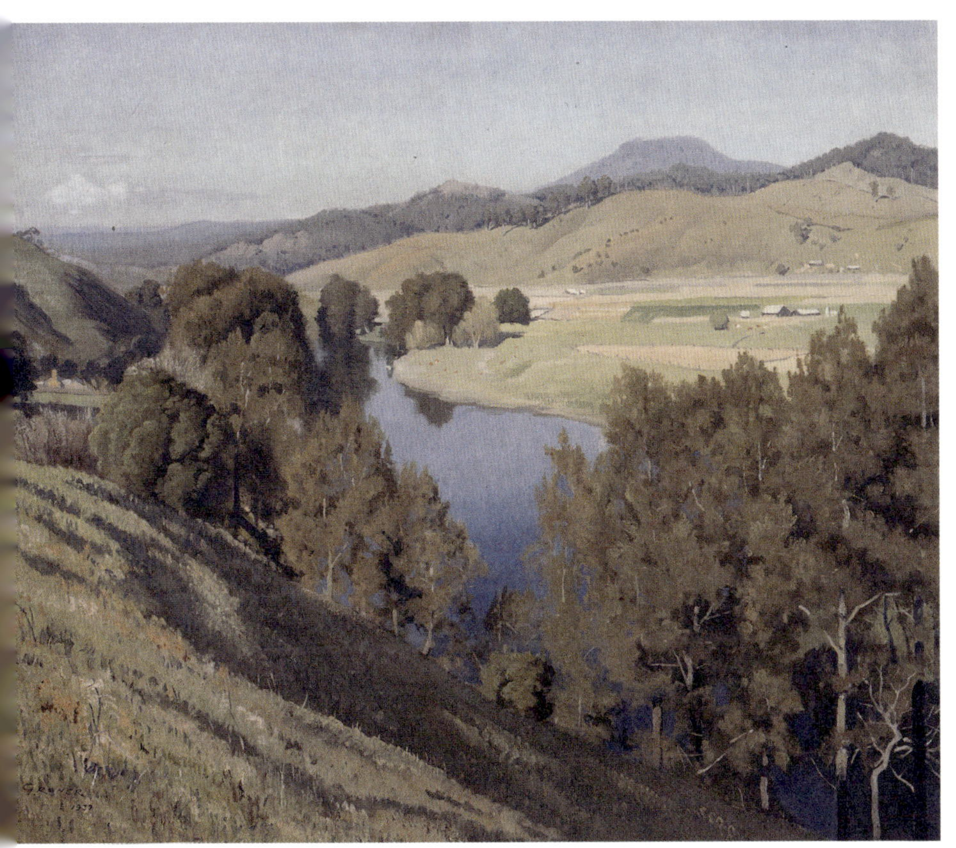

Top – *Omega pastoral*, 1950, oil on canvas, Lloyd Rees (Australian)

Bottom – *Bellinger pastoral*, 1937, oil on canvas, Elioth Grüner (Australian)

Following – *It Was Blue and Green*, 1960, oil on linen, Georgia O'Keeffe (American)

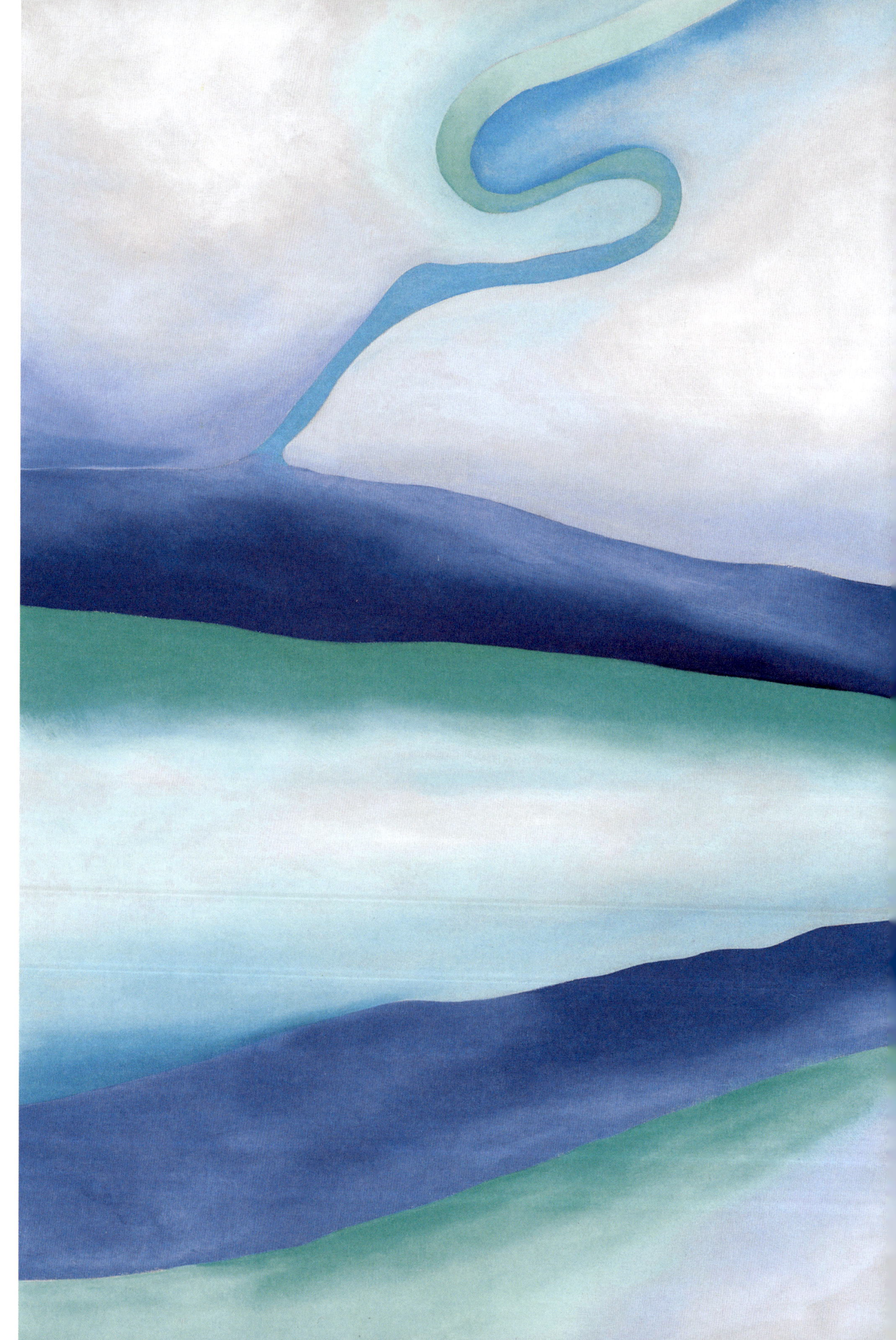

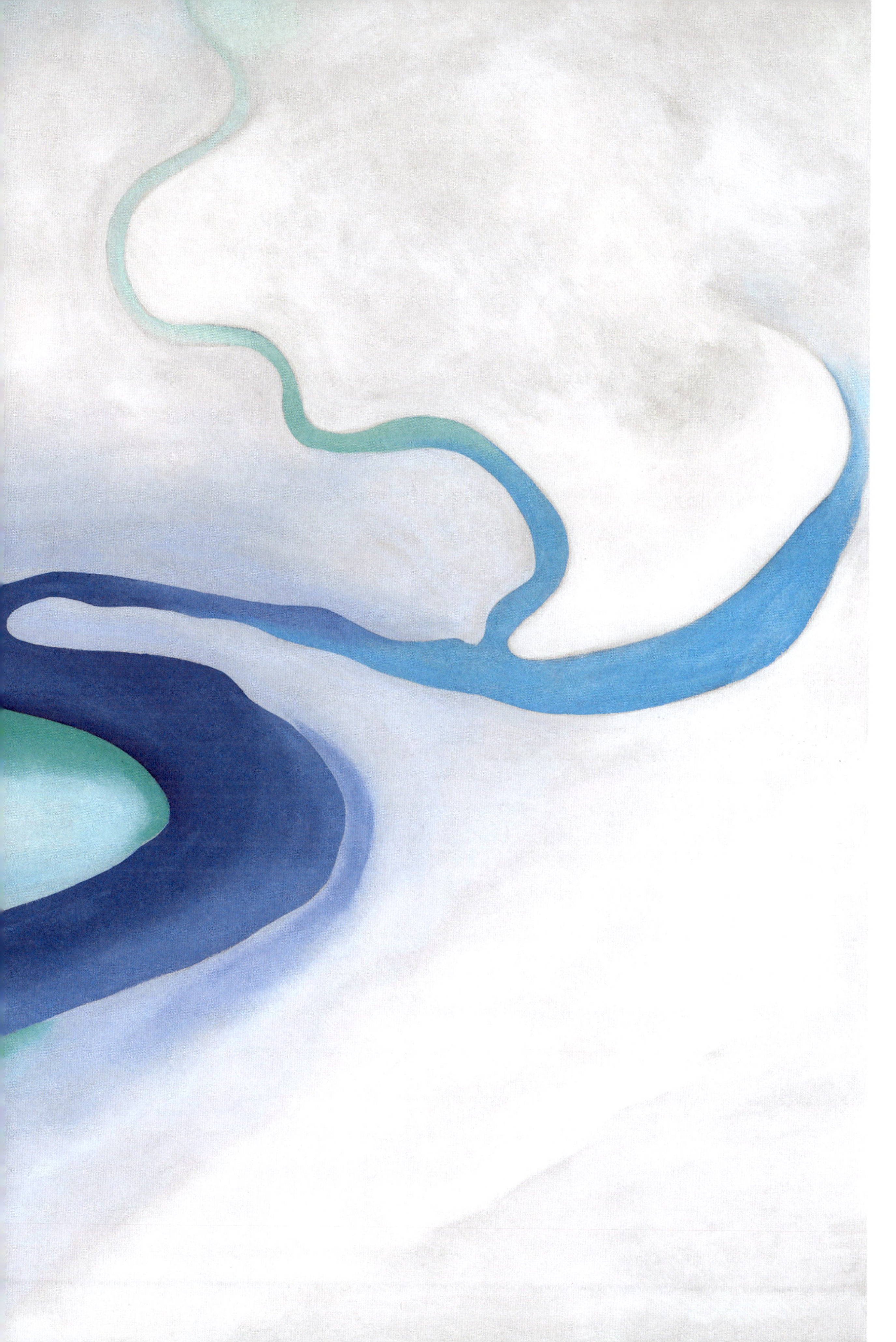

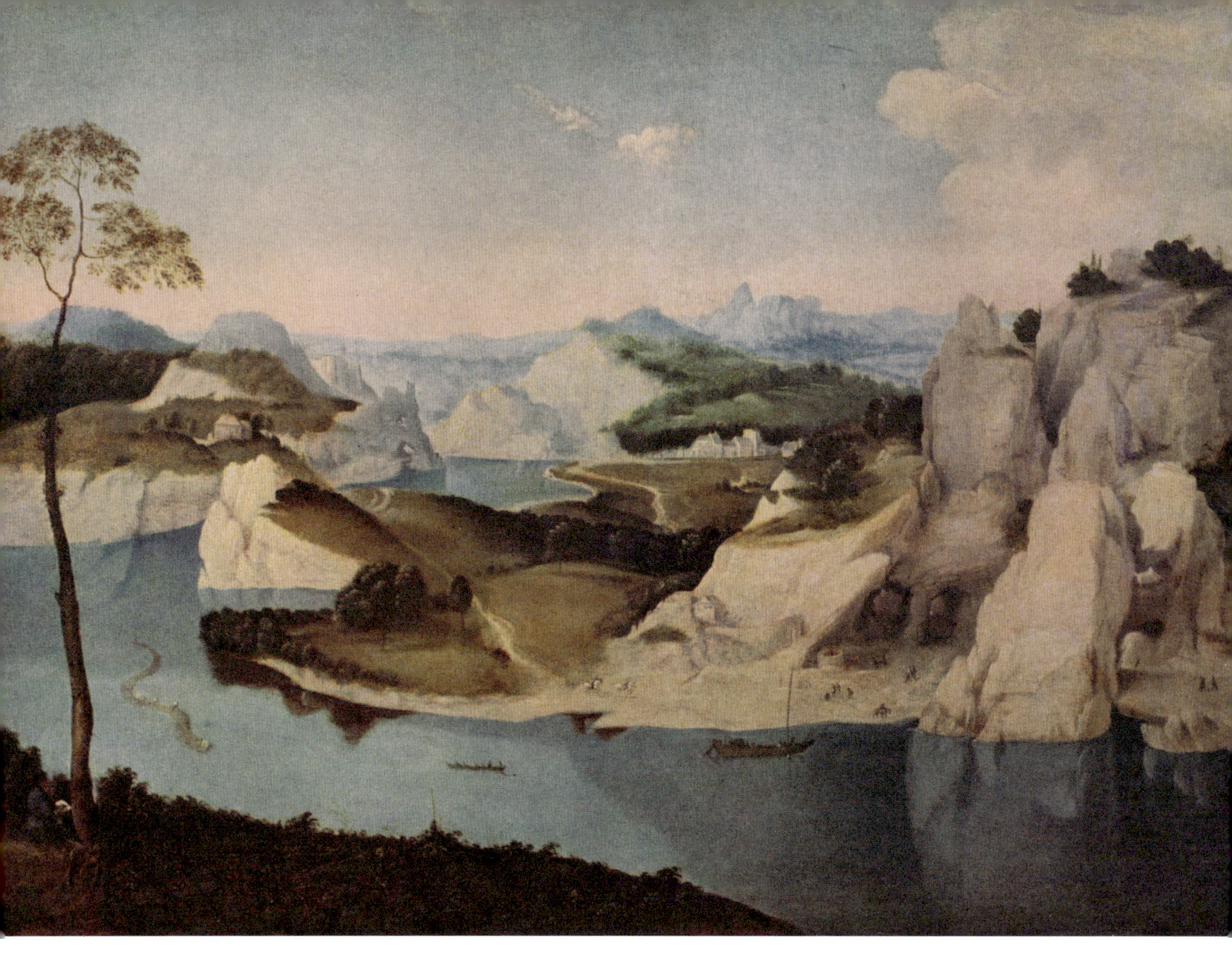

Above – *Landscape: A River among Mountains*, c. 1600, oil on poplar, Pieter Bruegel the Elder (imitator of) (Dutch)

Opposite – *Njirrakarpa, Finke River, James Ranges*, c. 1948, painting in watercolour, over drawing in black pencil, Albert Namatjira (Western Arrarnta people, Australian)

Following – *Ice Pattern* (detail), 1948, watercolour and graphite pencil on board, Henry Schnakenberg (American)

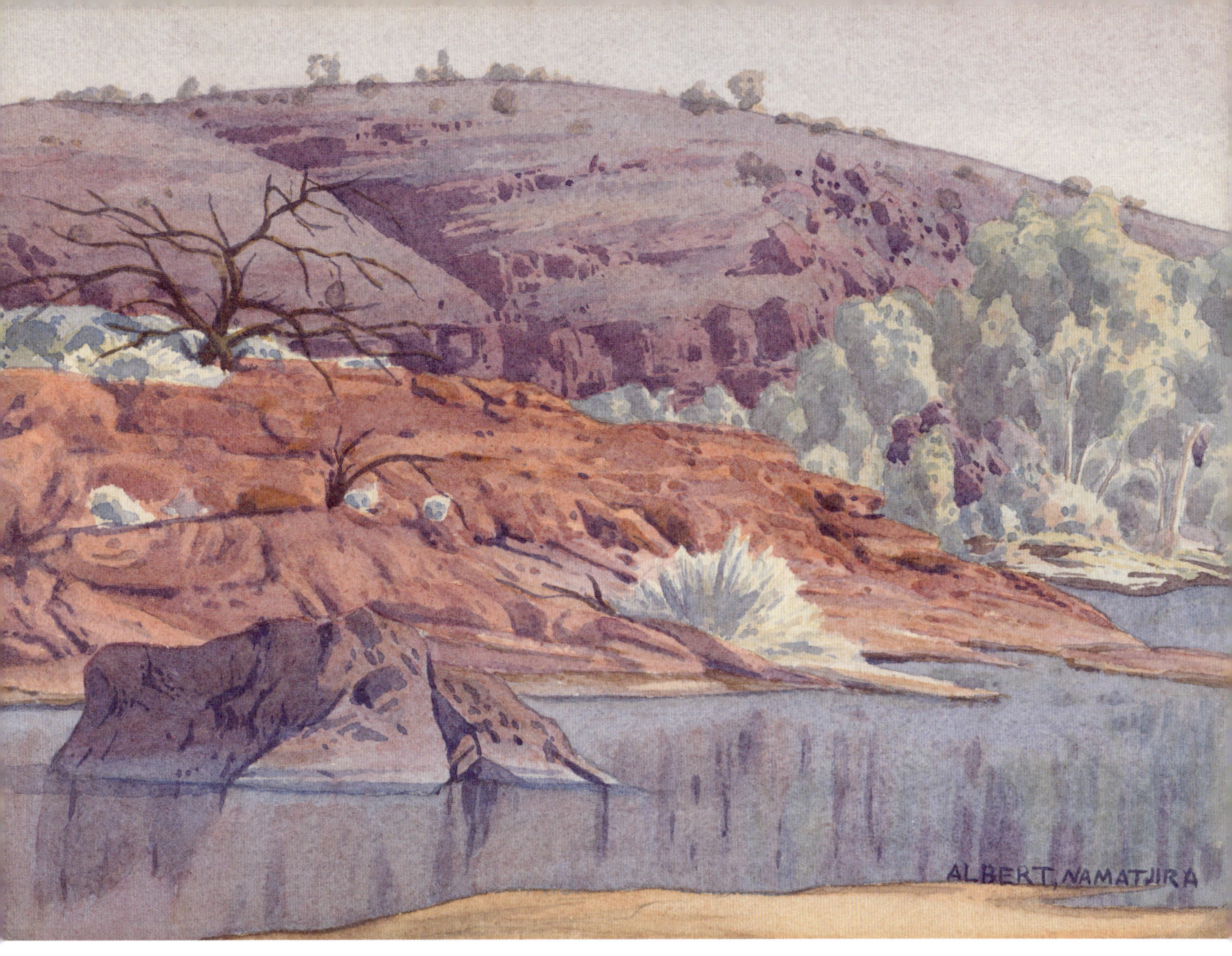
ALBERT, NAMATJIRA

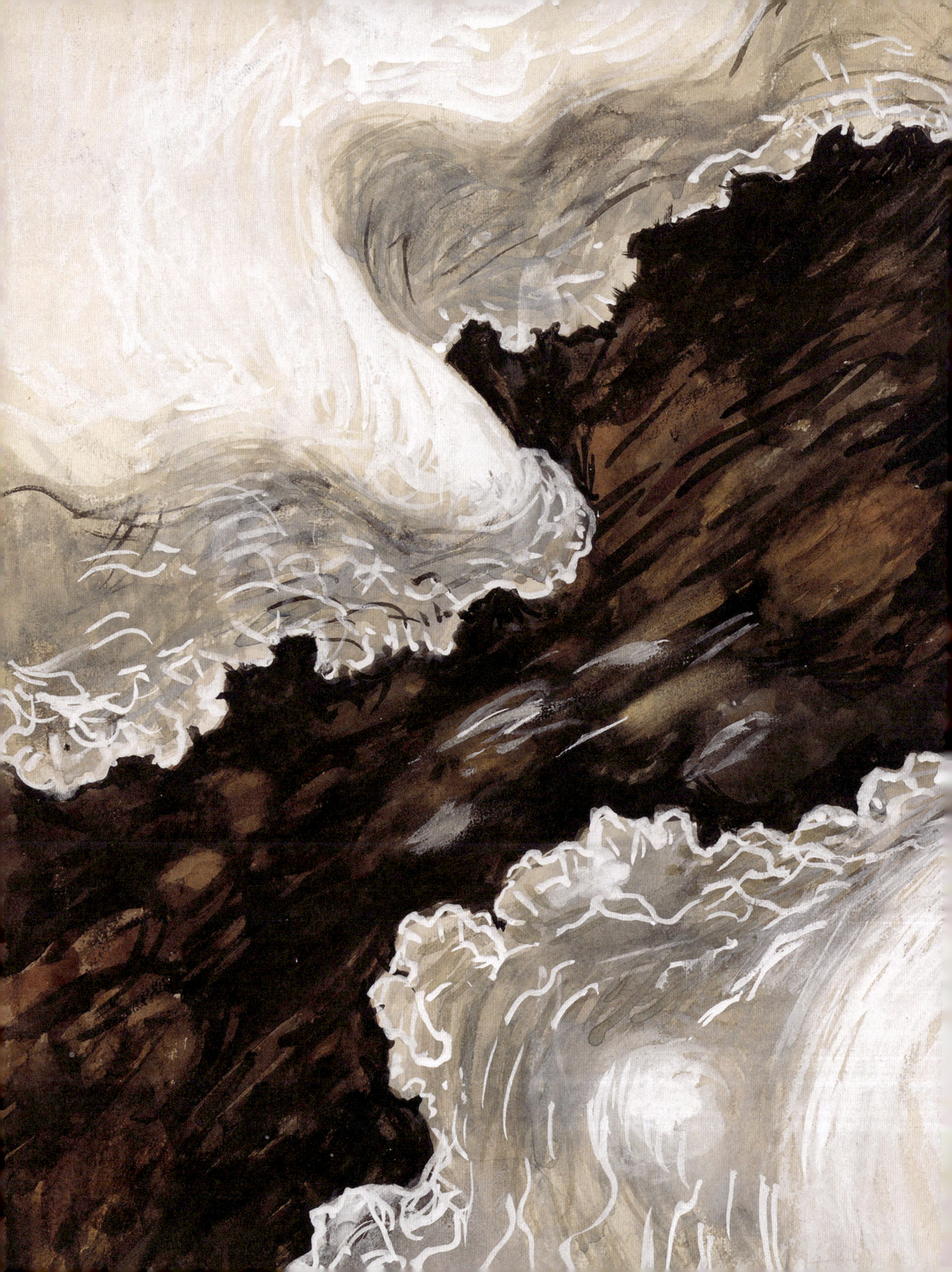

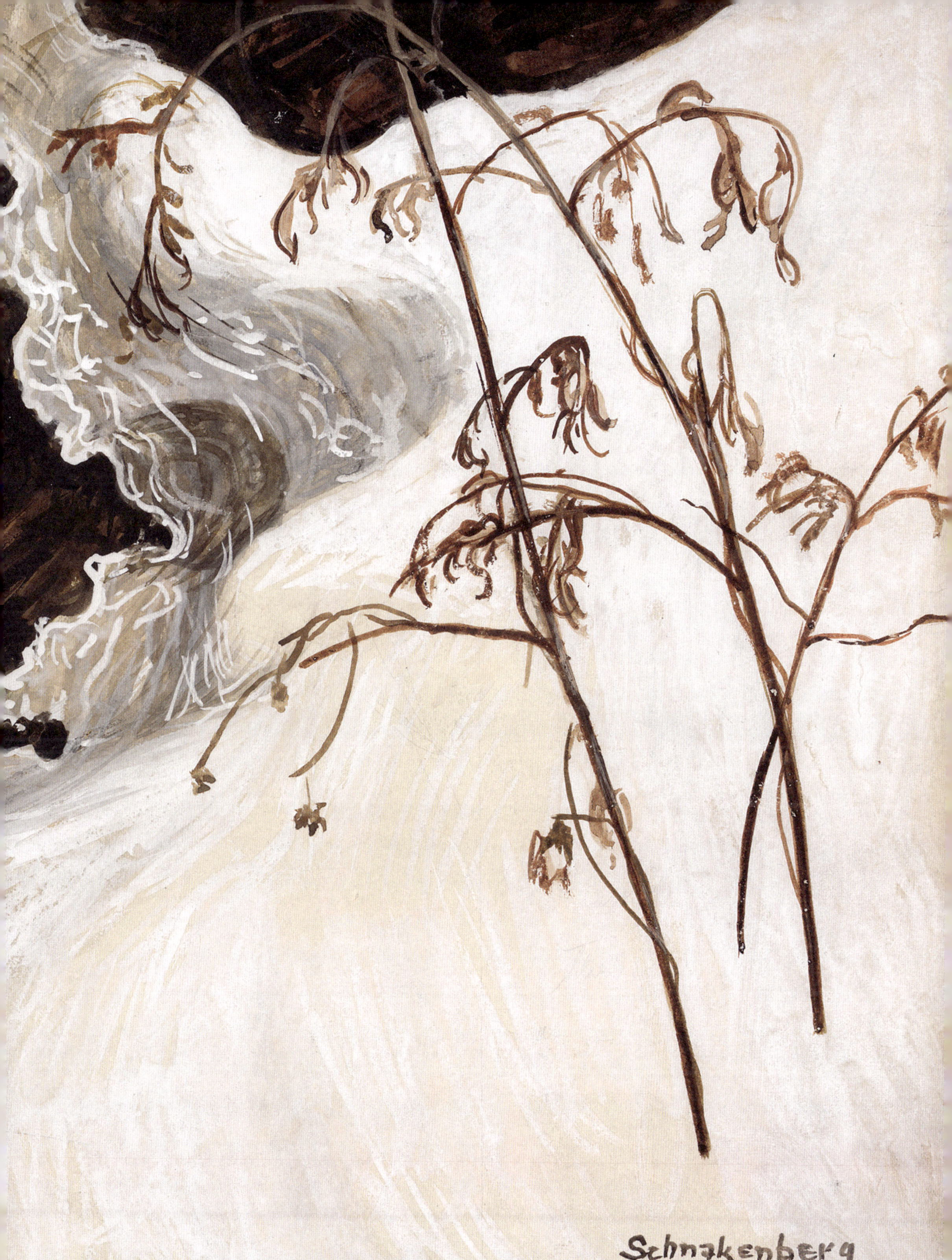
Schnakenberg

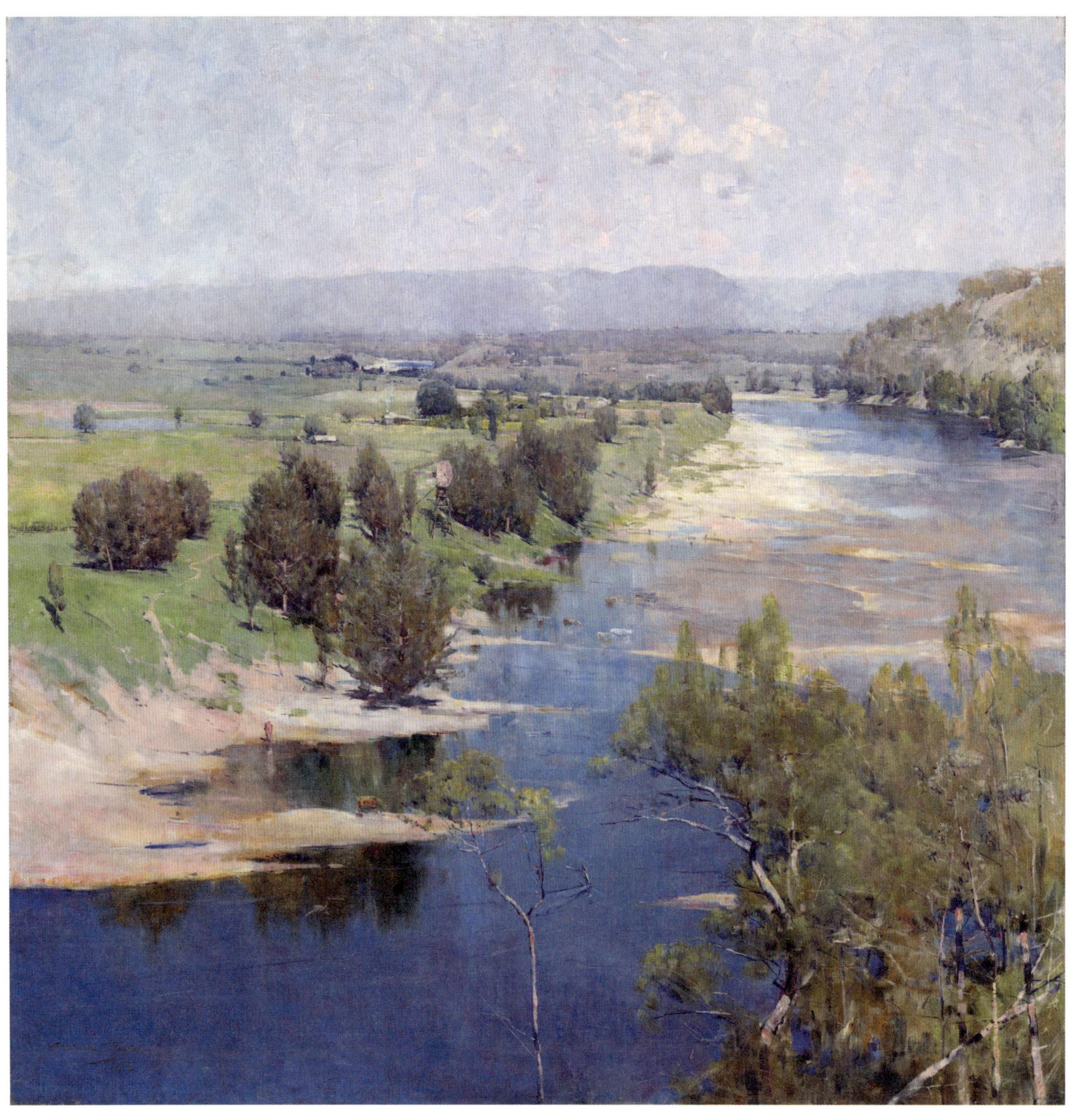

ARTHUR STREETON PERFECTLY CAPTURES THE HEAT HAZE OF THE MIDDAY SUN THAT DRIFTS DOWNWARDS FROM THE TOP REGISTER OF THE PICTURE PLANE, STOPPING SHORT AT THE MIDDLE GROUND WHERE THE RIVER IS AT ITS WIDEST POINT. THE DEEP COBALT BLUE OF THE WATER APPEARS LIKE AN OASIS IN THE DRY DESERT. STREETON HAS ADDED A STROKE OF RED ON THE EMBANKMENT – A TRICK HE USED IN HIS PAINTING TO DRAW THE EYE CLOSER AND ADD INTRIGUE.

Above – *'The purple noon's transparent might'*, 1896, oil on canvas, Arthur Streeton (Australian)

Opposite – *Molonglo River from Mount Pleasant, Canberra*, 1927, oil on canvas on board, Hilda Rix Nicholas (Australian)

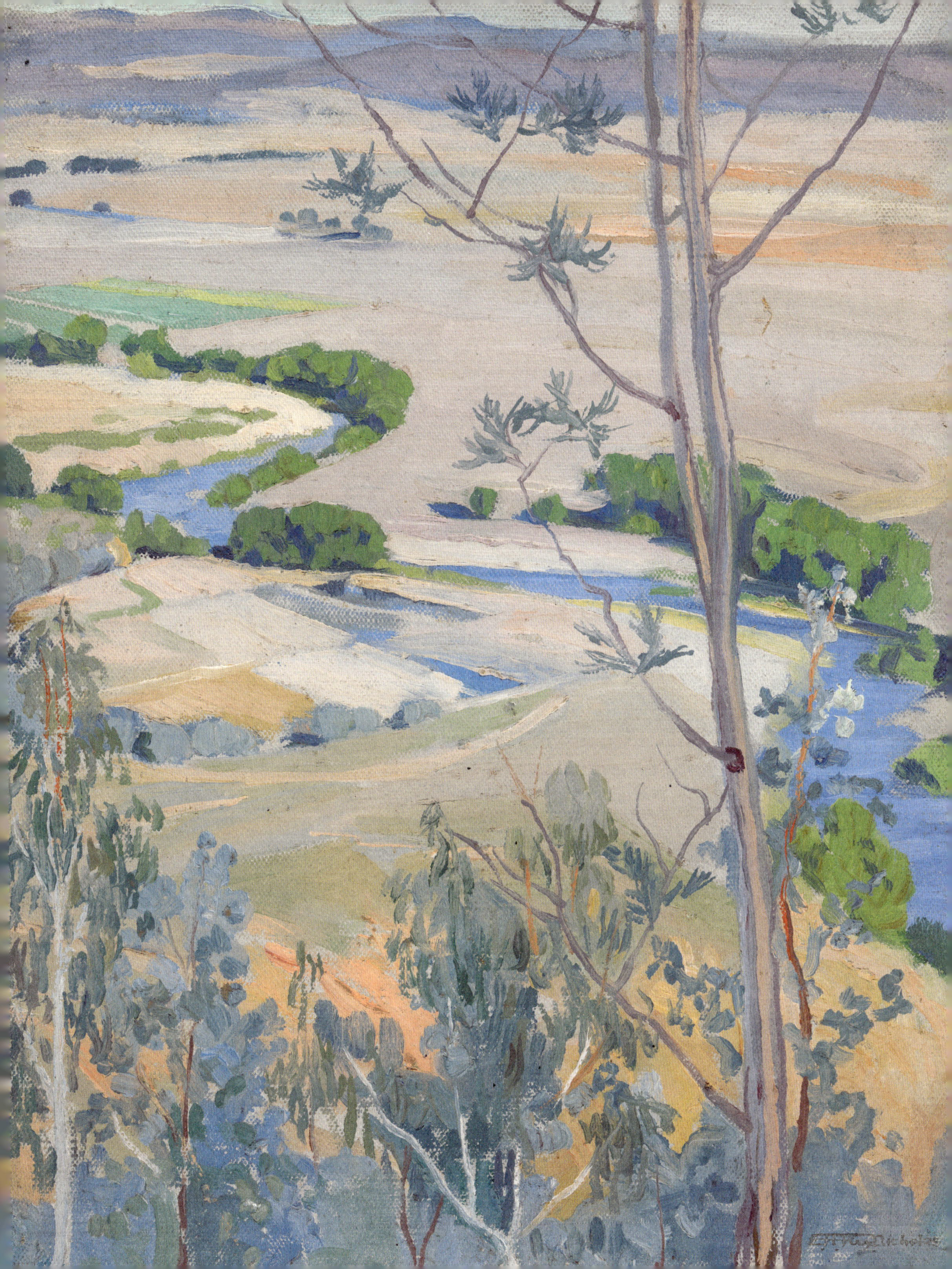

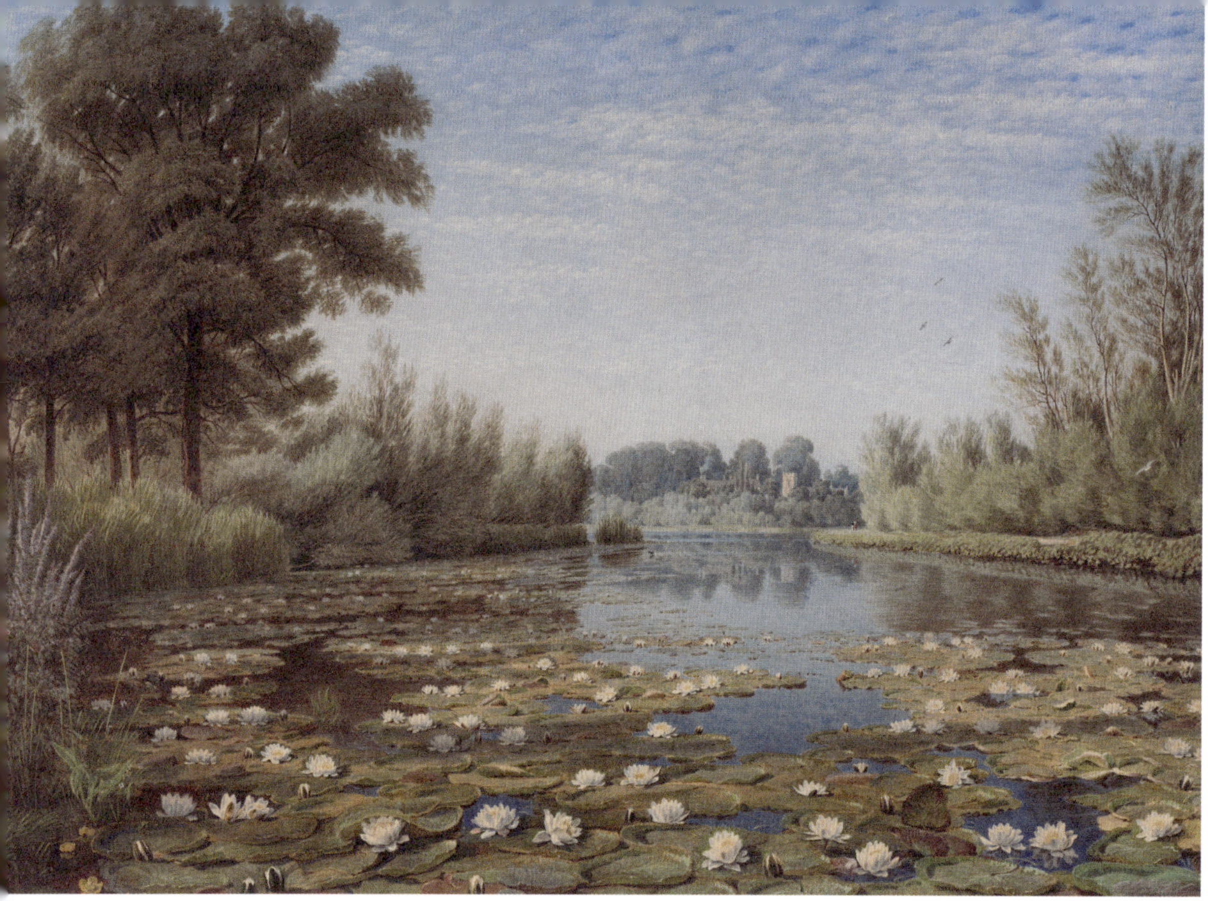

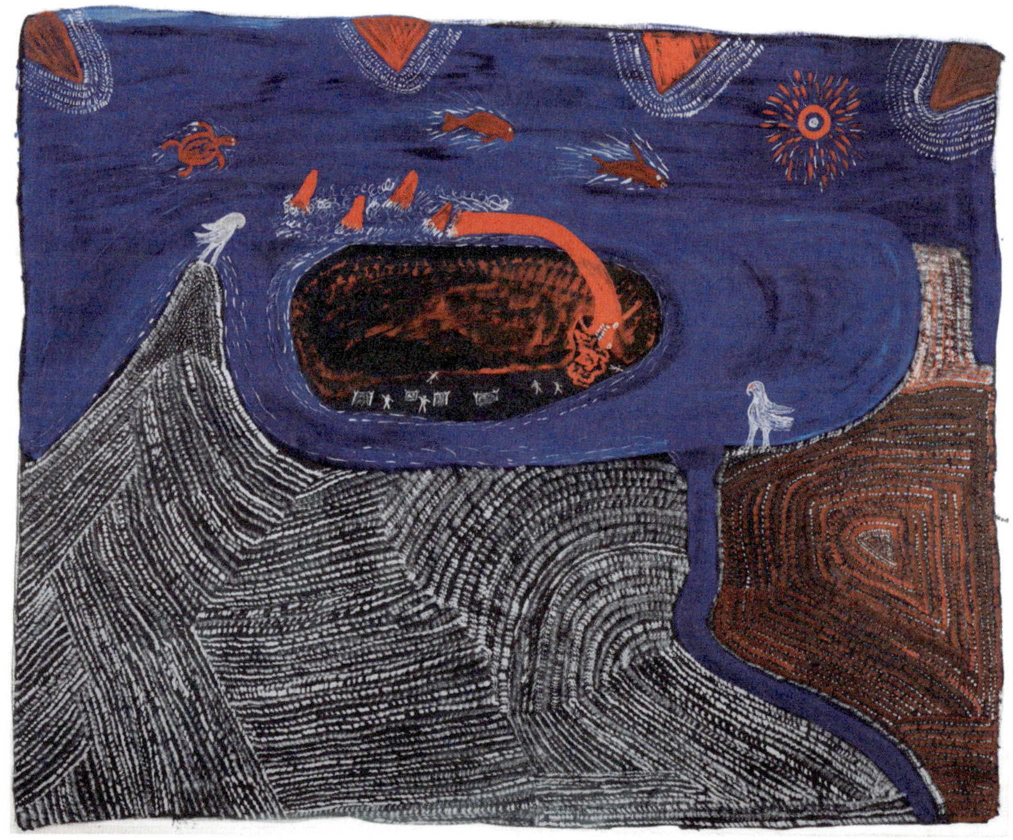

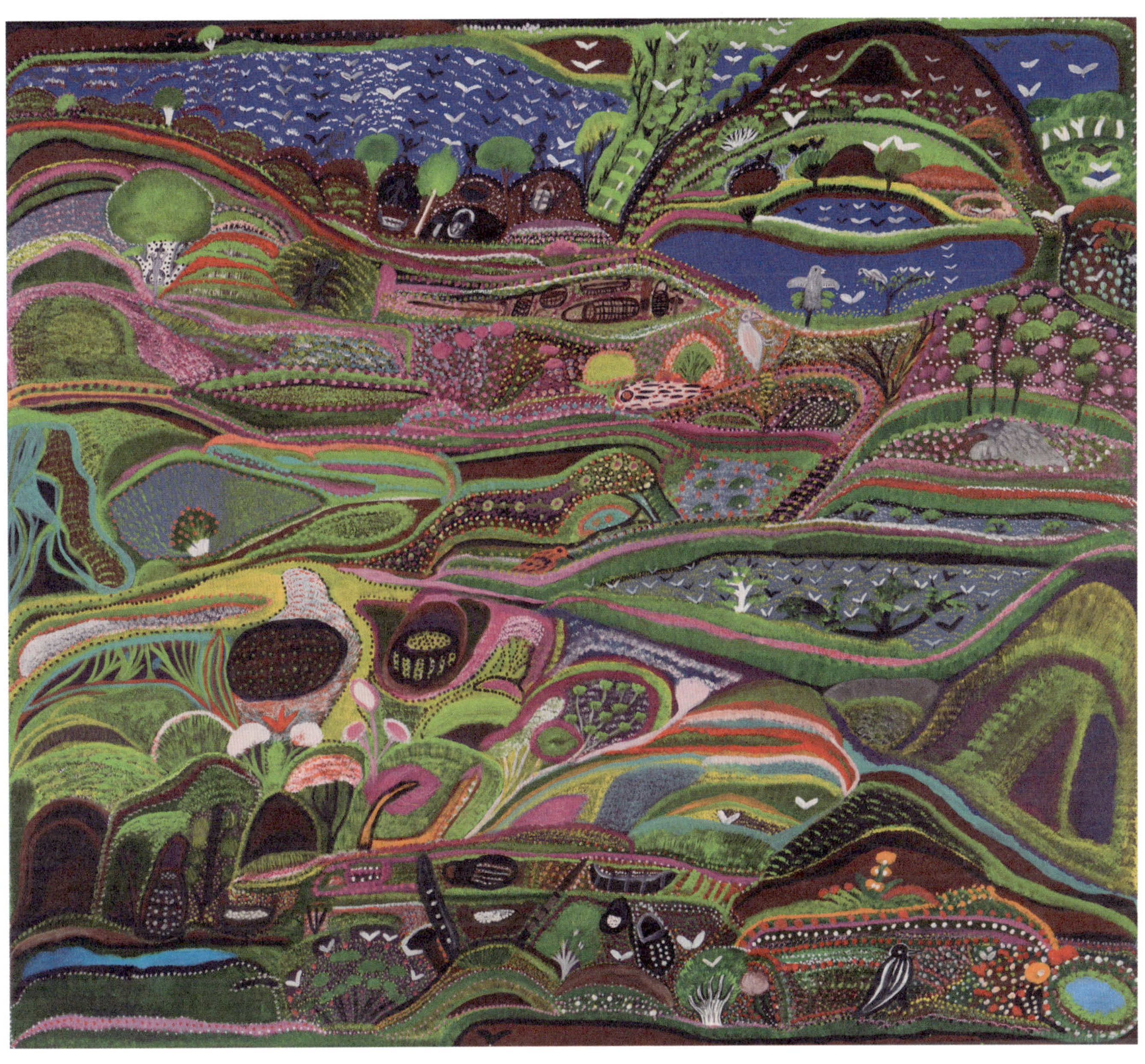

Opposite top – *Scene near Shipton on Cherwell, Oxfordshire*, 1835, watercolour, gouache and brown ink over graphite on laid paper, William Turner of Oxford (British)

Opposite bottom – *The Limmen Bight River,* 1990, synthetic polymer paint on canvas, Ginger Riley Munduwalawala (Marra people, Australian)

Above – *We All Share Water*, 2001, synthetic polymer paint on canvas, Gertie Huddleston (Wandarang/Mara people, Australian)

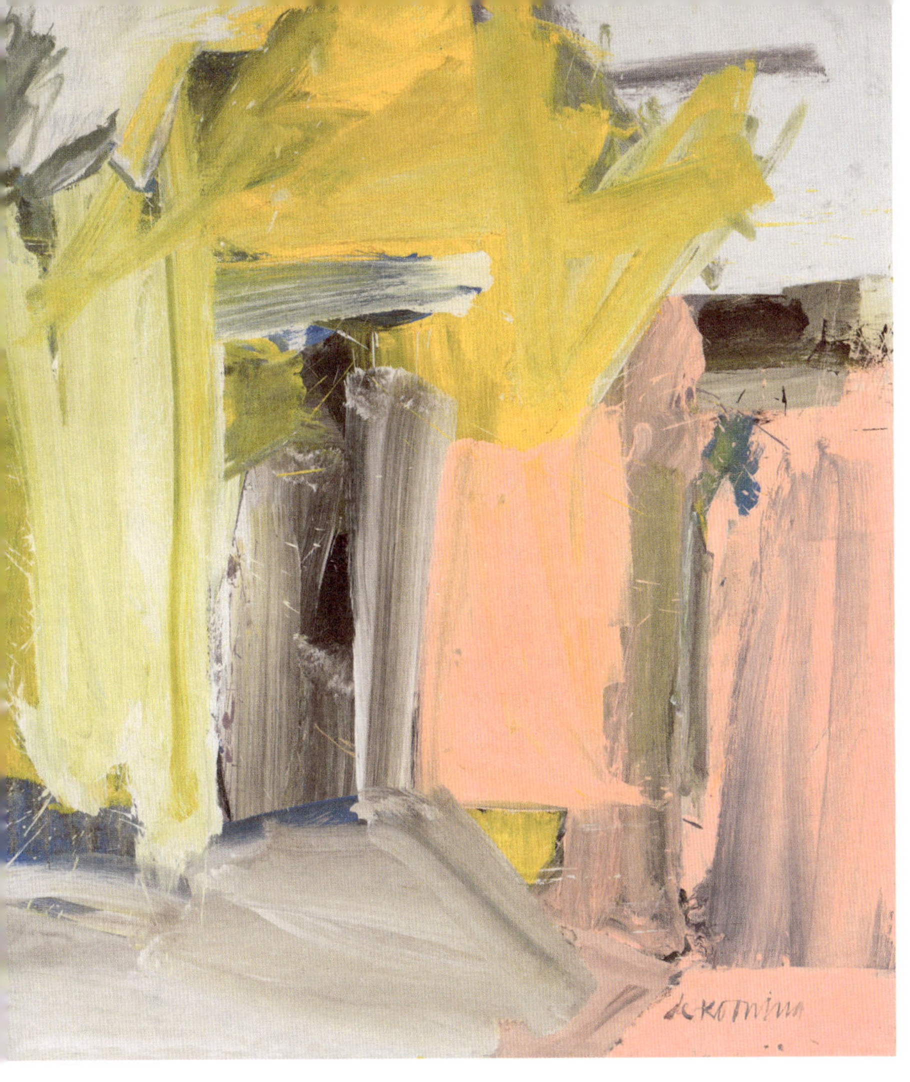

Opposite – *River Test – Trees at Water's Edge*, 1989, oil on linen, Ellen Phelan (American)

Top – *Door to the River*, 1960, oil on linen, Willem de Kooning (Dutch/American)

Bottom – *Lake of the Ozarks*, 1970, coloured pencil, chalk and ballpoint pen on paper, Joseph Yoakum (American)

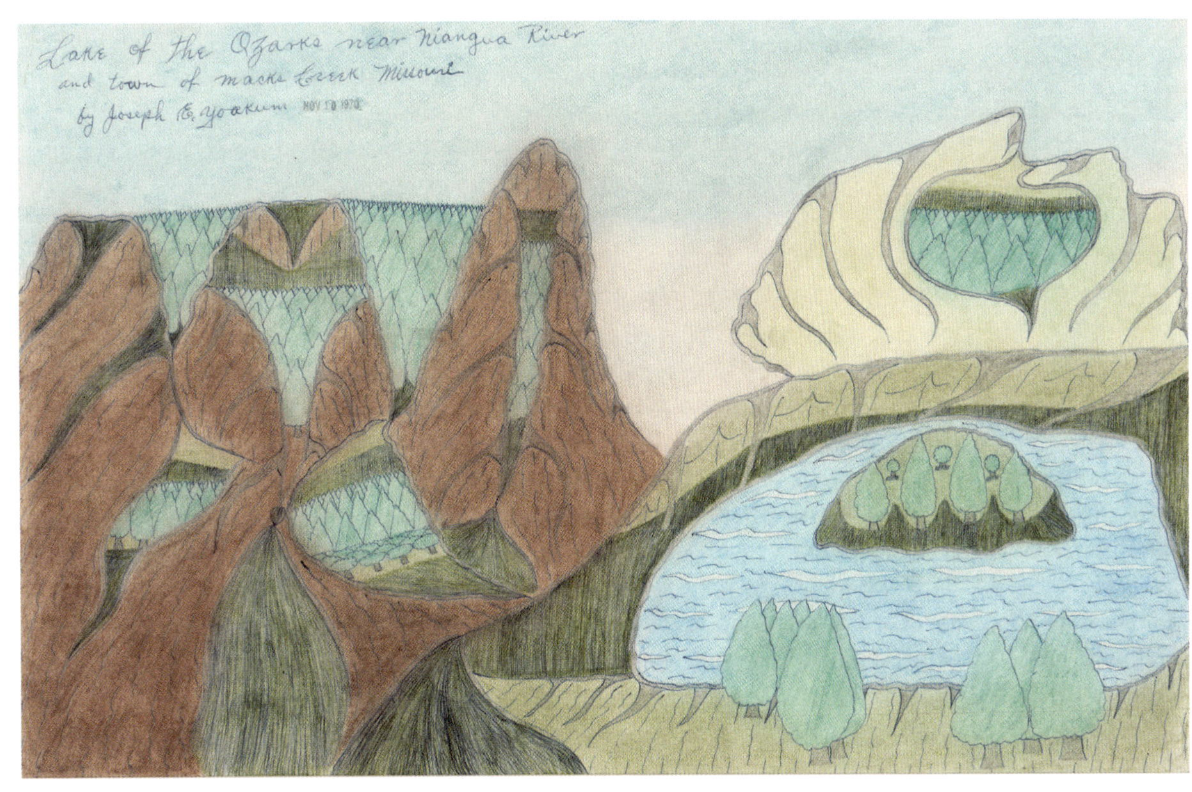

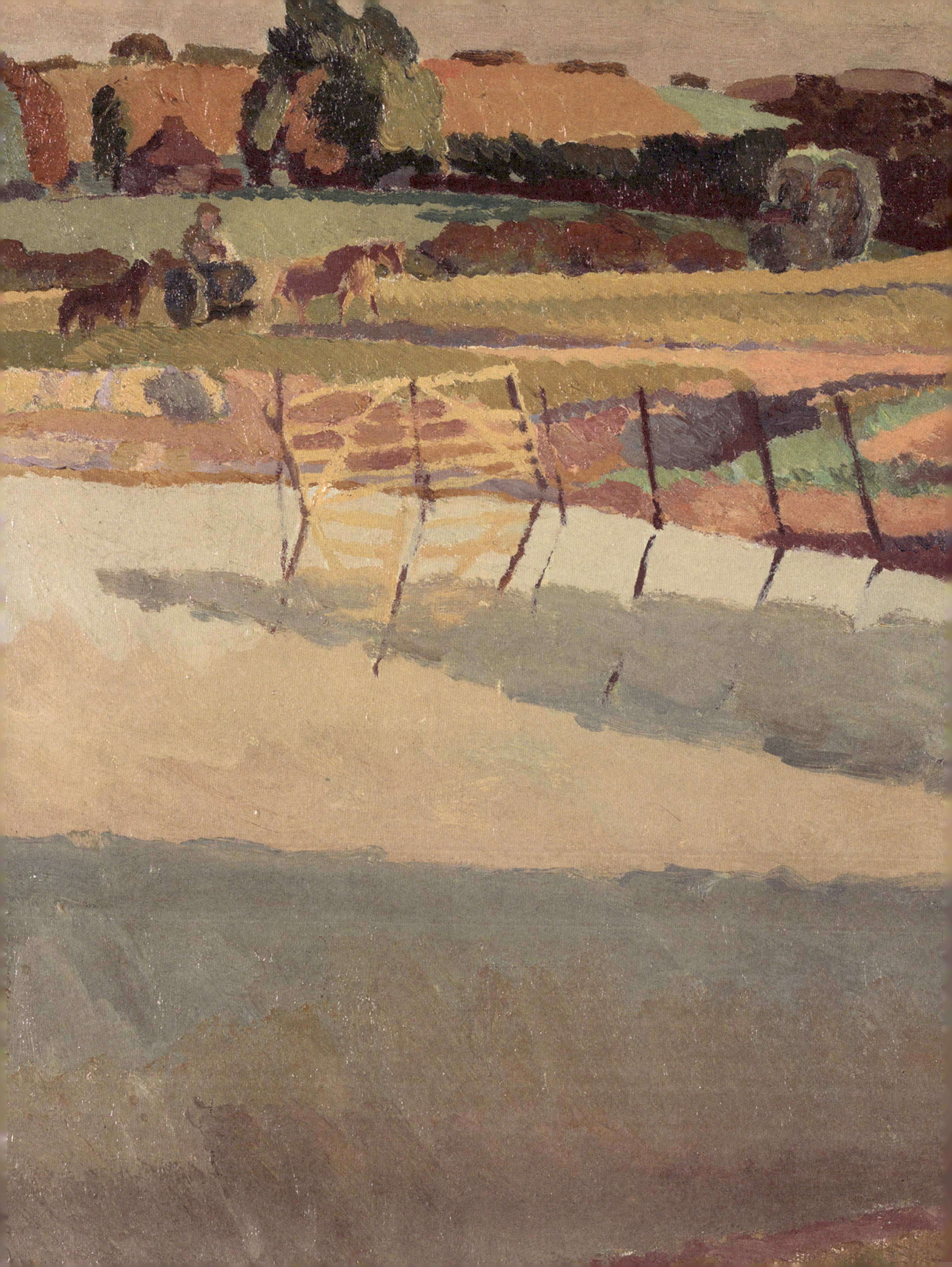

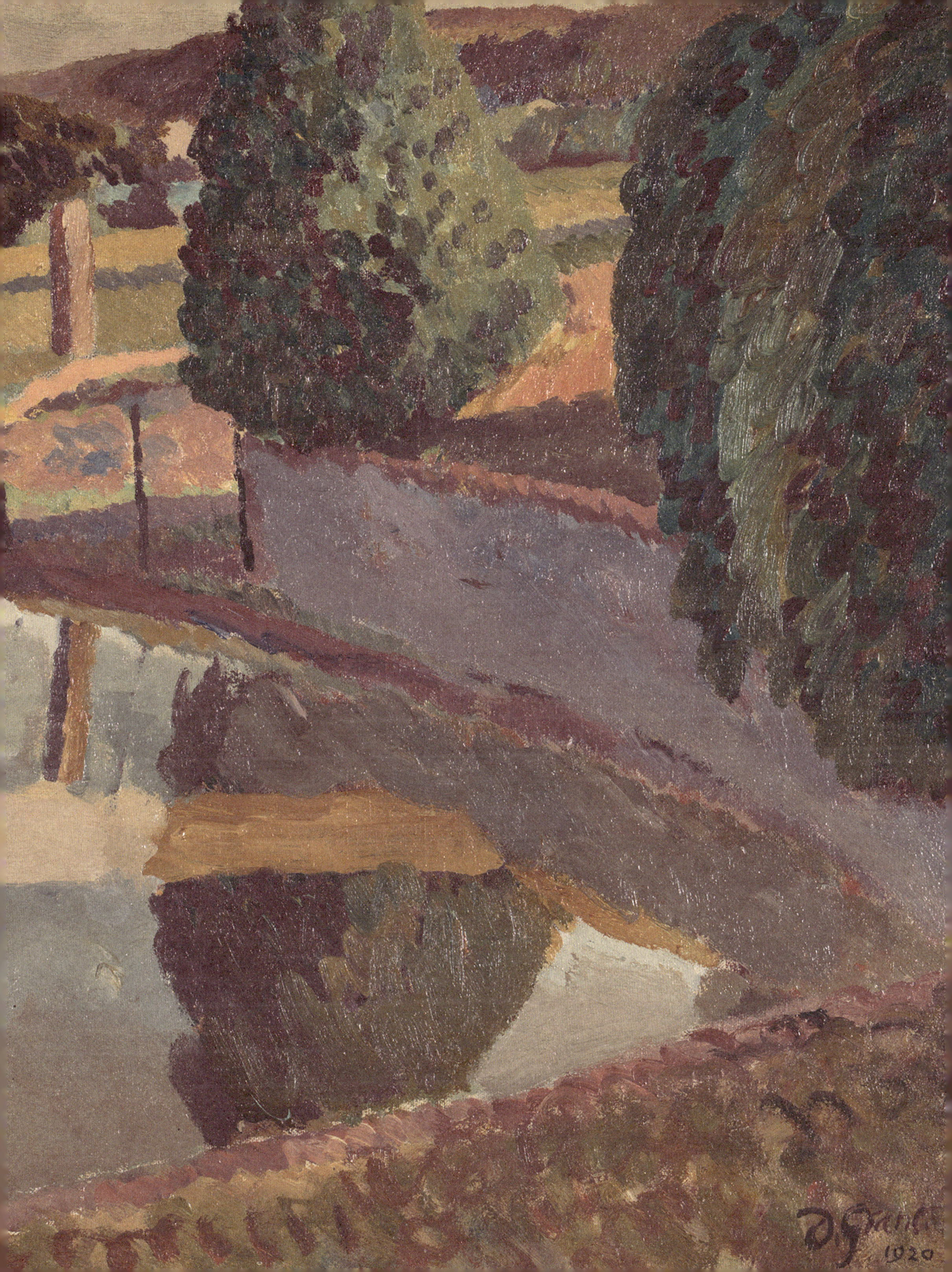

LAKES & PONDS

LAKES AND PONDS ARE SITES FOR GATHERING, SWIMMING AND PAINTING. THE STILL SURFACE OF THE WATER REFLECTS THE SEASONS AND THE SKY PERFECTLY, PROVIDING INSPIRATION FOR PAINTERS AND WRITERS ALIKE. THESE OPEN BODIES OF WATER ARE OFTEN DISTINGUISHED BY THEIR LUSH SURROUNDING HABITAT. NOTICE THE ACTIVITIES AND LIVELINESS IN AND AROUND THE LAKES AND PONDS ON THE PAGES THAT FOLLOW.

Previous - *Landscape, Sussex* (detail), 1920, oil paint on canvas, Duncan Grant (British)

Opposite - *The Pond at Charleston, East Sussex*, c. 1916, oil on canvas, Vanessa Bell (British)

Following left - *Lake Baker* (detail), 2021, synthetic polymer paint on linen, Timo Hogan (Pitjantjatjara people, Australian)

Following right - *Highland Landscape* (detail), 1920, pastel on paper, Simon Bussy (French)

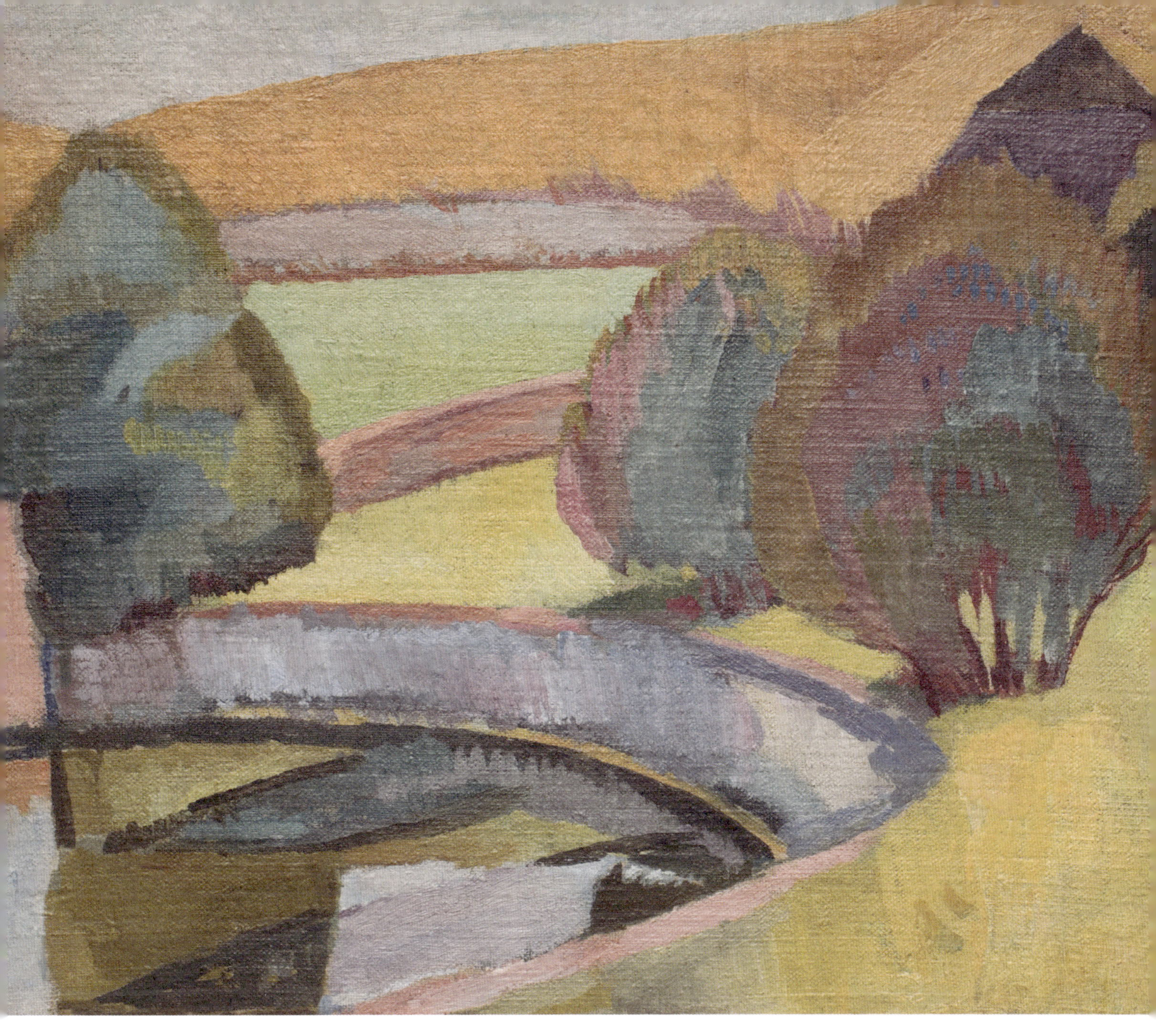

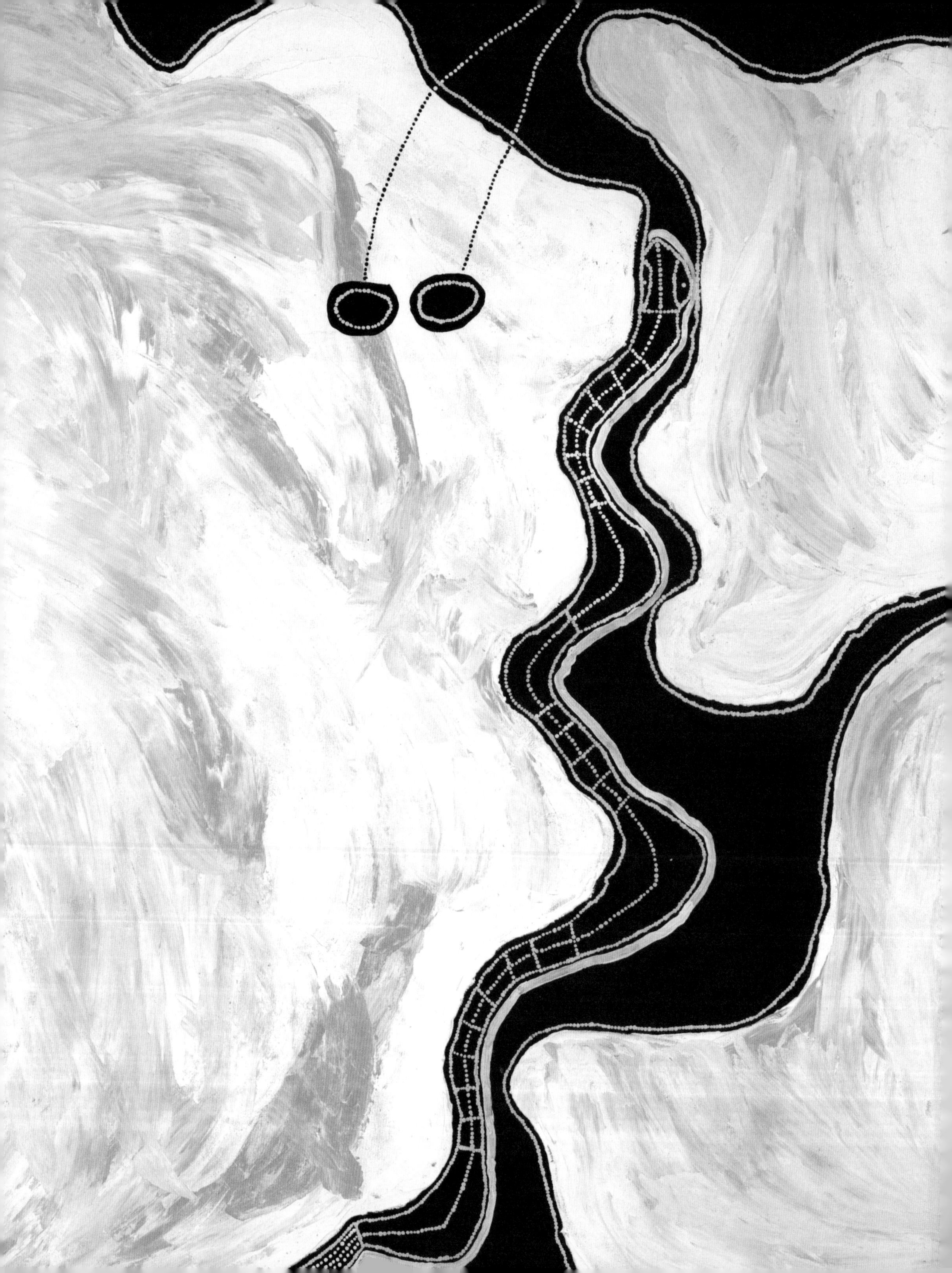

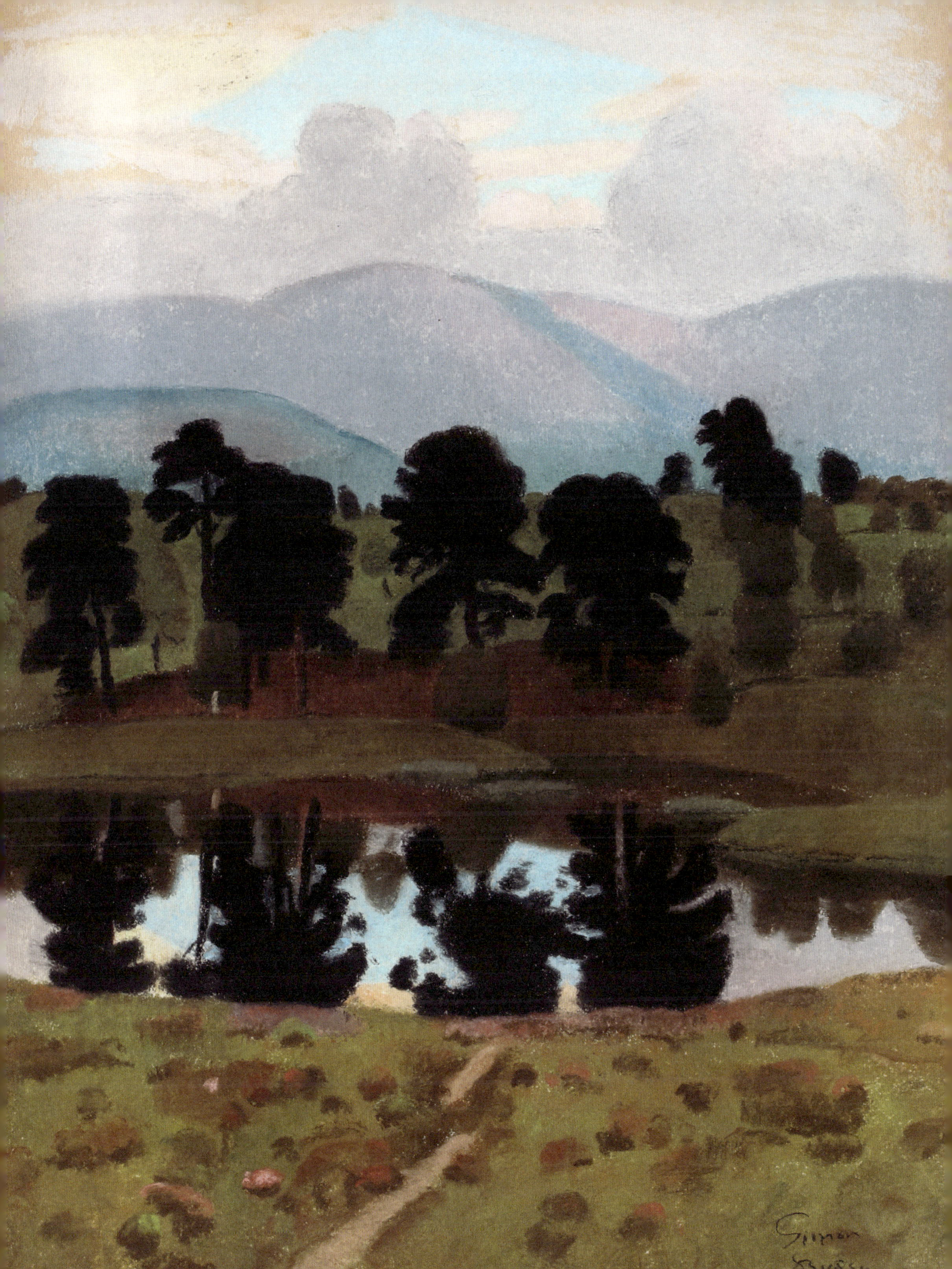

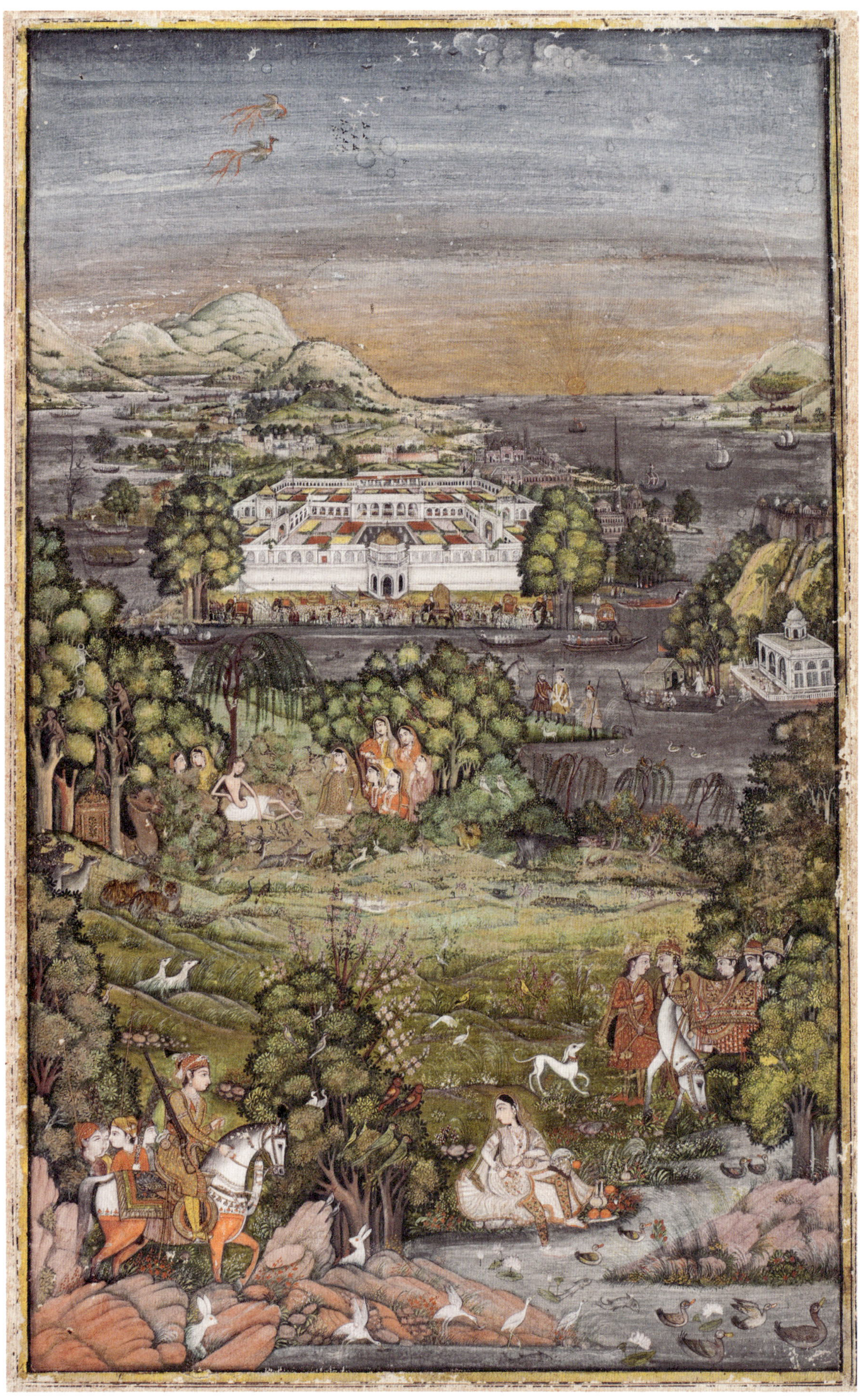

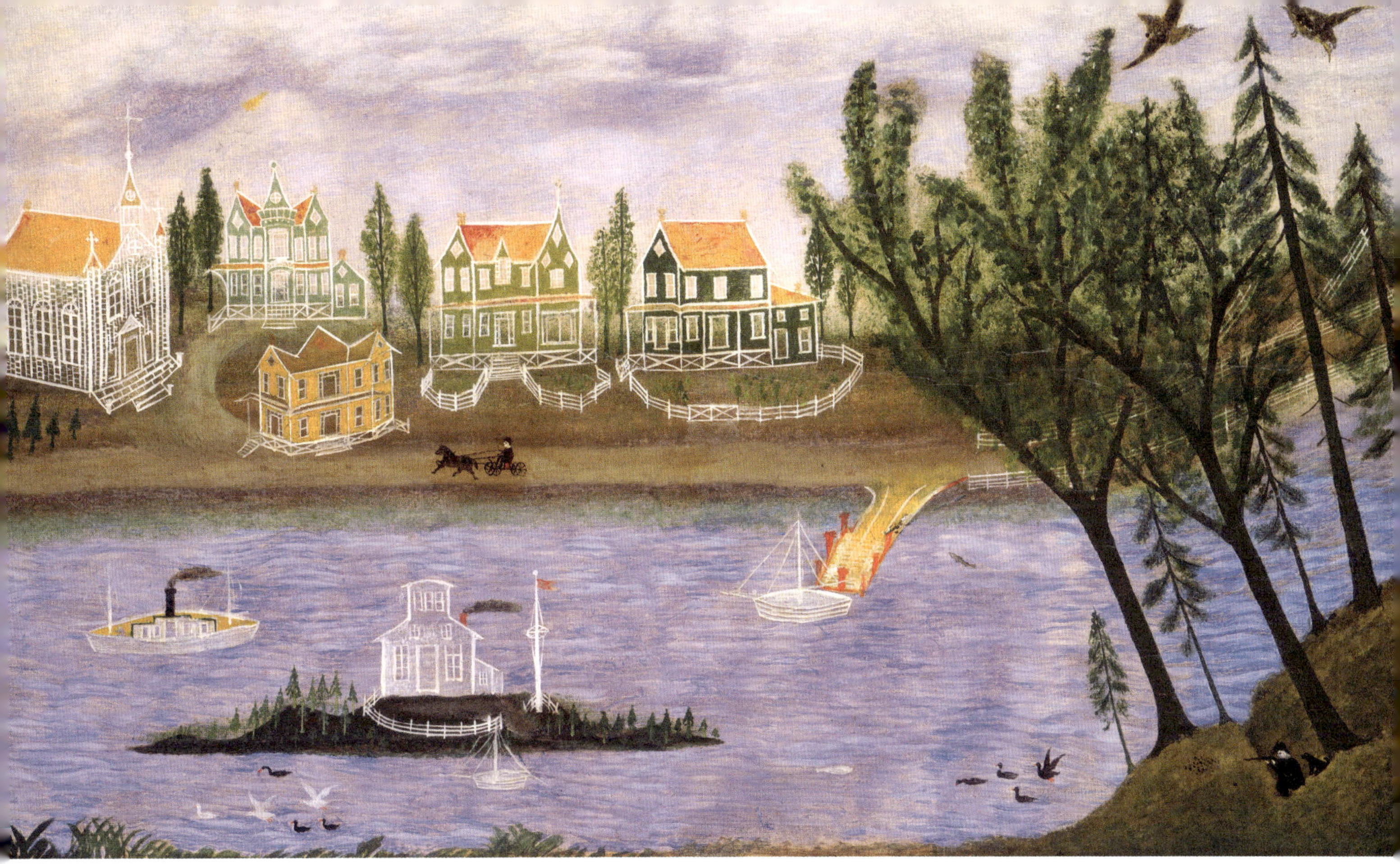

Opposite – *Layla and Majnun, and Khusraw and Shirin, Illustrations of Themes from Persian Poetry*, c. 1775, opaque watercolour and gold on paper, Unknown artist (Indian)

Top – *Village by the River*, c. fourth quarter of 19th century, oil on canvas, Unknown artist (American)

Bottom – *Udaipur 1916*, 1916, colour woodblock print on wove paper, Charles W Bartlett (British)

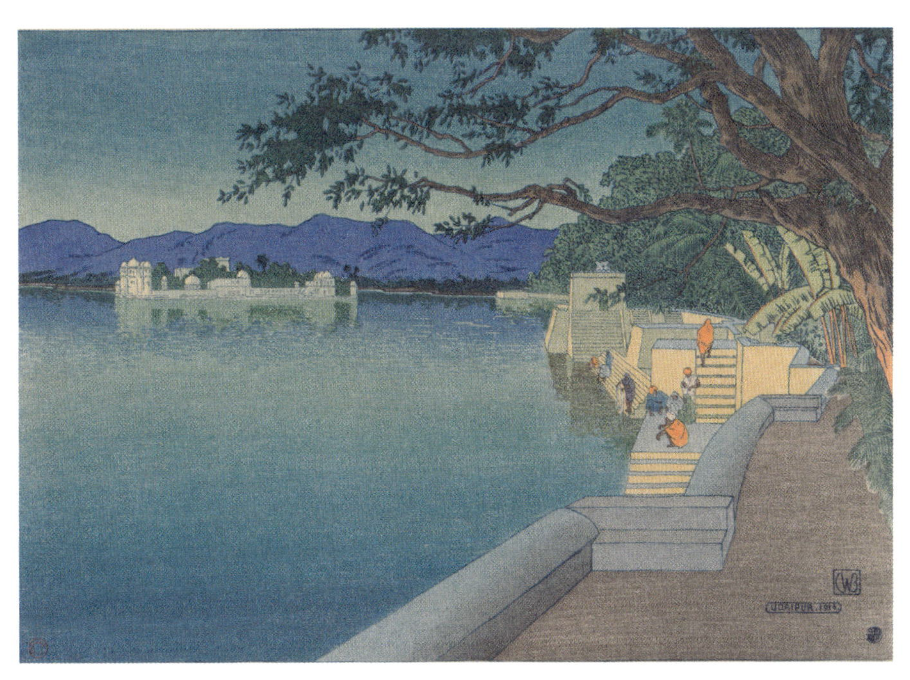

SWIMMING IN PONDS

ALICE VINCENT

To swim in a pond is to confront the outside world on a different level. It is rare to be able to see the bottom of one; these ecosystems are their own small worlds, full of plantgrowth and animal life, and to enter into it is to embody that. And so entering it – perhaps plunging, perhaps diving, perhaps gingerly making your way down the steps, lowering more of your body in with each one – is to change a state. From air to liquid. From earth to water.

I spent the first really warm day of summer at Charleston House, the Sussex country home of artists Vanessa Bell and Duncan Grant and their many Bloomsbury Group-oscillating friends and lovers. There, in the early afternoon, my young son and I sought shelter from the sun beneath the trees on the edge of the old orchard. He was newly upright on his feet and independent with them, and while I let him explore I followed him as he headed towards the large swimming pond that stretches out in front of the house.

My son was fascinated by the water. He knelt at the edge of it, trying to make sense of its glinting surface. I sympathised with him; it was hot, we were sweaty, the water looked cool and inviting. But we couldn't go in. There's still a rowing boat tied up on the water, but most of the living things that breach the surface these days are wild ducks and fish.

Perhaps he was always meant to be drawn in by the water; ponds have held him from the beginning. Almost exactly two years before, on the day I found out I was pregnant, I swam in a pond tucked away on an estate in Berkshire. It took me a few days to process that my body was harbouring something that would grow into another, and the one place where I didn't feel strange about my body was in the water, where my ankles tangled with weeds. As the baby grew I kept plunging myself into these spaces, where the line between earth and liquid blurred and thinned. A space that shifted with the seasons as my own body was.

As you swim you share the space with others. Ducks dive, their tailfeathers at a level with your forehead. Moorhens and coots putter by. Perhaps there are fish, perhaps a heron watching them. All this life is going on regardless of human voyeurism. Foliage that is usually viewed from an elevation of sitting or standing is now at water-level; willow leaves drape their fingertips upon the surface. It forces you to examine the familiar anew.

I think this is why the best ponds feel otherworldly, as in, a world removed from the one you usually inhabit. I first went to Kenwood Ladies' Pond – one of several in Hampstead Heath, although the only one that excludes men – when I was in my mid-twenties and relatively new to London. It was a scruffier thing then, short of the architecturally stylish changing rooms with their James Turrell-style open roof, where women of nearly every decade would bathe and lounge naked across the surrounding lawn. I could barely believe it existed, this hidden paradise of women just being; being with their friends, being with their bodies, being with themselves.

Many things have changed in London since then, but in spite of the new infrastructure and the controversial booking system (you used to turn up and queue, often for hours in a heat wave), the Ladies' Pond still feels like a place

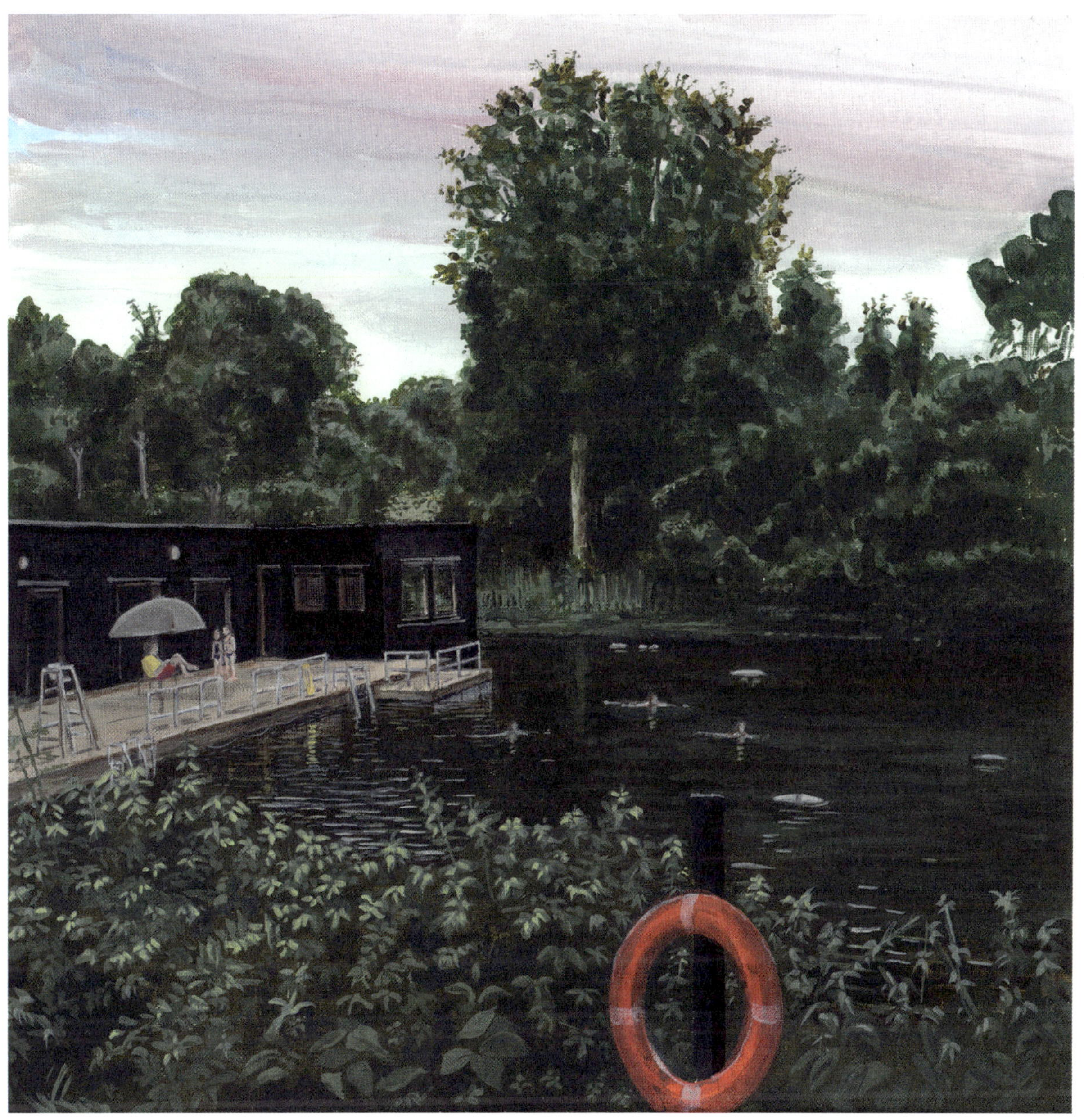

from decades, if not centuries, ago. It is not easy to get to: there is no vehicular access and the path isn't paved. The nearest Tube stations are over 20 minutes' walk away. There's no phone signal, and the rules about phones are strict in any case – they are to be switched off, and no photos are to be taken. There are no clear signposts to them; instead you must trust your instinct or your memories or your wavering map and await the evidence that you have reached your destination: Women Only. This water is deep and cold. Competent swimmers only. From this officious signage the ponds are a further 100 metres ahead. You must walk past ancient oak trees and tall horse chestnuts. You are entering into an enclave; it necessitates a little journeying.

And as a result, the ponds draw people harbouring attention. The heartbroken and the weary, the habitual and the novice, the exercisers and the escapees. When the water is shared by this many ducks, it is cleansing in unexpected ways.

Hampstead Heath, Womens Pond at Dusk, 2023, giclée print, Laura Price (British)

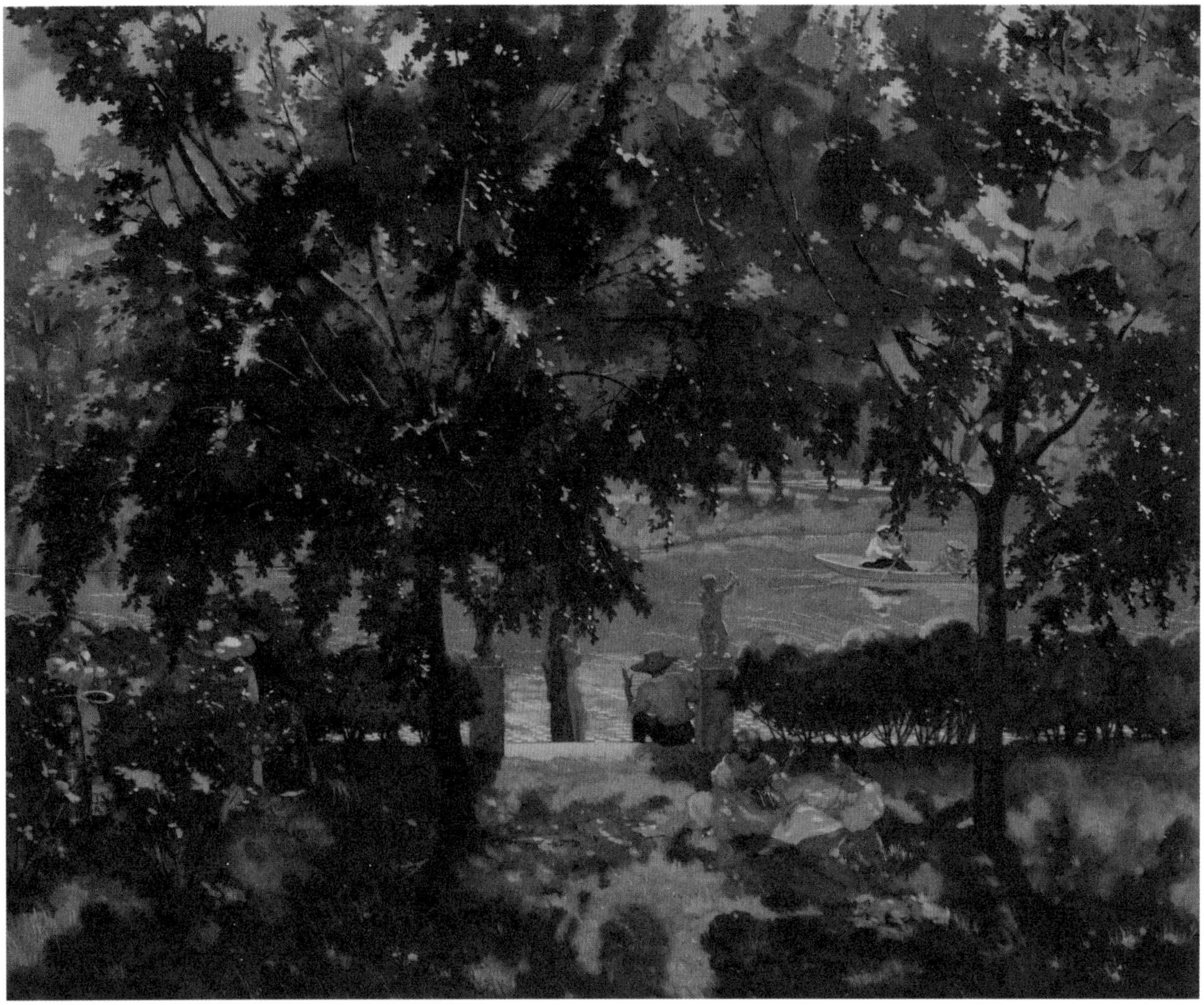

Top – *River Scene*, 1929, gouache on paper on board, Konstantin Andreyevich Somov (Russian)

Bottom – *The Bathers*, c. 1847, etching, Charles François Daubigny (French)

Opposite – *Women of a zenana bathing at night*, c. late 18th century, opaque watercolour, possibly Datia style, Unknown artist (Indian)

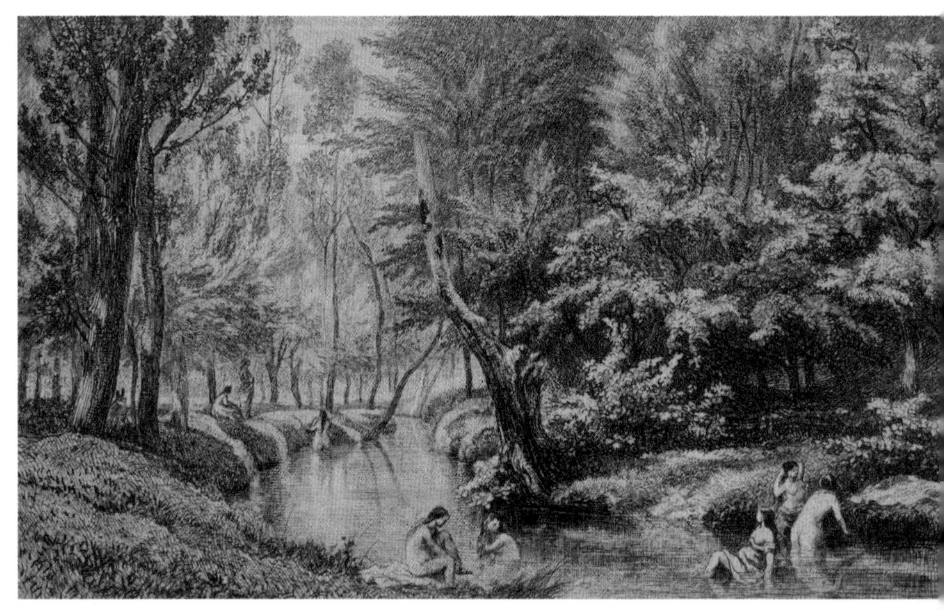

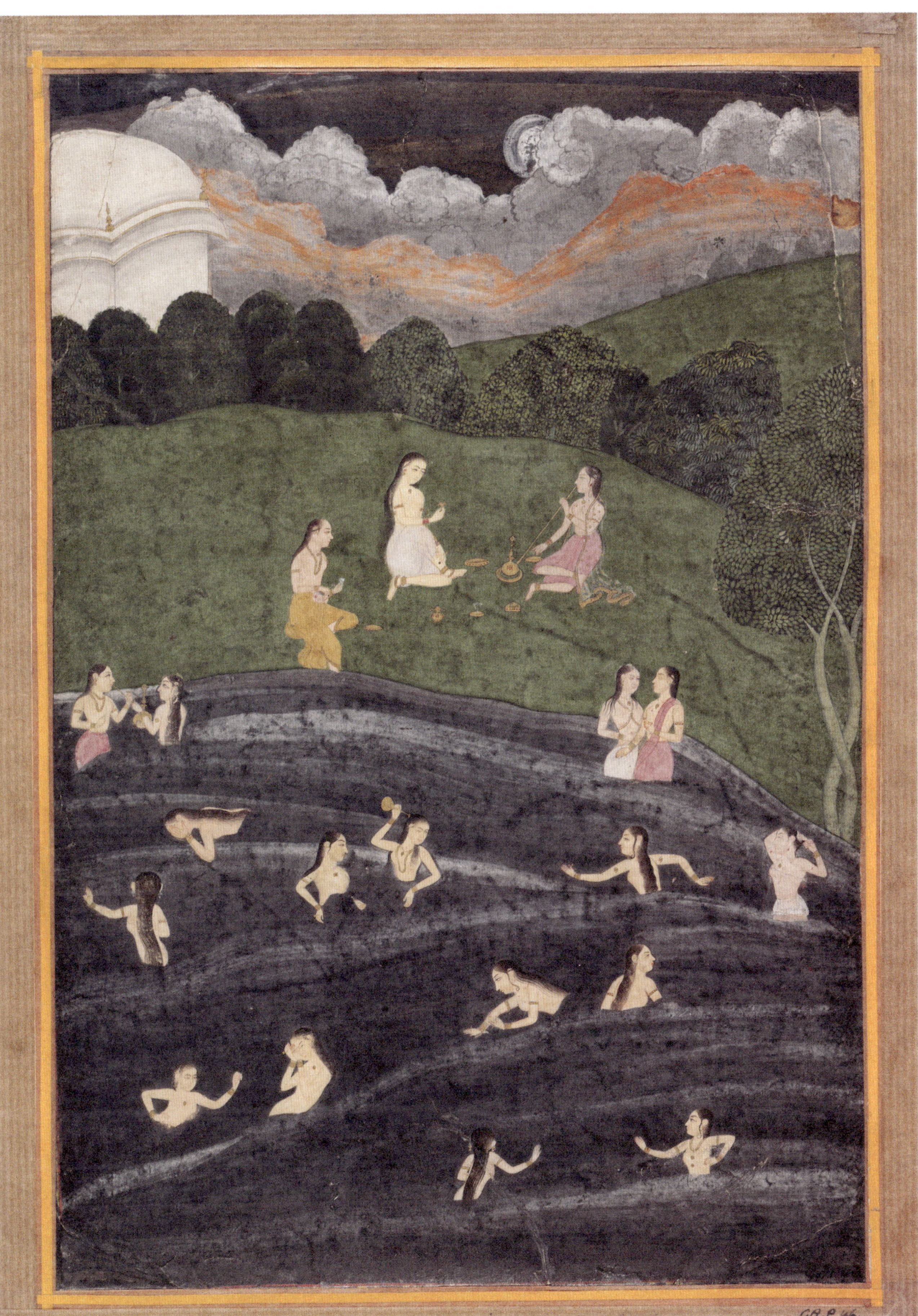
GM.P.46

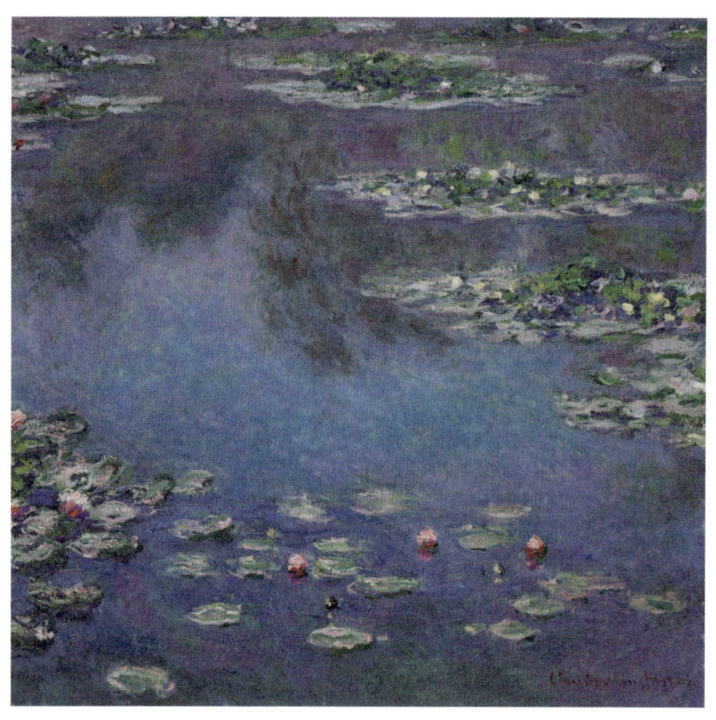

LOVINGLY OBSERVED AND PAINTED BY MANY ARTISTS ACROSS CULTURES, WATER LILIES OR NYMPHAEA DECORATE THE SURFACES LIKE LANTERNS ON THE WATER.

Top – *Water Lilies*, 1906, oil on canvas, Claude Monet (French)

Bottom – *Benten Pond, Shiba*, 1929, colour woodblock print, Kawase Hasui (Japanese)

Opposite – *Prince Dara Shikoh (1615–1659) Visits a Sage*, c. 1750, opaque watercolour and gold on paper, attributed to Hunhar II (Indian)

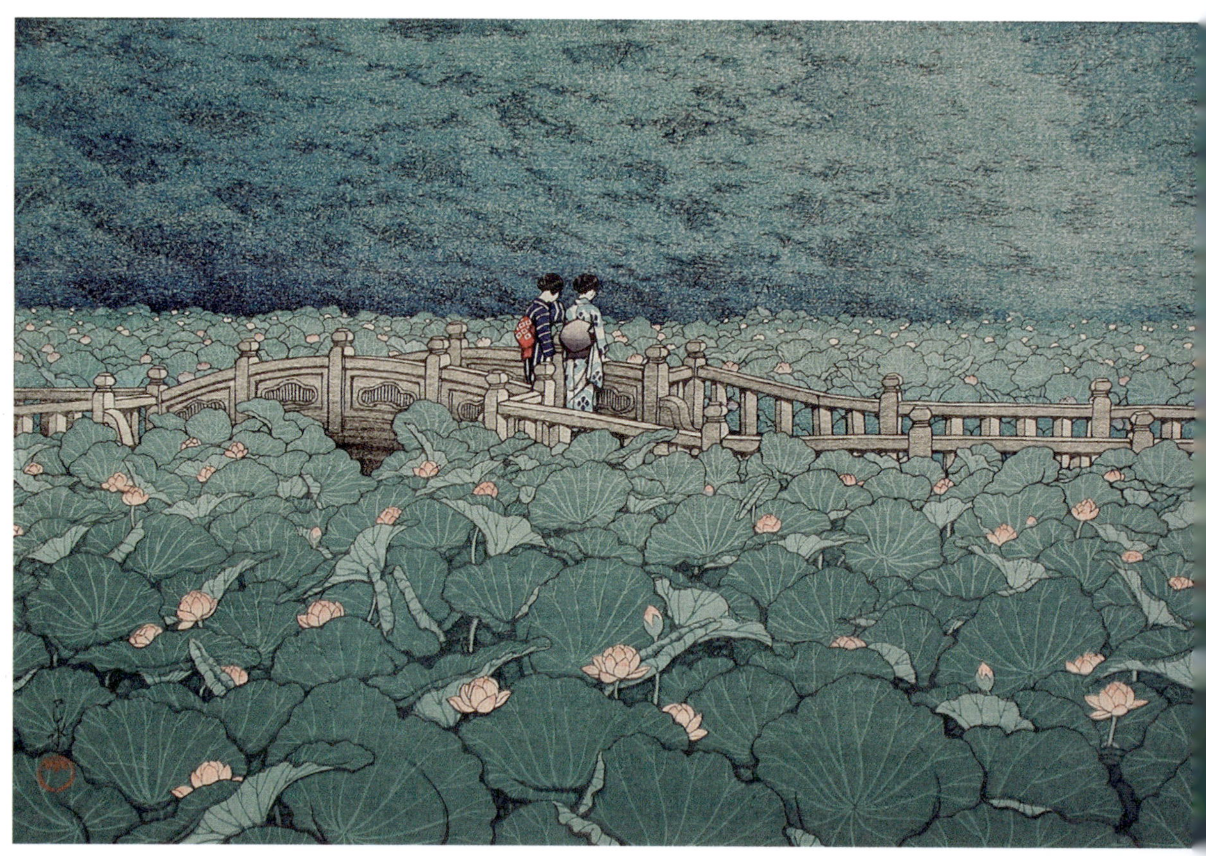

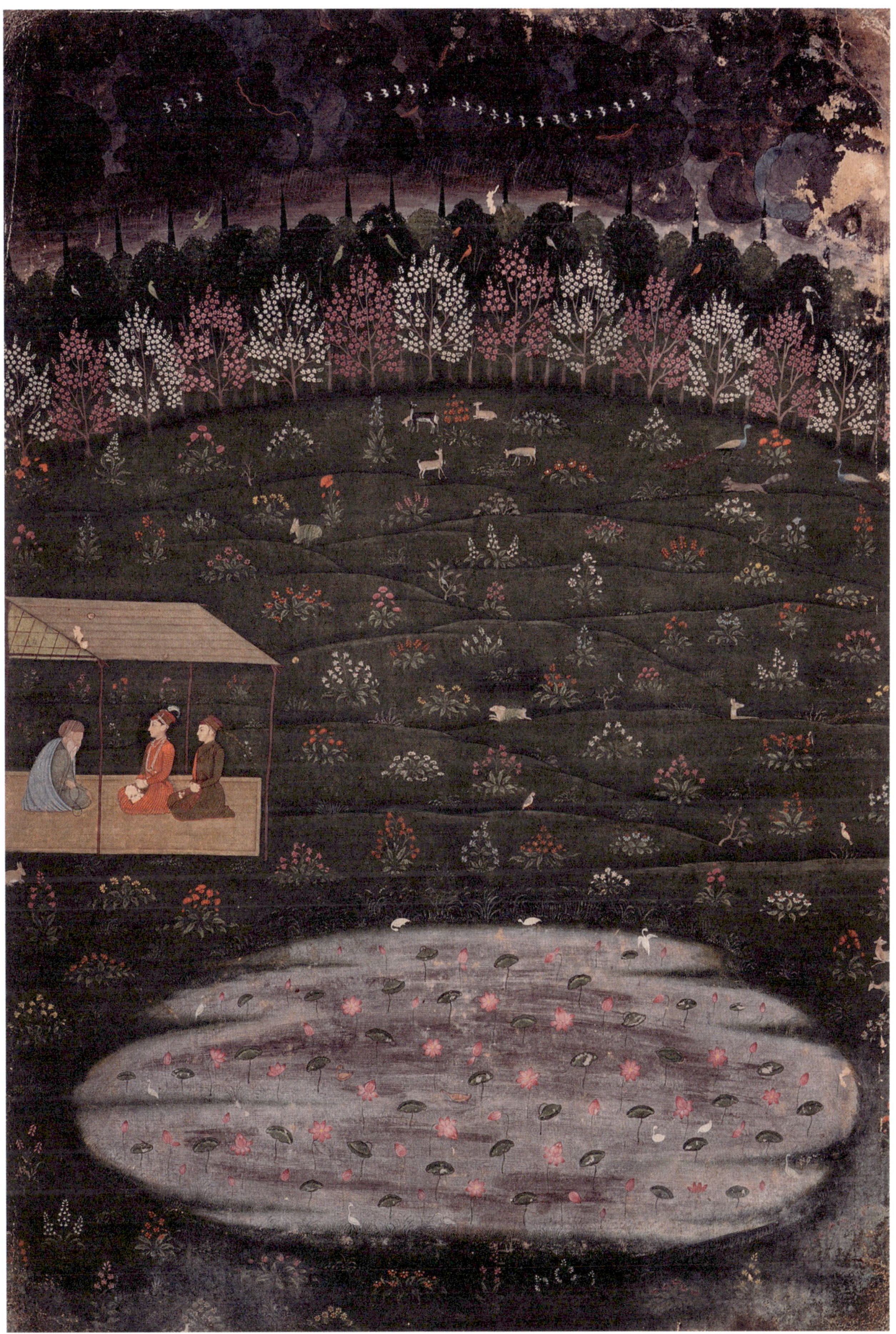

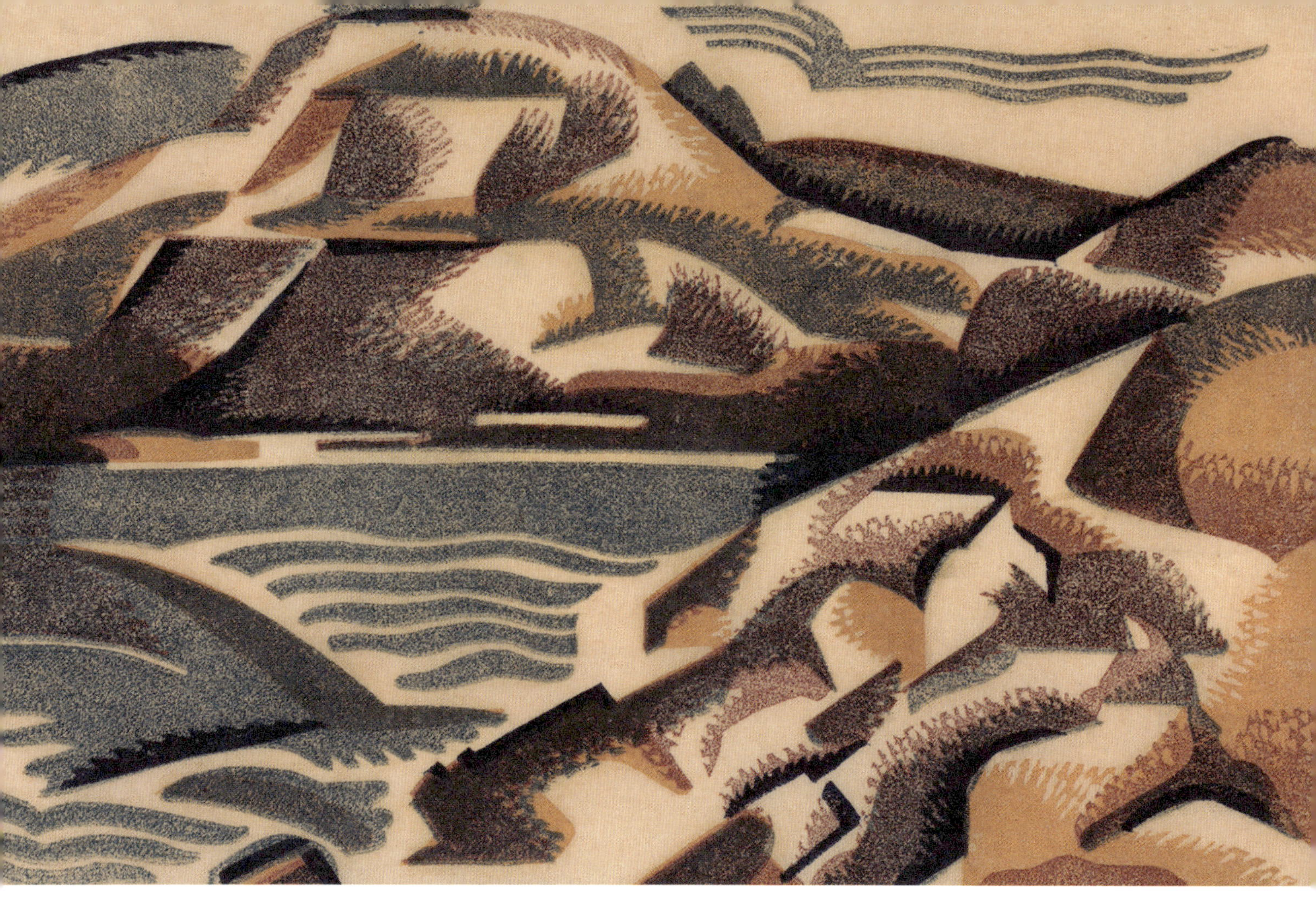

202 *Chapman's Pool*, 1935, colour linocut on Oriental paper, Dorrit Black (Australian)

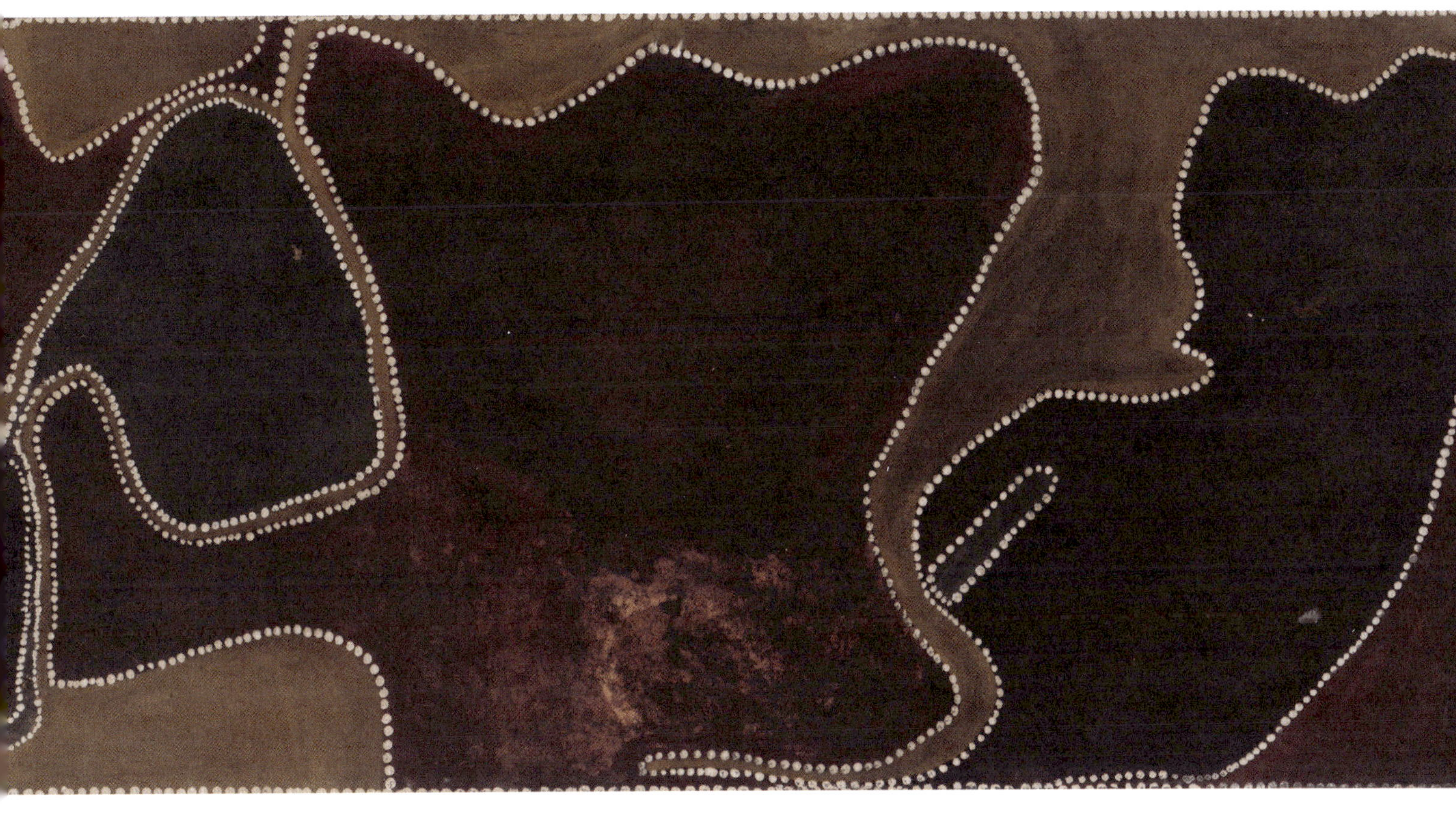

OCHRE AND BROWNS HAVE BEEN USED TO REFLECT WATER COUNTRY IN THESE PAINTINGS. THE WATERING HOLES AND WATERWAYS MAPPED IN ROVER JOOLAMA THOMAS'S PAINTING CONTINUE TO CONVEY KNOWLEDGE AND THE STORY OF HIS PEOPLE. TAKE A CLOSE LOOK AT THE LINES AND PERSPECTIVES USED TO EXPRESS THE COLOURS OF WATER.

Lurinjipungu (Clara Springs) (detail), 1984, natural pigments, binders on plywood, Rover Joolama Thomas (Kukatja/Wangkajunga people, Australian)

Glass mosaic bowl fragment, c. late 1st century BCE–early 1st century CE, glass; cast, Unknown artist (Roman)

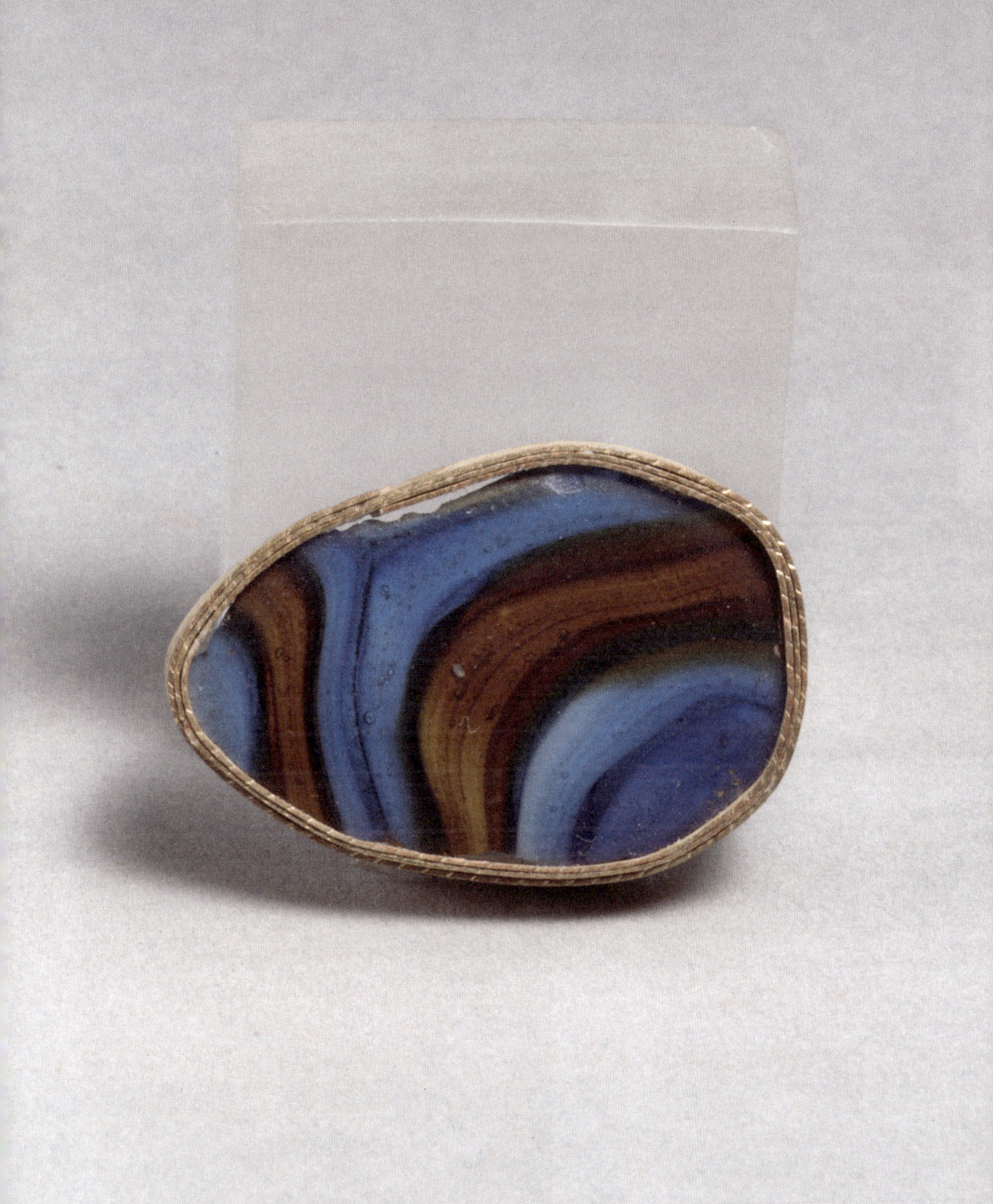

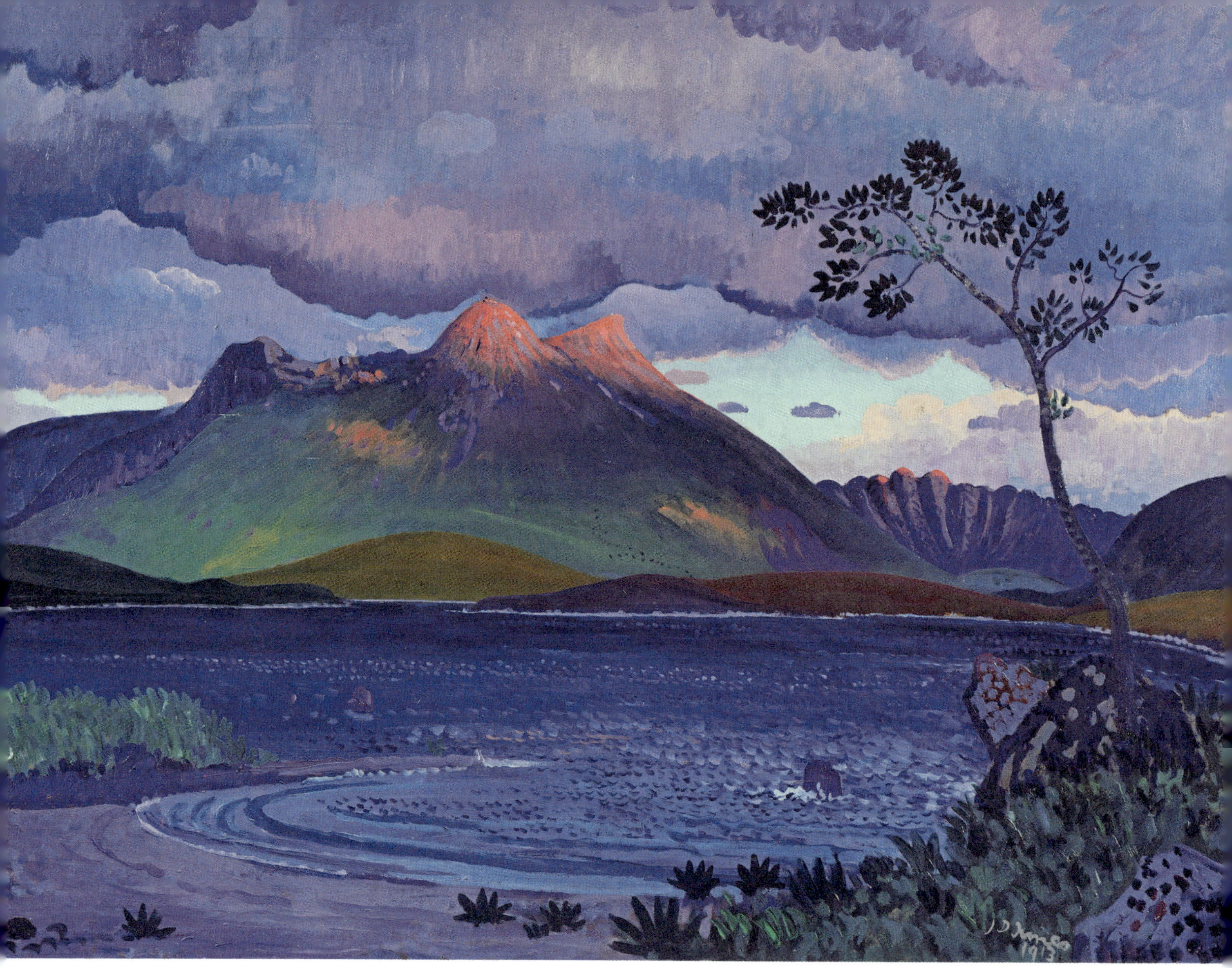

Top – *Arenig, North Wales*, 1913, oil paint on plywood, James Dickson Innes (Welsh)

Bottom – *Mt. McKinley and Wonder Lake, Mt. McKinley National Park, Alaska*, 1947, gelatin silver photograph, Ansel Adams (American)

Opposite top – *Vista Lake*, 1932, wood engraving on laid paper, Walter Joseph Phillips (Canadian)

Opposite bottom – *Lake and Mountains*, 1928, oil on canvas, Lawren S. Harris (Canadian)

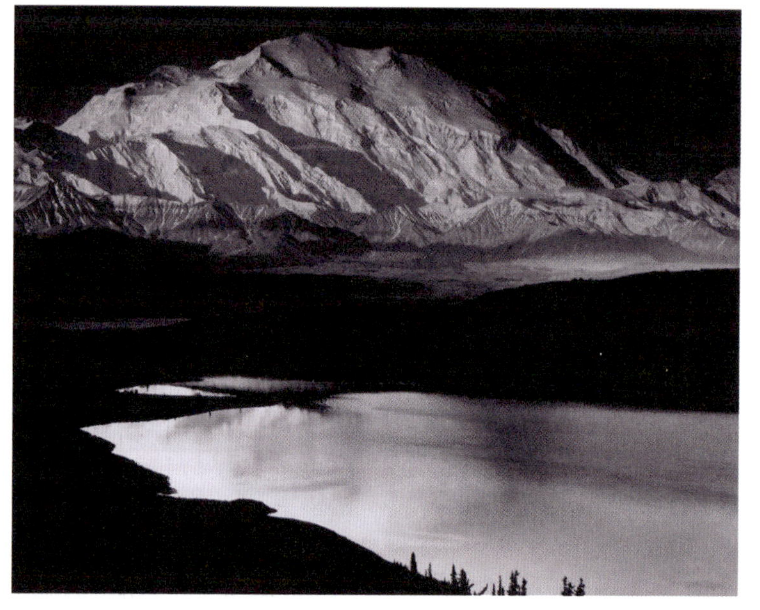

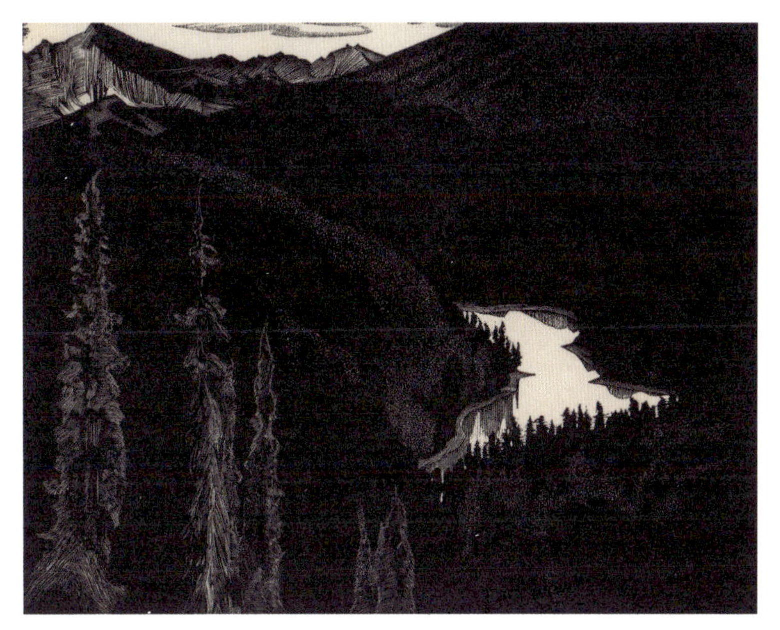

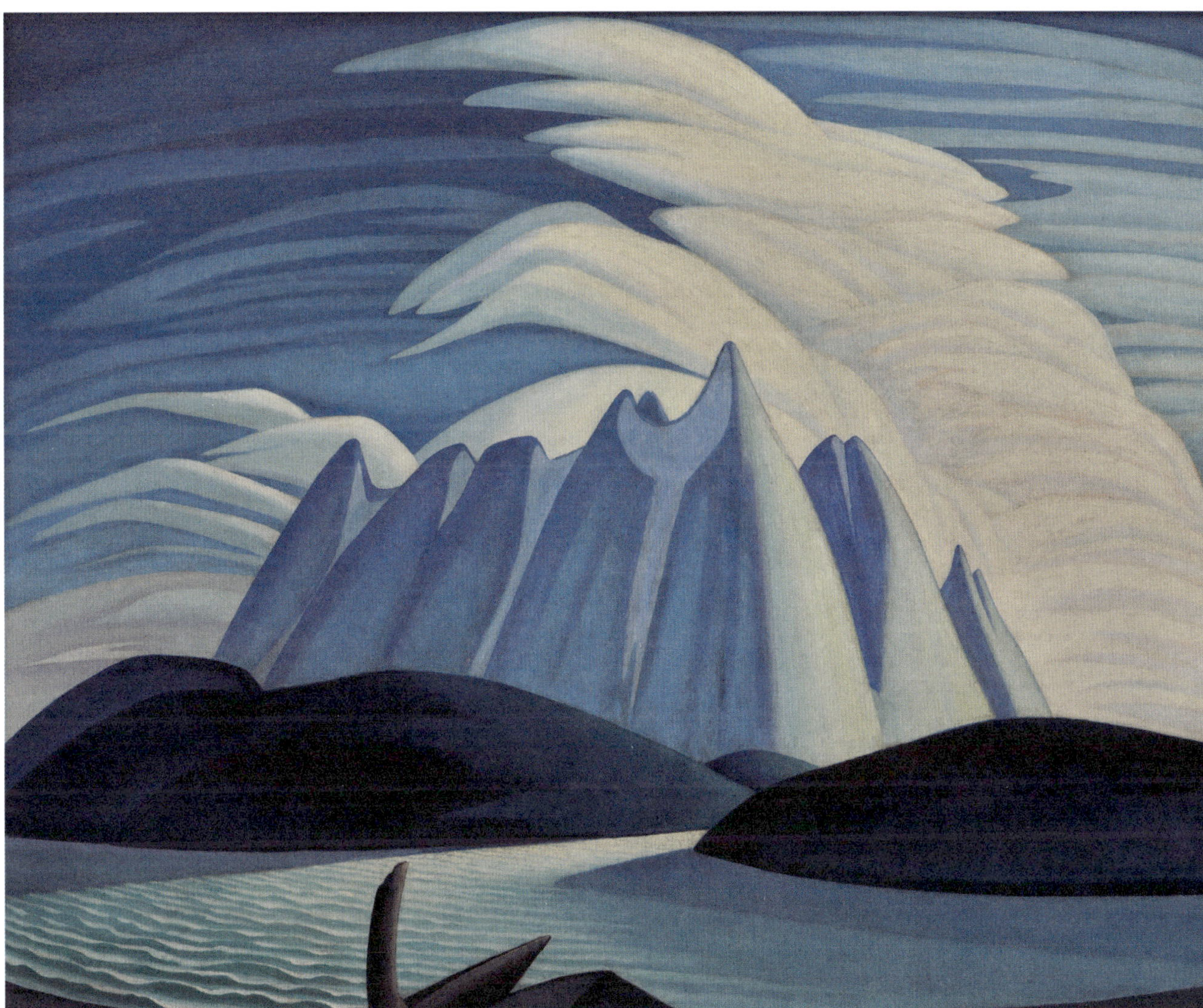

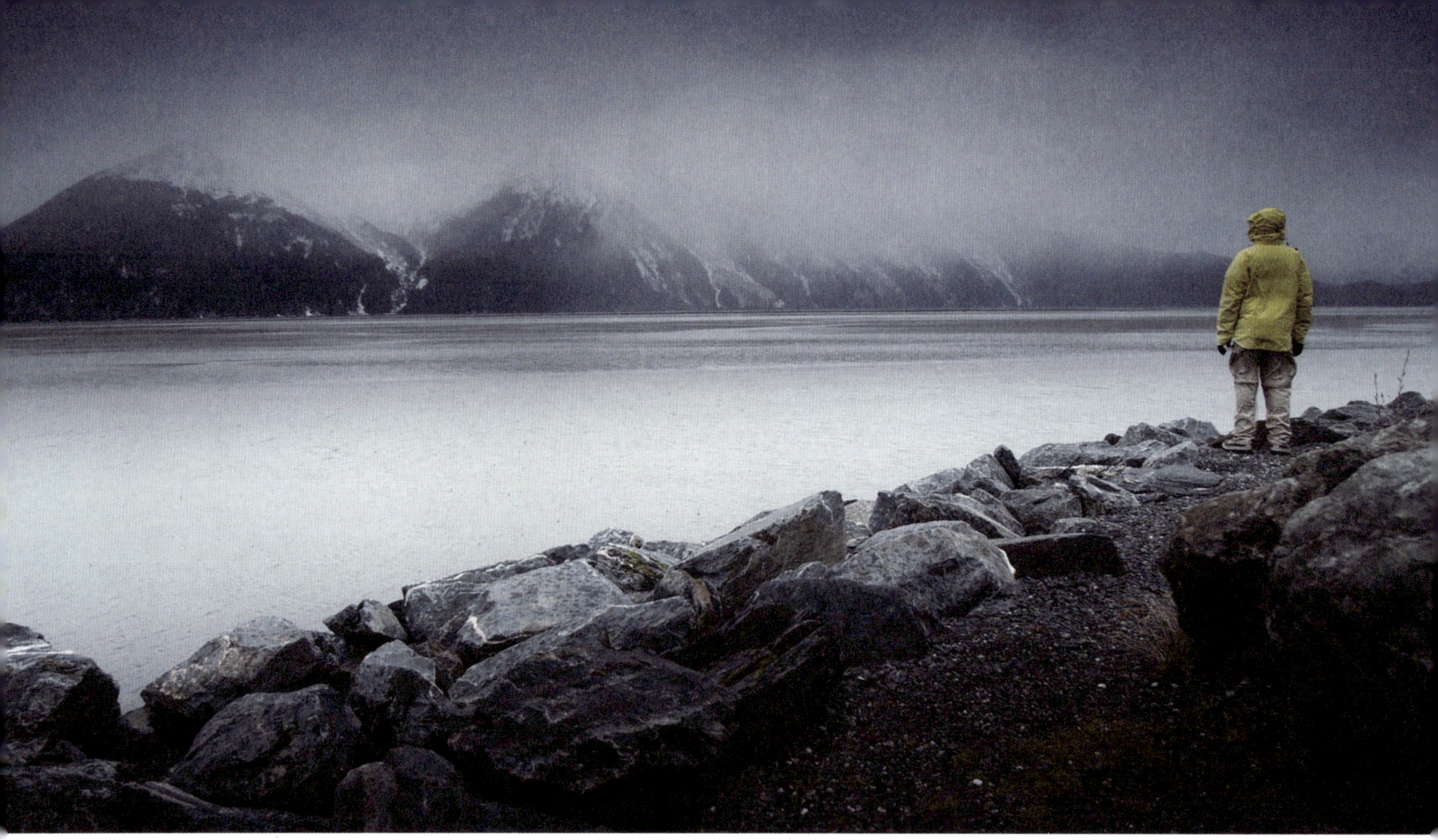

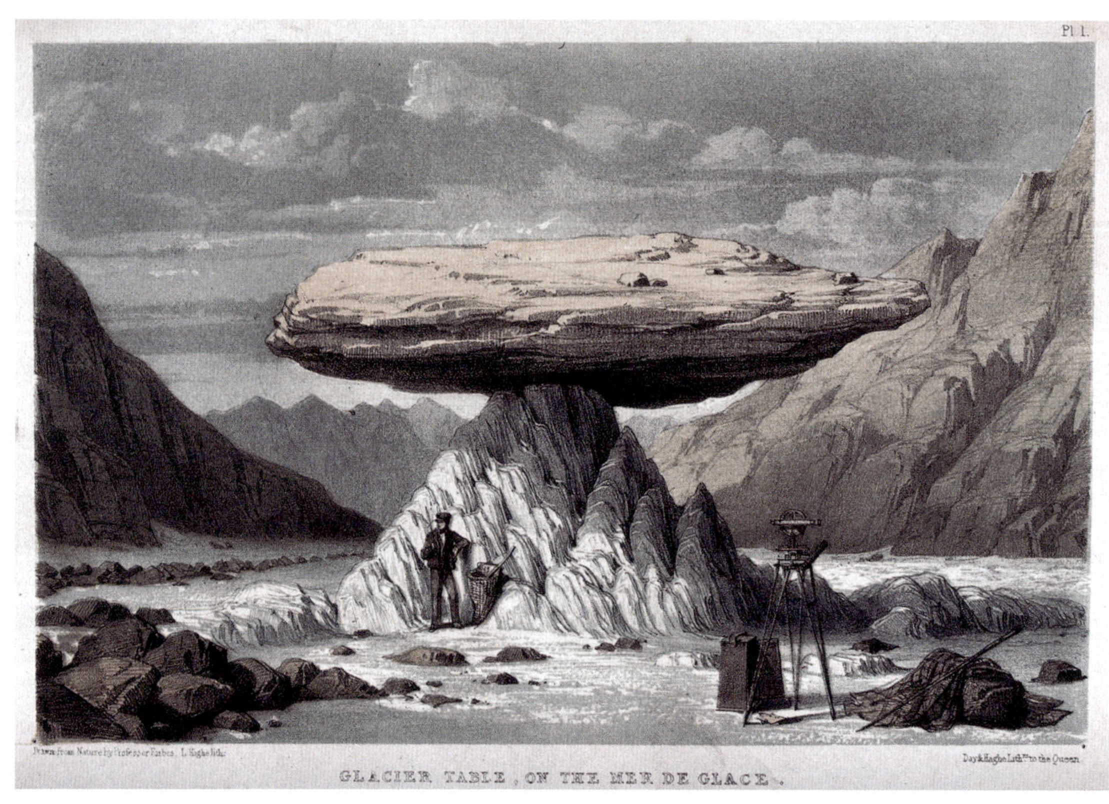
Pl. I.
Drawn from Nature by Professor Forbes. L. Haghe lith.
Day & Haghe Lithrs to the Queen
GLACIER TABLE, ON THE MER DE GLACE.

GLACIERS & ICEBERGS

ARTISTS WHO HAVE CAPTURED GLACIERS HAVE OFTEN ALSO REMARKED ON THE SURROUNDING ATMOSHPHERE. SCOTTISH ARTIST WILHELMINA BARNS-GRAHAM (SEE PAGES 210–11) WROTE THE FOLLOWING NOTE UPON HER VISIT TO THE GRINDELWALD GLACIERS IN SWITZERLAND IN 1949 '[THE] MASSIVE STRENGTH AND SIZE OF THE GLACIERS, THE FANTASTIC SHAPES, THE CONTRAST OF SOLIDITY AND TRANSPARENCY, THE MANY REFLECTED COLOURS IN STRONG LIGHT, THE WARMTH OF THE SUN MELTING AND CHANGING THE FORMS, IN A FEW DAYS A THINNESS COULD BECOME A HOLE ... A PIECE COULD DISINTEGRATE AND FALL OFF, BREAKING THE SILENCE WITH A SHARP CRACK AND ITS ECHOES. IT SEEMED TO BREATHE!'

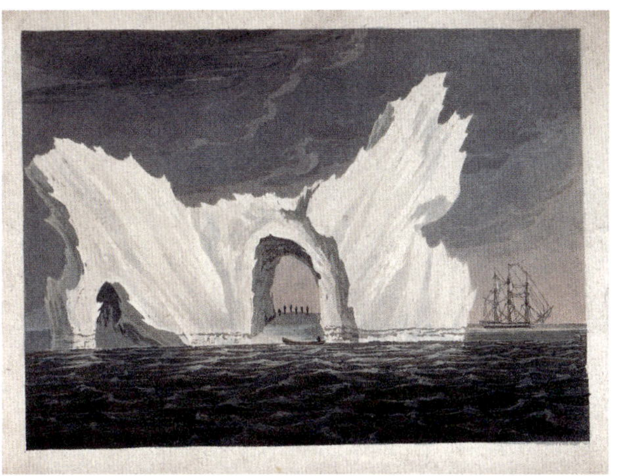

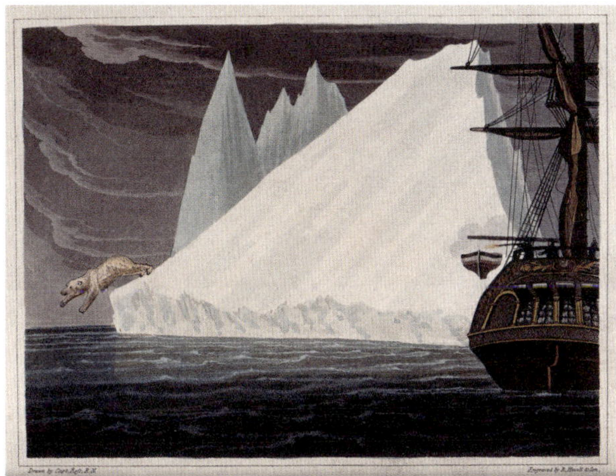

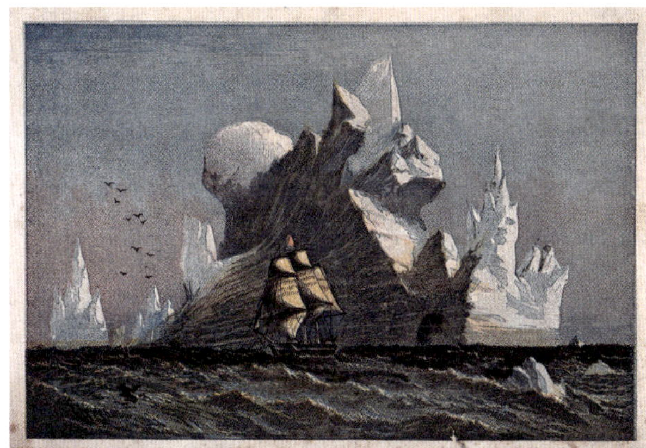

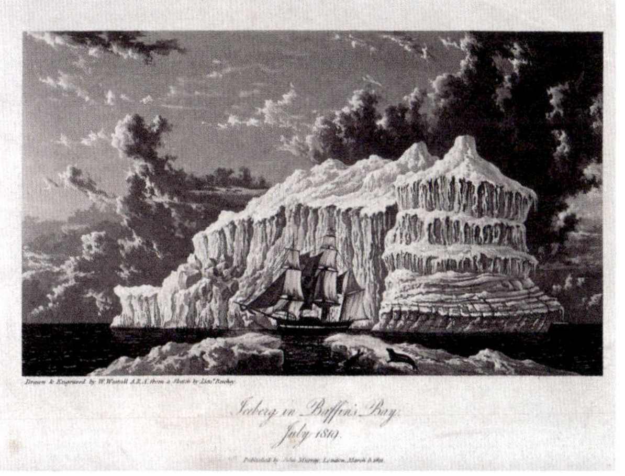

Opposite top – Movie still from *Mnemosyne*, 2010, film still, Sir John Akomfrah RA (director) (Ghanaian/British)

Opposite bottom – *Mont Blanc: a flat boulder raised on a pinnacle of ice*, 19th century, coloured lithograph, Louis Haghe (Belgian) after James David Forbes (British)

This page, top to bottom – *Meteorology: a large iceberg including an arch within which people are standing*, 19th century, coloured aquatint with watercolour, Unknown artist (British)

A polar bear plunges into the sea from a very steep iceberg while fishermen look on from a nearby trawler, 1819, engraving with etching, engraving by R Havell after J Ross (British)

A large iceberg with a ship sailing past it, c. 1800–99, engraving with etching, engraving by or after Edwin Weedon (British)

Geology: a large iceberg in Baffin Bay, 1821, aquatint with etching, engraved by W Westall after F W Beechey (British)

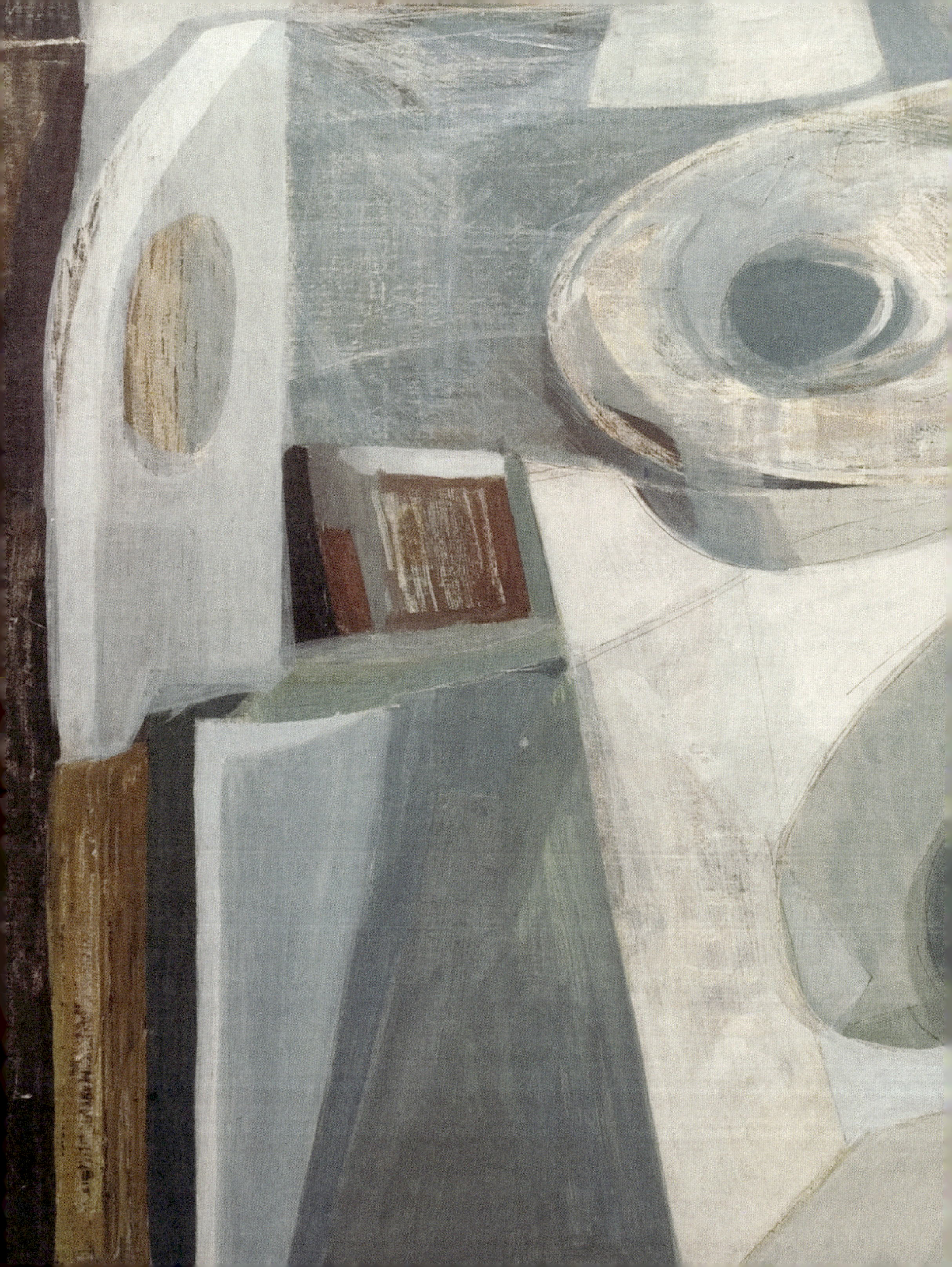

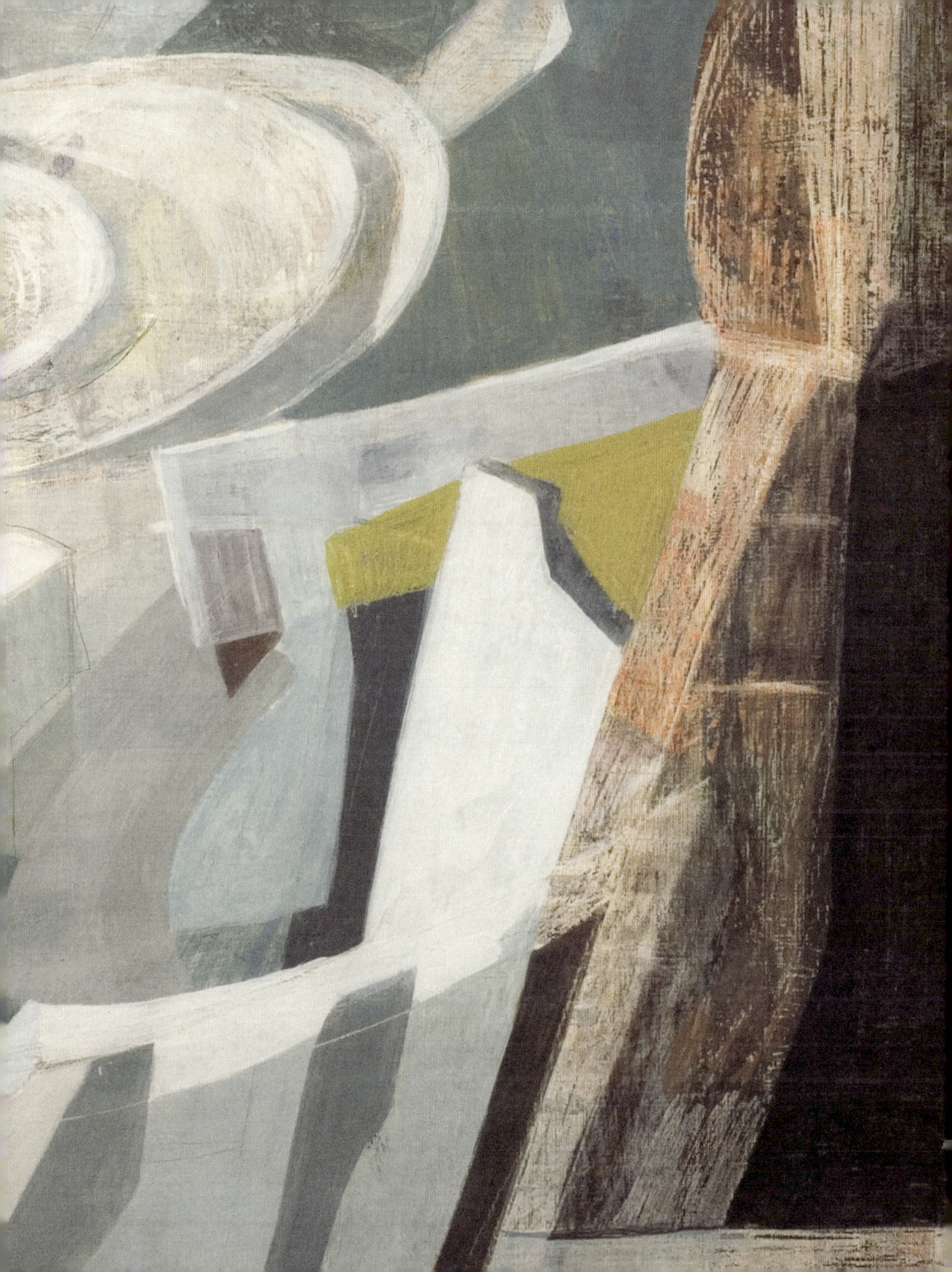

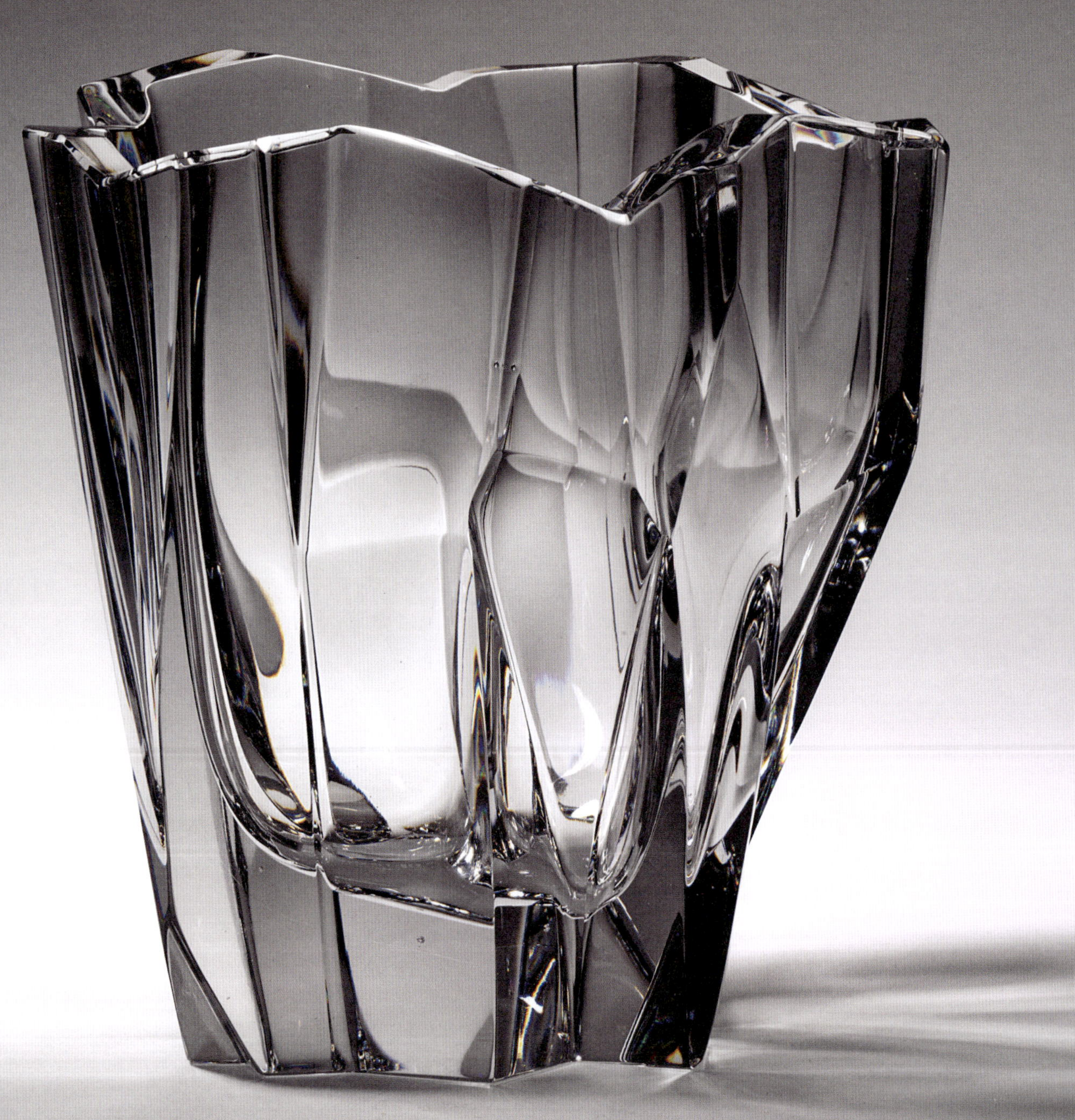

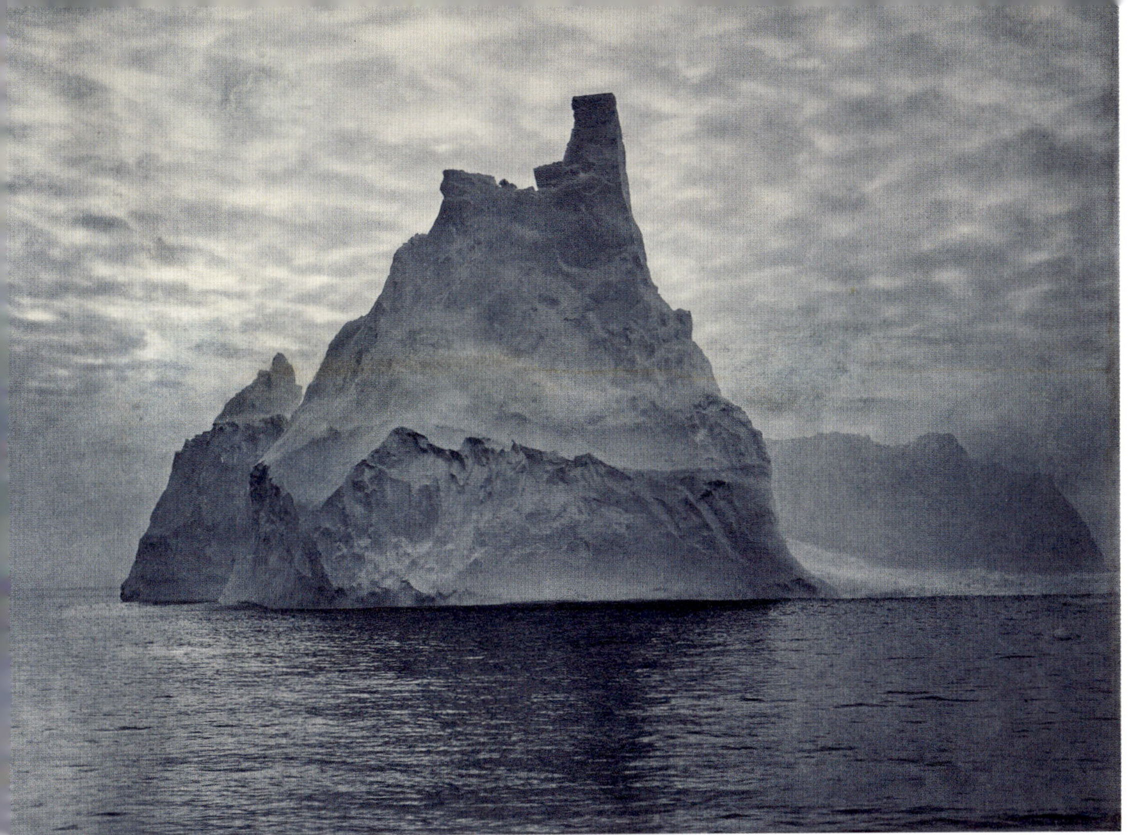

OBSERVE THE SHARP AND LUMINOUS QUALITY OF THE ICEBERG, WHAT VISUAL EFFECT DOES THE ARTIST USE TO CREATE THE IMPRESSION OF ICE-COLD AIR? IF WE ONLY SEE THE TIP OF THE ICEBERG IMAGINE THE SCALE OF WHAT LIES BENEATH.

Previous – *Glacier Vortex* (detail), 1951, oil on canvas, Wilhelmina Barns-Graham (Scottish)

Opposite – *Iceberg*, 1950 (designed), 1962–63 (made), mould-blown glass, Tapio Wirkkala (Finnish)

Top – *No title (A turreted berg)*, 1913, carbon print, Frank Hurley (Australian)

Bottom – *Icebergs in the Southern Ocean, January and February 1861, Leaf 6*, 1861, watercolour, pen and ink, Arthur Dobree (Australian)

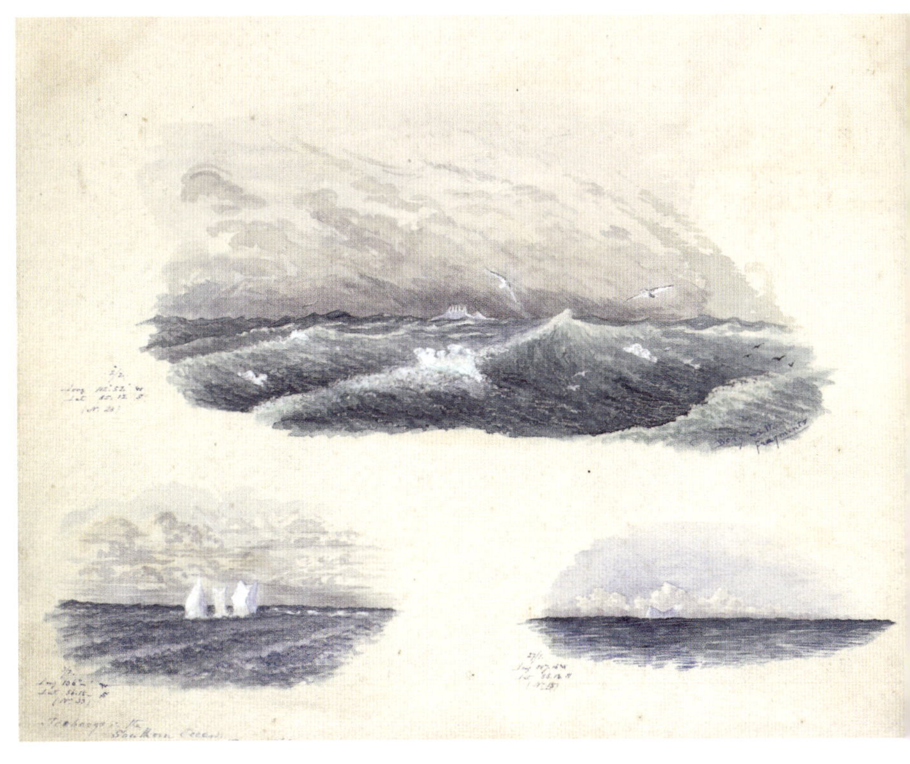

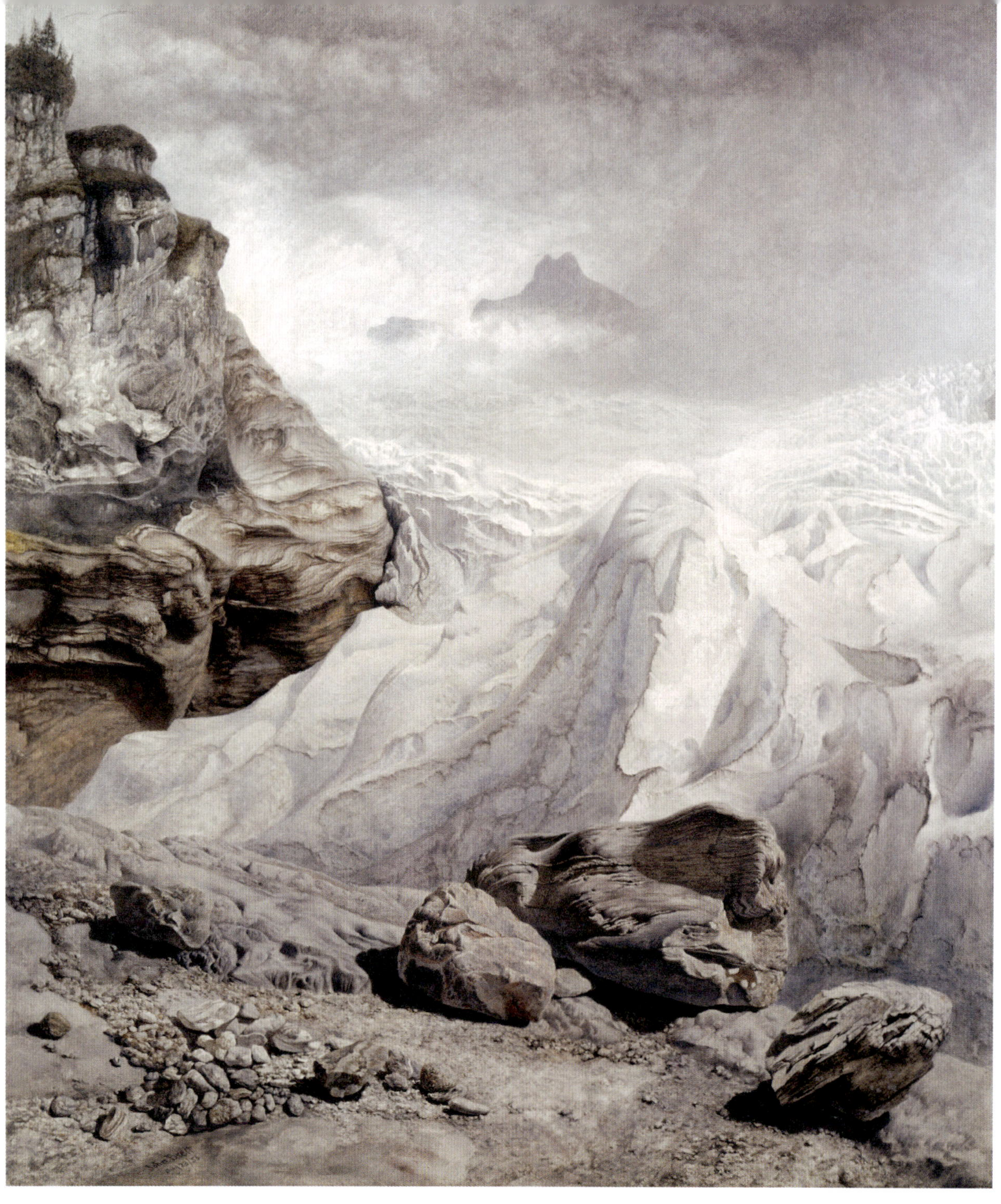

Above – *Glacier of Rosenlaui*, 1856, oil paint on canvas, John Brett (British)

Opposite top – *The Glacier of Simmenthal*, 1774, watercolour and graphite on paper, Samuel Hieronymous Grimm (Swiss)

Opposite bottom – *The Source of the Arveyron below the Glacier du Bois and Mer de Glace*, 1802, graphite, watercolour and gouache on paper, Joseph Mallord William Turner (British)

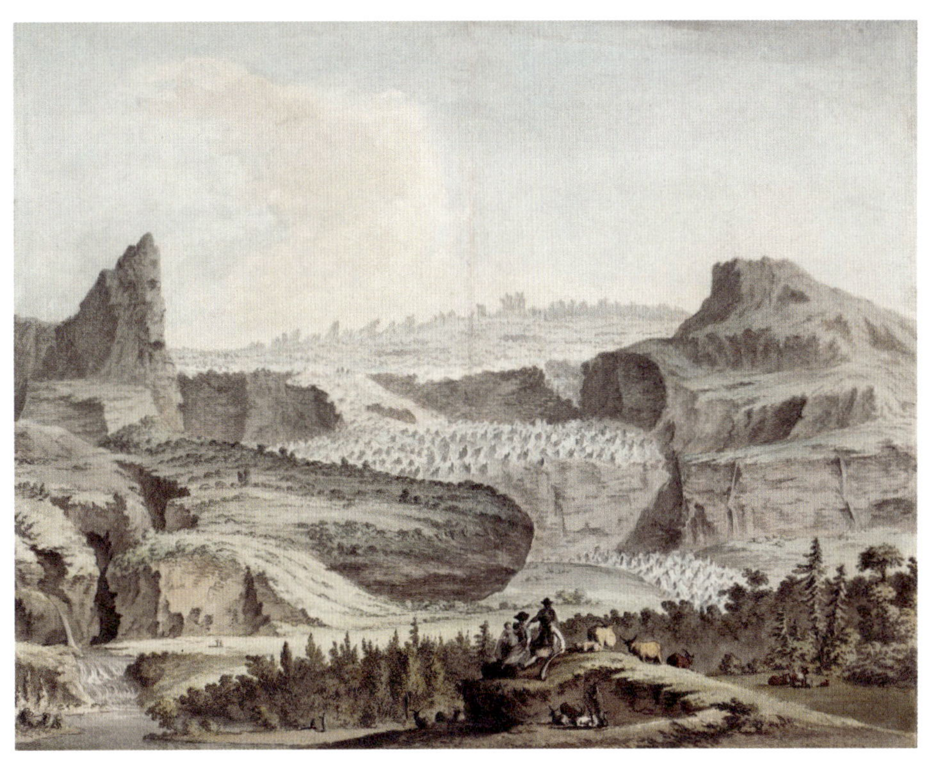

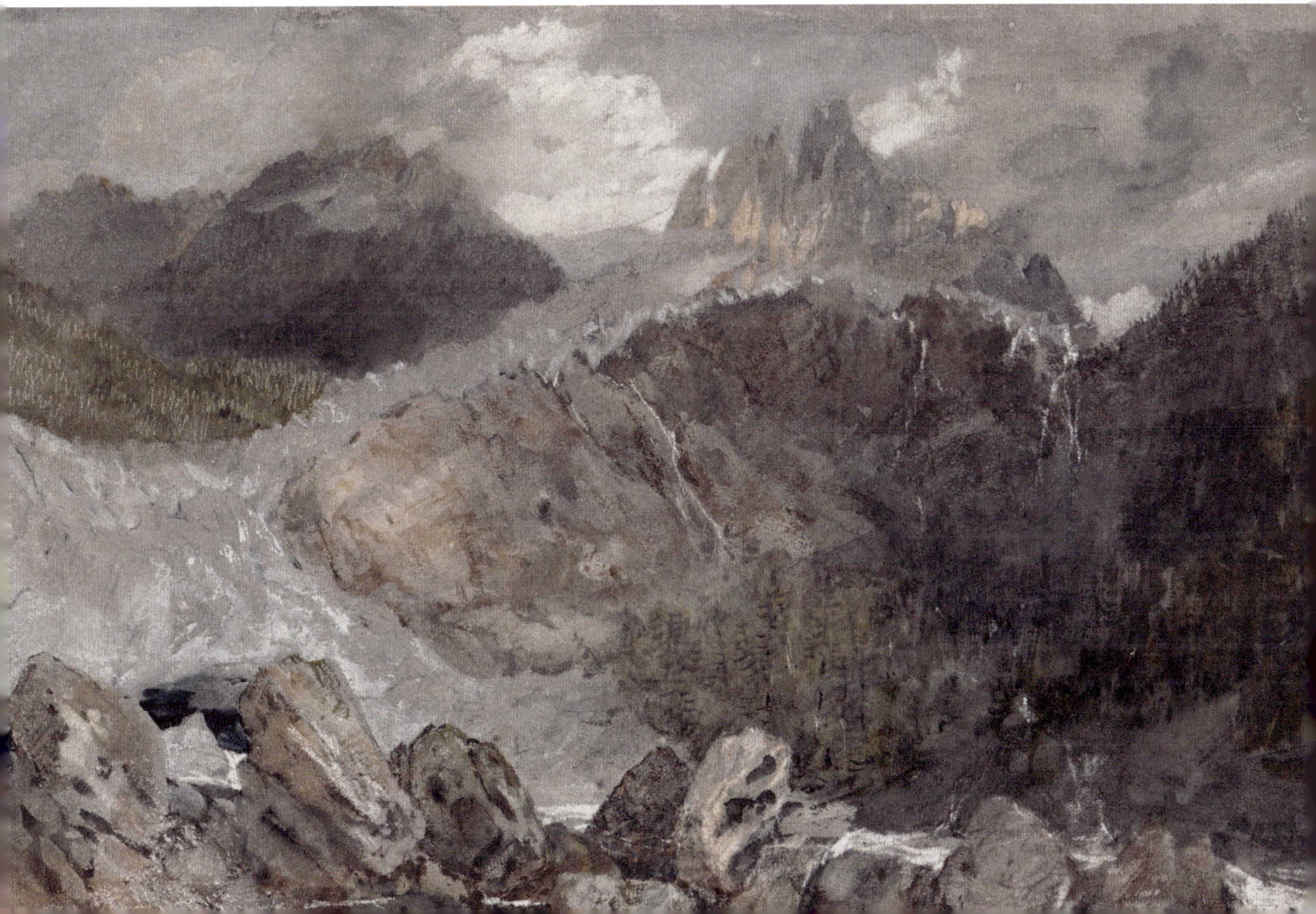

SKY

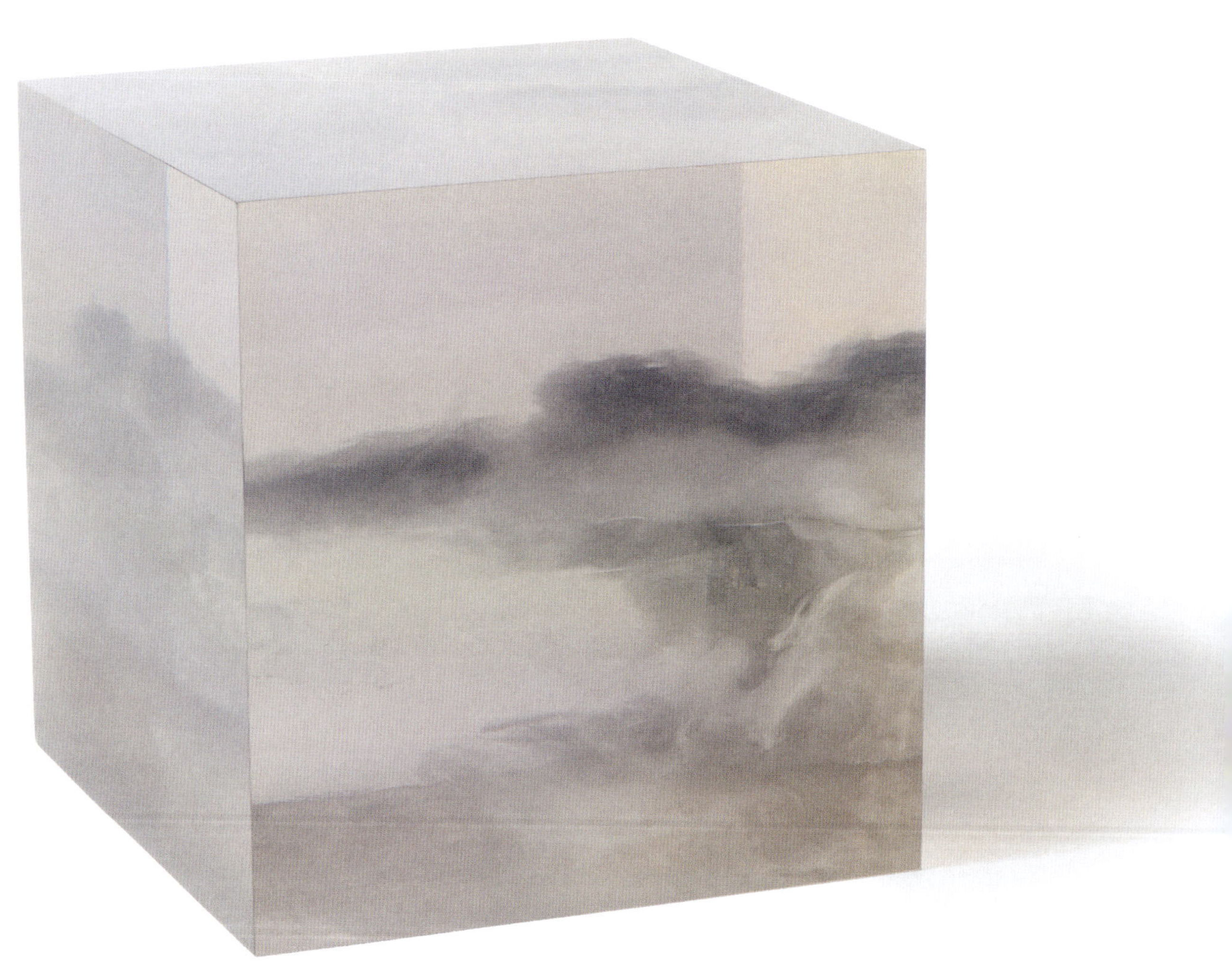

SKY

THE ELEMENTS OF THE SKY CAPTURE OUR IMAGINATION IN CURIOUS WAYS: THE PASSING CLOUDS, A CANOPY OF STARS, A NORTHERLY WIND, THE FULL MOON, A RADIANT SUN. ARTISTS ACROSS MILLENNIA HAVE DEMONSTRATED VARIOUS WAYS OF ILLUSTRATING ATMOSPHERE IN THEIR WORKS. TO RENDER THE NIGHT SKY, RAYS OF SUNSHINE OR A SOFT BREEZE REQUIRES INGENUITY AND CREATIVE SKILL. THE OBSERVATIONS MADE ON A MOONLIT WALK HAVE FOUND THEIR WAY INTO THE WORK OF MANY INSPIRED ARTISTS, WRITERS AND POETS.

Sitting quietly, sometimes silently, beneath the surface of works of art, are the stories of innovation and sometimes rebellion or even accident. Uncovering the stories is one of the great benefits of slower, deeper looking. The Korean Moon jar, for instance, a porcelain vessel that resembles the shape the moon, gained the attention of collectors in the later stages of the Joseon dynasty (1392–1910) (see page 287). Due to their large size, the jars are made by joining two half spheres, a process which inevitably results in subtle imperfections. These irregularities were revered by scholars and collectors who, through deep contemplation, observed an understated beauty and uniqueness in every jar created.

Since ancient times, the sky has been associated with the divine as it plays host to gods from various cultures and faiths. Evelyn De Morgan's (1855–1919) monumental pre-Raphaelite-style painting *Night and Sleep* (1878) shows the personification of Night (Nyx) listlessly moving across a dusk sky with her son Sleep (Hypnos) (see page 242). They soar above the landscape in a somnolent state, as their billowing crimson robes form a cloud-like shape. Night gently guides Sleep, as he scatters poppies from a great height in the hope of inducing a drowsy state into the mortals below. The entwined bodies of the pair recall the arrangement of Zephyrus and Aura featured in Botticelli's *The Birth of Venus* (c.1480).

When we think about the weather, we look to the sky for clues. English landscape painter John Constable (1776–1837) worked within the artistic and intellectual realms of Romanticism. In the early 1800s he began to take significant steps towards a new way of conceiving clouds and sky in his painting and sketches (see page 225). He was strongly influenced by the young chemist and amateur meteorologist Luke Howard, who in 1802 suggested a system for classifying clouds by identifying three key groups: cirrus, cumulus and stratus. This was a revelation for Constable, who took to observing the changing nature of clouds and conducting extensive studies outdoors in the Suffolk countryside – a practice he termed 'skying'. His approach was a departure from the formal expectations posited by the Royal Academy of Arts where clouds in paintings behaved in a manner that was convenient for the composition. Constable's oil sketches of storm fronts and driving rain from blackened clouds appear to be rendered from within the weather cell, unedited from direct observation, as opposed to a prescribed blueprint for skies.

The sky can be uplifting with its stunning range of hues. It reminds us that we are part of an infinite and astounding universe, its changing state often impacting our mood and outlook. In modern times the dark night sky has increasingly eluded us. It requires a trip beyond densely packed and brightly lit urban environments to truly see the stars and appreciate a moonlit landscape. As a result, we have made a profound impact on the nocturnal habits of animals and birdlife, and even our own circadian rhythms. We have become subservient to systems and algorithms that mean we are less likely to observe subtle changes in the environment, taking pause only when a catastrophic system threatens to impinge on our self-designed daily lives.

Previous – *Small Cloud Box*, 1966, cast polyester resin, Peter Alexander (American)

By engaging in the practice of slow looking in nature we also need to be prepared for the grief it may yield as it will inevitably reveal the impact of our actions. Works of art that have the natural world as their subject matter celebrate the beauty, expose the devastation, and defend the majesty of nature. They provide us with an insight into ourselves, both individually and collectively. Some of the artists and writers featured here used their practice to raise critical awareness of the changing nature of the environment. They started by looking at the world around them.

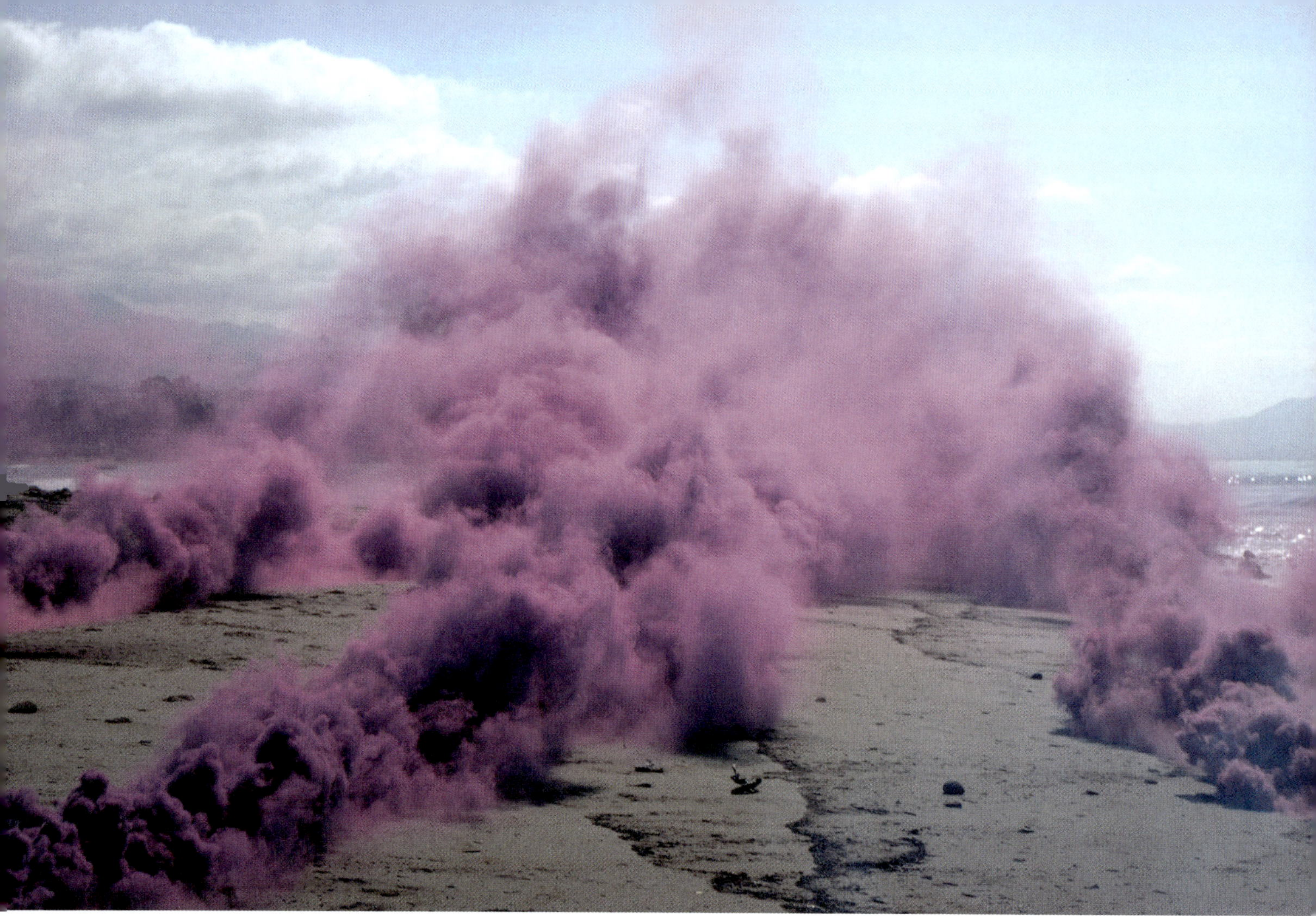

CLEAR BLUE SKIES HAVE AN UPLIFTING EFFECT ON OUR MOOD, BUT ARTISTS ARE MORE OFTEN DRAWN TO DRAMA AND CONTRAST. JUDY CHICAGO'S WORK OF A STRETCH OF ROLLING PURPLE CLOUDS RELEASES A SOFTNESS INTO THE ENVIRONMENT, TO FEMINISE IT RATHER THAN IMPOSE ANY PERMANENT FIXTURE ON THE LAND.

 Purple Atmosphere from the On Fire Suite, 2013, archival pigment print on paper, Judy Chicago (American)

CLOUDS

ON A OVERCAST DAY, OBSERVE THE SPEED WITH WHICH THE CLOUDS MOVE. DO THEY OBSCURE THE SUN, SUDDENLY CASTING A GLOOMY AMBIANCE? DO THEY RESEMBLE ANOTHER FORM OR SHAPE? QUIETLY EXAMINE THE CLOUDSCAPES IN PICTURES, NOTING ANY FAMILIAR OR UNUSUAL PATTERNS THAT COME INTO VIEW.

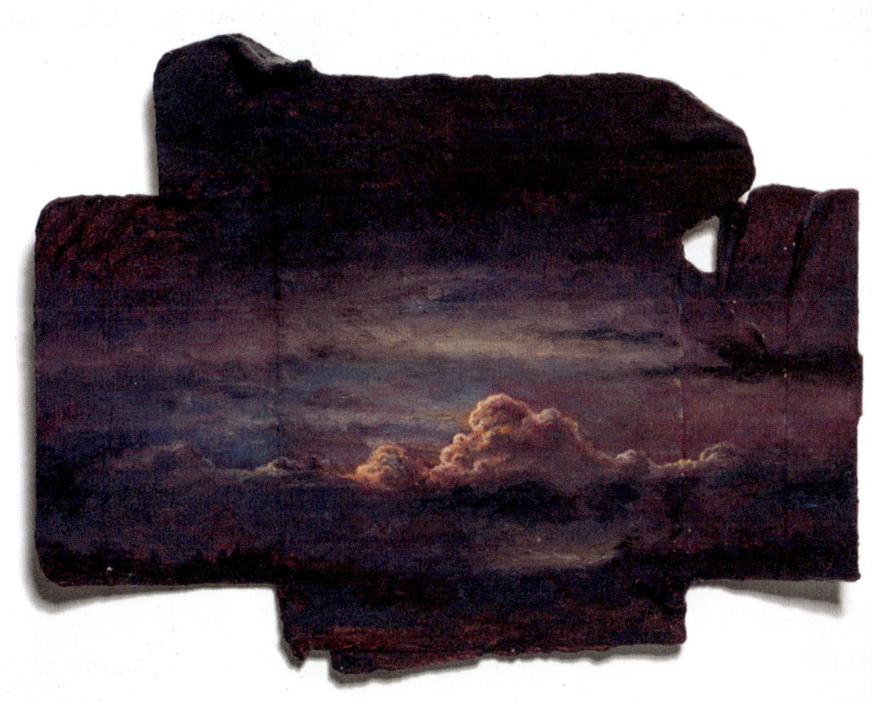

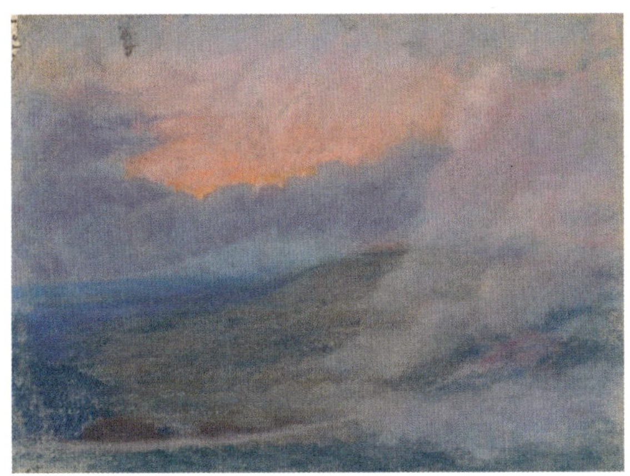

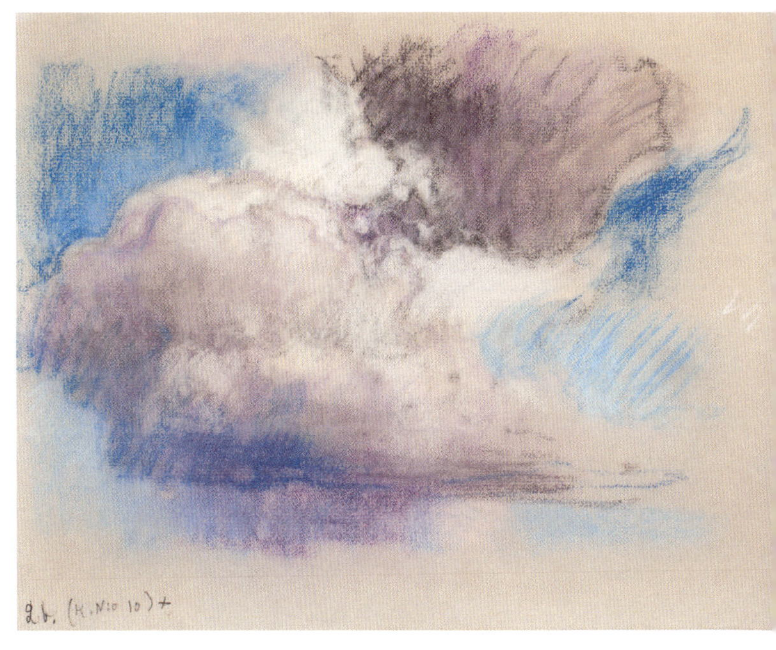

Top – *New York Trash Recycled 13*, 2007, oil on trash found on the street, Petri Ala-Maunus (Finnish)

Middle – *Paysage de montagne au soleil couchant avec effets de nuages*, c. 1896–1914, pastel laminated on recycled cardboard, François Garas (French)

Bottom – *Clouds*, c. 1910–12, page from sketchbook, watercolour and pastel on paper, Eero Järnefelt (Finnish)

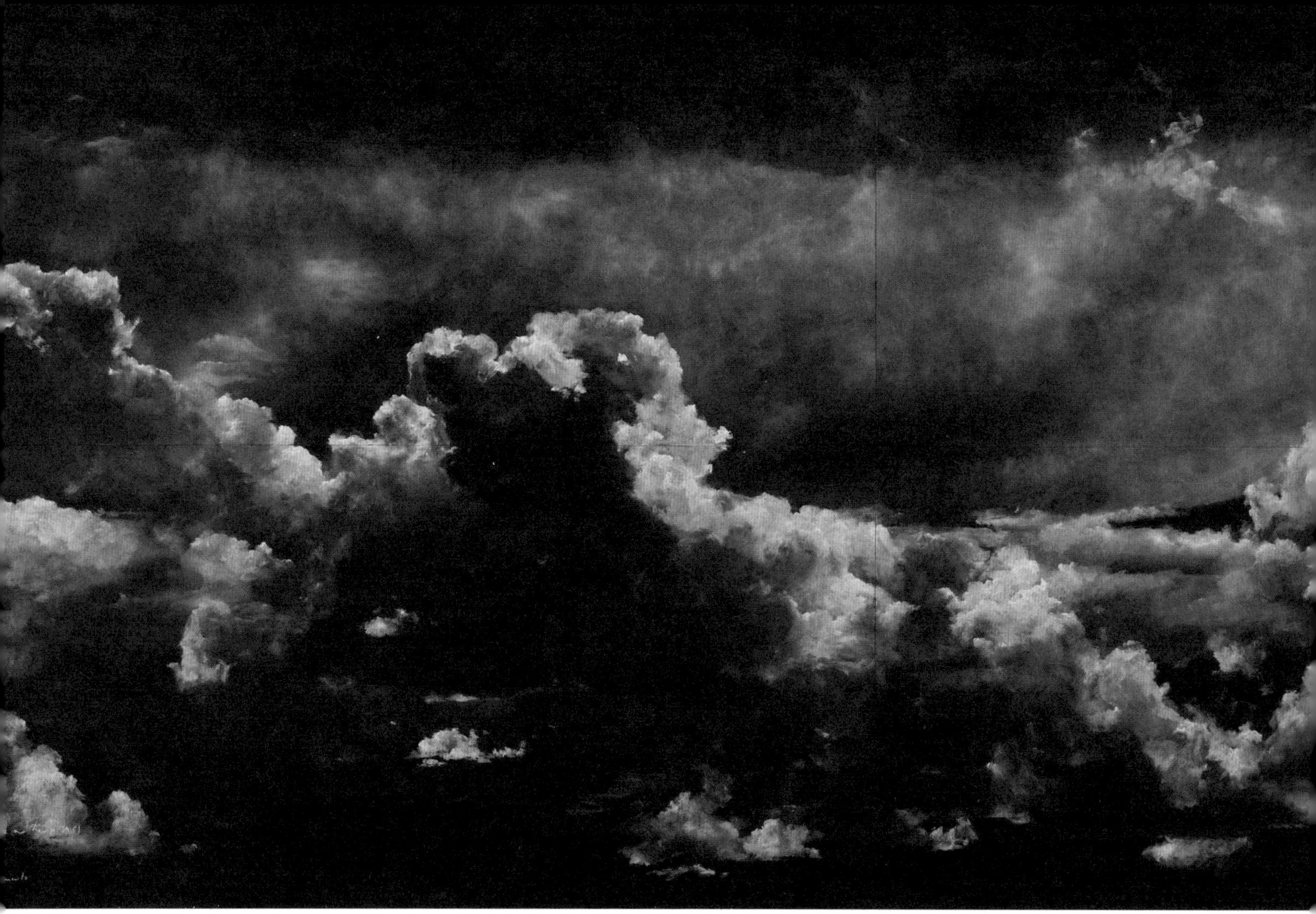

PICTURES ENTIRELY DEDICATED TO THE SKY CAN HAVE A PARTICULAR EFFECT ON A VIEWER. WHETHER THE LITTLE PATCH OF CLOUDS SEEN HERE BY JOHN CONSTABLE SKETCHED IN SOFT BLUE AND WISPY WHITE OR TACITA DEAN'S MONUMENTAL CHALKBOARD WORK OF LOW ALTITUDE, FLUFFY CUMULUS CLOUDS, THEY CREATE A SKY-HIGH FEELING OF BEING IN A MOVING CLOUDSCAPE.

Above – *Cúmulo*, 2016, chalk on blackboard, Tacita Dean (British)

Opposite – *Study of Cirrus Clouds*, c. 1822, oil on paper, John Constable (British)

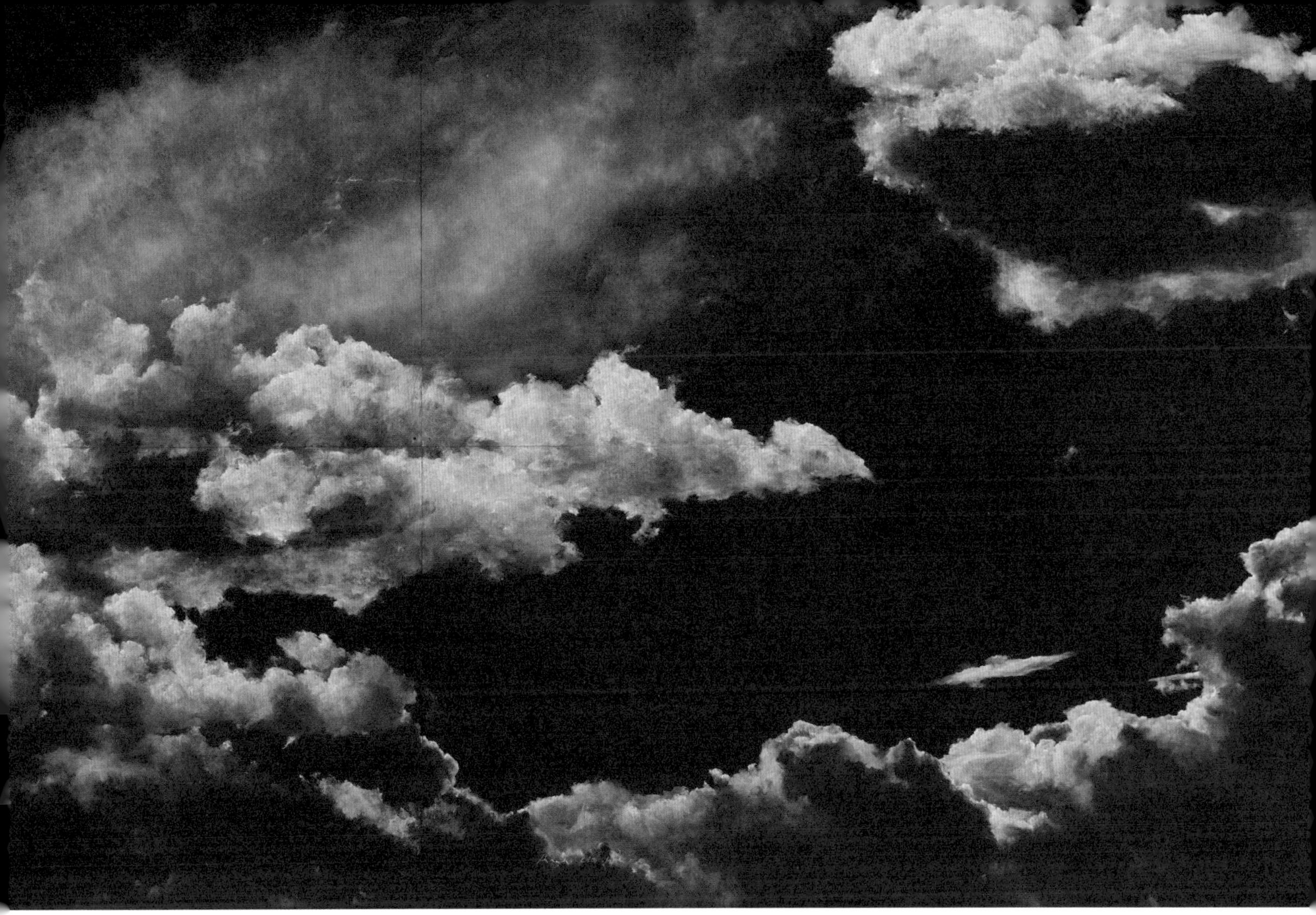

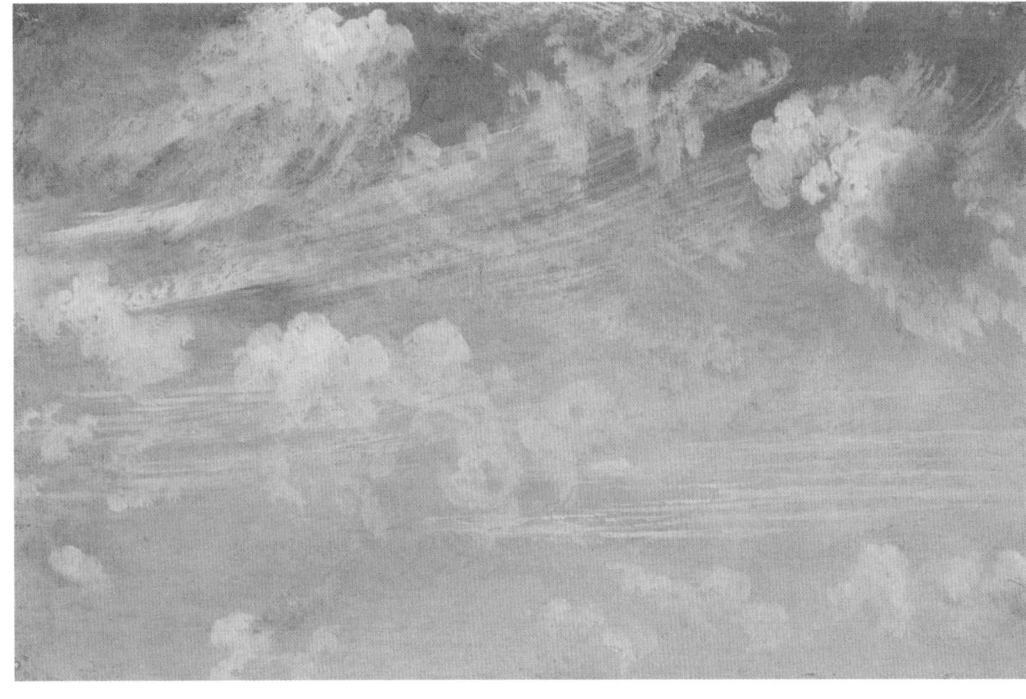

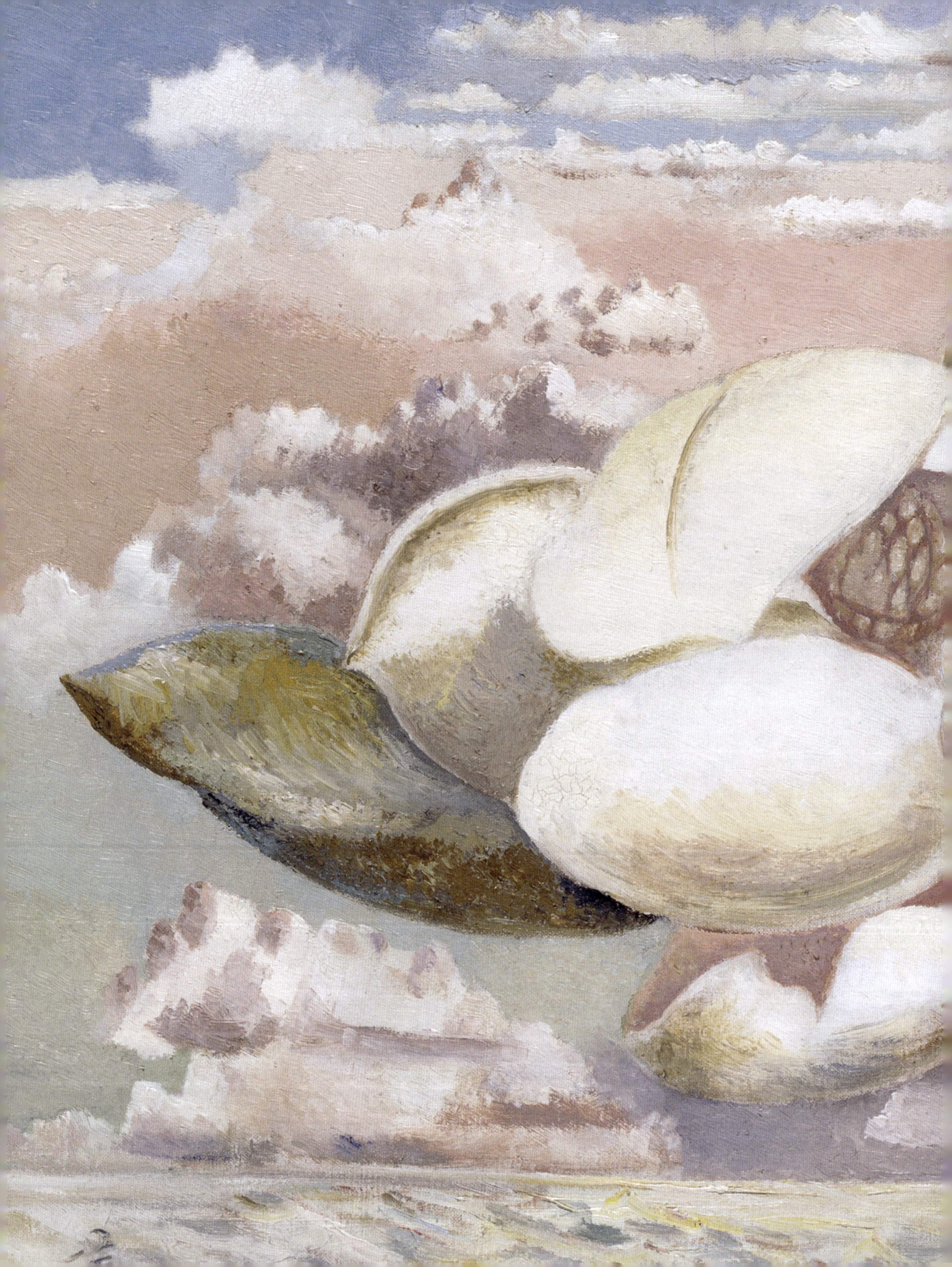

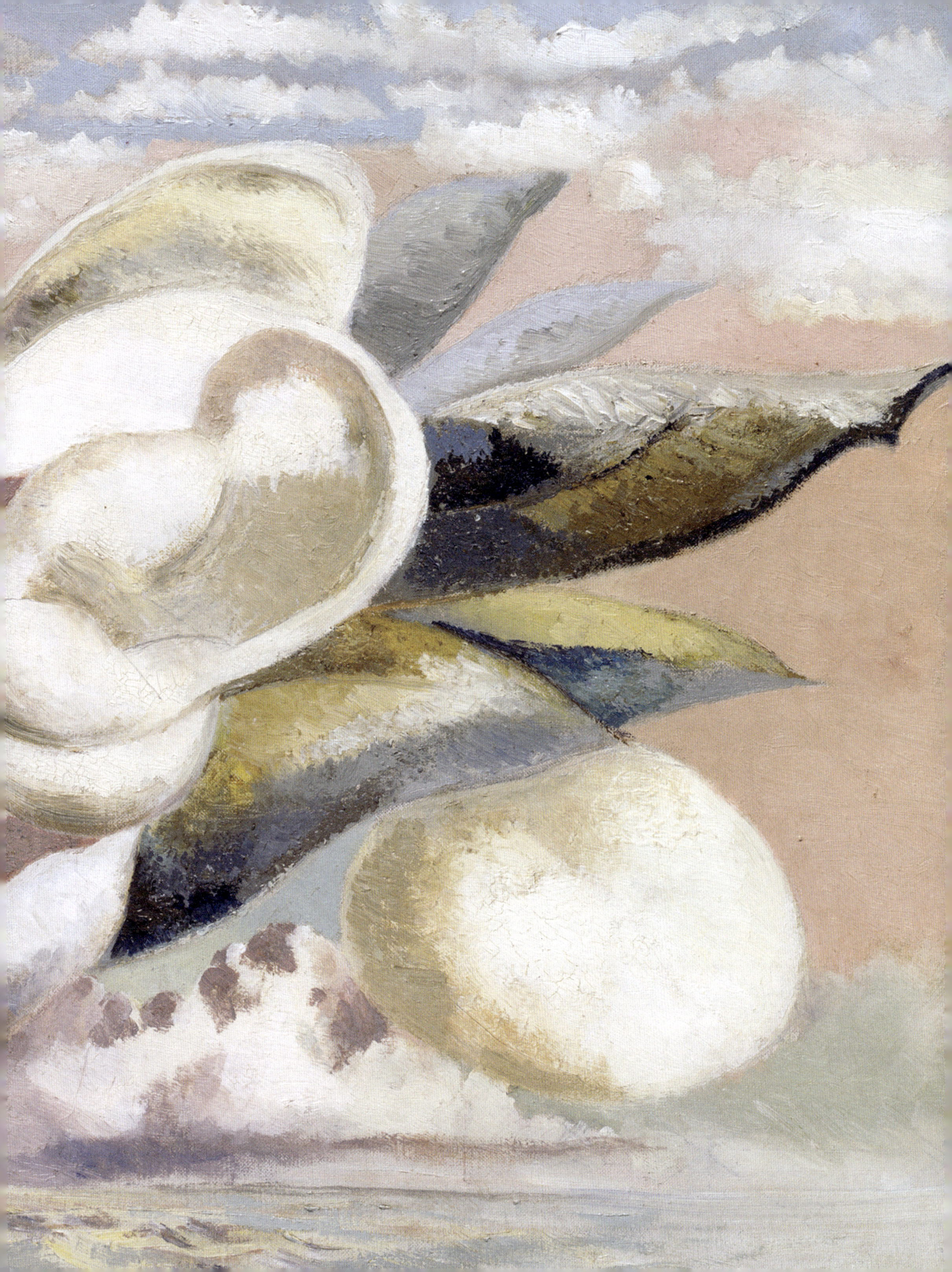

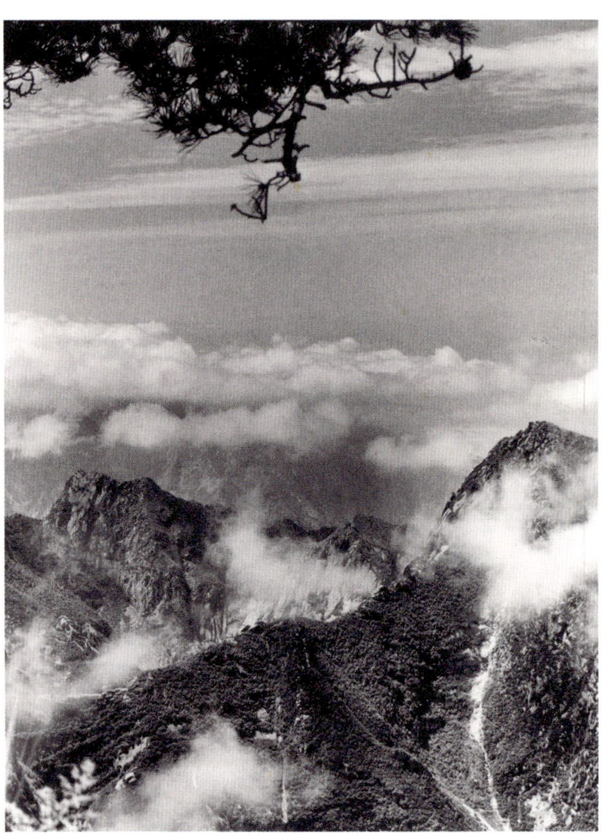

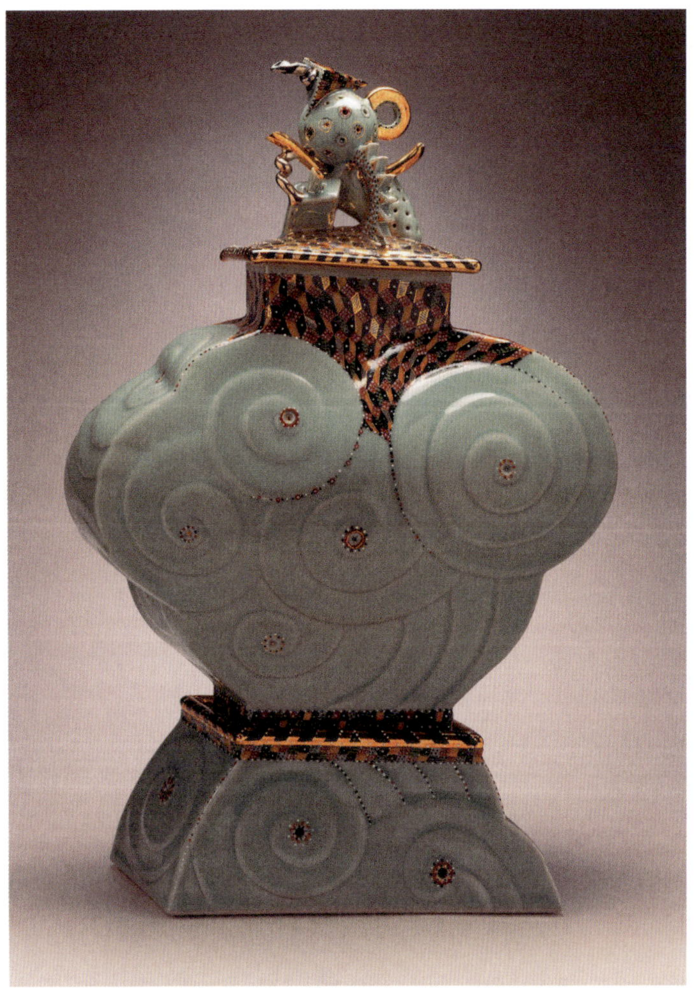

Previous – *Flight of the Magnolia*, 1944, oil paint on canvas, Paul Nash (British)

Top – *North Peak Ridge of Hua Mountain*, 1935 (printed 1970s), gelatin silver photograph, Hedda Morrison (German)

Bottom – *Untitled Cloud Vessel*, 1997, porcelain, Ralph Bacerra (American)

Opposite – *Study of Clouds with a Sunset near Rome*, c. 1786–1801, oil on paper, Simon Alexandre Clément Denis (Flemish)

THE AUSPICIOUS CLOUD, FIVE-COLOURED CLOUD, OR LUCKY CLOUD, IS A RECURRING MOTIF IN CHINESE ART AND CULTURE SYMBOLISING GOOD FORTUNE AND PEACE. THE STYLISED PATTERN OF THE CLOUD FORM HAS EVOLVED OVER MILLENNIA AND HOLDS SIGNIFICANCE WITHIN THE REALMS OF CHINESE COSMOLOGY, CHINESE IMMORTALS AND AGRICULTURAL SOCIETY.

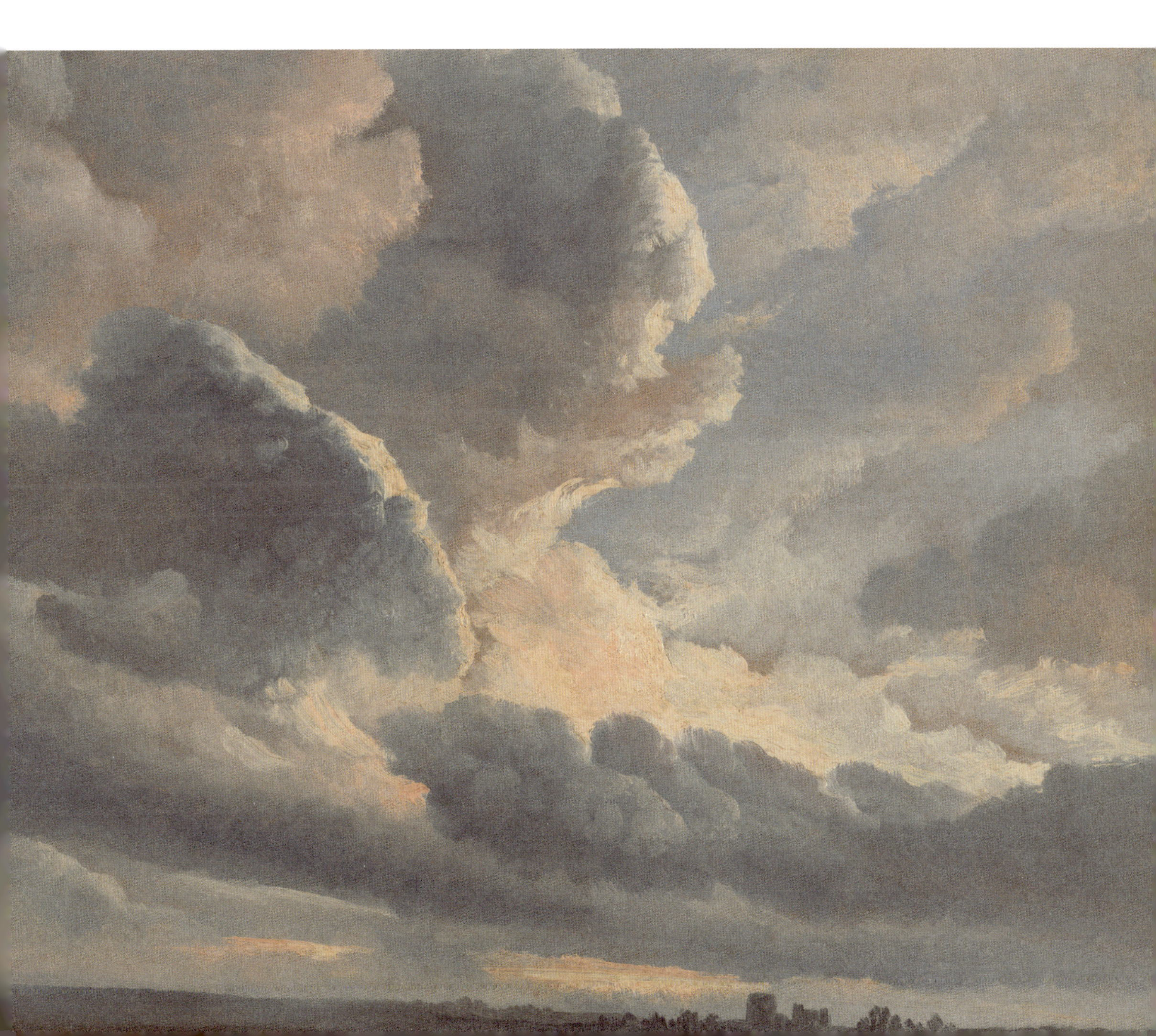

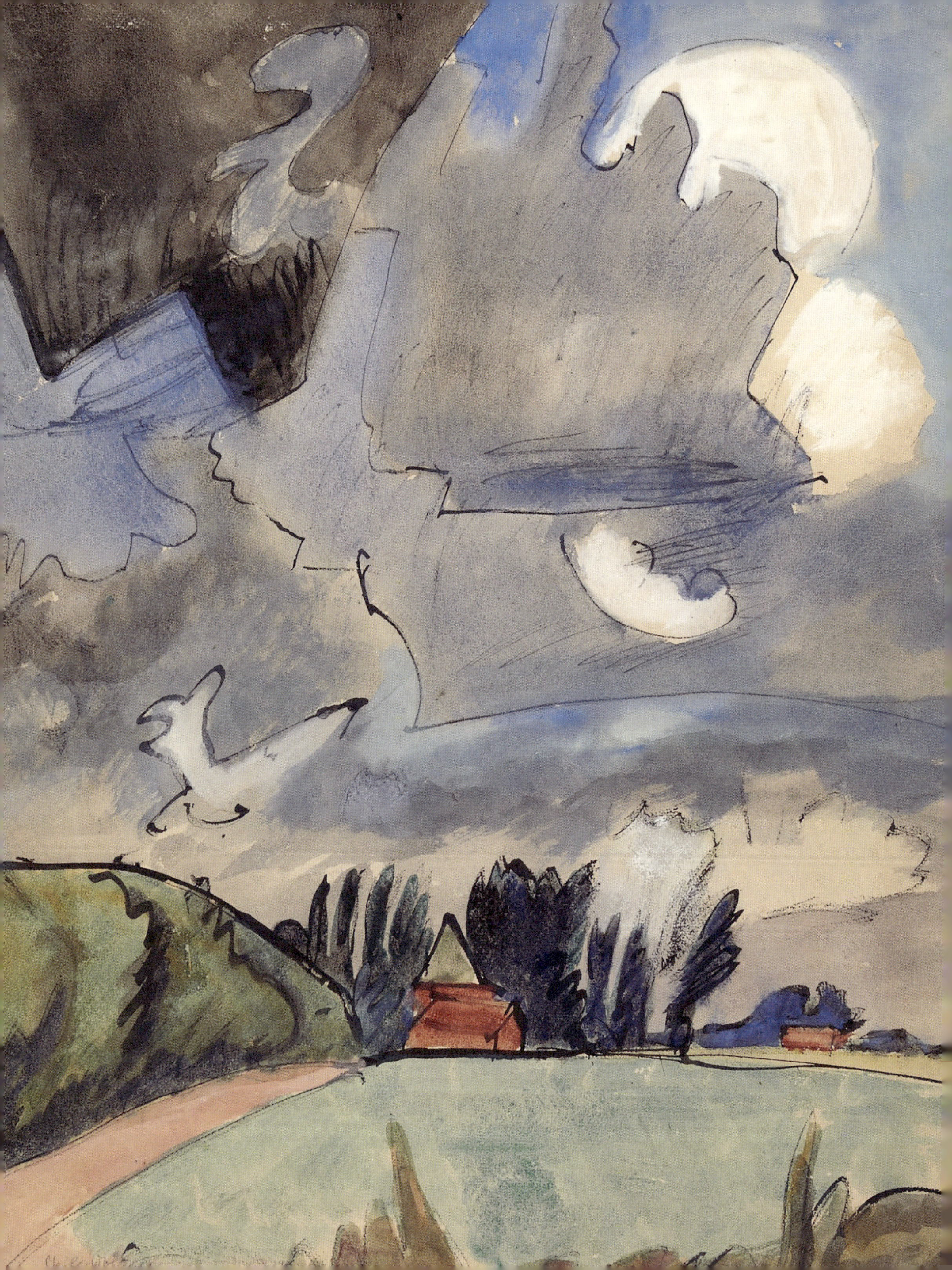

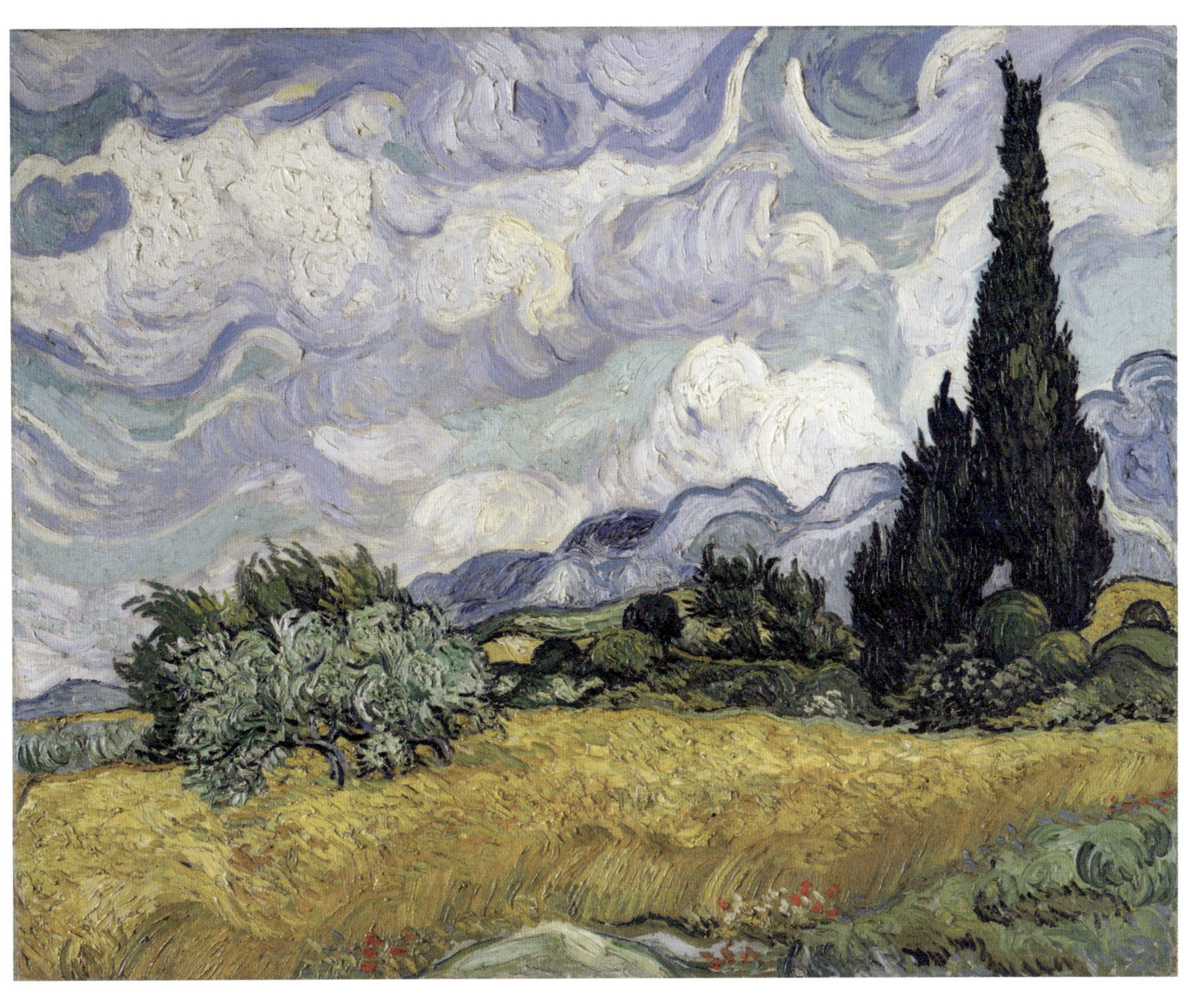

Opposite – *Steep Clouds* (detail), 1913, watercolour, Erich Heckel (German)

Above – *Wheat Field with Cypresses*, 1889, oil on canvas, Vincent van Gogh (Dutch)

CLOUDS, AIR AND WEATHER SYSTEMS IN PRINT

MIYA TOKUMITSU

Air meets air – an incipient encounter. When a printed atmosphere is separated from its matrix on the press bed or, in the case of screenprint, when the final mesh film is lifted from the sheet below, the image of air comes into direct contact with its prototype. As evident in works from horizon-piercing Gothic spires to John Constable's luminous cloud paintings, air and its systems have long beckoned to makers as things to be moulded, represented, infused into their art. In print, a distinct tension is embedded in these processes, for print's many techniques, all entailing direct touch of sheet and matrix, are emphatically airless. Yet atmosphere and print communicate in intriguingly parallel ways, through contact and changing pressure. The line etchings of clouds in Alexander Cozens's treatise, *A new method of assisting the invention in drawing original compositions of landscape* (1785) (see page 234), and *Cirrus* (2017) (see page 235), a screenprint with embossing by Victoria Burge – prints of different eras – take celestial phenomena as their subjects. Both works evoke the ways that air itself functions as a medium while also calling forth the atmospheric qualities of print.

The aim of *A new method* was to serve as a practical guide for artists by systematising the rendering of landscape. Within the pamphlet, a set of twenty illustrations depicts the sky in different moods. These sky images are arranged in a progressive sequence with terse captions explaining their contrasts, for instance: 'The same as the last, but darker at the bottom than the top.' Working in line etching, Cozens crafted his monochrome skies solely through the orchestration of contrasts between printed lines and unprinted paper. Simply by varying the density of lines and their hatching, he achieved lyrical tonal variations within each sheet. The unprinted paper poking through the etched lines becomes light shining through the clouds or dancing across their surfaces. Each composition is a fleeting vision; as Cozen's lines come together and then apart, clouds appear and disappear, and light flickers. His etchings show the sky to be a channel, communicating obscurity and revelation, reflections and refractions, and an array of temperaments.

There is a poetic contravention – indeed another kind of contrast – between the message and the medium in Cozen's sky etchings. In each sheet, Cozens has stilled the sky twice, first encoding various arrangements of sky, light, and clouds through the careful placement of lines on his etching plates, then sending his plates to print, where his images were forcefully fixed to paper. But clouds and vapor are perhaps the most palpable natural examples of evanescence. Cozens acknowledges as much. His construction,

'The same ..., but ...', repeated throughout the sky etchings, bows to one of the atmosphere's essential qualities: its mutability.

Burge's *Cirrus* is also concerned with celestial systems and entropy. Its circuitry of lines and points draw from the stabilising visual language of cartography and age-old human efforts to map the sky. At the same time, these marks, so often employed in the service of orientation and wayfinding, seem subsumed into the print's wafting nebulae. Grid and atmosphere seem to dissolve into one another. As with Cozens's lines, the density of marks and hues fluctuates irregularly across the pictorial field, evocative of the fluid, and sometimes surprising, pressure changes of weather.

Cirrus is not an etching but a screenprint; its image is built up with four successive layers of ink squeezed through mesh stencil screens, one screen for each colour in the print. It may seem counterintuitive for screenprinted marks, in their matte opacity, to represent air and clouds, but again a tension in the technique proves illuminating: the ink, like air, passes through screens, coming into contact with matter on either side. The image produced is an effect of its displacement under pressure.

Of particular note is the fact that the inked portion of *Cirrus* does not comprise the entire print. A platemark frames the image, registering the blind embossment of the paper subsequent to the screenprinting, a highly unusual combination of printing methods. Platemarks are depressions in paper produced by passing it through a press together with a printing plate. Sheets with platemarks are objects in relief; in other words, they allow for the intrusion of air into the dented portions. *Cirrus*'s inked image thus sits behind a shallow pocket of air within the sheet itself. Unlike with screenprinting, platemarks always occur when printing copperplate etchings and therefore are not typically understood as carriers of meaning in those prints. However, considered together with *Cirrus*, the platemarks of Cozens's etchings take on significance as infusions of actual air into his illustrations.

In *The Marvelous Clouds: Toward a Philosophy of Elemental Media*, scholar John Durham Peters encourages us to understand environments as media; like television, the internet, paintings, sound recordings and poetry, natural elements like air are also repositories of readable data and processes. The sky etchings in *A new method* and *Cirrus* are in one sense, ledgers of the information that their artists have gleaned from the atmosphere. But more than this, through print, Cozens and Burge engage with the very ways that air communicates: Cozens, by puzzling through the coding of translucency and shadow through only the placement of lines; and Burge, by articulating the expansion and compression of airflow through the layering of inks squeezed through screens.

Cozens's sky etchings and Burge's *Cirrus* have released themselves from the horizon. As prints, both works are images fixed to (and indented on) paper, but as depictions of the natural world, they are unattached to the ground-tethered grids of Renaissance-era perspective. They are readings of the atmosphere's messages as well as material and technical emulations of its communicative processes. They are gloriously ungrounded, fully in, and of, the air.

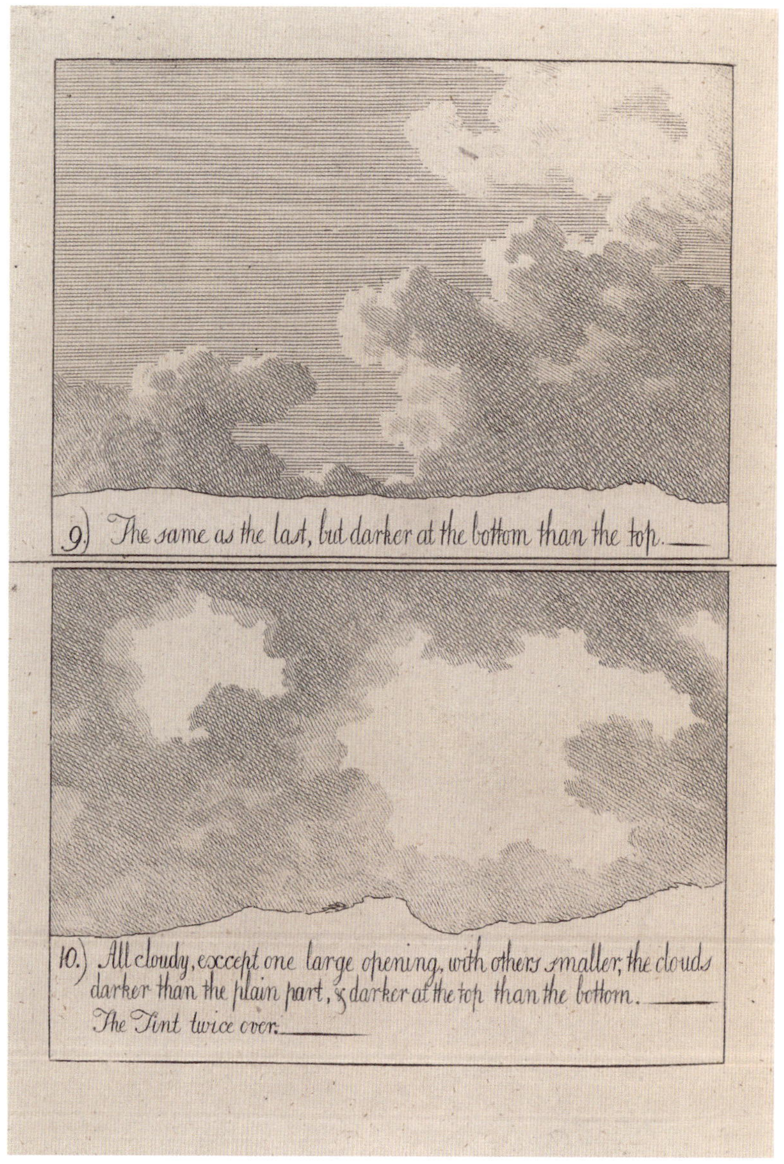

A new method of assisting the invention in drawing original compositions of landscape (Plates 25–26), 1785, part of manuscript, Alexander Cozens (British)

Cirrus, 2017, screenprint with embossing, Victoria Burge (American)

NOTICE THE PRONOUNCED BAND OF COLOUR USED BY ARTISTS HERE TO DELINEATE THE SKY FROM LAND, SEA AND CLOUDS.

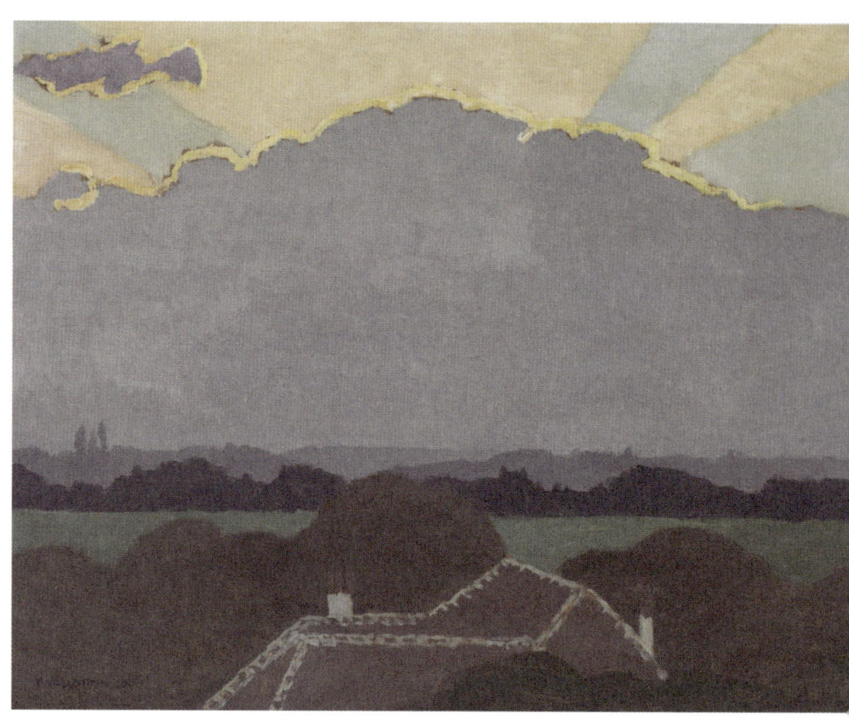

Top – *The Great Cloud*, 1900, oil on cardboard, Félix Vallotton (Swiss–French)

Bottom – *Yellow Sky*, 1958, oil paint on canvas, Milton Avery (American)

Opposite – *Land and sky from sea 2*, 2005, oxides and ink on canvas, Julie Gough (Australian)

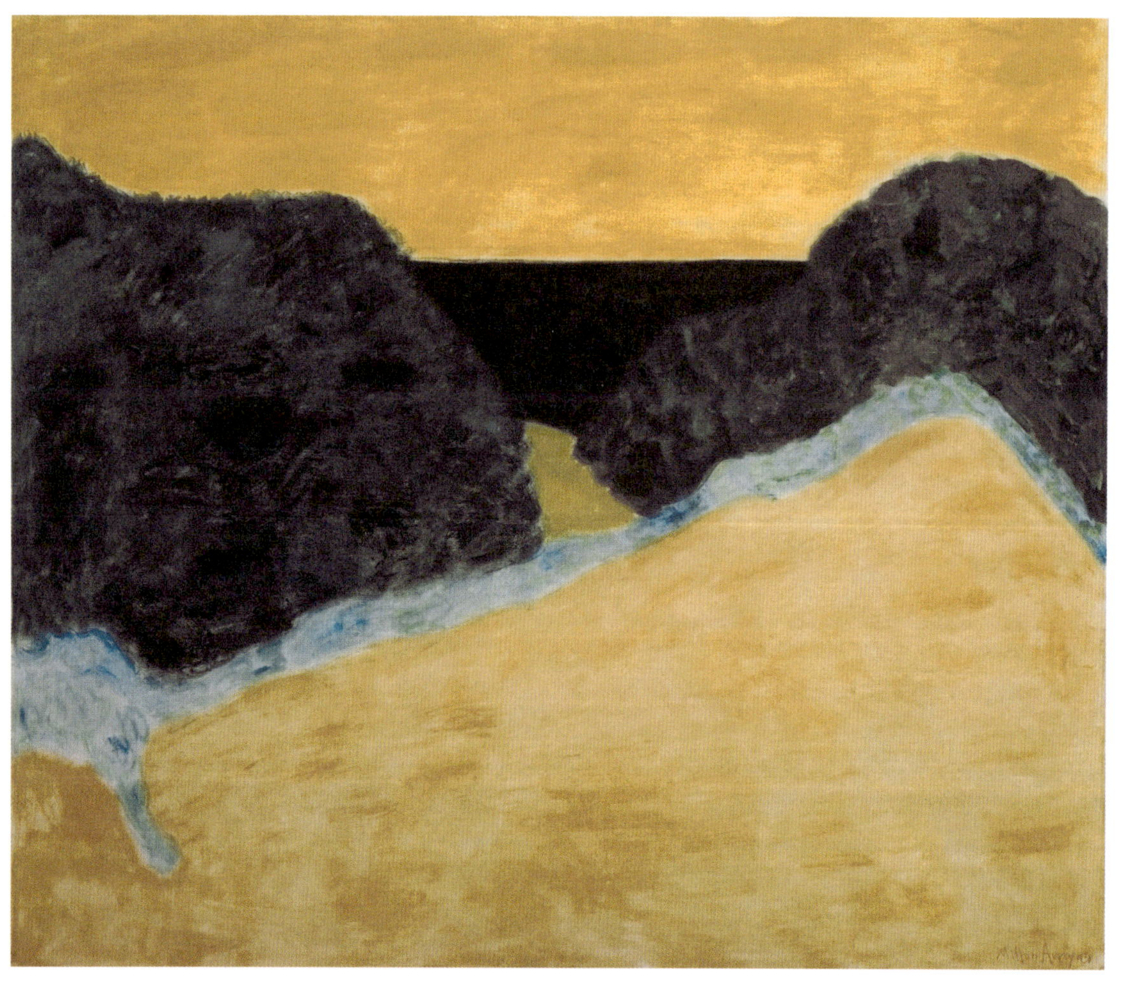

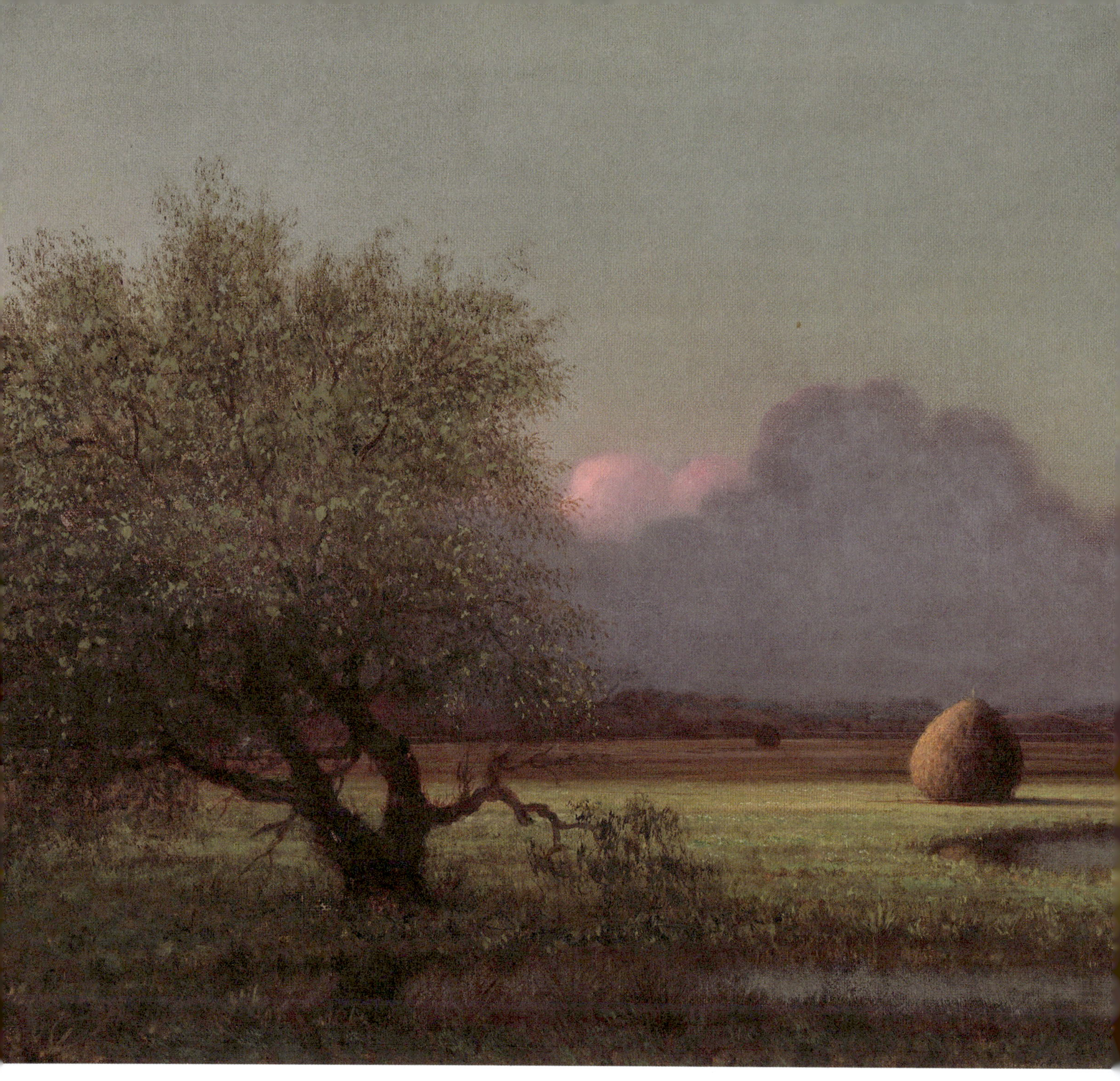

 Sunlight and Shadow: The Newbury Marshes, c. 1871–75, oil on canvas, Martin Johnson Heade (American)

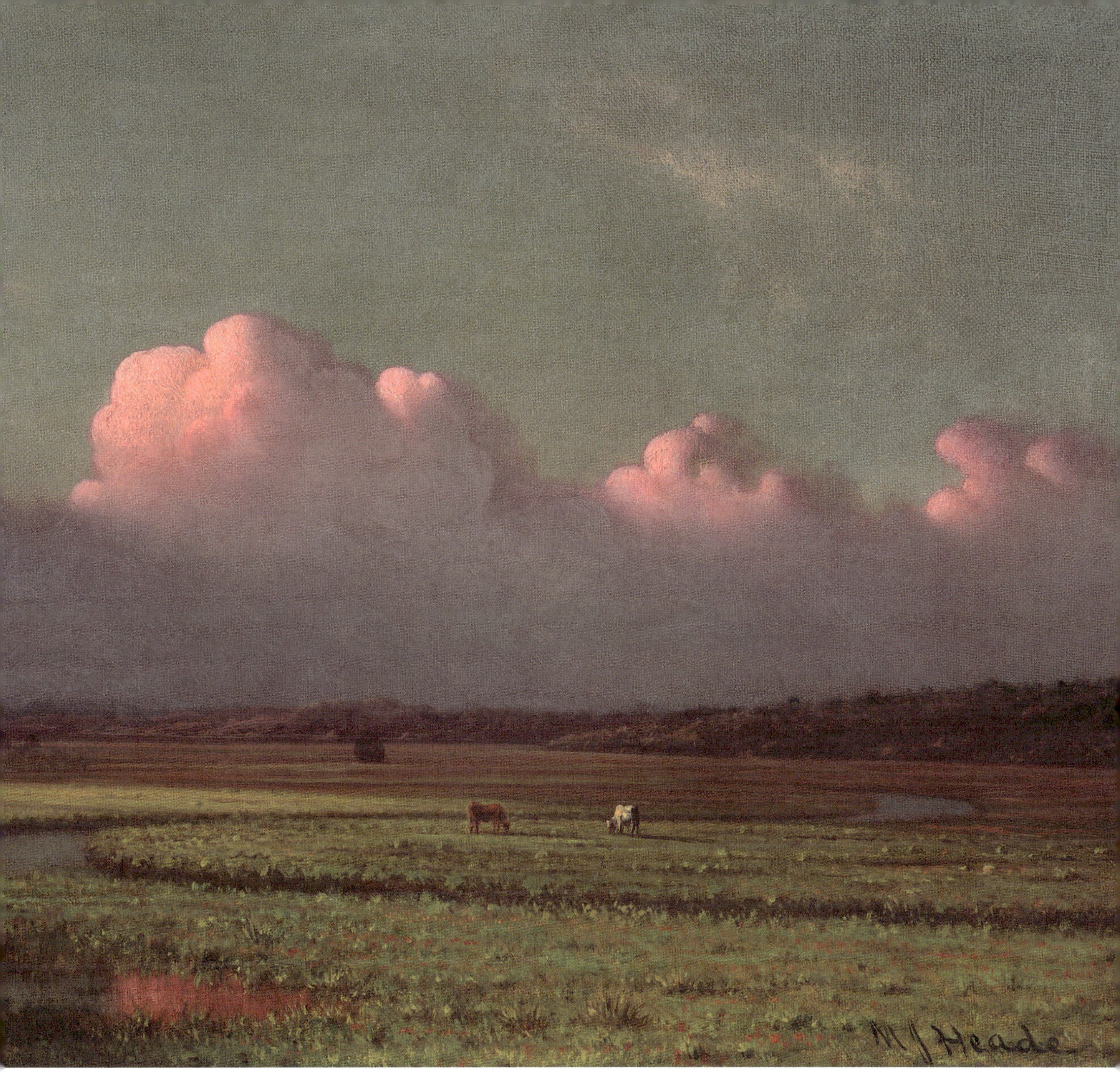

AMERICAN LANDSCAPE PAINTER MARTIN JOHNSON HEADE OBSERVED THE CHANGING WEATHER CONDITIONS OF THE SALT MARSHLAND AROUND NEW ENGLAND. HE WAS PARTICULARLY FASCINATED BY THE TIDAL RANGE AND THE EFFECT OF LIGHT ON THE SURROUNDING LANDSCAPE. IN SUNLIGHT AND SHADOW: THE NEWBURY MARSHES THE SILHOUETTE OF THE LOW ROLLING CLOUD IS COUNTERBALANCED BY THE APPLE TREE IN THE FOREGROUND AND THE WATERWAY THAT MEANDERS THROUGH THE LANDSCAPE. THE ROSE-PINK TINTED CLOUDS ARE A STRIKING CONTRAST TO THE SOFT AQUA TONES OF THE SKY.

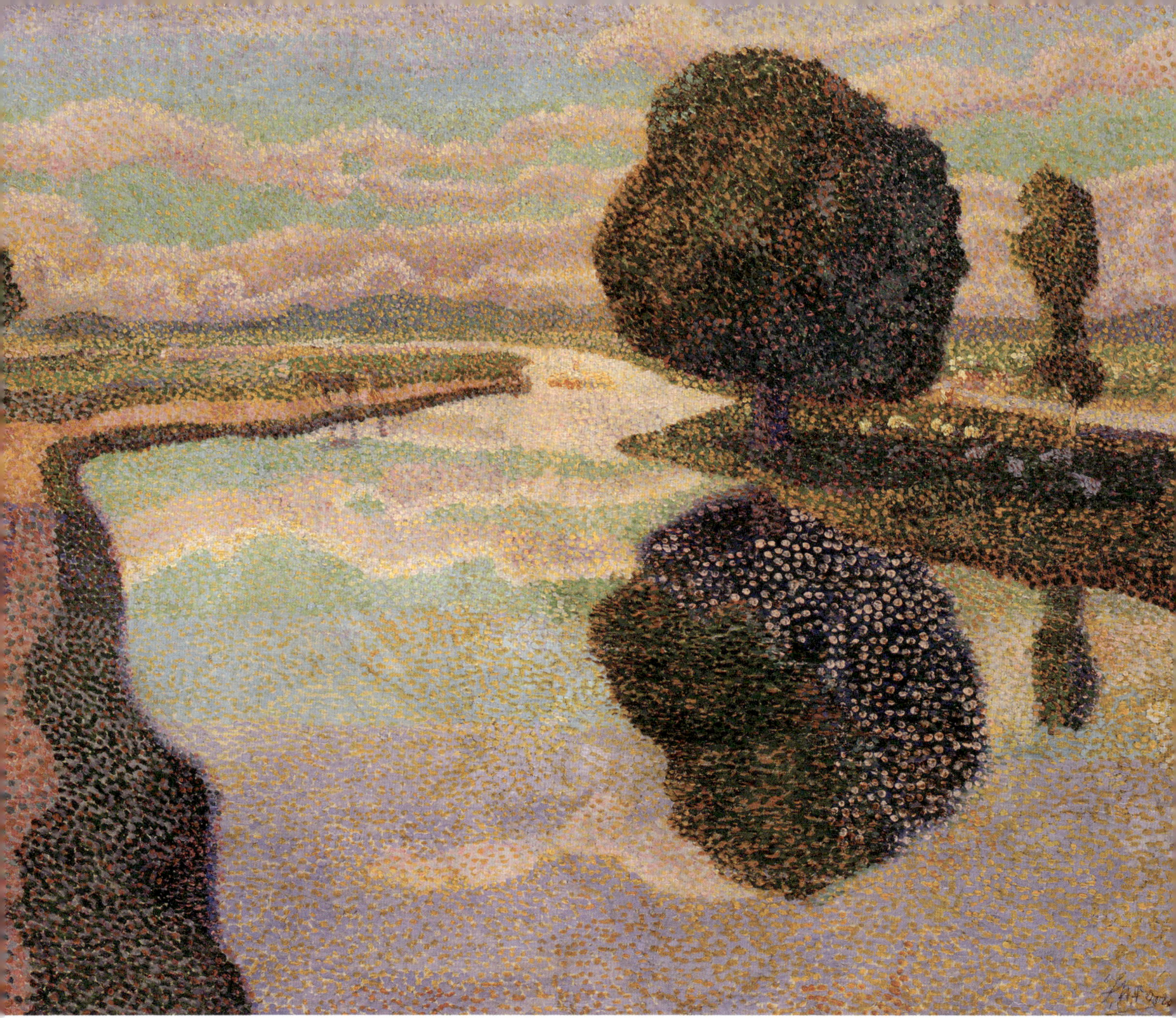

THE POINTILLIST STYLE OF PAINTING ALLOWED ARTISTS TO EXPERIMENT WITH THE PLACEMENT OF PURE COLOUR SIDE-BY-SIDE, APPLIED WITH SMALL BRUSH STROKES OR DOTS. CENTRED AROUND COLOUR THEORY AND SCIENTIFIC UNDERSTANDING OF OPTICAL EFFECTS, IT IS THOUGHT THAT THE VIEWER'S EYE WILL MIX THE COLOUR. A PAINTING WITH THIS TECHNIQUE DEMANDS A SLOW LOOKING PRACTICE.

 Landscape with Canal, 1889, oil on canvas, Jan Toorop (Dutch)

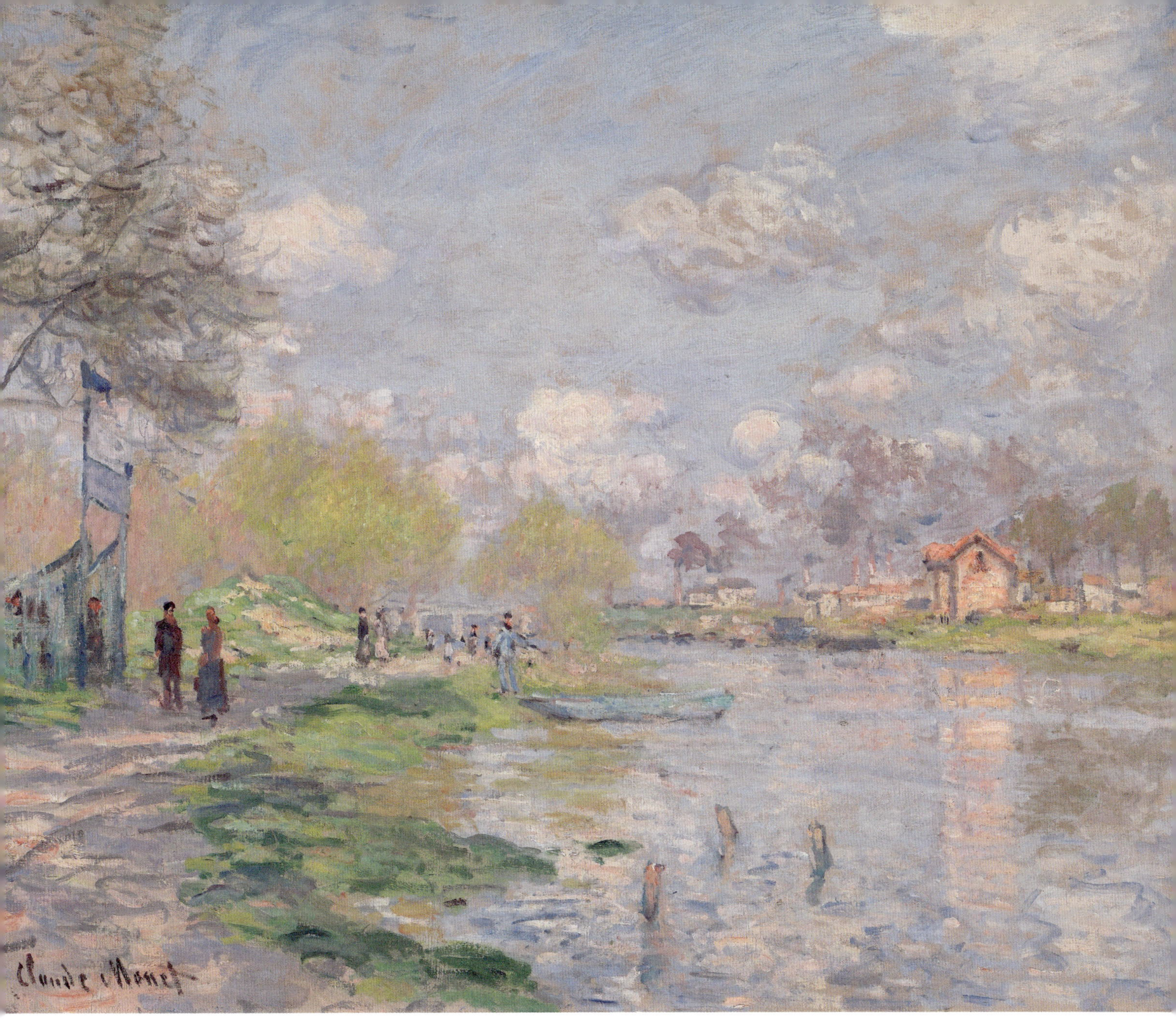

Above – *Springtime on the Ile de La Grande Jatte*, 1878, oil on canvas, Claude Monet (French)

Following – *Night and Sleep* (detail), 1878, oil on canvas, Evelyn De Morgan (British)

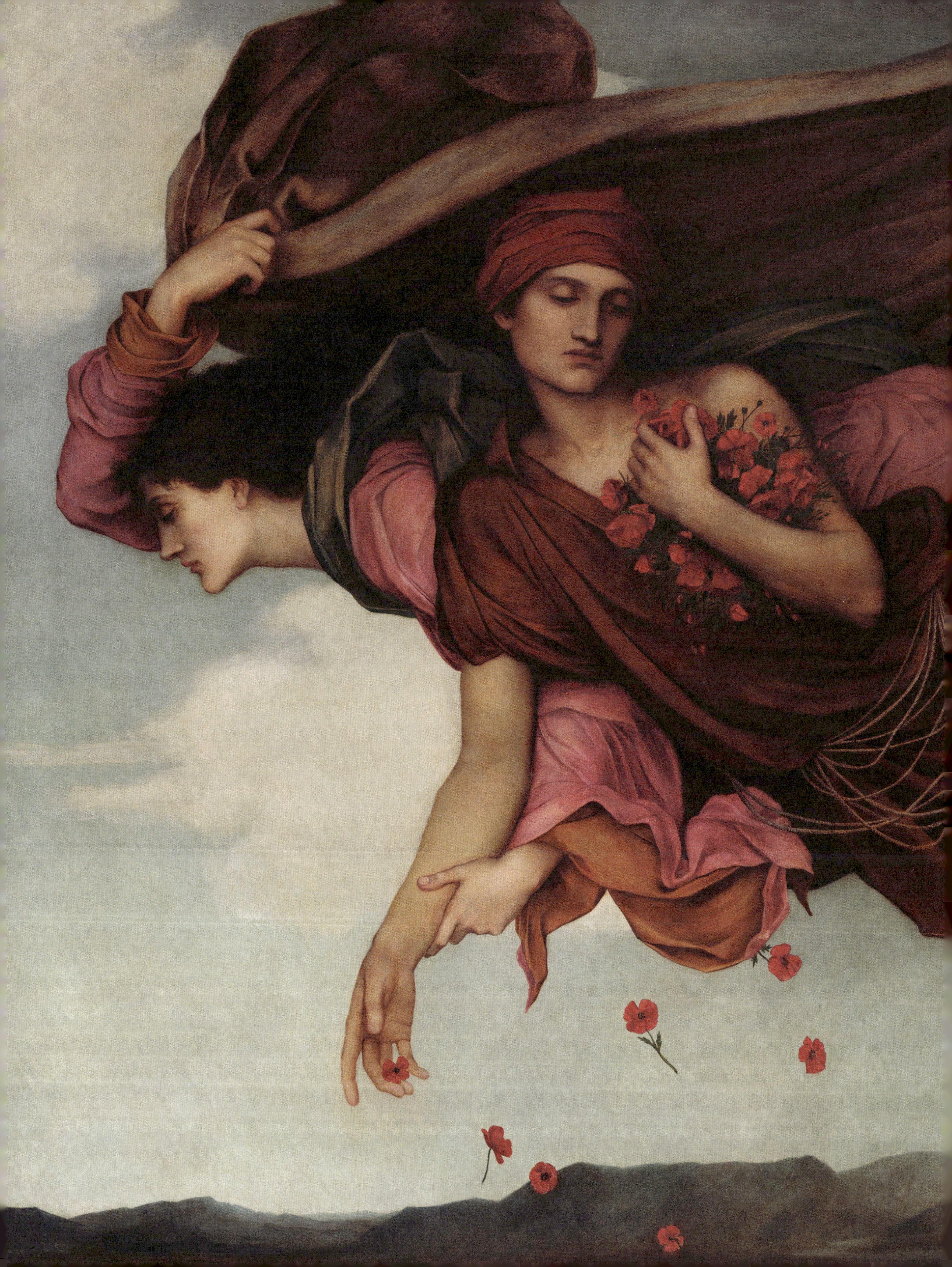

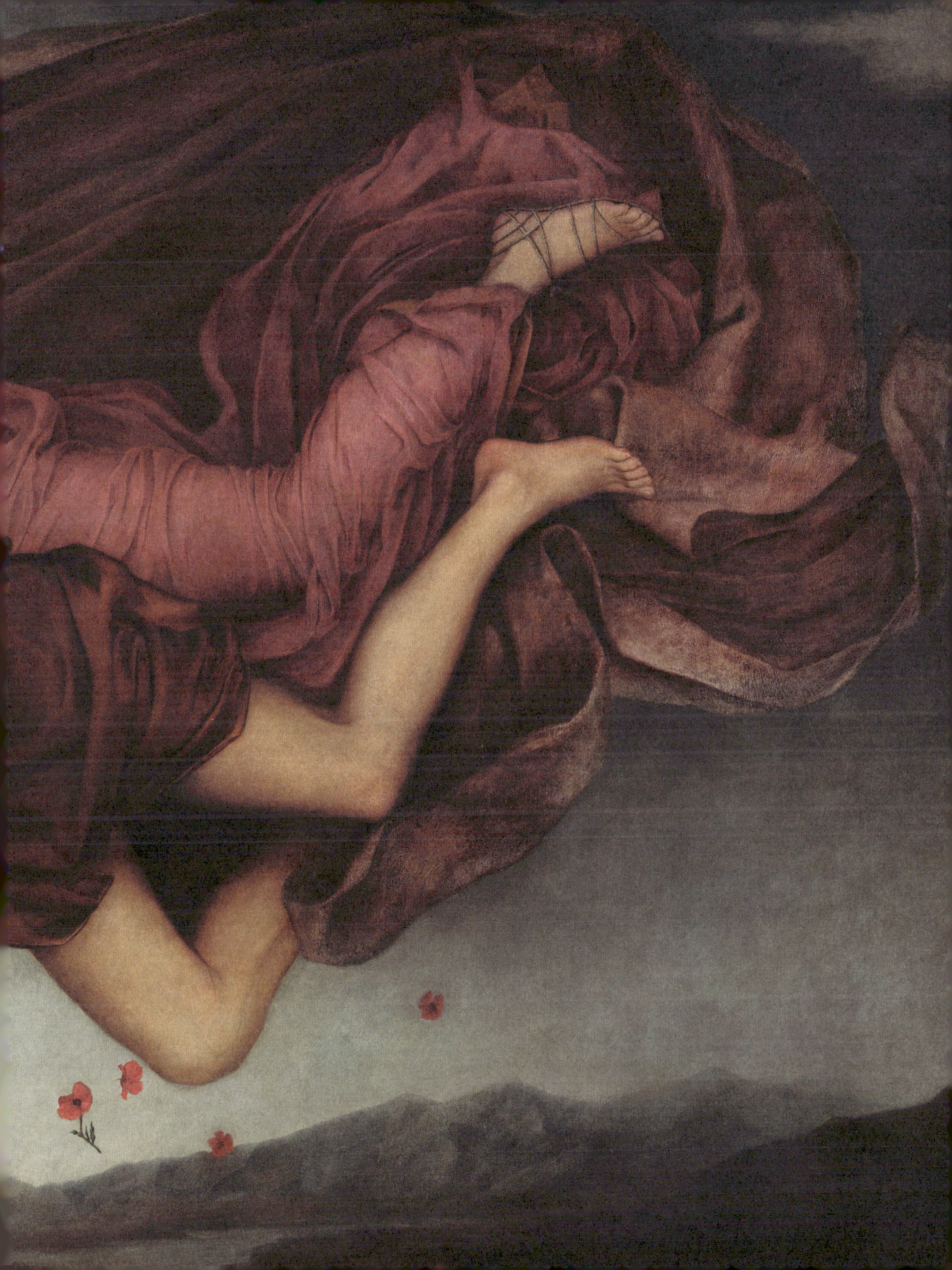

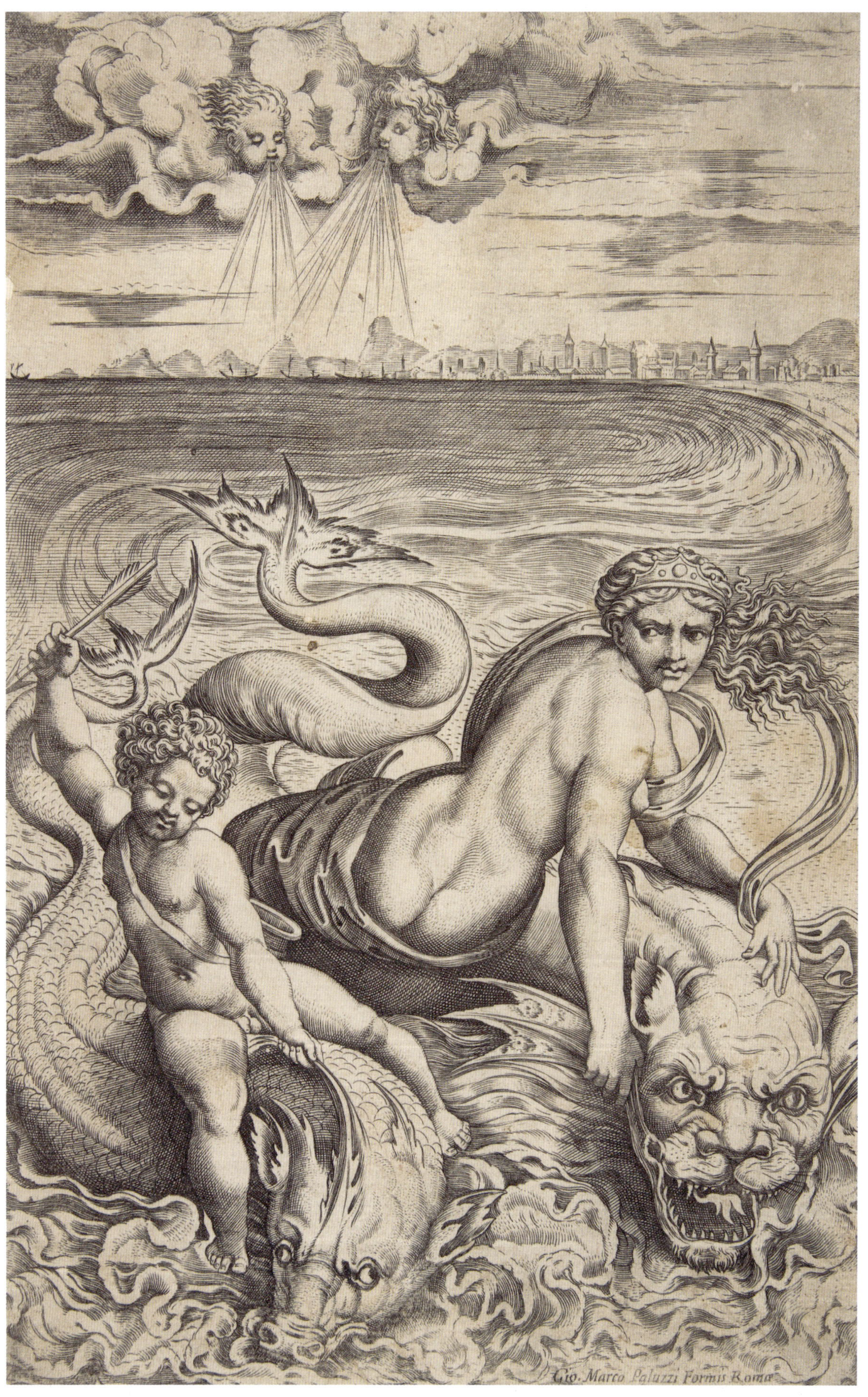
Gio. Marco Paluzzi Formis Roma

WIND

AIRSTREAMS CAN BEHAVE IN MIGHTY AND FIERCE WAYS. DEMONSTRATING THE FORCE OF NATURE THROUGH STRONG WINDS CAN ALSO PROVIDE AN OPPORTUNITY TO SHOW A MASTERFUL COMMAND OF SKILL AND TECHNIQUE, AND ALSO GREAT WIT. ZEPHYRUS IS THE PERSONIFICATION AND GOD OF THE WEST WIND. HE CONNOTES SPRINGTIME, AND IS OFTEN SEEN IN THE TOP CORNER OF A PICTURE WHERE HE IS PORTRAYED WITH FULL CHEEKS AND A VISIBLE STREAM OF AIR BEING EXPELLED FROM HIS PERFECTLY PURSED LIPS.

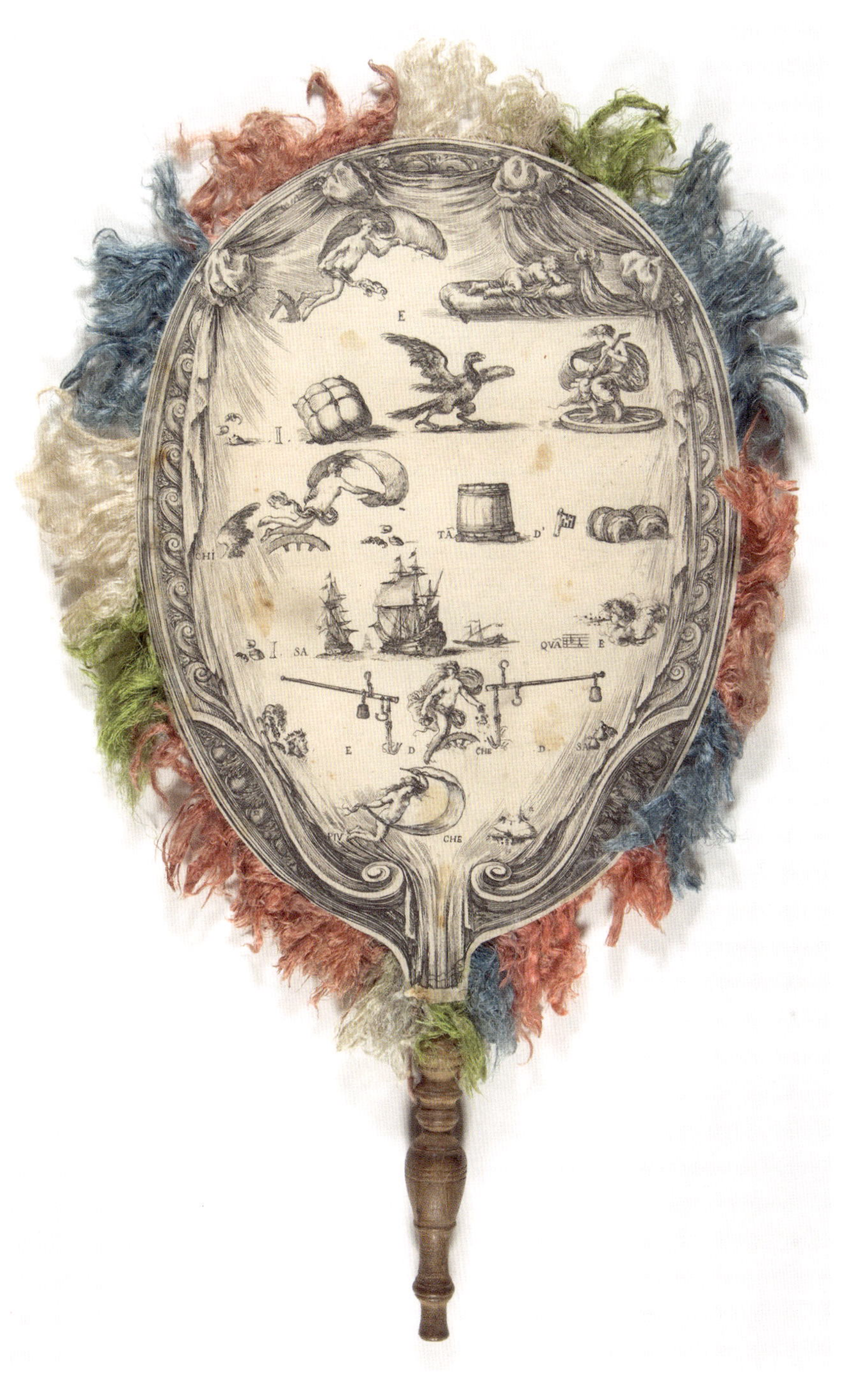

Opposite – *Venus and Cupid riding two sea monsters, Cupid raises an arrow in his right hand, two heads representing wind in the clouds above*, c. 1515–27, engraving, Marco Dente after Raphael (Raffaello Sanzio or Santi) (Italian)

Above – *A fan with a rebus on Love on one side Fortune on the other*, c. 1639, etching fashioned to form a fan with fringe around the edges and wooden handle, Stefano della Bella (Italian)

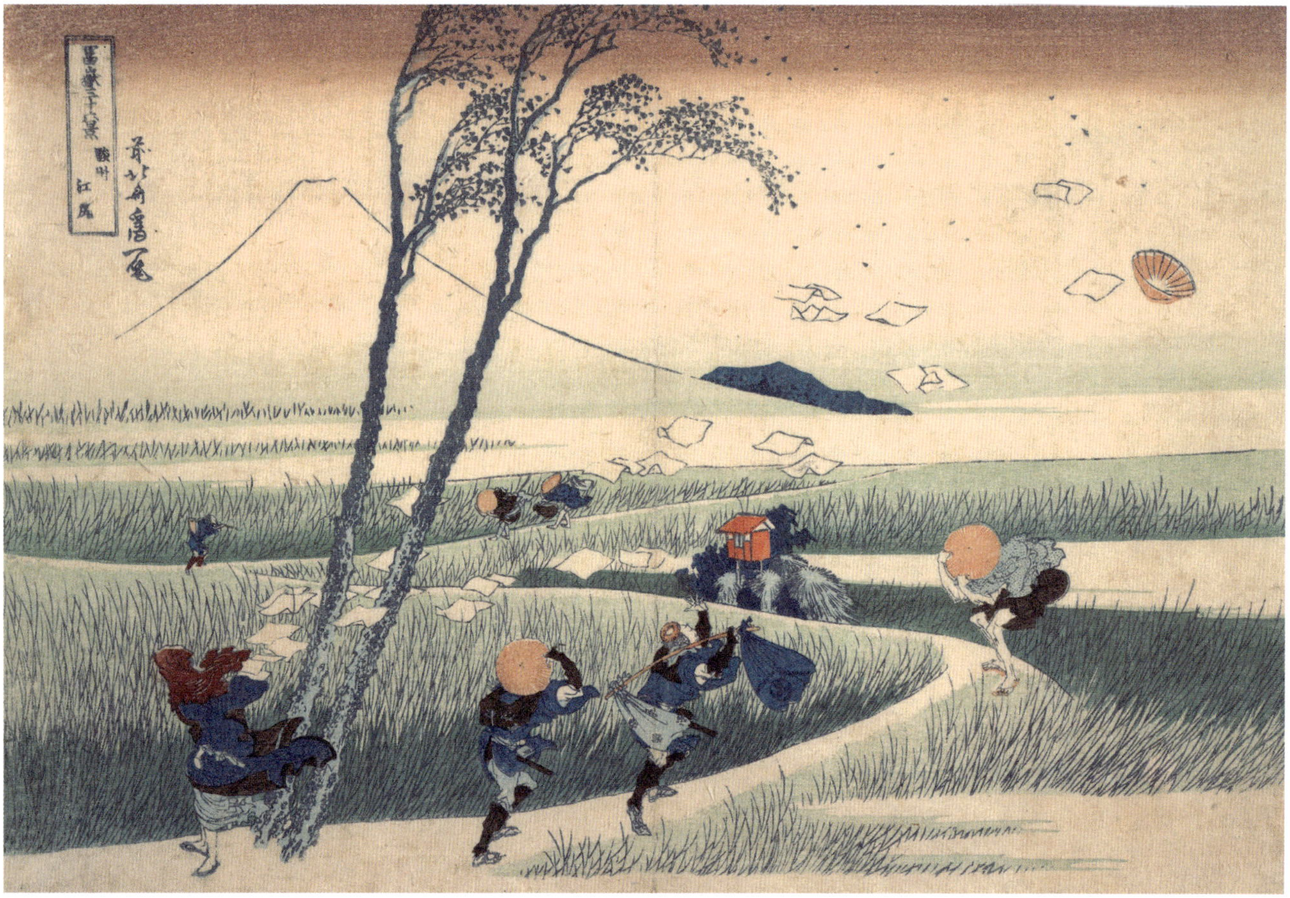

KATSUSHIKA HOKUSAI'S PRINT SHOWS THE STILL MOUNT FUJI WATCHING OVER A BLUSTERY SCENE. A PATHWAY SNAKES THROUGH THE LANDSCAPE AND IS POPULATED WITH FIGURES, HOLDING ONTO THEIR STRAW HATS, AND VISIBLY BEING BLOWN IN ONE DIRECTION, WHILE OTHERS BATTLE IN THE OPPOSITE DIRECTION AGAINST THE WIND. NOTICE HOW HOKUSAI HAS ADDED SMALL AND PLAYFUL DETAILS TO CREATE A GREAT SENSE OF MOVEMENT; PAPERS CAUGHT IN THE CURRENT MAKE UNDULATING WAVE-LIKE SHAPES AS THEY FLOAT UP AND AWAY. THE TRIALS OF TRAVELLING ON FOOT IN EARLY SPRING WEATHER!

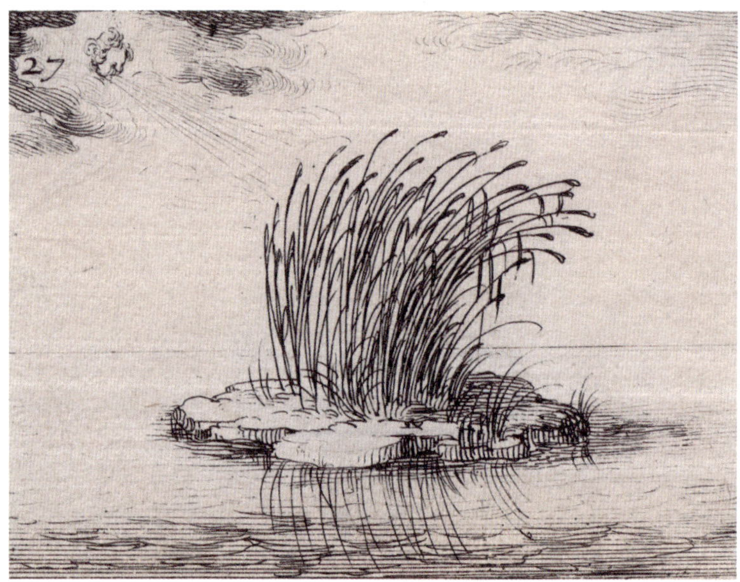

Top – *Ejiri in Suruga Province (Sunshū Ejiri)*, c. 1830–32, woodblock print; ink and colour on paper, Katsushika Hokusai (Japanese)

Bottom – *The Reed and The Wind*, c. 1621–35, etching, Jacques Callot (French)

Opposite top – *Windswept Landscape*, c. 1740–1806, watercolour and gouache, over traces of red and black chalk, Louis Gabriel Moreau (French)

Opposite bottom – *South Wind Cools in the Himalayas: Folio from the Second Guler Gita Govinda Series*, c. 1775, opaque watercolour on paper, First Generation after Manaku (Indian)

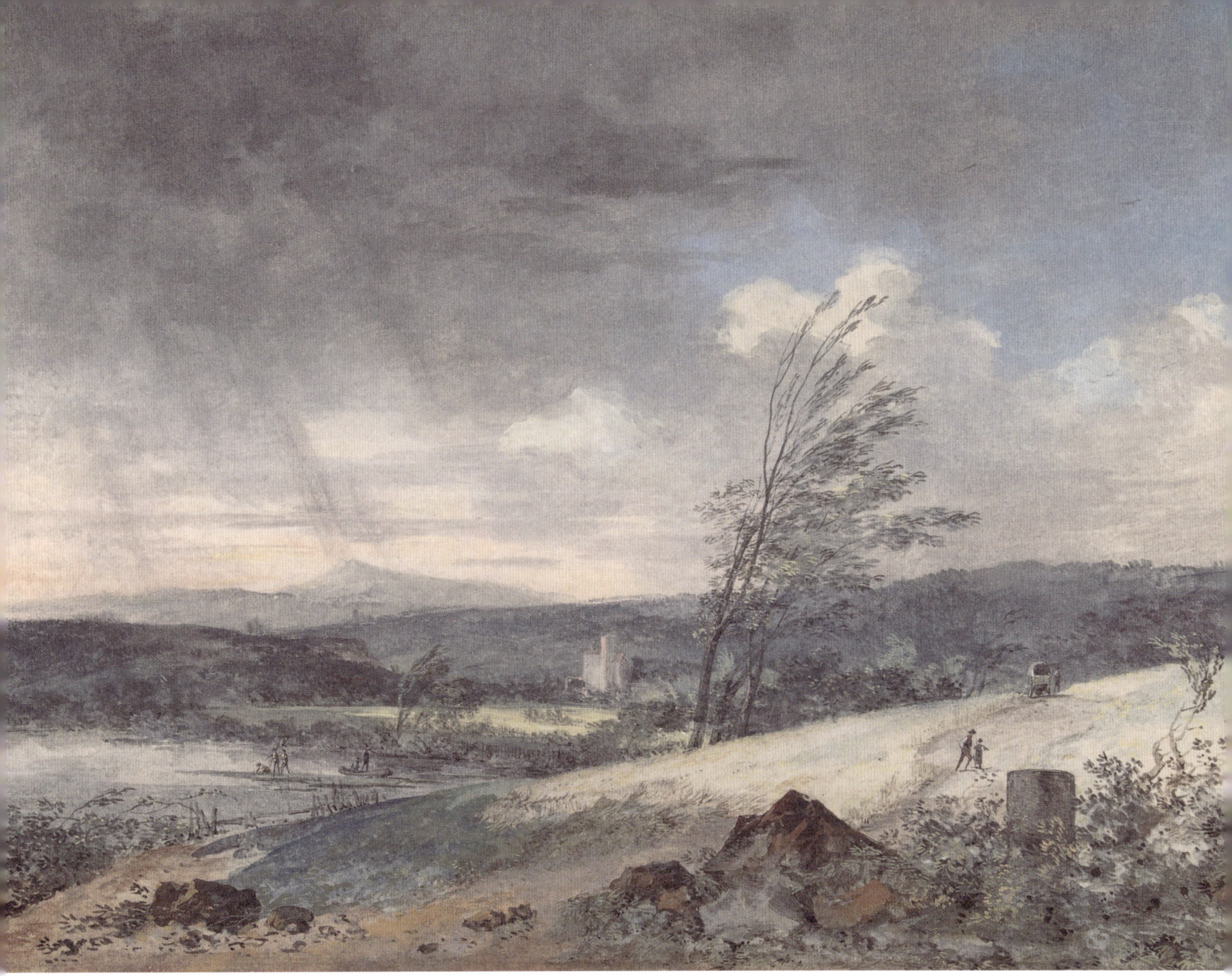

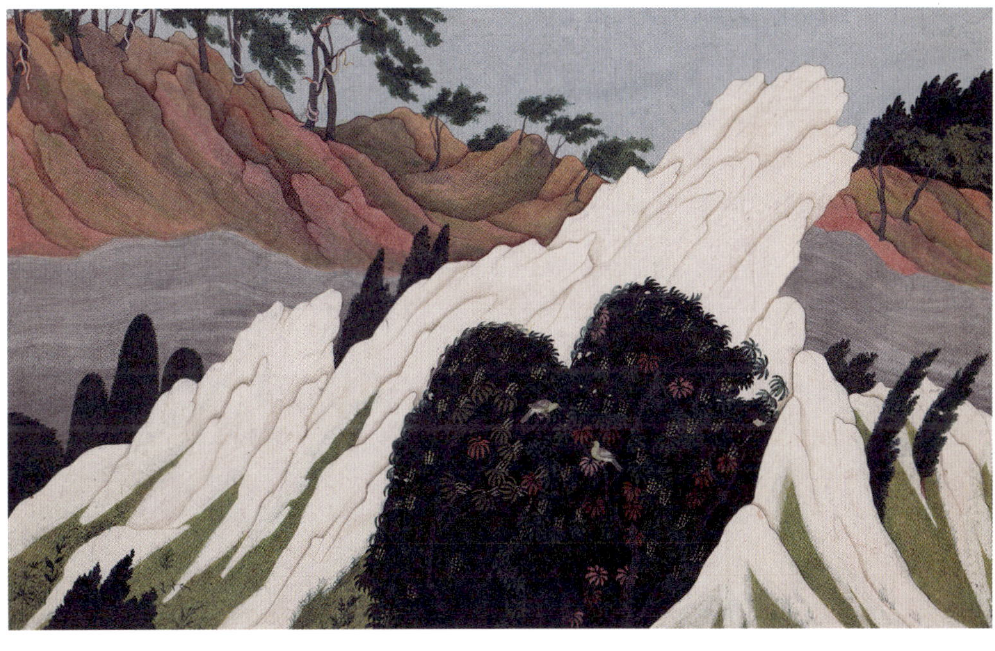

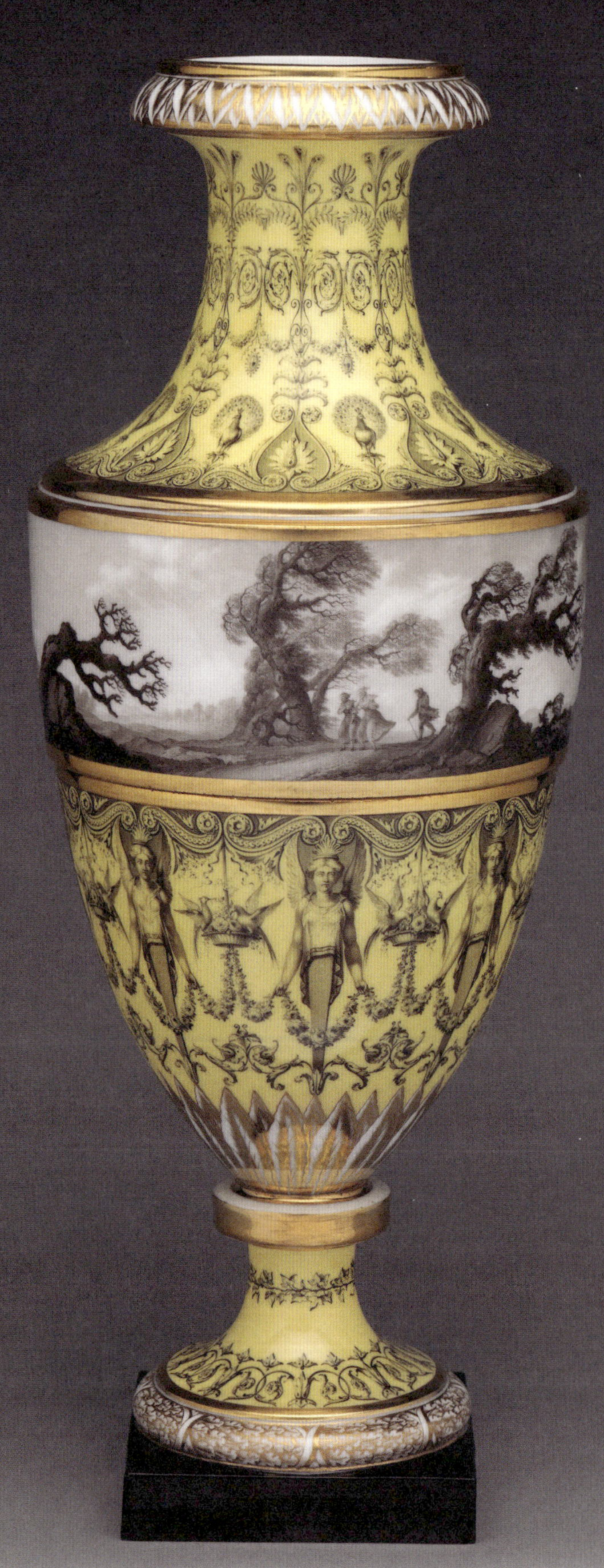

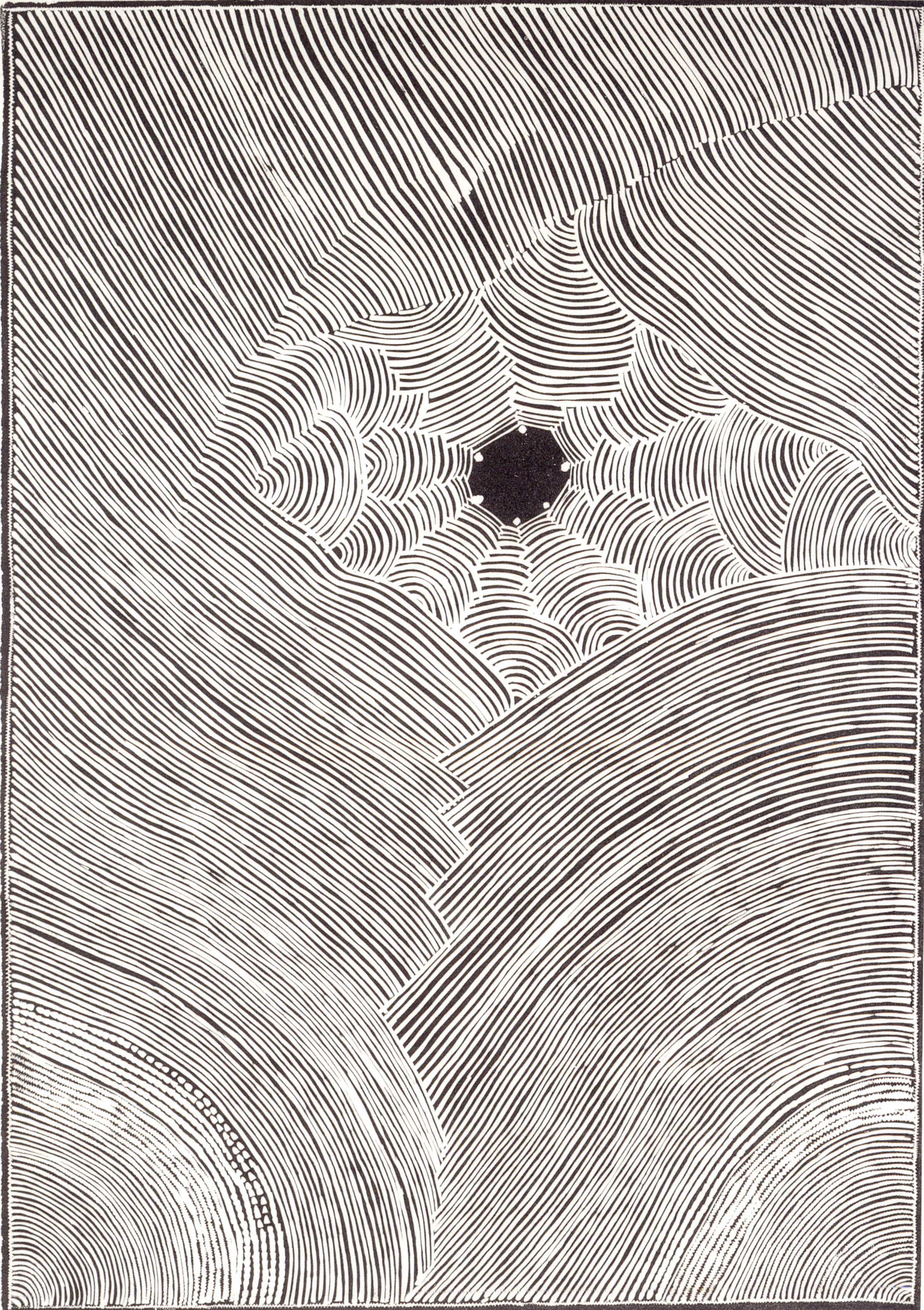

WILD WEATHER

THERE IS A DISTINCT CHANGE IN ATMOSPHERE WITH THE ONSET OF WILD WEATHER. OBSERVE THE RAPID PACE OF A CHANGING SKY AND THE NUANCE OF PATTERN IN LIGHTNING, CLOUDS AND RAIN.

Previous left – *Vase with scenes of storm on land*, c. 1797–98, hard-paste porcelain decorated in polychrome enamels, gold, manufactured by Dihl et Guérhard, possibly painted by Jean-Baptiste Coste (French)

Previous right – *Willy willy 1*, 1995, linocut, Janangoo Butcher Cherel (First Nations Australian)

Opposite – *Tunic,* early 20th-century, cotton with glass beads, Baba Adesina (Nigerian)

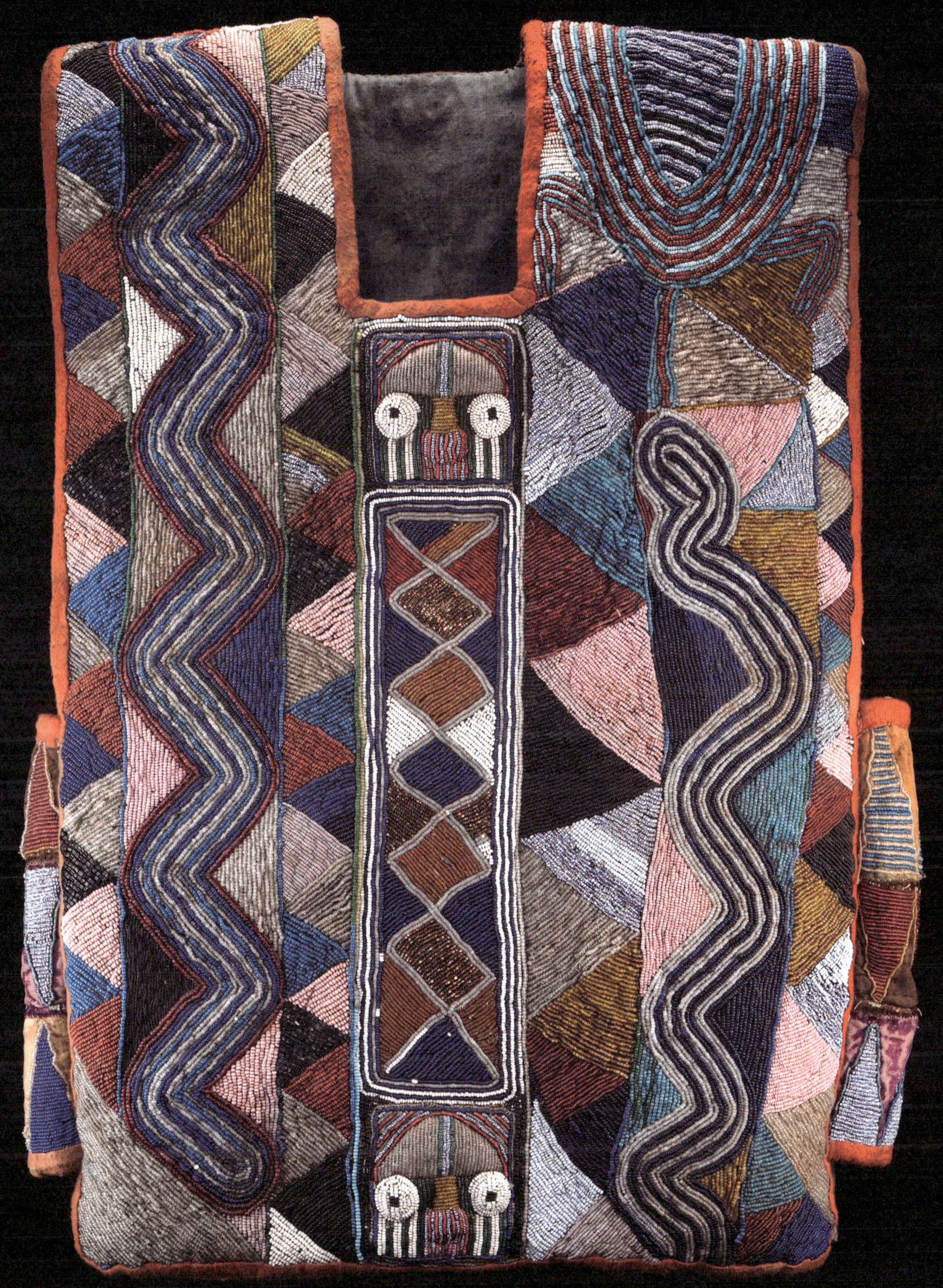

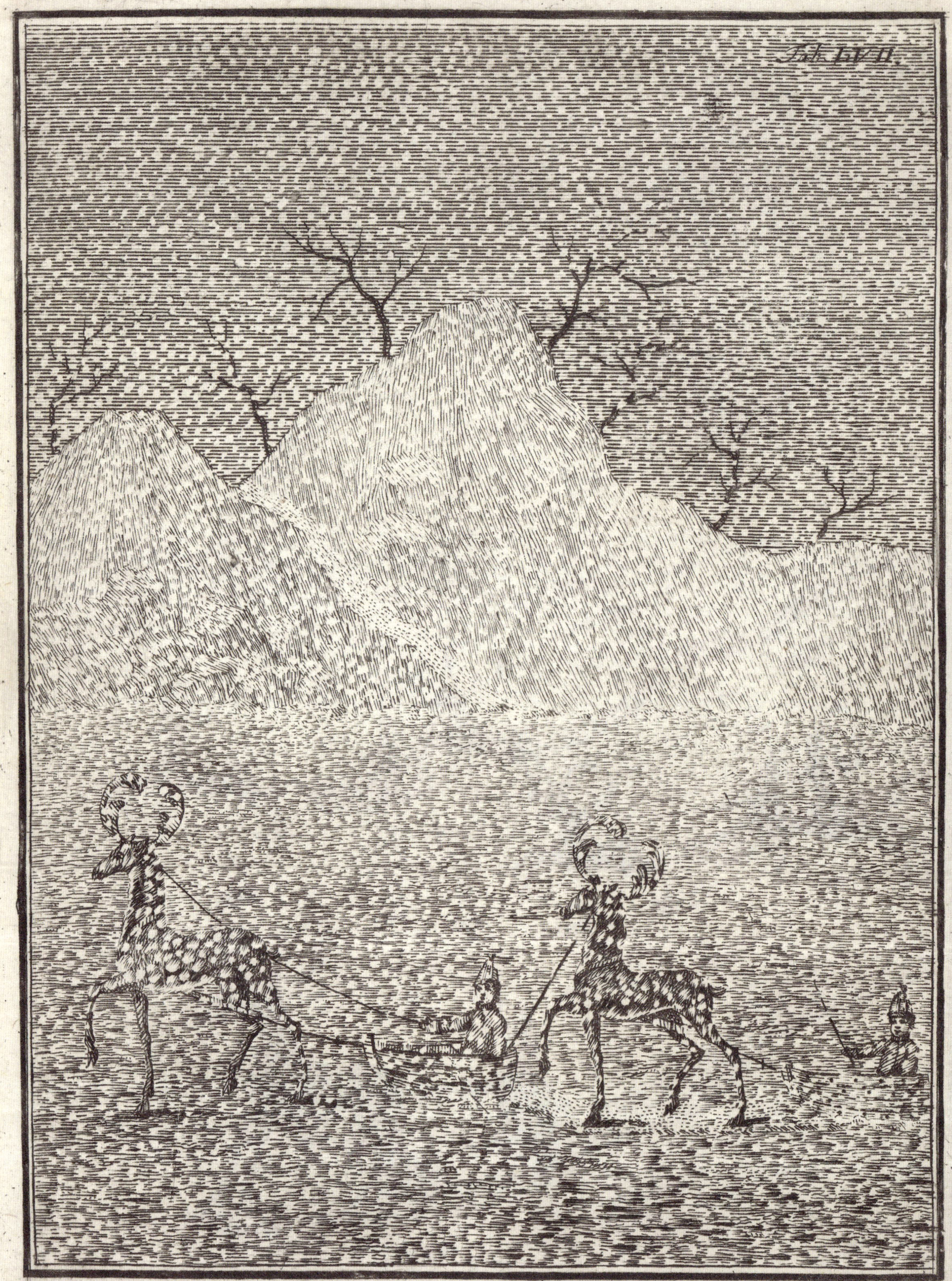
Tab. LVII.

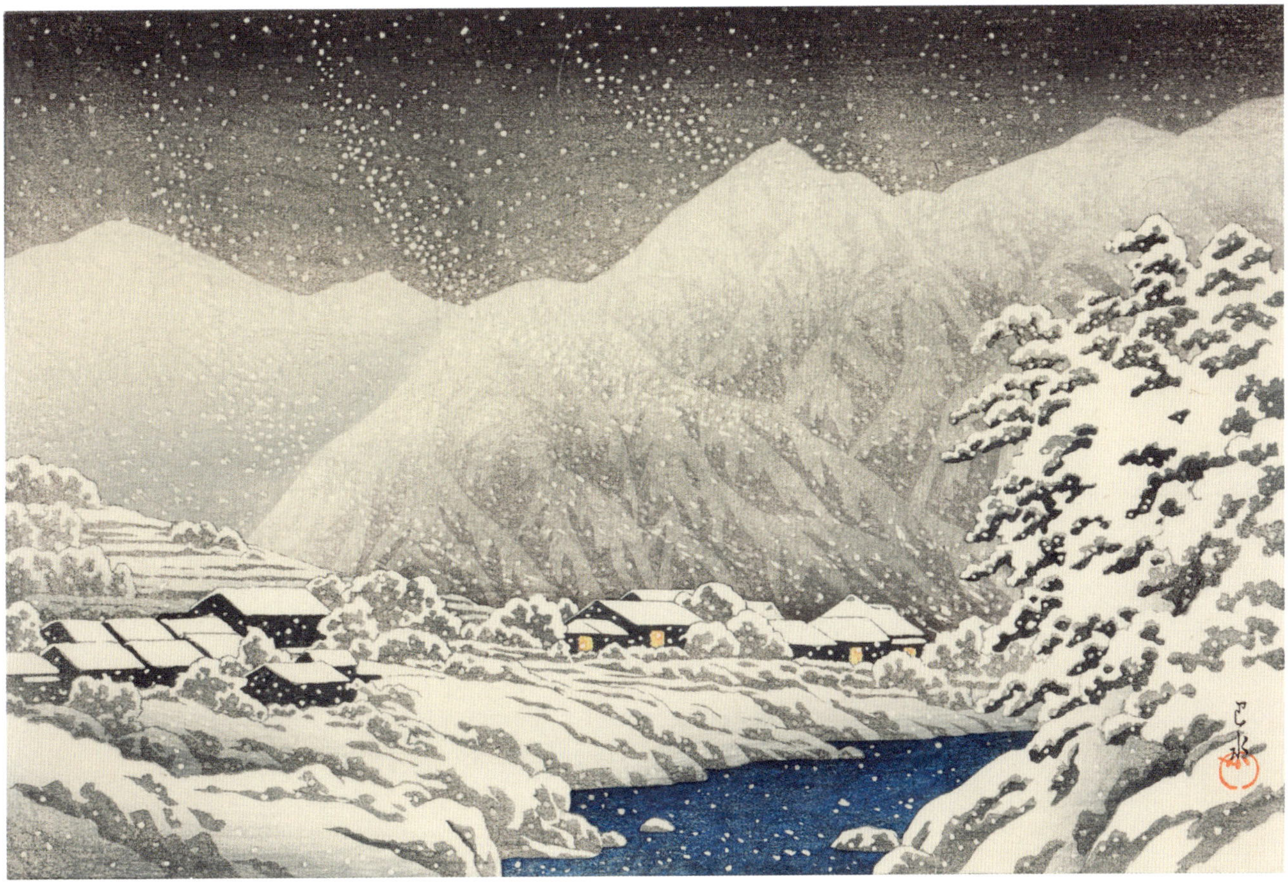

CONSIDER THE VISUAL LANGUAGE USED BY ARTISTS DEPICTING DIFFERENT SNOW CONDITIONS. FALLING SNOW, A DUSTING OF SNOW, DRIFTING SNOW, HEAVY SNOW, POWDERY SNOW, SNOW FLURRY AND NIGHT SNOW ALL CONTRIBUTE TO A GLISTENING AND SUPERBLY WHITE COVERED LANDSCAPE.

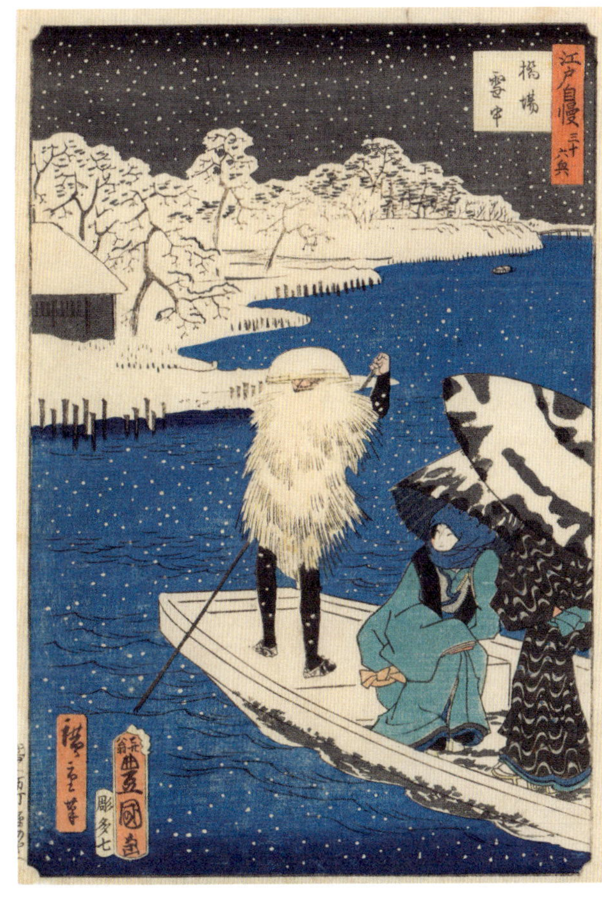

Opposite – *Sledge Driving in Drifting Snow,* 1767, line drawing with copper engraving on paper, Knud Leem (Norwegian), Johannes Rach and Odvardt Helmodt de Lode (Danish)

Top – *In the Snow, Nakayama-Shichiri Road in Hida Province*, 1924, colour woodblock print; oban, Kawase Hasui (Japanese)

Bottom – *Ferryboat in the snow on the Sumida River*, 1864, colour woodblock print on paper, Utagawa Kunisada and Utagawa Hiroshige II (Japanese)

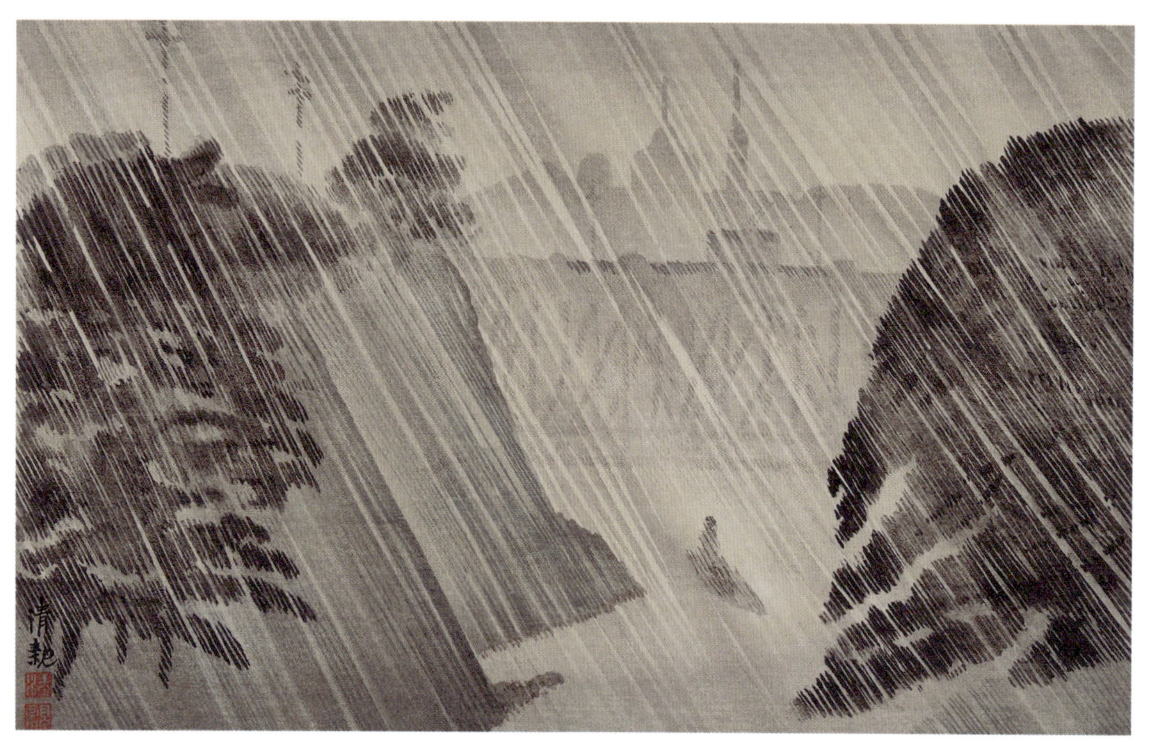

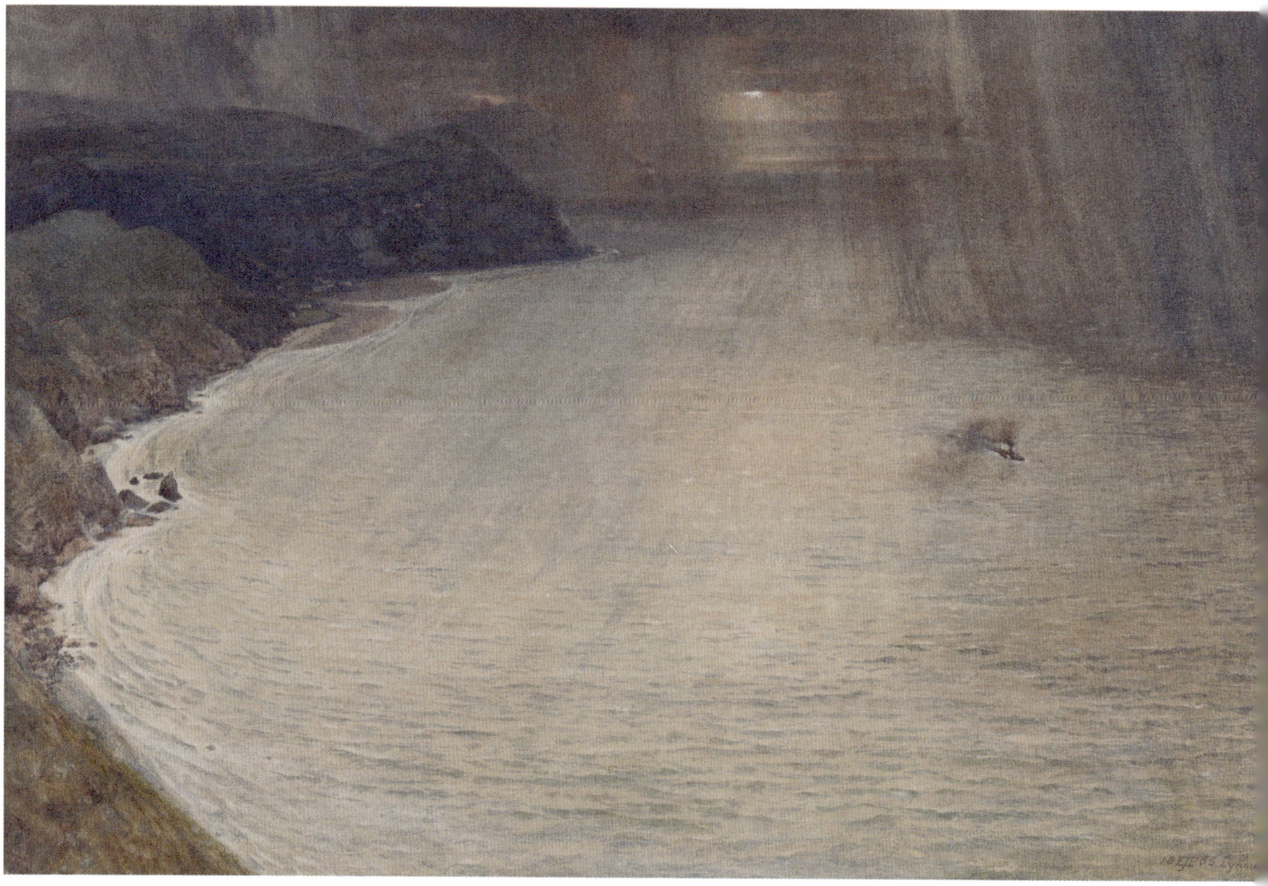

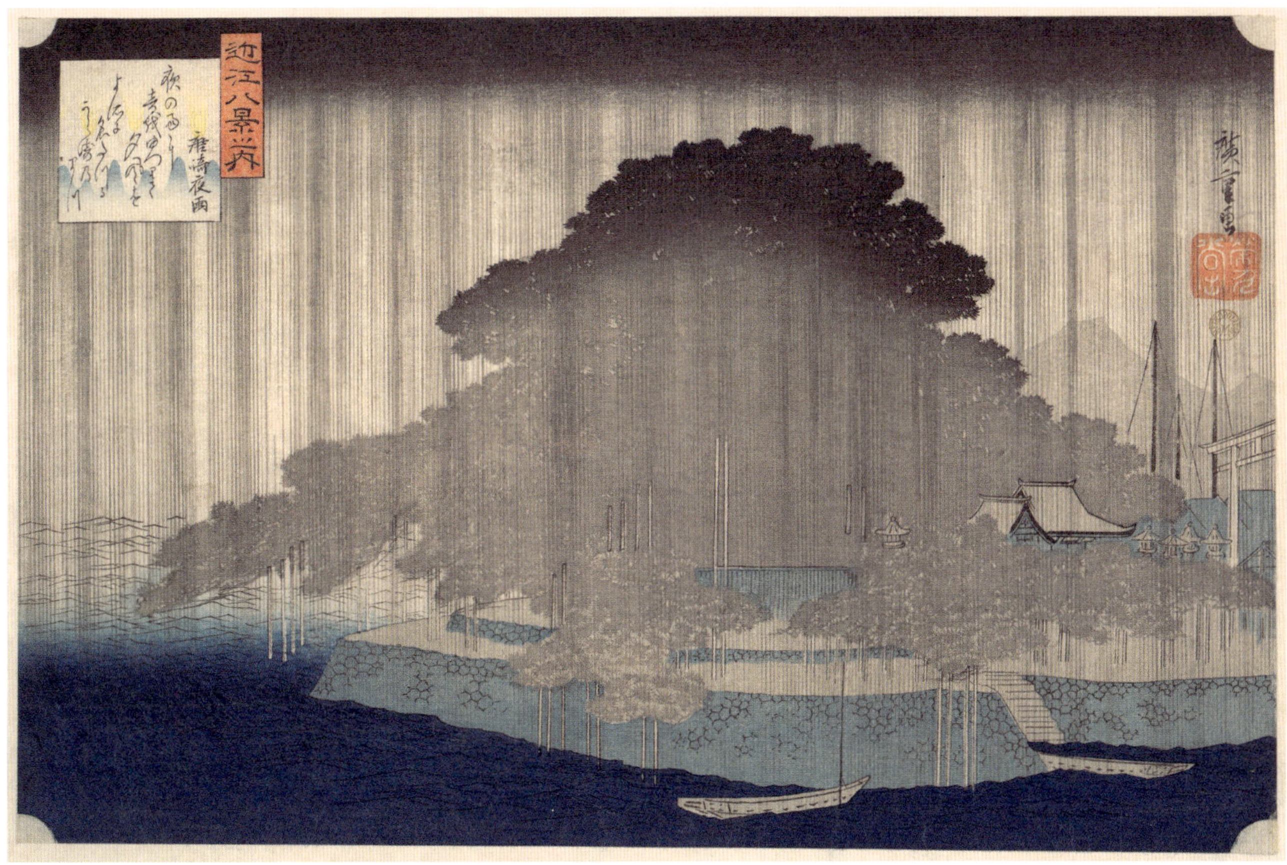

BEING CAUGHT IN A DOWNPOUR, ESPECIALLY IN HORIZONTAL SHEETS OF RAIN, CAN ELICIT A FEELING OF BOTH EXHILARATION AND FEAR. IN HEAVY RAINS IT CAN BE DIFFICULT TO SEE FAR AHEAD. IN THESE IMAGES OF DELUGE, THE ARTISTS RENDER A CURTAIN OF RAIN IN THE FOREGROUND WITH INTERMITTENT VIEWS THROUGH TO THE SCENE BEYOND.

Opposite top – *Heavy Rain at Ochanomizu Bridge*, c. 1915, woodblock print, ink and colour on paper, Kobayashi Kiyochika (Japanese)

Opposite bottom – *The West Wind, Lynmouth*, 1866, watercolour and gouache, Sir Edward John Poynter (British)

Above – *Night Rain at Karasaki*, c. 1835, woodblock print, ink and colour on paper, Utagawa Hiroshige (Japanese)

Following – *Maharana Fateh Singh's hunting party crossing a river in a flood* (detail), 1893, opaque watercolour on paper, Shivalal (Indian)

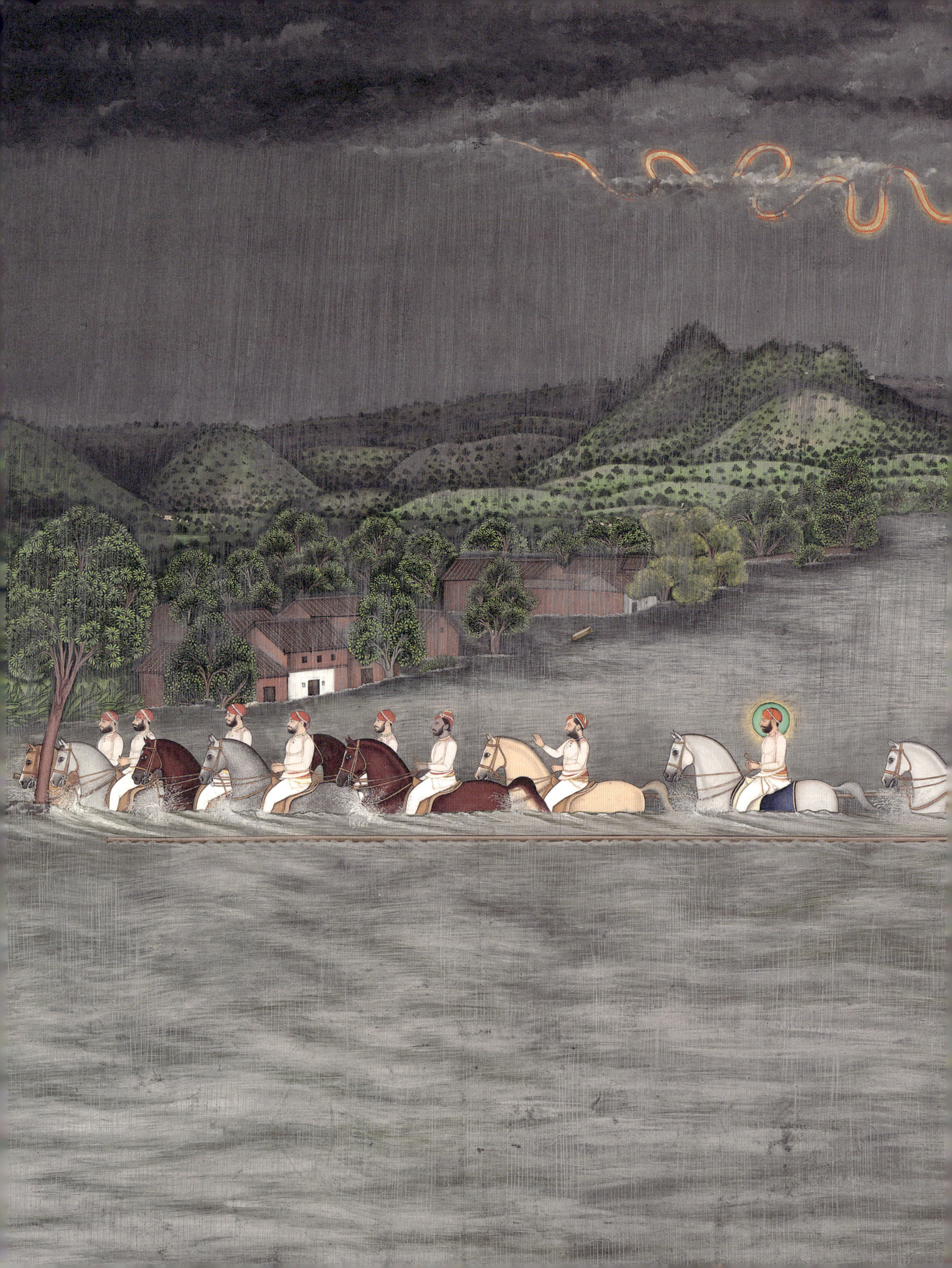

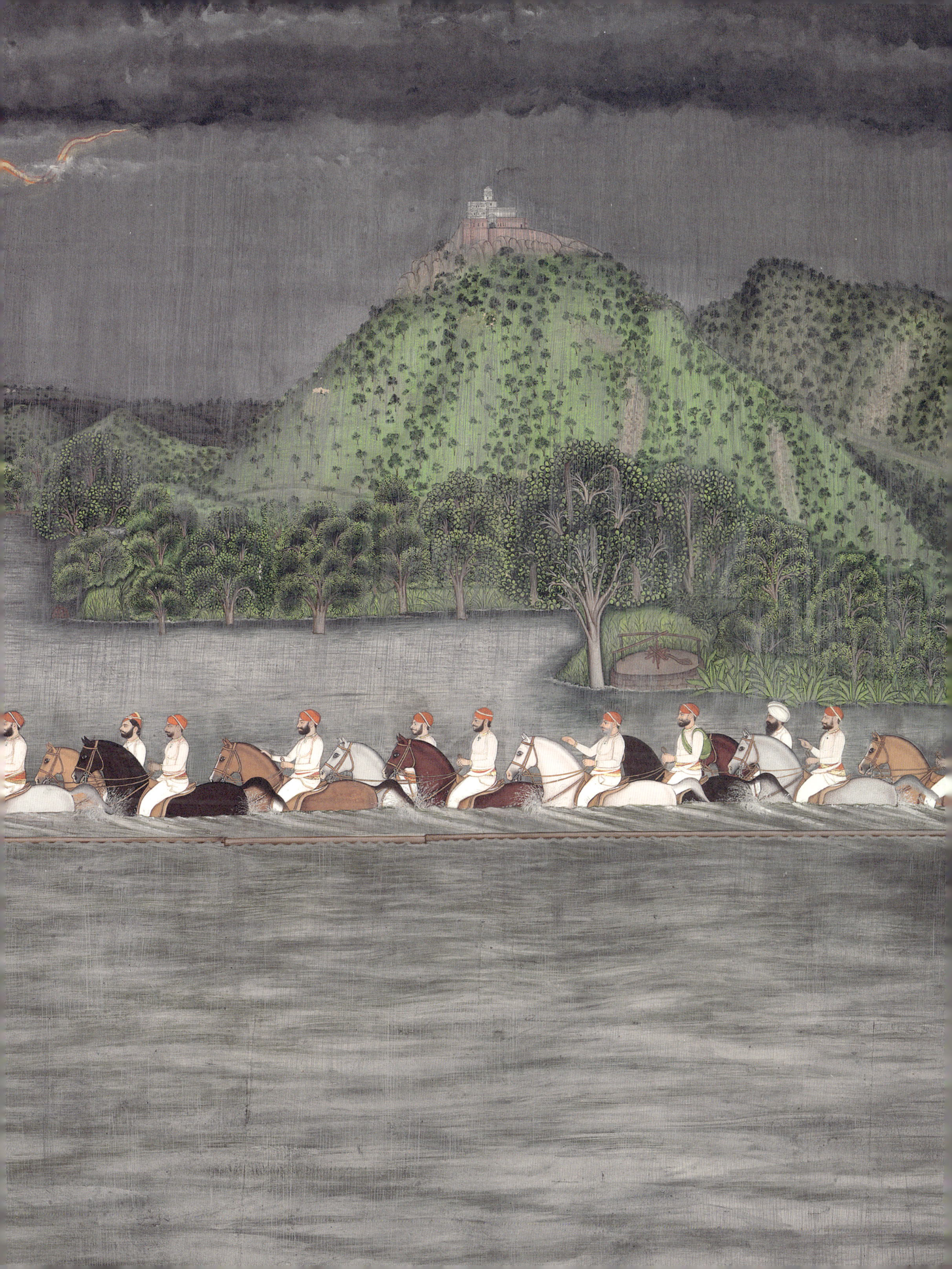

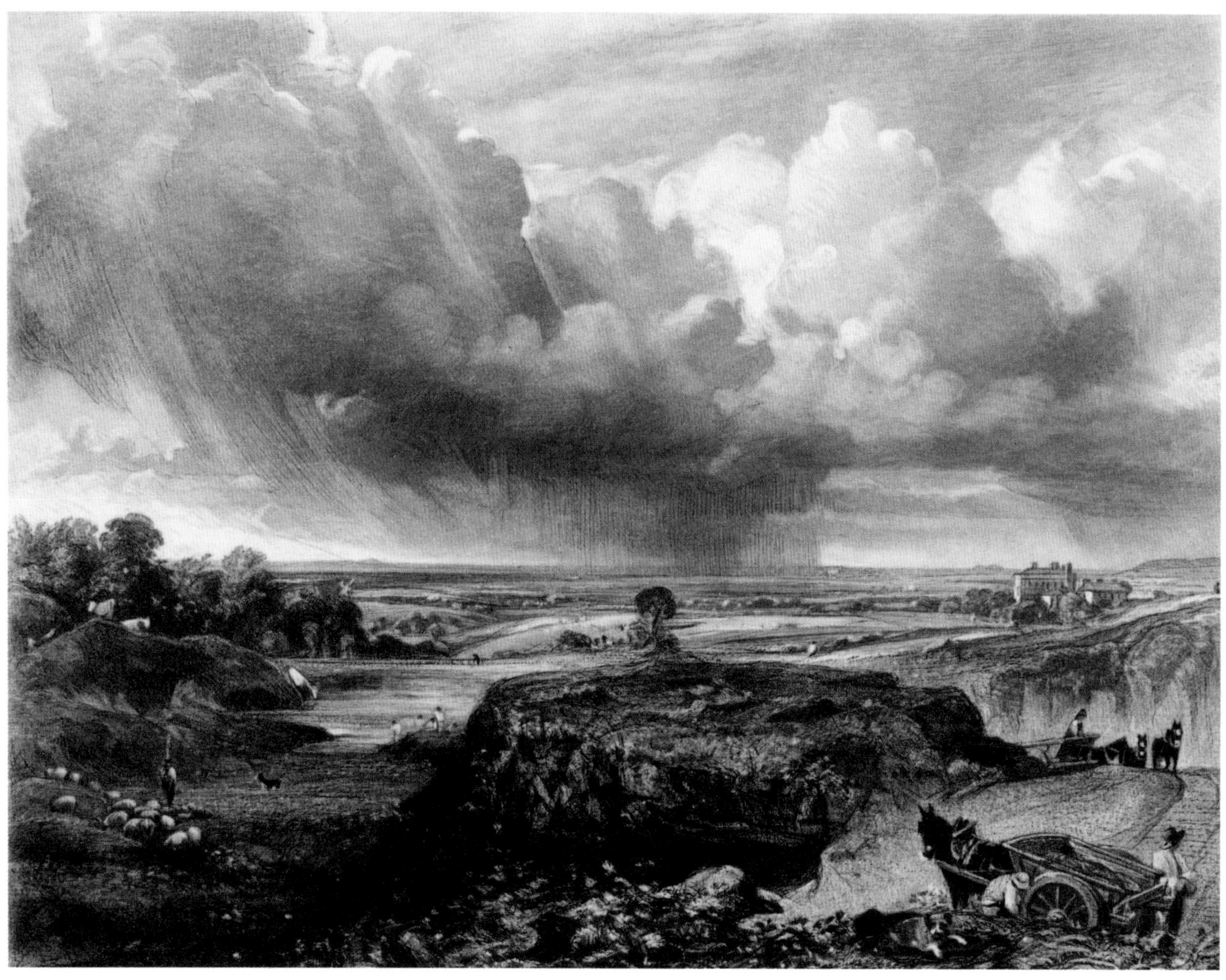

THERE IS A REAL BUZZ AND COMMOTION GENERATED WITH THE ONSET OF A STORM. AS THE SKY CONJURES A SCENE OF RAPIDLY CHANGING LIGHT AND COLOURS, WE IMMEDIATELY SEEK SHELTER, EVEN PAUSING FOR THE WEATHER TO PASS.

 Hampstead Heath, 1855, mezzotint on paper, John Constable and David Lucas (British)

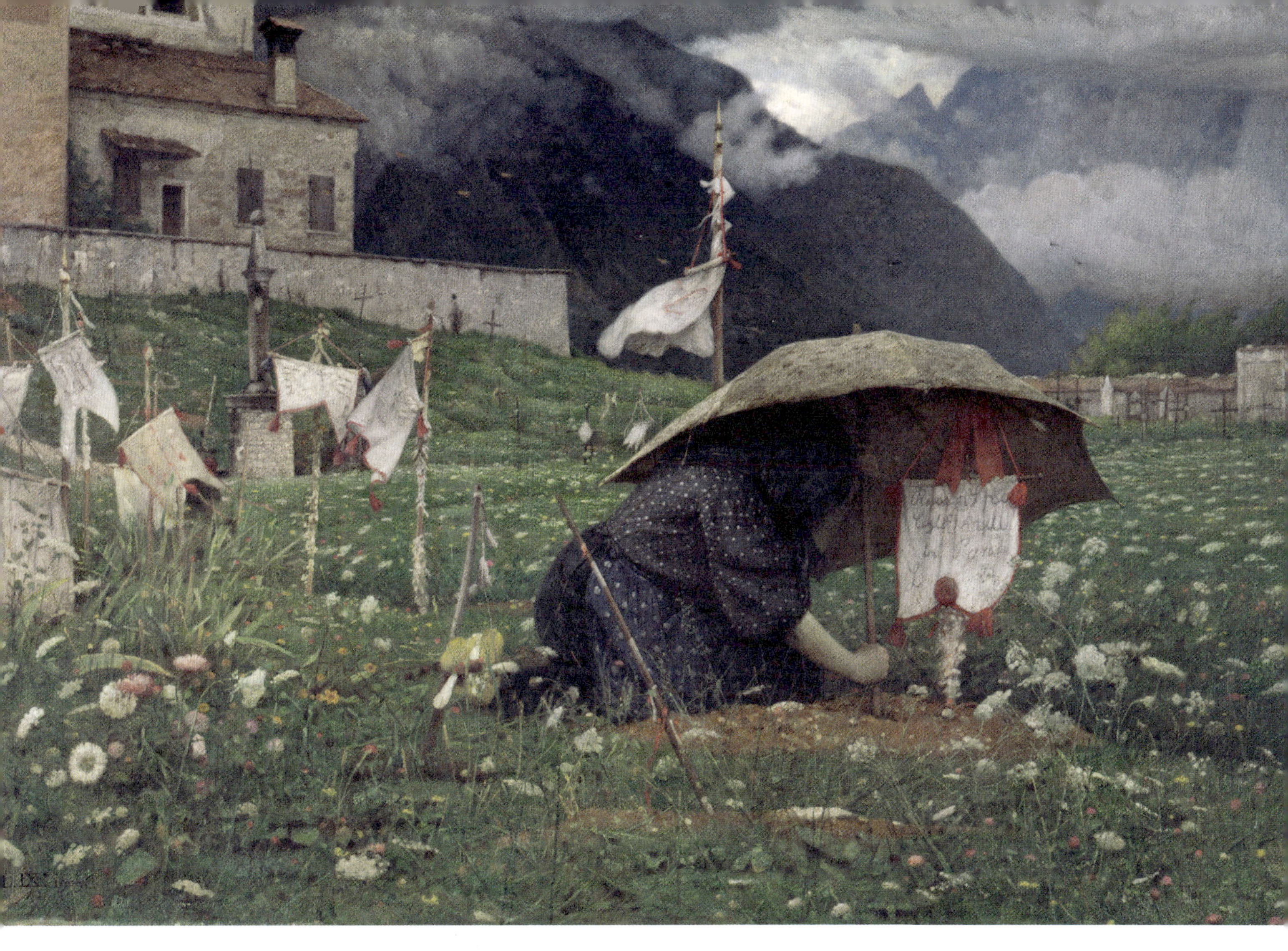

Above – *The first rain*, 1909, oil on canvas, Luigi Nono (Italian)

Following – *Returning storm*, 2001, etching, Rick Amor (Australian)

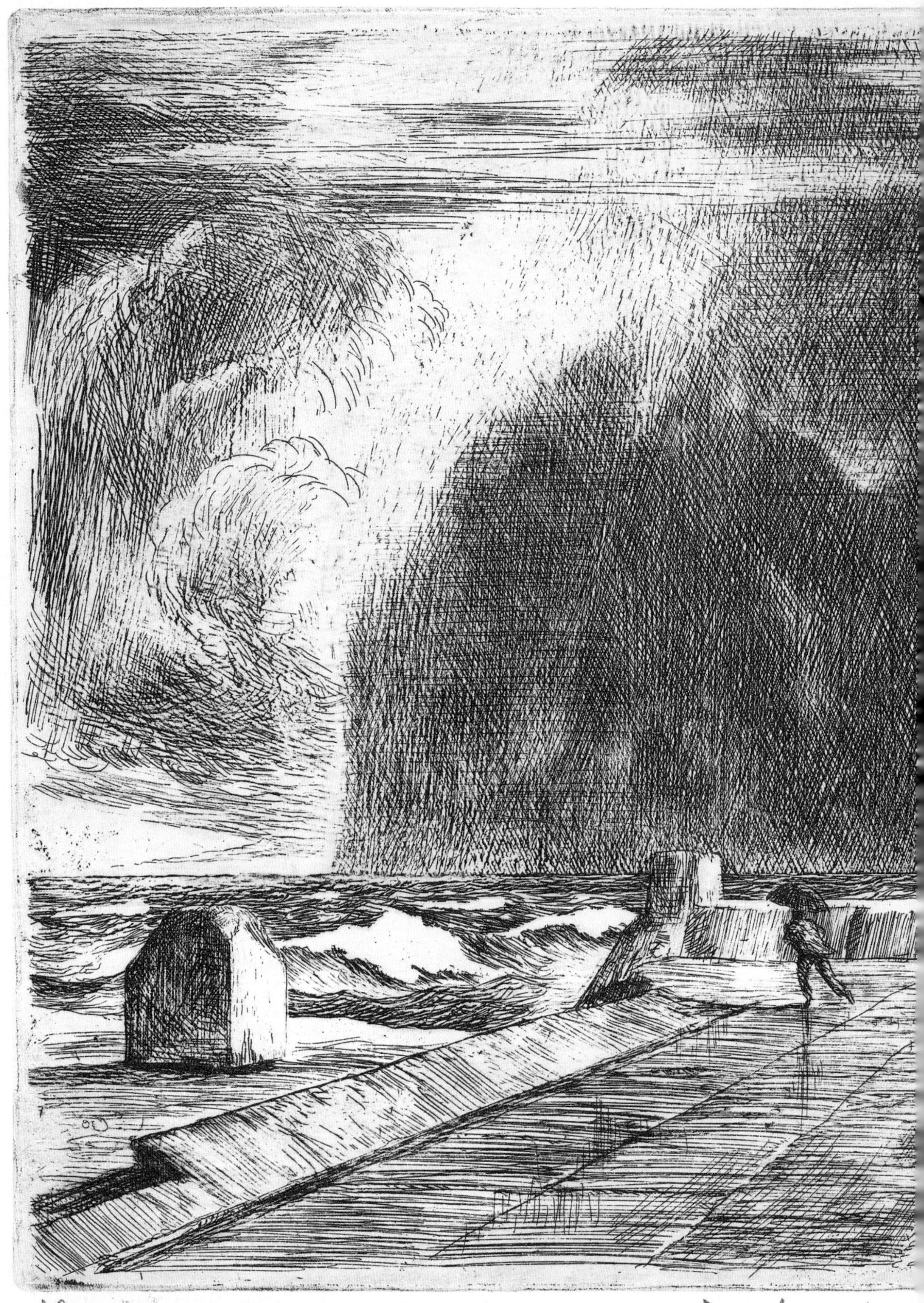
10/10

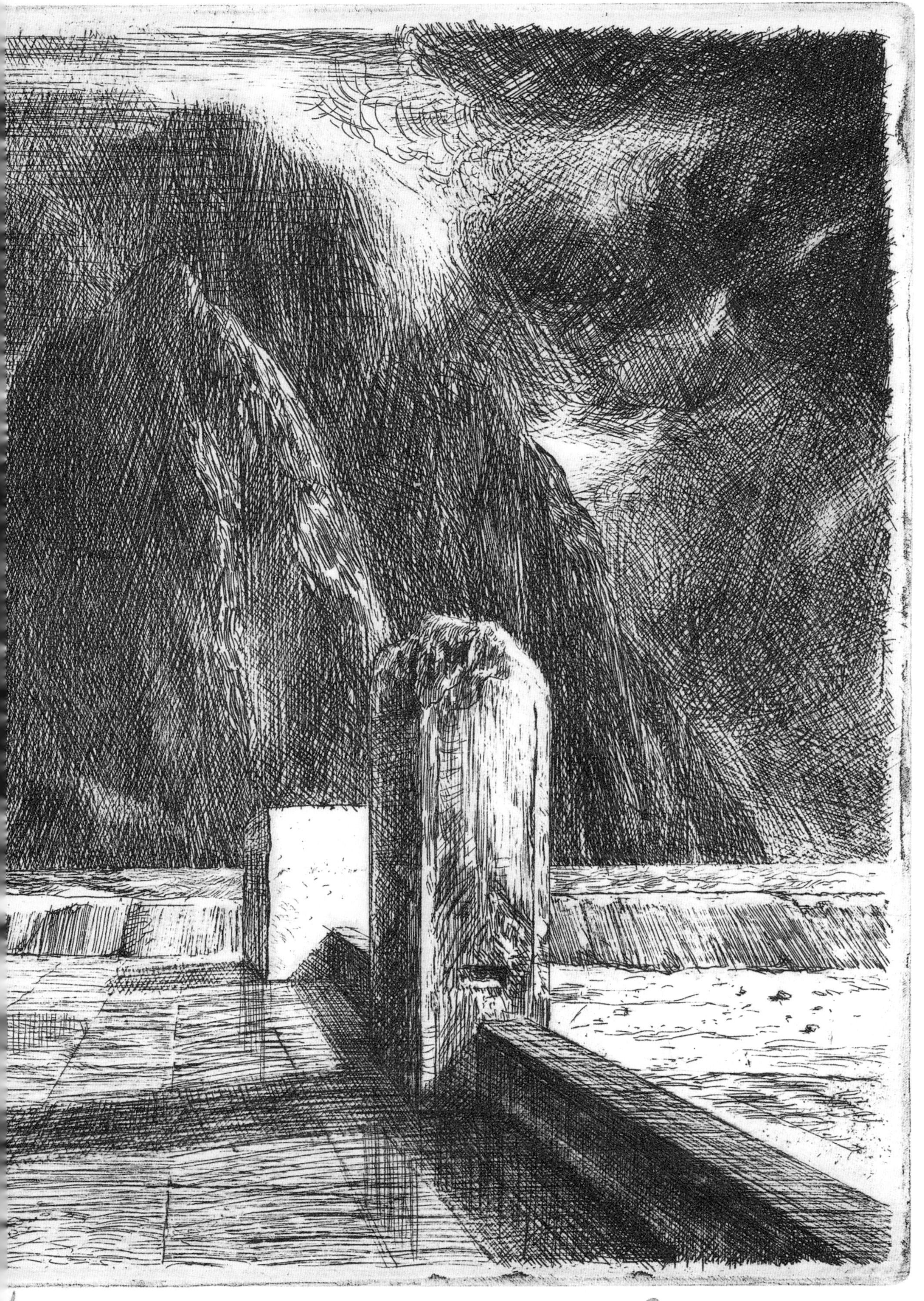

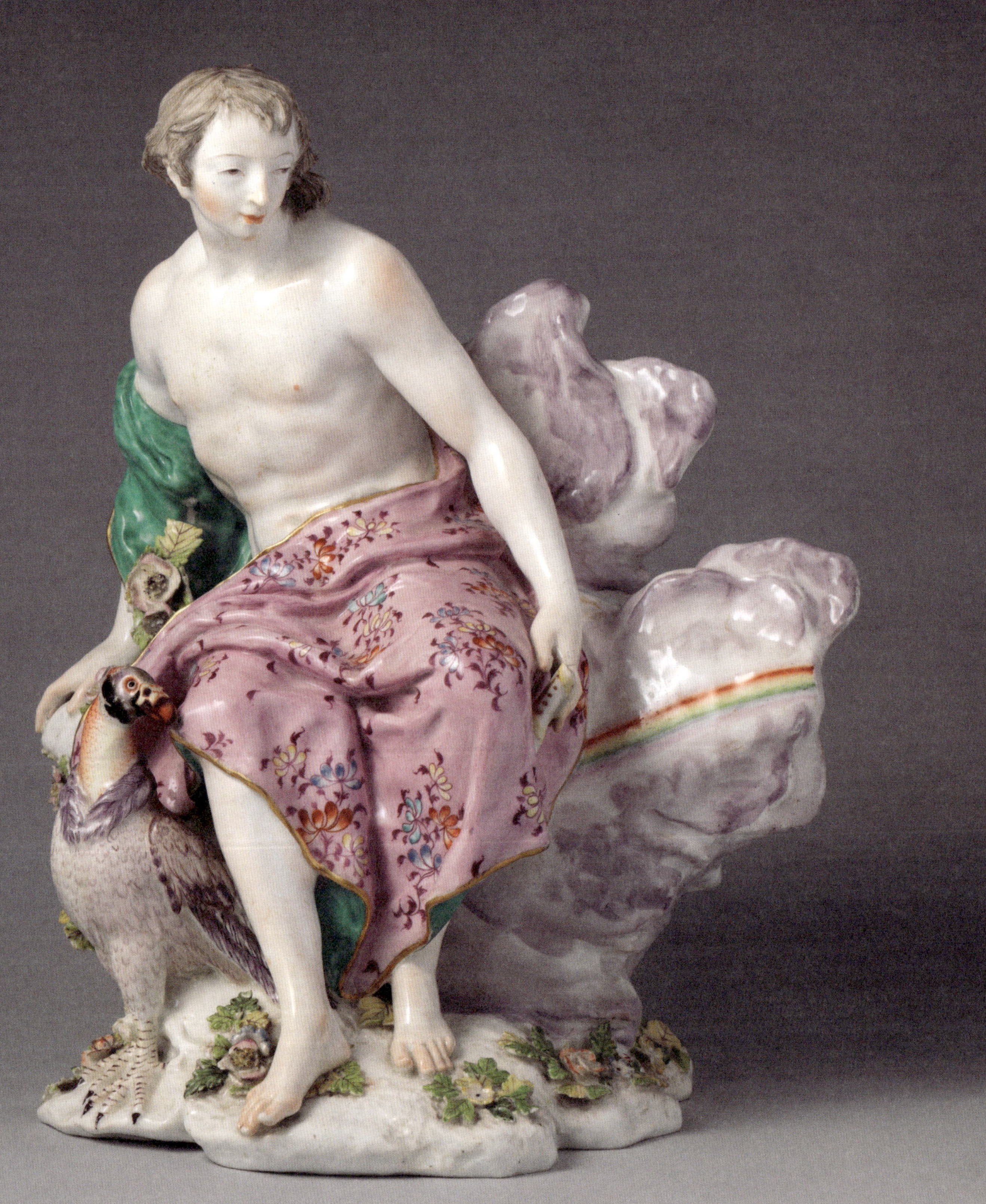

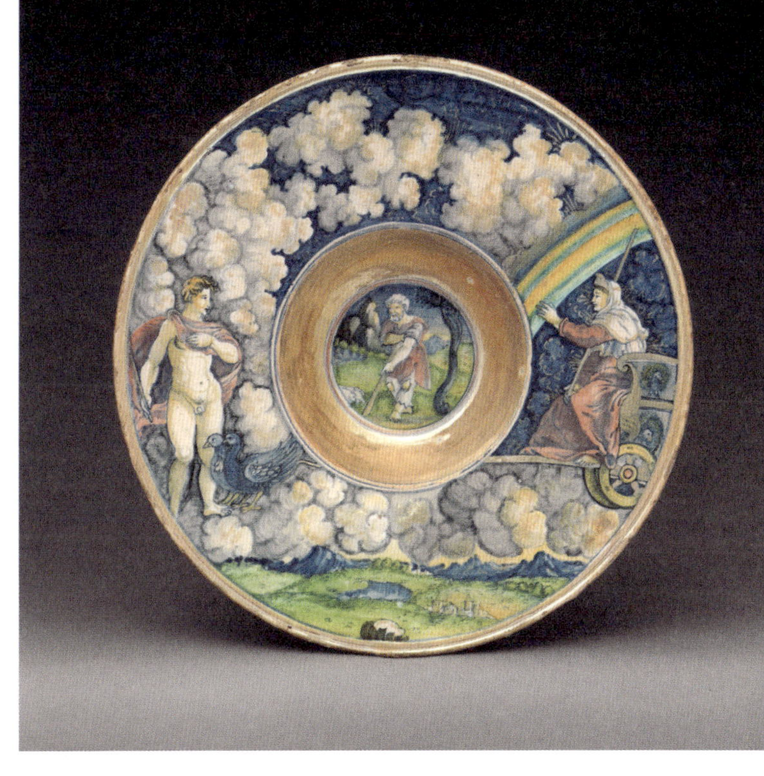

RAINBOWS

RAINBOWS IN ART CAPTURE A FLEETING SPECTACULAR OCCURRENCE. THERE IS A PARTICULAR MAGIC IN WITNESSING A RAINBOW APPEAR IN THE SKY – JUST LIKE A DREAM, THE HARDER YOU TRY TO SEIZE IT, THE QUICKER IT SLIPS OUT OF VIEW.

Opposite – *Sight (one of a pair)*, c. 1755, Chelsea Porcelain Manufactory (British), soft-paste porcelain with enamel decoration and gilding, modelled by Joseph Willems (Flemish)

Top – Wide-rimmed bowl with figures from Virgil's Aeneid, 1525, maiolica (tin-glazed earthenware), lustered, various artists/makers (Italian)

Bottom – *Rainbow reflection*, c. 1970, oil on board, Sam Byrne (Australian)

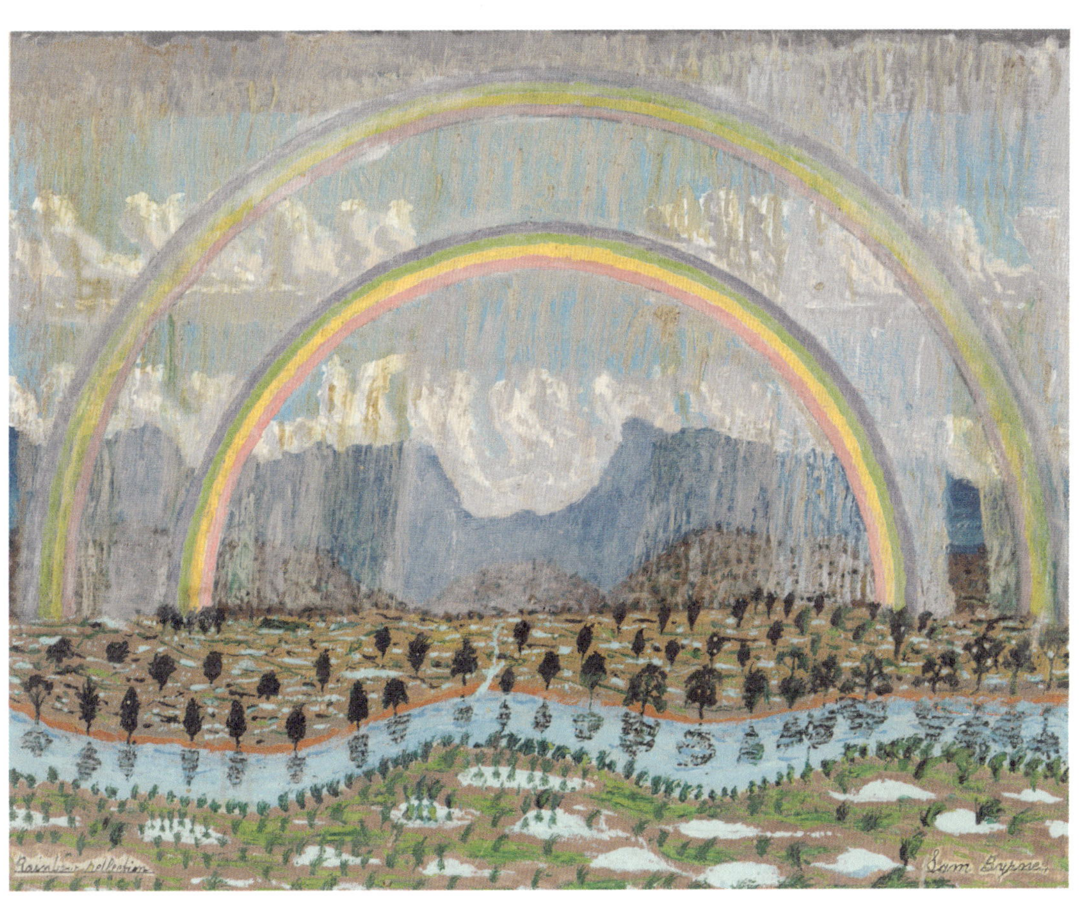

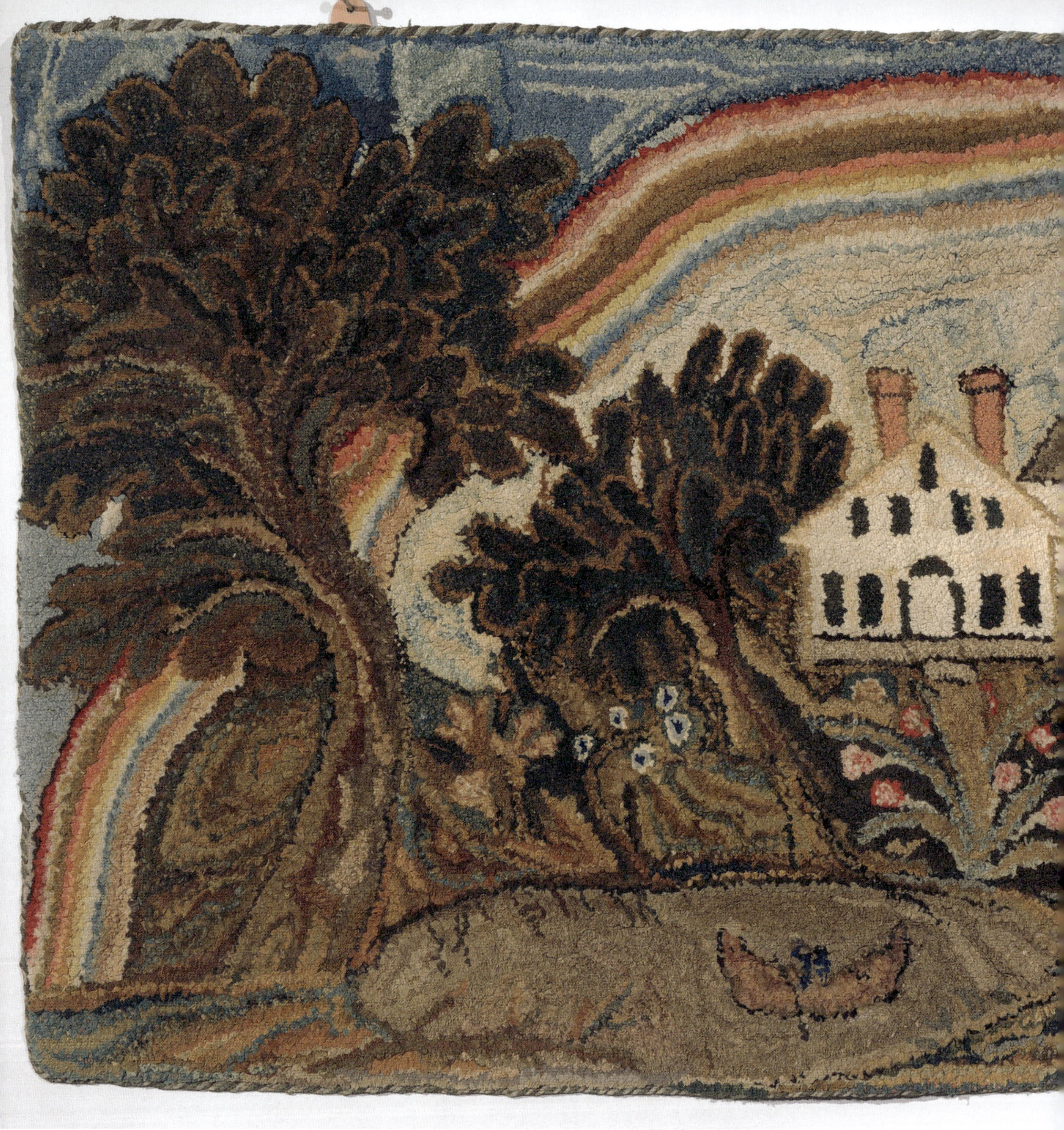

 Hooked Rug, c. 1860, wool, Lucy Trask Barnard (American)

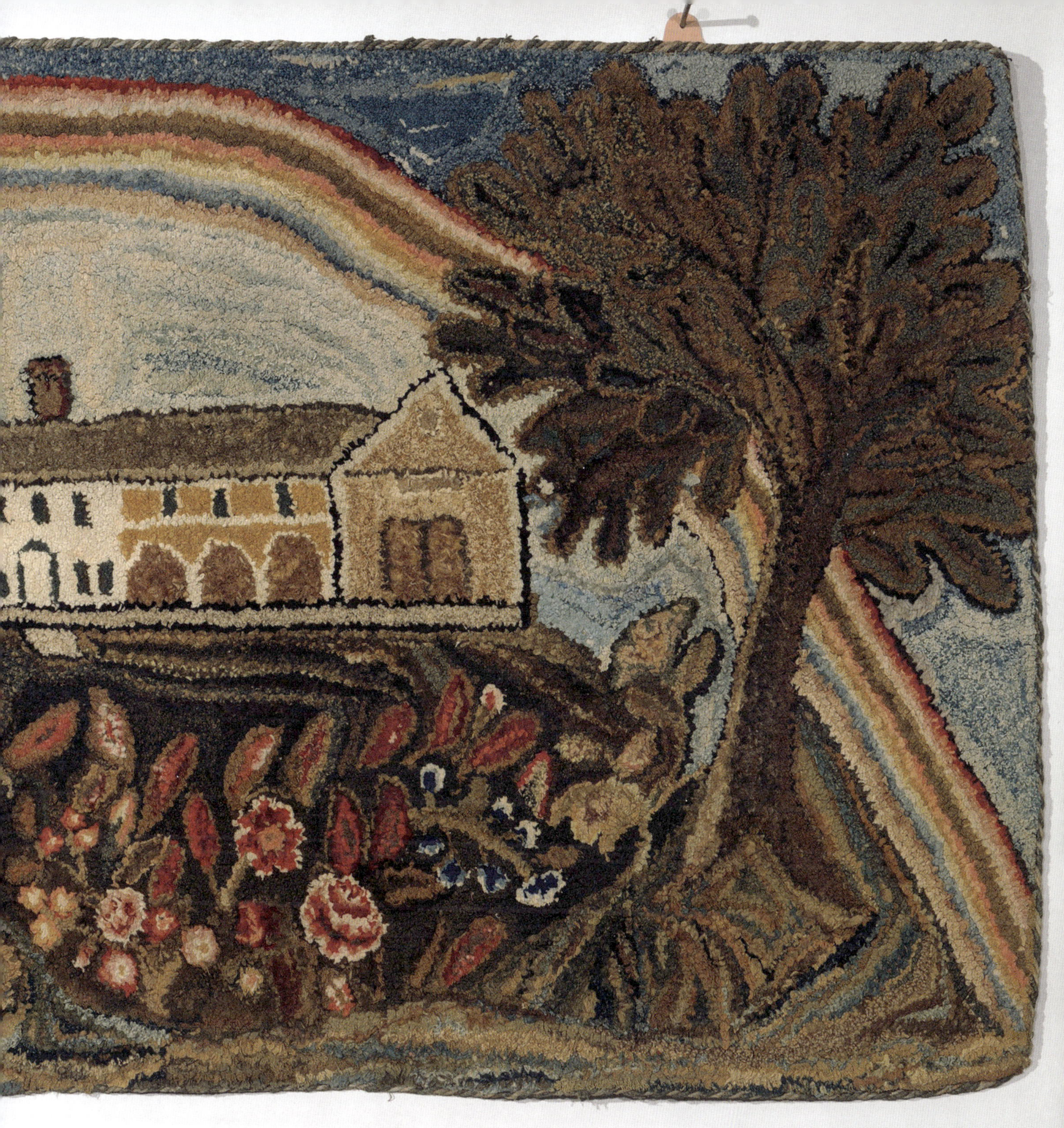

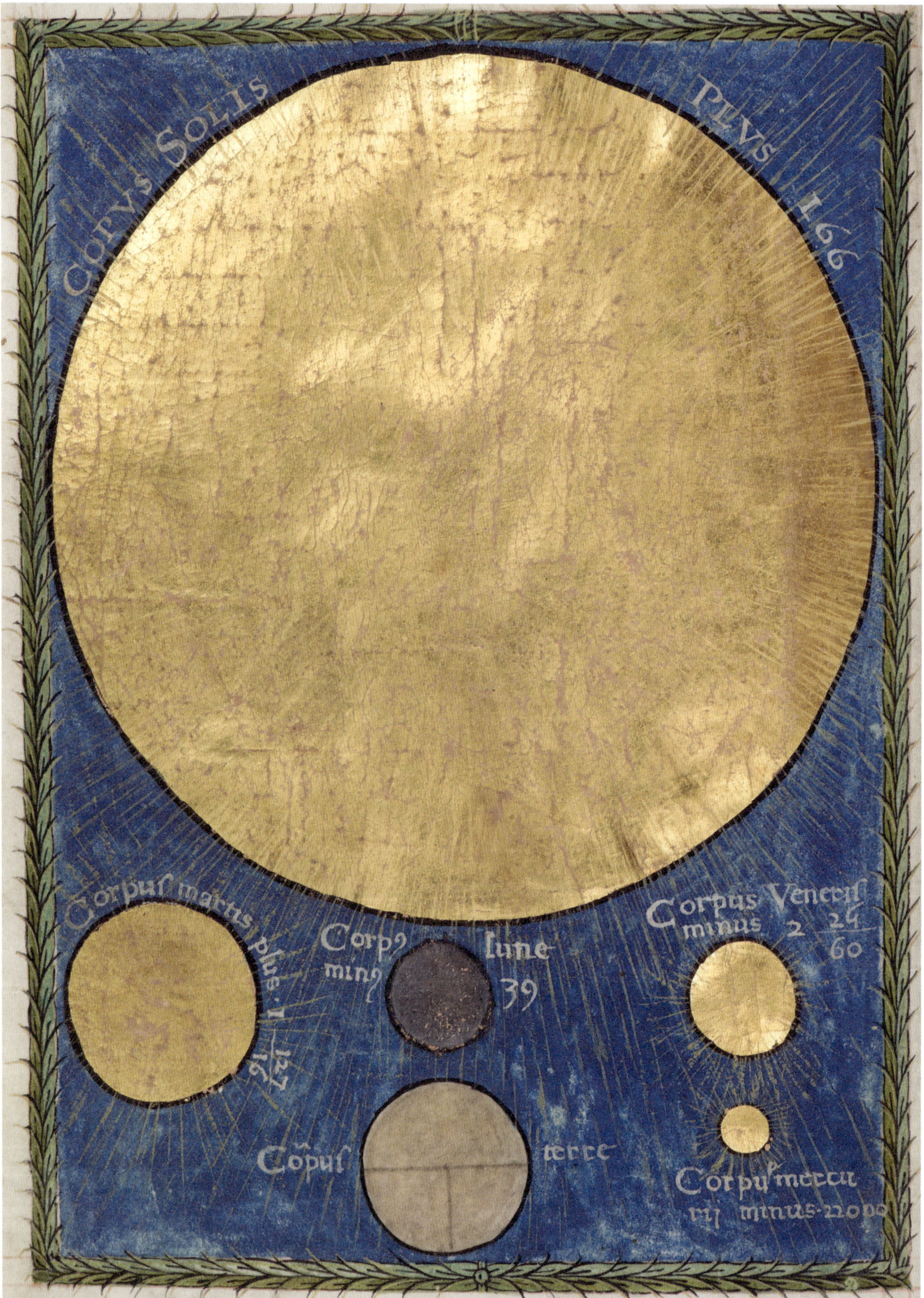
Corpus Solis
Plus 166
Corpus martis plus ·I· 127/16
Corp' lune
min' 39
Corpus Veneris
minus 2 24/60
Copus terre
Corpu' mercu
rij minus·22000

SUNS

SOME OF THE OLDEST SURVIVING OBJECTS AND ILLUSTRATIONS DEPICT THE SUN. JUST LIKE OTHER VITAL ELEMENTS OF NATURE, THE SUN NOURISHES ALL LIVING BEINGS. IN THE COOLER MONTHS WE SEEK ITS RADIANT, WARM EMBRACE AND IN THE HEIGHT OF SUMMER WE OFTEN TRY TO ESCAPE ITS POWERFUL, HOT RAYS. CONTEMPLATE HOW ARTISTS HAVE RENDERED SUNBEAMS AND THE MIGHTY AURA OF THIS BRILLIANT STAR.

Opposite – *Sun, Moon and Planets (shelfmark 'Latin MS 53', from 'Astronomia')*, c. 1470–80, codex, parchment, Joachinus de Gigantibus (German)

Below – *The Sun Chariot*, Nordic Bronze Age, c. 1500–1300 BC , bronze, clay cores, Unknown artist (Norwegian)

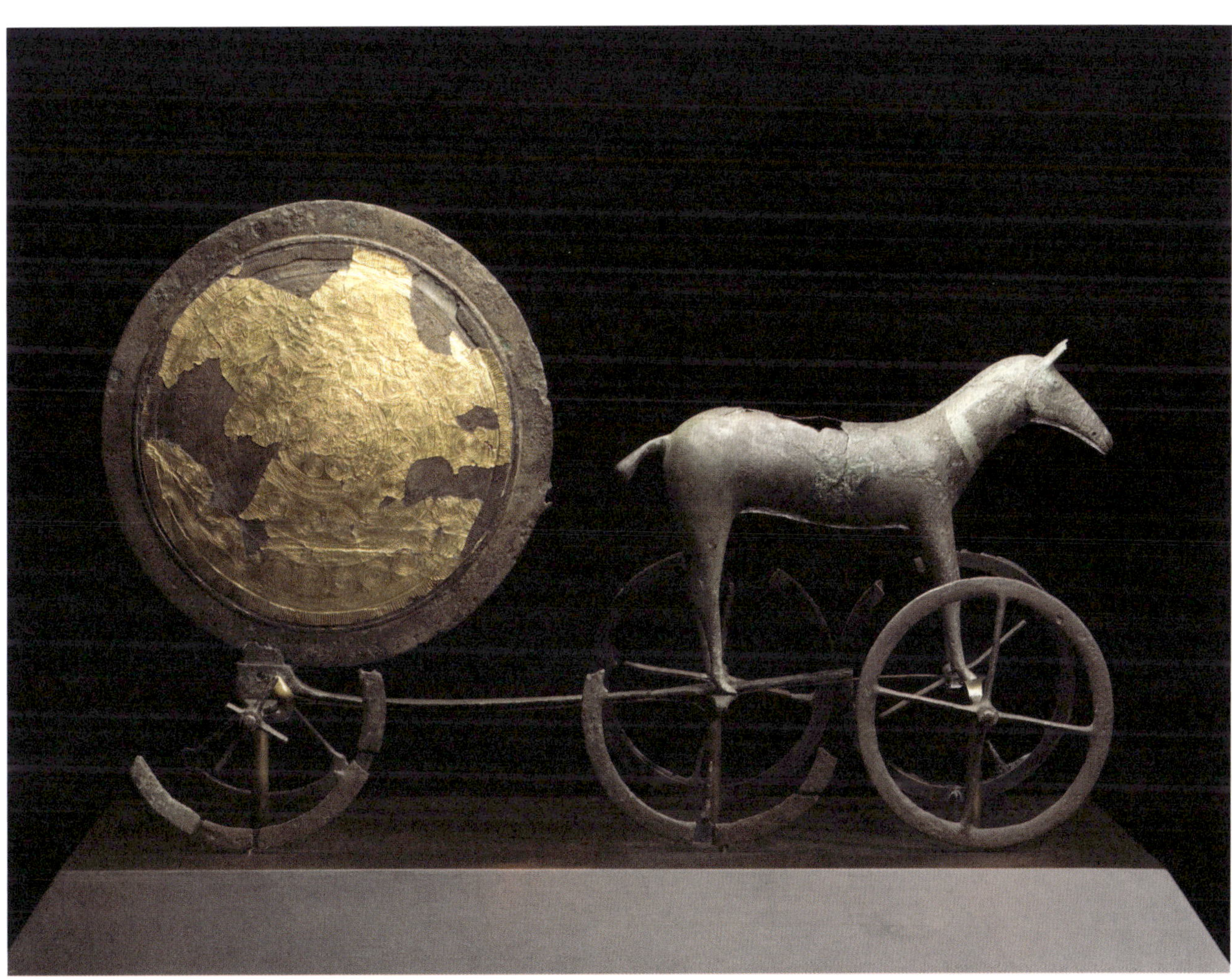

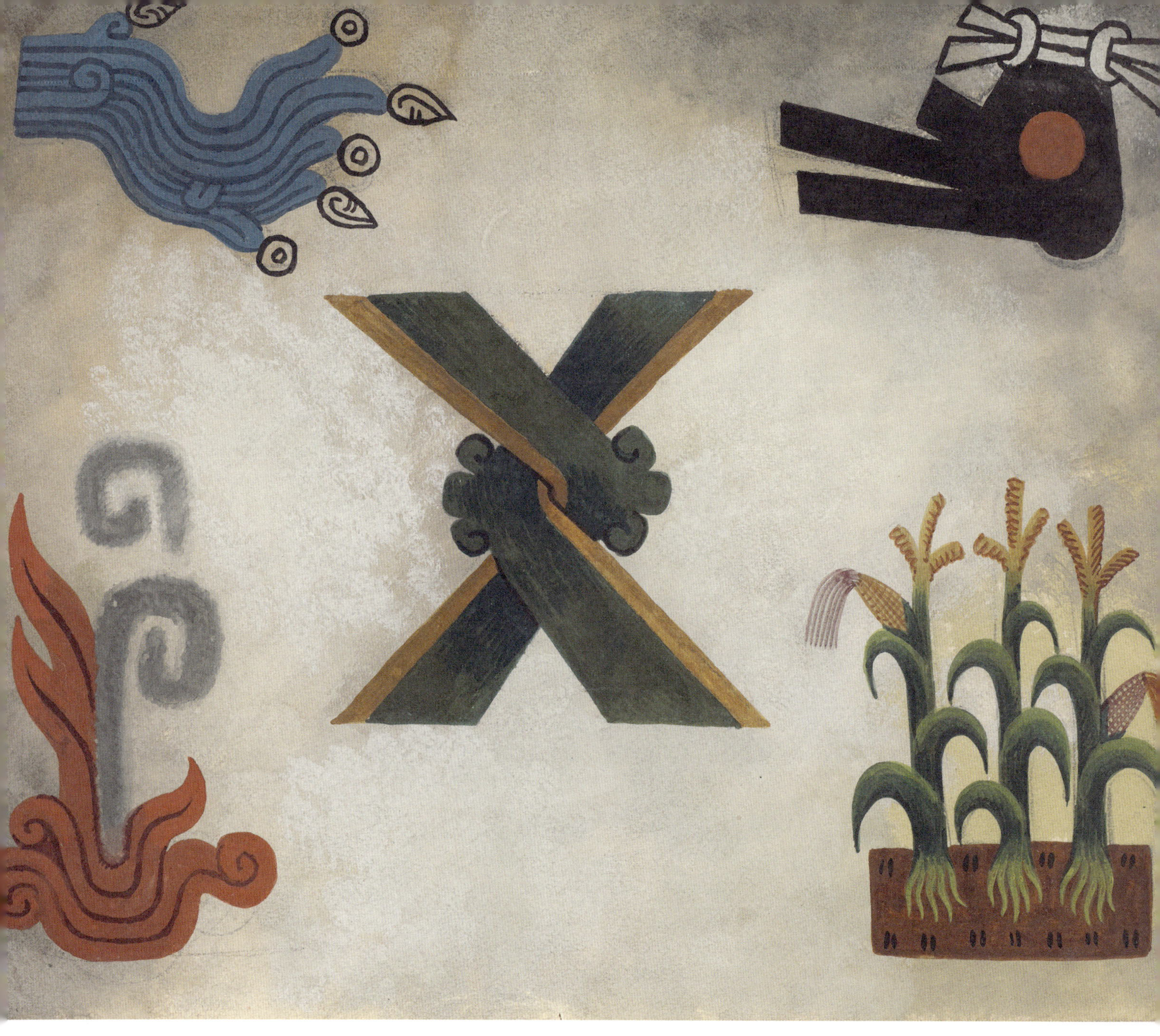

Design for a stage curtain, for the ballet Los cuatro soles (The Four Suns), c. 1927–33, gouache, Miguel Covarrubias (Mexican)

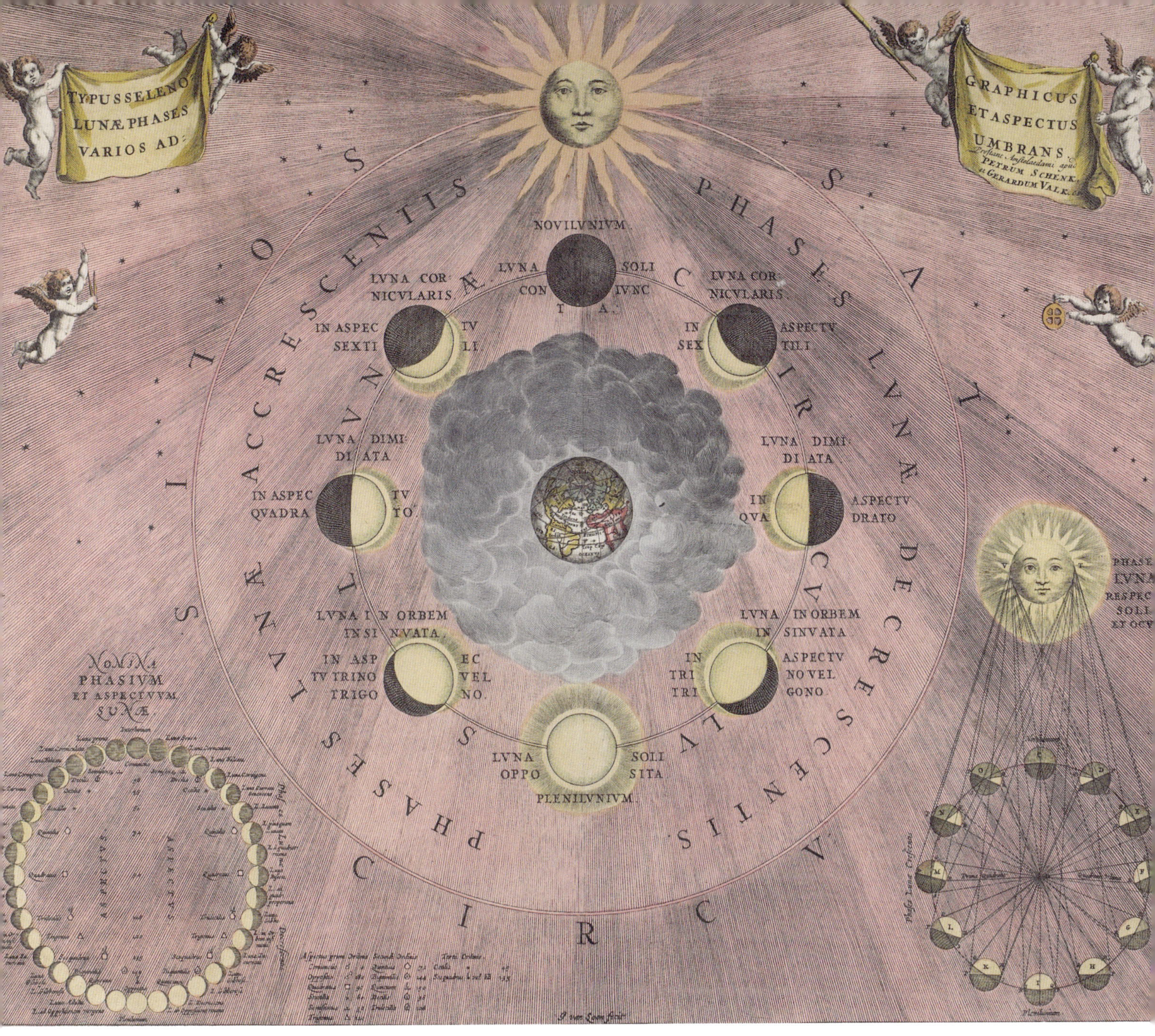

The Varying Phases and Appearances of the Moon, from Harmonia Macrocosmica, 1660, hand-coloured engraving with gold, Andreas Cellarius; Engraver, Johannes van Loon (Dutch)

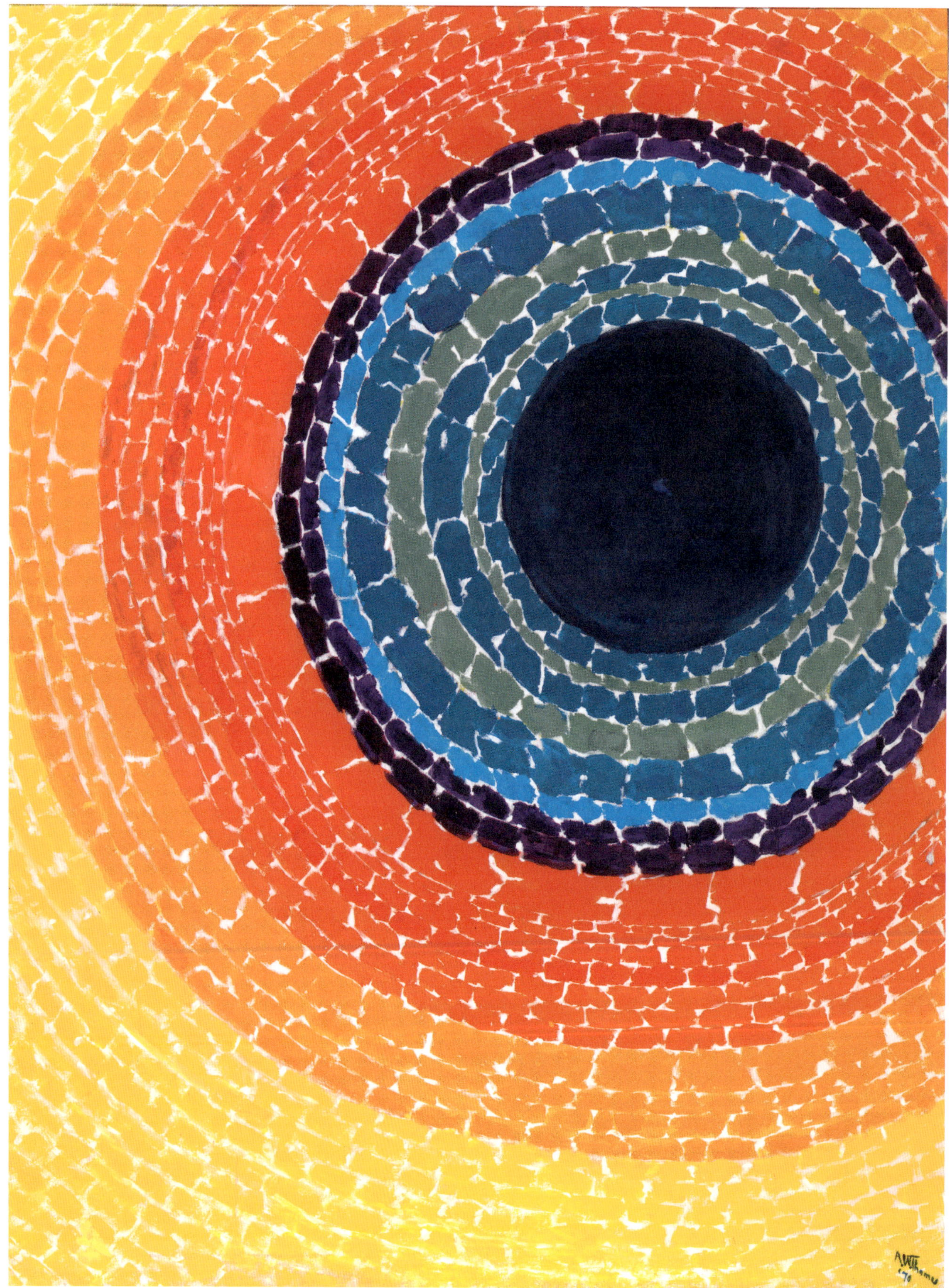

 The Eclipse, 1970, acrylic on canvas, Alma Thomas (American)

Top – *Solar Eclipse, Lompoc 1923*, 1923, oil on canvas, Howard Russell Butler (American)

Bottom – *Astronomy: eclipses (top), and the Moon's passage around the Earth*, 1851, engraving with watercolour, John Emslie (British)

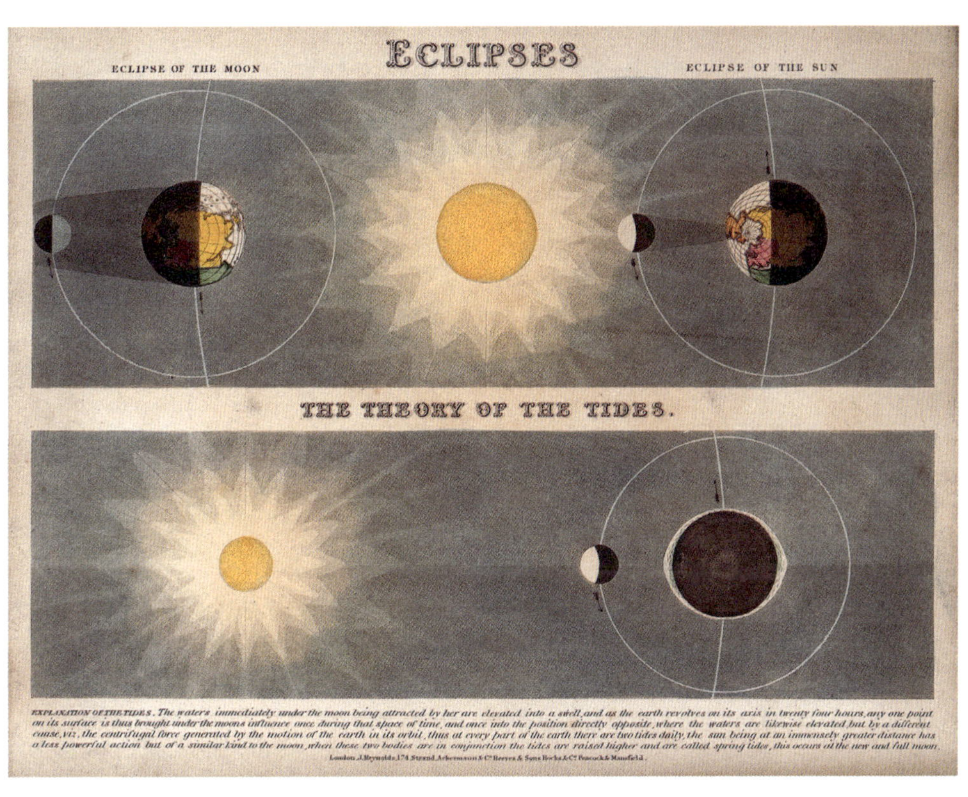

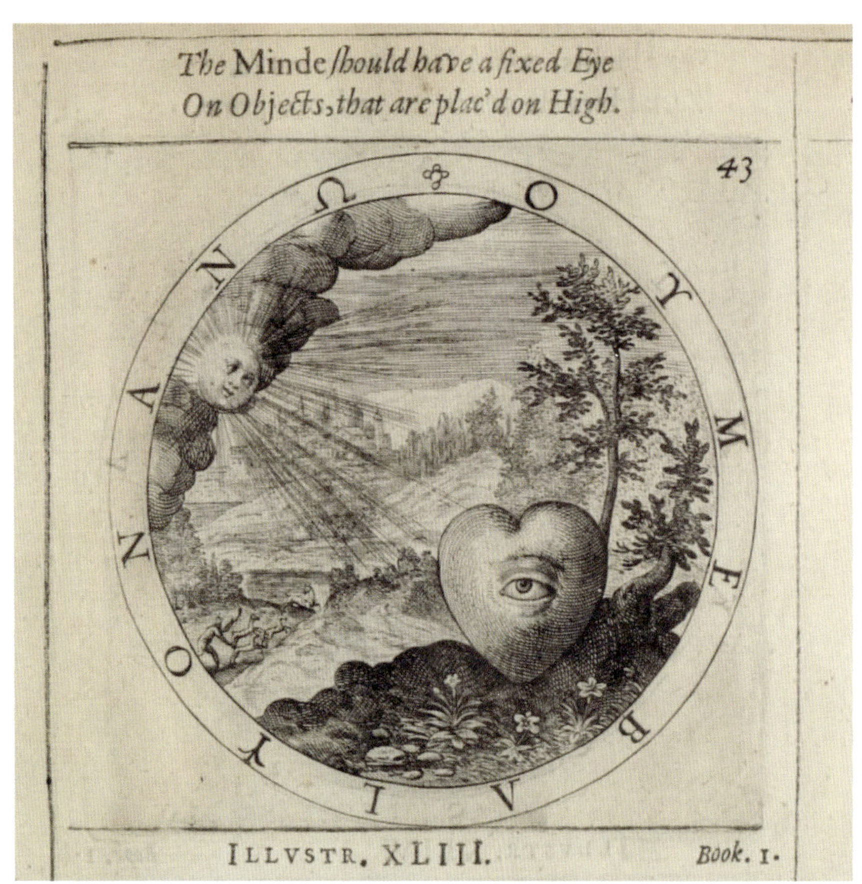

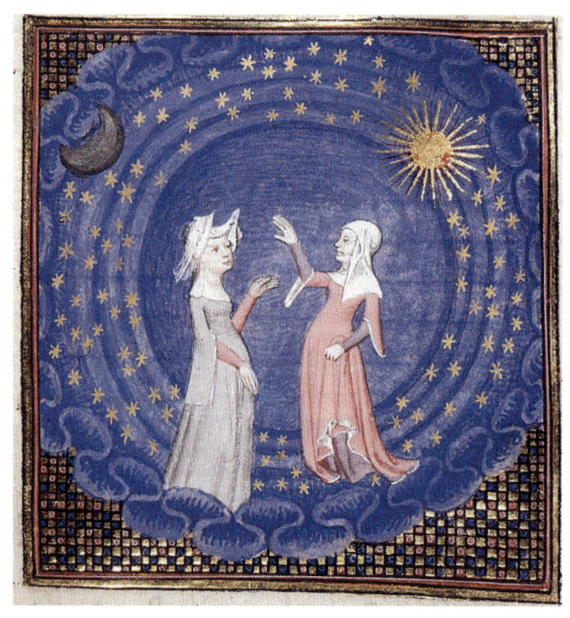

Top – Illustration from *A collection of emblemes, ancient and moderne quickened with metricall illustrations, both morall and divine: and disposed into lotteries*, 1635, illustration in a book, George Wither and Gabriel Rollenhagen (British)

Bottom – *Christine and the Sibyl standing in a sphere of the cosmos, with the moon, sun and stars surrounding them*, c. 1410–14, Christine de Pizan (French)

Opposite – *The dove, no 2* ,1915, oil on canvas, Hilma af Klint (Swedish)

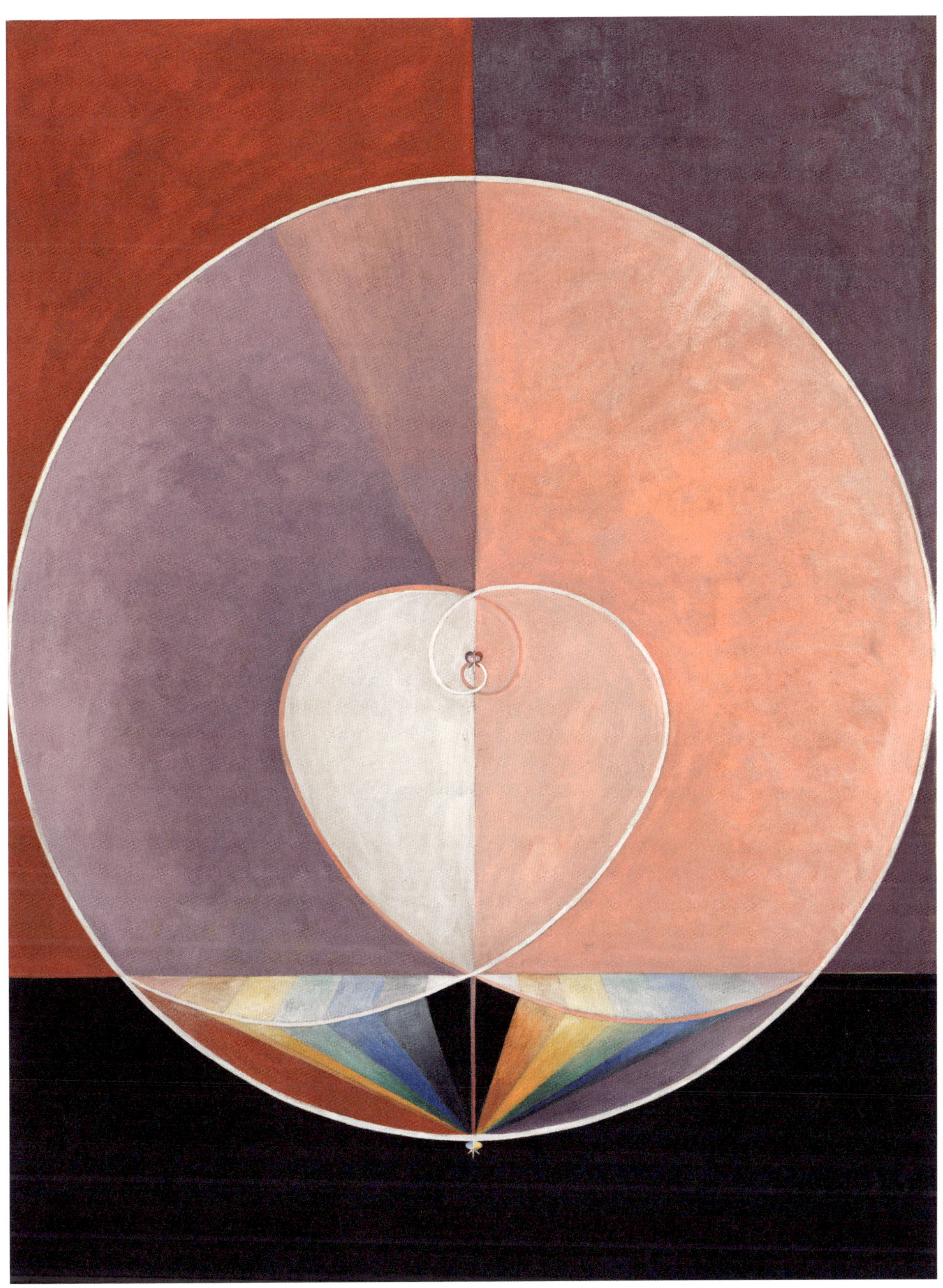

THE SPHERICAL ASPECT OF THESE WORKS CARRIES A QUALITY OF FEMININITY. COSMOLOGICAL FORCES AND THE ENERGY OF TRUTH PLAYED A ROLE IN THE WORK AND PRACTICE OF SWEDISH ARTIST HILMA AF KLINT. SHE WAS INTERESTED IN THE DOVE AS A CREATURE OF THE SKY AND THE LAND. HER DOVE SERIES REVEALS HER INTEREST IN COSMIC ICONOGRAPHY, RELIGIOUS SYMBOLISM, COLOUR THEORY AND SCIENTIFIC DISCOVERY.

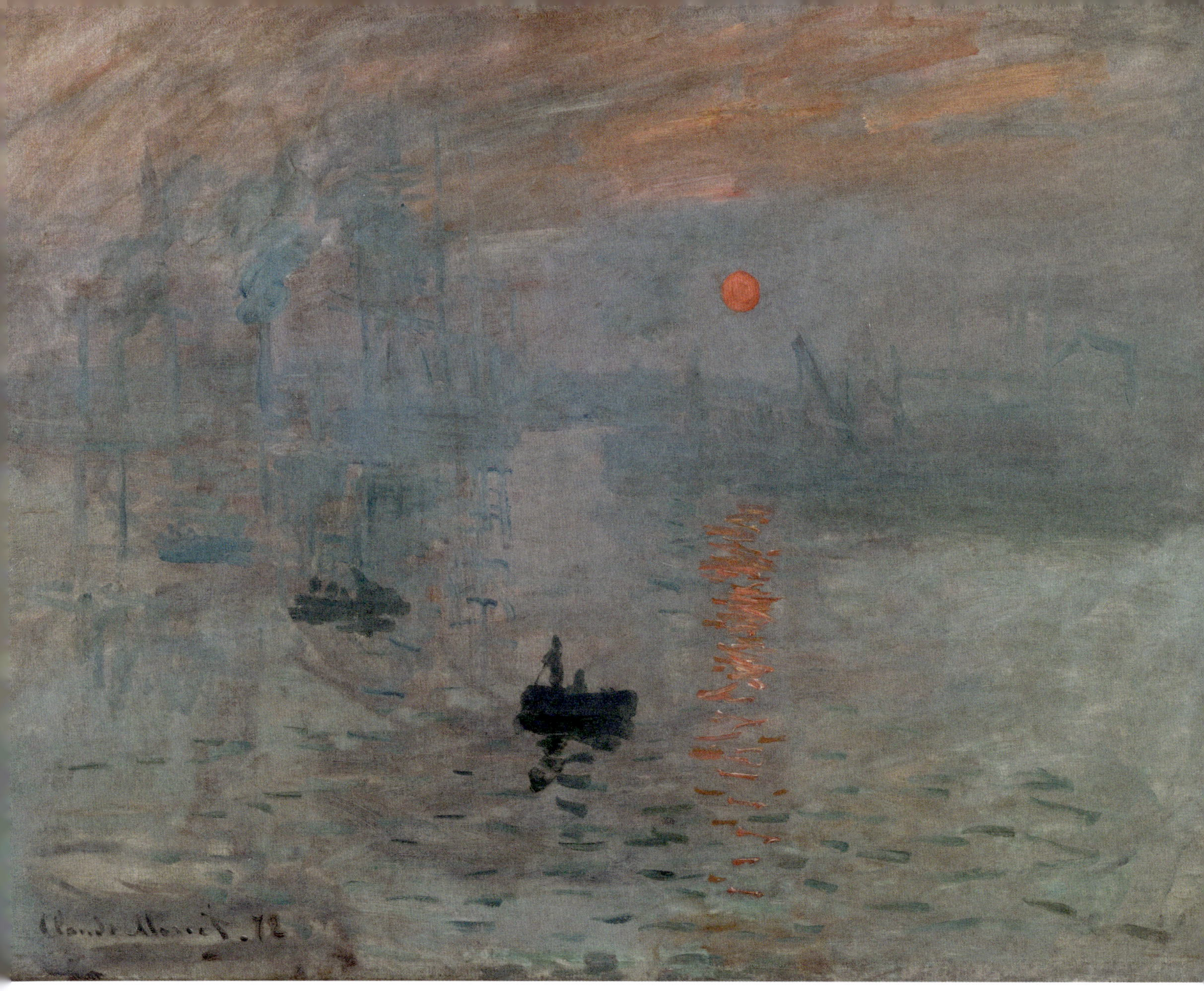

TAKE A CLOSER LOOK AT THE EFFECT OF COLOUR COMBINATIONS ON THESE TWO PAINTINGS OF RED SOLAR DISCS. CADMIUM RED SIDLES UP TO PINK AND BLUE VIOLETS WHICH ARE HIGHLIGHTED BY MARKS OF IRIDESCENT WHITE.

 Impression Sunrise, 1872, oil on canvas, Claude Monet (French)

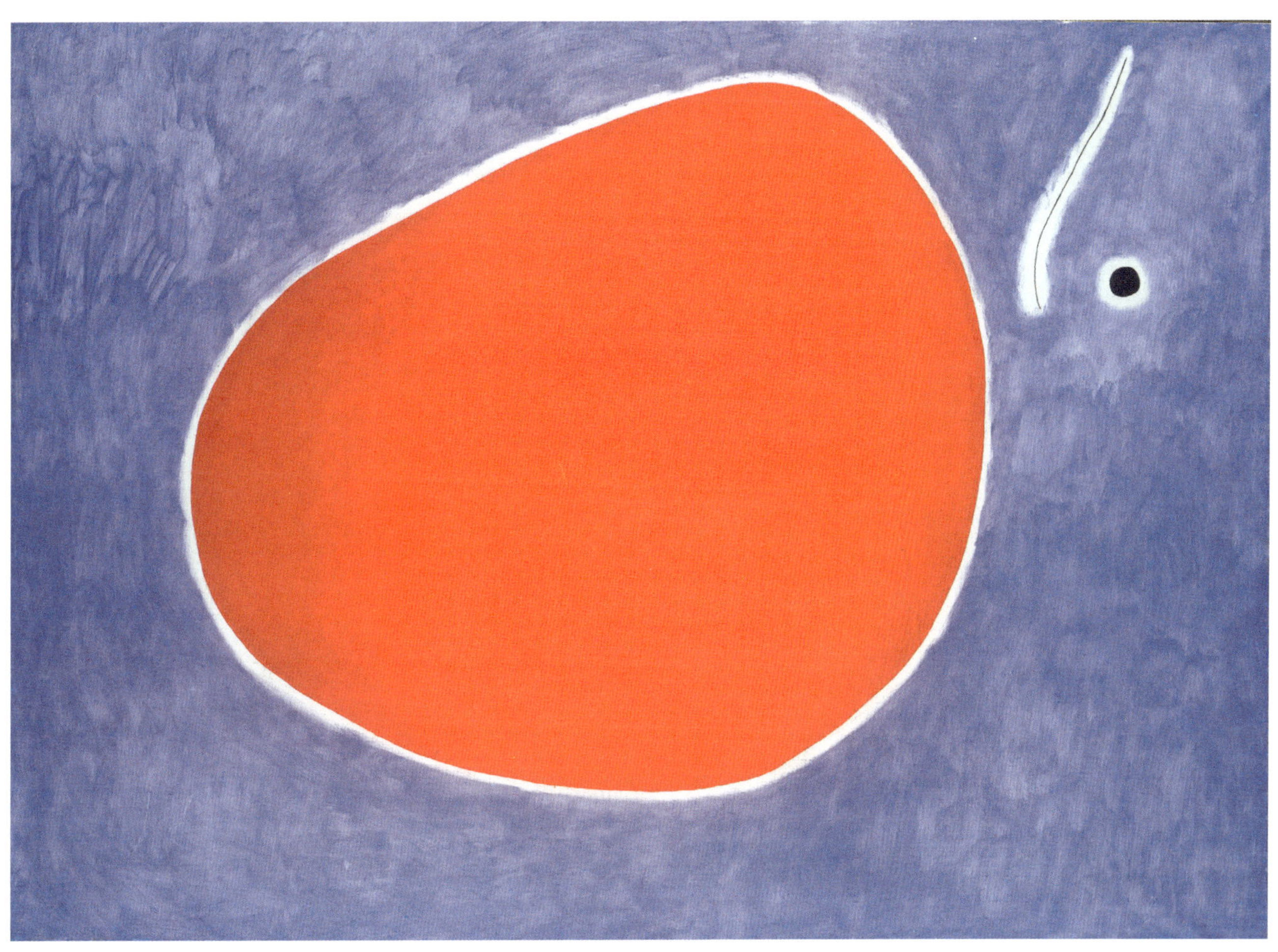

Above – *Flight of the Dragonfly in Front of the Sun*, 1968, oil on canvas, Joan Miró (Spanish)

Following left – *Untitled (Red)*, 1956, glue, oil, synthetic polymer paint and resin on canvas, Mark Rothko (American)

Following right – *Setting Sun on Sacramento Valley, California*, U.S.A, 1930, ink and colours on paper, Chiura Obata (American)

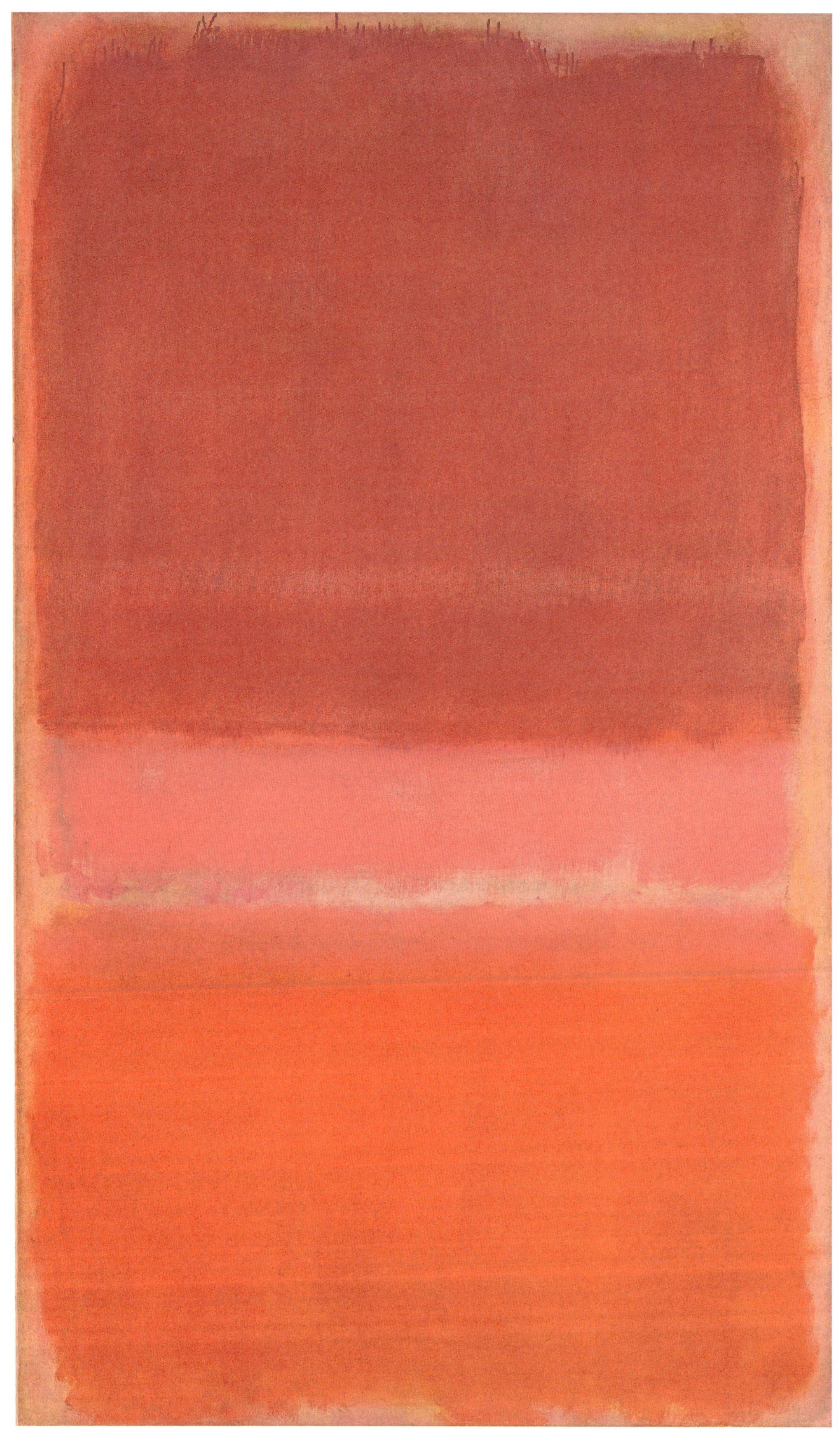

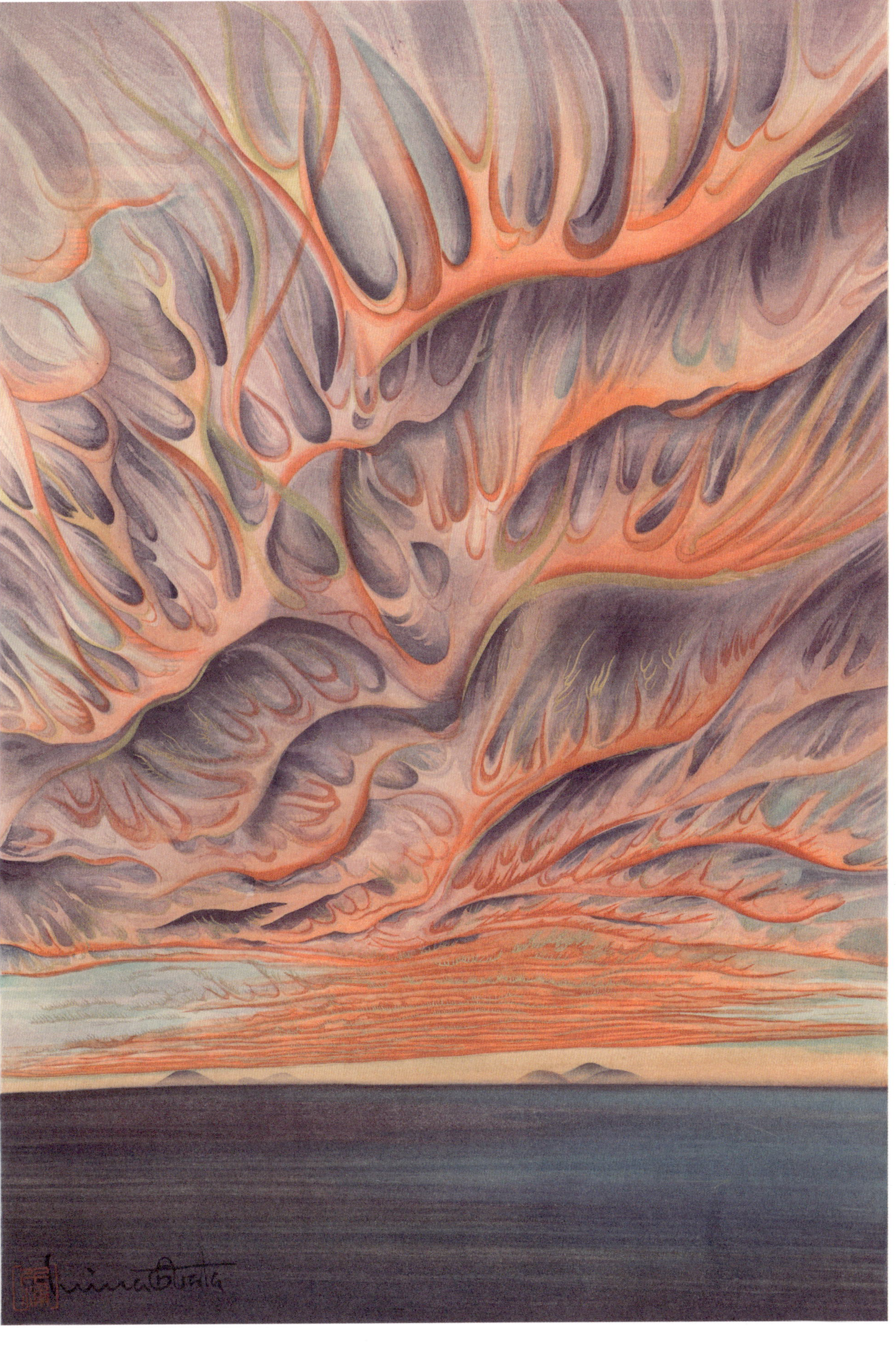

MOONS

THE PHASES OF THE MOON, AND DUSK OR TWILIGHT, FREQUENTLY PRESENT UNIQUE AND MAGICAL LIGHT EFFECTS. LILACS AND ROSES TOUCH THE LANDSCAPE AND WATER, CREATING A SOFTNESS IN THE AIR, WHICH CAN BE COUNTER TO THE DROP IN TEMPERATURE AS THE SUN SETS AND THE MOON RISES.

THE MOON HOLDS SPECIAL RESONANCE ACROSS CULTURES. IT HAS THE CAPACITY TO ILLUMINATE OUR NIGHT SKY AND TO PLUNGE US INTO COMPLETE DARKNESS. THE TIDES ARE SYNCHRONISED WITHIN ITS ORBIT AND AGRARIAN SOCIETIES DESIGNED THE LUNISOLAR CALENDAR IN ACKNOWLEDGMENT OF ITS FORCE. THE MOON CONTINUES TO FASCINATE AND INSPIRE US.

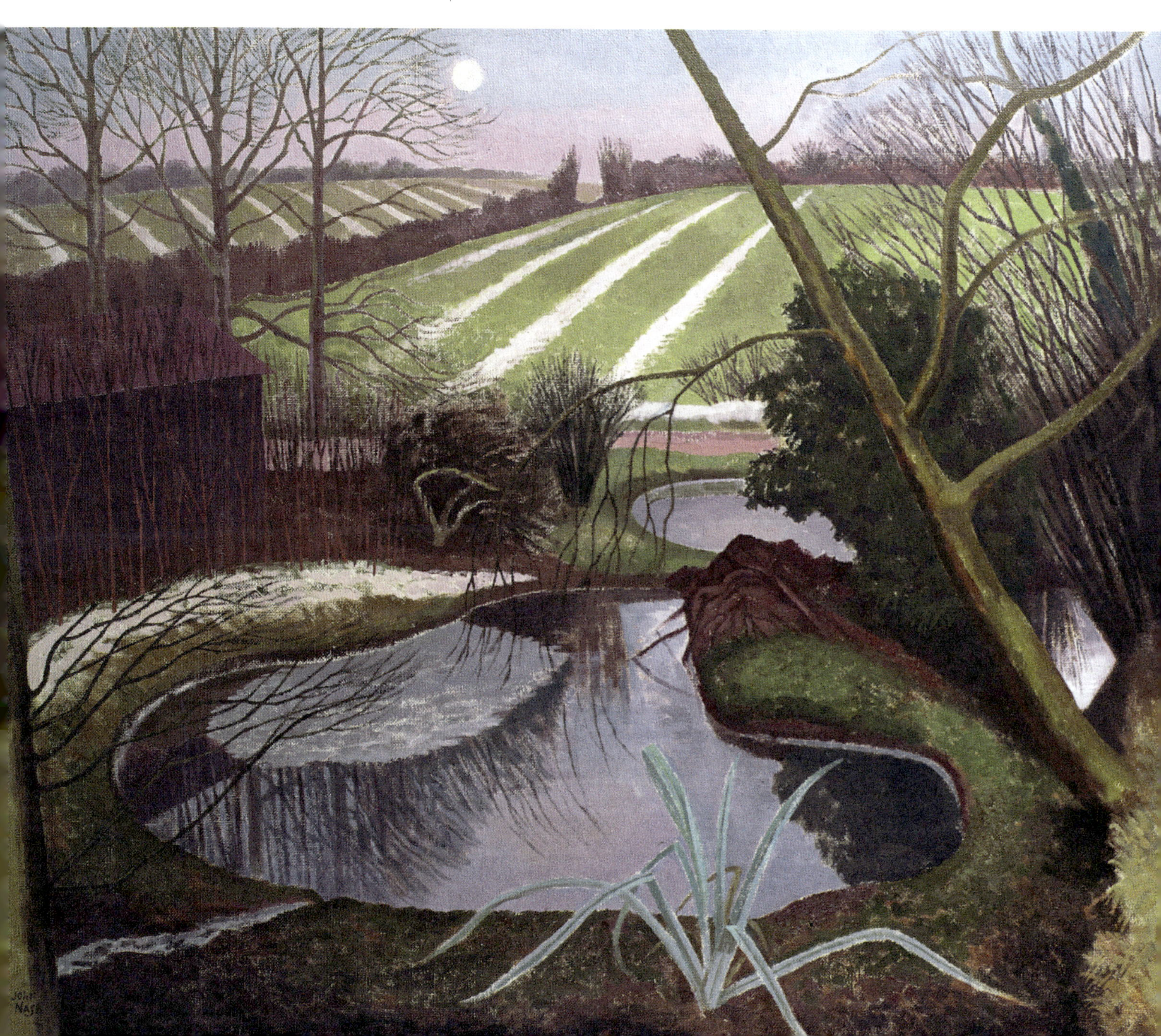

Opposite – *Winter Evening*, 1960, oil on canvas, John Nash (British)

Below – *Landscape of the Moon's First Quarter*, 1943, oil on canvas, Paul Nash (British)

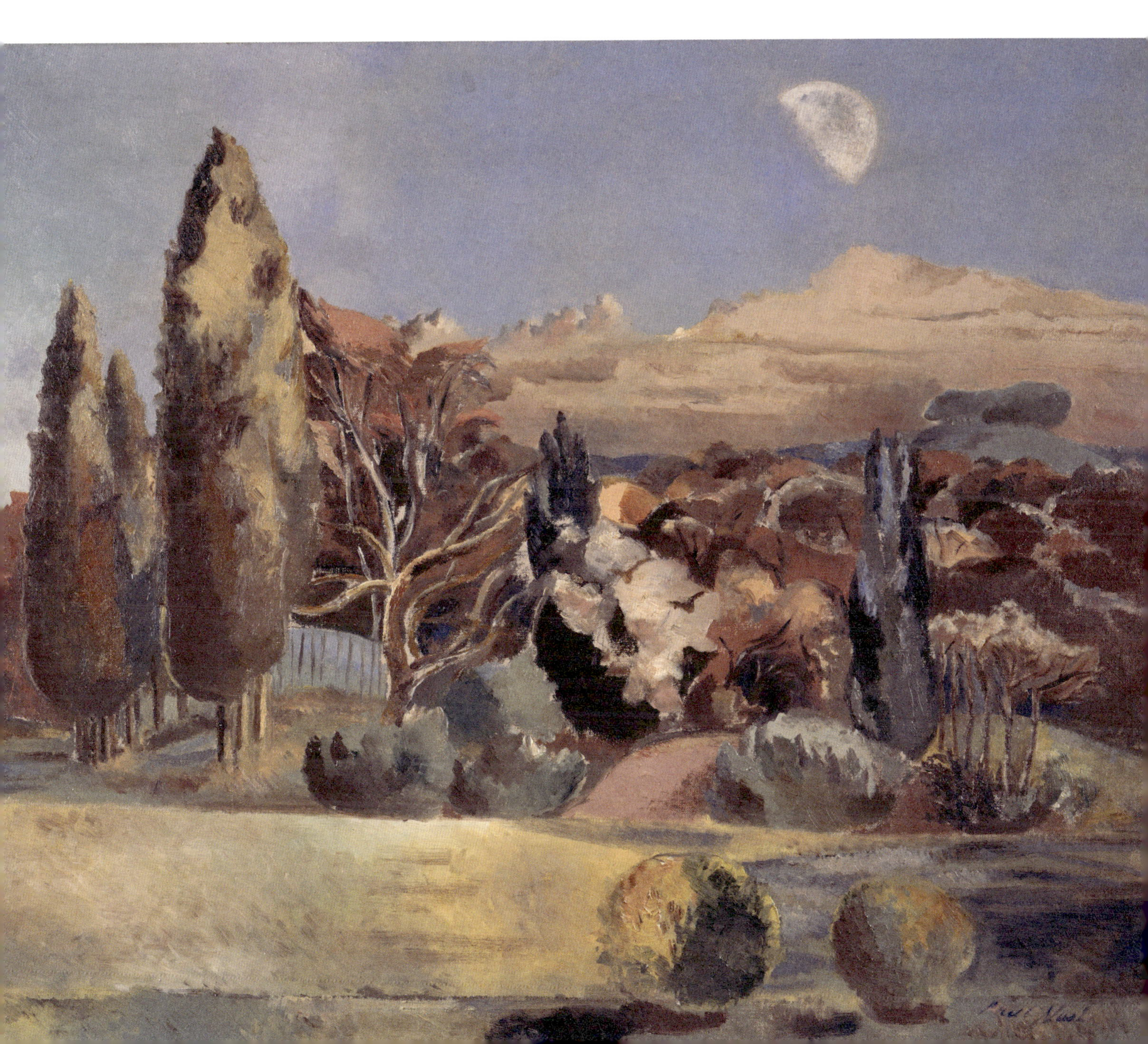

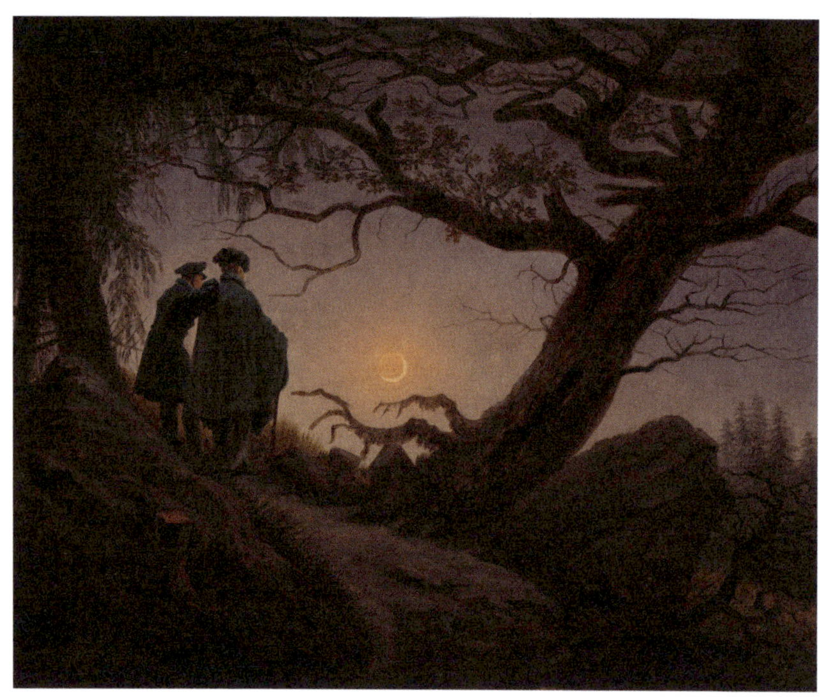

Top – *Two Men Contemplating the Moon*, c. 1825–30, oil on canvas, Caspar David Friedrich (German)

Bottom – *Nocturne – Hydrangea Terrace, Chateaux Ledoux*, 1907, three colour relief halftone, Edward Steichen (American)

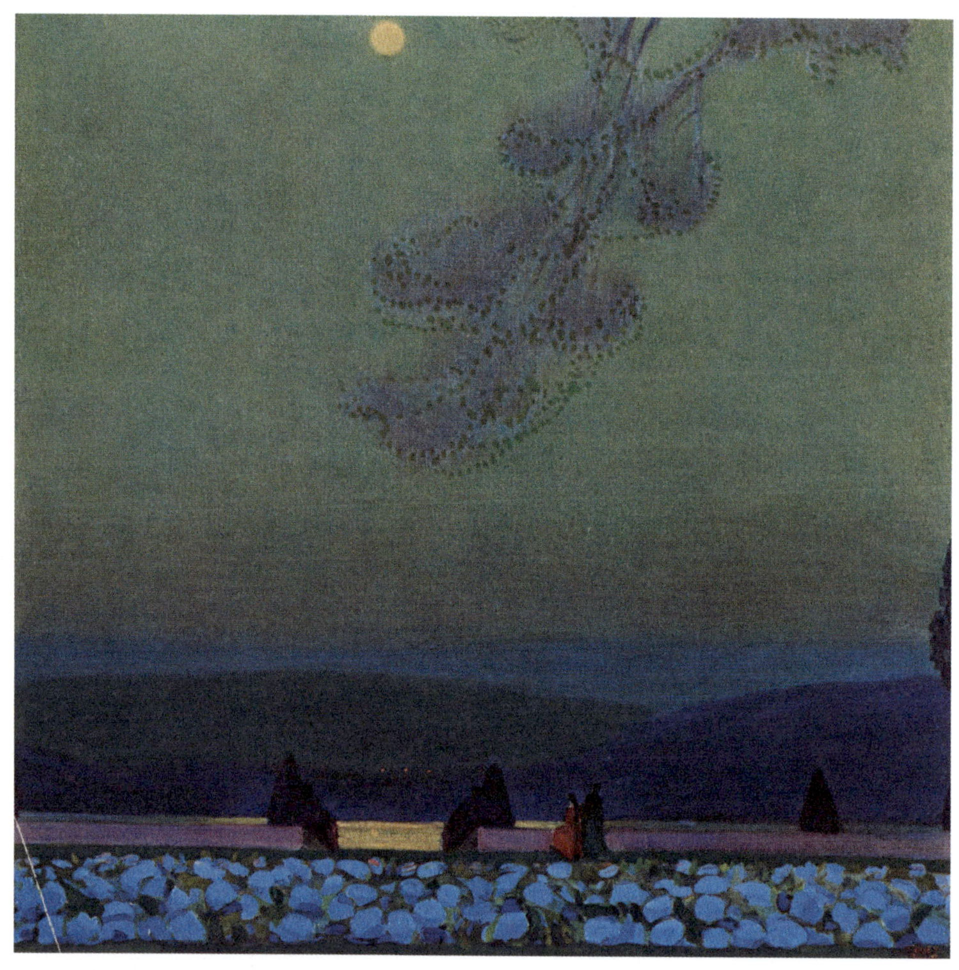

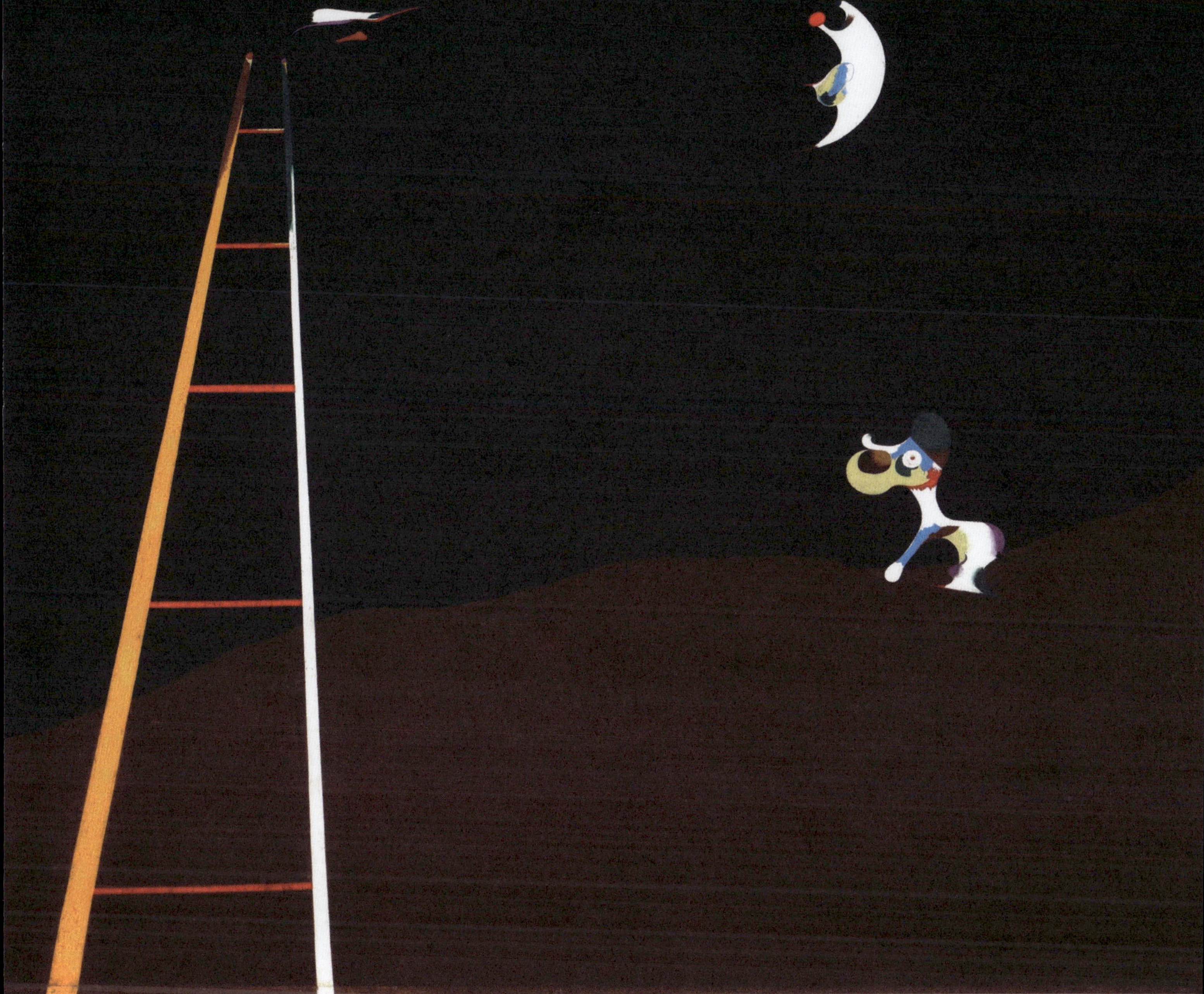

MOON VIEWING IS A POPULAR PASTIME THAT ENDURES THE WORLD OVER. IT INSPIRES LATE-NIGHT WALKS IN SEARCH OF AN ELEGANT CRESCENT-SHAPED OR STRIKING FULL MOON. NOTICE THE ATTENTIVE GAZE OF THE SMALL FIGURES AS THEY GAZE UP TO THE NIGHT SKY.

Dog Barking at the Moon, 1926, oil on canvas, Joan Miró (Spanish)

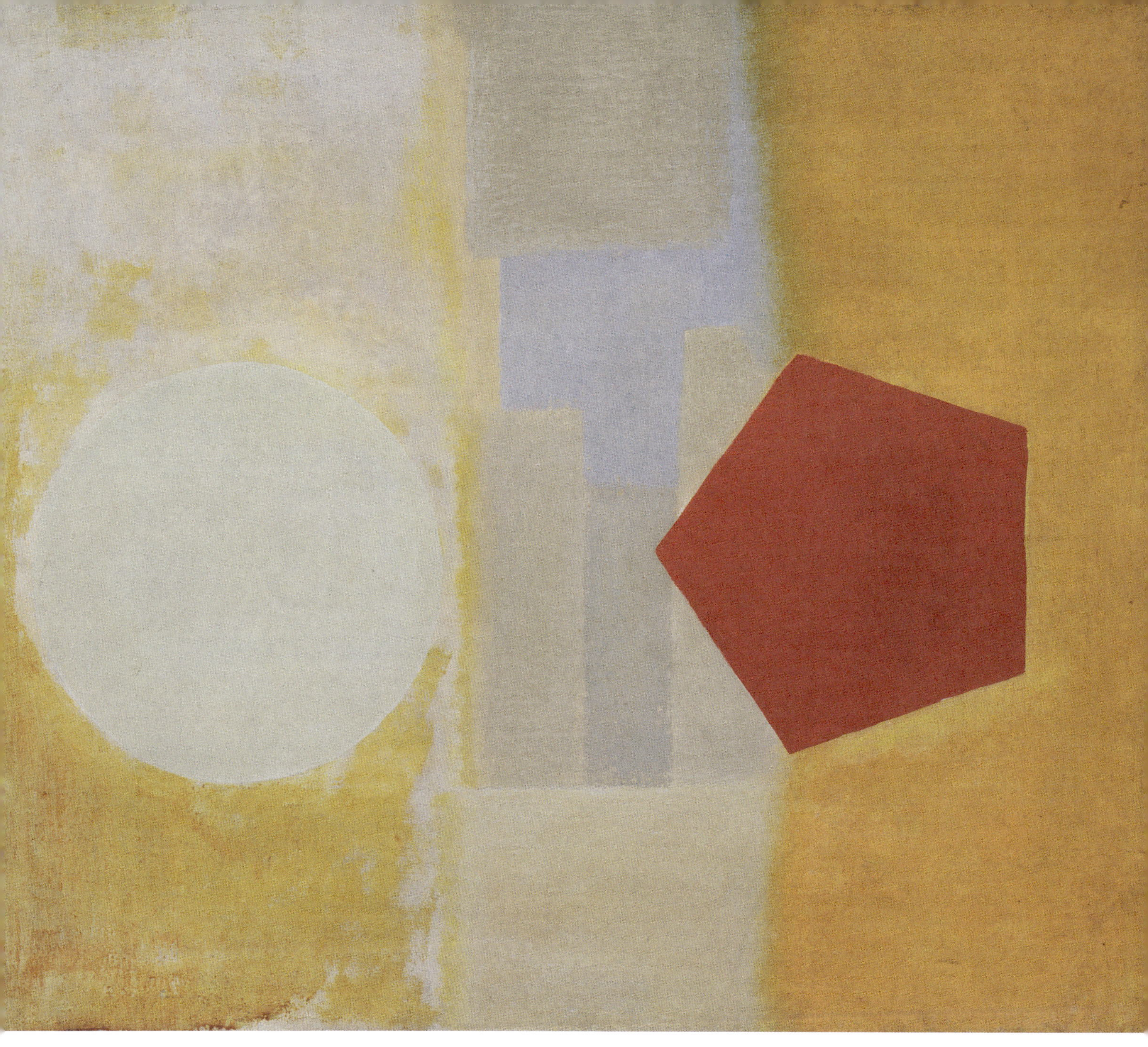

Above – *Moonlight and Lamplight*, 1937, oil paint on canvas, Winifred Nicholson (British)

Opposite top – *Moon 1*, c. late 1990s, lithograph; ink and colour on paper, Maki Haku (Japanese)

Opposite bottom – *Moonlight*, 1926, lithograph on zinx, Wanda Gág (American)

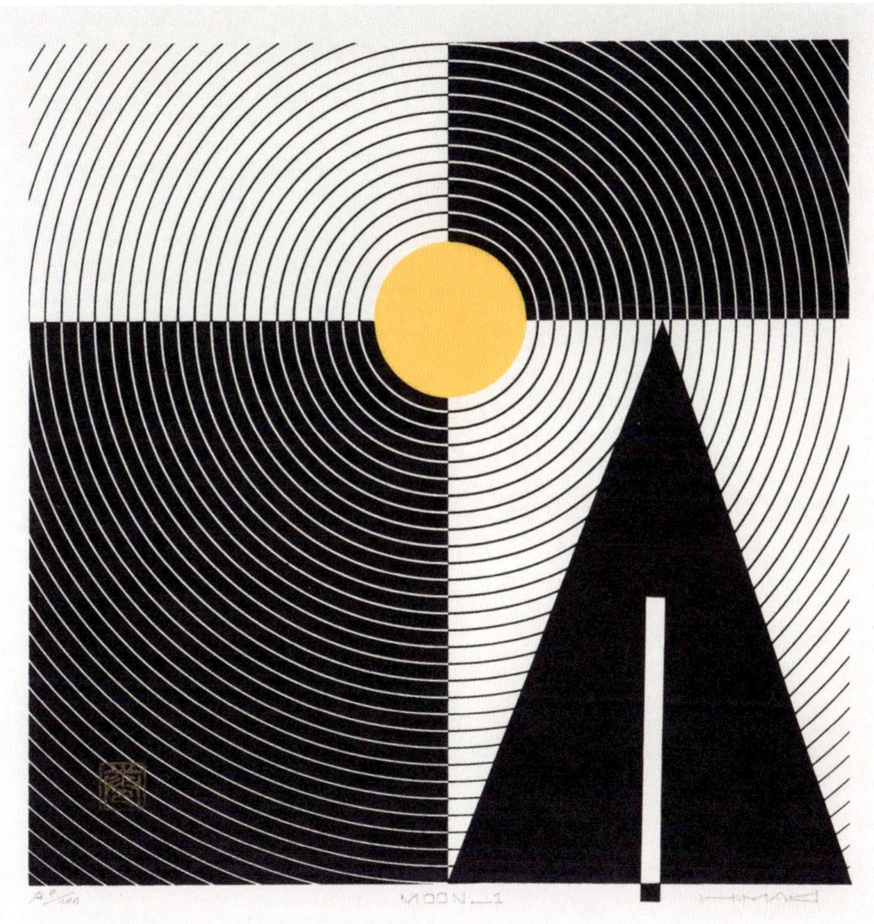

TAKE A CLOSER LOOK AT THE SHAPES AND PATTERNS PROJECTED BY THE RADIANT FULL MOON.

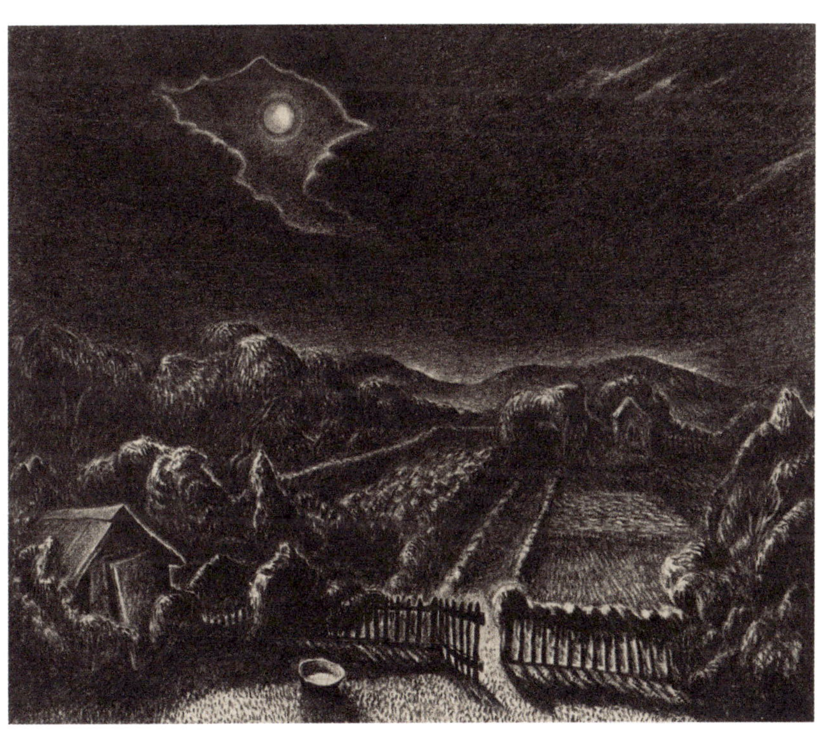

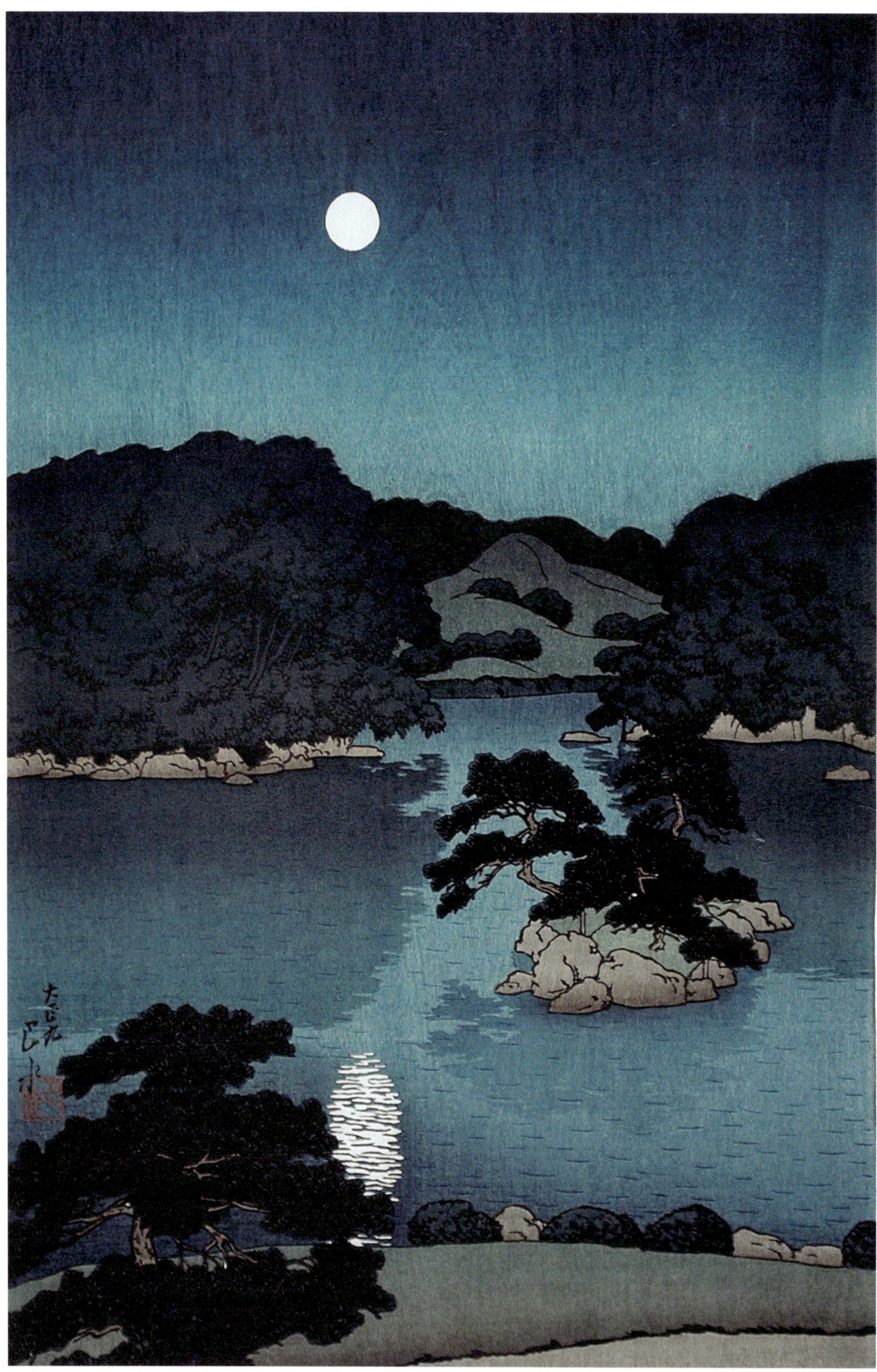

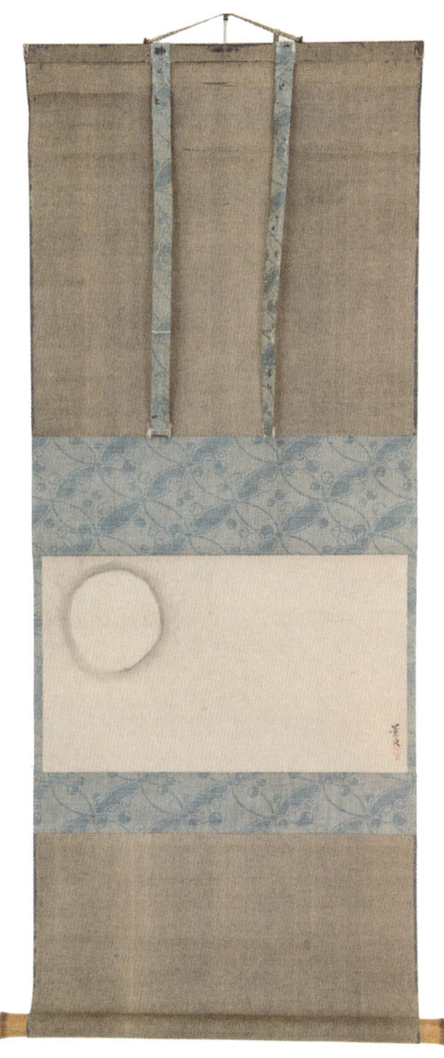

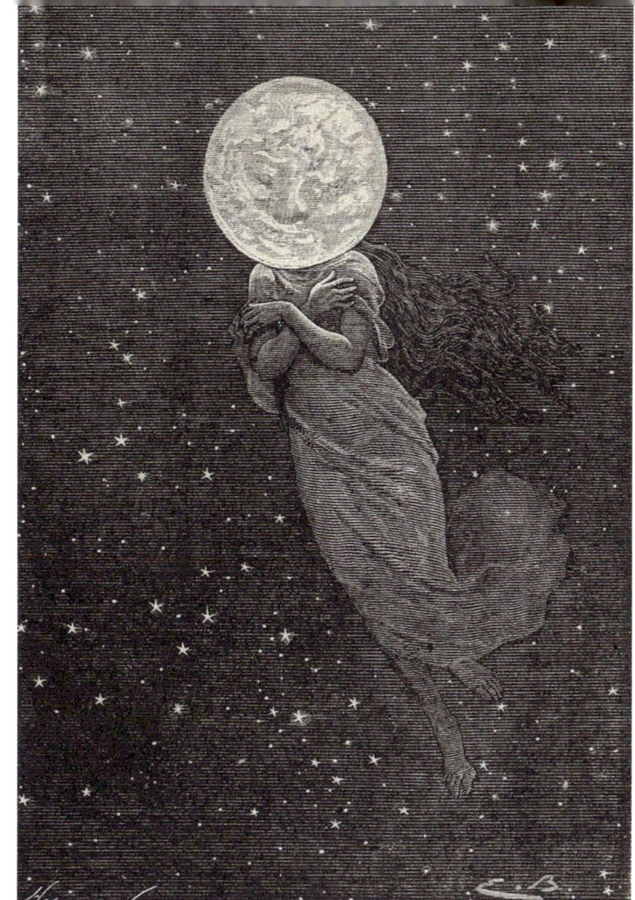

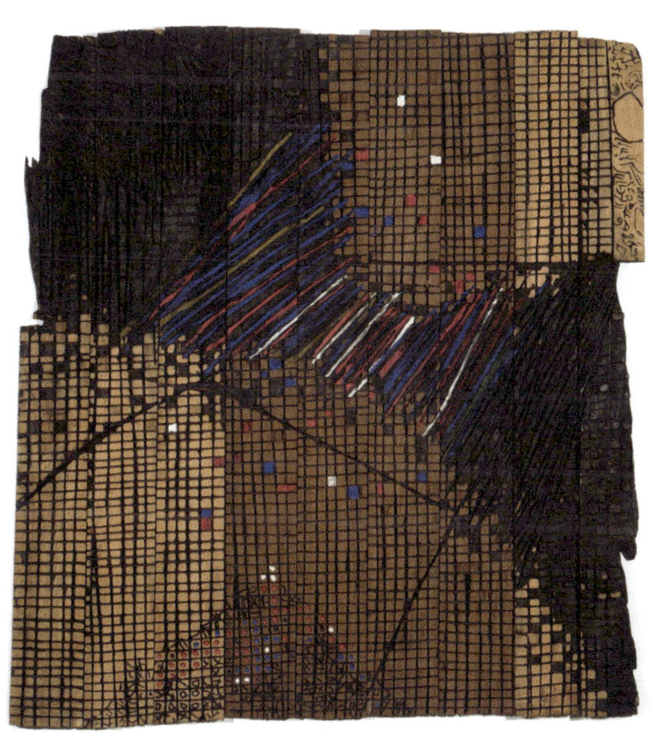

Opposite – *Moonlit Night (Daisensui Pond)*, 1920, colour woodblock print, Kawase Hasui (Japanese)

Top – Illustration from Jules Verne's book *From the Earth to the Moon*, 1865, Émile-Antoine Bayard and Alphonse-Marie-Adolphe de Neuville (French)

Middle – *Full Moon*, early 19th century, ink on paper, Matsumura Keibun (Japanese)

Bottom – *Earth-Moon Connexions*, 1993, wood, paint, El Anatsui (Ghanaian)

Following left – *The moon traversed by two thin clouds in a purple sky* (detail), 1967, watercolour with pencil, Mary Bishop (Mary Cecil Hamilton) (British)

Following right – *Moon jar*, second half of 18th century, porcelain, Unknown artist (Korean)

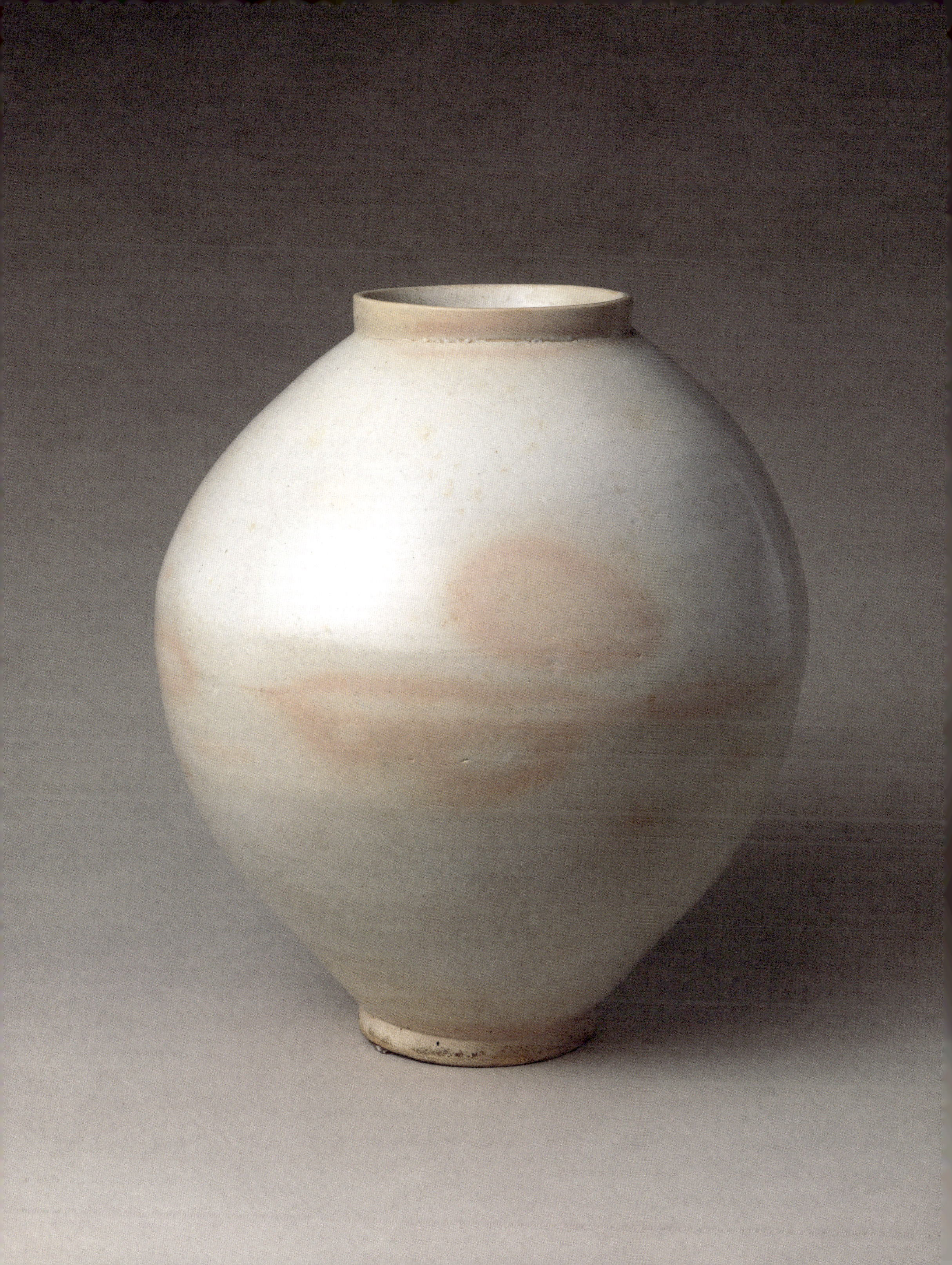

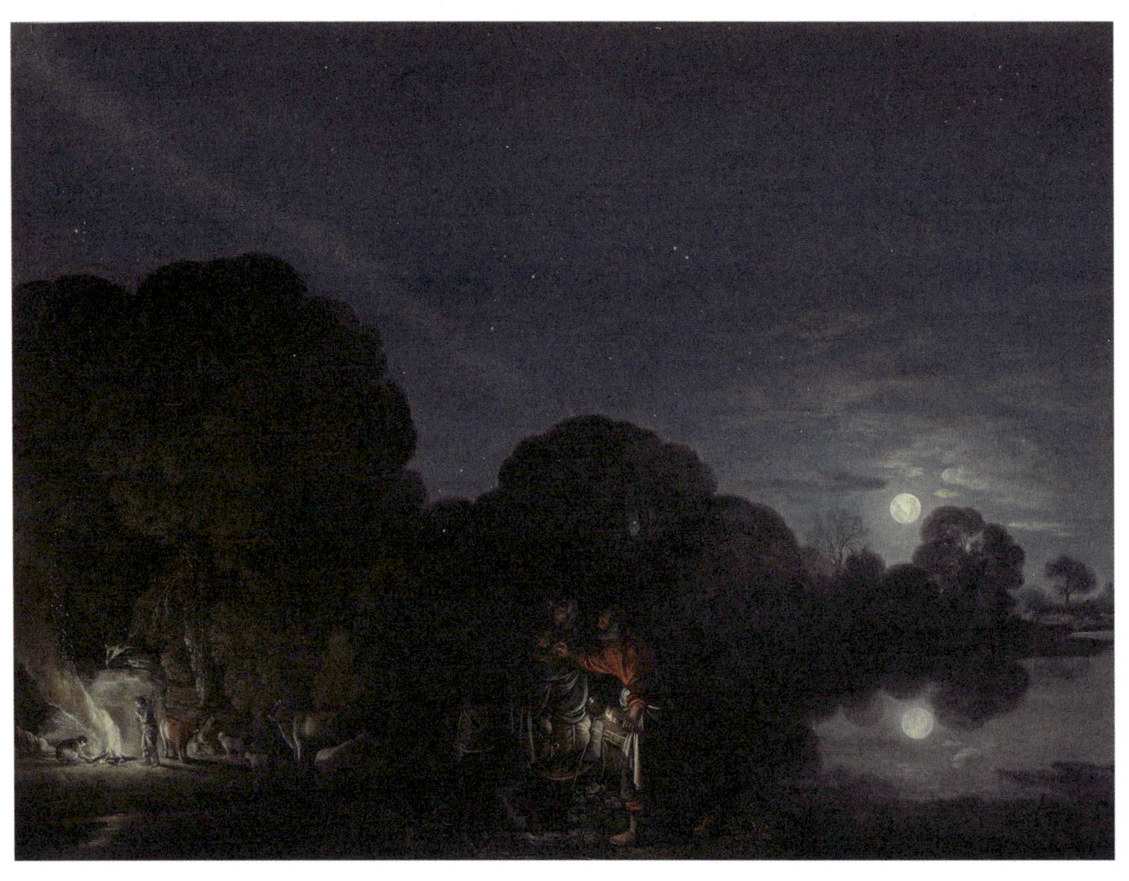

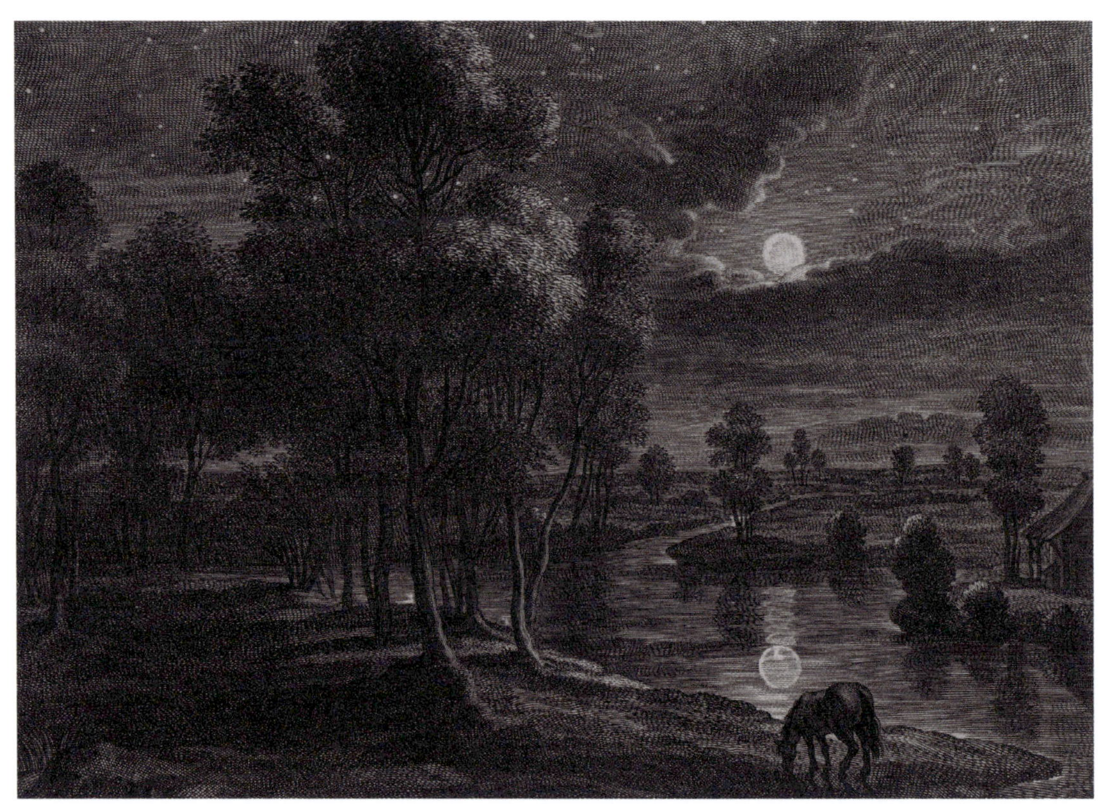

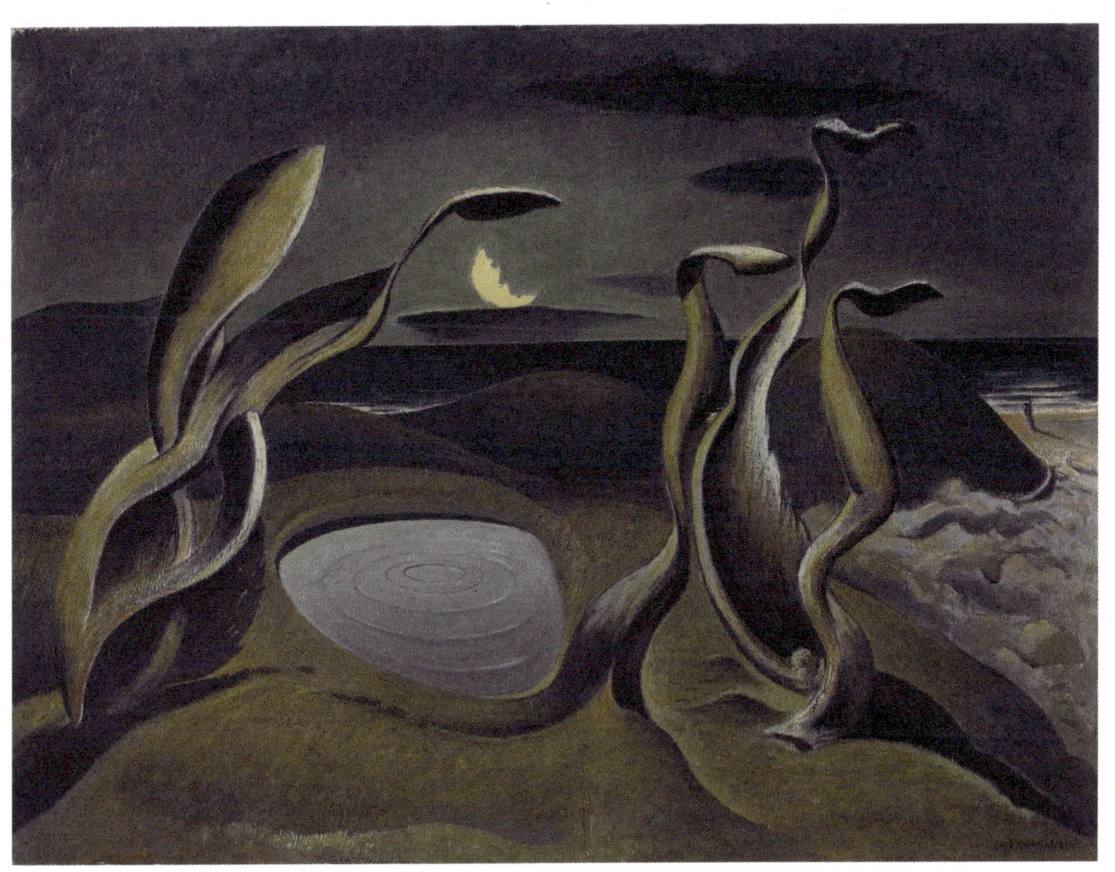

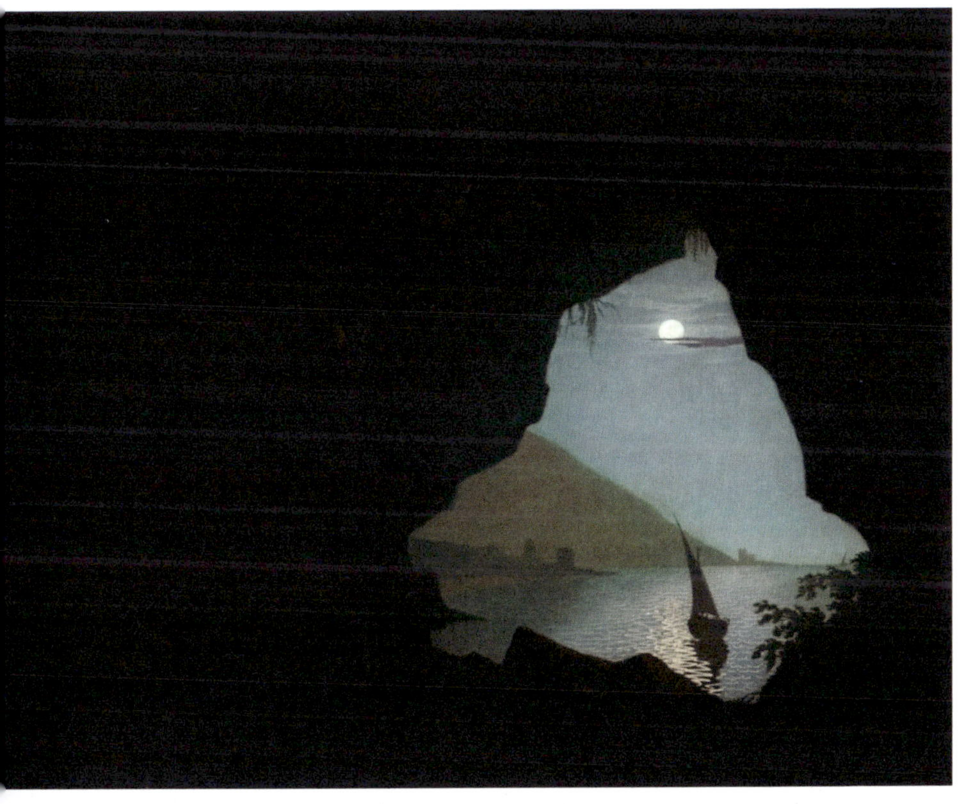

Opposite top – *The Flight into Egpyt*, 1609, copper, Adam Elsheimer (German)

Opposite bottom – *Landscape by moonlight*, 1635–40, engraving, Peter Paul Rubens (Flemish)

Top – *Circles and Moon*, 1950, oil on ply panel, Ralph Maynard Smith (British)

Bottom – *Grotto in the Gulf of Salerno, Italy, Moonlight*, c. 1780–90, oil on canvas, Joseph Wright of Derby (British)

Following – *Clair de lune* (detail), 1895, oil on canvas, Félix Vallotton (French)

CELESTIAL BODIES & THE NORTHERN LIGHTS

THE GALACTIC AND LIVELY CHARACTERISTIC OF THE SKY COMMUNICATES IN SACRED WAYS. A STARRY NIGHT SKY IS OFTEN USED IN FIRST NATIONS ART TO REPRESENT ANCESTRAL STORIES PASSED DOWN OVER CENTURIES THROUGH VISUAL MEANS OR SPOKEN WORD. CONSIDER THE RANGE OF PICTORIAL DEVICES USED TO CONVEY STORIES, BEAUTY AND THE MAPPING OF CONSTELLATIONS AND CELESTIAL ACTIVITY.

Below – *The Origin of the Milky Way*, c. 1575, oil on canvas, Jacopo Tintoretto (Italian)

Opposite – *Milŋiyawuy (River of Stars)*, 2020, earth pigments on Stringybark (Eucalyptus sp.), Naminapu Maymuru-White (First Nations Australian)

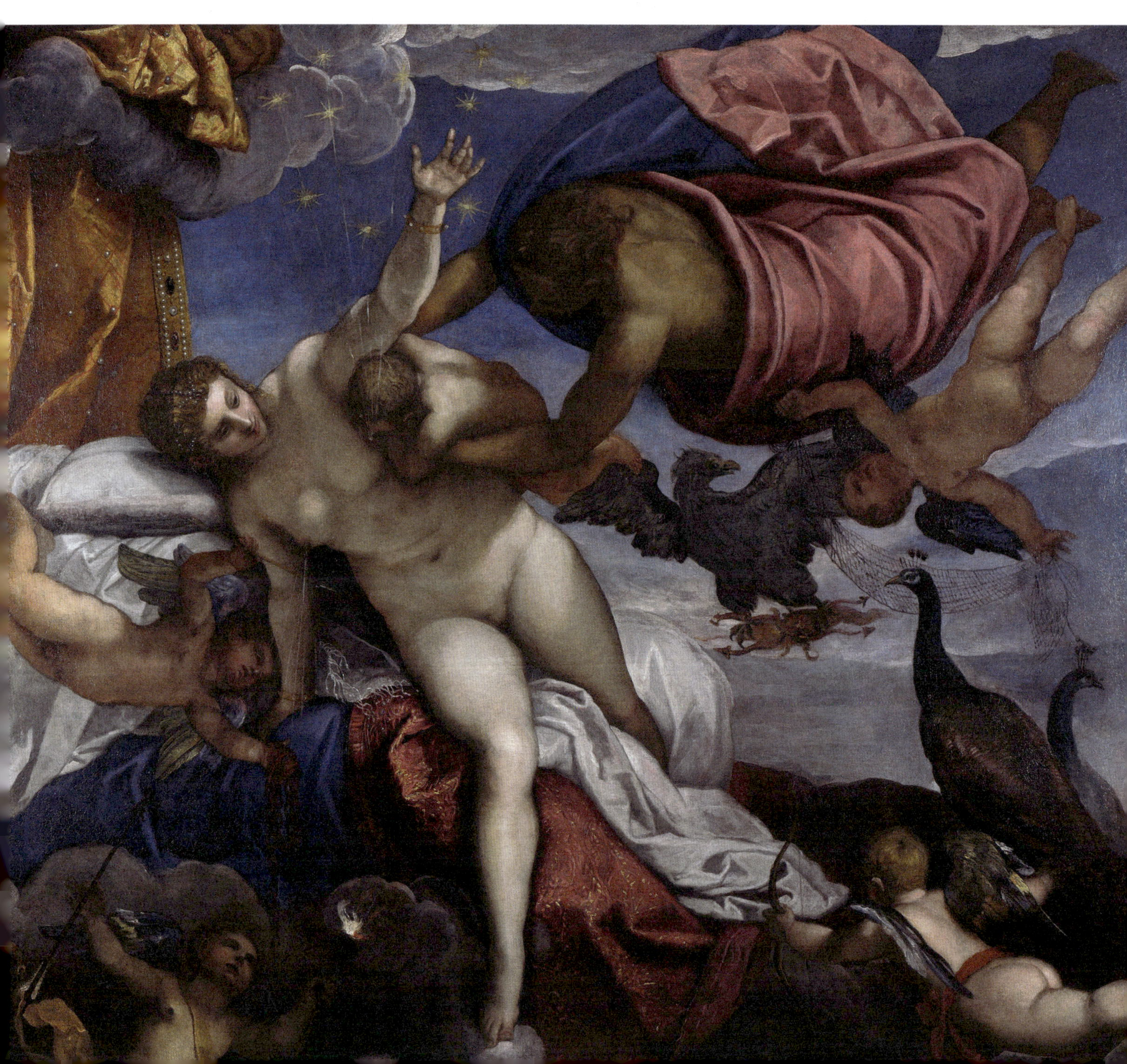

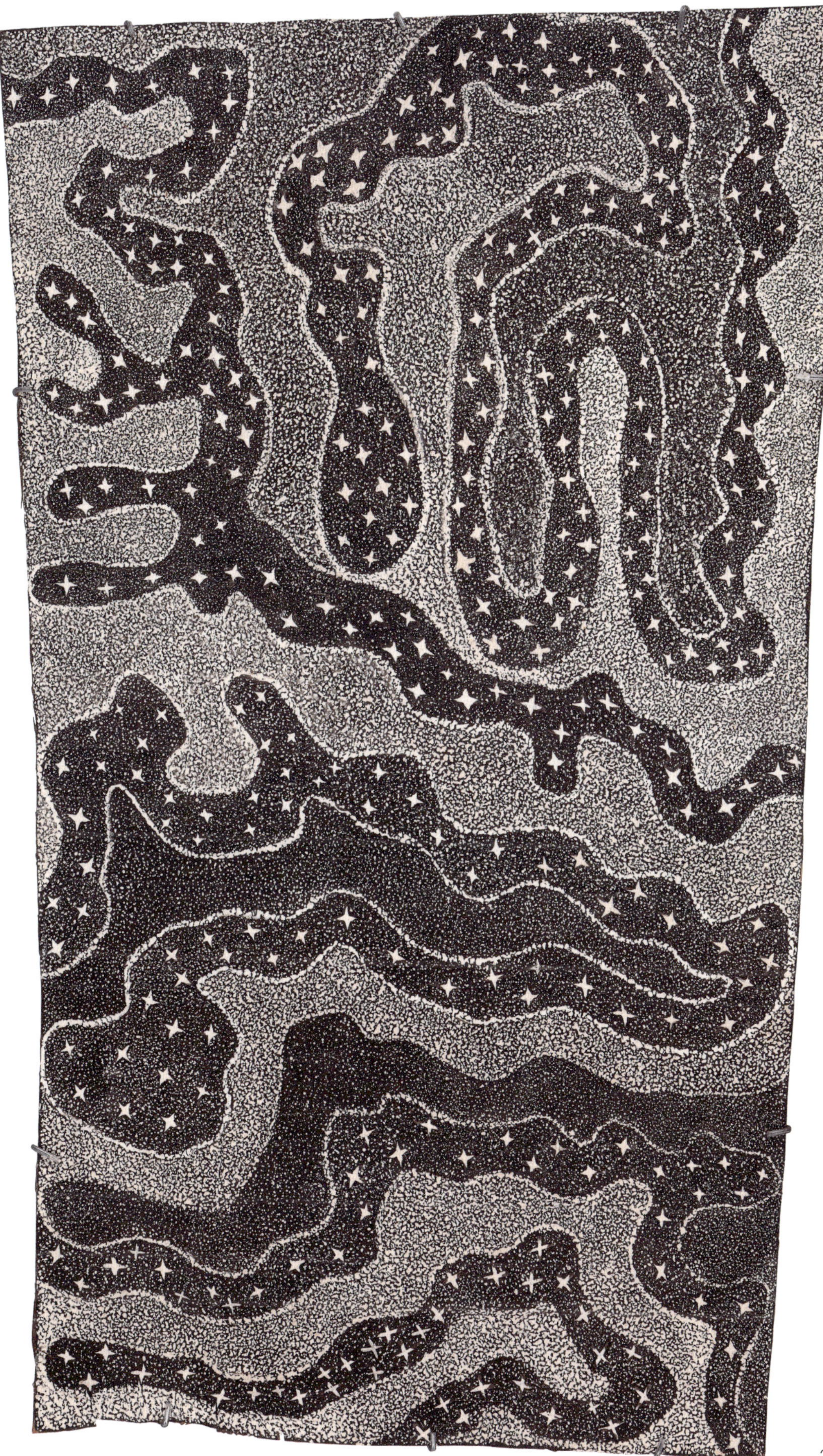

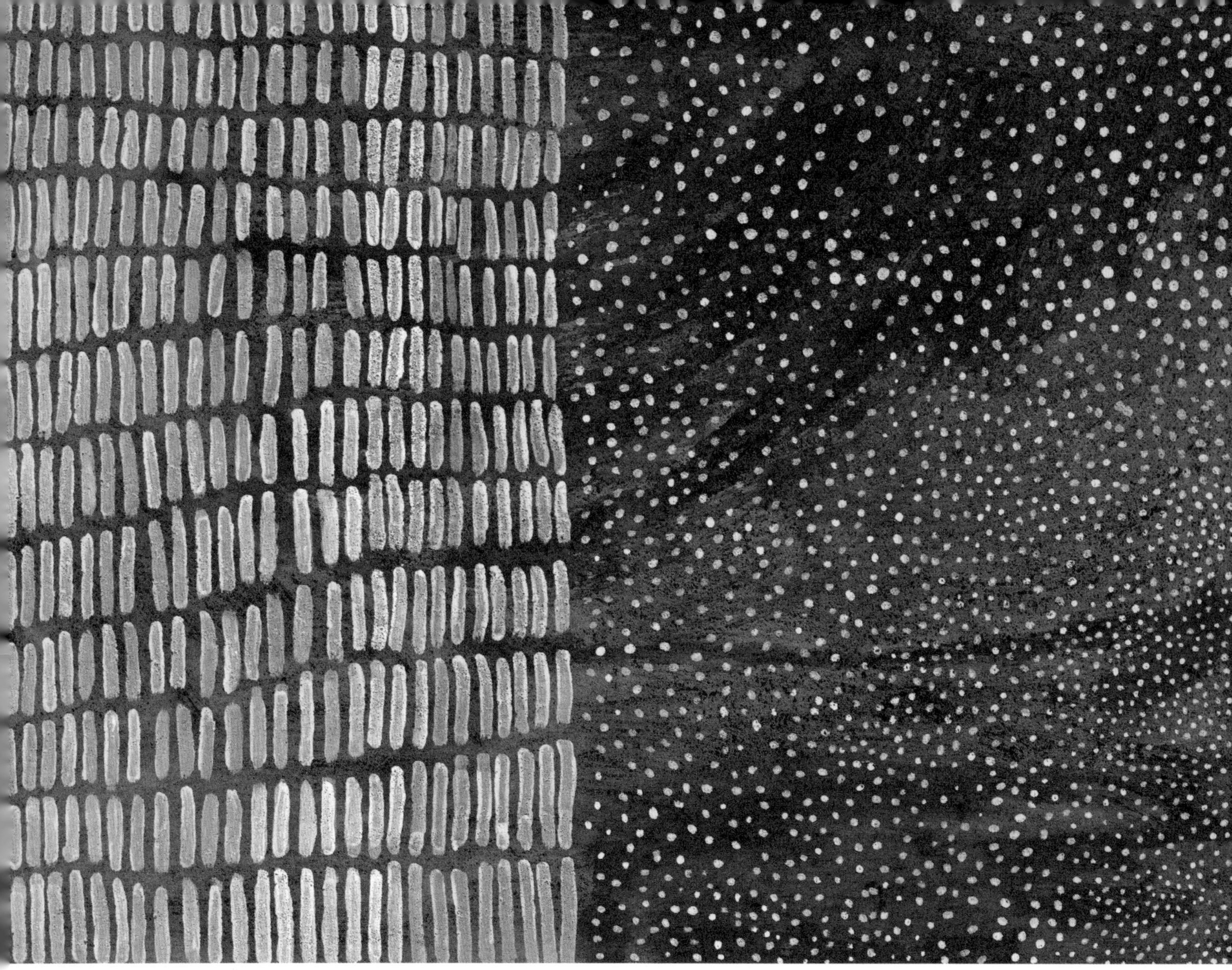

Above – *Starry night in Jimbirla country*, 2000, earth pigments on canvas, Lena Nyadbi (Australian)

Opposite top – *The Starry Night*, 1889, oil on canvas, Vincent van Gogh (Dutch)

Opposite bottom – *Landscape with Stars*, c. 1905–08, watercolour on white wove paper, Henri-Edmond Cross (Henri-Edmond Delacroix) (French)

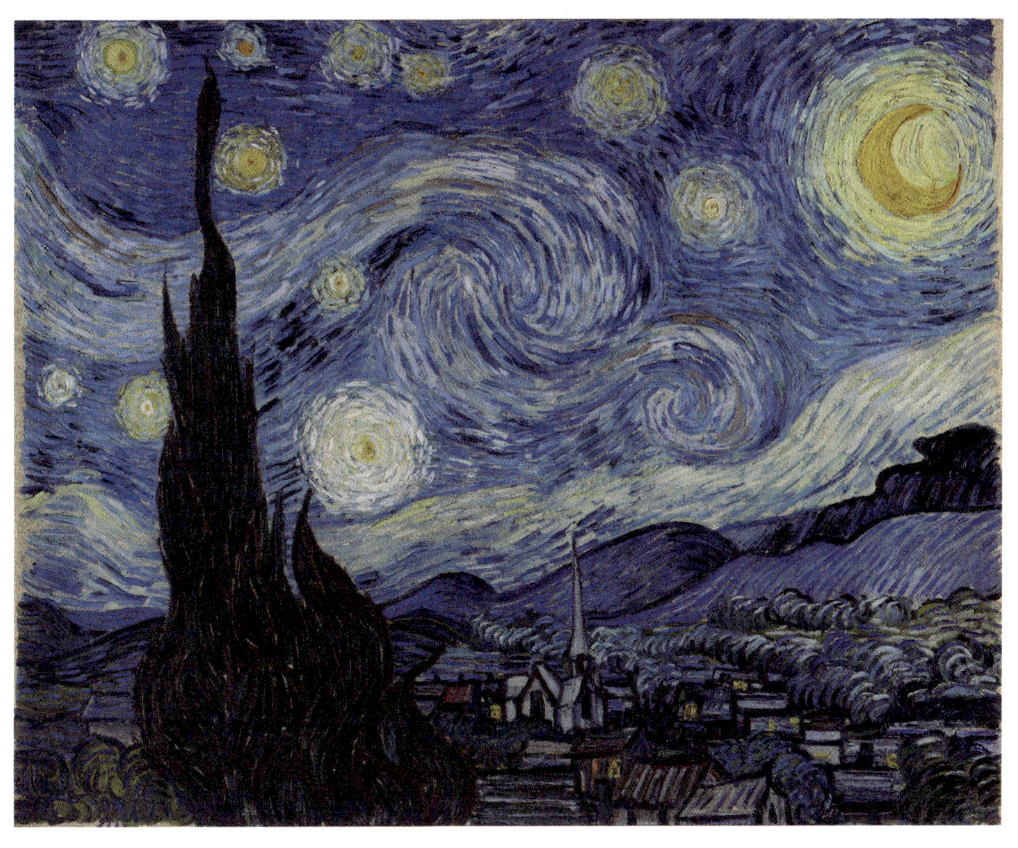

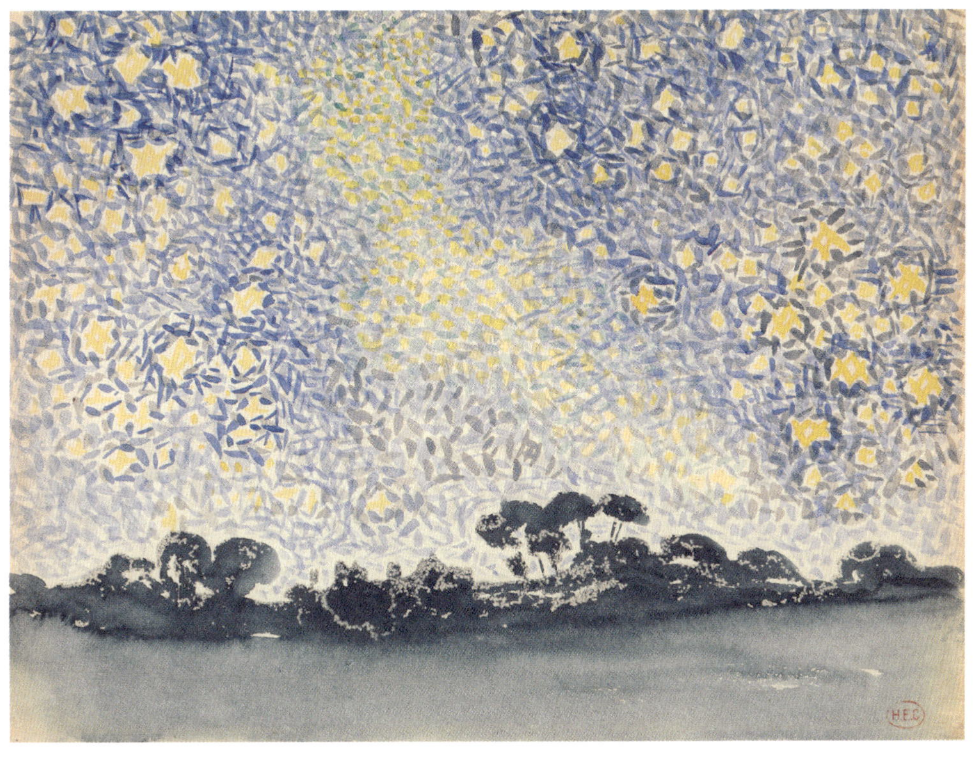
H.E.C

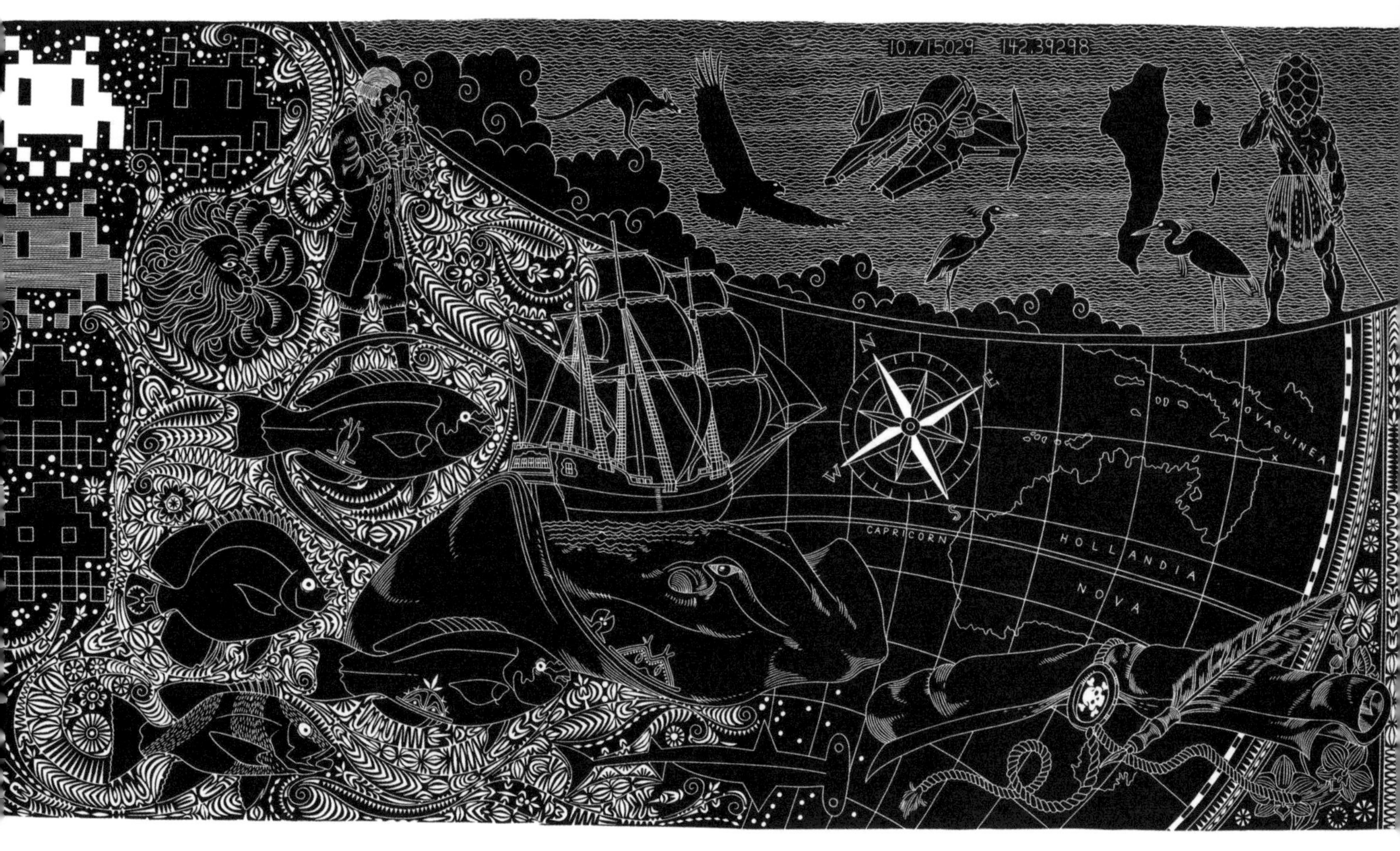

Above – *Bedhan Lag: Land of the Kaiwalagal,* 2019 (detail), linocut, Brian Robinson (Maluyligal, Wuthathi and Dayak people, Australian)

Opposite – *Chart of the Zodiac, including the stars of the 4th magnitude, between the Parallels of 24°½ declination North & South,* c. 1831, engraving, aquatint, printed in black ink, Thomas L Mitchell (after) (Scottish), John Carmichael (engraver) (Australian)

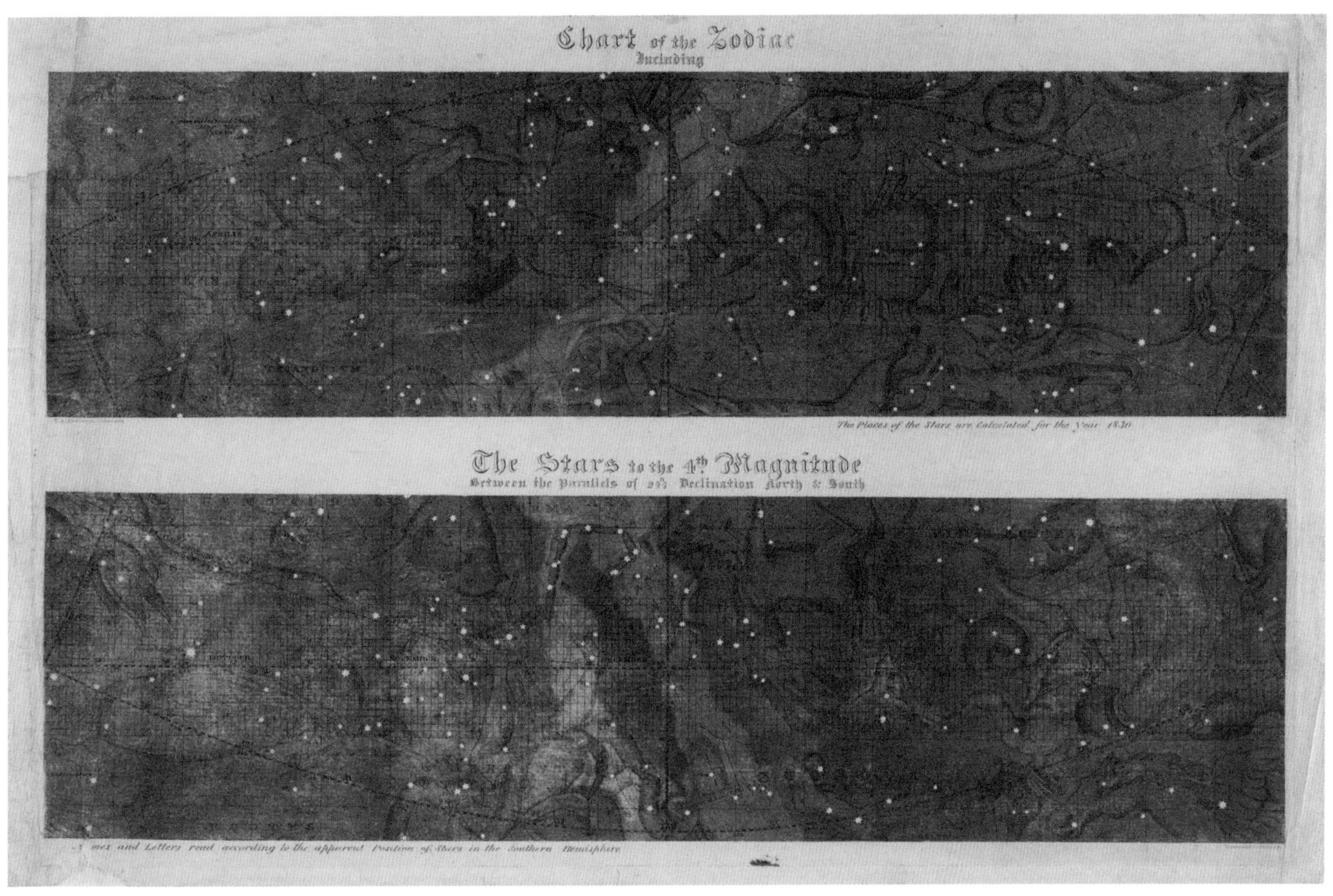

Following left – *Comet of March 1843, seen from Aldridge Lodge, V.D. Land* (detail), 1843, lithograph printed in black ink on wove paper, Mary Morton Allport (Australian)

Following right – *The November meteors: As observed between midnight and 5 o'clock A.M. on the night of November 13–14 1868* (detail), c. 1881–82, chromolithograph, Étienne Léopold Trouvelot (French)

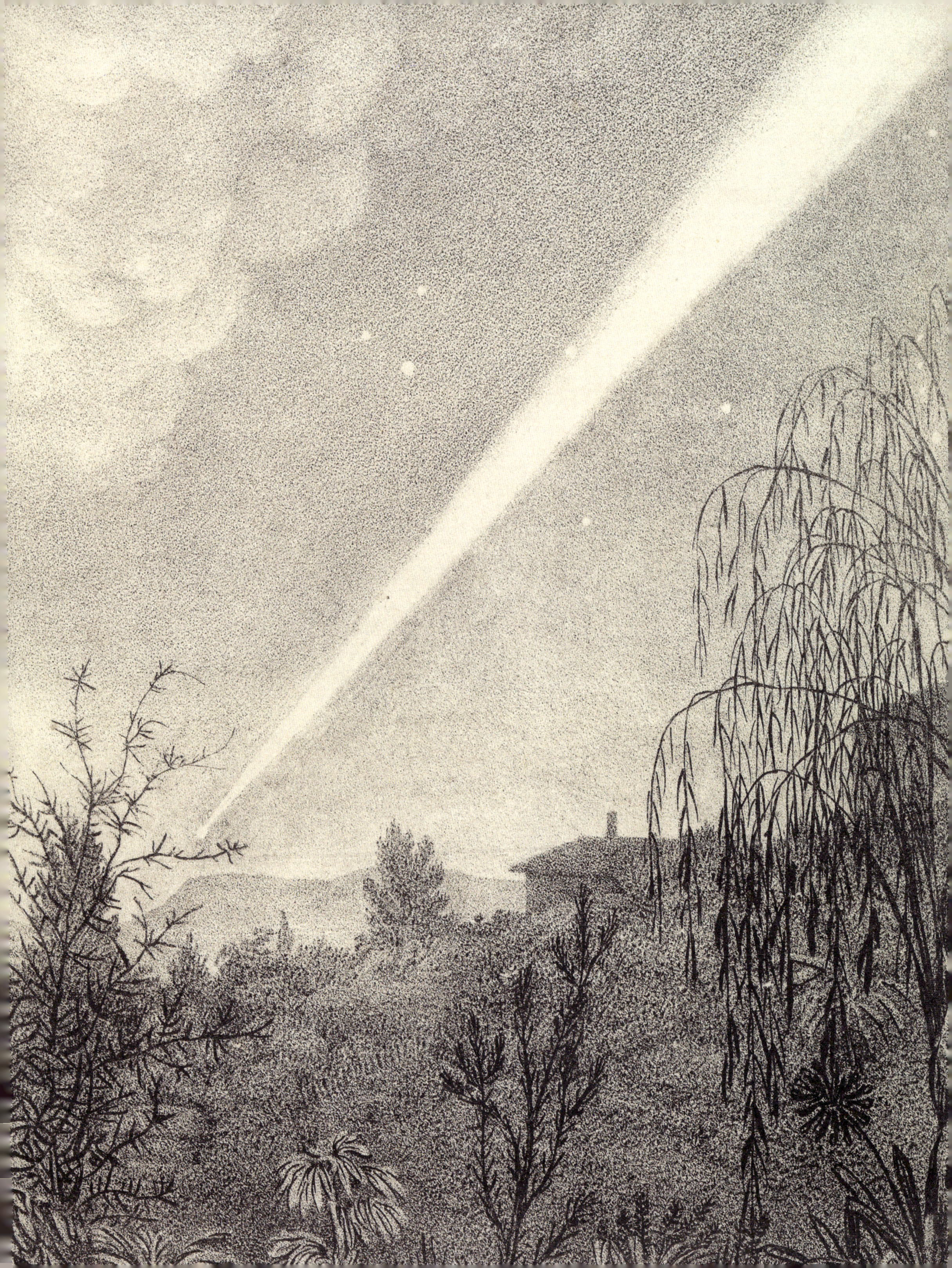

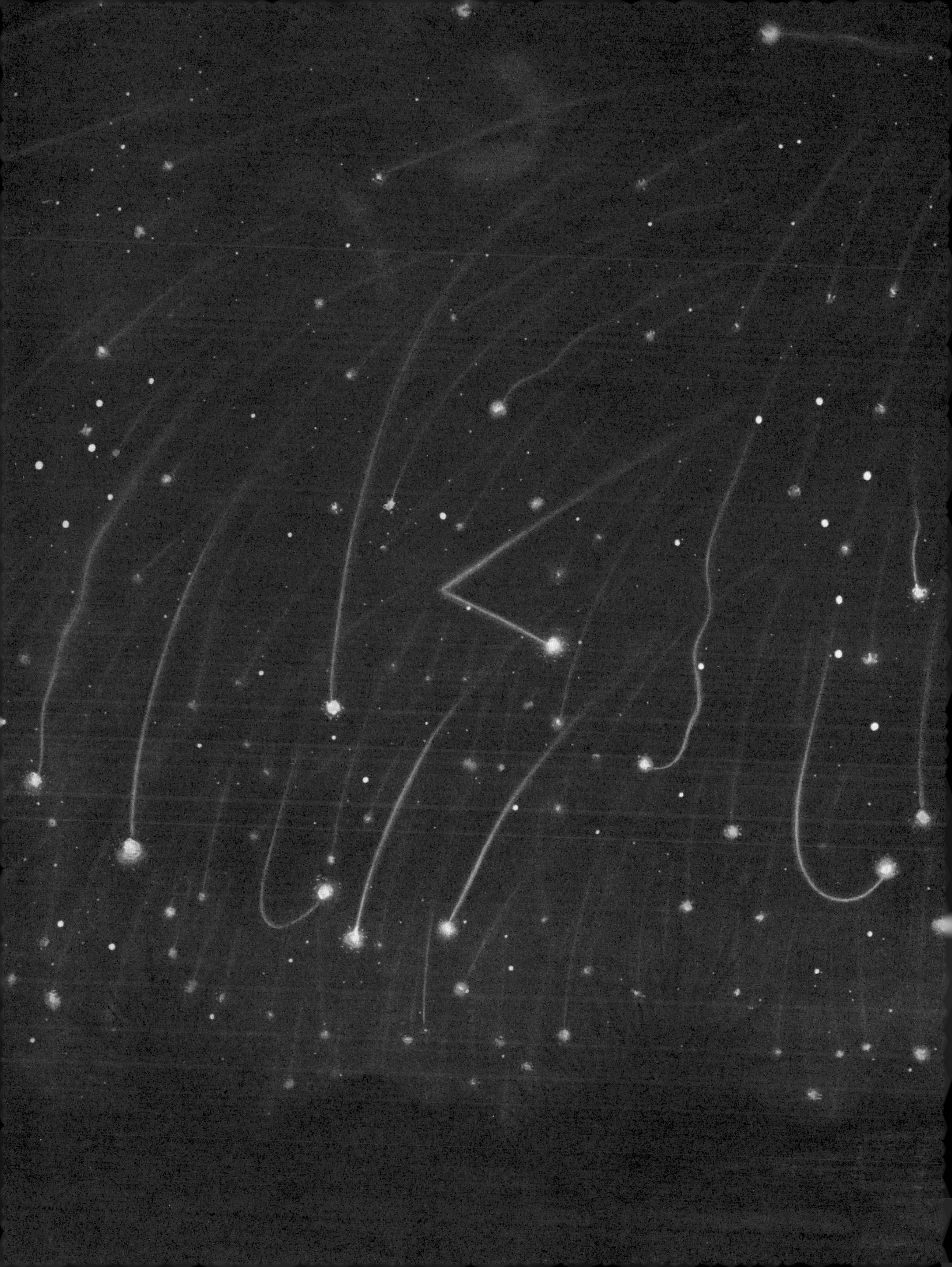

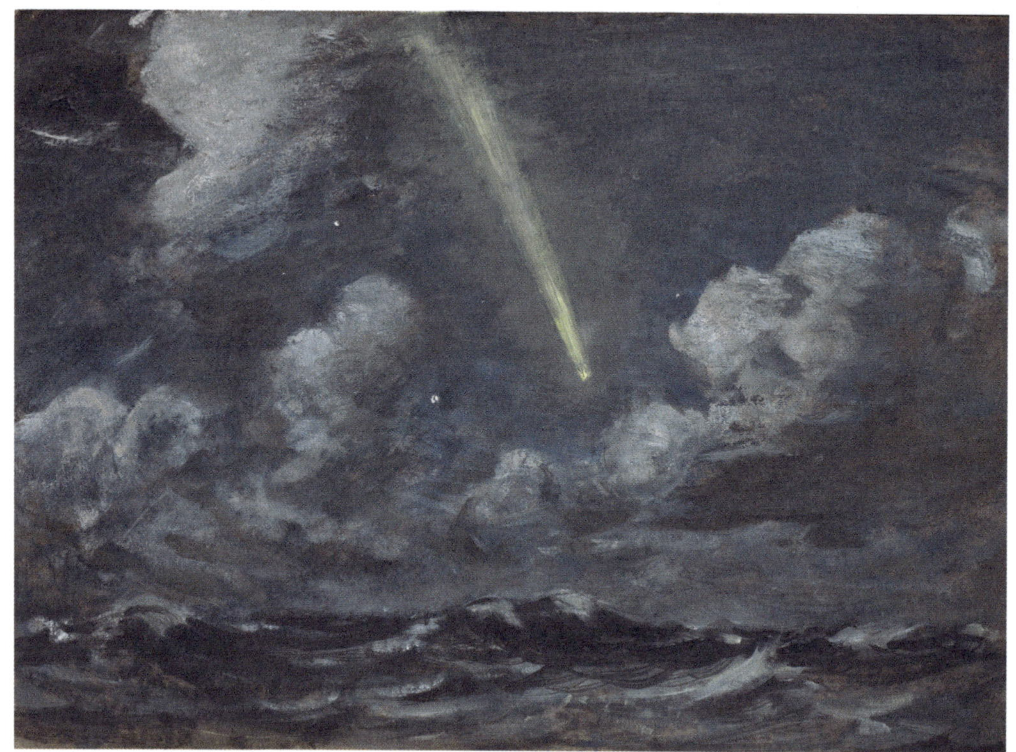

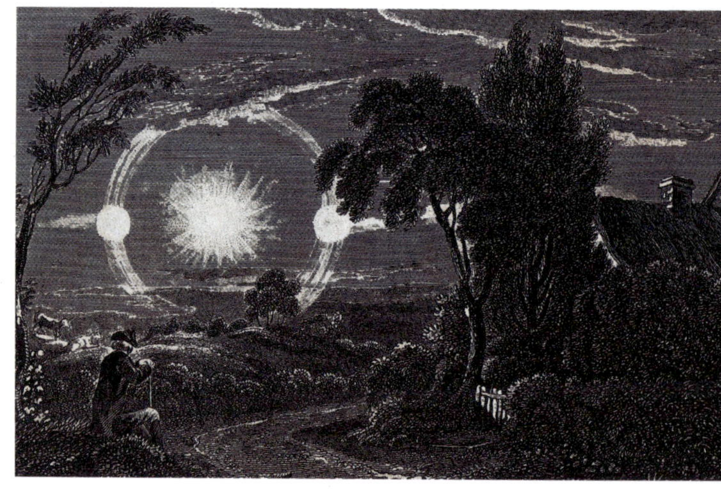

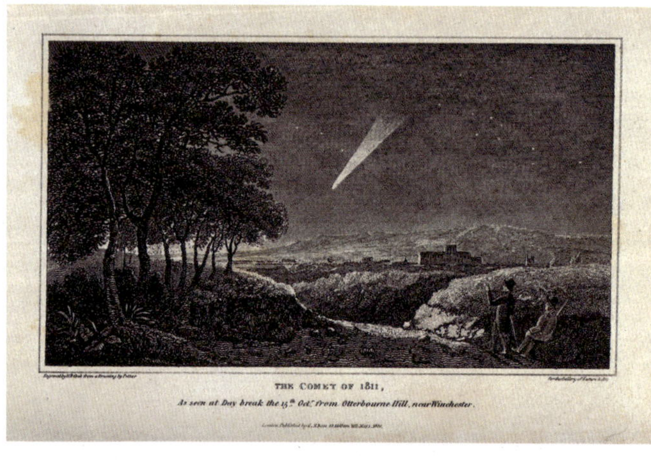

Top – *A Comet*, c. late 19th century–mid 20th century, oil on paper, John Everett (British)

Middle – *Astronomy: an atmospheric condition producing sun dogs, giving the effect of two suns*, 1820, engraving with etching, William Marshall Craig (British)

Bottom – *Astronomy: a large, bright, comet in the night sky over Winchester, being observed by two men*, 1820, engraving by H R Cook after Pether (British)

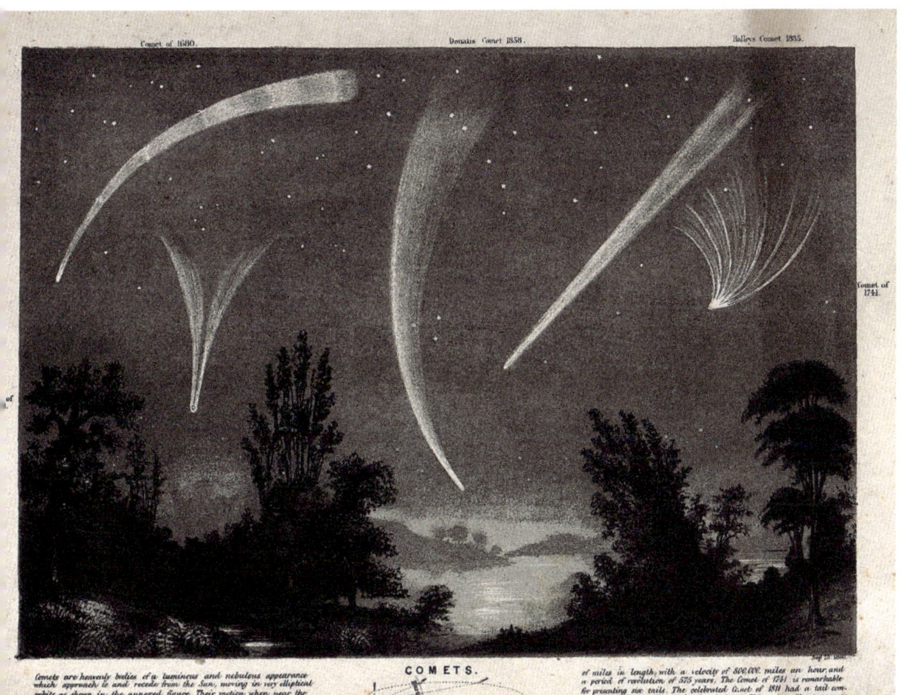

THE SOLAR SYSTEM HOSTS COMETS AND CONSTELLATIONS THAT SPEND HUNDREDS OF THOUSANDS OF YEARS IN ORBIT. THERE IS A MYSTICAL AND EXALTING FEEL TO IMAGES THAT SHOW COSMIC ACTIVITY AND SPACE WEATHER.

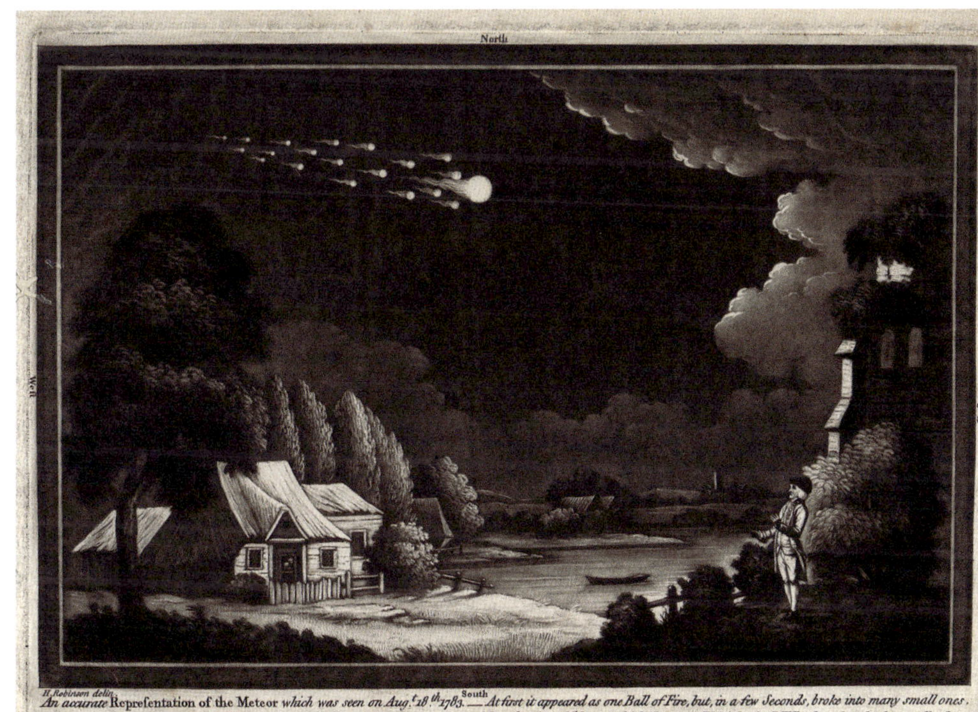

Top – *Astronomy: comets in a night sky*, 1860, engraving, Unknown artist (British)

Bottom – *Astronomy: a meteor shower in the night sky*, c. 1783, mezzotint, Henry Robinson (Canadian)

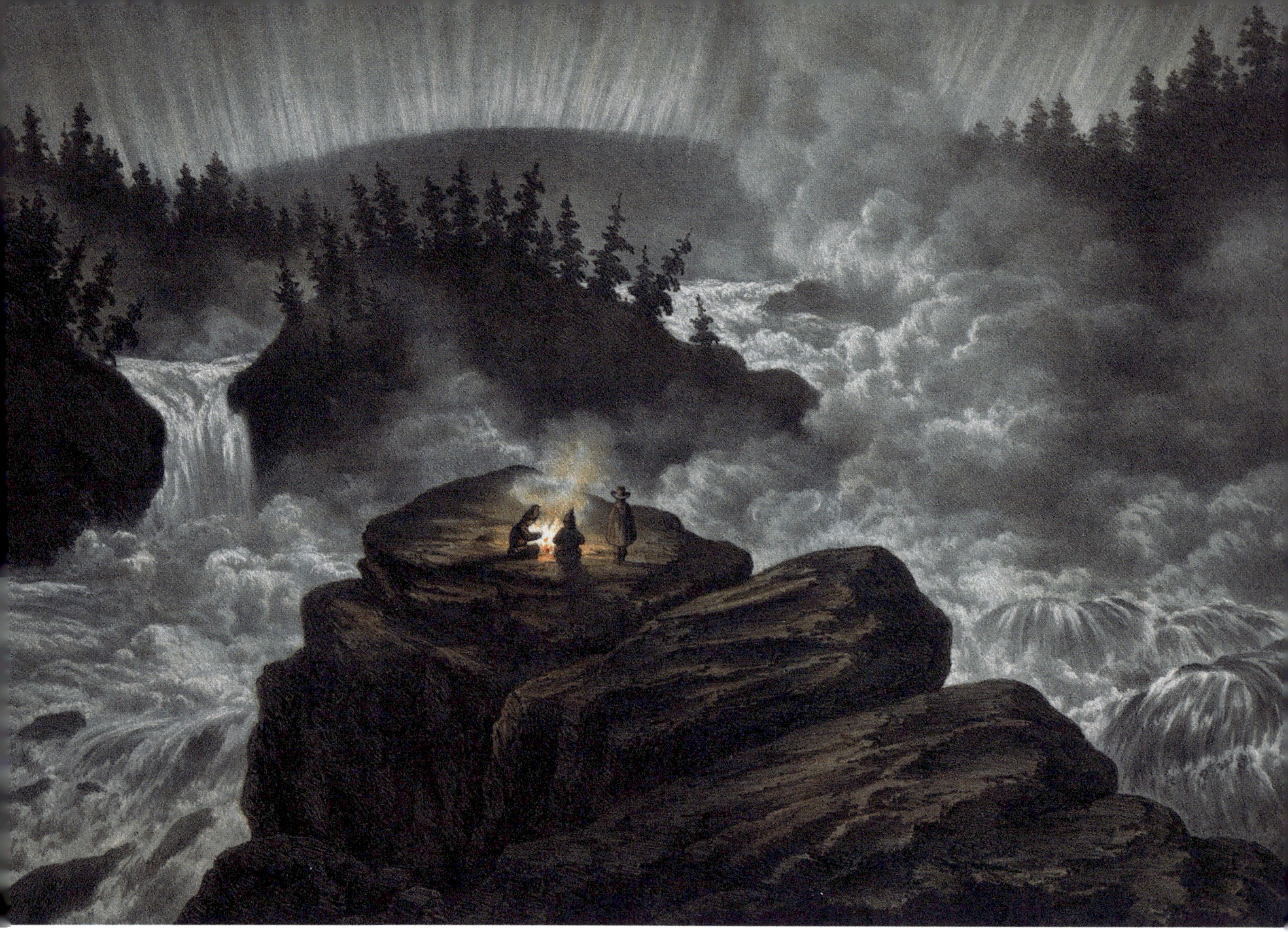

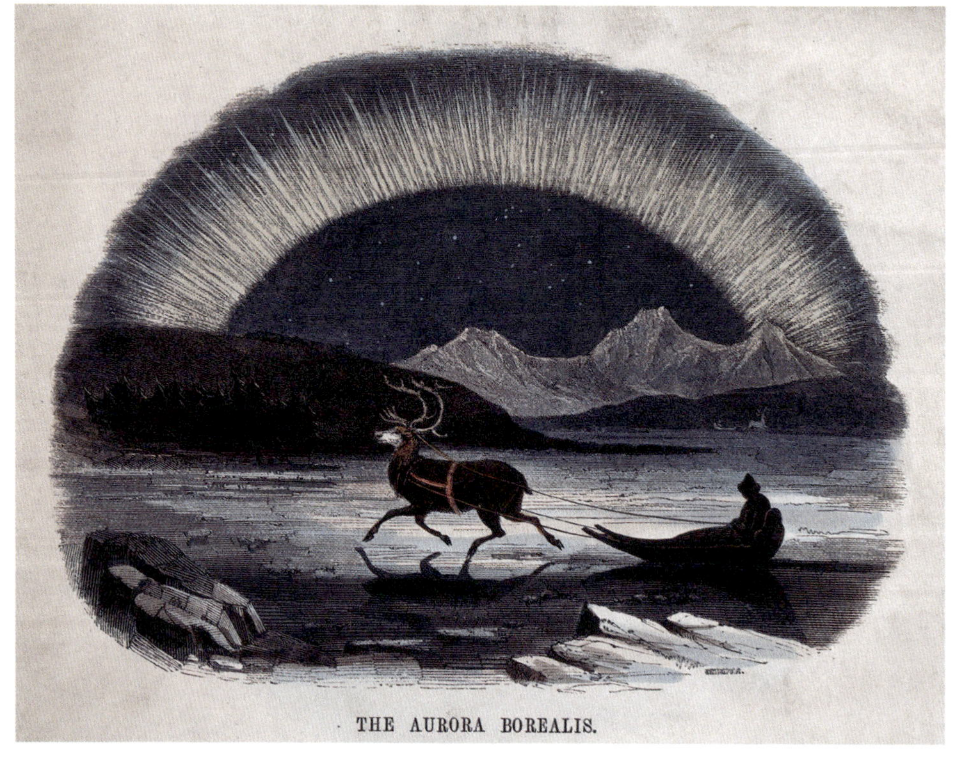
THE AURORA BOREALIS.

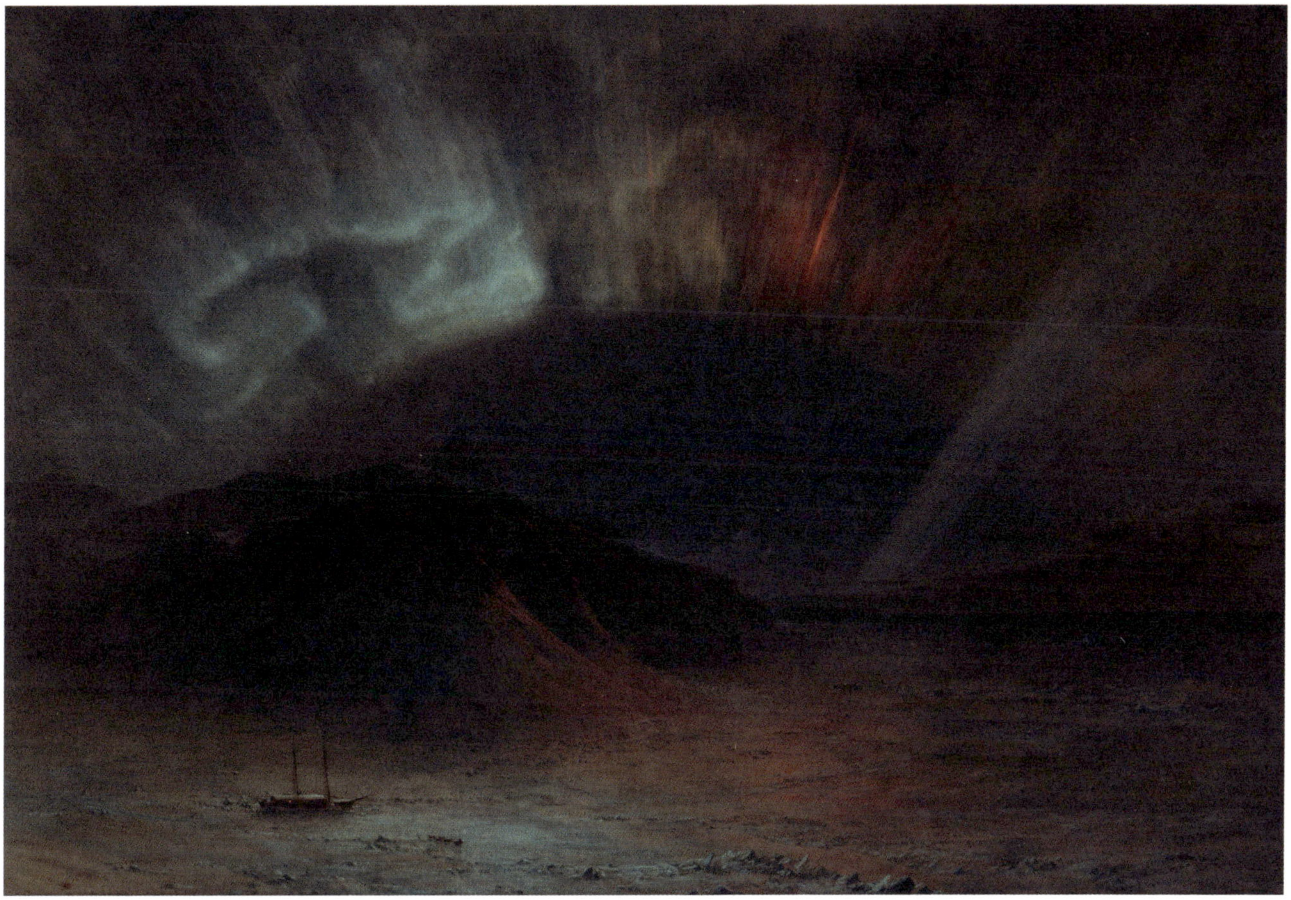

THE MIDNIGHT SUN AND THE NORTHERN LIGHTS HAS MADE A LASTING IMPRESSION ON ARTISTS. NOTICE THE VERTICAL FORMAT OF THESE PAINTINGS AND HOW IT SERVES TO AMPLIFY THE BOUNDLESSNESS OF THE ARCTIC SKY AND THE SPECTACULAR PHENOMENON OF COLOURED LIGHT.

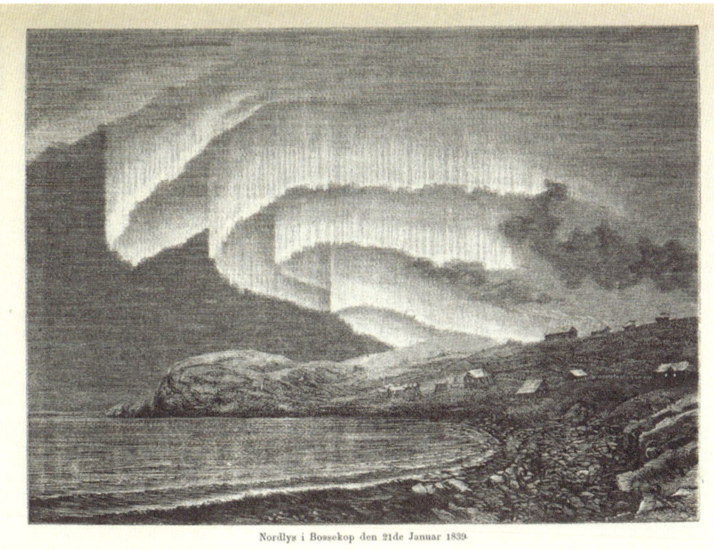

Nordlys i Bossekop den 21de Januar 1839

Opposite top – *Njommelsaska i Lappland*, 1856, chromolithograph, Carl Svante Hallbeck (Swedish)

Opposite bottom – *Astronomy: the Aurora Borealis, with a reindeer-drawn sledge in the foreground*, 1880, coloured wood engraving with watercolour, Charles H Whymper (British)

Top – *Aurora Borealis*, 1865, oil on canvas, Frederic Edwin Church (American)

Bottom – *Nordlys I Bossekop dec 21de Januar 1839*, 1885, from the book *Under Nordlysets Straaler, Skildringer fra Lappernes Land*, Sophus Tromholt (Danish)

304 *Northern Lights. Study from North Norway*, c. 1901, oil on canvas, Anna Boberg (Swedish)

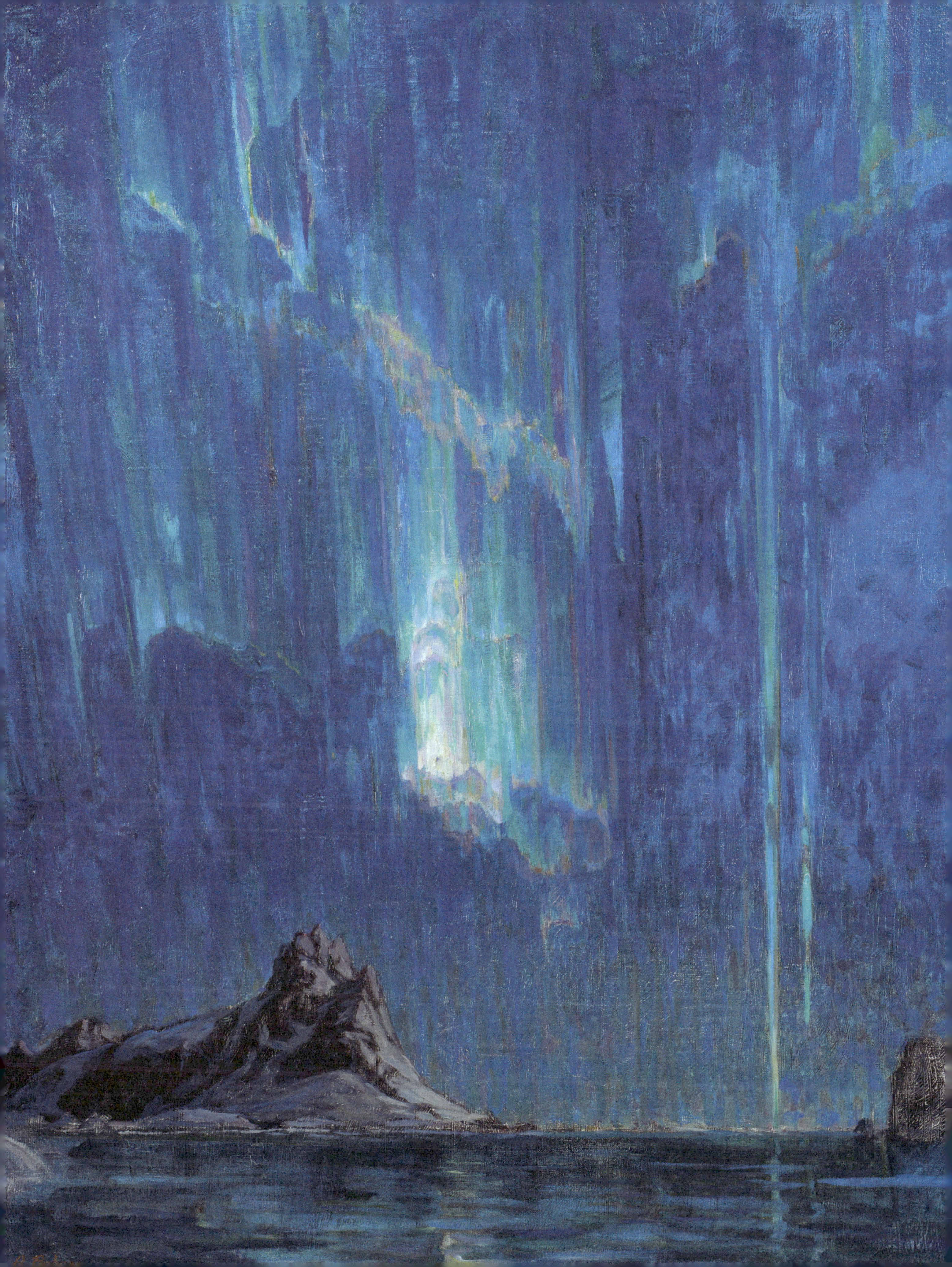

ARTWORK CREDITS

2–3 Harald Sohlberg, *Winter Night in the Mountains*, 1914
Oil on canvas, 160.4 x 180 cm (detail)
Courtesy of The National Museum of Norway Art, Architecture and Design, Norway
Photo: Børre Høstland

6–7 Rosslynd Piggott, *Upside-down landscape*, 1989
Oil on linen, 136 x 183 cm
Monash University Museum of Art, Melbourne
© Rosslynd Piggott/Copyright Agency, 2025

8 Caspar David Friedrich, *Chalk Cliffs on Rügen*, 1818
Oil on canvas, 90.8 x 70.6 cm
Kunst Museum, Winterthur
Oskar Reinhart Foundation, 1930
Photo: SIK-ISEA, Zürich, Philipp Hitz

12–3 Formerly attributed to Zhao Bosu, *Springtime Mountains*, c. 1644–1911
Ink and colour on silk, 35.2 x 295.6 cm
National Museum of Asian Art, Smithsonian Institute, Freer Collection
Gift of Charles Lang Freer, F1909.196

20–1 Georgia O'Keeffe, *Untitled (Red and Yellow Cliffs)*, 1940
Oil on canvas, 61 x 91.4 cm
Georgia O'Keeffe Museum, Santa Fe
© Georgia O'Keeffe Museum. ARS, New York/Copyright Agency, Australia, 2025
Photo: Georgia O'Keeffe Museum, Sante Fe/Art Resource, NY

LAND

24 Emily Carr, *Trees in the Sky*, 1939
Oil on canvas, 111.6 x 68.7 cm
Courtesy of Art Gallery of Ontario, Toronto
Gift of Richard M Ivey, 2008
Photo: © AGO

28–9 Charles-François Daubigny, *Apple Trees in Blossom*, 1874
Oil on canvas, 85 x 157 cm
Courtesy of Scottish National Gallery, Edinburgh

30 René Magritte, *The Sixteenth of September*, c. 1956–58
Gouache over graphite on paper, 35.6 x 27.6 cm
© René Magritte. ADAGP/Copyright Agency, 2025

31 (Top) Utagawa Hiroshige, *Moon Pine, Ueno*, 1857
Woodblock print; ink and colour on paper, 36 x 23.5 cm
Courtesy of Honolulu Museum of Art

(Bottom) Cedric Savage, *Laurel tree*, c. 1930
Oil on board, 42 x 48 cm
Courtesy of Auckland Art Gallery Toi o Tāmaki, Auckland

32 Design after Karl Gustav Forrer, produced by Allan, Cockshut & Co., *Portion of wallpaper from a woodland scene design*, 1906 (made)
Wallpaper, 101.7 x 50.5 cm
Courtesy of Victoria and Albert Museum, London
Photo: © Victoria and Albert Museum, London

33 (Top) John Crome, *Forest scene with oak trees*, early 19th century
Oil on canvas, 74 x 61.6 cm
Courtesy of Victoria and Albert Museum, London
Photo: © Victoria and Albert Museum, London

(Middle) Unknown artist (Japanese), *Jar with pine tree*, c. 1900
Stoneware, overglaze, 27.8 x 29 cm
Courtesy of Art Gallery of South Australia, Adelaide
Bequest of R H Longden, 1994

(Bottom) Georgia O'Keeffe, *The Lawrence Tree*, 1929
Oil on canvas, 78.7 x 101.6 cm
Courtesy of Wadsworth Atheneum Museum of Art, Connecticut
The Ella Gallup Sumner and Mary Caitlin Sumner Collection Fund
© Georgia O'Keeffe Museum. ARS/Copyright Agency, 2025

34 Jacob George Strutt, *A gnarled and hollow old oak tree (Quercus robur L.) sheltering a shepherd and his sheep*, 1823
Etching, 28.9 x 36.2 cm (detail)
Courtesy of Wellcome Collection, London

35 Tacita Dean, *Majesty*, 2006
Gouache on photograph mounted on paper, 300 x 420 cm
Courtesy of the artist, Frith Street Gallery, London and Marian Goodman Gallery, New York/Paris/Los Angeles
© Tacita Dean

36 (Top) Tacita Dean, *Small Sakura Study (Jindai II)*, 2023
Coloured pencil on handprinted Foma matte silver gelatin photograph mounted on paper
Courtesy of the artist, Frith Street Gallery, London and Marian Goodman Gallery, New York/Paris/Los Angeles
© Tacita Dean
Photo: Simon Hanzer

(Middle) W Stoker (1811) after James Forbes (1778), *Banyan Tree (Ficus benghalensis L.) with many trunks*, 1811
Lithograph, 23.3 x 20.5 cm
Courtesy of Wellcome Collection, London

(Bottom) Unknown artist (Chinese), *Pair of miniature trees in enamelled basins*, second half of 18th century
Painted enamels on copper, coral, ivory and various stones, 40 x 37 x 21.5 cm
© Royal Collection Enterprises Limited 2024 | Royal Collection Trust

37 (Top) Henrik Immanuel Wigström, *Pine tree in bowl*, c. 1896–1908
Painted matt gilt, with wire and diamonds, 8.2 x 9.1 x 3.5 cm
Donated for Queen Mary's Doll's House, 1924
© Royal Collection Enterprises Limited 2024 | Royal Collection Trust

(Bottom) Yamamoto Baiitsu, *Three Friends of Winter [right of a pair]*, first half of 19th century
Ink with flecks of gold pigment on paper, 157 x 360 cm
Courtesy of Minneapolis Institute of Art, Minneapolis
Gift of Elizabeth and Willard Clark

38–9 Jacob van Ruisdael, *The Forest Stream*, c. 1660
Oil on canvas, 99.7 x 129.2 cm
The Metropolitan Museum of Art, New York
Marquand Collection, Gift of Henry G. Marquand, 1889

40 Paul Gauguin, *Martinique Landscape*, 1887
Oil on canvas, 117 x 89.8 cm
National Galleries of Scotland, Edinburgh
Presented by Sir Alexander Maitland in memory of his wife Rosalind, 1960

41 (Top) Paul Sandby (etcher) & David Allan (draughtsman), *Peggy and Jenny*, 1758
Etching, illustration for *The Gentle Shepherd* by Allan Ramsay, published by John Robertson jnr., 23.6 x 18.1 cm
National Gallery of Victoria, Melbourne
Gift of John H Connell, 1917

(Middle) Sheng Mao, *Recluse Fisherman, Autumn Trees*, c. 1349
Fan mounted as an album leaf; ink and colour on silk, 26.7 x 33.7 cm
The Metropolitan Museum of Art, New York
Ex coll: C C Wang Family, Purchase, Florance Waterbury Bequest and Gift of Mr and Mrs Nathan Cummings, by exchange, 1973

(Bottom) Arthur Lismer, *Little Island, MacGregor Bay*, 1929
Oil on wood-pulp board, 32.9 x 41 cm
Courtesy of the Art Gallery of Ontario, Toronto
The Thompson Collection at the Art Gallery of Ontario, 2017
© Estate of Arthur Lismer
Photo: AGO

42 Ruth Burgess, *Winter forest*, 2006
Wood engraving, printed in black ink on white wove paper, 12.6 x 10 cm
Courtesy of Art Gallery of New South Wales, Sydney
Arthur Boyd Acquisition Fund, 2006
© Ruth Burgess

43 (Top) Sheroanawe Hakihiiwe, *Shereka hemoshi*, 2020
Acrylic on handmade cotton paper, 99.5 x 70.3 cm
Courtesy of Art Gallery of New South Wales, Sydney
Purchased with funds provided by the Patricia Lucille Bernard Bequest 2022
© Sheroanawe Hakihiiwe

(Bottom) Eugene von Guérard, *Ferntree Gully, Dandenong Ranges, Victoria*, 1867
Colour lithograph, 32.8 x 51.4 cm
National Gallery of Victoria, Melbourne
Felton Bequest, 1960

44–5 Paul Klee, *Light over former times*, 1933
Watercolour, 20.8 x 32.8 cm
Princeton University Art Museum, Princeton
Laura P Hall Memorial Collection
Photo: Princeton University Art Museum. Licensed by Art Resource, NY

46 (Top) Piero del Pollaiuolo, *Apollo and Daphne*, c. 1470–80
Oil on wood, 29.5 x 20 cm
Courtesy of The National Gallery, London

(Bottom) Oliver Messel (designer), *Theatre costume (headdress for the Cavalier of the Fairy of the Woodland Glades in The Sleeping Beauty, Sadler's Wells Ballet, Convent Garden)*, 1960
Millinery
Victoria and Albert Museum, London
Given by the Royal Academy of Dance

47 Royal Porcelain Manufactory, Berlin, *Vase*, c. 1820–25
Hard-paste porcelain, 43.7 x 29.8 x 28.9 cm
Courtesy of The Metropolitan Museum of Art, New York

49 Gustav Klimt, *The Park*, c. 1910 or earlier
Oil on canvas, 110.4 x 110.4 cm
Courtesy of The Museum of Art, New York
Gertrud A. Mellon Fund

50 J & J Parkin, *Three flowering plants: a garden dahlia (Dahlia cultivar), a calamint (Calamintha coccinea) and a verbena (Verbena tweediana)*, c. 1833–59
Coloured engraving
Courtesy of Wellcome Collection, London

51 (Top) Mary Delany, *Geranium Inquinans, from an album (Vol. IV, 72)*, 1778
Collage of coloured papers with bodycolour and watercolour on black ink background, 34.2 x 23.7 cm
Courtesy of The British Museum, London
Bequeathed by Augusta Hall, Baroness Llanover

(Middle) Unknown (Sudanese), *Bowl with floral and geometric designs*, c. 1st–3rd century
Pottery and paint, 6.7 x 10.8 cm
Courtesy of The Metropolitan Museum of Art, New York
Rogers Fund, 1913

(Bottom) Robert Jacob Gordon, *Gorteria diffusa*, c. 1777–86
Drawing, 28.2 x 17.7 cm
Courtesy of Rijksmuseum, Amsterdam
Purchased with support of private collectors

52–3 Unknown (Japanese), *Seven flowering plants, one possibly a kingcup and six pinks (Dianthus species)*, c. 1870
Watercolour
Courtesy of Wellcome Collection, London

54 Theodor Josef Petter, *Alpine Flora*, 1853
Oil on canvas, 89 x 72 cm
Courtesy of Belvedere Museum, Vienna
Taken over from the Kunsthistorisches Museum Wien, Vienna

55 (Top) Unknown (likely American or British), *Brooch*, c. 1880–1900
Gold, silver, diamond and enamel brooch, 6.3 x 3.2 x 1.9 cm
Victoria and Albert Museum, London

(Bottom) Josef Sudek, *Untitled [flower in forest]*, 1968
Gelatin silver print, 16.9 x 22.7 cm
Courtesy of Minneapolis Institute of Art, Minneapolis
© Josef Sudek. OOA/S/Copyright Agency, 2025

57 Gordon Mortensen, *Beach Flowers*, 1990
Reduction woodcut, 101.6 x 73.66 cm (detail)
Courtesy of the artist and Davidson Galleries, Seattle
© Gorden Mortensen

58 Gustav Klimt, *Farm Garden with Sunflowers*, 1906
Oil on canvas, 110 x 110 cm
Belvedere Museum, Vienna
Purchase of Galerie Sanct Lucas, Vienna, 1939

59 (Top) Unknown (Japanese), *Plate with autumn grasses*, c. 17th–19th century
Nabeshima ware; porcelain with underglaze cobalt blue and celadon glaze, 5.72 x 20.32 x 20.32 cm
Courtesy of Minneapolis Institute of Art, Minneapolis
Mary Griggs Burke Collection, Gift of the Mary and Jackson Burke Foundation

(Middle) Unknown (Dutch), *Four Egyptian plants in a landscape, including purging cassia, French jujube or Chinese date, and a taro species*, c. 1676
Line engraving
Courtesy of Wellcome Collection, London

(Bottom) Daniel Shipp, *Restricted Storage Area* (from the series *Botanical Inquiry*), 2019
Pigment ink-jet print, various
© Daniel Shipp
Private collection

61 Vanessa Bell, *A Conversation*, c. 1913–16
Oil on canvas, 86.6 x 81 cm
Courtesy of The Courtauld, London (Samuel Courtauld Trust)
© Vanessa Bell. All rights reserved, DACS/Copyright Agency, 2025

62 John Brack, *Flowers (Shasta daisies)*, 1959
Oil on composition board, 88.9 x 56.1 cm
National Gallery of Victoria, Melbourne
Gift of Frank and Yvonne Nicholls, 2008
2008.252
© Helen Brack
Photo: National Gallery of Victoria, Melbourne

63 Unknown (Indian), *Two ladies carry flowers*, c. 19th century
Opaque watercolour and gold on paper, 38.8 x 25.6 cm
Courtesy of National Museum of Asian Art, Washington
Smithsonian Unrestricted Trust Funds, Smithsonian Collections Acquisition Program, and Dr Arthur M. Sackler

64–5 Antonio Vivarini (studio of), *The Garden of Love*, c. 1465–70
Oil, tempera and gold on spruce panel, 152.5 x 239 cm
National Gallery of Victoria, Melbourne
Felton Bequest, 1948

66 Jacques Le Moyne de Morgues (formerly attributed to John White), *A Young Daughter of the Picts*, c. 1585
Watercolour and gouache, touched with gold on parchment, 26 x 18.7 cm
Yale Center for British Art, Paul Mellon Collection, New Haven

67 Bow Porcelain Works, London (manufacturer), *Figures*, c. 1760
Porcelain
National Gallery of Victoria, Melbourne
The Colin Templeton Collection. Gift of Mrs Colin Templeton, 1942
Photo: National Gallery of Victoria, Melbourne

69 Balthasar van der Ast, *Flowers in a Wan-Li Vase, with Shells*, c. 1640–50
Oil on canvas, 53 x 43 cm (detail)
Mauritshuis, Netherlands
Bequest of J H Loudon to the Friends of the Mauritshuis Foundation, 1996

70 Abraham Mignon, *Still Life with Flowers and a Watch*, c. 1600–79
Oil on canvas, 75 x 60 cm
Courtesy of Rijks Museum, Amsterdam

71 Rachel Ruysch, *Vase with Flowers and an Ear of Corn*, 1742
Oil on canvas, 50.6 x 40.2 cm
National Gallery of Ireland, Dublin

72–3 Evelyn Dunbar, *A Land Girl and the Bail Bull*, 1945
Oil paint on canvas, 91.4 x 182.9 cm
Tate Modern, London
Presented by the War Artists Advisory Committee, 1946

74 Raoul Dufy, *The Wheatfield*, 1929
Oil paint on canvas, 130 x 162 cm
Tate Modern, London
Bequethed by Mrs A F Kessler, 1983

75 (Top) Utagawa Toyokuni II, *Harvest time in autumn*, c. 1826–35
Colour woodblock
National Gallery of Victoria, Melbourne
Felton Bequest, 1909
Photo: National Gallery of Victoria, Melbourne

(Bottom) Francis Vivares, Peter Paul Rubens (after), *Harvest-Time*, 1775
Etching, engraving, 41.2 x 51.4 cm
Courtesy of The British Museum, London
Felton Bequest, 1926
Photo: © Trustees of the British Museum

76 Unknown, *Gauri Ragini, Folio from a Ragamala*, c. 1650
Opaque watercolour and gold on paper, 21.6 x 19.3 cm
National Museum of Asian Art, Washington

77 (Top) Vincent van Gogh, *Women Picking Olives*, 1889
Oil on canvas, 72.7 x 91.4 cm
The Metropolitan Museum of Art, New York
The Walter H and Leonore Annenberg Collection, Gift of Walter H and Leonore Annenberg, 1995, Bequest of Walter H Annenberg, 2002

(Bottom) Unknown, *Hand Clutching an Olive Branch*, c. 1353–23 BC
Limestone, paint, 22 cm
Courtesy of The Metropolitan Museum of Art, New York
Gift of Norbert Schimmel, 1981

78–9 Unknown (Roman), *The painted garden from the Villa of Livia*, c. 40–20 BC
Photo: Luisa Ricciarini / Bridgeman Images

80–1 Paul Cézanne, *Mont Sainte-Victoire and the Viaduct of the Arc River Valley*, c. 1882–85
Oil on canvas, 65.4 x 81.6 cm
Courtesy of The Metropolitan Museum of Art, New York
H. O. Havemeyer Collection, Bequest of Mrs. H. O. Havemeyer, 1929

82 Charles Rennie Mackintosh, *Mont Alba*, c. 1924–27
Watercolour on paper, 38.7 x 43.8 cm
Courtesy of Scottish National Gallery, Edinburgh

83 (Top) Johann Wilhelm Tischbein, *An Idyllic Landscape: the sun shining on a meadow with a river and hills in the distance*, 1809
Black chalk, pen and brown ink, brown and grey wash and watercolour, 27.6 x 43.8 cm
Courtesy of Scottish National Gallery of Modern Art, Edinburgh

(Bottom) Joan Williams, *Algarve*, 1971
Coloured lithograph, 17 x 21 cm
Courtesy of The Women's Art Collection, London
Donated by Jean Owen-Jones
© The Estate of Joan Williams

84 (Top) Barbara Bosworth, *Untitled*, from the series *Meadow, Carlisle, Massachusetts*, 2004
Chromogenic print, sheet and image, 81.3 x 101.6 cm
Courtesy of the artist and Smithsonian American Art Museum, Washington
Gift of Haluk and Elisa Soykan, 2008
© Barbara Bosworth

(Bottom) Alexis Jean Fournier, *September*, 1889
Oil on canvas, 69.7 x 126 cm
Courtesy of Minneapolis Institute of Art, Minneapolis
Gift of Don and Diana Lee Lucker

85 Richard Long, *A Line Made by Walking*, 1967
Photograph, gelatin silver print on paper and graphite on board, 37.5 x 32.4 cm
Courtesy of Tate Modern, London
© Richard Long. DACS/Copyright Agency, 2025

86 Théodore Rousseau, *A Meadow Bordered by Trees*, c. 1845–60
Oil on wood, 41.6 x 61.9 cm
Courtesy of The Metropolitan Museum of Art, New York
Bequest of Robert Graham Dun, 1900

87 Jean-Baptiste Camille Corot, *Ville-d'Avray: Entrance to the Wood*, c. 1823–25, with later reworking, probably early 1850s
Oil on canvas, 46 x 35 cm
Courtesy of Scottish National Gallery
Purchased with the aid of A E Anderson in memory of his brother Frank, 1927

88 Gustave Courbet, *Deer in the Forest*, 1868
Oil on canvas, 130.81 x 97.79 cm
Courtesy of Minneapolis Institute of Art, Minneapolis
Gift of James J Hill

89 Katayama Bokuyō, *Forest*, 1928
Two-panel folding screen, ink and mineral pigments on silk, 189.23 x 237.49 cm
Courtesy of Minneapolis Institute of Art, Minneapolis
The William Hood Dunwoody Fund, 2007

90–1 Unknown (South Netherlandish), *Shepherd and Shepherdess Making Music*, c. 1500–30
Wool warp, wool and silk wefts, 234.9 x 292.1 cm
The Metropolitan Museum of Art, New York
Bequest of Susan Vanderpoel Clark, 1967

92–3 David Hockney, *A Bigger Grand Canyon*, 1998
Oil on sixty canvases, 207 x 744.2 cm
National Gallery of Australia, Canberra
Purchased with the assistance of Kerry Stokes, Carol and Tony Berg and the O'Reilly family 1999
© David Hockney

94 Henri Bastin, *Opal miner's camp*, 1958
Synthetic polymer paint on composition board, 54.8 x 71.3 cm
National Gallery of Australia, Canberra
Purchased 1973
© The Estate of Henri Bastin

95 (Top) Dora Carrington, *Spanish Landscape with Mountains*, c. 1924
Oil paint on canvas, 55.9 x 66.7 cm
Tate Museum, London
Bequeathed by Frances Partridge, 2004

(Bottom) Sidney Nolan, *Desert*, 1950
Oil and enamel on composition board, 90 x 120 cm
National Gallery of Victoria, Melbourne
Presented through the NGV Foundation by Mr Jason Yeap, Founder Benefactor, 2003
© The Sidney Nolan Trust. All rights reserved. DACS/Copyright Agency, 2025

96–7 Russell Drysdale, *The rabbiters*, 1947
Oil on canvas, 76.6 x 102.5 cm
National Gallery of Victoria, Melbourne
Purchased 1947
© Courtesy Russell Drysdale Estate

98 Isamu Noguchi, *To Intrude on Nature's Way*, 1971
Basalt with Japanese pine base, 168.9 x 48.9 x 45.1 cm
Collection of The Isamu Noguchi Foundation and Garden Museum, New York. The Noguchi Museum Archives
© The Isamu Noguchi Foundation and Garden Museum, New York/ARS/Copyright Agency, 2025
Photo: Kevin Noble

99 Emily Carr, *Vanquished*, 1930
Oil on canvas, 92 x 129 cm
Vancouver Art Gallery, Vancouver
Photo: Trevor Mills

100 (Top) John Coburn, *Landscape*, 1958
Oil on composition board, 45.8 x 76.5 cm
Gift of the Trustees of the Museum of Modern Art and Design of Australia, to the National Gallery of Victoria 1981. Transferred to Heide Museum of Modern Art by the Council of Trustees of the National Gallery of Victoria, 2005
© John Coburn/Copyright Agency, 2025

(Bottom) George Elbert Burr, *The Edge of the Desert, Arizona*, after 1924
Etching and drypoint on paper, 24.9 x 30.2 cm
Smithsonian American Art Museum, Washington
Bequest of Carolann Smurthwaite in memory of her mother, Caroline Atherton Connell Smurthwaite

101 Uta Kögelsberger, from the *Antipodes* series, 2014
Stills from film
© Uta Kögelsberger

102 Ansel Adams, *Antelope House ruin, Canyon de Chelly National Monument, Arizona*, 1942
Gelatin silver photograph, 49.9 x 38.8 cm
National Gallery of Australia, Canberra
Purchased 1977

103 (Top) Unknown (Chinese), *Seated luohan (arhat) in a grotto*, c. 18th–19th century
Lapis lazuli, 18.1 x 25.4 cm
The Metropolitan Museum of Art, New York
Gift of Heber R Bishop, 1902

(Middle) Derek Jarman, *Avebury Series 4*, 1973
Acrylic on canvas, 120 x 120 cm
Presented by the Contemporary Art Society, 1977
© Estate of Derek Jarman
Photograph reproduced with the kind permission of Northampton Museums and Art Gallery

(Bottom) Sesshū Tōyō, *Autumn and Winter Landscapes* (one panel), c. late 15th–early 16th century
Ink on washi paper, 47.6 x 30.2 cm
Tokyo National Museum, Tokyo

104 (Top) Jack Hutchison, *South Island lake and mountain*, c. 1910–87
Watercolour, 26.4 x 36.5 cm
Courtesy of Auckland Art Gallery Toi o Tāmaki
© Prudence Theobold

(Bottom) J E H MacDonald, *Lake O'Hara*, 1930
Oil on canvas, 53.6 x 66.5 cm
Courtesy of Art Gallery of Ontario, Toronto
The Thompson Collection at the Art Gallery of Ontario
Photo: © AGO

105 (Top) Formerly attributed to Qiu Ying (c. 1494–1552), *Travelers on the Road to Shu*, c. 16th–17th century
Ink and colour on silk, 53.1 x 170 cm (detail)
Courtesy of National Museum of Asian Art, Washington
Gift of Charles Land Freer

(Bottom) Ithell Colquhoun, *Kerry Landscape*, 1949
Oil on board, 29.5 x 39.5 cm
Courtesy of Private Collection and Ben Hunter, London
Photo: Jack Elliot Edwards

106–7 Ernst Ludwig Kirchner, *Mountain with Cattle*, 1918
Oil on canvas, 118.7 x 149.2 cm
Courtesy of Minneapolis Institute of Art, Minneapolis
The John R Van Derlip Fund and gift of funds from Mary Ingebrand-Pohlad; purchase from the collection of Alfred and Ingrid Lenz Harrison

108 Kawase Hasui, *Asahi Peak Seen from Mt. Hakuba*, 1924
Woodblock print, ink and colour on paper, 25.9 x 38.5 cm
Museum of Fine Arts Boston
Gift of L Aaron Lebowich

109 (Top) Charles Howorth (1856–1945), *Mt Sefton from near the Hermitage*, n.d.
Watercolour, 36.8 x 30.5 cm
Courtesy of Auckland Art Gallery Toi o Tāmaki
Bequest of Maye Lambert, 1935

(Bottom) Grace Butler (1886–1962), *Glaciers, Rolleston Mountains*, n.d.
Oil on canvas, 94.7 x 123.5 cm
Courtesy of Auckland Art Gallery Toi o Tāmaki
Gift of Messrs W R and F W Wilson, 1922

110 Eileen Agar, *Rocks at Ploumanach, Brittany*, 1936
Photograph, gelatin silver print, 15.5 x 15.5 cm
National Galleries of Scotland, Edinburgh
Presented by Mrs Virginia Zabriskie of Zabriskie Gallery, New York, 2000
© The Estate of Eileen Agar. All Rights Reserved 2017 / Bridgeman Images

111 Paul Cézanne, *Rocks at Fontainebleau*, c. 1890s
Oil on canvas, 73.3 x 92.4 cm
Courtesy of The Metropolitan Museum of Art, New York
H O Havemeyer Collection, Bequest of Mrs H O Havemeyer, 1929

112 Unknown (Chinese), *Scholar's rock*, c. 19th century
Limestone, wood stand, 61.9 x 41.3 x 28.6 cm
Courtesy of The Metropolitan Museum of Art, New York
Gift of Richard Rosenblum Family, 2008

113 (Top) Pietro Fabris, *Lava, scoriae and pumice from Mount Vesuvius*, 1776
Coloured etching with gouache, 21.3 x 39.2 cm
Courtesy of Wellcome Collection, London

(Bottom) Henry Moore OM, CH, *Dante Stones, Stone II*, 1977
Etching on paper, 29.2 x 19.7 cm
Courtesy of Tate, London
© The Henry Moore Foundation. All Rights Reserved. DACS/Copyright Agency, 2025

114 Pietro Fabris, *The Eruption of Mount Vesuvius in the Night of 8 August 1779*, 1779
Coloured etching on gouache, 38.8 x 21 cm
Courtesy of Wellcome Collection, London

115 (Top) Unknown (Japanese), *Case (Inrō) with Design of Deer and Maple Trees (obverse); Mount Fuji (reverse)*, c. 1820
Case: lacquer with pottery plaques; Fastener: coral; Toggle: red lacquer carved with design of Chinese figure and plant, 7 x 5.7 cm
Courtesy of The Metropolitan Museum of Art, New York

(Bottom) Unknown (Italian), *A volcanic eruption in Herculaneum, showing the advance of lava flow over walls, with Vesuvius visible in the background*, 1861
Painting, gouache
Courtesy of Wellcome Collection, London

116–7 Erica McGilchrist, *Volcano*, 1955
Acquarell pencil on card, 23 x 34.5 cm
Courtesy of Heide Museum of Modern Art, Melbourne
Gift of Erica McGilchrist, 1999
© Estate of Erica McGilchrist

WATER

120 Sigrid Granfelt, *Pines by the Sea*, 1895
Oil on canvas, 85 x 53 cm (detail)
Finnish National Gallery/Ateneum Art Museum
Photo: Finnish National Gallery/Hannu Pakarinen

124 Hiroshi Sugimoto, *Five Elements: Sea of Japan, Hokkaido, 1986*, 2011
Optical-quality glass with black-and-white film, 15.2 x 7.6 x 7.6 cm
Courtesy of The Metropolitan Museum of Art, New York
Gift of Sylvan Barnet and William Burto, in honor of John T. Carpenter, 2012
© Hiroshi Sugimoto

125 Paul Nash, *Winter Sea*, c. 1925–37
Oil on canvas, 71 x 96.5 cm
Courtesy of York Museums and Gallery Trust
Gift from Mrs C Grey, 1956

126 Unknown (Chinese), *Fan with Dragon*, c. 17th century
Silk tapestry, 26 x 25.7 cm
Courtesy of The Metropolitan Museum of Art, New York
From the Collection of A. W. Bahr, Purchase, Fletcher Fund, 1947
Photo: © The Metropolitan Museum of Art. Licensed by Art Resource, NY

127 (Top) Dame Barbara Hepworth, *Sea Form (Porthmeor)*, 1958
Bronze on wooden base, 80 x 109.2 x 24.1 cm
Courtesy of Yale University Art Gallery
Barbara Hepworth © Bowness

(Bottom) Johan Christian Dahl, *Waves and Breakers in the Bay of Naples*, 1821
Oil on cardboard, 36 x 22.5 cm
The National Museum of Norway Art, Architecture and Design, The Fine Art Collections, Oslo
Photo: Jacques Lathion

128 David Hockney, *The Wave, A Lithograph*, 1990
Lithograph on paper, 68.8 x 96.6 cm
© David Hockney/Tyler Graphics Ltd.
Photo: Richard Schmidt

129 (Top) Dame Barbara Hepworth, *Pelagos*, 1946
Elm and strings on oak base, 43 x 46 x 38.5 cm
Courtesy of Tate, London
Barbara Hepworth © Bowness

(Bottom) C R W Nevinson, *The Wave*, 1917
Oil on canvas, 50.8 x 76.2 cm
Yale Center for British Art, Paul Mellon Fund, New Haven

130 (Top) Utagawa Kuniyoshi, *Concise Illustrated Biography of Monk Nichiren: Calming the Stormy Sea at Tsunoda in Exile to Sado Island*, c. 1835–36
Woodblock print; ink and colour on paper, 22.5 x 34.9 cm
Courtesy of The Metropolitan Museum of Art, New York
Henry L Phillips Collection, Bequest of Henry L Phillips, 1939

(Bottom) Théodore Géricault, *Sailboat on a Raging Sea*, c. 1818–19
Brush and brown wash, watercolour over black chalk, on brown laid paper, 15.2 x 24.7 cm
Getty Museum, Los Angeles
Private Collection

131 (Top) Katsushika Hokusai, *The Great Wave off Kanagawa*, c. 1830
Colour woodblock, 25.7 x 37.7 cm
National Gallery of Victoria, Melbourne
Felton Bequest, 1909
Photo: National Gallery of Victoria, Melbourne

(Bottom) Pieter Jansz van der Croos, *Sailing ships in a storm*, c. 1609–70
Oil on wood, 32 x 48 cm
Courtesy of Finnish National Gallery, Helsinki
Owner: Suomen valtio
Photo: Finnish National Gallery/Jenni Nurminen

132 Tawaraya Sotatsu, *Waves at Matsushima*, c. 17th century
Pair of folding screen paintings; ink, colour, gold, and silver on paper, 166 x 369.9 cm (each)
Courtesy of National Museum of Asian Art, Washington
Gift of Charles Lang Freer

133 Gustave Courbet, *Marine: The Waterspout*, 1870
Oil on canvas, 68.9 x 99.7 cm
Courtesy of The Metropolitan Museum of Art, New York
H O Havemeyer Collection, Gift of Horace Havemeyer, 1929

134–5 Hiroshi Sugimoto, *Ligurian Sea, Riomagio*, 1993. Neg# 391.
Gelatin-silver print, 50.8 x 61 cm
Courtesy of Lisson Gallery
© Hiroshi Sugimoto

136 Helen Frankenthaler, *Cape, (Provincetown)*, 1964
Synthetic polymer paint and resin on canvas, 278.5 x 237.2 cm
National Gallery of Victoria, Melbourne
Purchased with the assistance of the National Gallery Society of Victoria, 1967
© Helen Frankenthaler Foundation, Inc. ARS/Copyright Agency, 2025

137 Edward Hopper, *(Rocks and Sea)*, c. 1916–19
Oil on wood, 29.8 x 40.8 cm
Whitney Museum of American Art, New York
Josephine N Hopper Bequest
© Edward Hopper. ARS/Copyright Agency, 2025

138–9 Edward Bawden, *Coast scene*, c. late 1920s–early 1930s
Watercolour over pencil, laid down, 29.4 x 37.7 cm
National Gallery of Victoria, Melbourne
Felton Bequest, 1955
© Estate of Edward Bawden

140 Christo and Jeanne-Claude, *Wrapped Coast, Little Bay, Sydney, Australia, 1968–1969*, 1969
Colour photograph by Harry Shunk mounted on aluminium panel, 40 x 50.2 cm
Dorothy and Herbert Vogel Collection
National Gallery of Art, Washington
© Christo Javacheff. ADAGP/Copyright Agency, 2025

141 Bea Maddock, *Terra Spiritus … with a darker shade of pale* (Sheet I), c. 1993–98
Stencil, printed in hand-ground Launceston ochre, from multiple hand-cut mylar stencils; letterpress text blind printed; hand-written script, 28.4 x 76 cm (each)
National Gallery of Australia, Canberra
Gordon Darling Australasian Print Fund, 1998
© Estate of Bea Maddock

142 Ben Nicholson, *July 15 1949 (St Ives harbour)*, 1949
Oil and pencil on canvas, 35.2 x 40.3 cm
Yale Center for British Art, Paul Mellon Collection, New Haven
© Ben Nicholson. DACS/Copyright Agency, 2025

143 Ogata Kenzan, *Japanese incense container*, c. 1799
Stoneware with glaze, 12 x 11 x 2.1 cm
Courtesy of The Fitzwilliam Museum, Cambridge
Photo: © The Fitzwilliam Museum, Cambridge

144 Lawrence W Ladd, *The Blue Grotto*, c. 1880
Watercolour on paper, 45 x 71.1 cm
Smithsonian American Art Museum, Washington
Gift of Bates and Isabel Lowry

145 Brett Whiteley, *Evening coming in on Sydney Harbour*, 1975
Oil on cotton on canvas, 228.2 x 190 cm
National Gallery of Victoria, Melbourne
Presented by Mrs Adrian Gibson as the winner of the 1975 Sir William Angliss Memorial Art Prize, 1976
© Wendy Whiteley/Copyright Agency, Australia, 2025

146 (Top) Edward Lear, *Abu Seer*, 1867
Watercolour, graphite, pen and black ink on medium, slightly textured, blue laid paper, 8.6 x 16 cm
Yale Center for British Art, Conneticut
Gift of Donald C Gallup

(Bottom) Eugène Delacriox, *The Sea at Dieppe*, c. 1852–54
Watercolour on laid paper, 26.7 x 44.6 cm
Courtesy of The Metropolitan Museum of Art, New York
Gift from the Karen B Cohen Collection of Eugène Delacroix, in honour of Jill Newhouse, 2014

147 Vanessa Gardiner, *Blue Coast 20*, 2006
Acrylic on board, 36 x 46 cm
Courtesy of The Women's Art Collection, Cambridge
© Vanessa Gardiner
Photo: The Women's Art Collection

148 Willem de Kooning, *Beach scene*, 1970
Lithograph, 93.7 x 72 cm
National Gallery of Victoria, Melbourne
Purchased through The Art Foundation of Victoria with the assistance of Henry and Dinah Krongold, Founder Benefactors, 1984
© The Willem de Kooning Foundation, New York. ARS/Copyright Agency, 2025

149 Yves Tanguy, *Old horizon*, 1928
Oil on canvas, 100 x 73 cm
National Gallery of Australia, Canberra
© Yves Tanguy. ARS/Copyright Agency, 2025

150 Claude Monet, *Rough weather at Étretat*, 1883
Oil on canvas, 65 x 81 cm
National Gallery of Victoria, Melbourne
Felton Bequest, 1913
Photo: National Gallery of Victoria, Melbourne

151 (Top) John Constable, *Weymouth Bay*, 1816
Oil on canvas, 45.2 x 24.7 cm
Courtesy of Victoria and Albert Museum, London
Given by Isabel Constable, 1888

(Bottom) David Lucas (engraver) and John Constable (after), *Weymouth Bay, Dorsetshire*, 1830
Mezzotint and drypoint on chine collé, 14.2 x 18.3 cm
National Gallery of Victoria, Melbourne
Felton Bequest, 1970
Photo: National Gallery of Victoria, Melbourne

152 Piero della Francesca, *Madonna and Child with Saints (Montefeltro Altarpiece)*, c. 1472–74
Tempera on panel, 251 x 172 cm
© Pinacoteca di Brera, Milano – MiC

153 (Top) Dihl et Guérhard, *Plate with marine subject*, c. 1789–97
Porcelain, 3.8 x 24.1 cm
Courtesy of The Metropolitan Museum of Art, New York
Purchase, Sidney R. Knafel Gift, in honor of Jeffrey Munger, 2018

(Bottom) Unknown (Chinese), *Snuff Bottle*, c. 19th century
Hair crystal, coral stopper, 8.7 cm
Courtesy of The Metropolitan Museum of Art, New York
Bequest of Mary Stillman Harkness, 1950

154 Judy Watson, *two halves with bailer shell*, 2002
Pigment, synthetic polymer paint on canvas, 194 x 108 cm
National Gallery of Australia, Canberra
Purchased 2003
© Judy Watson/Copyright Agency, 2025

155 (Top left) Unknown, *Hand axe knapped around a fossil shell, located centrally on one face, identified as the Cretaceous bivalve mollusc Spondylus spinosus*, Lower Palaeolithic Acheulean c. 500,000–300,000 BCE
Stone, flint, shell, 7.9 x 3.5 x 13.2 cm
Museum of Archaeology and Anthropology, Cambridge

(Top right) Unknown (Chinese), *Hai-Lo*, c. 19th century
Sea shell, 26.7 cm
Courtesy of The Metropolitan Museum of Art, New York
The Crosby Brown Collection of Musical Instruments, 1889
Photo: © The Metropolitan Museum of Art. Licensed by Art Resource, NY

(Middle) Unknown (Japanese), *Conch-Shaped Clay Object*, Jōmon period, 2000–1000 BC
Found at the Uenoyama Site, Niigata
Courtesy of Tokyo National Museum, Tokyo

(Bottom) Ellen José, *The bu (Trumpet shell)*, 1996
Woodblock print on unryushi paper, 47.1 x 32.5 cm
Courtesy of Queensland Art Gallery | Gallery of Modern Art
© Ellen José Memorial Foundation
Photo: QAGOMA

156 Naum Gabo, *Red Stone*, c. 1964–65
Stone, 21 x 41 x 46 cm
Courtesy of Tate, London
The Work of Naum Gabo © Nina & Graham Williams/Tate, London 2023

157 Georgia O'Keeffe, *Shell No. 2*, 1928
Oil on board, 24 x 18 cm
Georgia O'Keeffe Museum, Santa Fe
Gift of the Burnett Foundation, 1997
© Georgia O'Keeffe Museum. ARS/Copyright Agency, 2025
Photo: Malcolm Varon

158 Andreas Feininger, *Broken Conch Shell*, c. 1977
Gelatin silver print, 25.8 x 20.2 cm
The Montreal Museum of Fine Arts
Wysse E Feininger Bequest, 2010
© Estate of Andreas Feininger
Photo: MMFA

159 (Top) Barbara Morgan, *City shell*, 1938, printed 1972
Gelatin silver photograph, 34.4 x 25.1 cm
National Gallery of Victoria, Melbourne
Gift of Krystyna Campbell-Pretty AM and Family through the Australian Government's Cultural Gifts Program, 2022Courtesy of Barbara and Willard Morgan photographs and papers, UCLA Library Special Collections
© The Barbara Morgan Estate

(Bottom) Olive Cotton, *The shell*, c. 1935
Gelatin silver photograph. 37.6 x 30 cm
National Gallery of Australia, Canberra
Purchased 2012

161 Marguerite Mahood, *Figure of a mermaid with seal*, c. 1947
Modelled earthenware, 25 x 14.5 x 10.3 cm
National Gallery of Australia, Canberra
Purchased 1979
© Estate of Marguerite Mahood

162 Partly designed and perhaps made by Reinhold Vasters or Alfred André, *Pendant with Venus and Cupid on a Dolphin*, c. 1865–90
Enamelled gold, rubies and pearls, 11 x 8.5 cm
Courtesy of The Metropolitan Museum of Art, New York
Robert Lehman Collection, 1975

163 (Top) Unknown (Iranian), *'Jonah and the Whale', Folio Probably from a Jami al-Tavarikh (Compendium of Chronicles)*, c. 1400
Ink, opaque watercolour, gold, and silver on paper, 33.7 x 49.5 cm
Courtesy of The Metropolitan Museum of Art, New York
Purchase, Joseph Pulitzer Bequest, 1933

(Middle) Engraved by Anonymous, after Battista Franco, *Female Nude with Two Seahorses*, c. 1599–1622
Engraving; third state, 8.8 x 12.4 cm
Courtesy of The Metropolitan Museum of Art, New York
The Elisha Whittelsey Collection, The Elisha Whittelsey Fund, 1949

(Bottom) Unknown (Burmese), *Parabaik. Burmese court manuscript*, c. 1857–85
Paint on paper, 21 x 92.4 x 53.5 (detail)
Courtesy of The British Museum, London
© The Trustees of the British Museum
Photo: © The Trustees of the British Museum

164–5 Sandro Botticelli, *Birth of Venus*, c. 1485
Tempera on canvas, 172.5 x 278.5 cm
Courtesy of Gallery Uffizi, Florence

166 Keisai Eisen, *The Kegon Falls, One of the Three Waterfalls*, c. 1845
Woodcut, nishiki-e (full colour) technique, 34.2 x 22.8 cm
Courtesy of Auckland Art Gallery Toi o Tāmaki, Auckland
Mackelvie Trust Collection, Auckland Art Gallery Toi o Tāmaki

167 Georges Fouguet, *'Cascade' Pendant*, c. 1900
Gold, open enamel on spangles, opals, diamonds and baroque pearl, 12 x 5 cm
Courtesy of Petit Palais – Fine Arts Museum of Paris
© ADAGP, Paris, 2025

168 Eddie Clemens, *The End of the Waterfall (No. 2)*, 2007
Ink on paper (found receipt role ends), 157 x 104 cm (detail)
Courtesy of Auckland Art Gallery Toi o Tāmaki, Auckland
Chartwell Collection, Auckland Art Gallery Toi o Tāmaki, 2009
© Eddie Clemens

169 Georgia O'Keeffe, *Waterfall—End of Road—'Iao Valley*, 1939
Oil on canvas, 48.3 x 40.6 cm (detail)
Collection of Honolulu Museum of Art
Purchase, Allerton, Prisanlee and General Acquisition Funds and with a gift from *The Honolulu Advertiser*, 1989
© Georgia O'Keeffe Museum. ARS/Copyright Agency, 2025

170 Gustave Courbet, *A River in a Mountain Gorge*, c. 1864–65
Oil on canvas, 81.4 x 64.7 cm
National Galleries of Scotland, Edinburgh
Presented by Sir Alexander Maitland in memory of his wife Rosalind, 1960
Photo: Antonia Reeve

171 (Top) Camille Corot, *Waterfall at Terni*, 1826
Oil on paper, laid down on wood, 26.7 x 30.8 cm
Courtesy of The Metropolitan Museum of Art, New York
The Whitney Collection, Gift of Wheelock Whitney III, and Purchase, Gift of Mr and Mrs Charles S McVeigh, by exchange, 2003

(Bottom) Balthazar Nebot, *Aysgarth Falls, Yorkshire*, c. 1750–62
Oil on canvas, 76.2 x 111.8 cm
Yale Center for British Art, Paul Mellon Collection, New Haven

172 Jacob van Ruisdael, *A Landscape with a Waterfall and a Castle on a Hill*, c. 1660–70
Oil on canvas, 101.x 86 cm
The National Gallery, London
Photo: The National Gallery, London

173 Joseph Mallord William Turner, *Drawing of the Clyde (Liber Studiorum, part IV, plate 18)*, 1809
Etching and mezzotint; first state of three, 18.3 x 26.7 cm
Courtesy of The Metropolitan Museum of Art, New York
H O Havemeyer Collection, Bequest of Mrs. H O Havemeyer, 1929

174 Ginger Riley Munduwalawala, *Nyamiyukanji, the river country*, 1997
Synthetic polymer paint on canvas, 185.3 x 201.8 cm
Art Gallery of New South Wales, Sydney
© Reproduced courtesy of the Estate of Ginger Riley Munduwalawala & Alcaston Gallery, Melbourne

175 (Top) Lloyd Rees, *Omega pastoral*, 1950
Oil on canvas, 78.8 x 106.8 cm
National Gallery of Victoria, Melbourne
Felton Bequest, 1950
© Alec and Jancis Rees/Copyright Agency, 2025

(Bottom) Elioth Grüner, *Bellinger pastoral*, 1937
Oil on canvas, 64 x 76.2 cm
National Gallery of Victoria, Melbourne
Felton Bequest, 1940
Photo: National Gallery of Victoria, Melbourne

176–7 Georgia O'Keeffe, *It Was Blue and Green*, 1960
Oil on linen, 76.5 x 101.6 cm
Whitney Museum of American Art, New York; Lawrence H Bloedel Bequest
© Georgia O'Keeffe Museum. ARS/Copyright Agency, 2025

178 Pieter Bruegel the Elder (imitator of), *Landscape: A River among Mountains*, c. 1600
Oil on poplar, 50.8 x 68.6 cm
Courtesy of The National Gallery, London
Photo: The National Gallery, London

179 Albert Namatjira, *Njirrakarpa, Finke River, James Ranges*, c. 1948
Painting in watercolour, over drawing in black pencil, 27.5 x 37 cm
National Gallery of Australia, Canberra
Gift of Gordon and Marilyn Darling, celebrating the National Gallery of Australia's 25th Anniversary, 2008. Donated through the Australian Government's Cultural Gifts Program
© Namatjira Legacy Trust/Copyright Agency, 2025

180–1 Henry Schnakenberg, *Ice Pattern*, 1948
Watercolour and graphite pencil on board, 38.3 x 55.7 cm (detail)
Whitney Museum of American Art, New York
© Estate of Henry Schnakenberg

182 Arthur Streeton, *'The purple noon's transparent might'*, 1896
Oil on canvas, 123 x 123 cm
National Gallery of Victoria, Melbourne
Purchased, 1896
Photo: National Gallery of Victoria, Melbourne

183 Hilda Rix Nicholas, *Molonglo River from Mount Pleasant, Canberra*, 1927
Oil on canvas on board, 41 x 32 cm
National Gallery of Australia, Canberra
John Hindmarsh AM and Rosanna Hindmarsh OAM Fund 2013, 100 works for 100 years
© Bronwyn Wright

184 (Top) William Turner of Oxford, *Scene near Shipton on Cherwell, Oxfordshire*, 1835
Watercolour, gouache and brown ink over graphite on moderately thick, moderately textured, cream laid paper, 54.6 x 75.2 cm
Yale Center for British Art, Paul Mellon Fund, Connecticut

(Bottom) Ginger Riley Munduwalawala, *The Limmen Bight River*, 1990
Synthetic polymer paint on canvas, 156 x 202 cm
National Gallery of Australia, Canberra
Purchased with Funds from the Moet & Chandon Australian Art Foundation
© Reproduced courtesy of the Estate of Ginger Riley Munduwalawala & Alcaston Gallery, Melbourne

185 Gertie Huddleston, *We All Share Water*, 2001
Synthetic polymer paint on canvas, 141.5 x 160.5 cm
National Gallery of Australia, Canberra
Purchased 2010
© Estate of Gertie Huddleston

186 Ellen Phelan, *River Test – Trees at Water's Edge*, 1989
Oil on linen, 127 x 79.4 cm
Whitney Museum of American Art, New York
Gift from the Emily Fisher Landau Collection
© Ellen Phelan. ARS/Copyright Agency, 2025

187 (Top) Willem de Kooning, *Door to the River*, 1960
Oil on linen, 203.5 x 178.1 cm
Whitney Museum of American Art, New York
Purchased with funds from the Friends of the Whitney Museum of American Art
© The Willem de Kooning Foundation New York. ARS/Copyright Agency, 2025
Photo: Licensed by Scala

(Bottom) Joseph Yoakum, *Lake of the Ozarks*, 1970
Coloured pencil, chalk and ballpoint pen on paper, 30.3 x 48.4 cm
Whitney Museum of American Art, New York
Purchased with funds from the Drawing and Print Committee
© Estate of Joseph Yoakum

188–9 Duncan Grant, *Landscape, Sussex*, 1920
Oil paint on canvas, 45.7 x 76.2 cm (detail)
Courtesy of Tate, London
Bequeathed by Frank Hindley Smith, 1940
© Tate

191 Vanessa Bell, *The Pond at Charleston, East Sussex*, c. 1916
Oil on canvas, 29.5 x 34.8 cm
Courtesy of The Charleston Trust
© Vanessa Bell. All rights reserved. DACS/Copyright Agency, 2025
Photo: Charleston

192 Timo Hogan, *Lake Baker*, 2021
Synthetic polymer paint on linen, 200 x 137 cm (detail)
Courtesy of Queensland Art Gallery, Brisbane
Purchased with funds from the Future Collective through the Queensland Art Gallery | Gallery of Modern Art Foundation, 2022
© Timo Hogan/Copyright Agency, 2025
Photo: QAGOMA

193 Simon Bussy, *Highland Landscape*, 1920
Pastel on paper, 30 x 22 cm (detail)
Courtesy of Philip Mould & Company, London

194 Unknown (Indian), *Layla and Majnun, and Khusraw and Shirin, Illustrations of Themes from Persian Poetry*, c. 1775
Opaque watercolour and gold on paper, 36.5 x 22.5 cm
Los Angeles County Museum of Art (LACMA), Los Angeles
From the Nasli and Alice Heeramaneck Collection, Museum Associates Purchase

195 (Top) Unknown (American), *Village by the River*, c. fourth quarter of 19th century
Oil on canvas, 51 x 85.1 cm
National Gallery of Art, Washington
Gift of Edgar William and Bernice Chrysler Garbisch

(Bottom) Charles W Bartlett, *Udaipur, 1916*, 1916
Colour woodblock print on moderately thick, slightly textured, beige wove paper, 28.9 x 40.5 cm
Yale Center for British Art, Paul Mellon Fund, New Haven

197 Laura Price, *Hampstead Heath, Womens Pond at Dusk*, 2023
Limited edition gicleée print, 40 x 40 cm
Laura London Art, London
© Laura Price

198 (Top) Konstantin Andreyevich Somov, *River Scene*, 1929
Gouache on paper on board, 36.2 x 44.8 cm
Courtesy of Tate, London
Bequeathed by Peter Provatoroff, 1964

(Bottom) Charles François Daubigny, *The Bathers*, c. 1847
Etching, 22.1 x 31.3 cm
The Cleveland Museum of Art, Cleveland
Gift of Ralph King, the Frederick Keppel Memorial, 1920

199 Unknown (Indian), possibly Datia style, *Women of a zenana bathing at night*, c. late 18th century
Opaque watercolour, gold, 31.3 x 21.5 cm
National Gallery of Australia, Canberra
The Gayer-Anderson Gift 1954

200 (Top) Claude Monet, *Water Lilies*, 1906
Oil on canvas, 89.9 x 94.1 cm
The Art Institute of Chicago
Mr and Mrs Martin A Ryerson Collection

(Bottom) Kawase Hasui, *Benten Pond, Shiba*, 1929
Colour woodblock print, 25.1 x 37.1 cm
Los Angeles County Museum of Art (LACMA), Los Angeles
Gift of Mr and Mrs Felix Juda
© Estate of Kawase Hasui
Photo: © 2025 Museum Associates/LACMA. Licensed by Art Resource, NY

201 Attributed to Hunhar II, *Prince Dara Shikoh (1615–1659) Visits a Sage*, c. 1750
Opaque watercolour and gold on paper, 40.3 x 27.9 cm
Los Angeles County Museum of Art (LACMA), Los Angeles
Gift of the Michael J Connell Foundation

202 Dorrit Black, *Chapman's Pool*, 1935
Colour linocut on Oriental paper, 22.7 x 32.4 cm
Courtesy of Queensland Art Gallery | Gallery of Modern Art, Brisbane
Purchased by Queensland Art Gallery Foundation Grant, 2002
Photo: QAGOMA

203 Rover Joolama Thomas, *Lurinjipungu (Clara Springs)*, 1984
Natural pigments, binders on plywood, 90 x 180 cm (detail)
National Gallery of Australia, Canberra
Purchased from Gallery admission charges, 1984
© Rover Thomas/Copyright Agency, 2025

205 Unknown (Roman), *Glass mosaic bowl fragment*, c. late 1st century BCE–early 1st century CE
Glass; cast, 2.5 x 3.8 cm
Courtesy of The Metropolitan Museum of Art, New York
Edward C Moore Collection, Bequest of Edward C Moore, 1891
Photo: © The Metropolitan Museum of Art. Licensed by Art Resource, NY

206 (Top) James Dickson Innes, *Arenig, North Wales*, 1913
Oil paint on plywood, 85.7 x 113.7 cm
Courtesy of Tate, London
Presented by Rowland Burdon-Muller 1928

(Bottom) Ansel Adams, *Mt. McKinley and Wonder Lake, Mt. McKinley National Park, Alaska*, 1947
Gelatin silver photograph, 39.2 x 48.8 cm
National Gallery of Australia, Canberra
Purchased 1980

207 (Top) Walter Joseph Phillips, *Vista Lake*, 1932
Wood engraving on laid paper, 14 x 18 cm
National Gallery of Victoria, Melbourne
Gift of Mr. Peter Lindsay, 1963
© Estate of Walter Joseph Phillips

(Bottom) Lawren S. Harris, *Lake and Mountains*, 1928
Oil on canvas, 130.8 x 106.7 cm
Courtesy of Art Gallery of Ontario, Toronto
Gift from the Fund of the T Eaton Co. Ltd. for Canadian Works of Art, 1948
© Family of Lawren S. Harris
Photo: AGO

208 (Top) Sir John Akomfrah RA (director), Movie still from *Mnemosyne*, 2010
45 minutes, English, Colour, DVD
© John Akomfrah. DACS/Copyright Agency, 2025
Photo: Royal Academy of Arts, London

(Bottom) Louis Haghe (Belgian) after James David Forbes, *Mont Blanc: a flat boulder raised on a pinnacle of ice*, 19th century
Lithograph, printed in colours, 13 x 20.1 cm
Courtesy of Wellcome Collection, London

209 (Top to bottom) Unknown, *A large iceberg including an arch within which people are standing*, 19th century
Coloured aquatint with watercolour
Courtesy of Wellcome Collection, London

Engraving by R Havell after J Ross, *Meteorology: a polar bear plunges into the sea from a very steep iceberg while fishermen look on from a nearby trawler*, 1819
Engraving with etching, 14.7 x 20.3 cm
Courtesy of Wellcome Collection, London

Engraving by or after Edwin Weedon, *A large iceberg with a ship sailing past it*, c. 1800–99
Engraving with etching
Courtesy of Wellcome Collection, London

Aquatint by W Westall after W Beechey, *Geology: a large iceberg in Baffin Bay*, 1821
Aquatint with etching, 8.2 x 14.2 cm
Courtesy of Wellcome Collection, London

210–1 Wilhelmina Barns-Graham, *Glacier Vortex*, 1951
Oil on canvas, 60 x 71.5 cm (detail)
© Wilhelmina Barns-Graham Trust
Photo: Southampton City Art Gallery/ Bridgeman Images

212 Tapio Wirkkala, *Iceberg*, 1950 (designed), 1962–63 (made)
Mould-blown glass, 20.2 x 16 cm
Courtesy of Victoria and Albert Museum, London
© Tapio Wirkkala. KUVASTO/Copyright Agency, 2025
Photo: Victoria and Albert Museum, 2024

213 (Top) Frank Hurley, *No title (A turreted berg)*, 1913
Carbon print, 43.4 x 59.4 cm
National Gallery of Victoria, Melbourne
Purchased, 1999

(Bottom) Arthur Dobree (attributed to), *Icebergs in the Southern Ocean, January and February 1861, Leaf 6*, 1861
Watercolour, pen and ink
National Gallery of Victoria, Melbourne
Purchased, 1994

214 John Brett, *Glacier of Rosenlaui*, 1856
Oil paint on canvas, 44.5 x 41.9 cm
Courtesy of Tate, London

215 (Top) Samuel Hieronymous Grimm, *The Glacier of Simmenthal*, 1774
Watercolour and graphite on paper, 29.5 x 37.1 cm
Courtesy of Tate, London

(Bottom) Joseph Mallord William Turner, *The Source of the Arveyron below the Glacier du Bois and Mer de Glace*, 1802
Graphite, watercolour and gouache on paper, 31.3 x 46.8 cm
Courtesy of Tate, London

SKY

218 Peter Alexander, *Small Cloud Box*, 1966
Cast polyester resin, 12.7 x 12.7 x 12.7 cm
Los Angeles County Museum of Art (LACMA), Los Angeles
Gift of Eleanor and Ted Congdon, by exchange, and purchased with funds provided by the Ducommun and Gross Endowment
© The Estate of Peter Alexander
Photo: © 2025 Museum Associates/LACMA. Licensed by Art Resource, NY

222 Judy Chicago, *Purple Atmosphere from the On Fire Suite*, Printed 2013 and 2018
Archival pigment print on paper, 50.8 x 60.9 cm
© Judy Chicago. ARS/Copyright Agency, 2025

223 (Top) Petri Ala-Maunus, *New York Trash Recycled 13*, 2007
oil on trash found on the street, 19 x 24.5 cm
Finnish National Gallery/Museum of Contemporary Art Kiasma
© Petri Ala-Maunus
Photo: Finnish National Gallery/Petri Virtanen

(Middle) François Garas, *Paysage de montagne au soleil couchant avec effets de nuages*, c. 1896–1914
Pastel laminated on recycled cardboard, 33 x 44.8 cm
Courtesy of The Orsay and Orangerie Museums, Paris
© Musée d'Orsay, Dist. RMN-Grand Palais/RMN

(Bottom) Eero Järnefelt, *Clouds*, c. 1910–12
Page from sketchbook, watercolour and pastel on paper
Finnish National Gallery/Ateneum Art Museum
Photo: Finnish National Gallery/ Tero Suvilammi

224–5 Tacita Dean, *Cúmulo*, 2016
Chalk on blackboard, 244 x 723 cm
Foundation Beyeler, Riehen/Basel
Courtesy of the artist, Frith Street Gallery, London and Marian Goodman Gallery, New York/Paris/Los Angeles
© Tacita Dean
Photo: Stephen White

225 John Constable RA, *Study of Cirrus Clouds*, c. 1822
Oil on paper, 114 x 178 cm
Courtesy of Victoria and Albert Museum, London
Given by Isabel Constable, 1888

226–7 Paul Nash, *Flight of the Magnolia*, 1944
Oil paint on canvas, 51.1 x 76.2 cm
Courtesy of Tate, London

228 (Top) Hedda Morrison, *North Peak Ridge of Hua Mountain*, 1935 (printed 1970s)
Gelatin silver photograph, 30.5 x 22.8 cm
National Gallery of Victoria, Melbourne
Purchased, 1976
© Harvard-Yenching Library, Harvard University
Photo: Harvard-Yenching Library of the Harvard College Library, Harvard University

(Bottom) Ralph Bacerra, *Untitled Cloud Vessel*, 1997
Porcelain, 49.5 x 33 cm
Los Angeles County Museum of Art (LACMA), Los Angeles
Purchased with funds provided by Friends of Clay and Decorative Arts Council Fund
© Estate of Ralph Bacerra
Photo: © 2025 Museum Associates/LACMA. Licensed by Art Resource, NY

229 Simon Alexandre Clément Denis, *Study of Clouds with a Sunset near Rome*, c. 1786–1801
Oil on paper, 3.8 x 39.4 cm
Getty Museum, Los Angeles

230 Erich Heckel, *Steep Clouds*, 1913
Watercolour, 52.8 x 45.3 cm
Princeton University Art Museum, Princeton
Bequest of Sophie Goldberg Bargmann and Valentine Bargmann

231 Vincent van Gogh, *Wheat Field with Cypresses*, 1889
Oil on canvas, 73.2 x 93.4 cm
Courtesy of The Metropolitan Museum of Art, New York
Purchase, The Annenberg Foundation Gift, 1993

234 Alexander Cozens, *A new method of assisting the invention in drawing original compositions of landscape (Plates 25–26)*, 1785
Part of manuscript, printed for the author, by J Dixwell, in St Martin's Lane: and sold by Mr A Cozens, no. 4, Leicester Street, Leicester Fields; and J. Dodsley
Yale University Library, New Haven

235 Victoria Burge, *Cirrus*, 2017
Screenprint with embossing, 50 x 57 cm
Published by Planthouse
© Victoria Burge 2025

236 (Top) Félix Vallotton, *Le grand nuage, The Great Cloud*, 1900
Oil on cardboard, 35 x 46 cm
Cantonal Museum of Fine Arts, Luasanne
Acquisition with the participation of the Société Vaudoise des Beaux-Arts, 1952
© Musée cantonal des Beaux-Arts de Lausanne

(Bottom) Milton Avery, *Yellow Sky*, 1958
Oil paint on canvas, 156.2 x 184.1 cm
Courtesy of Tate, London
Presented by Mr and Mrs Philip G Cavanaugh through the American Federation of Arts 1963
© Milton Avery/ARS/Copyright Agency, 2025

237 Julie Gough, *Land and sky from sea 2*, 2005
Oxides and ink on canvas, 80.4 x 54.2 cm
National Gallery of Victoria, Melbourne
Purchased with funds donated by Supporters and Patrons of Indigenous Art, 2005
© Butcher C Janangoo/Copyright Agency, 2025

238–9 Martin Johnson Heade, *Sunlight and Shadow: The Newbury Marshes*, c. 1871–75
Oil on canvas, 30.5 x 67.3 cm
National Gallery of Art, Washington

240 Jan Toorop, *Landscape with Canal*, 1889
Oil on canvas, 63 x 75 cm
Jan Toorop, Landschap met vaart (de kastanjeboom) / The chestnut tree, 1889
DM/912/304
Dordrechts Museum, donation Hidde Nijland, 1912

241 Claude Monet, *Springtime on the Ile de La Grande Jatte*, 1878
Oil on canvas, 61.8 x 50.3 cm
The National Museum, Oslo
Photo: Anne Hansteen Jarre

242–3 Evelyn De Morgan, *Night and Sleep*, 1878
Oil on canvas, 108 x 157.8 cm (detail)
De Morgan Collection, England

244 Marco Dente after Raphael (Raffaello Sanzio or Santi), *Venus and Cupid riding two sea monsters, Cupid raises an arrow in his right hand, two heads representing wind in the clouds above*, c. 1515–27
Engraving, 26.5 x 17.2 cm
Courtesy of The Metropolitan Museum of Art, New York
Bequest of Phyllis Massar, 2011

245 Stefano della Bella, *A fan with a rebus on Love on one side Fortune on the other*, c. 1639
Etching fashioned to form a fan with fringe around the edges and wooden handle
Courtesy of The Metropolitan Museum of Art, New York
Estate of Florance Waterbury, 1970

246 (Top) Katsushika Hokusai, *Ejiri in Suruga Province (Sunshū Ejiri)*, c. 1830–32
From the series *Thirty-six Views of Mount Fuji (Fugaku sanjūrokkei)*
Woodblock print; ink and colour on paper, 25.1 x 37.5 cm
Courtesy of The Metropolitan Museum of Art, New York
Henry L Phillips Collection, Bequest of Henry L Phillips, 1939

(Bottom) Jacques Callot, *The Reed and The Wind*, c. 1621–35
Plate 27 from *The Light of the Cloisters*
Etching; second state of two (Lieure)
Courtesy of The Metropolitan Museum of Art, New York
Bequest of Edwin De T Bechtel, 1957

247 (Top) Louise Gabriel Moreau, *Windswept Landscape*, c. 1740–1806
Watercolour and gouache, over traces of black and red chalk, 39.9 x 52.6 cm
Courtesy of The Metropolitan Museum of Art, New York
Bequest of Walter C. Baker, 1971

(Bottom) First Generation after Manaku, *South Wind Cools in Himalayas: Folio from the Second Guler Gita Govinda Series*, c. 1775
Opaque watercolour on paper, 17.8 x 27.4 cm
Museum Rietberg Zürich, Collection of Eva and Konrad Seitz
Photo: Rainer Wolfsberger

248 Manufacturer Dihl et Guérhard, possibly painted by Jean-Baptiste Coste, *Vase with scenes of storm on land*, c. 1797–98
Hard-paste porcelain decorated in polychrome enamels, gold, 46.2 x 18.4 x 18.4 cm
Courtesy of The Metropolitan Museum of Art, New York
Wrightsman Fund, 2014

249 Janangoo Butcher Cherel, *Willy willy 1*, 1995
Linocut, 73.5 x 52.8 cm
National Gallery of Victoria, Melbourne
Purchased, 1997
© Butcher C Janangoo/Copyright Agency, Australia, 2025

251 Baba Adesina, *Tunic*, early 20th-century
Cotton, glass beads
National Museum of African Art, Washington

252 Knud Leem, Johannes Rach and Odvardt Helmodt de Lode, *Sledge Driving in Drifting Snow*, 1767
Line drawing with copper engraving on paper
The National Museum of Art, Architecture and Design, The Fine Art Collections, Oslo
Photo: Andreas Harvik

253 (Top) Kawase Hasui, *In the Snow, Nakayama-Shichiri Road in Hida Province*, 1924
From the series Souvenirs of Travel, Third Series
Colour woodblock print; oban, 26.4 x 38.7 cm
The Art Institute of Chicago, Chicago
Clarence Buckingham Collection
© Estate of Kawase Hasui
Photo: The Art Institute of Chicago/Art Resource, NY

(Bottom) Utagawa Kunisada and Utagawa Hiroshige II, *Ferryboat in the snow on the Sumida River*, 1864
Colour woodblock print on paper, 36 x 24.2 cm
Courtesy of Queensland Art Gallery | Gallery of Modern Art
Purchased 1997 with funds from the International Exhibitions Program
Photo: QAGOMA

254 (Top) Kobayashi Kiyochika, *Heavy Rain at Ochanomizu Bridge*, c. 1915
Woodblock print, ink and colour on paper, 19.5 x 31.4 cm
Princeton University Art Museum, Princeton
Museum purchase, The Anne van Biema Collection Fund

(Bottom) Sir Edward John Poynter, *The West Wind, Lynmouth*, 1866
Watercolour and gouache, 30.5 x 46.4 cm
Courtesy of The Metropolitan Museum of Art, New York
Harry G Sperling Fund, 2015

255 Utagawa Hiroshige, *Night Rain at Karasaki*, c. 1835
From the series Eight Views of Ōmi
Woodblock print; ink and colour on paper, 22.2 x 34.6 cm
Courtesy of The Metropolitan Museum of Art, New York
Rogers Fund, 1914

256–7 Shivalal, *Maharana Fateh Singh's hunting party crossing a river in a flood*, 1893
Opaque watercolour on paper, 85 x 159 cm (detail)
Courtesy of Maharana of Mewar Charitable Foundation, The City Palace Museum, Udaipur
Photo: The City Palace Museum, Udaipur
© MMCF

258 John Constable and David Lucas, *Hampstead Heath*, 1855
Mezzotint on paper, 14 x 18.2 cm
Courtesy of Tate, London

259 Luigi Nono, *The first rain*, 1909
Oil on canvas, 137 x 202 cm
Courtesy of The Orsay and Orangerie Museums, Paris
© Musée d'Orsay, Dist. RMN-Grand Palais/Patrice Schmidt

260–1 Rick Amor, *Returning storm*, 2001
Etching, 21.8 x 32.4 cm
National Gallery of Victoria, Melbourne
© Rick Amor/Copyright Agency, 2025

262 Modelled by Joseph Willems, Chelsea Porcelain Manufactory, *Sight (one of a pair)*, c. 1755
Soft-paste porcelain with enamel decoration and gilding, 28.3 cm
Courtesy of The Metropolitan Museum of Art, New York
Bequest of John L. Cadwalader, 1914

263 (Top) Various artists/makers, *Wide-rimmed bowl with figures from Virgil's Aeneid*, 1525
Maiolica (tin-glazed earthenware), lustered, 5.1 x 28.3 cm
Courtesy of The Metropolitan Museum of Art, New York
Gift of George Blumenthal, 1941

(Bottom) Sam Byrne, *Rainbow reflection*, c. 1970
Oil on board, 59.4 x 74 cm
National Gallery of Australia, Canberra
Purchased 1973
© Estate of Sam Byrne

264–5 Lucy Trask Barnard, *Hooked Rug*, c. 1860
Wool, 152.4 x 73.7 cm
Courtesy of The Metropolitan Museum of Art, New York
Sansbury-Mills Fund, 1961

266 Joachinus de Gigantibus, *Sun, Moon and Planets (shelfmark 'Latin MS 53', from 'Astronomia')*, c. 1470–1480
Codex, parchment, 21.2 x 14 cm
Courtesy of John Rylands Research Institute and Library, Manchester
Image provided by The John Rylands Research Institute and Library, The University of Manchester

267 Unknown, *The Sun Chariot*, c. 1500–1300 BC
Bronze, clay cores, 59 cm x 35 x 29 cm
The National Museum of Denmark, Copenhagen
Photo: The National Museum of Denmark

268 Miguel Covarrubias, *Design for a stage curtain, for the ballet Los cuatro soles (The Four Suns)*, c. 1927–33
Gouache, 23 x 28 cm
Princeton University Art Museum, Princeton
Bequest of Gillett G Griffin

269 Andreas Cellarius; Engraver, Johannes van Loon, *The Varying Phases and Appearances of the Moon, from Harmonia Macrocosmica*, 1660
Hand-coloured engraving with gold, 42.8 x 50.8 cm
Courtesy of Minneapolis Institute of Art, Minneapolis
The Minnich Collection, The Ethel Morrison Van Derlip Fund, 1966

270 Alma Thomas, *The Eclipse*, 1970
Acrylic on canvas, 157.5 x 126.4 cm
Courtesy of Smithsonian American Art Museum, Washington
Gift of the artist, 1978

271 (Top) Howard Russell Butler, *Solar Eclipse, Lompoc 1923*, 1923
Oil on canvas, 122.5 x 82.5 cm
Princeton University Art Museum, Princeton
Gift of Howard Russell Butler Jr

(Bottom) John Emslie, *Astronomy: eclipses (top), and the Moon's passage around the Earth*, 1851
Engraving with watercolour
Courtesy of Wellcome Collection, London

272 (Top) George Wither and Gabriel Rollenhagen, Illustration from *A collection of emblemes, ancient and moderne quickened with metricall illustrations, both morall and divine: and disposed into lotteries*, 1635
Emblem Books, 1635

(Bottom) Christine de Pizan, Christine and the *Sibyl standing in a sphere of the cosmos, with the moon, sun and stars surrounding them*, c. 1410–14
From the *Book of the Queen*
British Library, Harley MS 4431, f.1898v

273 Hilma af Klint, *The dove, no 2* ,1915
Oil on canvas
Courtesy of the Hilma af Klint Foundation
© Hilma af Klint Group IX/UW
Photo: The Moderna Museet, Stockholm, Sweden

274 Claude Monet, *Impression Sunrise*, 1872
Oil on canvas, 48 x 63 cm
Musee Marmottan Monet, Paris, France
Photo: © Bridgeman Images

275 Joan Miró, *Flight of the Dragonfly in Front of the Sun*, 1968
Oil on canvas, 173.9 x 243.8 cm
National Gallery of Art, Washington
Collection of Mr and Mrs Paul Mellon
© Successió Miró. ADAGP/Copyright Agency, 2025

276 Mark Rothko, *Untitled (Red),* 1956
Glue, oil, synthetic polymer paint and resin on canvas, 209.5 x 125.3 cm
National Gallery of Victoria, Melbourne
Purchased through The Art Foundation of Victoria with the assistance of the Helen M. Schutt Trust, Governor, the Commonwealth Banking Corporation, Fellow and The Signet Group, Fellow, 1982
© Kate Rothko Prizel & Christopher Rothko/ARS/Copyright Agency, 2025

277 Chiura Obata, *Setting Sun on Sacramento Valley, California, U.S.A*, 1930
Ink and colours on paper, 45.7 x 33.3 cm
Asian Art Museum, San Francisco (detail)
Gift of Dr Stephen A Sherwin and Merrill Randol Sherwin

278 John Nash, *Winter Evening*, 1960
Oil on canvas, 63.5 x 76 cm
Worthing Museum and Art Gallery
© Estate of John Northcote Nash
Photo: © Worthing Museum and Art Gallery/ © Estate of John Northcote Nash. All rights reserved 2025/Bridgeman Images

279 Paul Nash, *Landscape of the Moon's First Quarter*, 1943
Oil on canvas, 63.3 x 70.1 cm
Courtesy of Birmingham Museums Trust
Photo: Birmingham Museums Trust

280 (Top) Caspar David Friedrich, *Two Men Contemplating the Moon*, c. 1825–30
Oil on canvas, 34.9 x 43.8 cm
Courtesy of The Metropolitan Museum of Art, New York
Wrightsman Fund, 2000

(Bottom) Edward Steichen, *Nocturne – Hydrangea Terrace, Chateaux Ledoux*, 1907
Three colour relief halftone, 15.2 x 15.7 cm
Philadelphia Museum of Art, Philadelphia
From the Collection of Dorothy Norman, 1973-267-320
© The Estate of Edward Steichen. ARS/Copyright Agency, 2025

281 Joan Miró, *Dog Barking at the Moon*, 1926
Oil on canvas, 73 x 92.1 cm
Philadelphia Museum of Art, Philadelphia
A E Gallatin Collection, 1952-61-82
© Successió Miró. ADAGP/Copyright Agency, 2025

282 Winifred Nicholson, *Moonlight and Lamplight*, 1937
Oil paint on canvas, 76.2 x 88.9 cm
Tate Modern, London
© The Trustees of Winifred Nicholson

283 (Top) Maki Haku, *Moon 1*, c. late 1990s
Lithograph; ink and colour on paper, 25.4 x 25.4 cm
Collection of the Honolulu Museum of Art
Gift from the Family of James Kiyoto Imai, Keith, Corbin, Steven and Janis Dedrick in memory of Mariko Mochizuki Imai, 2018

(Bottom) Wanda Gág, *Moonlight*, 1926
Lithograph on zinx, 35.8 x 42.7 cm
Courtesy of Minneapolis Institute of Art, Minneapolis
Gift of the Estate of Wanda Gág

284 Kawase Hasui, *Moonlit Night (Daisensui Pond)*, 1920
Colour woodblock print, 36.5 x 24.1 cm
Los Angeles County Museum of Art (LACMA), Los Angeles
Gift of Mr and Mrs Felix Juda
© Estate of Kawase Husui
© 2025 Museum Associates/LACMA. Licensed by Art Resource, NY

285 (Top) Émile-Antoine Bayard and Alphonse-Marie-Adolphe de Neuville, Illustration from Jules Verne's book *From the Earth to the Moon*, 1865
Published by J Hetzel Paris

(Middle) Matsumura Keibun, *Full Moon*, early 19th century
Painting, ink on paper, 102.2 x 47.6 cm
Collection of Honolulu Museum of Art
Bequest of John Gregg Allerton, 1991

(Bottom) El Anatsui, *Earth-Moon Connexions*, 1993
Wood, paint, 90 x 84.4 cm
National Museum of African Art, Washington
© El Anatsui

286 Mary Bishop (Mary Cecil Hamilton), *The moon traversed by two thin clouds in a purple sky*, 1967
Watercolour with pencil, 56 x 45 cm
Courtesy of Wellcome Collection, London
© Estate of Mary Bishop

287 Unknown (Korean), *Moon jar*, second half of 18th century
Porcelain, 38.7 x 33 x 14 cm
Courtesy of The Metropolitan Museum of Art, New York
The Harry G C Packard Collection of Asian Art, Gift of Harry G C Packard, and Purchase, Fletcher, Rogers, Harris Brisbane Dick, and Louis V Bell Funds, Joseph Pulitzer Bequest, and The Annenberg Fund Inc. Gift, 1975

288 (Top) Adam Elsheimer, *The Flight into Egypt*, 1609
Copper, 30.6 x 41.5 cm
Bevarian State Painting Collections – Alte Pinakothek, Munich
From the collection of Elector Johann Wilhelm of the Palatinate

(Bottom) Peter Paul Rubens, *Landscape by moonlight*, c. 1635–40
Engraving, 32 x 44.5 cm
The Courtauld, London (Samuel Courtauld Trust)
Bequest of Count Antione Seilern, 1978

289 (Top) Ralph Maynard Smith, *Circles and Moon*, 1950
Oil on ply panel, 34.9 x 46.3 cm
The Fitzwilliam Museum, Cambridge
Given by The Friends of the Fitzwilliam Museum, 2003
© Courtesy of The Ralph Maynard Smith Trust

(Bottom) Joseph Wright of Derby, *Grotto in the Gulf of Salerno, Italy, Moonlight*, c. 1780–90
Oil on canvas, 101.6 x 127 cm
Derby Museum and Art Gallery
Photo: Derby Museums

290–1 Félix Vallotton, *Clair de lune*, 1895
Oil on canvas, 27 x 41 cm (detail)
Courtesy of The Orsay and Orangerie Museums, Paris
© RMN-Grand Palais (Musée d'Orsay)/ Michel Urtado

292 Jacopo Tintoretto, *The Origin of the Milky Way*, c. 1575
Oil on canvas, 149.4 x 168 cm
Courtesy of The National Gallery, London

293 Naminapu Maymuru-White, *Milŋiyawuy (River of Stars)*, 2020
Earth pigments on Stringybark (Eucalyptus sp.), 140.5 x 84.5 cm
National Gallery of Victoria, Melbourne
Purchased with funds donated by Lisa Fox, 2021
2021.192
© Naminapu Maymuru-White, courtesy of Buku-Larrŋgay Mulka Centre, Yirrkala
Photo: National Gallery of Victoria, Melbourne

294 Lena Nyadbi, *Starry night in Jimbirla country*, 2000
Earth pigments on canvas, 90.1 x 121 cm
National Gallery of Victoria, Melbourne
Purchased through the NGV Foundation with the assistance of the Joan Clemenger Endowment, Governor, 2001
DC16-2001
© Lena Nyadbi/Copyright Agency, 2025
Photo: National Gallery of Victoria, Melbourne

295 (Top) Vincent van Gogh, *The Starry Night*, 1889
Oil on canvas, 73.7 x 92.1 cm
Museum of Modern Art (MoMA), New York
Acquired through the Lillie P Bliss Bequest (by exchange). Conservation was made possible by the Bank of America Art Conservation Project

(Bottom) Henri-Edmond Cross (Henri-Edmond Delacroix), *Landscape with Stars*, c. 1905–08
Watercolour on white wove paper, 24.4 x 32.1 cm
Courtesy of The Metropolitan Museum of Art, New York
Robert Lehman Collection, 1975

296 Brian Robinson, *Bedhan Lag: Land of the Kaiwalagal*, 2019
Linocut, edition 5/10; printed by Theo Tremblay, Editions Tremblay, 100 x 185 cm
Courtesy of the artist and Geelong Gallery, Geelong
Ursula Hoff Institute award, 2019
© Brian Robinson
Photo: Michael Marzik

297 Thomas L Mitchell (after) John Carmichael (engraver), *Chart of the Zodiac, including the stars of the 4th magnitude, between the Parallels of 24°½ declination North & South*, c. 1831
Engraving, aquatint, printed in black ink, from one copper plate, 16.1 x 59.8 cm
National Gallery of Australia, Canberra
Purchased 2004

298 Mary Morton Allport, *Comet of March 1843, seen from Aldridge Lodge, V.D. Land*, 1843
Lithograph printed in black ink on wove paper, 23 x 18 cm (detail)
Courtesy of Libraries Tasmania, Hobart

299 Étienne Léopold Trouvelot, *The November meteors: As observed between midnight and 5 o'clock A.M. on the night of November 13–14 1868*, c. 1881–82
Chromolithograph, 16.5 x 21.7 cm (detail)
The New York Public Library Digital Collections, New York

300 (Top) John Everett, *A Comet*, c. late 19th century–mid 20th century
Oil on paper, 35.5 x 50.8 cm
National Maritime Museum, Greenwich, London
Bequeathed by the artist 1949
Photo: National Maritime Museum, Greenwich, London

(Middle) William Marshall Craig, *Astronomy: an atmospheric condition producing sun dogs, giving the effect of two suns*, 1820
Engraving with etching
Courtesy of Wellcome Collection, London

(Bottom) H R Cook, *Astronomy: a large, bright, comet in the night sky over Winchester, being observed by two men. Engraving by H.R. Cook, 1811, after Pether*, 1820
Engraving
Courtesy of Wellcome Collection, London

301 (Top) Unknown (British), *Astronomy: comets in a night sky*, 1860
Engraving
Courtesy of Wellcome Collection, London

(Bottom) Henry Robinson, *Astronomy: a meteor shower in the night sky*, 1783
Mezzotint, 20 x 16.1 cm
Courtesy of Wellcome Collection, London

302 (Top) Carl Svantje Hallbeck, *Njommelsaska i Lappland*, 1856
Chromolithograph, 19.7 x 27.4 cm

(Bottom) Charles H Whymper, *Astronomy: the Aurora Borealis, wirht a reindeer-drawn sledge in the foreground*, 1880
Coloured wood engraving with watercolour
Courtesy of Wellcome Collection, London

303 (Top) Frederic Edwin Church, *Aurora Borealis*, 1865
Oil on canvas, 142.3 x 212.2 cm
Smithsonian American Art Museum, Washington
Gift of Eleanor Blodgett, 1911

(Bottom) Sophus Tromholt, *Nordlys I Bossekop dec 21de Januar 1839*, 1885
From the book *Under Nordlysets Straaler, Skildringer fra Lappernes Land*
Published Kjøbenhavn, 1885, British Library

305 Anna Boberg, *Northern Lights. Study from North Norway*, c. 1901
Oil on canvas, 97 x 75 cm
Courtesy of The National Museum, Sweden

BIOGRAPHIES

Dr Olivia Meehan is an art historian and object-based teaching specialist. She received her MPhil and PhD in the History of Art from the University of Cambridge. Her graduate research focused on the circulation of cultural material and ideas in early modern Europe and Japan. She has also trained at the V&A Museum, London in Creating Innovative Learning Programmes. Since graduating she has worked in museums and galleries in Australia and abroad, and as a lecturer in the History of Art at University of Cambridge, Australian National University and University of Melbourne. She also regularly contributes to *The World of Interiors*.

Alice Vincent is an internationally-published writer, broadcaster and multi-platform storyteller. Her books include *Hark* and the bestselling *Why Women Grow* and *Rootbound, Rewilding a Life*, with the later two longlisted for the Wainwright Prize. She is a columnist for *The Guardian* and *The New Statesman*, and writes for *Vogue, The Financial Times, The Sunday Times* and *The Observer*.

Dr Harriet Baker is a writer and critic. Her work has appeared in the *London Review of Books, Paris Review, The New Statesman, Financial Times, TLS* and *Apollo*. She is the author of *Rural Hours: The Country Lives of Virginia Woolf, Sylvia Townsend Warner and Rosamond Lehmann* (2024).

Dr Lizzie Marx is the Curator of Dutch and Flemish Art at the National Gallery of Ireland in Dublin. Marx received her doctorate from the University of Cambridge with the thesis 'Visualising, Perceiving and Interpreting Smell in Seventeenth-Century Dutch Art'. She has worked on exhibition projects in the UK, Ireland and the Netherlands, including *Fleeting – Scents in Colour* (2021) at the Mauritshuis, The Hague, and *Vermeer Visits* (2024) and *Turning Heads: Rubens, Rembrandt and Vermeer* (2024) at the National Gallery of Ireland, Dublin.

Dr Miya Tokumitsu is an art historian who has written extensively about the cultural values that work holds in the 21st century. A former Fulbright scholar, she holds a PhD from the University of Pennsylvania and is a contributing editor at *The Public Domain Review*. She is the author of *Do What You Love: And Other Lies About Success & Happiness* (2015).

Reverend Takafumi Zenryu Kawakami is the 24th head priest at Shunkoin Temple in Kyoto, Japan. He travels the world leading global workshops on the topics of Zen, Buddhism, philosophy, the self and meditation at various companies and institutions such as MIT, Brown University, Eton College, Microsoft and TEDx.

SUGGESTED SLOW READING

In the spirit of fostering a slow and meditative practice it seems fitting to suggest a short list of writing that promotes the closer examination of nature and art. In addition to the various titles mentioned throughout this book, the following authors offer descriptions, knowledge and ideas to savour.

Potawatomi botanist Robin Wall Kimmerer's *Braiding Sweetgrass: Indigenous Wisdom, Scientific Knowledge and the Teachings of Plants* (2020) widens the ecological study on relationships in the living world through indigenous insight and knowledge.

Rachel Carson's writing is as relevant and powerful today as when it was first published, especially her moving works on the sea, including *The Sea Around Us* (1951).

The poetry of place as examined by Wiradjuri poet and artist Jazz Money in *how to make a basket* (2021) shifts our thinking on land, language and love through their creative and visual prose.

In Sōetsu Yanagi's collection of thoughtful essays *The Beauty of Everyday Things*, translated by Michael Brase (2019) he proposes a notion of seeing and knowing that is challenging and something of a revelation.

David Hinton's translations of ancient Chinese literature especially *The Mountain Poems of Hsieh Ling-yü* (2014) exemplify the tradition of *Shanshui shi* 'rivers and mountain' poetry. His book Existence: *A Story* (2016) exquisitely describes the cosmos through Chinese landscape painter Shitao (1642–1707) and other poet wanderers.

An essential addition to any slow looking library are the writings of John Berger, in particular his *Selected Essays* (2001) for the richly intimate, descriptive text.

In an extraordinary act of contemplative looking, art writer Lily le Brun expands our horizons as she takes in one picture at time in *Looking to Sea: Britain Through the Eyes of its Artists* (2023).

Whether in paintings, in writings, or in real life, the pleasure of nature is everywhere, especially if you take it slowly.

ACKNOWLEDGEMENTS

Much of the work on this book was undertaken on the unceded lands of the Wurundjeri Woi-wurrung and Bunurong/Boon Wurrung peoples of the Kulin Nation. I recognise their continuing connection to lands, waters and community and pay my respect to all traditional custodians past, present and emerging.

This book would not have been possible without the passion and dedication of my publisher Kirsten Abbott. Her devotion to beauty, art and nature has been a driving force from the very first moment we connected; my heartfelt thanks to Kirsten for her belief in the project, her wisdom and her expertise. Also at Thames & Hudson Australia, very special thanks go to my editor Shannon Grey for her intelligence and guidance with words and images, and to Lisa Schuurman for her support and work throughout the process. I would like to acknowledge the entire team at Thames & Hudson Australia and in the UK for their commitment in realising the book. Thanks to Ashlea O'Neill for her beautiful design and her exceptional talent in working with colour. Ashlea's design delicately but deliberately extends the invitation for close looking.

Special thanks to contributors Alice Vincent, Harriet Baker, Lizzie Marx and Miya Tokumitsu, whose words, ideas, and intellect inspire a different way of seeing art and the world around us. Thanks also to Jazz Money, Nina Mingya Powles and Tiffany Francis-Baker for their valuable contribution and work towards to the book.

I extend my deep gratitude to Reverend Takafumi Zenryu Kawakami whose thinking first motivated me to develop a practice for close looking based on the Zen view of 'observation as experiment'. Taka's teachings have transformed my approach to meditative practice. His discerning approach to art and humanity has elevated my formal studies and training. I am so grateful for his friendship and generosity.

Thank you to all of the artists whose work energises the book in ways we could never measure. To the art galleries and museums worldwide for their support, and to the curators whose expertise allows us greater insight into the works of art. I have read, with careful attention, their research and writing in catalogues, both online and in print. Thanks especially to Harriet Loffler, Curator of the Women's Art Collection UK and Elspeth Pitt, Senior Curator Australian Art at the National Gallery of Australia for their distinctive writing on art, their friendship, and suggestions for the book, and to Dr Hannah Lucas whose work in the area of contemplative studies has truly enriched my thinking on reflection and observation.

Thank you to family, friends and colleagues including Juliana Engberg, Jacqueline Dutton, Steve Martin, Yasmeen Hassan, Ruby Lowe, Marty Cielens, Jean Michel and Ann Massing, and Colin Sindall for our enduring discussions about art, beauty, poetry and observation; you have each enlivened this project. Finally, deep thanks must go to my partner Robyn whose endless love provides the perfect space for ideas and words to flourish, and to Marcel, an excellent observer, for his care and good cheer. It is my hope that this book finds a special place in the hearts of the next generation of art and nature lovers, and slow looking practitioners – for Theodore and all the young ones in our orbit.

First published in Australia in 2025
by Thames & Hudson Australia
Wurundjeri Country, 132A Gwynne Street
Cremorne, Victoria 3121

First published in the United Kingdom in 2025
by Thames & Hudson Ltd
6–24 Britannia Street
London WC1X 9JD

First published in the United States of America in 2025
by Thames & Hudson Inc.
500 Fifth Avenue
New York, New York 10110

p 1: Extracted quote by Georgia O'Keeffe originally published in the exhibition catalog 'An American Place', and later cited in *Georgia O'Keeffe: The Poetry of Things* (Phillips Collection, 1999).

28 27 26 25 5 4 3 2 1

ISBN 978-1-760-76473-9
ISBN 978-1-76076-525-5 (U.S. edition)

EU Authorized Representative: Interart S.A.R.L
19 rue Charles Auray, 93500 Pantin, Paris, France
productsafety@thameshudson.co.uk
interart.fr

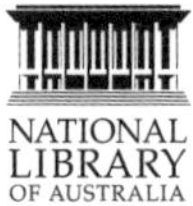

A catalogue record for this book is available from the National Library of Australia

A CIP catalogue record for this book is available from the British Library

Library of Congress Control Number 2024953042

Every effort has been made to trace accurate ownership of copyrighted text and visual materials used in this book. Errors or omissions will be corrected in subsequent editions, provided notification is sent to the publisher.

Front cover:
Gordon Mortensen
Beach Flowers, 2010
Reduction woodcut, 101.6 x 73.66 cm
Courtesy of the artist and Davidson Galleries, Seattle
© Gordon Mortensen

Back cover:
René Magritte
The Sixteenth of September, c. 1956–58
Gouache over graphite on paper, 35.6 x 27.6 cm
© René Magritte. ADAGP/Copyright Agency, 2025

Design: Ashlea O'Neill | Salt Camp Studio
Printed and bound in China by C&C Offset Printing Co., Ltd

Thames & Hudson Australia wishes to acknowledge that Aboriginal and Torres Strait Islander peoples are the first storytellers of this nation and the Traditional Custodians of the land on which we live and work. We acknowledge their continuing culture and pay respect to Elders past and present.

Be the first to know about our new releases, exclusive content and author events by visiting
thamesandhudson.com.au
thamesandhudson.com
thamesandhudsonusa.com